Building Accounting Systems Using Access 2007

Building Accounting Systems Using Access 2007

SEVENTH EDITION

JAMES T. PERRY

The University of San Diego School of Business

RICHARD NEWMARK

Monfort College of Business, University of Colorado

SOUTH-WESTERN
CENGAGE Learning

Australia • Brazil • Japan • Korea • Mexico • Singapore • Spain • United Kingdom • United States

Building Accounting Systems Using Access 2007, Seventh Edition

James T. Perry
Richard Newmark

V P Editorial Director: Jack W. Calhoun

Editor-in-Chief: Rob Dewey

Senior Acquisitions Editor: Matt Filimonov

Developmental Editor: Ted Knight, J. L. Hahn
Consulting

Editorial Assistant: Lauren Athmer

Senior Marketing Communications
Manager: Libby Shipp

Marketing Manager: Natalie King

Marketing Coordinator: Heather McAuliffe

Director, Content and Media Production:
Barbara Fuller-Jacobsen

Content Project Manager: Emily Nesheim

Production Technology Analyst: Adam Grafa

Media Editor: Bryan England

Senior Frontlist Buyer, Manufacturing:
Doug Wilke

Production Service: KGL

Senior Art Director: Stacy Jenkins Shirley

Internal Designer: Juli Cook

Cover Designer: cmiller design

Cover Images:

b/w photo: Getty Images/Rubberball

color image: iStockphoto

Senior Text Permissions Manager: Margaret
Chamberlain-Gaston

Senior Images Permissions Manager:
Don Schlotman

For product information and technology assistance, contact us at
**Cengage Learning Customer & Sales Support,
1-800-354-9706**

For permission to use material from this text or product, submit all requests online at **www.cengage.com/permissions**

Further permissions questions can be emailed to
permissionrequest@cengage.com

Library of Congress Control Number: 2009926876
ISBN-13: 978-0-324-66527-7
ISBN-10: 0-324-66527-X

South-Western Cengage Learning
5191 Natorp Boulevard
Mason, OH 45040
USA

Cengage Learning products are represented in Canada by Nelson Education, Ltd.

For your course and learning solutions, visit **www.cengage.com**
Purchase any of our products at your local college store or at our preferred online store **www.CengageBrain.com**

Printed in the United States of America
1 2 3 4 5 6 7 13 12 11 10 09

Brief Contents

Preface   xvii
Acknowledgments   xxiii
About the Authors   xxv

CHAPTER **1**   **Introduction to Microsoft Access**   1

CHAPTER **2**   **Databases and Accounting Systems**   51

CHAPTER **3**   **Creating, Populating, and Displaying Tables**   89

CHAPTER **4**   **Creating and Using Queries**   141

CHAPTER **5**   **Creating and Using Forms**   195

CHAPTER **6**   **Creating and Using Reports**   243

CHAPTER **7**   **Introduction to Data Modeling for Accounting Information Systems**   295

CHAPTER **8**   **Sales/Collection Process**   319

CHAPTER **9**   **Acquisition/Payment Process**   395

CHAPTER **10**   **Human Resources Process**   467

CHAPTER **11**   **Financing Process**   531

Index   587

Contents

Preface xvii
Acknowledgments xxiii
About the Authors.. xxv

CHAPTER 1

Introduction to Microsoft Access.. 1

Introduction   2
    What Is Microsoft Office Access?   2
    What Is a Relational Database?   2
    Starting Microsoft Access   3
    Obtaining Help   3
    Printing Help   4
    Exiting Access   4

Examining the Access Environment   5
    Access Work Surface   5
    Access Objects   9

Working with Databases and Tables   14
    Using Microsoft's Database Templates   14
    Opening a Database   16
    Creating a Backup of an Access Database   16
    Looking at Data through Different Tabs   17
    Opening a Table   18
    Moving around a Table   22
    Searching for a Value in a Column   22
    Changing a Table's Display Characteristics   23
    Sorting and Filtering Table Rows   24
    Printing a Table   26
    Printing a Table's Structure   26

Querying a Database   27
    Using a Query   28
    Creating a One-Table Query   29
    Saving a Query   30
    Sorting the Results   31
    Using More Complex Selection Criteria   32
    Creating Selection Criteria Using the "OR" Operator   34
    Including Expressions in a Query   36
    Printing Dynasets   37

Using Forms   38
    Viewing a Table through a Form   38
    Viewing a Query through a Form   40
    Creating a Form Quickly   40
    Saving a Form   41
    Editing Data with a Form   42
    Creating and Using a Split Form   42
    Printing a Form   43

Designing Reports 44
Previewing a Report 44
Creating a Report Quickly 44
Saving a Report 45
Printing a Report 47

Summary 47

CHAPTER 2
Databases and Accounting Systems... 51

Introduction 52

Database Accounting Systems 52
Events-Based Theories of Accounting 52
Double-Entry Bookkeeping Versus Database Accounting 53
Advantages of Database Accounting Systems 57
Disadvantages of Database Accounting Systems 58

Business Processes 59
Sales/Collection Process 60
Acquisition/Payment Process 61
Human Resources Process 62
Financing Process 62

Accounting Information Systems and Database Systems 63

Database Management Systems 64
Pre-DBMS Data Acquisition and Reporting 64
Functions of a Database Management System 65
Advantages of Database Management Systems 66
Disadvantages of Database Management Systems 66

Relational Database Management Systems 67
Database Objects 67
Primary and Foreign Key Attributes 68
Schema of a Relation 70
Data Dictionary 70
The Coffee Merchant Tables 70
Normalization 73

Fundamental Relational Database Operations 79
Select 79
Project 79
Join 79

Introduction to Database Design 82
Developing Entity-Relationship Models 83
Resources, Events, Agents (REA) Modeling 84

Summary 84

CHAPTER 3
Creating, Populating, and Displaying Tables................................... 89

Introduction to Tables 90

Creating a Table Using a Template 90

Creating a Table From Scratch 93
Adding a Column 94
Adding a Column Using a Lookup Field 95

Deleting, Renaming, or Moving a Table Column 98
Deleting a Column 98

Renaming a Column   98
Moving a Column   99

Establishing Intertable Referential Integrity   99

Editing and Removing Intertable Relationships   103

Deleting, Copying, Renaming, Hiding, and Showing Tables   104
Deleting or Copying a Table   104
Renaming a Table   104
Hiding or Showing a Table   104

Setting Field Properties   106
Field Size   106
Format   106
Input Mask   106
Caption   106
Default Value   107
Validation Rule and Validation Text   107
Required   107
Allow Zero Length *(text data type)*   107
Indexed Property   107
Lookup Properties   107

Establishing Table-Level Data Validation   108

Establishing a Primary Key   111

Examining and Setting Table Properties   113

Saving the Table Design   114

Printing Table Structure Information   115

Populating a Table   115

Modifying a Table's Datasheet   118
Resizing and Rearranging Columns   118
Hiding and Freezing Columns   119
Formatting the Datasheet   121
Displaying Column Totals   122

Printing Records   124

Organizing Tables in the Navigation Pane   125
Hiding and Revealing Object Names   127
Creating New Categories   127
Organizing Tables into Custom Categories   129

Separating Tables from Other Database Objects   131

Linking to External Access Tables   133

Summary   135

CHAPTER 4
Creating and Using Queries 141

Introduction to Queries   142

Types of Queries   142

Views   143

Creating a Basic Select Query   144

Retrieving Selected Rows from a Table   146

Working with a Dynaset   148
Producing Sorted Query Results   149
Altering the Order and Size of Columns   149
Altering Column Display Properties   150

Saving a Query and Printing Dynasets   151
   Saving a Query   151
   Printing Dynasets   151

Creating Queries with Query Wizards   151
   Creating Crosstab Queries   151
   Creating Find Duplicates Queries   153

Designing and Using a Parameter Query   153

Setting Query Properties   156
   Default View   156
   Output All Fields   156
   Top Values   156
   Unique Values   157
   Unique Rows   157
   Filter   157
   Order By   157
   Orientation   157

Working with Multiple-Table Queries   157

Understanding Table Relationships   158
   Understanding One-to-One Relationships   159
   Understanding One-to-Many Relationships   159
   Dealing with Many-to-Many Relationships   159

Using Expressions in a Query   160
   Using Operators   161
   Using the Expression Builder   162
   Introduction to Access Built-In Functions   164
   Using Math Functions   164
   Dealing with Null Fields Referenced in Expressions   166
   Using Date Functions   166
   Using Criteria in Queries   168

Grouping and Summarizing Data   173

Creating and Using an Outer Join Query   176

Building Pivot Table Queries   177
   What Is a Pivot Table?   178
   Pivot Table Terminology   178
   Creating One- and Two-Dimensional Pivot Tables   179

Working in SQL View   181
   Select Statement Syntax   182
   Self-Join Queries with SQL   183
   Using a Subquery to Find Customers Without Invoices   183
   Finding Employees with Longer than Average Tenure   185

Creating and Running Action Queries   186
   Make Table Query   187
   Update Query   187
   Delete Query   189
   Append Query   190

Summary   191

CHAPTER 5
Creating and Using Forms 195

Putting Forms to Work   196

Viewing Form Types   197

Building a Form   199
   Building a Standard Form   200
   Building a Split Form   203
   Building a Multiple Items Form   204

Guidelines for Good Form Design   205

Creating Basic Forms Using the Form Wizard   206

Creating a Form from Scratch in Design View   207
   Adding a Title to a Form   209
   Adding a Logo to a Form   209
   Navigating a Form   211
   Printing a Form   212

Modifying a Form in Layout View   214
   Modifying a Form's Default View   214
   Applying Conditional Formatting to a Control   216
   Understanding Control Layouts   217
   Sizing and Moving Controls   218

Enforcing Data Integrity and Consistency with Forms   220
   Using Data Validation to Avoid Errors   220
   Inserting Controls to Limit Choices: Buttons and List Boxes   222
   Creating a Behind-the-Form Query   225

Creating a Multitable Form and Subform   227
   Creating a Multiple-Table Form   227
   Creating a Subform From a Query   228

Creating Special Purpose Forms   230
   Creating a Mortgage Calculation Form   230
   Building a Switchboard   233
   Designating a Startup Form   235

Summary   237

CHAPTER 6
Creating and Using Reports 243

Creating a Basic Report Quickly   244

Modifying a Report in Layout View   245
   Adding a Logo and a Title   245
   Deleting, Moving, and Resizing Columns   246
   Modifying Column Titles   248
   Sorting and Grouping   249
   Formatting Reports   251
   Applying Conditional Formatting to a Control   252
   Previewing a Report   252

Building a Report Using the Report Wizard   253

A Few Guidelines for Good Report Design   257
   Use Existing Paper Reports When Needed   258
   Use Page Numbers, Dates, and Times   258
   Ensure Field Order Makes Sense   258
   Sorting and Grouping Are Always Welcome   258
   Keep it Simple   258

Creating a Report from Scratch in Design View   259
   Creating a Blank Report and Adding Fields   259
   Selecting Fields from Related Tables   260
   Creating a Tabular Control Layout   261
   Grouping and Sorting   261
   Adding Calculations to a Report   264

Adding Page Breaks Before Sections 266
Modifying Report Properties 267
Applying Conditional Formatting to a Control 268
Fine-Tuning the Report 269

Creating a Multitable Report Based on a Query 269
Examining a Query Supplying Report Data 269
Creating the First Draft of an Invoice Report 272
Manually Adding Fields 273
Rearranging and Reorganizing Fields 275
Saving a Report Under a New Name 277
Adding Calculated Controls 277
Adding Labels and Graphics 281

Publishing a Report 284
Printing a Paper Report 284
Exporting a Report to Word 285
Producing a PDF- or XPS-Format Report 285
Publishing to E-mail 287

Creating Mailing Labels 287

Summary 290

CHAPTER 7
Introduction to Data Modeling for Accounting Information Systems 295

Introduction to Data Modeling 296

Creating a Value System Model of an Enterprise 296

Creating a Value Chain Model of an Enterprise 298

Creating a Business Process Model of an Enterprise 301
Creating Events, Resources, and Agents and the Relationships Between Them 301
Adding Relationship Cardinalities to the Business Process Model 303
Adding Attributes to the Business Process Model 306

Converting a Business Process Model to a Logical Database 308

Creating the Access Database 309

Summary 316

CHAPTER 8
Sales/Collection Process 319

Introduction 320

Pipefitters Supply Company's Sales/Collection Business Process 320
Duality of Economic Events 321
Basic Sales/Collection Data Model 321
Completing the Sales/Collection Model 324

Customer Information 326
The Customer Table 326
Adding Controls to the Customer Table 327
The Customer Information Form 332
Maintaining Customer Records 334

Inventory Information 336
The Inventory Table 336
The Inventory Form 341

Sale Orders 347
Adding Employees to the Database 348
The Sale Order Table 348

The Sale Order-Inventory Table   351
The Sale Order Entry Form   353

Recording Sales   365
The Sale Table   365
The Sale-Inventory Table   366
The Sale Entry Form   367
Printing Invoices   371

Recording Cash Received From Customers   374
Cash Account Information   374
The Cash Receipt Table   375
The Cash Receipt Entry Form   377

Deriving Financial Statement Information   382
Sales   382
Accounts Receivable   383

Deriving Other Information Useful for Decision Making   385
Accounts Receivable by Customer   385
Open Sale Orders   387

Summary   390

CHAPTER 9

Acquisition/Payment Process 395

Introduction   396

Pipefitters Supply Company's Acquisition/Payment Business Process   397
Duality of Economic Events   397
Basic Acquisition/Payment Data Model   398
Completing the Acquisition/Payment Model   400

Vendor Information   402
The Vendor Table   402
The Vendor Information Form   403
Maintaining Vendor Records   404

Inventory Information   405
The Inventory Table   406
The Inventory Form   406

Purchase Orders   408
The Employee Table   409
The Purchase Order Table   409
The Purchase Order-Inventory Table   412
The Purchase Order Entry Form   413

Recording Purchases (Inventory Receipts)   430
The Purchase Table   431
The Purchase-Inventory Table   432
The Inventory Receipt (Purchase) Entry Form   433

Recording Cash Paid to Vendors   449
Cash Account Information   450
The Cash Disbursements Table   450
The Cash Disbursement Entry Form   452

Acquisition and Payment Process for Non-Inventory Items   457
Recording Information for Non-Inventory Resources with Short Useful Lives   457
Recording Information for Non-Inventory Resources with Long Useful Lives   458

Deriving Financial Statement Information   458
Accounts Payable   458

Deriving other Information Useful for Decision Making   460
   Accounts Payable by Vendor   461

Summary   462

CHAPTER 10
Human Resources Process 467

Introduction   468

Pipefitters Supply Company's Human Resources Business Process   468
   Duality of Economic Events   469
   Basic Human Resources Data Model   470
   Exemptions and Withholding Entities   473
   Completing the HR Model   473

Employee Information   474
   The Employee Table   476
   The Employee Type Table   480
   The Employee Information Entry Form   481
   Maintaining Employee Records   485

Recording Labor Acquisition (Time Worked)   487
   The Labor Acquisition Table   487
   The Labor Acquisition (Time Worked) Entry Form   491

Recording Cash Paid to Employees   495
   The Cash Disbursement Table   496
   Calculating Payroll   501
   The Cash Disbursement Entry Form for Payroll Checks   512

Deriving Financial Statement Information   517
   Wages and FWT Payable   517
   FICA and Medicare Payable   519
   Income Statement Items   520

Deriving Other Information Useful for Decision Making   521
   Employee Information Reports   521
   Time Worked Report   524

Summary   527

CHAPTER 11
Financing Process 531

Introduction   532

Pipefitters Supply Company's Financing Business Process   532
   Duality of Economic Events   533
   Basic Financing Data Model   534
   Commitment Events   535
   Completing the Financing Model   537

Creating Pipefitters' Financing Process in Access   538
   Stockholder and Creditor Information   538
   Recording the Loan Agreement Event   541
   Recording Cash Receipts from Debt Issues   550
   Recording Cash Paid to Creditors   558
   Recording the Stock Agreement Event   568
   Recording Cash Receipts from Stock Issues   573
   Recording Dividends (Cash) Paid to Stockholders   576

Summary   584

Index 587

Preface

To the Student

Traditional methods of recording economic events and accumulating accounting information have given way to database technology in today's accounting information systems. As we write this seventh edition of *Building Accounting Systems*, we find that organizations increasingly depend on databases that include accounting and other operating data for mission-critical information. Accounting information systems—or the accounting views of enterprise-wide databases—contain much of the information managers use to make decisions and control operations. These databases also store the information that accountants use to prepare formal accounting reports, such as year-end financial statements, that organizations issue to external users. As a professional accountant, you will play a central role in ensuring that the accounting systems you use, audit, and help design will deliver timely, accurate, and complete information. This book will help you learn how to perform that role effectively.

This text describes how database management systems provide design tools used by information systems professionals and accountants to build accounting systems. The text begins by explaining how database systems are a part of your everyday life. The text then helps you develop a basic understanding of the theory and practice of relational database management systems. The book then builds on that foundation and shows you how to build the elements of accounting systems using Microsoft Access, one of the most widely available database management software packages for personal computers.

Chapters 1 through 6 of the book provide a firm foundation in using Microsoft Access with an accounting application as the backdrop. Chapters 7 through 11 explain the accounting related to business processes and shows you how to use the database theory and tools you learned in the earlier chapters to build accounting system elements for each of the four main business processes of merchandising and service firms: sales/collection, acquisition/payment, human resources, and financing.

Chapter 1 introduces Microsoft Access database management software. You will learn the basics of using tables to store information, displaying database contents, finding answers to questions with database queries, using forms to enter data, and printing database reports. Chapter 2 introduces database accounting systems by defining business processes and explains the bridge between pre-DBMS accounting systems and today's use of relation database management systems found at the heart of accounting systems. Chapter 3 leads you through the use of database tables—the data storage mechanism. You will create tables from scratch, create them using a wizard, and add and delete table columns. Referential integrity rules available in Access establish intertable relationships, and you will learn how to establish those relationships. Chapter 3 describes how to print a table's structure, populate tables with data, and organize tables into custom groups in the Navigation Pane. Finally, you will learn the advantages of separating tables from other Access database objects into two separate databases and then maintain the linkage between tables and the objects such as reports or forms that refer to them. In Chapter 4, you will create several queries—tasks for which we provide step-by-step guidance. You will be happy to know that you can perform all of these database functions without writing a single line of program code. When you have finished Chapter 4, you will have the database skills you need to create queries—the fundamental database building blocks that deliver data to the remaining basic accounting system components. Chapter 5 provides an in-depth discussion of designing and creating Access forms. You will learn how to create forms based on one table and multiple tables. Similarly, you will learn how to modify form designs, manipulate forms in the new Layout view, and add data integrity rules to form controls. Chapter 6 describes how to create and use Access reports. You will create reports using the Report Wizard, create one from scratch without using a wizard, and build a report whose data is derived from a query.

Chapters 7 through 11 apply database concepts and techniques to the specific challenges of building accounting information systems, which include incorporating internals into the database design and implementation, as well as generating, financial statement information. Chapter 7 explains the basic concepts of designing accounting information systems—the steps you need to complete *before* you begin to build your accounting database in Access. In Chapter 8, you will begin your walk through the business processes with the sales/collection process. For example, you will learn how to use tables, queries, and forms to record sales and cash collections. Chapter 9 shows database applications in the acquisition/payment process, which include recording purchase orders and the receipt of goods ordered, and paying vendors. In Chapter 10, you will design and build the payroll-related elements of a human resources process. You will learn how to combine records of time worked with employee information to calculate gross pay, deductions, and net pay. Chapter 11 describes the financing process and shows you how to build accounting database elements for both equity and debt financing. The chapter explains how to record stock subscriptions and dividend payments as well as loan issuances and loan repayments. Since Chapters 8 through 11 are all based on the same company, you will learn how to integrate multiple business processes, especially in Chapters 10 and 11.

We hope you will become an active participant as you read the text and work through the step-by-step examples. You will best retain what you have read by working through the book on a computer. To reinforce your learning, we have included four types of review questions at the end of each chapter:

- *Multiple-choice questions, which refresh your memory about key points in a chapter.*
- *Discussion questions, which are more general and provide a basis for interesting small group discussions of the topics.*
- *Practice Exercises, which are short problems that require you to use Access to create a solution.*
- *Problems, which are more comprehensive problems that require you to use Access to create your own accounting databases or extend the examples in the text.*

By studying the text carefully, working through the examples, and using the end-of-chapter materials to reinforce your knowledge, you will learn how to use database management software to design and build accounting systems that deliver timely, accurate information to managers and financial statement users.

To the Instructor

Many accounting professors feel that the accounting information systems course is the greatest teaching challenge in the curriculum. One of our goals in writing this book was to help make your job of teaching accounting systems easier. Accounting practice has evolved from manual journals and ledgers to database accounting systems—even in very small firms. At the same time, many introductory accounting courses have shifted to financial statement user and managerial decision-maker orientations from the more traditional preparer orientations. Despite this decreased emphasis on the mechanics of accounting in the introductory courses, accounting majors still need to understand how accounting systems record, classify, and aggregate economic events. This book serves as a powerful tool that can help you to give your students a solid introduction to database principles and valuable hands-on experience in constructing accounting systems. By using Microsoft Access—object-based software that features an intuitive graphic user interface—this book vastly reduces the amount of class time you must spend on non-accounting systems matters. The text's step-by-step instructions can reduce your time and drudgery in the computer lab. The time you do spend with students in class or in the computer lab will not be wasted on mundane "click here and then click there" instructing, because we have filled this book with detailed instructions and examples to save you that kind of work.

We are convinced that there are at least as many different ways of teaching the accounting systems course as there are professors teaching it. Therefore, this book was designed to be flexible. In a junior- or senior-level course, the book can effectively supplement any accounting information systems text currently on the market. Most of these texts are organized around business processes (or transaction cycles) that are identical or similar to the business processes we use in this book. Adopters of this book's earlier editions have used it successfully with many different accounting information systems texts. This edition of the textbook includes more emphasis in four areas: (1) designing elements of database accounting systems, (2) discussion and implantation of internal controls, (3) creating queries to produce financial statement information, and (4) integrating individual business processes to create a comprehensive accounting system. Some instructors have used this book as the main course text, supplementing it with readings from the current literature on internal control and systems design, though the emphasis on these areas in the current edition will likely reduce instructors' need to supplement these areas. Instructors have incorporated the book into their courses in various ways. Some cover all or part of the book in class. Others assign the book as a series of computer lab assignments or as outside reading.

Many accounting systems courses include some type of systems design project. A number of instructors have used earlier editions of this book as an effective springboard for such projects. Students can extend the book's examples or use them as analogs for the real-world systems they design and build in their projects. Students will feel better prepared to take on the challenge of a systems design project after they have experienced successes with creating the example integrated accounting system in this book.

Although we designed this book to meet the needs of the undergraduate accounting major systems class, it is flexible enough to be used in other settings. Many community colleges now offer a computer accounting course. This book would serve well as either the main text or a supplement in such a course. Instructors of graduate accounting systems courses may wish to assign this book as a project for those students who lack undergraduate systems course work or for those students whose undergraduate systems exposure is dated. Instructors of information systems auditing courses at the graduate level have also found the book to be a useful supplement in those courses. The book includes a number of features that will make your teaching easier:

- *A concise introduction to database theory that includes thorough discussions of normalization and entity-relationship modeling.*
- *An exposition of the database approach to accounting systems that includes a comparison to double-entry bookkeeping procedures.*
- *Step-by-step instructions in all chapters that guide the student through each example.*
- *Numerous figures that show the computer screen at key points in each task and that show finished forms and printed reports.*
- *A Companion Web site that contains tables, files, queries, forms, reports, and other information to help students complete the exercises and follow along with the examples in the text.*

We have taken special care to include database tables, forms, queries, and reports so that students can use any chapter independently of other chapters. You will find that many of the tables include comprehensive examples of significant size. By including these very large tables, we hope to give students an experience that resembles working with real-world databases.

An Instructor's Manual is available to adopters. It includes detailed lecture suggestions for each chapter and solutions to all end-of-chapter questions and exercises. The Instructor's Manual also indicates where instructors can go on the Web to get support, including a solution database for each chapter, which contains solutions to all computer exercises in the form of Microsoft Access tables, forms, queries, and reports. Other materials available on the protected instructors' resource Web site include the text of the Instructor's Manual in both Microsoft Word 2007 and Adobe PDF formats, to help you create customized lecture notes, transparencies, and presentation software slide shows for classroom use.

Organization of the Book

The text contains eleven chapters. The first six chapters introduce Microsoft Access and basic database modeling. The next five chapters show students how to use the database theory and tools from the earlier chapters to design, build, and integrate functional accounting system database elements.

Chapter 1 familiarizes students with the Microsoft Access database management system. The chapter illustrates all major database elements, including tables, queries, forms, and reports. Chapter 2 presents a brief history of databases; describes the requirements for databases to be in first, second, and third normal forms; and describes how database accounting differs from double-entry bookkeeping and why firms are using database accounting systems. Chapter 3 provides students with hands-on experience in building and populating database tables. Chapter 4 describes the role of queries in an accounting system. Chapter 5 contains a thorough discussion about designing and building Access forms for data entry, modification, and viewing. Chapter 6 describes Access reports, which can be used to supply management with hard copy output.

The next five chapters of the book show students how to apply the tools and techniques from the first six chapters to the specific tasks of designing and building accounting system elements for a single company. We use four business processes to organize these four chapters: sales/collection, acquisition/payment, human resources, and financing. The four individual business process chapters are preceded by a chapter on data modeling—Chapter 7. In this chapter, students learn a design methodology that employs a set of common elements that students can use to design and implement any business process. The first section of each of the four business process chapters begins with a description of the example company's business process and provides step-by-step instructions to construct a data model using an entity-relationship diagram. We expanded the data model feature in this edition in response to requests from many users of previous editions.

We define the sales/collection process to include cash receipts and the acquisition/payment process to include cash disbursements. Chapter 8 shows students how to track customer information, sale orders, sales, and cash receipts in the sales/collection process. In Chapter 9, students get to see the acquisition/payment process as a mirror image of the sales/collection process. They learn how to track vendor information and record purchase orders, receipt of goods ordered, and cash disbursements. They also become aware of integration issues by using and sometimes altering tables that are common to both business processes. Chapter 10, the payroll portion of the human resources process, is another place where we increased our coverage. The data model includes work schedule and labor operation tables to increase student knowledge of a complete payroll system (even though these elements are not included in the example company's database). We also show students how to compute withholding allowances based on the current gross pay to increase the realism of the example. In Chapter 11, the final business process chapter, we chose to cover the financing process instead of the conversion process so that we can show students a complete accounting system for a merchandising firm. Because financing includes separate sets of events for both debt financing and equity financing, it provides more opportunities to discuss system integration issues.

When Chapter 11 is completed, students will have a comprehensive accounting system. Because students produce financial statement information related to each business process, instructors can extend the textbook database by having students generate external financial reports such as income statements and balance sheets. This will require students to apply their knowledge to derive financial statement queries that are not in the textbook. These queries will span multiple business processes and will derive financial statement information such as cash balances, ending inventory, cost of goods sold, and retained earnings.

In addition to the 11 chapters in the textbook, we provide a capstone chapter online after publication as a special web enrichment module. This module includes financial statement queries that span multiple business processes as well as financial statement reports.

Paths Through the Book

You can follow several paths through the book. Chapters 1 and 2 should be read first. Chapter 1 is a great introduction to Access without requiring students to create anything on their own, and it is a good place to start. Chapter 2 establishes the link between database systems and accounting systems and helps students to understand that linkage early on. Chapter 3 should be read next, because tables are the fundamental building block of all database systems upon which other database objects—queries, forms, and reports—depend. Chapter 4 probably should be next, because forms and reports optionally can depend on the existence of queries as their foundation. Chapters 5 and 6 need not be read in that order. However, it is important to read the first six chapters *before* reading later chapters.

Many instructors will want to cover all of the business process chapters, assigning Chapters 7, 8, 9, and 10 in sequence. Some instructors prefer to focus on one or two business processes each semester. Chapters 7, 8, and 9 are ideal candidates for such a focus. Chapter 7 introduces students to data modeling, and Chapters 8 and 9, the sales/collection and acquisition/payment processes, are the most common and straightforward of the businesses processes to design and build. You can go directly to Chapter 10 from Chapter 7 if you wish. Although Chapters 10 and 11 can be used without first working through Chapters 8 or 9, students will find Chapters 10 and 11 easier if they have first worked through Chapter 8 or 9.

Acknowledgments

Creating a successful book is always a collaborative effort between the authors and publisher. We work as a team to provide the best book possible. We would like to thank the many professors who have used previous editions in their classes and have provided us with valuable insights and suggestions for this edition.

The authors especially want to acknowledge the work of the professionals at Cengage. We extend special thanks to Matt Filimonov, our acquisitions editor, and to the other members of the Accounting Team at Cengage. We appreciate the care and attention to detail with which everyone at Cengage handled the development and production of this edition.

If you would like to contact us about the book, we would enjoy hearing from you. We welcome comments and suggestions that we might incorporate into future editions of the book. For the latest information about Building Accounting Systems and related resources, please visit our Web site, www.cengage.com/accounting/perry.

We hope our textbook is error free, but that is rarely the case with any textbook. If you wish to report any errors that you find in the textbook, then please do the following:

- *Give the page number and the location on the page (for example, "page 347, 21st line from the top").*
- *Write an explanation for the correction with any screen shots if they help explain the error.*
- *E-mail the preceding information to: PerryErrata@gmail.com*

Trademark List

The following trademarks and registered trademarks appear in this book:

1. Microsoft, Windows, Access, Word, Excel, Exchange, Internet Explorer, Office, and The Microsoft Network are registered trademarks of Microsoft Corporation. Any reference to Microsoft Windows, Access, Word, Excel, Exchange, Internet Explorer, Office, or The Microsoft Network refers to this note.
2. Adobe is a registered trademark of Adobe Systems Incorporated. Any references to Adobe refer to this note.

About the Authors

Jim Perry is a Professor of Information Systems in the School of Business at the University of San Diego. He is the author or co-author of over 80 textbooks and trade books and over a dozen articles on computer security, database management systems, multimedia delivery systems, and chief programmer teams. Jim is a charter member of the Association for Information Systems. He holds a Ph.D. in computer science from the Pennsylvania State University and a Bachelor of Science in mathematics from Purdue University. Jim has worked as a computer security consultant to various private and governmental organizations, including the Jet Propulsion Laboratory. He was a consultant on the Strategic Defense Initiative ("Star Wars") project and served as a member of the computer security oversight committee.

Rick Newmark is a Professor of Accounting in the Kenneth W. Monfort College of Business at the University of Northern Colorado. He is the author or co-author of over a dozen articles and three dozen presentations on accounting information systems, teaching pedagogy, distance learning, technology in the classroom, and taxation. Rick has served on the Board of the AIS Educators Association for the past six years and is currently Research Committee Chair for the American Accounting Association's Strategic and Emerging Technology Section. He holds a Ph.D. in accounting from the University of Miami, a Master of Science in Taxation from the University of Miami, and a Bachelor of Science in Finance from the University of Florida. Rick has worked as a CPA for international and local CPA firms prior to entering academia.

CHAPTER 1

Introduction to Microsoft Access

CHAPTER OBJECTIVES

This chapter introduces you to using the Microsoft Office Access database. You will use existing databases to browse data, use Microsoft Access menus, and create several types of information forms. The purpose of this chapter is to provide you a level footing in using Access. If you have used Microsoft Access extensively, then you can skip this chapter. Important topics covered in this chapter include:

- **Understanding the Access work environment.**
- **Creating and using Access objects including tables, queries, forms, and reports.**
- **Customizing the Access environment.**
- **Opening and displaying tables.**
- **Retrieving information with queries.**
- **Modifying tables' contents with action queries.**
- **Creating and using forms to display data.**
- **Designing and using database reports.**

The backdrop application we use for this chapter is a database for a small bakery that specializes in cheesecakes and muffins. The database illustrates how a typical business organization uses a database to manipulate and store crucial business information. The fictitious business, called the Incredible Cheesecake Company, maintains tables, forms, queries, and reports about customers, invoices, bakery products that they make fresh daily, and shipping companies that deliver their products. More importantly, this chapter demonstrates the central role of databases to track and maintain critical business information and economic events.

Introduction

Modern computer-based systems, including most accounting systems, have a database system. An accounts receivable program, for example, frequently stores its information in a special system known as a database. The information is subsequently extracted, summarized, and displayed by a program especially adept at storing, organizing, and quickly retrieving facts that are stored in a database. Such systems are known as database management systems.

What Is Microsoft Office Access?

You will study and use one such database management system written for microcomputers, called Microsoft Office Access. Once you learn the fundamentals of Microsoft Office Access, you will be able to create your own accounting systems with this powerful database system. (In this textbook, we usually use the shorthand term "Access" rather than the longer term "Microsoft Office Access.")

What Is a Relational Database?

Access is a relational database management system. A relational database system is founded on the rules, created and published by Dr. E. F. Codd that collectively defines a relational database management system. Of the several database management system types, the relational database management systems are the most widely used today. We will uncover some of Codd's rules for relational database systems in upcoming chapters.

The fundamental storage entity for a relational database system is easy to visualize—it is a two-dimensional object having rows and columns called a table. A table holds data, and each row corresponds to one instance of data. Each of a table's columns corresponds to a different characteristic, called an *attribute*. For example, consider a table holding employee information. A particular row of the table represents an individual employee. There are as many rows in an employee table as there are employees in the company, its divisions, or its departments. The employee table's columns typically contain employees' first names, last names, hire dates, social security numbers, genders, birth dates, and so on. Each column holds only one type of data. For instance, a given column always contains employees' hire dates and nothing else; another column holds only employees' last names. Never are these two mixed together in one column, for instance.

A database usually has more than one table. For instance, an employee table might be only one of several tables that collectively describe a company's employees, their skills, and products they sell or manufacture. In other words, a collection of tables that are related and collectively describe an entity is known as a database. You can imagine that an accounts receivable database contains many tables that are related to one another: a customer table, a salesperson table, an inventory table (you sell goods from inventory), and so on. Although most databases contain several tables, the terms *database* and *table* frequently are used interchangeably. *Flat file* is the term given for a database consisting of one table—a very rare occurrence in business.

Most databases used in business and government are large, often consisting of hundreds of tables containing thousands and even millions of rows each. We will not subject you to such a large system in our examples or exercises. However, our databases do contain more than one table, and some of those tables have several hundred rows. Manipulating several, larger tables will give you an idea of what real corporate databases entail. The reason for using multiple tables to represent related information will become clear as you continue to read.

To better understand the concept of tables and their relationships, begin by launching Access and looking at a few tables we have prepared.

Starting Microsoft Access

To use Access, you must execute or launch it. Often, Access is represented as an icon on the computer screen desktop or in the Start menu. An alternative way to launch Access in Windows XP, for example, when icons are absent is to click Start, click Run, type *Msaccess.exe*, and press Enter. Launch Access now using its representative icon or the Run dialog box as described here.

The *Getting Started with Microsoft Access* window appears (see Figure 1.1). In the left panel are local and remote Access database templates from which you can choose when creating a new database. The middle section of the window shows a blank database option at the top and graphical representations of specific types of empty databases with predefined tables. In the right panel are a list of recently opened databases and paths to them for the computer you are using. At the top of the list is a "More..." hyperlink that displays, when clicked, the Open dialog box showing files on your computer. In the upper-right corner of the window is a question mark icon. That opens Access help. Take a moment to examine the *Getting Started with Microsoft Access* window (the *Getting Started* window, for short) shown in Figure 1.1.

Fig. 1.1 Getting Started with Microsoft Access opening window.

Obtaining Help

It is important to know how to get help when you get stuck or would just like to know more about a particular aspect of Access. Let's see what help is available on creating forms. Make sure the *Getting Started with Microsoft Access* window is active, and then do the following exercise.

EXERCISE 1.1: DISPLAYING HELP

1. Click the question mark (help) icon in the upper-right corner (or press the F1 function key). The Access Help dialog box opens.
2. Click Forms in the list of topics.
3. Click Create a form from the list of topics. Help about creating forms. Scroll through the topic to familiarize yourself with using help (see Figure 1.2).
4. After you have examined the help screen for a moment, click the Close button (the X) on the Access Help title bar.

Printing Help

Occasionally, you may wish to jot down some especially important information you found in Help. You can print a help screen. By printing a few of the important help screens, you will have a handy reference within easy reach—even if you aren't near a computer. Once you have located the help screen you want to print, click the Help page Print button (see Figure 1.2), then select a printer, determine whether you want to print the entire help page(s) or a smaller number of pages, and click the Print button. Windows prints the help screen information. That is all there is to it.

Exiting Access

After completing all of your database work, you should always exit Access. If you are using a database stored on a removable memory device such as a thumb drive, it is especially important to remember to exit Access before removing the memory device. Otherwise, you risk losing data. Exiting Access signals the program to do its housekeeping chores such as posting any changes you have made to your database on your disk, closing other information sources, and returning to Windows. Click the Exit icon (the X) in the Access title bar. Access quickly closes any open databases and returns to Windows. (If you have Access open on the "Getting Started…" window, keep it open for exercises that follow. If not, then launch Access.)

Fig. 1.2 **Displaying help on a particular topic.**

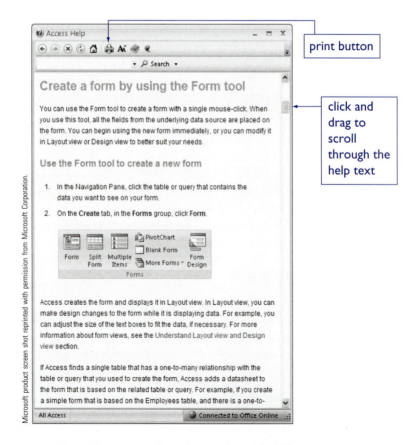

Examining the Access Environment

With the Getting Started window displayed, let's open the database associated with Chapter 1 as we describe the database environment further. Follow the steps in Exercise 1.2. *Note:* When you open an Access database, it often displays a Security Warning bar above the database window and Navigation Pane. Click the *Options* button and then click the *Enable this content* radio button to allow otherwise blocked content. You have to do this each time you open a database. Step 4 in Exercise 1.2 reminds you to do this.

EXERCISE 1.2: OPENING THE CHAPTER 1 DATABASE

1. If necessary, launch Access to display the Getting Started window.
2. Click the More... hyperlink in the *Open Recent Database* panel on the right side of the screen.
3. In the Open dialog box, locate the supplied database Ch01.accdb by using the Look in list box. Click the database Ch01.accdb name in the Open panel (the "accdb" extension may not appear if your system has that file extension display option turned off), and click the Open button. The database opens and probably displays a security warning in a bar above the list of database objects.
4. Click the Options button appearing in the Security Warning message, click the Enable this content radio button, and click OK to permit full access to the database and dispatch the warning bar.

Access Work Surface

The Microsoft database interface is vastly improved in its Access 2007 product. After some practice with the new interface, you probably will agree that it is more intuitive and easier to use. The interface consists of the Access ribbon, the Navigation Pane, the Quick Access Toolbar, and the large, open window in which objects are displayed in full view. Notice that the Access title bar displays the custom title "Incredible Cheesecake Company (Chapter 1)." Setting an application title into the Access title bar is one of the options available when you click the Office button and the click Access Options. We'll describe more about that option later.

The Access Ribbon

Access provides a ribbon interface, also known as *Office fluent* interface, displaying commands through a tabbed interface. The ribbon occupies the top portion of the main Access screen. It replaces menus and toolbars from Access 2003 and earlier versions, and it simplifies working with Access. The ribbon contains command tabs. Each command tab contains command *groups*, and the groups contain individual controls. Figure 1.3 shows the Home tab selected and open—the default when you open a database. The Home tab contains the groups *Views, Clipboard, Font, Rich Text, Records, Sort & Filter,* and *Find.* These groups allow different views of the database, allow you to modify display characteristics via the Font group, provide record sorting and filtering tools, and allow you to do search and replace operations on data. Other tabs contain different groups. Instead of explaining the use of the various tabs and groups, we defer that discussion until we actually use them.

There are a couple of shortcuts that help you manage the interface. Press Alt+F11 (press and hold down the Alt key and then tap the F11 function key) to collapse the Access ribbon when you want more screen real estate. Tap the shortcut again to

Fig. 1.3 The Access Ribbon interface and the Chapter 1 database.

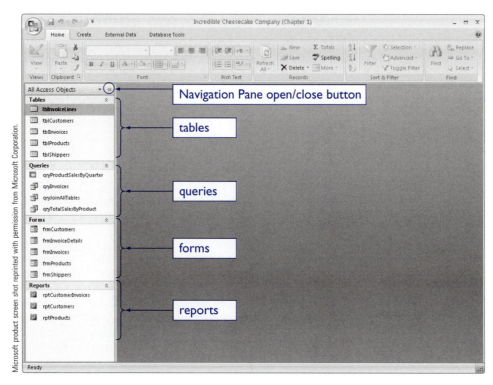

display the ribbon. The Alt+F11 sequence is a *toggle*. To quickly open the tabs on the ribbon, move the mouse into the ribbon and scroll the mouse wheel.

Understanding the Navigation Pane

On the left side of the database window is the Navigation Pane. The Navigation Pane is your primary tool for switching between Access objects. It is the main location from which you open tables, modify queries, run reports, display forms, and perform other operations on your database objects. The Navigation Pane replaces the Database window from earlier Access versions. At the top in the upper-right corner of the Navigation Pane is the Open/Close button. When you need more screen space in the open window, click the Open/Close button to reduce the Navigation Pane. Only its shutter bar appears. To reopen the Navigation Pane, click its shutter bar.

The Navigation Pane in Figure 1.3 shows database objects grouped by object type. At the top of the Navigation Pane are the database's tables; beneath tables are all the queries followed by forms. Reports are at the bottom of the database's Navigation Pane in this example. You can organize the Navigation Pane with *categories*, and you can filter what appears in the categories with *groups*. You can create custom categories in the Navigation Pane by clicking on the drop-down list in the Navigation Pane's title bar to reveal its options (see Figure 1.4). The options are *Custom, Object Type*, and *Tables and Related Views*. When open, the Navigation Pane indicates the current choices with check marks.

Custom. This creates a new tab in the Navigation Pane that you can rename from its default Custom Group 1 to any meaningful name. Drag and drop objects into the custom group to populate it. Custom groups are particularly handy when you want to group together tables, queries, and other objects that logically belong together. For example,

Fig. 1.4 Customization options for the Navigation Pane.

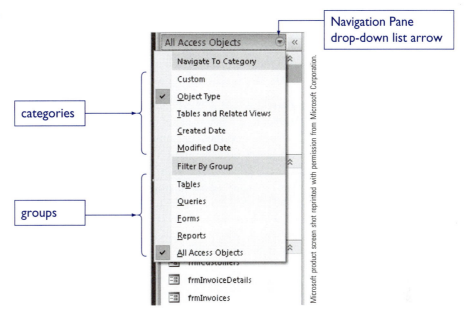

Navigation Pane drop-down list arrow

categories

groups

Microsoft product screen shot reprinted with permission from Microsoft Corporation.

you could create custom groups such as "Customers," "Products," or "Invoices" to hold tables, queries, forms, and reports related to customers, products, and so on. We'll create custom groups later to illustrate this convenient organization option.

Object Type.   The Object Type setting is the familiar grouping available in earlier versions of Access. It is the organization displayed in Figure 1.3 in which objects are grouped together by type: Tables, then Queries, and so on.

Tables and Related Views.   This setting automatically groups queries, forms, and reports with the tables on which they depend. Figure 1.5 shows an example of the Chapter 1

Fig. 1.5 *Tables and Related Views* option.

Microsoft product screen shot reprinted with permission from Microsoft Corporation.

database objects grouped by its tables and the objects, in each group, referring to their respective tables. For example, the objects under the *tblProducts* group name include the like-named table, four queries, two forms, and two reports (*rptCustomerInvoices* and *rptProducts*). This view of database objects reveals the relationships between objects. Prior to Access 2007, it was difficult to determine inter-object relationships.

Created Date and Modified Date. These two views, although handy, are not emphasized in this text. They permit you to group objects by their creation or latest modification dates. We find these options of marginal value and will discuss them no further.

While categories organize the Navigation Pane, groups, headed by the title "Filter By Group" in the Navigation Pane, let you filter the categorized items. With the default "Object Type" category selected, you can click Tables, Queries, Forms, or Reports to display only Tables, Queries, Forms, or Reports, respectively. The *All Access Objects* choice displays all objects. Hiding selected groups is simple. Simply click a group's header to hide its contents. Click again to display it. For example, clicking an open Tables group hides all its members. Clicking it again reveals them. Hiding or displaying selected groups in the Navigation Pane gives you more control over whether or not objects' names are listed in the Navigation Pane.

Setting Access Options

Although you may not need to do much with the look and feel of the Access program, it is handy to ensure that we all have the same view of our objects throughout this book. So, we'll examine a few database options that affect the entire Access database and ensure that selected options are set.

You can customize Access, itself, by clicking the Office button and then clicking the Access Options button. The Access Options dialog box contains a large number of Access database options, compartmentalized into 10 categories. The next exercise ensures that your view of the Chapter 1 database is the same as you see in the figures.

EXERCISE 1.3: SETTING ACCESS OPTIONS

1. Launch Access, if necessary, and open the Ch01.accdb database accompanying this book.
2. Click the Office button, click Access Options, and click the Popular category, if needed.
3. Click the Default file format list box, and click Access 2007 (if necessary).
4. Click the Current Database category in the left panel.
5. Click the Tabbed Documents radio button, and place a check mark in the Display Document Tabs check box, if needed. Both these options are near the top of the Current Database options.
6. Click the Compact on Close check box, if needed, to place a check mark in it.
7. Click the Remove personal information from file properties on save check box to place a check mark in it (see Figure 1.6).
8. Click the OK button near bottom of the dialog box to confirm.

You may have to close and reopen Access, if directed, for the new options to take effect.

The Quick Access Toolbar

In the upper-left corner of the main Access screen and to the right of the Office Button is the Quick Access Toolbar. Remaining visible at all times, the Quick Access Toolbar is a handy toolbar in which you place icons for often-used Access commands. You can

Fig. 1.6 Changing Access options.

easily add commands that you use most frequently. In a school computing environment, the Quick Access Toolbar may be locked down so it cannot be changed or, if changed, may reset to its default three icons (Save, Undo, and Redo) when you open Access later. Let's add a couple of icons to the Quick Access Toolbar.

TRY IT

Click the *Office* button, click the *Access Options* button, click *Customize* in the left panel of the Access Options dialog box, click the *Open* icon in the Popular Commands list, and click the *Add* button. Access copies the Open command over to the list of Quick Access Toolbar commands. Add another command to the Quick Access Toolbar: Click the drop-down list beneath "Choose commands from," click *Home Tab*, drag the scroll box down until you see the Design View icon (they are in alphabetical order by toolbar). Click *Design View* and click the *Add* button in the center of the dialog box. Click *OK* to confirm your new additions to the Quick Access Toolbar. Look at your Quick Access Toolbar. It displays the two new commands to the right of the original three. Anytime you want to open a new database, simply click the Open command in the Quick Access Toolbar.

Access Objects

Access provides many ways to store, display, and report your data. The structures and methods you employ to store and display your data are called objects. Access objects include tables, queries, forms, reports, macros, and modules. (Pages disappeared in Access 2007.) This text explains how to use these objects, placing emphasis on the first four of them—tables, queries, forms, and reports. This section contains an overview of four of these six important object classes, and it shows how you can use each to build accounting information systems. The sections that follow use existing tables, queries, forms, and reports contained in the Chapter 1 database. Exploring the objects illustrates how information is organized and retrieved with a database system located at the heart of an accounting information system. At various points in the chapter, we ask you to create some small tables, short queries, simple forms, and small reports for practice.

Tables

Tables are the fundamental storage structures for data and the *only* place where data is stored in the database management system. Tables are two-dimensional objects with columns and rows. Each row contains all available information about a particular item. (We use the term *record* interchangeably with *row*.) All rows contain exactly the same number of columns, although not every column of every row necessarily has a value. Sometimes an entry is empty. An empty value is called *null* in database parlance. Null values are very important and indicate a value is "not known."

Consider a table holding customer information. A small company having 67 customers stores customer data—name, address, credit limit, and so on—in table. Each customer column would be a particular information field. (The terms *field* and *column* are used synonymously in this and other texts.) Each column contains one type (or category) of information. For instance, one column contains each customer's street address; another column holds each customer's company name, and yet another column holds each customer's city and state. Figure 1.7 shows an example of a small Access table that stores customer data. (Some columns are resized to make their column names and values completely visible.) The main difference between this customer table and an industrial-strength table is size—most customer tables contain thousands, if not millions, of rows. Moreover, customer data tables usually have many columns. This example is purposefully small so you can understand the principles of database tables without the added complexity of large data volumes.

Fig. 1.7 Example table containing fundamental customer data.

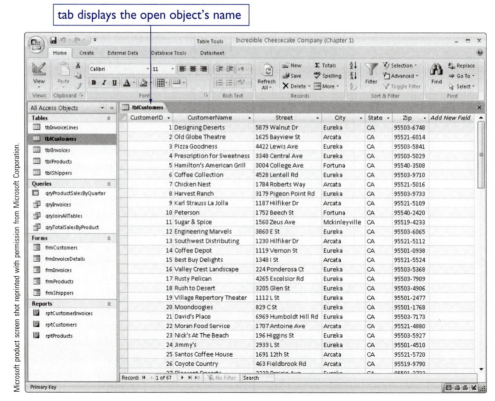

Observe that each column holds only one type of data. This is an important rule to keep in mind when you create your own tables. Each row contains information about a customer, and only one customer's data is stored in a given row. Although the customer table contains only integer and character data, Access tables can hold Memo, Date/Time, Currency, AutoNumber, Yes/No, OLE Object, Hyperlink, and Attachment data types. (We'll discuss these in detail later.)

At the top of each column is the column's name, called an ***attribute***, which uniquely identifies a column. Each row corresponds to one customer. A row is indivisible. That is, the data in a row remains with the row, even if the rows are sorted or displayed in a different order. Though the rows are unsorted, they can be organized into a more meaningful arrangement whenever necessary. This is one of the advantages of a relational database system: the order of rows in a table is unimportant. In other words, you do not have to be worried about inputting data into a table in an orderly way. No row is more important than another.

The order of table columns is unimportant also. They are placed in an arbitrary order left to right. We have designed the *tblCustomers* table so that the customer identification number is first—a common practice places a row's unique identification as the first column, though doing so is *not* required. In other words, no implicit meaning or significance exists in the columns' arrangement. The field *CustomerID* contains mutually unique values. No two customers share the same identification number. This type of field is called a table's ***primary key***. You will learn more about primary keys later.

Queries

There are several types of queries, but the most common query is called a ***selection query***. A selection query is a question you can ask about your database. (Because selection queries are the most commonly used type, they are simply called ***queries***.) For instance, a query stated in English is "Which customers live in Fortuna, CA?" or "Which customers' invoices are over 60 days past due?" (The latter query cannot be answered with only one table. We'll have to connect it to another table to answer that question.) Queries are especially helpful for combining information from several related tables into a single, cohesive result. Queries also provide a way to reduce the data volume by returning and displaying only the subset of table rows in which you are interested. You can use queries to summarize data, displaying only the aggregate results. For instance, you can ask Access to total all outstanding invoices from an invoice table (stored in the table *tblInvoices* shown in Figure 1.7). Other types of queries insert new data into a table, delete unwanted data from a table, or change values in one or more table columns. Queries facilitate selecting which tables are the subjects of your questions, designating the columns you would like to see, and specifying which table rows to fetch.

The structure of a query is called its ***design***. The query result, called the ***dynaset***, is displayed in a Query window. Figure 1.8 shows an example of a query's design and its dynaset, each in its own window. (You have to change the *Document Window Options* value to "Overlapping Windows" to permit multiple, overlapping windows. However, it is best to not change that option on your computer.) Only the columns appearing in the query design show in the dynaset. Check marks (two of them in this example) in the query grid's *Show* row prescribe which columns appear in the dynaset. The second field is actually an expression that totals sales by unique product name and rounds the result to two decimal places. The *Sort* row in the second column of the query design contains "Descending," which means the results are sorted in high to low order on the field values. The expression >8765, called a ***selection criterion***, filters the rows thereby restricting returned rows to those that meet the conditions specified by the criteria—in this case, rows whose total sales value is greater than $8765.

Fig. 1.8 Example query and dynaset.

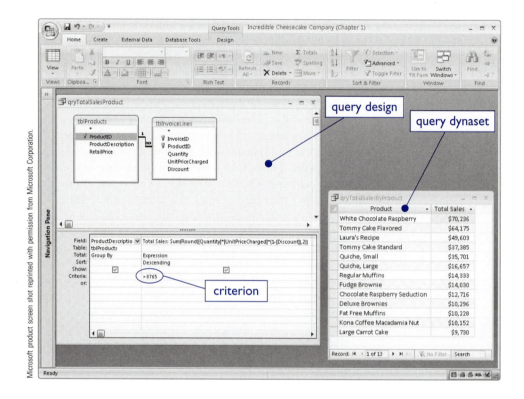

Forms

Frequently, it is better to work with table data one row at a time. Tables are not an intuitive interface for many people, especially those who are not accustomed to working with databases. Access forms solve this problem. Forms display data from a table or a query in a format that is easier to understand. You can see one row or many rows of a table. Figure 1.9 shows an example of a form displaying the customer information, from the table *tblCustomer*, in an attractive and intuitive layout.

A form may be an easier way to view and change data stored in your databases. One of several records appears in the form. You can move to the next record, the previous record, or the first or last record by clicking the navigation buttons located in the lower-left corner of the window. You can move directly to a specific record by pressing F5, typing a record number, and pressing Enter. The single, right-pointing arrow button moves one record at a time, displaying the next record in the form. The right-pointing arrow button with a vertical line to its right moves directly to the last record. The opposite actions take place for the left-pointing navigation buttons. The words *Primary key* appearing in the lower-left corner are text that was typed in the comment column of the underlying table when it was created. Comments in the table can provide helpful information to users about the highlighted field of a form.

Reports

Imagine trying to show several people in a meeting a financial statement displayed on your notebook computer's screen. That would be awkward and unprofessional. Hard copy output—an Access report—is a better solution. By having reports available, you can distribute them easily to any assembled group. Access provides a comprehensive report-producing facility, and you will examine it in depth in Chapter 6.

Fig. 1.9 Example form displaying a customer's information.

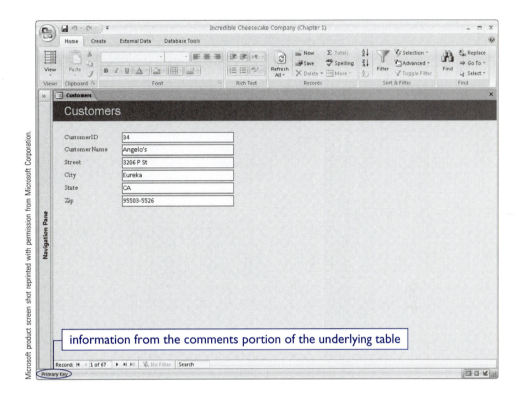

Access reports are often the most significant output produced by a database system. While it is important to store accounts receivable information in a database and to query that database for answers, an equally important activity is to produce printed results. For instance, you might want a list of all customers whose payments are over 60 days past due. If there are more than a few dozen of those customers, then a printed report is the most useful output. You can scan the list, marking accounts that deserve special attention. You can also make copies of a hard copy output for distribution to appropriate departments and managers.

You can use Access's report design features and tools to customize a report to look any way you would like. A report can display data from one table or from several tables that have been linked together. Figure 1.10 shows an example of a simple report containing a company logo, attractive column headings, and sorted customers grouped by city name. All of the report data comes from the customer table called *tblCustomers*. The simple report is easy to create, and the results are professional-looking. Unlike using Access, it might take several hours to create an equivalent report using a programming language such as Java or C++ and require many lines of code and programming skill to produce results.

The sections that follow describe the process of using and creating tables, queries, forms, and reports. We encourage you to participate in the exercises, because the remainder of the chapter is interactive. You will learn the most if you duplicate the steps we present and actually use and create the objects that we do. To help you in this process, we have supplied many of the required tables, queries, forms, and reports so that you can try them out. In addition, you will create a few of your own.

Fig. 1.10 Example report.

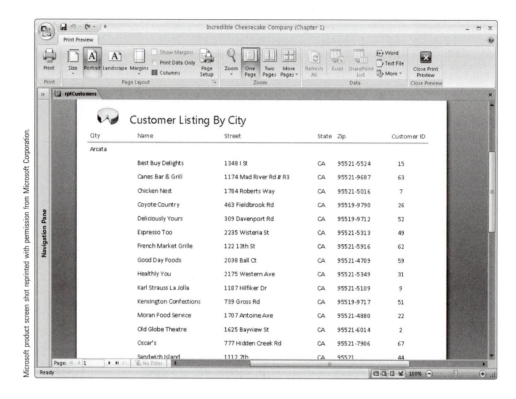

Working with Databases and Tables

The foundation of any database system rests on its tables. Tables hold the data that is transformed into information. In this section you will learn how to use tables that we have provided, create your own tables, modify the order in which table columns are displayed, and link tables together.

The only database you'll need to complete the in-text exercises in this chapter you have already located and opened: Ch01.accdb. It is available as a download from the publisher's Web site (South-Western Cengage Learning). The Web location of files and other digital materials are found in this book's preface. You can choose to create a brand new database from scratch, create a database from several of Microsoft's supplied templates, or open an existing database from the *Getting Started with Microsoft Office Access* window. First, let's briefly examine templates.

Using Microsoft's Database Templates

When the initial Access welcome screen appears when you launch Access, it displays local and online templates in the left panel headed by the label "Template Categories." The online templates change from time to time as Microsoft updates and adds to the collection. Templates provide partially complete database solutions to common applications such as assets tracking, inventory control, marketing projects, and so on. The templates contain prebuilt tables without data and other objects such as forms and reports to accompany the base tables. It is instructive to look at an example of one of the supplied, local database templates before moving on. In preparation for this next exercise, close any open databases and launch Access, if necessary.

EXERCISE 1.4: USING A MICROSOFT-SUPPLIED TEMPLATE

1. Click Local Templates in the *Template Categories* panel, and then click Assets in the *Featured Online Templates* section.
2. Click the folder icon the right of the File Name text box and then use the Save in list box of the File New Database dialog box to navigate to a folder on your computer where you want to store the database.
3. Change the suggested database name from *Assets*, if you wish, and then click the Create button. Access builds and opens the new database and displays the Asset List form.
4. Click the Navigation Pane shutter, if needed, to open it (see Figure 1.11).
5. Double click any objects you want in the Navigation Pane to open them in the tabbed interface.
6. Right-click any tab in the database window, and click Close All to close all the open windows.
7. Click the Microsoft Office button and then click Exit Access to close Access.

Fig. 1.11 Assets database.

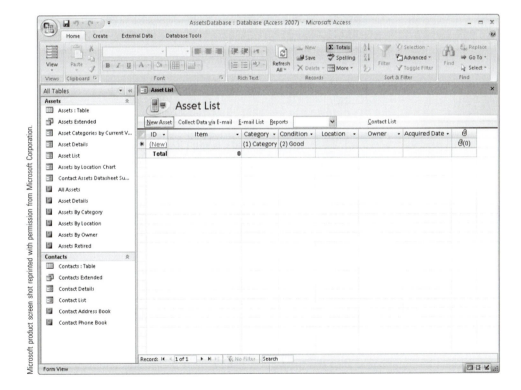

Microsoft product screen shot reprinted with permission from Microsoft Corporation.

You may wish to explore the Microsoft online databases also. If so, then open Access and click any of the template categories in the left panel under the *From Microsoft Office Online* heading. One particularly useful online database is the ubiquitous Northwind 2007 database. It is a rich, full database containing tables with hundreds of rows, more than 19 tables, more than 30 forms and subforms, and many reports. You can learn a lot about Access databases by perusing the content, structure, and implementation of the fully functioning Northwind database. We suggest you download and save it.

Opening a Database

Once you have created a database, you can close it and later reopen it to make changes or simply run reports. Access stores all the objects of a particular database—tables, queries, forms, and reports—within one file. The Microsoft Access database management system fetches and stores information in whichever database is open, but only one Access database may be open at a time.

EXERCISE 1.5: OPENING THE CHAPTER 1 DATABASE

1. Launch Access; click the More... hyperlink in the *Open Recent Database* panel (see Figure 1.1 from earlier in the chapter).
2. Click the Look in list box, and navigate to the disk drive and folder containing Ch01 (see Figure 1.12).
3. In the large list box displaying folder names and file names, click Ch01, and click the Open button. (Alternatively, you can double-click the database file name to open it.) Microsoft Access displays the Ch01 Database window (see Figure 1.3).

Fig. 1.12 Open dialog box.

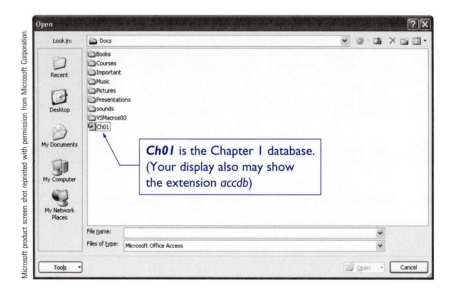

Microsoft product screen shot reprinted with permission from Microsoft Corporation.

In the Navigation Pane, Access 2007 displays objects in categories such as Tables, Queries, Forms, and Reports. Within each category objects are sorted by their names. If the Navigation pane is closed, then click its shutter to open it. You can drag the right edge of the Navigation Pane to widen it to reveal longer object names.

Creating a Backup of an Access Database

As a matter of safe computing, you should regularly back up your database to provide protection against data loss and other inadvertent mistakes. A backed-up database provides protection such as system failures and mistakes that the usually reliable Undo command cannot fix. Examples of instances where Undo will not work are following any of the several action queries whose job it is to modify table data. Modified table data, except for row-at-a-time modifications, are not reversible with a simple Undo command. However, if you have a backup, you can simply restore the damaged table from its backup copy. (You will learn how in a later chapter when the Import and Export commands are described.)

Besides providing protection from data loss, database backups serve as a convenient way to save your database in a different folder after you open it. More times than we can count, people create a new database in its default location and then cannot find it later. By simply opening it and then creating a backup in a known location provides a convenient database-level "save as" command. If you want to practice the steps, follow these steps. Otherwise, simply read the steps.

TRY IT

Click the *Microsoft Office Button*, point to *Manage* in the pop-up menu, and click *Back Up Database*. The *Save As* dialog box opens. In the *Save in* list box, navigate to the disk and folder where you want to copy your database. Optionally, change the name of your database file in the *File name* list box. However, the suggested database name captures the original database name and date stamp. That's convenient. Finally, click the *Save* button to save the database in the new location.

Looking at Data through Different Tabs

Access provides several ways to view your data. You can inspect your data in a Table, which displays data in columns and rows called a Datasheet view—just like a spreadsheet's data. Or you can use a Form to display one or more rows in a nontabular format. Forms provide an attractive way to view and change data, because they can be designed to resemble paper forms with which you are already familiar. New to Access is the ability to view data through a split form. A ***split form*** displays a Datasheet table view in one half of the screen and a form in the other half. Moving from one record to another in one window of the split causes the data in the other window to move automatically. Alternatively, you can view your data in a report format with the Report. Reports provide a preview so that you can review a report prior to printing it.

Because each view usually opens in separate tabbed windows, you can review multiple objects simply by clicking the appropriate tab. Figure 1.13 shows the table *tblProducts* contents displayed as in Datasheet view on the *tblProducts* tab, as a form on the *frmProducts* tab, and in a report on the *rptProducts* tab. Of course, you click each tab to open the respective view, or you can set the Access option to display document windows in *Overlapping Windows* to see multiple views simultaneously. The older overlapping window views often lead to confusion when windows obscured other views, so we favor the cleaner and easier to navigate *Tabbed Documents* database window organization.

The Chapter 1 database contains information about a San Diego bakery that produces cheesecakes and related baked goods. The small database consists of five interrelated tables: customers (*tblCustomers*), invoices (*tblInvoices*), invoice detail lines (*tblInvoiceLines*), products (*tblProducts*), and shipping companies (*tblShippers*). Throughout this text, we follow the object naming convention that all tables begin with the prefix *tbl* (followed immediately by the rest of the object name). Queries begin with *qry*, forms begin with *frm*, and reports begin with *rpt*. The customers table contains information about 67 customers (companies, really) that purchase products from the Incredible Cheesecake Company. The invoice table contains master information about each invoice including the date, the company, selected shipper, and so on. Linked to the invoice table is the invoice detail lines table. Each row in the invoice detail lines table (or simply, invoice lines table) contains the item ordered, the quantity, the price charged, and any applicable discount. The shippers table contains a small list of four typical shippers. (We have

Fig. 1.13 Product inventory objects in datasheet, form, and report tabs.

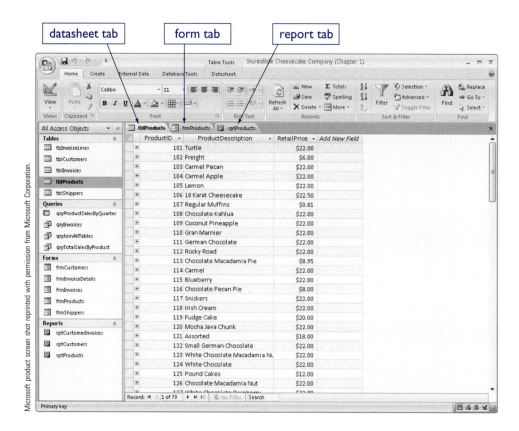

included only the names of the shippers and omitted phone and address information for them in the interest of simplicity. Such information is based on location and highly variable anyway.) The products table contains a list of the 79 products that the Incredible Cheesecake Company sells. Figure 1.14 shows the relationships among the five tables in the database. They appear in the Relationships window. All the tables and the connections between them are added manually. You will learn later how to establish these permanent, inter-table relationships.

All of these tables are smaller than those encountered in a database for a typical business. We want you to comprehend the process of extracting meaningful information from the data, not marvel at the size of the database. It is easier to understand database concepts using several small tables. Therefore, we have limited the number of rows in these tables but kept them sufficiently large to be interesting. We begin our active, hands-on exploration of Access by examining the use of Access tables, the elemental building block of all database applications.

Opening a Table

The most fundamental building block of a database—and the only one that actually contains data—is the table. We begin by examining tables. When you open a table, it appears in the Datasheet window, also called the *Access work area*. The Datasheet view displays data in rows and columns, much like a spreadsheet. There are several ways to open a table, and the best method is a matter of personal taste. You can open any object, including tables, by using any of these methods: (1) Double-click any object's name in the Navigation Pane to open it in the Access work area; (2) right-click any object's name and click Open from the pop-up menu; or (3) click and drag the object's name to the Access work area.

Fig. 1.14 Table relationships for the Chapter 1 database.

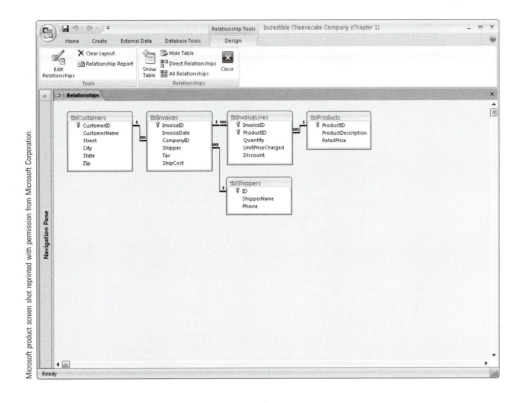

Microsoft product screen shot reprinted with permission from Microsoft Corporation.

It's easier to understand this process if you open an existing table and experience firsthand how some of the toolbar buttons and menus operate. In preparation for the exercise that follows, launch Access and open the Chapter 1 database. Now you are ready to follow the steps in the next exercise to open one of the tables in the database.

EXERCISE 1.6: OPENING A TABLE

1. Ensure that all database objects are categorized by type and showing by clicking the Navigation Pane list arrow and then clicking Object Type from the *Navigate to Category* group. Click the Navigation Pane list arrow again and click All Access Objects Group located at the bottom of the menu. Doing so ensures all existing access objects' names appear in the Navigation Pane.
2. If the Tables category is closed, then click the Tables shutter to open the list of tables.
3. Double-click tblCustomers in Tables category. (Alternatively, you can right-click *tblCustomers* and click Open in the pop-up menu.) Access opens the customers table in Datasheet view and displays a new command tab on the ribbon—Datasheet (see Figure 1.15).

Take a moment to examine the customers table. Notice the Datasheet navigation buttons located in the Navigation bar found at the bottom edge of the Table window. The ribbon contains a *contextual command tab* called *Datasheet*. (A contextual command tab appears when selected windows are selected and only then.) It is context sensitive and therefore available only while a table is displayed in Datasheet view. Clicking the Datasheet contextual tab opens new groups on the ribbon including *Views, Fields and Columns, Data Type & Formatting,* and *Relationships*. The groups and commands that

Fig. 1.15 The
customers table in
Datasheet view.

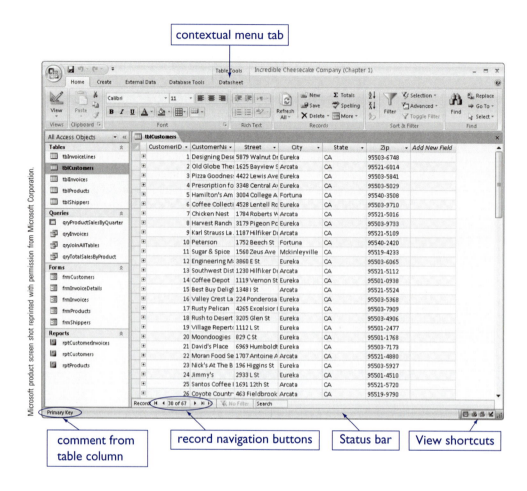

appear in the ribbon depend on the menu command tab you click. By default, the Home tab is open when you open a table in Datasheet view. Below the record navigation buttons at the bottom of the window is the Status bar. In Datasheet view, the Status bar displays any comment that is in the selected table column. Notice in Figure 1.15 that the status bar displays the string "Primary Key," because that is the comment created for the CustomerID column.

You can customize the status bar by right-clicking it and selecting the options you want. Take a moment to experiment with customizing your status bar.

TRY IT

Right-click the status bar. The *Customize Status Bar* dialog box appears. Click *Caps Lock* to remove its check mark. Click *View Shortcuts* to remove its check mark. Click outside the dialog box to close it. Notice that the shortcuts that were in the lower-right corner no longer appear. Put them back by right-clicking the status bar and then clicking *View Shortcuts*. Notice that the shortcuts reappear. (The shortcuts are convenient ways to switch between the four table views of Datasheet, PivotTable, PivotChart, and Design.)

Most ribbon tabs and groups are familiar, because they are similar to those found in the ribbon of other Windows products. Beginning on the left end of the Home tab (on the ribbon) is the View group. It contains four views mentioned in the Try It above. You can quickly switch from Datasheet view to design view by simply clicking the displayed Datasheet view icon in the View group—you need not drop down the list of views. The Clipboard group contains the familiar Cut, Copy, Paste, and Format Painter icons. The Font group contains a rich set of formatting commands allowing you to modify various display characteristics. The Rich Text group allows you to set the direction of text to be displayed from right to left or vice versa and to create bulleted and numbered lists. The Records group contains commands to add new records, delete one or more existing records, check spelling in a table, and display totals for one or more table columns at the end of the table. Sort & Filter provides ways to filter a table so it displays only records matching a set of criteria. Find contains the record find, find and replace, and go to commands.

If you prefer to use the keyboard instead of a mouse to launch commands, the ribbon interface provides a comprehensive collection of keyboard shortcuts called ***KeyTips***. To use keyboard shortcuts, press and release the Alt key. Access then displays KeyTips for each feature that is available—in this case, the tabs including the KeyTip *H* for Home, *C* for Create, and so on (see Figure 1.16). When you press a shortcut key, the keyboard shortcut keys appear for each of the commands within that command tab's groups. Figure 1.17 shows the shortcut keys for the Home tab. To cancel the action being taken and to hide the KeyTips, tap the Alt key again.

Fig. 1.16 Datasheet view tab shortcut keys.

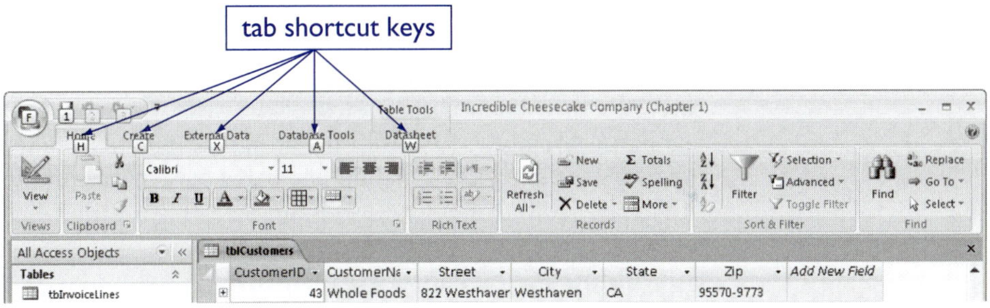

Fig. 1.17 Datasheet view group shortcut keys.

TRY IT

With the *tblCustomers* displayed in Datasheet view, press *Alt*. Tab shortcuts appear. Press *A* to open the Database Tools command tab. Press *E* to open the Relationships window. Press *Alt* to redisplay the shortcut keys on the Design context menu. Press *S* and then press *C* to close the Relationships window.

When a horizontal scroll bar appears along the bottom of the Table window, it indicates that some table columns are out of view. The scroll bar works like any other Windows scroll bar: Drag the scroll box to the right and the window pans to the right; click the scroll arrows and the window shifts for each click in the indicated direction. Vertical scroll bars appear whenever any rows of the table cannot be seen, as is frequently the case. The vertical scroll bar, located on the right side of the Table window, operates similarly to the horizontal scroll bar.

Moving around a Table

When you open an Access database table, only the first 20 plus rows display on the screen. There are several ways to move through a table to view all its rows. You can select one of the movement choices from the Go To command of the Find group on the Home tab, for example. It contains the selections: *First*, *Previous*, *Next*, *Last*, and *New*. You can also use the keyboard: the up arrow, down arrow, PgUp, and PgDn keys move up one row, down one row, up one screen, and down one screen, respectively. Perhaps the easiest way to scroll through a table's rows is to use the navigation buttons (see Figure 1.15). Left to right, the record navigation buttons move to the top of the table, up one row, to a specific numbered record (the text box in which you type a value and press Enter), down one row, to the last record in the table, or add a new row to the table. The rightmost button opens a new record that is placed immediately following the last record in the table. The *New (blank) record* button is a convenient way to add a new record to a table. Try the navigation buttons. With the customers table still displayed in a Table window, first click the *Last record* navigation button to go to the last row in the table. Then, click the *First record* navigation button to go to the first record. (We use the term *record* interchangeably with the term *row*.)

Notice that the record selector is highlighted for the currently selected row. The record selector column is to the left of the table's leftmost column (see Figure 1.15). As you move around the table with the navigation buttons, the record selector moves to another row. Pressing the right and left arrow keys moves the cursor to a different column in the same row.

Searching for a Value in a Column

Searching for a particular record in a table based on the value of one of its columns while in Datasheet view is straightforward. Though nearly half the data is visible in this small customer table example, most corporate tables contain hundreds of thousands and millions of rows. Finding a particular customer's record in such a large table would be extremely difficult without a database system. Imagine that the customer table contains many rows and you want to find the customer whose street address contains the partial word "railroad" but you do not remember the rest of the street name. Your task, in the next exercise, is to locate the customer's record. If necessary, open the table *tblCustomers*.

EXERCISE 1.7: SEARCHING FOR A ROW CONTAINING A PARTICULAR STRING

1. With the *tblCustomers* datasheet displayed, click the topmost street in the Street column. That action moves the cursor to the column you will ask Access to search.
2. Click the Home tab. Click the Find button (it looks like a pair of binoculars in the Find group on the right end of the Home ribbon) and type *railroad* in the Find What text box. Be sure to include an asterisk, a wildcard, on both ends of the string. (This allows the word *railroad* to be found anywhere in the street name.)
3. Select Down from the *Search* drop-down list.

4. Click the Find Next button to start the search process. Access searches the Street column for a match and moves the record selector to the row containing the Pizza Nova Hillcrest customer—record 48. Access highlights the street name of the first record matching the criteria.

5. Close the Find and Replace dialog box. This provides an unrestricted view of your table and the record that Access located.

6. Move the record pointer to the first record in the *tblCustomers* table by using the appropriate navigation button. Notice that the Street value in the first row is highlighted. (Leave the customer table open for the next set of steps.)

Changing a Table's Display Characteristics

You can change the visual properties of any table you are viewing. For instance, you can move table columns left or right, alter individual column display widths, remove the grid lines that separate the rows and columns, and alter fonts and their characteristics. When you make these Datasheet view changes, they do not affect the table's structure or contents. For instance, if you move a column from its current position, the underlying table structure is unaffected. Only the *display* characteristics of the table are affected. When you close a table whose Datasheet view display characteristics you changed, Access displays a dialog box asking "Do you want to save changes to the layout of the table…?" Clicking *No* cancels any display characteristic changes you made since the last save. Clicking *Yes* preserves those table display (Datasheet views) changes.

The easiest way to change a table's display characteristics is to view the table in Datasheet view and then make format selections from the Datasheet contextual command tab. Let's change a few display properties for the customers table. Before starting the exercise, make sure Access is active and the Chapter 1 database is open.

EXERCISE 1.8: CHANGING A TABLE'S DISPLAY PROPERTIES

1. In the Tables category, right-click tblInvoices and then click Open in the pop-up menu. The invoices table opens in Datasheet view.

2. Click the Datasheet contextual command tab to display its groups and commands.

3. Click any cell in the Tax column and then click the Apply Currency Format button in the *Data Type & Formatting* group. Repeat this step for the ShipCost column. Now both the currency columns display currency symbols for their column entries.

4. Move the mouse pointer to the Shipper *field selector* (column heading). When the mouse pointer is over the column heading, it changes to a down-pointing arrow. Click the column to select it.

5. Click inside the darkened column's field selector (*not* the data below the field selector), drag to the leftmost position in the table, and release the mouse button. (The column remains darkened after you release the mouse.)

6. With the Shipper column still selected, right-click the mouse anywhere within the column. A pop-up menu appears.

7. Click Column Width from the list of pop-up menu choices.

8. Click the Best Fit button. The column resizes to the smallest width that will display both the column label and the widest entry in the column.

9. Repeat step 5 above to move the InvoiceDate column to the second column, just to the right of the Shipper column you just moved. Click any data value to deselect the column (see Figure 1.18).

Fig. 1.18 Changing a table's display properties.

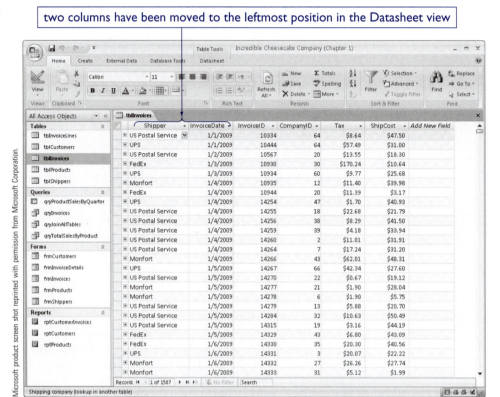

two columns have been moved to the leftmost position in the Datasheet view

Microsoft product screen shot reprinted with permission from Microsoft Corporation.

Sorting and Filtering Table Rows

For small tables, it is often easy to scan a table to locate a particular record or group of records when the table is sorted. For instance, it is somewhat difficult to scan the invoices table, as small as it is, and determine quickly which shippers were used on, say, March 15. You can imagine how difficult searching for shipments by shipper on particular dates is on a much larger invoice table with thousands of records, especially when the records are not sorted by shipper or date. The *tblInovices* table is sorted in order by its primary key column, InvoiceID. This is not useful for manual searching.

By default, tables are automatically organized on their primary key field(s). The Invoices table, for instance, is organized on the InvoiceID field because that field was designated the table's primary key field during its creation. (Primary key fields ensure that each row of a particular table is unique and uniquely identifiable.) In the next exercise, you will sort and filter the table to display only invoices issued on March 15 sorted by shipper name. In preparation for the exercise, ensure that Access is still running and that the Ch01 database is open. Double-click *tblInvoices* in the Tables category list, if needed, to open it in Datasheet view.

EXERCISE 1.9: SORTING AND FILTERING TABLE ROWS

1. With the *tblInvoices* table displayed in Datasheet view, right-click any data value in the Shipper column.
2. Click Sort A to Z in the pop-up menu. Now the invoice records are alphabetized by the shippers' names.
3. Click the list selector arrow in the InvoiceDate column found on the right portion of the column selector. Sorting options and a list of unique column values appears in a drop-down menu.
4. Click the (Select All) check box to clear its check mark and all the check marks on unique values displayed below it.
5. Using the scroll box in the drop-down menu, locate and click 3/15/3009 (see Figure 1.19).
6. Click OK to apply the newly created filter. Only the eight records whose date matches the filter date appear in Datasheet view. They are sorted by shipper name.

Fig. 1.19 Filtering records.

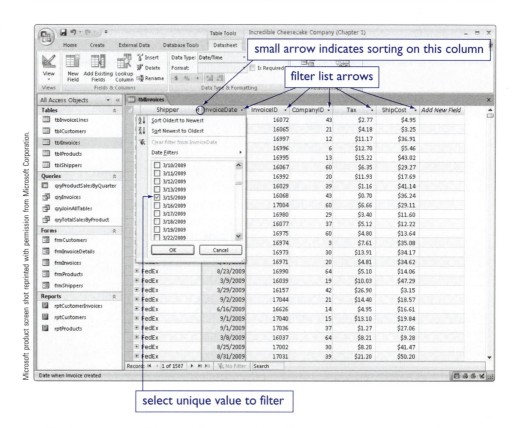

Notice that the Shipper column contains the up-pointing arrow on the column header indicating the sort order; the InvoiceDate column shows a small funnel—a filter—indicating the column is filtered. The status bar displays the word "Filtered" as a further indication that table row filtering is in effect.

Another way to sort a table is to create an Advanced Filter/Sort from the Advanced Filter Options command in the Filter & Sort group on the Home tab. If you do, you can select multiple sort columns (for instance, ascending order by Shipper and then ascending order by ShipCost for each shipper group). You can select column names from a list, place each sort column into a sort grid, and select either an Ascending or Descending sort order for each column. You redisplay the datasheet in its original order by clicking the Clear All Sorts button and clicking the Toggle Filter button. Experiment a bit with these. They can do no harm, because the table's actual record order is unaffected. Only a datasheet displayed row order is changed.

After you are done experimenting with sorting and filtering, close the invoices table by right-clicking its tab and clicking Close or Close All in the drop-down menu that appears. When the dialog box displays asking if you want to save the changes to the design of the table, click No.

Printing a Table

To print a database table, select the table (it need not be open) or display the table in Datasheet view, click the Microsoft Office Button, hover over Print, and click Print. When you select Print from the Office menu, the familiar Print dialog box appears. You can choose to print all pages or a range of pages. Select a page range by entering *From* and *To* page numbers. Alternatively, you can click the Selected Record(s) radio button to print only the record(s) you have highlighted in the table—only one row if you have not specifically selected more than one row. Normally, you need only one copy of the report. However, simply alter the value in the *Number of Copies* spin control box. You can click the Setup button on the Print dialog box to make limited choices for the four margins and whether or not to print headings. When you are ready to print the table, click the OK button. Otherwise, click the Cancel button to nullify the print process.

A printed table is created using a default format. The table's contents are printed in columns with horizontal and vertical table grid lines. Normally, today's date appears in the upper-right corner of the report, and the table's name appears centered above the table. At the bottom center of the page is a page number. Access prints additional pages whenever a table's columns are wider than can be printed on a single page.

The table report is functional but far from beautiful. Access provides tools for producing high quality, attractive reports replete with fonts, specialty features such as underlining and boldface, etc. Later in this chapter we describe how to create and use Access reports. Table printouts are quick and easy to produce and allow you to quickly check values in various columns.

Printing a Table's Structure

Printing information about the structure and definition of any table is a bit more complicated. First, ensure the table whose structure you want to print is closed. Click the Database Tools command tab and then click Database Documenter in the Analyze group. The Documentor dialog box opens. Check the box corresponding to the name of the object(s), *tblCustomers*, for instance (see Figure 1.20). Click OK. The table's structure appears in a preview window whose tab is labeled *Object Definition*. Click the Print button in the Print group of the Print Preview contextual command tab, and then make selections in the Print dialog box before clicking the OK button to print the structure. Be aware that the structure is typically several pages long. A hard copy of a table's definition provides good system documentation.

Fig. 1.20 Printing a table's structure information.

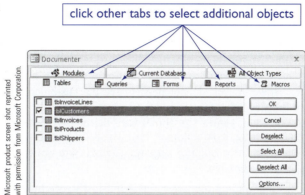

click other tabs to select additional objects

Microsoft product screen shot reprinted with permission from Microsoft Corporation.

Querying a Database

One of the very powerful capabilities of relational databases is the ability to ask questions that return interesting and meaningful answers derived from a database. Relational database systems make asking questions particularly easy, and Access is no exception. A *query*, the usual name for a question, can be simple or complex and can involve one table, dozens of tables, or even hundreds of tables. In a query, you specify which tables are involved in the data retrieval operation, which columns are to be retrieved, which records are to be returned, how to sort the returned rows, and what calculations should be performed. The result is also a table. Relational database systems are closed systems, because queries use tables as input and return tables as answers. Simply stated, you put tables in and get tables out. A very important distinction between tables and queries, though both appear similar, is that tables are the only database objects that actually hold data. Queries *do not* hold data. They are merely stored definitions that tell the database system how to extract and display data from tables.

One of the most popular types of queries is called a selection query. A *selection query* retrieves rows from one or more related tables. There are other types of queries that do not retrieve answers. Instead, they alter tables by inserting new records, deleting existing records, updating data, or creating new table columns.

All of the examples and discussion in this section illustrate selection queries. The section called *Creating Action Queries* describes the other types of queries—those that alter table data.

What are examples of the kinds of information you could retrieve with a query, and why not simply print a table? Consider a larger version of the customers table. Suppose it contains over 50,000 customer rows and you need to know how many customers live in San Diego, California. Or perhaps your manager wants to know how many customers have placed an order within the last six months. You probably would not print a 50,000-row customer table and then manually look for the answers. That could take hours and be fraught with error and frustration. To compound the problem, the Print command does not allow you to regulate which rows or which columns print.

Queries give you flexibility to decide which rows and columns of a table should be printed and provide an easy way to sift through large volumes of data. That is, queries provide a straightforward way to pose ad hoc questions that return subsets of table rows, columns, or both.

Access uses a query creation methodology called *Query by Example*, or *QBE*. QBE is a method of stating a query whereby you give Access an example of the result you want, and Access uses that model to return a result in a table-like structure called a *dynaset*.

Using a Query

Suppose you are in the marketing department of the Incredible Cheesecake Company and you want a list of all customers who live in Arcata, California. Furthermore, you want the list sorted by zip code. Because you are planning to mail literature to those customers, you want to see the customers' name and address fields (including zip code). However, you do not need to see the customers' identification numbers. To extract the needed information, you create a query by showing Access an example of what you want. Figure 1.21 shows both the query's design and the resulting dynaset. Recall that to show both windows, you'd have to change the tabbed interface to "Overlapping Windows" in the Access Options dialog box. Again, we suggest you use the tabbed interface.

Let's try running the preceding query just to see how the question formation process works. The query shown in the Query window of Figure 1.21 has been saved in the Chapter 1 database under the name *qryArcataCustomers*. By using the "qry" prefix on all query names[1], we can easily distinguish queries from other database objects.

Fig. 1.21 A query design and resulting dynaset.

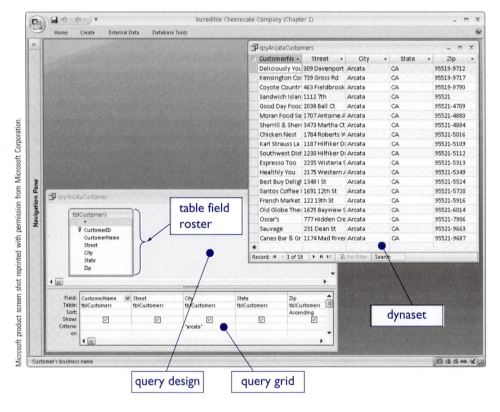

In the next section you will build a new query from scratch. The next exercise illustrates using an existing query. First, launch Access, if necessary, and ensure that database Ch01 is open. Then, complete the following exercise to open and run a query.

---

[1]*A note about naming objects:* We follow the convention that query names have the prefix *qry* followed by the query name. No object name contains embedded blanks. Blanks in object names can be troublesome, and you should avoid them. For instance, the name *qryNewCustomers* is preferable to the name *qry New Customers*, with blanks between the words. Squash the separate words together and distinguish them by using initial capital letters for each word except the prefix (tbl, qry, frm, and rpt). This format is called *camel case* and is used throughout the industry.

EXERCISE 1.10: RUNNING A QUERY

1. In the Queries category of the Navigation Pane double-click qryArcataCustomers. (Double-clicking a database object's name in the Navigation Pane is the fastest way to open it in nondesign view.) Alternatively, you can right-click the query name and then click Open in the pop-up menu that appears. A dynaset appears displaying the query's result.
2. After you have examined the results, right-click the query's tab and click Close in the pop-up menu.

The preceding dynaset displays customers living in Arcata, California, sorted by zip code. Candidate rows are drawn from a table called *tblCustomers*. If you are curious about how the query is structured, right-click the query name in the Navigation Pane and click Design View in the pop-up menu.

Creating a One-Table Query

You can create new queries using the Query By Example (QBE) method. For instance, suppose you want to see a list of all customer invoices that are over 60 days past due. Printing or displaying the invoices table would not produce the answer you want because Access would print *all* invoices in the table. What you need is a way to sift through all the invoices, locating and displaying only those whose invoice date is older than 59 days.

The best way to construct the required display is to create a query. There are several ways to create a query. You can forge a query from scratch or you can use a Query Wizard. Query construction begins by clicking the Create command tab. Then, you click either the Query Wizard button or the Query Design (to build a query manually) in the group labeled *Other*. If you create a query manually, then the query grid opens (see Figure 1.21, for example) and you proceed to add fields and criteria to instruct Access to search through the invoices table for all invoices more than 59 days old. Rows that satisfy the age condition will appear in the dynaset when you run the query.

Let's go through the process of creating a simple selection query that searches the *tblInvoices* table, returning a portion of the rows. You will create a query that lists all invoice rows in which the shipper is FedEx and the invoice date is between 2/16/2009 and 2/28/2009. You want to locate those rows because you have found out that FedEx has made a mistake in its shipping costs during that 13-day period. This gives you a simple way to check the rows for that subset of the invoices table. Prepare for the exercise by closing any open tabs by right-clicking any tab and clicking Close All in the pop-up menu.

EXERCISE 1.11: CREATING A ONE-TABLE QUERY

1. Click the Create command tab and then click Query Design in the *Other* group. The Show Table dialog box opens. (If it doesn't, then click Show Table in the Query Setup group of the Design contextual command tab.)
2. Double-click tblInvoices on the Tables tab of the Show Table dialog box; click the Close button on the Show Table dialog box.
3. Double-click the title bar of the field roster, which is found in the upper half of the query design window. The field roster fields are highlighted. Click inside the highlighted column names and drag them to the left-most cell in the Field row of the query grid. Six Field cells fill with the six field roster names.

4. Click the cell in the Criteria row under the InvoiceDate column and type the following expression. After you finish typing it, press Enter to complete the expression.

between #2/15/2009# and #2/28/2009#

(Enclosing dates in # symbols ensures that Access recognizes the enclosed values as dates rather than arithmetic expressions.)

5. Click the cell in the Sort row of the InvoiceDate column, click its list box arrow on the right end of the cell, and select Ascending from the list to sort the rows by the InvoiceDate column.

6. Click the Criteria cell under the Shipper column—the same row that the date criteria is in. Here is a slightly tricky part: Type 2 (without any other punctuation) in the cell. This seems counterintuitive, but the Shipper column actually contains a numeric value that corresponds to a shipper name in another table. The criteria must match a value, not a text string such as "FedEx." The value 2 corresponds to the FedEx shipping company. Figure 1.22 shows the completed query design. (The Invoice Date is wider so you can see the entire criteria expression.)

7. Click the Datasheet View button in the Results group of the Design contextual command tab to view the dynaset. The dynaset, shown in Figure 1.23, displays the results of this query—the FedEx shipments that took place in the second half of March 2009.

Fig. 1.22 Query design with criteria and sorting.

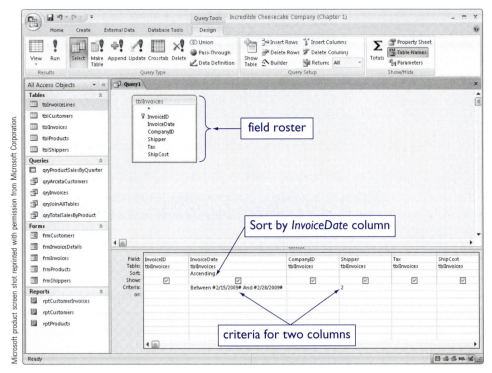

Saving a Query

You may wonder why save a query if it never changes. Although a query's definition may never change (unless you change it), the rows that a query retrieves may change. For example, once you craft a query to retrieve customers whose invoices are greater than 59 days past due, the dynaset result will change over time; the query will not,

Fig. 1.23 One-table query dynaset.

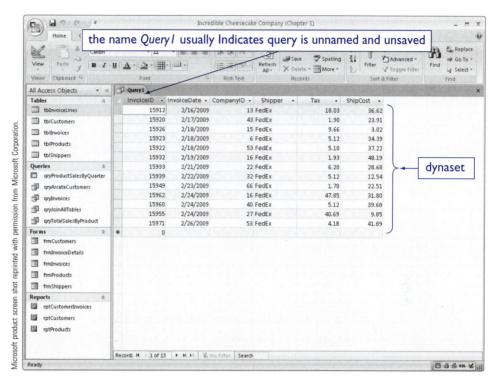

however. That's why it is a good idea to save your queries for use later. By saving a query, you can later rerun it to obtain accurate, timely information about changing data. *Note*: You cannot save the dynaset, because it is not an object. A dynaset merely displays data from the underlying table that pass the criteria test. (You can create a special query, called a *Make Table* query, which can save the dynaset as a table. We explore this and other special query types later in the chapter.)

You save a new or changed query by selecting either *Save* or *Save As* from the Office Button menu (or by clicking the *Save* button on the Quick Access Toolbar).

TRY IT

With the new query open (Design or Datasheet view), click the *Save* button on the Quick Access Toolbar. Type the name *qryMarchFedEx* in the Query Name text box. Click *OK*. The query is saved. Right-click the *qryMarchFedEx* tab and click *Close* to close the window.

Sorting the Results

Normally, Access displays a dynaset in order by the primary key of the underlying table. (For instance, the *tblInvoices* table's key column is CustomerID.) If the table referenced by a query has no primary key, then the dynaset's rows display in no particular order. However, you can specify your own sort requirements—as you did in the previous exercise—so that dynaset rows display in a more meaningful and useful order. You select a sort order by selecting either Ascending or Descending beneath the appropriate column(s) in the QBE grid Sort row. There can be multiple columns that specify sorting.

In that case, the second and subsequent sort columns, left to right, become tiebreakers for sort columns to their left.

TRY IT

Display in Design view the query *qryMarchFedEx,* and click in the Sort row beneath the first column. Select either Ascending or Descending from the dropdown list. Continue selecting, if desired, other columns to the right in the QBE grid. You can select *Ascending* or *Descending* for any number of columns, but the leftmost column having the Sort row cell filled is the primary sort column. The significance of other sort columns are determined by their relative position in the QBE sort grid, left to right. You may wish to drag one or more columns to the left to enhance their influence on the final sort order. Better yet, you can add columns to the right specifying sort orders for each column. Clear the Show check box of any duplicate columns so they are used to sort, but are not displayed, in the dynaset.

Using More Complex Selection Criteria

Suppose the manager of the Incredible Cheesecake Company wants to isolate all invoice rows in which the discount is nonzero but less than 11%. Customer invoice lines with any discount that is less than 11% will be audited to ensure that the quantities represented by those rows are adequate. Although the actual invoices are not subject to change, any returned rows will help the financial people either reinforce the business rules they have established for discounts or revisit and revise the quantity discount rules.

To answer the preceding request, the manager can formulate a query that returns all *tblInvoiceLines* table rows for which the value in the discount column is greater than zero and less than 11%. The criteria clearly involves two conditions—two different percentages in this case. Furthermore, both conditions must be true for a row to be returned in the dynaset. For situations like this, the criteria use an AND logical operator. In fact, you can use the AND operator in the criteria whenever you select rows based on a range of values for a single column of a table. The date criteria you used earlier (*between #2/15/2009# and #2/28/2009#*) contained the AND operator along with the word "between" to filter rows.

For this query not all columns in the *tblInvoiceLines* column will be listed. It is sufficient to list only the quantity, price charged, and discount columns. In this example, we include a subset of the invoice table's columns in the query's dynaset. In preparation for the next exercise, close all windows except the Database window by right-clicking any object's display tab and clicking Close All.

EXERCISE 1.12: WRITING A QUERY WITH AN "AND" OPERATOR

1. Click the Create command tab and then click Query Design in the *Other* group.
2. Double-click the tblInvoiceLines table name in the Show Table dialog box, and click the Close button.
3. Click Quantity in the *tblInvoiceLines* table field roster, hold down the Ctrl key, and click, in turn, UnitPriceCharged and Discount. Release the Ctrl key.

4. Click inside any of the selected fields in the table field roster, drag the list to the first cell in the Field row, and release the mouse. When you release the mouse, Access places the three fields in separate Field row cells in the QBE grid.
5. Click the Criteria cell below the Discount column and type >0 and <0.11 to establish the selection criteria. (Place a blank preceding and following the word *and*. No blanks are needed following the > symbol or the < symbol.) Press Enter or Tab to complete the entry. Notice that Access automatically capitalizes the word *And* if you have typed everything correctly. If you do make a typing mistake, click the criterion cell, correct the mistake, and press Enter.
6. Click the Ascending in the Sort cell below the Quantity column to sort the results by the Quantity column.
7. Click the View button (*not* the View button list arrow) in the Results group of the Design contextual command tab to see the query's result (see Figure 1.24).
8. When you are finished examining the dynaset, right-click the new query's tab and click Close All to all open windows.
9. Click No when you are asked if you want to save the newly created query.

Fig. 1.24 Using an *and* operator in a criterion expression.

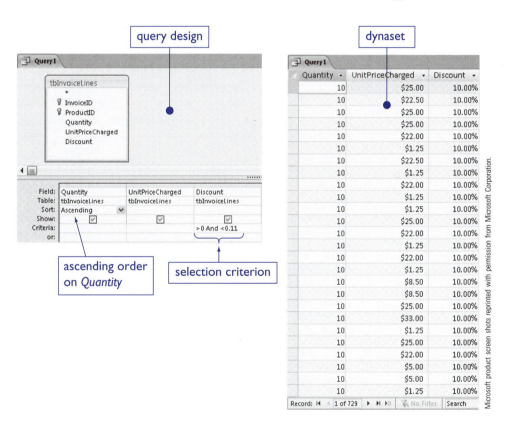

Look carefully at the expression in the QBE grid in Figure 1.24 in the Criteria row of the Discount column. That expression filters rows, selecting only those rows whose Discount value falls within the specified range.

Three new symbols and a logical operator are introduced in the criteria. The *and* operator separates two expressions. This indicates that the conditions to its left and right must be met simultaneously. In other words, rows are displayed only if the discount value is greater than zero and less than 0.11. An alternative way to write this criterion expression is *between 0.0 and 0.11*. Most people prefer to use this form when dealing with a contiguous range of values.

You probably are already familiar with the greater than (>) and less than (<) symbols. These are just two of the comparison operators that Access provides. A complete list of comparison operators appears in Figure 1.25. Among the logical operators is *And*. The list of logical operators is given in Figure 1.26.

Fig. 1.25 Comparison operators.

Operator	Meaning
<	Less than
>	Greater than
=	Equal to
<=	Less than or equal to
>=	Greater than or equal to
<>	Not equal to

Fig. 1.26 Logical operators.

Operator	Meaning
And	Conditions on both sides must be true for the statement to be true. Otherwise, the statement is false.
Or	The statement is true if a condition on either side is true or if both conditions are true. Otherwise, the statement is false.
Not	A unary operator, it negates the logic it precedes.

When you want to use criteria on two or more fields simultaneously, you place those conditions under the respective column names in the same query grid Criteria row. For instance, suppose you want to list all invoices involving a particular shipper during a particular month of a given year. This query involves a combination of criteria in a single query that are similar to queries you created in previous exercises.

Creating Selection Criteria Using the "OR" Operator

You are likely to encounter queries similar to the following: "List the customers who have ordered something in the last 30 days or who have purchased more than $500 worth of products in the last 90 days." Another example is: "List all of the products we sell that have the word *chocolate* in their description or products that sell for less than $10." Both of the preceding questions involve two conditions, either of which is reason enough to list the record. That is, the criteria are called OR conditions. Unlike AND conditions, in which all conditions must be true to select and return a row to the dynaset, OR conditions require that only one of the conditions need be true for a row to be returned.

How do you form a query involving OR conditions? There are two basic ways to formulate OR criteria, depending on whether the criteria concern one field or different fields. If two different fields are involved (product description and product price in our example), then you create a query containing two Criteria rows—one row for each condition. If a criterion involves only one field, then you can place alternate acceptable values in one field, separating them with the word *Or*.

The next exercise uses the first method, since two different fields are involved. Close any open Access windows, but leave the Chapter 1 database open.

EXERCISE 1.13: FORMING A QUERY WITH "OR" CRITERIA

1. Click the Create command tab and click Query Design in the *Other* group.
2. Double-click the tblProducts table in the Show Table dialog box and then click the Close button.
3. Double-click the * (asterisk) in the *tblProducts* field roster to place it in the first cell of the Field row in the QBE grid.
4. Double-click the ProductDescription and RetailPrice fields in the field roster to automatically place them in the second and third columns in the Field row.
5. Clear the check boxes under the ProductDescription and RetailPrice columns so Access does not display those columns twice in the dynaset.
6. Click the Criteria cell under the ProductDescription column in the QBE grid, press Shift+F2 to open the Zoom box and thereby enlarge the Criteria cell (this action is called "invoking the Zoom window"). In the Zoom box type the criterion like "*choc*" (type the quotation marks) and click OK to close it. Access ignores capitalization when searching for text strings.

   (Strictly speaking, the Zoom box is not needed here. However, we want you to know that you can display this text box whenever you need to give you an enlarged view of Field cells or Criteria cells as you type in them.)
7. Click the second row Criteria row under the RetailPrice column. (Make sure this criterion is in a different row than the ProductDescription criterion.) Type the expression <10.
8. Click the Datasheet View button to see the query's dynaset.

The dynaset returns rows sorted low to high on the primary key, ProductID. Both the dynaset and underlying query are shown in Figure 1.27. Normally, you can see either the query or the dynaset but not both, because they are opposite sides of the same "coin."

Fig. 1.27 Using *or* criteria in a query.

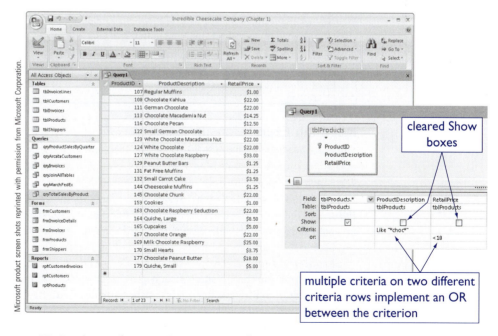

Notice that to form an OR query, you have as many Criteria rows in the QBE query grid as there are independent selection criteria. Each row contains characters, a value, or an expression below a single column. When OR conditions involve only one field, there is an alternative way to write the criteria. For instance, suppose you want to display product table rows for product descriptions that contain *chocolate* or *peanut*. Because both criteria involve the same field, ProductDescription, you can write both criteria in one criteria row, separating the criteria with the reserved word OR (either uppercase or lowercase):

Like "*peanut*"Or Like "*chocolate*"

Although most other database systems consider character string capitalization important, Access does not. Access ignores capitalization and locates matching rows based on spelling alone. Character matching rules vary from one database product to another, however. Be sure to experiment with it first. *Chocolate Fudge* in a query may not match *chocolate fudge* in the database if you are not using Microsoft Access.

The asterisk preceding and following the word *chocolate* is one of the *wildcard* characters. Asterisk can stand for none or for any number of letters. This allows a match on a string such as *Dutch German Chocolate, Chocolate Creme*, and so on. The asterisk can be used on either or both ends of any query string. Whenever you use a wildcard with a character string, Access automatically inserts the word *Like* ahead of it. Of course, the order of the strings separated by OR does not matter.

What would happen if you formed a query with only one row and placed the expression **<10** beneath RetailPrice and (in the same criteria row) placed **Like "*choc*"** beneath ProductDescription? No rows would be returned in the dynaset because no table rows satisfy both criteria simultaneously. The latter query is an example of specifying AND criteria. Simply stated, each Criteria row states conditions that must all be satisfied before any rows are selected by those particular criteria for inclusion in the dynaset. Of course, if there are other Criteria rows, they too may select rows to be retrieved.

TRY IT

Modify the query you created in Exercise 1.13 previously by moving the *<10* criteria to the same Criteria row as the *Like "*choc*"* criteria (using the standard Windows cut/paste method). Click the *Datasheet View* button. What appears in the dynaset? An empty row! That means that no rows satisfy the criteria. Right-click the *Query1* window tab, click *Close* on the pop-up menu, and click *No* when asked if you want to save changes.

Including Expressions in a Query

For most applications, it is informative to calculate values that are not stored in the database. Accounting applications are no exception. For instance, the manager usually keeps a watchful eye on total amounts invoiced. One way to tally invoiced sales is to record the total value of each invoice line found in the *tblInvoiceLines*. However, the *tblInvoiceLines* table does not record that value—as it should not if the table is to follow accepted database and table design standards. There are two approaches to solving this problem; one is correct and the other is wholly incorrect.

An *incorrect* solution would be to create a new *tblInvoiceLines* table column that holds the total purchase value of each purchased item. Although this might be an acceptable solution when using a spreadsheet product, doing this with a database can lead to inconsistencies in the database and trouble later on. Why? Suppose that the total purchase price is calculated as the product of the Quantity and UnitPriceCharged columns (that is, purchase price is the product of the quantity of each item purchased and its purchase price). Now, suppose someone discovers a mistake made in transcribing the quantity purchased for a particular item. Instead of recording the quantity of

20 (twenty) for a particular product sold, someone recorded the quantity as 200 (two hundred). Discovering the mistake, the value is corrected to 200 in the *tblInvoiceLines* Quantity column.

Even though the Quantity value is now correct in the database record for a particular errant transaction, the total purchase price is not. Unlike a spreadsheet, a field value in a database row does not change automatically when other values on which it depends change. Here's an important rule covering this situation: *Never store in a table any value (field) that is functionally dependent on two or more fields in the record.* That's a simplification of a rule that will be described in Chapter 2, but it merely states you shouldn't store in any table a value you can calculate or derive from one or more tables in the database.

So, what is the correct way to arrive at the total purchase price for each invoice line item? The correct way is to include an *expression* in the query that calculates the desired value dynamically—each time the query is executed. Instead of your creating such a query, we have provided an example for you to execute. You will find this query containing the calculation described here in the Chapter 1 database. In the Queries category, it is called *qryInvoices*.

TRY IT

Double-click the query *qryInvoices*. The query displays rows from two tables: *tblInvoiceLines* and *tblProducts*. (The *tblProducts* table is not needed to illustrate calculations, but adding the second table allows us to show the product name in the dynaset.) Examine the query in Figure 1.28 as well as the dynaset showing the retrieved and calculated results. The expression calculated and displayed in the *Extended* column is actually a tiny bit more complex than a simple product of two numbers. It also takes into account any discount applied to the item and then rounds the entire expression to two decimal places. Ignore all the rounding and discount for now. Leave the query open for subsequent use.

Click the Design View button, and examine the query's design. Pay particular attention to the expression in the Field row. (You may have to click the horizontal scroll bar to bring the field into view.) The expression

Extended: Round([Quantity]*[UnitPriceCharged]*(1-[Discount]),2)

computes the extended price for each row in turn and creates a new column in the dynaset. The word *Extended* followed by a colon and a space is the column's name (also called an *alias*). The expression variables [Quantity] and [UnitPriceCharged] reference table field names and get their values from them for each individual row.

Printing Dynasets

Before printing, always check the dynaset to make sure it contains the results you expected. For example, you may pose a query that is too broad and encompasses too many database records. Or perhaps you inadvertently omitted a needed column. Prior to printing a dynaset, open it (this is not strictly required but guarantees you'll print the correct object). Then, click the Microsoft Office Button, hover the mouse over the Print command, and click Print or Print Preview. Clicking Print directly displays the Print dialog box. Clicking Print Preview displays a preview of your output. In this latter case, click the Print button in the Print group to display the Print dialog box. Make the appropriate choices in the Print dialog box and then click OK to print the dynaset.

Fig. 1.28 A query
containing an
arithmetic expression.

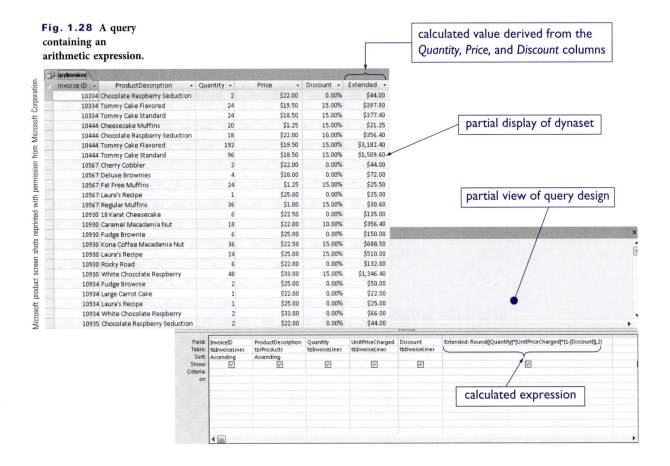

calculated value derived from the
Quantity, Price, and *Discount* columns

partial display of dynaset

partial view of query design

calculated expression

Caution: Many tables are long and the printout may go on for pages. It is best to preview
the output and then specify the start/end pages to print.

Using Forms

A form provides a convenient, less-cluttered work surface through which you can enter,
modify, or simply view information in your tables. A form can display information from
one or more tables. Additionally, a form can display information from a query (that is,
the query's dynaset).

One of the advantages of using a form to enter or modify data is that the form can
resemble a paper form with which you or your clients are already familiar. When the
form on the screen mimics a paper form, those using the form will intuitively know
what information goes where, and they usually feel more comfortable with a familiar interface. Entering data directly into a table can be more confusing and error-prone, especially for anyone not familiar with databases in general or Access in particular. Another
advantage of a form is that you can enforce a medley of validation checks on values that
are entered in a table through a form.

Viewing a Table through a Form

To help you better understand Access forms, we have created several, and they are in
your Chapter 1 database. For example, the products form is based on the *tblProducts* table and is called *frmProducts*. Following the conventions stated earlier in the chapter, all

our form names, with very few exceptions, have the prefix *frm*. Work through the next exercise to open the products form.

EXERCISE 1.14: OPENING AN EXISTING FORM

1. Close all open windows by right-clicking any open window's tab and clicking Close All
2. If the Forms shutter in the Navigation Pane is closed, click it to open the list of forms in the Chapter 1 database.
3. Double-click the form frmProducts. The products form appears.
4. Click the Last record navigation button near the bottom of the form to advance to the last form record. Although this is a very simple form, you can see that the presentation is less cluttered and more intuitive to use (see Figure 1.29).
5. Click the First record navigation button to move back to the first record in the table.
6. Right-click the frmProducts tab and then click Close to close the form.

Fig. 1.29 A simple but handy product form.

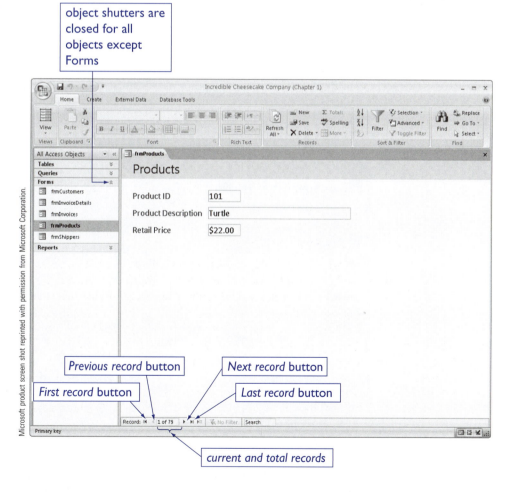

Microsoft product screen shot reprinted with permission from Microsoft Corporation.

Familiar navigation buttons, which you used in Exercise 1.14, appear along the bottom edge of the form. Those buttons perform the usual actions: move to the top of the table, move up one row, and so forth. As you navigate using the button, you probably notice that the form displays records in order by Product ID. The form is built from the *tblProducts* table whose primary key, ProductID, maintains the table (and thus the form) rows in order by the ProductID field. If you want rows displayed in the form in product description (name) order, you could create a query that returns rows sorted on ProductDescription column of the *tblProducts* table (specify Ascending sort in the QBE grid under ProductDescription). Then you can build a form based on the query. We illustrate a query-based form next.

Viewing a Query through a Form

You can create forms from queries as well as tables. It makes no difference whether the form displays a table's contents or a query's contents. Figure 1.30 shows a form based on the query *qryMarchFedEx* you created earlier in Exercise 1.11 in this chapter. Notice that the Form window status line displays the current record and the total number of records. In this case, the total number of records depends on how many rows are selected by the query on which the form is built. It is likely that you will create and use many forms based on queries.

Fig. 1.30 Form data supplied by the *qryMarchFedEx* query.

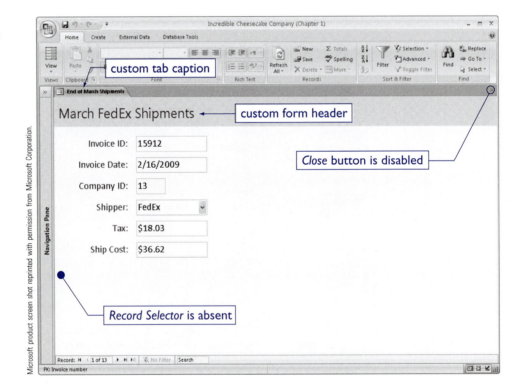

Microsoft product screen shot reprinted with permission from Microsoft Corporation.

Creating a Form Quickly

The best way to enter or modify data is through a form. Making modifications to data through a table's Datasheet view is sometimes daunting to anyone unfamiliar with Access, but a form provides an intuitive, uncluttered interface to even the novice. We illustrate how easy it is to create a functional and attractive form by simply choosing a table and clicking a button.

TRY IT

Click the *Create* command tab and then click *tblCustomers* to select (but *not* open) the customers table. Click the *Form* button in the Forms group. (It is the left-most icon in the group.) A Form and its associated subform appear in Layout View. Click the *Form* button in the Views group of the Home command tab to display it in Form view—the way a user normally interacts with forms (see Figure 1.31).

Access creates a form and its associated subform because of relationships that exist between the *tblCustomers*, *tblInvoices*, and *tblInvoiceLines*. The form links all three tables together allowing you to make changes in any of the related tables by using the form—a "window" into the three tables. The form's header displays *tblCustomers* which is assigned from the name of the original table you selected before creating the form. You can easily change that text to something more suitable as well as make any number of cosmetic changes. You'll do that later.

Fig. 1.31 An automatically created form.

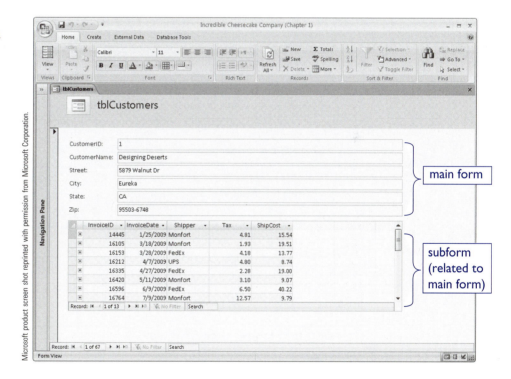

Microsoft product screen shot reprinted with permission from Microsoft Corporation.

Leave the Form open, because you will save it in a few moments. You probably agree that the form and its subform are attractive and functional.

Saving a Form

You can save a form design by clicking the Save icon in the Quick Access Toolbar. Then you type the form's name in the Save As dialog box. Doing so saves the newly created form, not the data. Any new or modified data is *automatically* saved in underlying table (s) by Access when you move to a new record in the form or close the form.

TRY IT

With the newly created form still displayed in Form view, select Save in the Quick Access Toolbar. Type the name *frmCustomersAutoForm* in the Form Name text box of the Save As dialog box. Click *OK* to complete the form save operation. Right-click the form document's tab and click *Close All* to close the form and any other open windows.

Editing Data with a Form

It is often easier to alter data in a table using a form. Because only one table row is usually displayed on the form, you are less likely to make mistakes. Editing table data through a form is simple. While looking at a form in Form view (not Design view), you click the field that you want to change and make any needed changes. Try editing a record in the Broker table through the form.

EXERCISE 1.15: EDITING DATA WITH A FORM

1. Double-click the form name frmCustomers found in the Forms category of the Navigation Pane. The form opens in Form view.
2. Move to the record for customer name *Caffe Tazza* by pressing PgDn keyboard key three times or by using the navigation buttons.
3. Press Tab repeatedly to move to the Street field. (The entire value is highlighted if you use Tab or the arrow keys to move to the selected fields instead of the mouse.)
4. Type 24 Oak Street to correct the street name.
5. Click the Next Record navigation button to cause Access to post the change to the underlying table. Then, click the Previous Record navigation button to verify the change you made has been posted.
6. Right-click the form's document tab and click Close to close the form.

Recall that Access does not post changes to a table until you move to another record, close the table, or close the database. Keep in mind that the form merely displays table data. The form itself is not changed. Only the table data is actually changed. You never need to save a form again unless you change its *design*.

Creating and Using a Split Form

A form allows you to view data provided by a table or generated by a query one record at a time. A form is intuitive and can be designed to mimic paper forms familiar to any business. Navigation buttons on the form's bottom edge allow easy form navigation. However, an advantage of viewing a table in Datasheet view is that you can navigate quickly and easily throughout the records using scrollbars or keyboard navigation keys—PgUp and PgDn for example. A ***split form***, introduced in Access 2007, provides the speedy navigation available via a Datasheet view of a table along with the nicer layout provided by a form. It does this by dividing the document window into two halves: The top half is a form and the bottom half is a datasheet. The idea behind a split form is that you use the datasheet to locate the record you want and the record's data is simultaneously displayed in the form. Split forms are a snap to create. You do that next.

EXERCISE 1.16: CREATING A SPLIT FORM

1. Click the tblCustomers table found in the Tables category on the Navigation Pane. (You do not need to open the table.)
2. Click the Create command tab and then click Split Form (in the Forms group). Access builds a split form and displays it in Layout View.
3. Click the Form View button in the Views group of the Format contextual tab.
4. Provide more room for the datasheet portion by hovering the mouse over the divider between the two halves, which is called the *splitter bar*. When the mouse pointer becomes a double-headed arrow, click and drag the splitter bar up toward the last form field, Zip. Be careful to not obscure any fields in the form portion of the split form.
5. Click the Shutter Bar Open/Close button on the Navigation Pane to reduce the Navigation Pane to just its shutter bar (see Figure 1.32).

Fig. 1.32 Example split form.

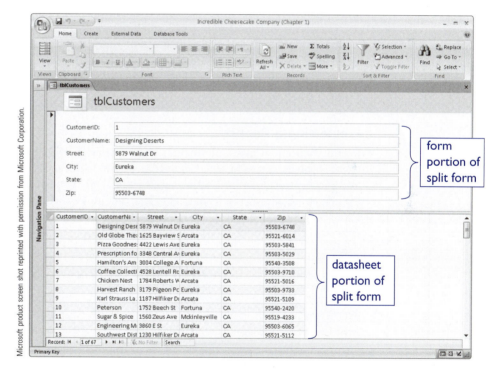

When you have finished examining the split form, you can close it and discard it. We will not refer to it anymore in this chapter.

Printing a Form

Though forms are best suited for onscreen work, you can print them too. To print one record displayed in a form, open the form, locate the record, and click the Microsoft Office Button, hover over Print, and click Print. When the Print dialog box appears, click the Selected Record(s) radio button to print only the displayed form. (If you forget to click that radio button, then Access prints all forms for all the records—something you probably do not want to do.) You will notice that neither the form's title bar nor its navigation buttons appear on the printout.

Printing a range of records via a form is not quite as simple because multiple forms print on each page. Invoke the Print dialog box in the same way as above. This time, however, click the Pages radio button, enter the beginning and ending page numbers in the page range boxes, and click OK. Access prints table rows in the format of the displayed form. However, you probably will not want to print more than a few records this way. There is a better way to print larger amounts of information from tables. An Access report is the most efficient way to design and produce tabular output of the records in a table or a query result. Access reports are introduced next.

Designing Reports

Frequently, you will want either to preview a report onscreen or to produce a printed report, which you can pass around at a meeting or keep as a permanent record. Access reports are just that—reports. You cannot enter data or edit data in a report. Reports range from simple, utilitarian designs to professional-looking reports complete with attractive typefaces, drop shadows, and graphics.

Reports can be displayed in four different views: Report View, Print Preview, Layout View, and Design View. The latter two views allow you to make structure changes to the report, whereas Report View and Print Preview display the report onscreen and disallow any changes to it.

Previewing a Report

Reports typically display information from a table, a collection of related tables, or a query. We have created a report derived from two tables and a query with results similar to the query you examined earlier (see Figure 1.28). Though a lot can be gained from looking at the query's results onscreen, it is even more useful to review the results in an attractively formatted report. First, let's learn how to open a stored report definition and preview the report prior to actually printing it.

EXERCISE 1.17: LOADING AND PREVIEWING A REPORT

1. Open a Navigation Pane object using a different method: Right-click rptCustomerInvoices and then click Open in the shortcut menu. The report opens in Report View.
2. Use the vertical scroll bar to review several of the report's pages. Figure 1.32 shows the top few lines of the report in Report View. The four report views also are represented by buttons in the right end of the status bar (see Figure 1.33).
3. Close the report (right-click the report window tab, click Close). You don't have to save the report.

Creating a Report Quickly

Creating a report from a table is similar to creating a form from a table. You select a table name in the Navigation Pane, click the Create command tab, and click Report in the Reports group. A default-format report appears. In the following exercise you will create a report based on the *tblCustomers* table.

Fig. 1.33 A customer and invoice report.

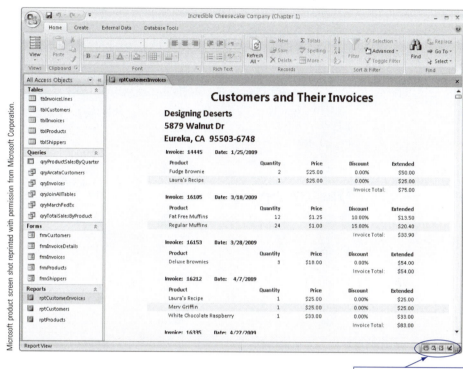

Microsoft product screen shot reprinted with permission from Microsoft Corporation.

report view buttons

EXERCISE 1.18: CREATING A REPORT QUICKLY

1. Click tblCustomers in the Tables category of the Navigation Pane to highlight its name.
2. Click the Create command tab and then click Report (in the Reports group). Access builds a report and displays it in Layout View. Notice that the report header displays the day, date, and time. The vertical dashed line on the right side indicates that the report is wider than the portrait-oriented physical page can display.
3. Click the Page Setup contextual tab and click Landscape in the Page Layout group.
4. Click the Print Preview button in the Access status bar (lower right corner) to get an accurate representation of the report. Reduce the Navigation Pane and use the Zoom scroll control to display an entire report's width in the window (see Figure 1.34).
5. After you examine the report, you can save it for later use. You do that in the next exercise.

Saving a Report

Reports are saved like any other objects described in this text—by clicking the Save command in the Quick Access Toolbar or selecting it from the Office Button menu. Later, if you choose to delete the report, you can simply right-click the report's name in the Navigation Pane and click Delete in the pop-up menu.

Fig. 1.34 A basic report.

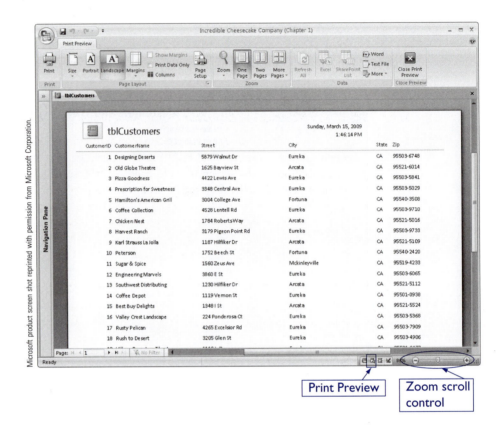

Print Preview

Zoom scroll control

EXERCISE 1.19: SAVING A REPORT

1. With the previously generated report open, right-click the report's document tab and then click Save in the shortcut menu.
2. Type rptCustomerTest in the Report Name text box of the Save As dialog box.
3. Click OK to complete the save operation.
4. Right-click the report's document tab, which now displays *rptCustomerTest*, and then click Close to close the report window.

When you no longer need an object such as a database table, query, form, or report, you can delete it to free up space. Regardless of the object type you choose, you can delete it by using any of several methods. Remove a report, for example, by clicking its name to highlight it and then press the Delete key. Another way is to right-click an object and then select Delete from the shortcut menu.

EXERCISE 1.20: DELETING A REPORT

1. Click rptCustomerTest in the Reports category in the Navigation Pane.
2. Press Del on the keyboard.
3. Click Yes when prompted with the dialog box message "Do you want to permanently delete the report..." to confirm your choice. Access deletes the report.

Printing a Report

The real reason to craft an attractive report is to produce a printed copy of it or some subset of it. Try printing a page or two of a report we have included with your Chapter 1 database.

TRY IT

Right-click the report *rptProducts* and then click *Print Preview* in the shortcut menu to display the report in Print Preview. Click the *Next Page* navigation button on the bottom of the screen to go to page 2. Click *Next Page* again to see the last of three pages. Finally, click the *First Page* navigation button to return to the first report page. Click the *Print* command in the Print group. Print only the first page by clicking the *Pages* radio button in the Print dialog box. Type *1* in the From text box. Click *OK* to print page 1 of the three-page report. Right-click the report document tab and then click *Close All* to close the report preview and any other open document windows.

If you follow the directions carefully in the preceding Try It exercise, then you produce a report showing Incredible Cheesecake Company products ranging from 18 Karat Cheesecake at the top followed by approximately 35 other product lines. Notice the alternating shaded lines in the report. They visually distinguish adjacent report lines from one another. This is but one of a huge number of report formats available. Finally, you are ready to close the Access database entirely.

EXERCISE 1.21: CLOSING THE DATABASE AND CLOSING ACCESS

1. Click the Microsoft Office Button.
2. Click Close Database, the bottom-most command in the menu. The database and Access close.

Summary

You have learned a great deal about database systems in general and the Access database system in particular. You understand what a relational database is and why it is the best choice for dealing with related sets of information.

Tables are the building blocks of a database system and consist of columns and rows. There are several ways to manipulate tables to produce the result you want. Access maintains table rows in order when a table has a primary key. The navigation buttons in the Datasheet view of a table window facilitate moving to various rows in a table. You can move a column in a table to another position by dragging its heading left or right. This alters the table's display characteristics but does not actually alter a column's position in the stored table.

In addition to tables, Access contains other objects including queries, forms, and reports. Queries, or questions, use the QBE method to pose questions about the data stored in one or more tables. Able to retrieve a subset of rows or columns, queries narrow the search for relevant information to just those elements of interest. You learned how to create queries using simple criteria as well as more complex expressions involving comparison operators. You created AND criteria in which two or more conditions must be simultaneously true. You saw that OR criteria are created by placing conditions on two or more rows of the query model.

Forms provide a simpler interface to tables, because only one row at a time is displayed. You used a form and quickly created a form from a table. Forms can be made to look like paper forms encountered in a business.

When a form resembles an existing paper—one already in use—the computer form is rather intuitive and easy to use. You learned that by merely clicking a form entry and typing, you can change a table's data. When you move to a new record, the change is then posted to the table. And you learned that you can filter data through a table, thereby restricting which table rows are shown in a form.

Finally, you got a brief look at the hard copy output facility of Access: an Access report. First, you previewed an existing report. Then, you created a default, quick report from a table. Reports provide a way to print and summarize information from one or more tables in a pleasant-looking format. Reports are output only, and you cannot change a table's contents with a report.

This chapter has given you the fundamental tools to begin using Access to build systems. In Chapter 2, we introduce more formal foundations of relational database management systems. In that chapter you will learn about some rules and techniques that will help you design and build accounting information systems using tables, which are well-suited for the purpose.

Questions and Problems for Review

Multiple-Choice Questions

1. Access is a _____ database management system.
   a. hierarchical
   b. helical
   c. relational
   d. rational

2. When you launch Microsoft Access, you can choose a prebuilt skeletal database called a(n) _____ from a wide variety of them available online and on your local computer.
   a. form
   b. template
   c. sample database
   d. download

3. The View menu lets you display different types of objects including forms, reports, macros, _____, and modules.
   a. favorites
   b. groups
   c. design
   d. tables

4. Only one object actually holds database data. This is the database's _____(s).
   a. table
   b. query
   c. database engine
   d. form

5. You can place filtering criterion into a _____ to produce a dynaset, which is a subset of one or more tables' rows.
   a. form
   b. view
   c. query
   d. attribute

6. When you use two *Criteria* rows of a query's QBE grid under the same column, you are using a(n) _____ operator.
   a. and
   b. not
   c. or
   d. filter
   e. between

7. A _____ form simultaneously displays a form in one panel and a table's Datasheet view in the other panel.
    a. columnar
    b. tabular
    c. relationships
    d. split

8. Suppose you want to review what queries, forms, and reports in the Chapter 1 database refer to the table *tblInvoiceLines*. In the Navigation Pane, you would view objects in the _____ category.
    a. Object Type
    b. Custom
    c. Tables and Related Views
    d. Filter By Group

9. You should never store in a table any value that is functionally _____ two or more fields in the same record.
    a. preceding
    b. dependent on
    c. opposed to
    d. linked with

10. Assume the sales tax charged on all purchases is 6.5 percent of the ExtendedPrice (price*quantity* (1-discount)) field available in a table called *tblSales*. What is the correct expression to compute sales tax— the expression you would place in a Field row of the query to display the tax?
    a. 6.5 *[ExtendedPrice]
    b. [ExtendedPrice]*0.065
    c. 0.065*[tblSales]
    d. 6.5%[tblSales]

Discussion Questions

1. Describe the Access work surface: its ribbon, tabs, shortcut keys, and so on. Be sure to use the correct terminology when describing them.
2. Discuss when it is advantageous to view your data through a table's Datasheet view and when a Form based on the table window is better. Explain your reasons. Is there a way to do both? How?
3. List at least two slightly different ways to open and display a table, assuming the Navigation Pane is open.
4. Discuss why you would use database queries to retrieve information.
5. Describe the different ways to design a database report, and discuss the possible situations where you might use these different designs.

Practice Exercises

Note: You might want to work with a *duplicate* copy of the Chapter 1 database in case you need to rescind an action. Databases have a nasty habit of not having an Undo command just when you need it. Review the section *Creating a Backup of an Access Database* to refresh your memory about how to create a copy of your database. Then, tackle some or all of the following practice exercises. All of these Practice Exercises use objects that are found in your Chapter 1 database.

1. In Datasheet view, sort the *tblCustomers* table on the City and CustomerName fields so that the rows are in order first by city (A to Z) and then CustomerName (A to Z) within each city. Print the sorted table directly from the table's Datasheet view window.
2. Create and execute a query based on the *tblCustomers* table that displays which customers live in the city of *Fortuna*. Display only the columns CustomerName, Street, and City (in that order, left to right). The query should sort the rows into ascending order by the customers' names (like a telephone book listing does). Ensure that the dynaset columns are wide enough to print the widest entry each holds. Save the

query as your last name followed by your first name so that your name appears in the top of the printed result. Print the resulting dynaset.

3. Open the *tblProducts* table in Datasheet view. Without using a query, display in Datasheet view only products whose retail price is greater than or equal to $25.00 (*Hint:* Use a *Number Filter* accessible through the column filter drop-down list) and sort the resulting rows from low to high on the ProductDescription. Widen all Datasheet columns as needed to ensure that the widest values in their columns are completely visible. Print the dynaset. (No need to save the changes to the design of the table when you close it, however.)

4. Create a form based on the query *qryMarchFedEx*. (You created the query in Exercise 1.11 that begins on page 29. If you skipped that exercise, then revisit it, create the query, and then continue with this problem.) Navigate to the third record. Open the Office Button, point to Print, click Print Preview, and click the Landscape button. Close the Print Preview. Now that the default printing is landscape, use the Office Button to print only the third form—the one with InvoiceID 15926. Be very careful *not* to print all 13 forms (*Hint:* Remember Selected Record(s)). Save the form with any name prefixed by "frm."

5. Create a report based on the query *qryTotalSalesByProduct* found in the Queries. In report layout view, click the header ("qryTotalSalesByProduct") twice so the mouse pointer turns to an I-beam. Then, drag through the title and type your first and last names as its replacement. Print only the first page of the report. Save the report with an appropriate name and the prefix "rpt."

Problems

Note: You might want to work with a *duplicate* copy of the Chapter 1 database in case you need to rescind an action. Databases have a nasty habit of not having an Undo command just when you need it. Review the section *Creating a Backup of an Access Database* to refresh your memory about how to create a copy of your database. Then, tackle some or all of the following practice exercises. All of these Problems use objects that are found in your Chapter 1 database. Remember to click the *Options* button, click the *Enable this content* radio button, and click *OK* when you open the database anew for any of the following problems.

1. This problem has three parts and three results labeled A, B, and C. Run the query *qryArcataCustomers* found in the Queries category in the Navigation Pane. It produces the sales in Arcata in ascending order by zip code. (A) Display the dynaset, make columns wide enough to show all values but not wider than necessary, and print the modified dynaset. (B) Switch to Design view and modify the sort order so that the dynaset is in descending order by the CustomerName column with no other sort columns (criterion is still "Arcata" customers only). Switch back to Datasheet view and ensure the columns are wide enough but not too wide ("just right") and print the dynaset. (C) Finally, change the design by filtering the results so that the dynaset shows only customers who live in Arcata or Fortuna. Remove the State and Zip columns from the query result (either by deleting them from the QBE or by doing what?). Sort the results in descending order by City. Ensure the dynaset columns are still wide enough but not too wide. Print the third dynaset. Remember to write your name on all three printed dynasets.

2. You can create a form based on a query in exactly the same way you do based on a table. Create a form for the query *qryJoinAllTables* found in the query list for the database Ch01. Click the query name (no need to open it) and click the Form button in the Forms group on the Create command tab. Save the form. Navigate to record 4321. (*Hint:* Use the navigation text box, not its buttons.) Select Print from the Office Button menu, click Print Preview, and select Landscape orientation. Print only the form for the *selected record*. Be very careful here. You do not want to print the entire 3,198-page report! Remember to write your name on the output.

3. Create a report based on the table *tblCustomers* found in your database. After highlighting the table, use the Report Wizard found in the Reports group of the Create command tab. In the first wizard step, double-click the following fields in the *Available Fields* list to place them in the *Selected Fields* list: CustomerName, Street, and City. Click Next to move to the second wizard step. Click City in the grouping level list box, then click the greater than symbol to add that grouping level. Click Finish to move to the end of the process. The report appears in a Print Preview window. The city name may be truncated. That's okay. Click the Print button in the Print group of the Print Preview contextual tab. Specify that you want to print only page 2 when the Print dialog box appears. Print your name on the report. Close the report and save it.

CHAPTER 2

Databases and Accounting Systems

CHAPTER OBJECTIVES

This chapter introduces database accounting systems and compares them to the double-entry bookkeeping systems with which you are already familiar. It also explains how accountants organize business activities into an interrelated chain of business processes and how database accounting systems use those business processes as organizing themes. This chapter covers the theoretical foundations for database accounting systems and contains practical examples of applying database theory. You will learn about the connection between accounting systems and database systems, why a relational database system is superior to double-entry bookkeeping for capturing accounting information, and some of the theory and history of relational database management systems. Enough theory is provided to aid you in creating efficient, optimal database objects, but the discussion avoids presenting more database theory than you need. In this chapter, you will learn about:

- **Differences between double-entry bookkeeping and database accounting systems.**

- **Advantages and disadvantages of database accounting systems.**

- **Business processes.**

- **The relationship between accounting systems and database systems.**

- **A brief history leading to the development of database management systems.**

- **Functions of database management systems.**

- **Theory and application of relational database management systems.**

- **The structure of database objects that store accounting events.**

- **The importance of normalizing tables.**

- **Performing database selections, projections, and joins.**

- **How accountants use the REA model when designing accounting databases.**

This chapter will help you understand the differences between double-entry bookkeeping and database accounting. The information about business processes will provide a framework that will help you apply your knowledge of Microsoft Access to the task of building accounting database components.

This chapter uses an accounting application—processing and maintaining invoice data—to illustrate the use of databases in accounting. The company used in our example, a coffee bean and tea wholesaler called The Coffee Merchant, purchases whole-bean coffees and teas at international auctions and sells the coffees and teas to a variety of coffee roasters. To begin, we will briefly examine the connection between accounting and database systems and explore how accounting came to use relational database management systems.

We urge you to download to your computer or other storage device the Access database from the book's companion Web site. The unzipped database is named *Ch02.accdb*. It contains all the objects that you will need to follow the illustrations in this chapter as well as to complete the end-of-chapter exercises and problems. It provides a place for you to store all of your Chapter 2 database work.

Introduction

Most accounting students learn the mechanics of accounting for economic transactions using the tools of manual double-entry bookkeeping such as journals and ledgers. This chapter begins with a discussion of the differences between database accounting systems and manual double-entry bookkeeping systems. We then explain the advantages and disadvantages of using a database approach to building accounting systems. Finally, the chapter describes business processes, which provide a way for accountants and others to classify economic events into related categories.

Many students have learned how to use Microsoft Access as a software application but have not learned much of the database theory that is essential for creating complex applications such as accounting systems. Chapters 3 through 6 describe how to use database software to build accounting system elements for a specific business process. In these chapters, you will learn how to create queries, forms, and reports to accomplish accounting tasks in any business process.

Database Accounting Systems

Much of the current interest in using databases for accounting systems arose out of businesses realizing the advantages of relational databases, such as Microsoft Access, for all their information processing needs. Rather than maintain separate files and programs for each business function, companies are trying to consolidate their data and data-handling operations. Some firms have created enterprise-wide databases that store all of the firm's information in one system.

Events-Based Theories of Accounting

Over the past 40 years, accounting researchers such as William McCarthy, Guido Geerts, Eric Denna, and George Sorter have developed and refined various events-based approaches to accounting theory. Their work provides a solid theoretical underpinning for accountants' increasing use of relational databases to perform accounting tasks. These events-based approaches argue that accountants should strive to store all relevant attributes of economic events in a readily accessible form. Relational database software products, such as Microsoft Access, provide tools that accountants can use to accomplish that objective. Events theories of accounting offer an alternative to the commonly used double-entry bookkeeping approaches that have been a part of accounting for more than five centuries. Although events approaches to accounting have been discussed for many years, few accounting systems were constructed using events principles until quite recently. Beginning in the early 1990s, advances in information technologies, especially in database management software and disk storage, allowed companies to start building accounting systems based on events theories of accounting.

Double-Entry Bookkeeping Versus Database Accounting

For the better part of 500 years, double-entry bookkeeping provided an excellent method for recording transactions. It satisfied accountants' need to capture the essence of each transaction. When double-entry bookkeeping was first developed over 500 years ago, the costs of gathering and storing information were very high. Recording transactions with pen and paper was a time-consuming task. Double-entry bookkeeping gave accountants a valuable tool that quickly identified essential elements of transactions. Therefore, double-entry bookkeeping let businesspersons capture and store key attributes of transactions in a highly aggregated form. This helped keep the cost of information gathering and storage at affordable levels. Also, the debit-credit balancing check provided an important internal control feature in manual accounting systems.

TRY IT

If you would like to see how far we have come in replacing manual accounting systems with database systems, go to your local office supplies store and try to find a pad of two-column accounting paper. If you have trouble finding it, ask a salesperson for help. He or she will probably look up the product's location—in the store's computerized inventory database.

Computerized transaction processing has released accountants from the limitations and drudgery of manual accounting systems. Using computers, we can now quite easily capture a wide variety of information about each transaction. For example, supermarkets and other retail stores routinely read bar codes at checkout stations to capture the date and time of purchase, the identity of the item purchased, the store location, the checkout station number, and the cashier number. Even more important is that they obtain all of this information with one quick swipe!

Technologies such as bar code readers and optical scanners have played a major role in reducing the cost of acquiring and storing multiple attributes of each economic event. To see more clearly how double-entry bookkeeping and database accounting differ, let's consider a simple sales transaction. Most sales transactions begin when a customer sends a purchase order. If the firm receiving the purchase order has the goods in stock and finds the customer's credit to be acceptable, the firm ships the ordered goods and invoices the customer. A double-entry bookkeeping system would record this transaction for the selling firm with the following journal entry:

DATE	ACCOUNT	DEBIT	CREDIT
Date	Accounts Receivable	Amount	
	Sales		Amount
	Explanation		

Note that this journal entry includes five items of information:

- *Transaction date*
- *Names of the accounts debited*
- *Names of the accounts credited*
- *Transaction amount*
- *Explanation of the transaction*

In a general journal entry such as the one shown above, the explanation might contain the name of the customer. Firms that use specialized journals and subsidiary ledgers can store one additional information item: the customer's name or account code. For example, if the above journal entry had been posted to a subsidiary ledger, the record-keeping process would store the customer's name or account code in the subsidiary ledger. If the sale had been recorded in a specialized sales journal instead of in a general journal as shown above, the format would differ. For example, the account names might be implied by the transaction appearing in the sales journal rather than being explicitly stated; the information recorded would be the same in both cases. To summarize, a double-entry bookkeeping system records five or six transaction attributes and records one of them, the amount, twice.

Now consider how a relational database accounting system might handle the same transaction. A database accounting system would record the transaction in a set of database tables similar to those that appear in Figure 2.1. This view of the tables is what you see in the relationships window in Access.

The database system shown in Figure 2.1 stores some attributes of the sales transaction in the Invoice table, which appears in the figure as *tblInvoice*. We use the "tbl" prefix in this book to indicate that the Access object is a table. We use similar prefixes for other Access objects, including "frm" for forms, "rpt" for reports, and "qry" for queries.

Note, however, that many other attributes of the sales transaction are stored in the eight other tables that appear in Figure 2.1. A database accounting system can store many more attributes of the sales transaction than a journal entry can store. Note that this database accounting system for sales information stores these attributes in an atomic

Fig. 2.1 Sales transactions stored in a database accounting system.

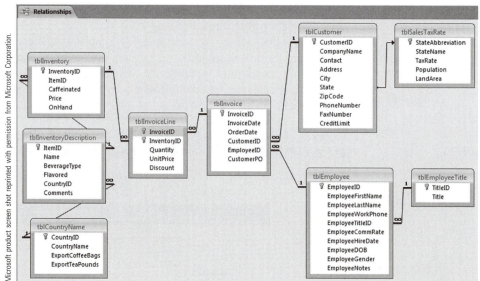

form, scattered throughout the tables. In Chapter 1 you learned a number of rules for designing effective database tables that store information attributes in multiple tables, yet allow the information to be pulled back together when needed. One of these rules requires you to establish a ***primary key*** for each table. The primary key consists of one or more fields in each table that provides a unique identifier for each row in the table. The primary key fields of the tables in Figure 2.1 have a key next to them.

The database system shown in Figure 2.1 stores 6 transaction attributes in the *tbl-Invoice* table and a virtually unlimited number of attributes in the other tables. For example, if the sale was for 20 different items, the *tblInvoiceLine* table would store 60 attributes (20 item quantities, 20 unit prices, and 20 discount percentages) for the transaction. Contrast this with the information stored in the double-entry bookkeeping journal entry. The journal entry does not even tell you how many items were on the invoice, much less tell you anything about those items.

Not only does the database accounting system store many more attributes than the double-entry bookkeeping system, it stores them more efficiently. A key feature of relational database software such as Microsoft Access is that it allows table designs that reduce or eliminate the storage of redundant information. For the sales information database in Figure 2.1, let's examine what is stored in each table, how the tables are linked, and how we might extract information from this sales system.

The primary key of *tblInvoice* is the InvoiceID field. The other attributes of the sale that are stored exclusively in this table include the invoice date, the customer's purchase order number, and the date the customer ordered the merchandise. The other two fields in *tblInvoice* are ***foreign key*** fields. Access, like many other relational database software packages, uses links between primary key fields and corresponding foreign key fields in other tables to maintain the connections among information attributes. The foreign keys in Figure 2.1 show the links from *tblInvoice* to other tables that contain information about sales.

Foreign key links help accountants avoid recording information more than once. For example, the first foreign key field in *tblInvoice* is CustomerID, which links *tblInvoice* to *tblCustomer*. Instead of storing customers' names, addresses, and other information in *tblInvoice* repeatedly for every invoice, this database design lets you store customer information once for each customer and link it to individual sales by including just one field, the CustomerID field, in *tblInvoice*. The other foreign key in *tblInvoice* is EmployeeID. The EmployeeID links each sale to a particular employee in *tblEmployee*.

In addition to linking tables, foreign keys can perform an error-control function. For example, the *tblSalestaxRate* contains the sales tax rates for each state. If the sales tax rate were entered directly in *tblInvoice*, each input clerk would have to look up the customer's state and then go to a sales tax table to obtain the correct tax rate. The use of foreign keys—State in *tblCustomer* and CustomerID in *tblInvoice*—eliminates opportunities to corrupt the sales database with incorrect data.

TRY IT

With several other members of your class, see how many different logical ways you can record employee titles with which you are familiar. You might be surprised at how many variations you can create.

The primary key of *tblInvoice,* InvoiceID, participates in a link to *tblInventory* as part of the primary key in *tblInvoiceLine*. Since this primary key includes two fields, it is called a ***composite primary key***. As you may know from your previous work with

Microsoft Access, the only way to link two tables that have a many-to-many relationship is through a *relationship table*. In a sales transaction, each invoice can have many inventory items. Also, each inventory item can appear on many different invoices. In this sales system, *tblInvoiceLine* is the relationship table that models the many-to-many relationship between *tblInvoice* and *tblInventory*. Its composite primary key includes two fields that link to the primary keys of the two tables that participate in the relationship.

Note that the database system directly records only some of the items that the double-entry bookkeeping system records. The database system records directly the date of the sale, the customer number, and the nature of the transaction as a sale. The database system does not record directly the transaction as an element of accounts receivable. Since sales transactions constitute the left side of the accounts receivable account, storing information about sales in the tables that appear in Figure 2.1 is sufficient in a database accounting system.

To calculate the amount of a particular invoice—the amount that the double-entry bookkeeping system recorded twice in the journal entry—an accountant using a database system would run a query that links *tblInvoice* with *tblInvoiceLine* and with *tblSalesTaxRate*. The query would obtain the Quantity and Price for each InventoryID in *tblInvoiceLine* for the InvoiceID. The query would also obtain the TaxRate from *tblSalesTaxRate*. The query would then multiply the Quantity by the Price for each InventoryID, often referred to as *line extensions*, and sum the line extensions. Then, the query would multiply the sum of the line extensions by the TaxRate for the customer's state from *tblSalesTax*. Finally, the query would add the sum of the line extensions to the sales tax amount to determine the amount of the invoice.

Although database theory argues against storing calculated fields in relational databases, accounting databases sometimes store intermediate calculation results such as this invoice amount calculation. Accountants intentionally violate the strict database rules to increase processing efficiency in databases that store large amounts of transaction data. Additionally, these intermediate amounts serve as an internal control by preserving the results of the calculations based on the information that was in the database at the time the transaction was processed. However, accountants do this reluctantly and avoid storing calculated fields when possible.

Accounting systems that use the database approach can do everything that double-entry bookkeeping does and more. Accountants can use the database tables in Figure 2.1 to calculate invoice amounts and generate the same accounts receivable records and financial statement amounts provided by journals and ledgers. However, the real power of using relational databases to store accounting information arises when managers need specific information that they did not know they would need when the system was created. For example, if a manager wanted to know how many green-colored inventory items were sold during March of last year, the journals and ledgers of double-entry bookkeeping would be virtually useless. However, by using a database accounting system, accountants could quickly provide the manager with an answer that includes number of items and sales in dollars. The database system could even generate subtotals by customer or geographic location for both number of items and sales in dollars.

TRY IT

Examine Figure 2.1 carefully. Identify interesting facts about the firm's sales and sales-related activities that you might find or calculate by searching the database tables and combining the information attributes they contain, a practice often referred to as *data mining*.

As you can see, relational databases record far more information for each transaction than a traditional double-entry bookkeeping system can record. A database accounting system also provides a flexible web of information relating a firm's economic events to each other. In the next two sections, we discuss some of the advantages and disadvantages of using database management systems in accounting applications.

Advantages of Database Accounting Systems

Manual double-entry bookkeeping systems can be very efficient; however, computer implementations of double-entry bookkeeping use a flat file processing design. In manual systems, the dual nature of the accounting debit and credit model provides a built-in error correction mechanism. In automated systems, this same duality is inefficient and serves no real control purpose.

Database accounting systems store data only once. This feature leads to a number of advantages over flat file double-entry accounting systems. A database accounting system can:

- *Reduce data storage costs.*
- *Eliminate data redundancy.*
- *Eliminate data inconsistencies.*
- *Avoid duplicate processing.*
- *Facilitate the add, delete, and update data maintenance tasks.*
- *Make data independent of applications.*
- *Centralize data management.*
- *Centralize data security.*

Database accounting systems offer greater flexibility in extracting data than flat file double-entry accounting systems. This flexibility leads to other advantages. For example, a database accounting system can:

- *Make report modifications and updates easier.*
- *Provide* ad hoc *query capabilities.*
- *Facilitate cross-functional data analysis.*
- *Permit multiple users simultaneous data access.*

Database accounting systems also provide data entry and integrity controls as part of the database management system. Accounting systems designers can embed these controls into the structure of the tables as they create them, which eliminates the need to program controls into every application that use the tables' data.

Because a database stores data only once, the storage costs will be lower than for a flat file system that requires redundant storage. By avoiding the need to store data in multiple locations throughout the system, a database accounting system prevents users from creating data inconsistencies. For example, when a customer's address changes in a database accounting system the change is made in only location, in the Customer table. Every application that uses customer addresses—which may include invoicing, billing, sales promotions, marketing surveys, and sales summaries—automatically begins using the updated address from the Customer table as soon as it is entered. Data inconsistencies can be a source of many potentially embarrassing problems for businesses. Since data are entered only once, the tasks of adding, deleting, and updating records can be accomplished more efficiently. By avoiding data redundancy, a database approach also ensures that the data items used in accounting applications will have the same field names, field lengths, and data types as other applications.

Centralizing data management and security lets businesses fix responsibility for these functions on one person or group. By concentrating this activity, a database approach enables the person or persons responsible for data management and security to develop valuable expertise in this function. When a firm adopts a database approach to manage its data, it usually hires a database administrator. The database administrator holds ultimate responsibility for the specifications and structure of all database tables in the information system. The database administrator is also responsible for enforcing security, making backups, and coordinating contingency plans for emergency situations.

Having the best collection of data in the world will not do managers any good if they cannot access it. A major advantage of database accounting systems is that they facilitate users' access to accounting data. By providing intuitive, graphically based report generators, database management software such as Microsoft Access allows accountants to easily change the structure and format of their reports.

One of the most difficult challenges of designing any accounting system has always been the task of creating reports. Designers found it very hard to anticipate every report that accountants and managers using the system might ever want because they had to do it before the system even existed. The powerful query languages built into Access and other database management systems make this task much easier. Queries let users ask database accounting systems for information by combining data tables and performing calculations in ways the systems' designers never imagined. Further, these user-designed queries and reports can access more than accounting data. For example, tables containing marketing and production information can be combined with accounting information tables to create truly cross-functional reports. This *ad hoc* querying and report-generating capability is one of the key advantages of using an accounting system built with relational database software.

Finally, database accounting systems implement many important data input and data integrity controls at the database level. In Chapter 3 you will learn how to include some of these controls in accounting data tables. By implementing these controls as part of the database, you avoid the need to include the controls in every application that uses the data.

Disadvantages of Database Accounting Systems

Despite the long list of advantages outlined in the previous section, database accounting systems have some disadvantages. The increased functionality of a database system does not come free—the higher price tag for a database system can include costs for items such as:

- *Greater hardware requirements.*
- *The database software itself.*
- *Employing a database administrator.*

Although centralizing management and security control functions in a firm can be advantageous, such centralization can create drawbacks such as:

- *The system operation becomes critical.*
- *Incorrect data entry corrupts many users' work.*
- *Territorial disputes over data ownership may arise.*

One last disadvantage that accountants occasionally note—a disadvantage that is more psychological than real—is accountants' distrust of single-entry accounting systems in general. Double-entry bookkeeping is so pervasive in accounting education and practice that most accountants automatically question and fear anything else.

The increased cost of a database accounting system is often offset by reduced needs for data storage and reduced programming costs. The elimination of data redundancy in a database system reduces the data storage capacity required. Since the data table structures can include many data entry and integrity controls, application programming is simplified—and simpler programming takes less time and costs less money.

The centralization of data and security control is a double-edged sword. Centralization puts all of a firm's information eggs in one basket, and that increases risk. However, it also allows a focusing of resources on contingency planning, security, backup, and recovery that can actually reduce risk levels.

Many firms have decided that the advantages offered by database accounting systems outweigh the disadvantages. Most new accounting system implementations are built using relational database systems. We expect this trend to continue as database management software becomes less expensive, more capable, and easier to use.

Business Processes

Most accounting information systems and auditing textbooks are organized around the primary business processes that add value to a firm. This framework, called a *value chain*, in which accounting systems are viewed in terms of processes rather than financial statement accounts, is consistent with a database approach to accounting systems. A common set of transactions, often referred to as *transaction cycles*, is associated with each business process. In this textbook we use the term *business process* rather than transaction cycle because a database accounting system gathers more than just the information necessary to record journal entries. A value chain diagram with common business processes appears in Figure 2.2.

Fig. 2.2 Value chain of business processes.

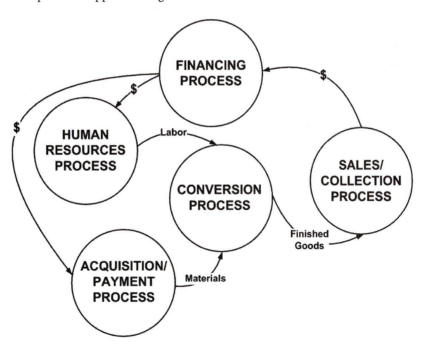

You can see how the business processes relate to each other in Figure 2.2. In the *sales/collection process*, firms sell finished goods for cash or the promise to pay cash. This cash enters the *financing process*. In the financing process, firms obtain cash by issuing equity and debt securities. They also pay dividends on the equity securities and the interest and principal repayments on debt securities in the financing process. Cash flows out of the financing process and into the acquisition/payment and human resources processes. In the *acquisition/payment process*, the firm exchanges cash for materials, supplies, and other expenses related to providing products or services to its customers. In the *human resources process*, the firm exchanges cash for salaries and related labor costs. The *conversion process* converts materials, labor, and other acquired resources into finished goods, completing the value chain.

Although most accountants use the process definitions shown in Figure 2.2, these exact definitions are not universally accepted. Some accountants and systems designers include human resources (HR) activities in the acquisition process since both HR and acquisition processes culminate in writing a check. However, most accounting information systems texts treat HR separately because HR transaction processing is more complex and requires tables and calculations that the acquisition/payment process does not require. You may also see the sales/collection process divided into separate sales and cash receipts processes. Similarly, the acquisition/payment process can be divided into separate acquisition and cash disbursement processes.

A firm may not have all of the business processes depicted in Figure 2.2. For example, service and merchandising firms usually do not have a conversion process. The acquisition/payment process in a merchandising firm acquires finished goods for resale; the acquisition/payment process in a manufacturing firm acquires raw materials and other resources for production. In many service firms, the acquisition/payment process is relatively unimportant, since the dollar amounts of materials and supplies purchased are small.

Many accounting information systems courses avoid extensive treatment of the transactions specific to the financing process because these transactions are few in number. However, auditing classes do spend significant time on financial cycle transactions because they are unusual and often involve large dollar amounts. The transactions that occur only in the financing process, such as stock issuances and large borrowings, are necessary for businesses to operate, so we will cover the financing process in this textbook.

Some accounting systems books describe a general ledger or financial reporting process. When a firm uses database accounting, its financial reporting activities do not require it to record a separate set of transactions. Accountants accomplish these reporting activities by querying and summarizing the data that the firm stores as it conducts its financing, acquisition/payment, HR, conversion, and sales/collection activities. Therefore, we do not treat financial reporting as a separate process in this book. The remainder of this chapter provides a brief introduction to the sales/collection, acquisition/payment, HR, and financing processes.

Sales/Collection Process

The sales/collection process includes all sales and cash collection activities. The three main transactions that we must record in the sales/collection process are customer orders, sales, and cash receipts from customers. We must also record the shipment of goods if it occurs separately from the sales transaction. The sales/collection process portion of an accounting system must be able to generate documents and reports that include:

- *Sales order reports*
- *Invoices*
- *Shipping documents*

- *Remittance advices*
- *Cash receipts summaries*
- *Sales analyses*
- *Balances owed by customers*

Manufacturing, merchandising, and service firms all have similar sales/collection processes. They all sell goods or services to customers, and they all expect customers to pay them. A typical sales/collection process portion of a database would include the following data tables:

- *Cash account*
- *Cash receipt*
- *Customer*
- *Finished goods inventory*
- *Sale*
- *Sale order*
- *Salesperson*

The database design should also include relationship tables, such as a Sales–Finished Goods Inventory table.

Acquisition/Payment Process

A manufacturing firm's acquisition/payment process includes all activities related to ordering raw materials from vendors, receiving the materials ordered, and paying for the materials. A merchandising firm's acquisition/payment process includes the activities related to ordering, receiving, and paying for goods acquired for resale. If a service firm has an acquisition/payment process in its accounting system, it will record the purchase of materials incidental to providing services, such as office supplies. All types of firms will also record the acquisition of long-term assets such as land, buildings, and equipment. The main transactions that we must record in the acquisition/payment processes are purchase orders, receipt of goods ordered, and payments to vendors. The acquisition/payment process portion of an accounting system must generate documents and reports that include:

- *Backorder reports*
- *Balances owed to vendors*
- *Checks*
- *Goods received summaries*
- *Purchase orders*
- *Purchase summaries*
- *Receiving reports*

The details included in the acquisition/payment process tables will vary depending on whether the firm is service, merchandising, or manufacturing. A typical acquisition/payment process portion of a database includes the following data tables:

- *Cash account*
- *Cash disbursement*
- *Purchase order*
- *Raw materials inventory*
- *Raw materials inventory receipt*
- *Vendor*

The database design would also include necessary relationship tables, such as a Purchase Order–Raw Materials Inventory table.

Human Resources Process

The HR process includes the system elements needed to calculate employees' gross pay, deductions, and net pay. The HR process must comply with a complex set of government regulations. The main transactions that occur in the HR process are employees earning pay, employer making payments to employees, and the employer making payments of payroll taxes and taxes withheld from employees' pay to various governmental entities. The HR process must generate documents and reports that include:

- *Checks*
- *Employee commission reports*
- *Employee earnings records*
- *Employee time reports*
- *Payroll registers*

Manufacturing, merchandising, and service firms all have similar HR processes since they all have employees. A typical HR process portion of a database would include the following data tables:

- *Cash account*
- *Cash disbursement*
- *Employee*
- *Time worked*

Financing Process

The financing process includes all cash receipts and cash payments related to both equity and debt financing activities. The main transactions that we must record related to equity financing are the issuance of stock, the receipt of cash from stock issues, the declaration of dividends, and payment of dividends. For debt financing, the main transactions we must record are the loan agreement, getting loan proceeds, and repaying interest and principal on loans. The financing process portion of an accounting system must be able to generate documents and reports that include:

- *Stock ownership by shareholder*
- *Dividends declared and paid*
- *Summary of outstanding loans*
- *Schedule of loan payments due*

Manufacturing, merchandising, and service firms have similar financing processes. They acquire money from owners/investors and distribute earnings, and they borrow money from creditors and repay their creditors. The differences in equity financing are based on business ownership structure: corporations issue stock and pay dividends; partnerships and sole proprietorships issue ownership interests and make distributions. A typical financing process portion of a database would include the following data tables:

- *Cash account*
- *Loan agreement*
- *Stock issue*
- *Dividend declaration*
- *Cash receipt*

- *Cash disbursement*
- *Investor*
- *Creditor*

The database design should also include relationship tables, such as a Loan Agreement–Cash Disbursements table.

Accounting Information Systems and Database Systems

Historically, accounting information has been captured in ledgers and journals. Information about credit sales, for instance, would be recorded in a sales journal. Each month, accountants would create financial statements such as income statements and balance sheets from the information in the ledgers. If a manager needed information about the firm's activities in the middle of the month, that manager had to wait until the books were closed at the end of the next month to obtain that information. In today's fast-paced and highly competitive business world, however, managers need more than the standard periodic accounting reports. Some information cannot be obtained easily, if at all, using traditional double-entry accounting software. For example, it would be difficult for a manufacturing manager to obtain data about total monthly inventory spoilage from a traditional accounting system. Other valuable aggregations of data that provide pictures of a company's current financial or labor situation are hard to obtain from traditional accounting systems. Conventional aggregation methods provided by accounting systems have buried valuable information.

Today's accounting systems use a different approach. Customized reports based on database queries are increasingly replacing traditional accounting reports. The advent of both inexpensive and widely available computer hardware and database management software has accelerated the move toward capturing accounting information in database systems. *Events accounting* consists of storing data about an economic event, such as a cash sale or receipt of a purchase order, in one or more database tables. Events accounting goes beyond merely recording the aggregate numbers associated with the event. Information recorded about an economic event can include who was involved (i.e., the customer's name), why the event occurred, when the event occurred, and what resources were affected by the event.

Events-based accounting systems are not bound by accountants' assumptions about how the information captured is to be aggregated, output, or used. Rather, the managers who will be making decisions based on the information are empowered to extract that information from the accounting events database. An inventory manager, for example, can create (or request the creation of) a report to display current stock levels and the percentage change in stock levels from the previous month.

This is a significant change from accounting information systems that made use of the debit and credit method of recording transactions in a highly aggregated form. If managers need information from the accounting system to help make crucial decisions, they simply request the data they need and then review the resulting report. Managers and other decision makers need no longer rely exclusively on the standard financial statements and other reports produced by traditional accounting systems. Although some of the standard financial statements can help managers make enterprise-wide decisions, much information is lost during the aggregation that takes place in traditional accounting systems when those systems generate financial statements.

In this book, you are learning about accounting information systems implemented using database management systems. Because database management systems can store anything an organization wants to record, they provide a wealth of information. Much useful business information can be generated from the data stored in a database's tables. As an emerging accounting information systems expert, you are on the leading edge of this significant shift to more useful accounting systems.

Next, you will learn about the evolution of database management systems and some advantages and disadvantages of using database systems. We begin with a brief look at what software business tools were available before the advent of database systems.

Database Management Systems

Database management systems (DBMSs) are valuable to business enterprises because they provide a way to store, retrieve, and modify crucial business data. DBMSs can be very cost effective, even though the software can be quite expensive. The next section briefly describes data management and reporting before the advent of database management systems. Subsequent sections describe the general capabilities of database management systems—what core services they typically provide—and the advantages and disadvantages of using database management systems.

Pre-DBMS Data Acquisition and Reporting

Before the availability of modern database management systems, corporate data acquisition and reporting were far different from today. Assume that it is the late 1960s and you are responsible for maintaining customer information for The Coffee Merchant, a small coffee wholesaler, on its medium-sized minicomputer. The data processing department has a staff of computer programmers and support personnel to supply all the company's data processing needs.

Flat files are data files containing information that is not explicitly linked to other information files. Flat files were an important part of business information processing in the early days of computerization. For instance, the accounts receivable department kept customer names and addresses in one file. When purchase orders were received, someone entered the coffee and tea order information into other flat files kept on disk. An orders file contained purchase order data such as the items ordered, quantity requested of each item, and whether the purchase was subject to tax—goods acquired for resale are not taxable until they are sold to a retail customer. Accounts payable kept its own set of files, which contained the names and addresses of vendors to which they owed money, invoice numbers, purchase order numbers, and similar information items.

Standard, frequently requested reports were readily available. These reports summarized data held in the files. When a manager wanted to see the latest sales figures for the previous month, he could place a request with the data processing department. The requested report would be on his desk by the next morning. Finding the current stock levels on all coffees and teas was a typical request that could be easily satisfied. Again, the data processing department would process the management request, run a program that accessed the appropriate files, and produce the report. This was typically how reports were generated for standard, traditional requests.

Requests for custom or unusual reports were a different matter. Although standard reports could be produced by scheduling and running programs written for that purpose, unusual report requests had to be custom-designed and written. For example, suppose the purchasing manager wanted to compare the inventory levels of the 20 most popular coffees and teas with the same period in the previous year. Such a report would require programmers to design and write a custom program. When a special request was received, a system analyst determined what files contained the information needed in the report. The analyst would also provide a program design. After the user(s) approved the design, one or more programmers wrote the program that would read the files, manipulate and summarize the data, and print a report. It was not unusual for a requested custom report to take several weeks before it was delivered to the requesting manager! Keeping a large pool of systems analysts and programmers on staff to supply the data processing needs of the company was expensive. Time is money, and managers could ill afford to wait weeks for critical reports.

Other problems existed in pre-DBMS days. Those problems included the creation of outdated and redundant data. Many departments and individuals created and maintained their own computer files, which resulted in the entry and storage of duplicated information. They would do this so they could access and examine data with their own programs quickly, rather than waiting for the overworked data processing department to respond to their requests. Duplicate data files led to occurrences of data redundancy and data inconsistency.

In many firms, the marketing department kept its own files of information about large customers so they could send out advertising and promotional mailings. The marketing department would hire a bright young programmer to maintain the files and write programs to produce mailing labels from them. Problems occurred when the independently maintained customer list fell out of date. Although the master list of customers was kept current by the data processing department using purchase orders received from customers each month, the marketing department did not have access to the updated data. As existing customers moved and new customers were added, the marketing department's customer list became outdated and, eventually, useless.

You can begin to see the types of problems that arose when businesses used separate information systems. A wall existed between the information consumers and the information itself. That wall was the data processing department, a necessary element in the information request and receipt cycle. Departments coped with unresponsive data processing departments by spawning separate islands of information that were independently maintained. These separate information islands created data redundancy and data inconsistency. In short, much time and money was expended to store and retrieve business data on computers before the arrival of database management systems and accounting information systems based on them.

Functions of a Database Management System

A database management system (DBMS) is a file management system that can store and manage different types of records within one integrated system. Using a DBMS's tools, a database administrator can create a sophisticated system that maintains company records, generates invoices, and in general keeps track of all a company's transactions. A *database* is the physical implementation of a particular set of records, and the DBMS controls access to those records. A *relational database management system*, one of three classical DBMS models, consists of tables containing data whose contents are related to one another through the data content of the tables. The capabilities that a DBMS provides in development of an information system are the following:

- *Efficient data maintenance: storage, update, and retrieval*
- *User-accessible catalog*
- *Concurrency control*
- *Transaction support*
- *Recovery services*
- *Security and authorization services*
- *Integrity facilities*

One of the most important DBMS abilities is its capacity to store, update, and retrieve data. Unlike a flat file system, you need not write and run a special program to store new data in a database. Likewise, when you want to extract information from various data files that are maintained by the DBMS, you can formulate a relatively simple report request in the database system's language. You need not enlist the support of a programmer to write lengthy and complicated programs to extract information. Besides, the DBMS hides all the file storage details from the user. Instead, the user is presented with an uncomplicated view of the data that the DBMS maintains.

Advantages of Database Management Systems

Some of the advantages that a DBMS provides should be clear from the preceding material. DBMSs have other advantages over the old file and programmatic access methods. Many larger database systems provide each user with an individual *view* of the database. Also known as a *subschema*, a view appears to the user to be the real table. It is a definition stored in the database that can extract information from one or more tables and exclude selected rows and columns from being displayed. For instance, a manager might have a view of the database that displays employee data for the employees who report to the requesting manager, but no others. Database systems implement views and provide a measure of security.

Data independence is another DBMS advantage. The term *data independence* refers to a DBMS's ability to hide the details of the physical storage of information from application programs that use the data. To extract information from a database, you merely request information by name and supply conditions that limit which rows are selected. The database system is responsible for translating the information request into data access statements that the database system can understand.

Changes to the structure of a database can be made transparent to the users. This is important because table designs can change over time and it becomes necessary to make changes to the internal structure of one or more tables. Frequently, table structure changes are made to provide significantly shorter database access times. When structure changes occur, using database views can mask those changes, since database views restrict what various users can retrieve from the database. The views mimic users' old perceptions of the affected tables' contents, and the database structure change causes no changes to users' access techniques or methods. On the other hand, imagine the degree to which programs would be affected in a flat file system if just a few changes were made to the structure of the files they access. Programmers would have to spend a great deal of time changing all the programs that reference the files whose structure was changed. In large systems it can be very difficult to find all programs that reference a particular file or set of files.

Finally, database systems help users share data with each other. Because corporate data are centrally stored, everyone has access to the same information and that information is always current and consistent, because there is only one copy of it. There are no duplicate versions of inconsistent data, as was often the case in the years prior to the advent of DMBSs.

Disadvantages of Database Management Systems

The DBMS's main disadvantage is that it can occupy a large amount of expensive disk storage space. You should consider the cost of disk storage when determining whether a database system is cost effective. Though database systems can occupy more than ten times the space required to hold the same data in flat files, DBMSs can still be a good value. Disk storage costs are much lower than the cost of maintaining data in flat files. Programming costs have gone up rapidly in the last 15 years, but prices of hardware such as disk drives have dropped sharply.

Large database systems often require additional people such as a database administrator to keep the system running smoothly. Other database experts may be hired to handle the information needs of the company. With few exceptions, these added costs are far less than the cost of not using a DBMS. Of course, smaller businesses using PC-based database management packages such as Microsoft Access can often avoid these additional personnel costs. In such cases, only the additional disk space cost is a factor in the decision.

Relational Database Management Systems

Database management systems can be implemented by following one of three data models in widespread use today. A *data model* is an abstract representation of a database system providing a description of the data and methods for accessing the data managed by the database. The three models in use are the *hierarchical model*, the *network model*, and the *relational model*. Throughout most of the late 1960s and early 1970s, most databases used the hierarchical or network model. IBM's IMS database system, which was widely used in the 1970s, is one example of a hierarchical DBMS. Cullinet's IDMS/R is a database built on the network model that was also popular in the 1970s. However, things changed rapidly during that decade. E. F. Codd, working in an IBM research laboratory, developed the relational model for database systems. Since that time, the relational model has evolved and the number of database systems based on the relational model has exploded. Today, the relational model is the overwhelming choice for database systems running on all kinds and sizes of computers.

The relational model provides several significant advantages over the hierarchical and network models. In the relational model, the logical and physical characteristics of the database are distinct; this provides users with a more intuitive view of the data. Using the relational model requires very little training. The relational model includes more powerful retrieval and update operators that allow complex operations to be executed with concise commands. Perhaps most importantly, the relational model provides powerful tools to let analysts know when a database has inherent design flaws.

The advantages of the relational model overwhelm the disadvantages of using database systems. From this point on in the text, when we refer to a DBMS, we specifically mean a *relational database management system*, or *RDBMS*.

Database Objects

The relational model is based in mathematical set theory, the theory of relations, and first-order predicate logic. The model defines the conceptual view that the user has all of the objects contained by the database system. Both the data objects and the relationships between them are represented as a collection of tables. All data in a relational database, including the database table definitions and information about database objects such as forms and reports, exist only in tables. This provides a simple and consistent view of the database.

A relational database is a collection of relations. The primary structure in a relational model database is a relation. A table is an example of a relation. For that reason, you will often see the terms *relation* and *table* used interchangeably. A table, or relation, consists of rows and columns, similar to a matrix or spreadsheet. The formal term for row is *tuple*, but most database experts use the less formal term *row*. The formal term for column is *attribute*, but most database experts use the term *column*. Alternative common terms used for relation, tuple, and attribute are *file*, *record*, and *field*, respectively. Figure 2.3 summarizes these three sets of terms.

Fig. 2.3 **Three sets of database terms.**

Formal Term	Common Term	Alternative Common Term
relation	table	file
tuple	row	record
attribute	column	field

You might have used spreadsheet software in some of your other accounting courses. A spreadsheet page resembles a database table in several ways. For example, a spreadsheet page has columns and rows. The columns in a spreadsheet page often have titles that describe the content of the columns. You might want to think of database tables as a special form of spreadsheet pages. The difference is that database tables must comply with very strict rules about what can be included in each row and column. The most important properties of database tables include the following:

- *The entries in each column of any row must be single valued.*
- *Each attribute (column) in a table has a distinct name, called the **attribute name**.*
- *Every entry in a column contains a value for that column only, and the values are of the same data type.*
- *The order of the rows is unimportant.*
- *The order (position) of the columns in relation to each other is unimportant.*
- *Each row is unique (i.e., it differs from all other rows in the table).*

The preceding table properties are very important. Later in this chapter, you will learn about each of these properties in detail. Figure 2.4 shows an example relation that is one of the tables included in The Coffee Merchant's database. Only the first 20 rows and the first seven columns are shown in the figure.

The Customer table contains hundreds of rows, in no particular order, one for each of The Coffee Merchant's customers. Because the row order is unimportant in a RDBMS, there is no implied meaning that one customer is more important than another. All you can tell from the row order is that the identification number field, called CustomerID, is in ascending order. In relational databases, a row's identity is determined by its content, not by its location within a table.

Primary and Foreign Key Attributes

The table that appears in Figure 2.4 contains ten columns, but only seven of these attributes appear in Figure 2.4: CustomerID, CompanyName, Contact, Address, City, State, and ZipCode. However, there is no theoretical reason to list the columns in that order. We have chosen to place the primary key column, CustomerID, as the first table column. Although Access does not require the primary key column to be first, most database designers follow this convention. We could, for example, place the Contact column in the second column, followed by the State and City columns.

Within each column you can see the attribute values for each row. For instance, the row identified as CustomerID 30121 contains "Fairfield Communities Inc." in its CompanyName value and "Best, F. Stanley" in its Contact value. Each row may store a different value for each attribute. In particular, the CustomerID value is unique for each row. This satisfies the rule that each row must be unique. A row is unique if any one of its columns is unique.

Fig. 2.4 The Customer relation, *tblCustomer*.

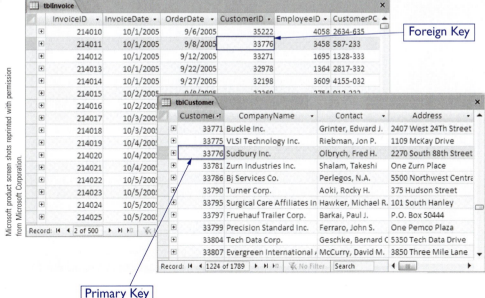

Microsoft product screen shot reprinted with permission from Microsoft Corporation.

	CustomerID	CompanyName	Contact	Address	City	State	ZipCode
⊞	30121	Fairfield Communities Inc.	Best, F. Stanley	2800 Cantrell Road	Little Rock	AR	72202
⊞	30125	Alamo Group Inc.	Maul, Duane A.	1502 East Walnut	Seguin	TX	78155
⊞	30129	Kiwi International Air Lines	Rigas, Alan J.	Demishpere Center	Newark	NJ	07114
⊞	30132	Republic Bancorp Inc.	Murray, T. Peter	1070 East Main Street	Owosso	MI	48867
⊞	30136	Browne Bottling Co.	Shelton, Carl E.	411 First Avenue South	Oklahoma City	OK	73102
⊞	30139	Cavco Industries Inc.	Golkin, David	422 Wards Corner Road	Phoenix	AZ	85012
⊞	30142	Bucyrus Erie Co.	Kostantaras, Jack R.	1100 Milwaukee Avenue	South Milwaukee	WI	53172
⊞	30144	U S Office Products Co.	Gerson, Terrence	2155 Monroe Drive No	Washington	DC	20005
⊞	30147	Ciatti S Inc.	Townes, Patrick J.	5555 West 78Th Street	Edina	MN	55439
⊞	30148	Tab Products Co.	Montrone, Frank A.	1400 Page Mill Road	Palo Alto	CA	94304
⊞	30149	Diversicare Inc.		105 Reynolds Drive	Franklin	TN	37068
⊞	30153	Audiovox Corp.	Choate, Robert	150 Marcus Boulevard	Hauppauge	NY	11788
⊞	30155	Twin Disc Inc.	Crist, Dennis P.	1328 Racine Street	Racine	WI	53403
⊞	30158	Bay State Gas Co.	Huff, Richard E.	300 Firebug Parkway	Westborough	MA	01581
⊞	30159	Fort Wayne National Corp.		110 West Berry Street	Fort Wayne	IN	46801
⊞	30163	Medusa Corp.	Hart, John M.	3008 Monticello Boule	Cleveland Heights	OH	44118
⊞	30164	Stv Group Inc.	Hill, Alex W.	11 Robinson Street	Pottstown	PA	19464
⊞	30168	Commercial Federal Corp.	McMeel, John D.	2120 South 72Nd Stree	Omaha	NE	68124
⊞	30170	Ketema Inc.	Crosley, Lynn H.	1000 East Main Street	Denver	CO	80222
⊞	30174	Thomas Nelson Inc.	Harber, L. H.	Nelson Place At Elm Hi	Nashville	TN	37214

Record: 23 of 1789 • No Filter   Search

Every relation must have a primary key that uniquely identifies each row in the table. The primary key can include one or more columns. When the primary key includes more than one column, the individual column values need not be unique, but the combined column values must be unique.

Every row in a RDBMS must be distinct from all other rows in that table, or else it cannot be retrieved easily. This is one of the fundamental rules of a RDBMS. To ensure uniqueness, a primary key is designated for a table. A primary key, as mentioned previously, is a column (or group of columns) that uniquely identifies a given row. Therefore, the system can distinguish one record (row) of a table from another. In the *tblCustomer* table, for instance, the CustomerID column—the customer's identification number—uniquely identifies a row. Thus, CustomerID is the primary key for the *tblCustomer* table.

Another important table field is a foreign key. A ***foreign key*** is an attribute in one table that matches the primary key field of another table. Figure 2.5 shows two of The Coffee

Fig. 2.5 Primary key and foreign key relationship.

Microsoft product screen shots reprinted with permission from Microsoft Corporation.

tblInvoice

	InvoiceID	InvoiceDate	OrderDate	CustomerID	EmployeeID	CustomerPC
⊞	214010	10/1/2005	9/6/2005	35222	4058	2634-635
⊞	214011	10/1/2005	9/8/2005	33776	3458	587-233
⊞	214012	10/1/2005	9/12/2005	33271	1695	1328-333
⊞	214013	10/1/2005	9/22/2005	32978	1364	2817-332
⊞	214014	10/1/2005	9/27/2005	32198	3609	4155-032
⊞	214015	10/2/2005	9/8/2005	32269	2754	912-332
⊞	214016	10/2/2005				
⊞	214017	10/3/2005				
⊞	214018	10/3/2005				
⊞	214019	10/4/2005				
⊞	214020	10/4/2005				
⊞	214021	10/4/2005				
⊞	214022	10/5/2005				
⊞	214023	10/5/2005				
⊞	214024	10/5/2005				
⊞	214025	10/5/2005				

Record: 2 of 500

Foreign Key

tblCustomer

	CustomerID	CompanyName	Contact	Address
⊞	33771	Buckle Inc.	Grinter, Edward J.	2407 West 24Th Street
⊞	33775	VLSI Technology Inc.	Riebman, Jon P.	1109 McKay Drive
⊞	33776	Sudbury Inc.	Olbrych, Fred H.	2270 South 88th Street
⊞	33781	Zurn Industries Inc.	Shalam, Takeshi	One Zurn Place
⊞	33786	Bj Services Co.	Perlegos, N.A.	5500 Northwest Centra
⊞	33790	Turner Corp.	Aoki, Rocky H.	375 Hudson Street
⊞	33795	Surgical Care Affiliates In	Hawker, Michael R.	101 South Hanley
⊞	33797	Fruehauf Trailer Corp.	Barkai, Paul J.	P.O. Box 50444
⊞	33799	Precision Standard Inc.	Ferraro, John S.	One Pemco Plaza
⊞	33804	Tech Data Corp.	Geschke, Bernard C	5350 Tech Data Drive
⊞	33807	Evergreen International	McCurry, David M.	3850 Three Mile Lane

Record: 1224 of 1789 • No Filter   Search

Primary Key

Merchant tables used to retrieve invoice data from the set of tables constituting the database. Many database designers use the same field name for related primary key and foreign key columns to indicate the two columns tie together two tables. For example, the foreign key CustomerID in the table *tblInvoice* is related to the identically named field in the table *tblCustomer*. Although many database designers follow this naming practice, Microsoft Access and other database management software packages do not require it.

The CustomerID column in the Invoice (*tblInvoice*) table is a foreign key, because it references a primary key found in one row of the *tblCustomer* table. The associations between foreign keys and primary keys are important because relational databases use them to establish connections between related tables.

Schema of a Relation

The schema of a relation is a set of information that includes the name of a relation and its attributes. Some database designers also call this set of information a **table structure**. A compact representation of the schema for the *tblCustomer* table, using the reduced number of columns in this illustration, is:

Customer(CustomerID, CompanyName, Contact, Address, City, State, ZipCode)

The table's attributes are enclosed in parentheses following the table name. In this notation, an underline indicates the primary key column(s). This is not the only way to write this schema, but it is one you will find in common use in many books on database design and in many accounting information systems textbooks. Though not shown here, a double underline or a line appearing over one or more fields indicates the field is a foreign key. Another common notation system uses bold type to indicate a primary key and italics to indicate a foreign key.

Data Dictionary

Relational database systems have a data dictionary. A data dictionary is a collection of tables containing the definition, characteristics, structure, and description of all data maintained by the RDBMS.

In addition to table descriptions, the data dictionary can store view definitions, database object owner names, database login names, and passwords. Fields in the data dictionary are automatically changed whenever an object's structure is changed. For example, if you delete a column from a table and rename another table, both operations cause changes to the data dictionary entries. A row in a table holding other tables' column names is deleted when you delete a column, and a row containing table names is updated when you rename a table. Having a data dictionary makes the job of the database management system and the database administrator easier, because all information needed about the system is contained in one place.

Unfortunately, Microsoft Access does not include a facility that automatically creates a data dictionary. You can create a data dictionary in a separate Access file, but it will not automatically update itself when you change the elements of the database.

The Coffee Merchant Tables

To understand how accounting information can be organized in a database system, let's look at an example. Several of the tables contained in the *Ch02.accdb* database include invoice data for customers of The Coffee Merchant. Figure 2.6 shows schema for each table used in the invoicing subsystem of The Coffee Merchant's database.

Fig. 2.6
Schemas of tables in the invoicing system.

tblCountryName	(CountryID, CountryName, ExportCoffeeBags, ExportTeaPounds)
tblCustomer	(CustomerID, CompanyName, Contact, Address, City, State, ZipCode, PhoneNumber, FaxNumber, CreditLimit)
tblEmployee	(EmployeeID, EmployeeFirstName, EmployeeLastName, EmployeeWorkPhone, EmployeeTitleID, EmployeeCommRate, EmployeeHireDate, EmployeeDOB, EmployeeGender, EmployeeNotes)
tblEmployeeTitle	(TitleID, Title)
tblInventory	(InventoryID, ItemID, Caffeinated, Price, OnHand)
tblInventoryDescription	(ItemID, Name, BeverageType, Flavored, CountryID, Comments)
tblInvoice	(InvoiceID, InvoiceDate, OrderDate, CustomerID, EmployeeID, CustomerPO)
tblInvoiceLine	(InvoiceID, InventoryID, Quantity, UnitPrice, Discount)
tblSalesTaxRate	(StateAbbreviation, StateName, TaxRate, Population, LandArea)

When bits of data from each of these tables are combined in the proper way, you can build and print an invoice. The *tblCustomer* table contains information about each customer. Each customer is assigned a primary key—a sequence of integers beginning with any number is sufficient—so that a customer can be uniquely identified. The Invoice table, *tblInvoice*, contains a history of invoices sent out by The Coffee Merchant. Each row is identified by the primary key, InvoiceID, and it holds each customer's invoice date (InvoiceDate), order date (OrderDate), customer identification number (CustomerID), identification number of the associated salesperson (EmployeeID), and the customer's original purchase order number (CustomerPO). Of course, an invoice shows more details than these held in the Invoice table *tblInvoice*, but those additional details (such as the customer's address) are contained in *tblCustomer*, which is linked to the Invoice table on the CustomerID attribute—the primary key in *tblCustomer* and a foreign key in *tblInvoice*. Figure 2.7 shows a Datasheet view of some *tblInvoice* rows.

Fig. 2.7 Example rows in the Invoice table, *tblInvoice*.

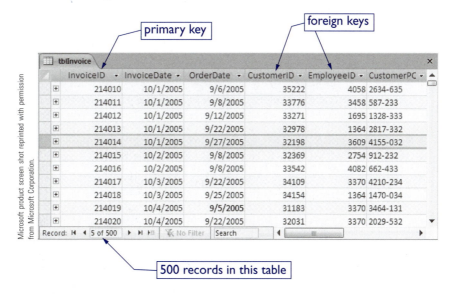

primary key

foreign keys

	InvoiceID ▾	InvoiceDate ▾	OrderDate ▾	CustomerID ▾	EmployeeID ▾	CustomerPC ▾
⊞	214010	10/1/2005	9/6/2005	35222	4058	2634-635
⊞	214011	10/1/2005	9/8/2005	33776	3458	587-233
⊞	214012	10/1/2005	9/12/2005	33271	1695	1328-333
⊞	214013	10/1/2005	9/22/2005	32978	1364	2817-332
⊞	214014	10/1/2005	9/27/2005	32198	3609	4155-032
⊞	214015	10/2/2005	9/8/2005	32369	2754	912-232
⊞	214016	10/2/2005	9/8/2005	33542	4082	662-433
⊞	214017	10/3/2005	9/22/2005	34109	3370	4210-234
⊞	214018	10/3/2005	9/25/2005	34154	1364	1470-034
⊞	214019	10/4/2005	9/5/2005	31183	3370	3464-131
⊞	214020	10/4/2005	9/22/2005	32031	3370	2029-532

Record: I◄ ◄ 5 of 500 ► ►I ►⁎ 🇽 No Filter   Search

500 records in this table

Order lines contain details about individual items ordered by the customer and included on the current invoice such as quantity ordered, unit price, and discount. These order line details are not stored in the Invoice table. Instead, those details are stored in three other tables: *tblInvoiceLine*, *tblInventory*, and *tblInventoryDescription*. Figures 2.8, 2.9, and 2.10 show sample rows from each of these tables. The *tblInvoiceLine* table may appear to be a bit unusual at first glance. It contains only five attributes: two fields that make up its composite primary key and three other fields that contain information about the items on each invoice. These information items include the quantity ordered, the quoted unit price (which can vary for a given product depending on the customer), and the discount percentage for each item on each invoice. A composite primary key consists of more than one attribute. In this table, InvoiceID and InventoryID combine to form the composite primary key. These two attributes identify the invoice and each inventory item number that will appear on a line of that invoice. The *tblInventory* and *tblInventoryDescription* tables store information about the coffees and teas available from The Coffee Merchant. Only a few of the over 100 items stored in the inventory tables appear in Figure 2.9. InventoryID identifies each inventory item uniquely, and other characteristics about the inventory item are stored in the *tblInventory* and *tblInventoryDescription* tables.

Fig. 2.8 Example rows in the Invoice Line table, *tblInvoiceLine*.

primary key · foreign key

InvoiceID	InventoryID	Quantity	UnitPrice	Discount
214010	1184	18	$6.90	5%
214010	1192	17	$13.30	10%
214010	1195	17	$3.90	0%
214010	1209	14	$6.20	15%
214010	1237	17	$10.90	5%
214011	1104	19	$5.30	5%
214011	1133	8	$7.90	0%
214011	1137	15	$7.00	15%
214011	1197	2	$7.10	0%
214011	1211	10	$14.70	15%

Record: 4 of 2192   No Filter   Search

Microsoft product screen shot reprinted with permission from Microsoft Corporation.

Fig. 2.9 Example rows in the primary Inventory table, *tblInventory*.

primary key · foreign key

InventoryID	ItemID	Caffeinated	Price	OnHand
1101	116	☑	$8.10	512
1102	422	☐	$5.30	3,190
1103	440	☐	$7.70	-130
1104	455	☐	$5.30	3,380
1105	449	☐	$7.60	3,300
1106	224	☑	$7.40	1,130
1107	113	☑	$8.80	315
1108	134	☑	$10.30	443
1109	275	☑	$8.00	354
1110	353	☐	$13.70	354

Record: 4 of 154   No Filter   Search

Microsoft product screen shot reprinted with permission from Microsoft Corporation.

These tables do not store the extended price, subtotal, and other information that normally appears on an invoice. The way to obtain these information items is to have Access calculate them when it prints invoices. Calculated values need not be stored in

Fig. 2.10 Example
rows in the secondary
Inventory table,
tblInventoryDescription.

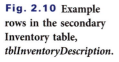
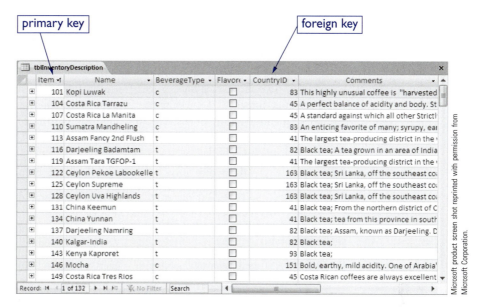

tables, because they can be obtained by multiplying each invoice line's quantity and
price attributes. It is generally undesirable to store values in a table that can be calculated from other table fields. Thus, the data in these four tables plus the Customer
table, *tblCustomer*, contain all of the information needed to produce invoices for The
Coffee Merchant.

Now that you understand the details of The Coffee Merchant's database tables, you
can learn about normalization. We will use The Coffee Merchant tables to illustrate the
reasons for and the definitions of normalized tables.

Normalization

In a relational table design, it is important to think carefully about where individual
pieces of data are stored. The process of determining the correct location for each attribute is called *normalization*. Another way of thinking about normalization is this: normalizing a database is storing data where it uniquely belongs. Unnormalized databases
can lead to redundant, inconsistent, or incorrect information being stored in tables.

There are many ways to arrange the invoice system attributes in sets of tables. Some
arrangements are better than others. A particular subset of the ways that attributes can
be organized into tables is called a *normal form*, and the basis of this arrangement is
called *normalization theory*.

Database theorists have identified seven normal forms. Like layers of an onion, each
normal form includes compliance with the rules of all lower normal forms. For example,
a table that is in third normal form is automatically in first and second normal forms and
complies with the rules for those three normal forms. The rules applied to achieve each
normal form are successively more stringent. The least restrictive is called the *first normal
form*, which is abbreviated as 1NF. Following that form are the *second*, *third*, *Boyce-Codd*,
fourth, *fifth*, and *Domain-Key* normal forms. Most accounting systems require use of only
the first three normal forms. Tables in third normal form are better than tables in second
normal form. Likewise, tables in second normal form are better than tables in first normal
form. The goal of the normalization process is to start with a collection of tables (or relations), apply normalization, and arrive at an equivalent collection of tables in a higher normal form. The process is repeated until all tables are in third normal form (3NF).

First Normal Form

A table that contains a repeating group is called an ***unnormalized table***. The relational model requires that all tables be in first normal form. To achieve this, repeating data must be removed from the table and stored elsewhere. For example, suppose that an invoice table held each invoice line for all invoices in the arrangement shown in Figure 2.11.

Notice that for each invoice in the Invoice table, there are several inventory item numbers, quantities, unit prices, and discounts. For instance, invoice number 214010 contains five items; each item corresponds to an invoice detail item on a printed invoice. The schema for this table is:

> tblInvoice (InvoiceID, InvoiceDate, CustomerID,
> InventoryID, Quantity, UnitPrice, Discount,
> InventoryID, Quantity, UnitPrice, Discount,...)

where the ellipsis indicates that InventoryID, Quantity, UnitPrice, and Discount can repeat any number of times—as many times as there are items listed on a single invoice.

Fig. 2.11 Example table containing repeating groups.

InvoiceID	InvoiceDate	CustomerID	InventoryID	Quantity	UnitPrice	Discount	
214010	10/01/05	35222	1184	18	$6.90	5%	
			1192	17	$13.30	10%	repeating group
			1195	17	$3.90	0%	
			1209	14	$6.20	15%	
			1237	17	$10.90	5%	
214011	10/1/2005	33776	1104	19	$5.30	5%	
			1133	8	$7.90	0%	repeating group
			1137	15	$7.00	15%	
			1197	2	$7.10	0%	
			1211	10	$14.70	15%	
214012	10/1/2005	33271	1127	17	$4.50	0%	
			1129	5	$8.40	0%	repeating group
			1189	14	$5.30	15%	
			1203	12	$8.10	15%	
			1249	2	$11.90	0%	
214013	10/1/2005	32978	1139	10	$5.30	15%	
			1198	17	$8.10	5%	
			1208	14	$4.50	15%	repeating group
			1216	19	$7.20	5%	
			1229	5	$12.90	0%	
			1249	5	$11.90	0%	
214014	10/1/2005	32198	1170	6	$44.50	10%	

To be in first normal form (1NF), a table cannot store repeating groups (multiple values) in one table column, nor can it store a variable number of {InventoryID, Quantity, UnitPrice, Discount} sets in each row. To convert the table shown in Figure 2.11 into first normal form, you can remove the repeating groups from the existing Invoice table and place them into a new table. However, you must add an additional column to the new table linking the rows of the newly formed table with the original Invoice table. An example of the structure of the two tables conforming to first normal form is this:

> tblInvoice(InvoiceID, InvoiceDate, OrderDate, CustomerID, EmployeeID, CustomerPO)
> tblInvoiceLine(InvoiceID, InventoryID, Quantity, UnitPrice, Discount)

The new table, *tblInvoiceLine*, contains five columns. The first two columns, InvoiceID and InventoryID, combine to form the new table's primary key. This is a ***composite primary key*** because the primary key includes two attributes.

Second Normal Form

Tables in first normal form can be placed into a relational database system, but in many cases first normal form is not sufficient to prevent problems. For example, Figure 2.12

shows an example of some rows of a Customer table in first normal form. The schema for this table is:

tblCustomer(<u>CustomerID</u>, CompanyName, PhoneNumber, Contact, <u>InvoiceID</u>, Total)

The Customer table contains customer information including the customer identification number, company name, telephone, and contact person. The last two columns indicate the customer's invoice number and amount. The two table columns, CustomerID and InvoiceID, form the table's primary key. Both are needed to access a row.

Several potential problems exist with the proposed 1NF Customer table. Suppose that the Customer table is the only place in which customer information such as address or name is stored. Further, suppose that a new customer has paid for an order in advance. The design would not allow such a customer to be added, because the InvoiceID value would be empty. When an attribute is empty, or has no value, it is *null*. The InvoiceID attribute cannot be null, because the primary key cannot be null or include a null attribute if it is a composite primary key. The inability to add a record is called an ***insertion anomaly***.

Consider this scenario. Cavco Industries pays for its two invoices, numbers 214123 and 214460 (see Figure 2.12, second and third rows), bringing its amount due to zero. The two rows corresponding to Cavco Industries are removed from *tblCustomer*. Not only are the two invoices removed, but the customer's identification number, name, phone, and contact person are deleted as well. So the deletion has a wider effect than desired; you lose knowledge of the customer entirely. Your mailing list is being destroyed! This predicament is known as a ***deletion anomaly***.

Finally, the *tblCustomer* table shown in Figure 2.12 contains much redundant information. For instance, the company identification number, name, phone number, and contact person are repeated for each new invoice that is issued for a particular customer. The customer name *Cavco Industries Inc.* is entered twice, as is *Golkin, David*, the contact person. It is pure luck that both the company name and contact person's name have been spelled correctly both times. To change the company name, you must find all occurrences of the name in the database and change each one. What a time-consuming task that could be! This small example illustrates that tables in first normal form can contain redundant data.

Fig. 2.12 Example rows of the Customer table in first normal form (1NF).

CustomerID	CompanyName	PhoneNumber	Contact	InvoiceID	Total
30125	Alamo Group Inc.	(210) 555-1483	Maul, Duane A.	214480	306.80
30139	Cavco Industries Inc.	(602) 555-6141	Golkin, David	214123	225.11
30139	Cavco Industries Inc.	(602) 555-6141	Golkin, David	214460	315.10
30174	Thomas Nelson Inc.	(615) 555-9079	Harber, L. H.	214390	491.96
30174	Thomas Nelson Inc.	(615) 555-9079	Harber, L. H.	214418	185.95
30206	Matlack Systems Inc.	(302) 555-2760	Gordon, W. Phil	214334	218.39
30212	Lilly Industries Inc.	(317) 555-6762	Choong, Jerry	214117	152.20
30221	Mcdonald & Co. Investments Inc.	(216) 555-2368	Bianco, Andrew R.	214249	297.34
30225	Krause S Furniture Inc.	(510) 555-6208	Woltz, Neil G.	214087	260.15
30228	F N B Corp. Pa	(412) 555-6028	Fancher, William R.	214284	98.35
30231	Everest & Jennings Internation	(314) 555-7041	Gray, Robert R.	214036	270.60
30231	Everest & Jennings Internation	(314) 555-7041	Gray, Robert R.	214256	165.96
30258	Lcs Industries Inc.	(201) 555-5666	Lebuhn, Eugene	214230	895.25
30258	Lcs Industries Inc.	(201) 555-5666	Lebuhn, Eugene	214308	541.97

Altering a table's structure and changing it into second normal form can prevent these anomalies. A table (relation) is in ***second normal form*** (2NF) if it is in first normal form and none of the nonkey attributes depend on only one portion of the primary key. That is, second normal form requires that each nonkey attribute depend on the entire primary key, not just part of it. This rule applies only when you have a composite primary key—one consisting of more than one table column.

The attribute Total in the Customer table in Figure 2.12 violates the 2NF definition. The value of Total is determined by the partial primary key InvoiceID. We say that Total is *functionally dependent* on InvoiceID, because a particular value of InvoiceID determines a single value of Total. On the other hand, Total does not depend on the attribute and partial primary key CustomerID, because the total invoice amount varies from invoice to invoice; no relationship exists between Total and a particular customer. On the other hand, the attributes CompanyName, PhoneNumber, and Contact each functionally depend on the partial primary key CustomerID. These two sets of functional dependencies are shown in Figure 2.13.

Fig. 2.13 Functional dependencies in the Customer table.

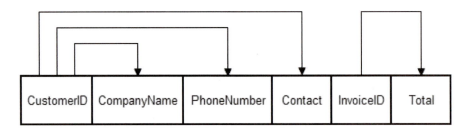

The arrows lead from a primary key to another attribute. For instance, the arrow leading from CustomerID to CompanyName means that CustomerID *determines* CompanyName (or CustomerID is a *determinant* of CompanyName). It is clear that we can correct this problem by breaking *tblCustomer* into two tables. Of course, we must note the relationship between these two tables by including an extra attribute—a foreign key—that links both tables on the CustomerID key. You can restructure *tblCustomer* and the related table *tblInvoice* so they are in second normal form by using a design such as this:

> tblCustomer(<u>CustomerID</u>, CompanyName, PhoneNumber, Contact)
> tblInvoice(<u>InvoiceID</u>, <u>CustomerID</u>, Total)

In this design, the CustomerID field in *tblInvoice* is a foreign key to *tblCustomer*. The double underline below CustomerID in *tblInvoice* indicates that it is a foreign key.

Third Normal Form

The design goal for relational databases is to create tables that are in third normal form. A table is in *third normal form* (3NF) if it is in second normal form and all transitive dependencies have been eliminated. A *transitive dependency* exists in a table if attribute B determines attribute C, and attribute C determines attribute D.

You have probably heard an expression that can help you understand and remember the difference between 2NF and 3NF. Part of the phrase used to swear in witnesses who are about to take the stand in a trial is: "… to tell the truth, the whole truth, and nothing but the truth." The second normal form is analogous to "the whole truth" part of the phrase—each attribute depends on the *whole* primary key. Similarly, the third normal form is analogous to "and nothing but the truth." Each attribute depends *only* on the primary key and on no other attribute in the relation. For example, consider the Invoice table shown in Figure 2.14.

The Invoice table's primary key is InvoiceID. Because only one customer may be assigned a particular invoice number (the value in the InvoiceID field), the invoice number uniquely determines the invoice date, order date, customer identification number, employee identification number, and company contact person. There are no repeating groups in the table. Therefore, it is in first normal form. Furthermore, it is in second normal form because all attributes depend on the single-attribute primary key. However, it is not in third normal form, because all attributes are not functionally dependent on only the InvoiceID attribute. There is a transitive dependency in this design. The InvoiceID determines the CustomerID value, and CustomerID, in turn, determines the Contact column. Figure 2.15 shows the dependency in the Invoice table.

Fig. 2.14 Invoice table in second normal form (2NF).

Microsoft product screen shot reprinted with permission from Microsoft Corporation.

InvoiceID	InvoiceDate	OrderDate	CustomerID	EmployeeID	CustomerPO
214010	10/1/2005	9/6/2005	35222	4058	2634-635
214011	10/1/2005	9/8/2005	33776	3458	587-233
214012	10/1/2005	9/12/2005	33271	1695	1328-333
214013	10/1/2005	9/22/2005	32978	1364	2817-332
214014	10/1/2005	9/27/2005	32198	3609	4155-032
214015	10/2/2005	9/8/2005	32369	2754	912-232
214016	10/2/2005	9/8/2005	33542	4082	662-433
214017	10/3/2005	9/22/2005	34109	3370	4210-234
214018	10/3/2005	9/25/2005	34154	1364	1470-034
214019	10/4/2005	9/5/2005	31183	3370	3464-131
214020	10/4/2005	9/22/2005	32031	3370	2029-532
214021	10/4/2005	9/29/2005	33312	1301	1580-633

Record: 15 of 500   No Filter   Search

Fig. 2.15 Transitive dependencies in the Invoice table shown in Figure 2.14.

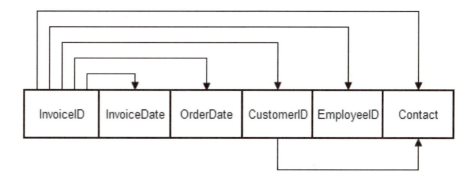

The arrows above the attribute boxes show the dependencies that exist between attributes and the table's primary key. Those relationships are fine. However, the arrow below the boxes shows a transitive dependency between CustomerID (the determinant attribute) and Contact. The easiest way to remove the transitive dependency is to create another table containing at least the determinant attribute and all attributes that are dependent on that determinant attribute. Once the transitive dependency is removed, the table will be in 3NF. The CustomerID field becomes a foreign key to link the invoice to individual customer information. The new tables could be structured as follows to bring them in compliance with 3NF:

> tblInvoice(<u>InvoiceID</u>, InvoiceDate, OrderDate, <u>CustomerID</u>, <u>EmployeeID</u>)
> tblCustomer(<u>CustomerID</u>, Contact)

Third normal form enforces an informal rule stating that a table should store one fact and one fact only. Prior to decomposing *tblInvoice* into two separate tables, it housed two facts: one fact about invoices (InvoiceDate, OrderDate, etc.) and one fact about customers (Contact). After two tables are created from a single table, each new table's structure (shown previously) holds only one fact.

Table Relationships

You have learned that the process of normalizing a database's tables usually produces several additional tables. Yet, the relationships between associated tables are maintained by the foreign key to primary key links. There are three fundamental types of relationships between related tables: *one-to-one (1–1)*, *one-to-many (1–M)*, and *many-to-many (M–M)*. The capital letter *M* indicates *many* records. Knowing about these three is important in understanding how to reconstruct information from data stored in constituent tables. Recall that rows from two tables are joined when the foreign key in one table's row matches the primary key in another table.

One-to-one relationships usually indicate unnecessary tables in the database design. You can usually combine tables with a one-to-one relationship into one table. Exceptions to this general rule can occur. For instance, the Customer table could have a one-to-one relationship with *tblCustomerNotes*, which might hold supplementary information about a few of The Coffee Merchant's customers. Because only a few customers have notes in the *tblCustomerNotes* table, you do not want to allocate an additional column for an occasional note. This would waste storage space. So, *tblCustomerNotes* would contain the foreign key CustomerID and a Notes column. CustomerID would serve both as the primary key for the *tblCustomerNotes* table and as a foreign key into the parent *tblCustomer* table. The following notation shows this relationship conveniently:

$$\text{tblCustomer } ^1\longrightarrow^1 \text{ tblCustomerNotes}$$

Databases often contain tables that have one-to-many relationships with each other. There are several examples in The Coffee Merchant's database. Look again at Figure 2.5. Consider the relationship between the *tblCustomer* table and the *tblInvoice* table. Each customer can have as many unpaid invoices as The Coffee Merchant permits (or none). On the other hand, an invoice row in the *tblInvoice* table can be associated with one and only one customer in the *tblCustomer* table. The relationship between the *tblCustomer* table and the *tblInvoice* table is said to be a one-to-many relationship (in that direction—customer to invoice). Although it is technically correct to talk about "many-to-one" relationships, most database designers indicate the "one" side of the relationship first and use the "one-to-many" phrasing. A one-to-many relationship is shown this way:

$$\text{tblCustomer } ^1\longrightarrow^M \text{ tblInvoice}$$

Finally, consider the relationship between invoices and the coffee and tea items found on individual invoice lines. Various coffees and teas can appear on the many lines of a single invoice. An invoice might contain a line for 10 pounds of Kona coffee and another line for 5 pounds of Zimbabwe. Similarly, the coffee and tea items in The Coffee Merchant's inventory can appear in several invoices. For example, many different invoices might include Kona coffee. This type of relationship between the Invoice table and Inventory table is called a many-to-many relationship. We depict this type of relationship as follows:

$$\text{tblInvoice } ^M\longrightarrow^M \text{ tblInventory}$$

Many-to-many relationships can be difficult to represent and maintain in a relational database system. Most database designers create a new table to represent the M–M relationship. This table is called a *relationship* table or a *junction* table, and it combines attributes from the tables that participate in the M–M relationship. The relationship table makes the connection between the two tables by converting the M–M relationship into two 1–M relationships. The relationship table in The Coffee Merchant's database is called Invoice Line (*tblInvoiceLine*); it preserves the relationship between invoices (*tblInvoice*) and inventory (*tblInventory*). You can represent this three-table relationship for the M–M relationship as:

$$\text{tblInvoice } ^{1}\!\longrightarrow^{M} \text{ tblInvoiceLine } ^{M}\!\longrightarrow^{1} \text{ tblInventory}$$

Thus, it is always possible to break a many-to-many relationship between two tables into two one-to-many relationships by using an intermediate relationship table. The following are some general rules governing relationships among tables.

1. Primary keys must not be null.
2. Create a foreign key from the primary key on the one side of the 1–M relationship.
3. Many-to-many relationships are handled by creating an additional table—the relationship table—that consists entirely of the parent tables' primary keys. (The relationship table can contain other columns as well.)
4. Most one-to-one relationships indicate unnecessary tables in the database design. In most cases, if your analysis results in a one-to-one relationship between two tables, you should merge the two tables into one table. The one-to-one relationship means that each row in the first table has one and only one row in the second table that is related to it. Thus, combining the tables makes sense. In some cases, however, such as when one group of fields is used more frequently than other fields or when some fields need a greater degree of security, keeping the fields in separate tables is better.

Fundamental Relational Database Operations

Relational database management systems provide several important and fundamental retrieval operations. Among the most significant are select, project, and join.

Select

The *select operation* chooses a set of rows from a table. Rows are selected based on a set of qualifying factors, often called *selection criteria*. The select operation creates a new, virtual table. There are several ways to implement a select operation. Some RDBMSs, such as Access, provide a Query by Example (QBE) graphical interface, in which you can choose example elements to specify selection criteria and check the attributes to be displayed.

Figure 2.16 shows a select operation and the resulting dynaset, another table. The query selects rows from a smaller version of an Employee table. Rows are selected in which the HireDate is after a particular date. Notice that the result returns all columns of the original table satisfying the selection criterion. The result is a table, because queries in relational database systems always deliver answers in table form.

Project

The *project operation* returns a subset of columns from one or more tables. Columns retrieved are a result of the user indicating them, not a result of specifying a selection criterion. Figure 2.17 shows an example of a projection of the Name and Gender columns of our example Employee table shown previously in Figure 2.16. Notice that a project operation does not specify which *rows* are retrieved. Projections indicate only which *columns* are retrieved in the result. Of course, you can combine the selection and project operations in one query to produce both a row and column subset of a table.

Join

The most important relational database operation is the *join operation*. It provides the ability to pull together data from associated tables into a single, virtual table. Usually,

Fig. 2.16 Select
operation.

Employee table:

ID	Name	Comm	HireDate	BirthDate	Gender
1301	Stonesifer	5%	07/06/96	03/10/66	F
1364	Pruski	4%	12/01/00	01/26/79	M
1528	Pacioli	6%	08/26/95	05/06/50	M
1695	Nagasaki	4%	01/28/00	04/10/77	M
2240	Stonely	15%	11/05/88	05/03/61	F
2318	Hunter	8%	11/16/93	01/26/54	F
2754	Kahn	5%	05/14/97	05/29/61	M
3370	Kole	9%	02/08/92	03/23/63	M
3432	English	8%	10/01/93	02/14/56	F
3436	Gates	6%	04/11/95	03/09/54	M
3458	Morrison	15%	12/13/89	07/04/56	F
3609	Chang	5%	09/16/97	03/30/77	F
...	...	...	...	...	...
4112	Goldman	11%	12/24/90	03/05/62	M

Result of selection operation: HireDate > 1/1/97

ID	Name	Comm	HireDate	BirthDate	Gender
1364	Pruski	4%	12/01/00	01/26/79	M
1695	Nagasaki	4%	01/28/00	04/10/77	M
2754	Kahn	5%	05/14/97	05/29/61	M
3609	Chang	5%	09/16/97	03/30/77	F

Fig. 2.17 Project
operation.

Employee table: **Projection:**

ID	Name	Comm	HireDate	BirthDate	Gender	Name	Gender
1301	Stonesifer	5%	07/06/96	03/10/66	F	Stonesifer	F
1364	Pruski	4%	12/01/00	01/26/79	M	Pruski	M
1528	Pacioli	6%	08/26/95	05/06/50	M	Pacioli	M
...	...	...	...	...	...	...	...
4057	Bateman	9%	02/16/92	05/01/58	M	Bateman	M
4058	Halstead	5%	06/16/96	12/22/73	F	Halstead	F
4082	Flintsteel	11%	03/21/90	08/22/58	F	Flintsteel	F
4112	Goldman	11%	12/24/90	03/05/62	M	Goldman	M

you join two tables together using a common attribute found in both tables. This is the role of the foreign and primary keys. In the most common form of the join operation, one table's foreign key value is used to locate a matching primary key in another table. Then, the selected data from the matching rows in both tables are combined. That is, rows of one table are concatenated with (placed next to) rows of the second table for which the common attribute matches.

For instance, suppose we want to join a slightly altered Employee table with the employee title information found in a table within *Ch02.accdb* called *tblEmployeeTitle*. In the Employee table is a number, which stands in place of an actual job title. The number is used so that the title is not misspelled when it is entered over and over in the Employee table. *tblEmployeeTitle* contains the numbers and actual job titles associated with the numbers. Normalization has produced the two tables rather than a single table with repeating job titles, which would violate 3NF rules. The tables are joined on title number columns found in both tables. In the Employee table, this column is called *EmployeeTitleID*, although the Caption property setting for that field has been shortened to *TitleID*. The *EmployeeTitleID* column in *tblEmployeeTitle* is the primary key and contains a corresponding title field, *Title*. Joining the two tables in TitleID produces the result shown in Figure 2.18. Note that the join column does not have to have the same name in both tables. In the illustration, TitleID is a foreign key in the *tblEmployee* table, whereas TitleID is the primary key in the *tblEmployeeTitle* table. Joining is a matter of matching foreign key and primary key values. The join illustration in Figure 2.18 is an example of the most common type of join. It is called an ***equijoin***, because rows from the two tables are placed next to each other (concatenated) on matching join column values, and the join column appears only once in the result.

Fig. 2.18 Join operation.

tblEmployee

ID	Name	TitleID	HireDate	Gender
1301	Stonesifer	2	07/06/96	F
1364	Pruski	1	12/01/00	M
1528	Pacioli	2	08/26/95	M
1695	Nagasaki	1	01/28/00	M
2240	Stonely	3	11/05/88	F
2318	Hunter	2	11/16/93	F
2754	Kahn	2	05/14/97	M
3370	Kole	2	02/08/92	M
3432	English	2	10/01/93	F
3436	Gates	2	04/11/95	M
. . .	. . .	. . .	. . .	. . .
4082	Flintsteel	3	03/21/90	F
4112	Goldman	3	12/24/90	M

tblEmployeeTitle

TitleID	Title
1	Sales Trainee
2	Sales Associate
3	Senior Sales Associate
4	Sales Manager
5	Senior Sales Manager
6	Division Sales Manager
7	Regional Manager
8	Division Manager
9	National Sales Manager

Result of join operation:

ID	Name	TitleID	HireDate	Gender	Title
1301	Stonesifer	2	07/06/96	F	Sales Associate
1364	Pruski	1	12/01/00	M	Sales Trainee
1528	Pacioli	2	08/26/95	M	Sales Associate
1695	Nagasaki	1	01/28/00	M	Sales Trainee
2240	Stonely	3	11/05/886	F	Senior Sales Associate
2318	Hunter	2	11/16/93	F	Sales Associate
2754	Kahn	2	05/14/97	M	Sales Associate
3370	Kole	2	02/08/92	M	Sales Associate
3432	English	2	10/01/93	F	Sales Associate
3436	Gates	2	04/11/95	M	Sales Associate
. . .	. . .	. . .	. . .	. . .	. . .
4082	Flintsteel	3	03/21/90	F	Senior Sales Associate
4112	Goldman	3	12/24/90	M	Senior Sales Associate

Another join operation type combines rows from two or more tables on the join column, but rows that do not match on the join column are included in the result. This type of join is called an ***outer join***. Outer joins are useful for creating reports that show information such as employees who have made no sales or students who have not signed up for a particular class.

There is no theoretical limit to the number of tables that may be joined. For instance, one of the results we can produce with a join operation is invoices. An invoice is created by a query that joins five of The Coffee Merchant's tables whose schemas are shown in

Figure 2.6. Tables joined to form an invoice are connected in pairs on common columns, but not all on the same columns. For instance, the *tblCustomer* table can be joined to the *tblInvoice* table via their common column, CustomerID. Continuing, the *tblInvoice* table can be joined to the *tblInvoiceLine* table (individual invoice lines) over the join column InvoiceID, an attribute found in both tables. The Inventory table, *tblInventory*, is joined to *tblInventoryDescription* to link the names of each invoiced item. *tblInventory* is joined to *tblInvoiceLine* on the common column InventoryID. Figure 2.19 illustrates how the join columns of all involved tables are connected to form the single result. All of the joins shown in Figure 2.19 are equijoins.

Fig. 2.19 Joining tables with primary key/foreign key relationships.

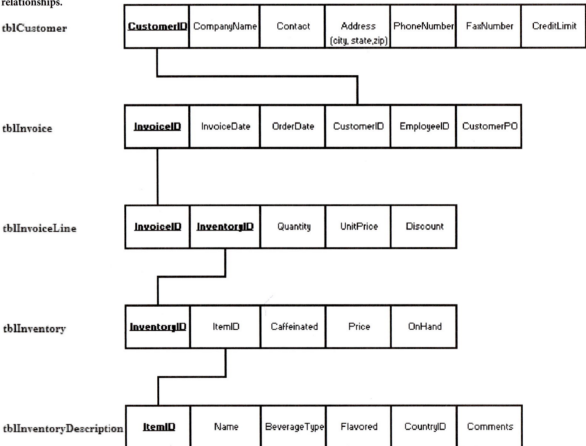

tblCustomer

tblInvoice

tblInvoiceLine

tblInventory

tblInventoryDescription

Introduction to Database Design

A well-designed database that accurately models an enterprise's operations is crucial to the success of any database system designed to maintain accounting information. A badly designed database can be worse than using no system at all; information can be misrepresented, difficult to find, or completely lost.

One important aspect of database design is carefully choosing the rows and attributes that you want to include in each table. This activity, often referred to as ***modeling***, can be accomplished using any of several methods. We introduce you to *entity-relationship* (abbreviated *E-R*) *modeling*, which is described in the context of The Coffee Merchant's invoice system.

Developing Entity-Relationship Models

Entity-relationship (E-R) modeling was introduced by Peter Chen in 1976. Since then, E-R modeling has gained wide acceptance as a graphical approach to database design.

Database designers often use three terms to describe a company's information: entities, relationships, and attributes. *Entities* are objects (people or things) that are important to the company (nouns such as customer, inventory, employee, or vendor) or important activities (nouns such as sale, purchase, or cash disbursement). *Relationships* describe the way in which entities interact or are related to one another. For example, the entity customer is related to the entity sale when the company sells something to a customer. *Attributes* describe the characteristics of entities and relationships. For example, a customer has a name and an address.

In the E-R model, diagrams represent entities and relationships. The diagrams contain three symbols: rectangles, diamonds, and lines. Rectangles represent entities, and diamonds represent relationships. Lines are the connections between the two. A digit or letter above the line indicates the degree of the relationship: one-to-one, one-to-many, or many-to-many. Figure 2.20 shows an example of an E-R diagram for The Coffee Merchant's invoice system. Attributes can be shown by a line leading from the entity or relationship to the attribute name.

Fig. 2.20 Entity-relationship diagram.

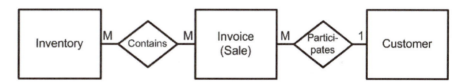

When a database includes many-to-many relationships, the relationship becomes a table. In this case, a new entity—shown with a diamond within a rectangle—is used to redraw two entities as three. The new entity reduces the many-to-many relationship to two relationships: a 1–M degree relationship on one side and an M–1 degree relationship on the other side (see Figure 2.21). 1–M signifies that one record from the table on one side may have many related records in the table on the other side of the relationship. For instance, an invoice can have a 1–M relationship to the items on the invoice: one invoice has many possible invoice lines *and* an invoice line participates with only one invoice.

Fig. 2.21 Revised entity-relationship diagram.

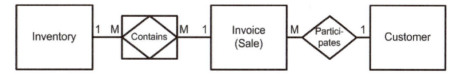

The newly created entity in the middle is implemented in a database as a *relationship table*, which includes the primary keys of the two joined entities as two elements in its composite primary key. A relationship table is sometimes called a *junction table* or a *bridge table*.

You can create tables for your database from the revised E-R diagram. One table is created for each entity. Primary keys for each table must be identified next. The relationships between entities, exemplified by lines connecting the entities, are maintained by foreign key/primary key linkages between tables. That is, a line from one entity to another is implemented by a key in one table (a foreign key) that matches one or more primary keys in the other table. In the case of a 1–M relationship, the "one" side of the relationship has a primary key matching possibly several rows on the "many" side of the relationship that contain the foreign key.

When a many-to-many relationship exists in the E-R diagram, such as the relationship between *tblInvoice* and *tblInventory*, a relationship table is created. The Contains table in Figure 2.21 contains the primary key from the *tblInvoice* table and the primary key from the *tblInventory* table. Once the relationship table is created, the three tables have a pair of one-to-many relationships.

A table can also be related to itself in a special case in which rows of a table are related to other row(s) in the same table. A typical example is an employee table in which the primary key identifies employees and a Supervisor column contains foreign keys pointing to each employee's supervisor. Supervisors are in the same table because they are themselves employees. When rows of a table are related to rows in the same table, it is a *recursive* relationship.

The last step is to normalize the individual tables. For best results, all tables should be at least in third normal form.

Resources, Events, Agents (REA) Modeling

William McCarthy drew on the principles of relational database theory developed by E. F. Codd and the entity-relationship modeling principles of Peter Chen to create a modeling approach specifically designed for accounting systems. In the late 1970s, McCarthy proposed an entity classification system that would allow accountants to use relational databases to handle accounting information efficiently and effectively.

McCarthy's approach, called the *REA (Resources, Events, Agents) model*, provides categories of entities that accountants can use to classify the entities that appear in accounting systems. In the REA model, resources are assets such as cash, inventory, and fixed assets. Events are transactions or other occurrences that have accounting effects and include things such as purchases and sales. Events can also be more subtle occurrences, such as the passage of time that causes interest to accrue on a loan or depreciation of a fixed asset to occur. Agents are humans or organizations that interact with resources and events. Agent entities commonly found in accounting systems include customers, suppliers, and employees.

REA modeling is a powerful tool that provides consistency between database models. This consistency makes it easier to expand a current database and to integrate multiple databases that have been designed using REA modeling. Chapter 7 provides a comprehensive overview of REA modeling and the subsequent chapters provide in-depth coverage of using REA modeling to build databases for individual business processes.

Summary

In this chapter, you have learned about database accounting systems, business processes, database management systems, database tables, relationships between tables, and database design. You learned why double-entry bookkeeping was an excellent system for organizing manual data gathering and storage tasks for many years but that database accounting systems can now offer significant advantages over computerized double-entry bookkeeping systems. Most firms today have concluded that the advantages of database accounting systems outweigh their disadvantages.

The chapter discussed value chain of business processes. It described the characteristics of database accounting systems for the sales/collection, acquisition/payment, human resources, and financing business processes.

This chapter also introduced database management systems and their application to accounting information. Database management systems are the basis of many accounting systems and provide several advantages over nondatabase approaches to managing data. High on the list of advantages are cost savings resulting from the centralization of all data management functions and the enforcement of data integrity and consistency by the database system. Relational database management systems provide the needed capabilities to represent accounting information. Data maintenance in a relational database management system does not require a programmer's help. Usually, people can learn to insert and delete database records and to query database systems. Valuable accounting information can be retrieved in a variety of formats and aggregation levels; information retrieval is not limited to a standard set of accounting reports.

The chapter also emphasized the importance of representing table objects in normalized form. First, second, and third normal forms have been described. First normal form precludes repeating groups; second normal form requires that all table attributes be dependent on the table's entire primary key, not just part of it. Third normal form includes all the characteristics of first and second normal forms. In addition, tables in third normal form do not contain attributes that depend on other nonkey attributes. Tables in third normal form avoid problems that can impair the integrity of accounting information.

The chapter closed with a brief overview of the REA model developed by William McCarthy. The REA model specifies three or more categories of entities that commonly occur in accounting information systems. The REA model helps accountants identify the entities that should be included in the E-R models for accounting databases.

Questions and Problems for Review
Multiple-Choice Questions

1. Bar code scanners are useful elements in accounting database systems because they can quite easily
   a. post journal entries to the general ledger.
   b. capture a wide variety of information about each transaction.
   c. prevent or detect cashier fraud.
   d. identify pricing errors in the database.
2. The events-based approach to accounting theory
   a. classifies businesses in terms of their complexity.
   b. requires the use of the REA model to classify entities.
   c. supports the use of double-entry bookkeeping systems.
   d. supports the use of relational database accounting systems.
3. A double-entry bookkeeping system records each transaction
   a. twice.
   b. as an abstraction.
   c. in a relational database.
   d. on the day it occurs.
4. Computerized accounting systems
   a. can be used to implement either a double-entry bookkeeping model or a database accounting model.
   b. always require the installation of expensive database management software.
   c. must be certified by the Internal Revenue Service and the American Institute of Certified Public Accountants before being sold.
   d. record all transactions in a general journal before posting them to special journals.
5. Database systems store data only once. This feature
   a. allows multiple users to have simultaneous data access.
   b. facilitates cross-functional data analysis.
   c. greatly reduces data inconsistencies within the system.
   d. makes it easier for managers to create their own customized reports.

6. The acquisition/payment process includes
    a. service companies ordering and receiving supplies used to provide services to customers.
    b. merchandisers' ordering and receiving of goods for resale.
    c. both a and b.
    d. none of the above.
7. A collection of tables that contain information about a database, including the database table structures and a list of all fields included in each table, is called a
    a. data dictionary.
    b. master data file.
    c. database index.
    d. database summary.
8. *Select* and *project* are two fundamental data retrieval operations that you can use in a relational database. Which of the following is a true statement regarding these operations?
    a. The select operation selects columns from a table.
    b. The project operation selects columns from a table.
    c. The project operation moves data from one table to another table.
    d. You must join two tables before using either the select or project operations.
9. A table that does not include any transitive dependencies
    a. cannot be in any normal form; all normal forms require at least one transitive dependency.
    b. is in first normal form or higher.
    c. is in second normal form or higher.
    d. is in third normal form or higher.
10. To represent a many-to-many relationship in a relational database, the designer must
    a. create four tables, each having a one-to-one relationship with the other three tables.
    b. create three tables, one for each of the entities and a third relationship table that includes the primary keys of the two entity tables.
    c. combine the two entity tables that share the many-to-many relationship into a single table.
    d. eliminate the many-to-many relationship; such relationships are not permitted.

Discussion Questions

1. Why is double-entry bookkeeping better suited to manual accounting systems than to computerized accounting systems?
2. What prevents accountants from using a database model to automate a double-entry bookkeeping system?
3. Discuss the problems that can arise from storing data in two different places.
4. What is a primary key, and why is it so important in a relational database management system?

Practice Exercises

1. Create a query for *tblInventory* in the *Ch02.accdb* file that combines three project operations and a select operation as follows: project the attributes InventoryID, Price, and OnHand; select rows in which the value for the Price attribute is between $4.00 and $5.00 per pound. Print your resulting datasheet.
2. Describe the tables that a grocery store would use in its sales/collection process. Be sure to include all necessary relationship tables and foreign keys.
3. Assume you are working for a service firm that operates 14 offices, each with 16 departments. What tables would you add to those listed in this chapter for the human resources process to track employee time worked by office and department?
4. Redraw Figure 2.2 for a merchandising firm.
5. Discuss the inherent problems of storing an employee's age as one of the attributes of a table. Discuss alternative solutions that would not cause inaccuracies in the database.

Problems

1. Create a query for *tblInventoryDescription* in the *Ch02.accdb* file that combines four project operations and two select operations as follows: project the attributes ItemID, Name, BeverageType, and Flavored; select rows in which the value for the Flavored attribute is Yes and for which the BeverageType attribute is "c" (these are the expressions you should place in the Criteria cells for those two attributes, respectively). Examine your results to ensure that they do not contain any rows with tea products, only coffee products. Print your resulting datasheet.

2. Carefully examine *tblInvoiceLine* in the *Ch02.accdb* database and answer the following questions: What type of table is *tblInvoiceLine*? What is the primary key of *tblInvoiceLine*? Unlike most printed invoices, which include quantity, the unit price, and an extension (quantity multiplied by unit price) for each inventory item, this table does not include an extension. Why not?

3. Suppose you are designing a database that contains information about university classes, students enrolled in classes, and instructors teaching various classes. The Catalog table lists all the courses that the university offers. The Classes table describes the classes offered during the semester and includes names of students currently enrolled in each class. The Students table contains one record for each student enrolled in the university. The Instructor table contains information about instructors including their names, phone numbers, and office telephone numbers. Discuss the relationship between the Instructor table and the Classes table. Is the relationship 1–1, 1–M, or M–M? Describe the relationship between the Students table and the Classes table. Finally, draw a diagram showing the tables Catalog, Classes, Instructor, and Students and how they might be linked. Use Figure 2.19 as a model of how to represent the tables. Include only the primary and foreign key fields in each table's representation.

CHAPTER 3

Creating, Populating, and Displaying Tables

CHAPTER OBJECTIVES

This chapter extends the knowledge that you gained in the introductory chapter with detailed information about Microsoft Access. You will learn about creating tables, using table templates, modifying table designs, implementing data constraints built into the tables by field properties, and entering data into tables. This chapter's exercises illustrate using Access techniques to create the foundations of any accounting information system—tables that hold the mission critical data. Like Chapter 1, this chapter is application-oriented and contains very little theory; however, we emphasize employing the theory we presented in Chapter 2. This chapter gives you the most important details about creating and maintaining tables including how to:

- Define a table's structure.

- Modify a table's structure and establish data integrity between related tables.

- Set table field properties including those restricting data ranges allowed for columns.

- Enter data into a table.

- Modify a table's datasheet display properties.

- Customize the Navigation Pane display to hide or display objects as well as create new Navigation Pane categories.

- Explain the advantages of separating tables from other database objects.

We introduce The Coffee Merchant database used here and in and many of the book's other chapters. We urge you to download to your computer or other storage device the Access database from the book's companion Web site. The unzipped database is named *Ch03.accdb*. It contains all the objects that you will need to complete the exercises in this chapter as well as the end-of-chapter exercises and problems. It provides a place for you to store all of your Chapter 3 database work.

Introduction to Tables

The term *Access objects* refers to several ways you can store and display information in your tables. Like most database systems, Access provides a rich variety of objects for your use. Beginning with the most fundamental, objects include tables, queries, forms, reports, macros, and modules. In this chapter, we discuss in depth only Access tables.

Database tables, in any relational database system, are the *only* objects that hold data. All other objects, such as queries, reports, and forms merely gather and display data from tables. Database information is stored in one or more tables comprised of rows and columns. A row contains all the information about a particular item in the table. Also called a record, a row's columns contain individual values for each attribute that characterizes the row. For instance, The Coffee Merchant's employee table, called *tblEmployee*, contains a row for each employee. Columns in the employee table hold information about eleven different attributes about each employee. For instance a column called EmpID contains a unique employee identification number; EmpFName is the field that stores each employee's first name; and EmpDOB stores each employee's birth date. The eleven values for each employee describe the characteristics about that employee that is important to the production of reports and other useful information used by management.

Each table column can contain only one data type. Though the exact names of these data types vary from one relational database management system (RDBMS) to another, they are all drawn from a small, common set. A column's data type provides a fundamental constraint on the type of information that can be entered into that column. For instance, declaring a column to have the data type Number prevents text data from occurring in that column. Access supports the data types listed in Figure 3.1. Of the listed types, you will use the Attachment, Currency, Date/Time, Hyperlink, Number, and Text data types for most of your data needs in this chapter and in general.

Creating and designing an Access table need not be complicated. You follow six basic steps in Access' Design view:

1. Create a table.
2. Select and type each field name corresponding to a table column and assign a unique data type to it.
3. Modify column properties and enter others for each column when needed.
4. Create indexes for selected columns to speed data access.
5. Select a primary key from one or more table columns.
6. Save the newly created table design

Once you have designed a table, then you display the table in Datasheet view and type data into each row's column to populate the table. In designing a table, you can choose to use predefined table templates that contain suggested field names and data types to speed table creation, or you can create and design your table by hand following the six steps listed above. First, you will learn how to create a table using an available template.

Creating a Table Using a Template

Table templates are predefined structures that contain columns and data types that may match your database application needs. If a table template is close but not exactly what you want, then you can modify it slightly to suit your needs. The advantage of using a table template over creating a table from scratch is avoiding the "blank table design" screen. A blank table design screen can be slightly intimidating. Having a prebuilt table that is close to what you need can speed you through the table design process by requiring just a few tweaks to make the table just right. This chapter emphasizes building tables from scratch because we think the greatest understanding will come from the table

Fig. 3.1 Microsoft
Access data types.

Data Type	Description and Use
Text	Holds from 0 to 255 characters consisting of anything you can type on the keyboard. Text data cannot be used in calculations.
Memo	Lengthy, variable-length text and numbers for comments or explanations. A memo field can contain from 0 to 65,535 characters.
Number	Numeric data used in calculations. Set the Field Size property to define the specific number type including byte, integer, long integer, single, double, replication ID, and decimal.
Date/Time	Holds date and time information. Several formats are available, or you can establish a custom format.
Currency	Holds monetary data of up to 19 significant digits (15 to the left of the decimal point and 4 to the right). Currency fields are formatted to display a currency symbol and two decimal places. Use currency to avoid rounding errors in financial calculations.
AutoNumber	A unique sequential number that Access automatically generates. This data type is often used for primary keys, because it guarantees unique values.
Yes/No	Yes/No, True/False, or On/Off are all examples of legitimate field values. Choose the Yes/No data type when only two values are possible (gender or invoice paid, for example).
OLE Object	Contains objects from another Windows application such as a picture, graph, sound, or spreadsheet. When you double-click an OLE object, the program that created the object is launched so you can modify or view the OLE object.
Hyperlink	Text or combinations of text and numbers constituting a World Wide Web hyperlink address.
Attachment	A special field that allows you to attach external data such as pictures, videos, sound, Word documents, and so on. (This field type is preferred over OLE Object, which will soon be deprecated.)
Lookup Wizard	A field that provides the mechanism to automatically look up a value from another table or list of fields by using a combo box or list box control.

building details. However, you should be familiar with the process for building tables with templates. Here is a description about that process.

After you launch Access and create a new, blank database or open an existing one, the Microsoft Fluent interface, or "ribbon" appears. The table templates are on the Create tab—in the first group called *Tables*. Click the Table Templates command to display the table templates. There are five table templates available: Contacts, Tasks, Issues, Events, and Assets. If these are not what you need and want to review others, then you may want to turn to database templates because they have an entire database of tables. If you use a database template (available on the opening Getting Started with Microsoft Office Access screen), then you can close the newly created and template-based database and import into your database only the tables that you want. In either case, once you select a table template or import one, then you can modify it. Figure 3.2 shows the five table template choices.

The steps to create a table using a template are outlined here. You do not need to follow these steps because you will be creating tables manually.

• *Click the Create tab.*

Fig. 3.2 Table
templates available.

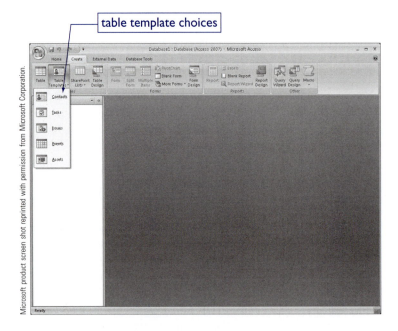

- *Click the Table Templates command found in the Tables group.*
- *Select one of the table templates that appear in the dropdown list. (The yet unnamed table appears in Datasheet view.)*
- *Enter data into the table.*
- *Close and save the newly designed and populated table.*
- *If necessary, make structure changes to the table in Design view and then resave it.*

Figure 3.3 shows the design of the Contacts table choice. Notice the primary key is assigned to the ID field. Almost all fields have the Text data type, but if you scroll down to the last field in the Design view, you will see Hyperlink, Memo, and Attachment fields. This is the assumed design of a contacts table. You can eliminate fields (columns) or modify them until they match your needs.

Fig. 3.3 *Contacts*
table template in
Design view.

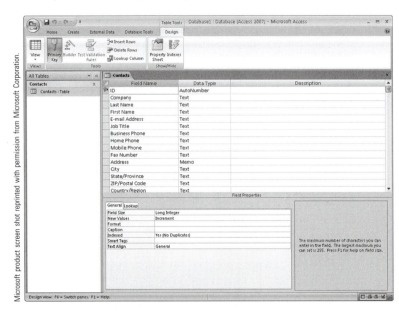

Creating a Table From Scratch

From here on in the chapter, you will be doing a lot of work with the Ch03 database. If you have not already done so, copy the database from this book's South-Western, Cengage Learning Web site, www.cengage.com/accounting/perry, to your storage device. Every change you make to the database occurs on the copy of the database you just created on your disk.

Prepare for the first exercise by launching Microsoft Access 2007. Follow the steps in the next exercise to create an employee table that is similar in structure to the table *tblEmployee* that is already in your Chapter 3 database. The number of fields in your version of the employee table will be less than that of *tblEmployee*, but you will use a variety of data types and techniques just the same.

EXERCISE 3.1: CREATING THE EMPLOYEE TABLE DESIGN

1. With Access open, click More (located in the upper right under the heading Open Recent Database), use the Look in list box to locate Ch03.accdb in the Open dialog box. Double-click Ch03.accdb to open the database. (Your Open dialog box may not display the database extension ".accdb" because that option—to display extensions of a known file type—may not be checked.) The Navigation Pane shows the names of three tables: *tblEmployee*, *tblEmployeeDivision*, and *tblEmployeeTitle*.
2. Click the Create tab, click Table found in the Tables group, and click the Design View command that appears in the Datasheet context tab. Access asks you to name the table.
3. Type tblMyEmployees in the Save As dialog box and then click OK to save the newly named table. Access displays the table, as yet undefined, in Design view.

Next, you will define the names, data types, and descriptions for each field in your table. When you complete Exercise 3.2, you will have a new table structure which you can populate with employee data. We instruct you to press Tab to move from one table definition column to another. There are other ways to move left to right and top down: you can click a column with your mouse, or you can use any of the arrow keys to move anywhere in the Design view grid—just like you would move the cursor in a spreadsheet. Tab is convenient, unlike other movement options, because the entire cell is selected (darkened). This allows you to replace all existing text by typing.

EXERCISE 3.2: DEFINING THE TABLE'S COLUMNS

1. With the table open in Design view, type EmpID (no spaces in any names, please) in the first row of the Field Name column. Press Tab, type N in the Data Type column (or select Number from its drop-down list), press Tab to move to the Description field, and type the description Employee identification number.

   Notice, by default, that the first row has a small key in the row selector column. That indicates the field EmpID is the table's primary key. You can set the primary key manually or change it to a different column. EmpID is, in fact, our table's primary key column so we will leave it as is.
2. Type EmpLName in the next empty Field Name cell, press Tab, press Tab again to accept *Text* as the default data type and move to the Description column, and type Last name to create the optional comment.
3. To change the maximum number of characters in any employee's last name, press F6 to jump to the Field Size property in the Field Properties panel found in

the lower half of the Design view window. (You can click the box to the right of *Field Size* to select it.) Type 25 in the Field Size cell.

4. Click the empty cell in the Field Name column of the third row, type EmpCommRate, press Tab, type N in the Data Type column (or select Number from its drop-down list), press Tab to move to the Description field, and type Commission rate.

5. Press Tab to move to the Field Name cell of the fourth row, type EmpHireDate, press Tab, click the Data Type drop-down list arrow, select Date/Time, press Tab, and type Hire date (with a space between the words *Hire* and *date*).

6. Press Tab to move to the Field Name cell of the next empty row, type EmpGender, press Tab, type T (to reaffirm the default choice, text, but unnecessary), press Tab, and type Gender.

7. Press Tab to move to the Field Name cell of the next empty row, type EmpNotes, press Tab, type M to select *Memo*, press Tab, and type Notes about performance, and press Tab to confirm the EmpNotes description column notes (see Figure 3.4).

8. There are several ways to save you changes. We pick a fast, keyboard method: Press Ctrl+S to save your table. Alternatively, you can click the Save icon in the Quick Access Toolbar or click Save in the Office button menu.

9. To close the saved table design, right-click the tblMyEmployees table tab and then click Close from the context menu. Access closes the table, and its name appears in the Navigation Pane list of table objects. (Alternatively, you can click the Close button on the table's Title bar.)

Fig. 3.4 Defining a table's structure.

new table appears in the list of objects

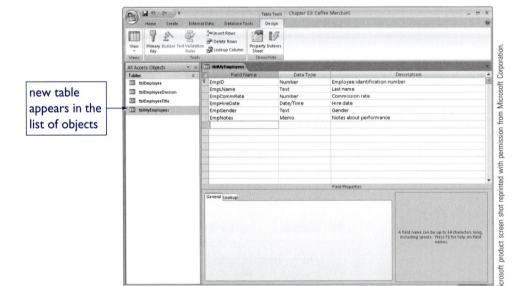

Microsoft product screen shot reprinted with permission from Microsoft Corporation.

Adding a Column

If you create and use a table and later—perhaps much later—discover you have left out an important column or two, you can add new columns to tables at any time. Relational database systems allow you to add and delete columns even when the table to be modified already is populated with data!

You can add a column to a table displayed in either Datasheet view or Design view. Adding a column in Design view is the best way, because you can add a column and define all of its characteristics in one window. On the other hand, you can add a column more quickly in Datasheet view.

You probably notice that we have left out a field for employees' first names. We add that column in the following exercise.

EXERCISE 3.3: INSERTING COLUMNS INTO AN EXISTING TABLE

1. Right-click tblMyEmployees in the Navigation Pane list of objects and click Design View.
2. Right-click anywhere in the second row, which corresponds to EmpLName, and click Insert Rows from the pop-up menu. Access opens up a row *above* the selected row, EmpLName.
3. Type EmpFName in the Field Name column, press Tab *twice* to accept Text as the default data type and move to the Description column, and type First name to enter an optional comment.
4. Limit the maximum number of characters in any employee's first name: Press F6 to jump to the Field Size property in the Field Properties panel and type 25 in the Field Size cell.
5. Click the Save icon in the Quick Access Toolbar to save the design changes.

Leave *tblMyEmployees* open in Design view for work you will perform in the next set of exercises. You will be adding two more columns to your table.

Adding a Column Using a Lookup Field

The Coffee Merchant's *tblEmployeeDivision* table contains the city and state in which each of The Coffee Merchant's divisions is located. It is useful to place often-repeated character strings such as cities or organization names in their own table along with a unique identification number. Then, you can refer to the cities with a number in place of the long string in the original table. Among other advantages, this prevents you from misspelling "Cincinnati" or other city names when they occur frequently in a table's columns. This is the purpose of the *tblEmployeeDivision* table. A related column, yet to be placed in the *tblMyEmployees* table, will contain a number that is related to ("points to") the company division number found in the *tblEmployeeDivision* table. Your next job will be to add a new table column to *tblMyEmployees*—a division number column—which is a foreign key field linked to the primary key of the *tblEmployeeDivision* table. A *foreign key* is a column whose values match identical values in another table's primary key column. A foreign key column in one table always corresponds to a primary key column in another table.

Access facilitates forging this linkage between two related tables with the Lookup Wizard available in the list of data types in Design view. Although not a data type per se, the Lookup Wizard establishes a foreign key-to-primary key linkage between two tables. More importantly, entering data into such a field becomes simple because Access displays the character string list of choices rather than a forgettable number when you populate the table column created with the Lookup Wizard.

Once the *tblMyEmployees* and *tblEmployeeDivision* tables are linked via the Lookup Wizard in Design view through their primary key/foreign key pairs, you will be able to select a city name from a restricted list of city names when you populate the *tblMyEmployees* table. This prevents mistyping a city name or selecting a city name that is *not* one of the allowed cities.

Each employee row should also have an entry indicating his title in the company. To avoid repetition, misspelling, or invalid title entry while populating an employee's title column, we'll use the Lookup Wizard to connect *tblMyEmployees* to another table with the list available company titles. The process of adding or deleting columns in a table is called altering the table's structure. Do not confuse this activity with adding or deleting *data* in a table's columns.

The next exercise shows you how to add two lookup columns to a table. In particular, you will add columns called EmpDivisionID and EmpTitleID to your *tblMyEmployees* table. Both of the previous columns are foreign keys because they refer to primary key values in other tables.

EXERCISE 3.4: ADDING A COLUMN TO A TABLE

1. With *tblMyEmployees* open in Design view, click the EmpCommRate row selector button (the blue button to the left of the Field Name column). Press and hold the Shift key and click the EmpHireDate row selector button. If you did this correctly, both the EmpCommRate and EmpHireDate rows are surrounded by a golden rectangle.
2. Click Insert Rows in the Tools group of the Design context tab. Access opens up two rows above EmpCommRate.
3. Click in the empty cell of the Field Name column just below the field name EmpLName. Type EmpDivisionID, press Tab, click the Data Type list box arrow and click Lookup Wizard. Access opens the first of a small number of wizard dialog boxes, which define the source of the column's data found in another table.
4. In the Lookup Wizard dialog box, click Next because you want to Access to look up values found in another table.
5. Ensure that the Tables radio button is selected (in the View panel). Click the entry Table: tblEmployeeDivision from the list of choices. This tells Access which table contains the text string corresponding to each employee's division name. Click Next to continue.
6. Click the >> button (select all fields) to slide all the fields over to the Selected Fields panel (see Figure 3.5). This permits all three fields to appear, although the primary key, DivisionID usually is hidden when you are populating the field.
7. Click Next.
8. Let's sort the choices by state and then by city within state (in case there are duplicate states): Click the drop-down list arrow in the first list box and click DivisionState.
9. Click the drop-down list arrow in the second list box and click DivisionCity. Click Next.

    Notice that the values from the *tblEmployeeDivision* table appear sorted in state and then city order (see Figure 3.6). Also note that the *Hide key column* checkbox is checked. This hides the primary key field, DivisionID, when the EmpDivisionID column is being populated. However, the primary key is stored in the EmpDivisionID column, not the displayed city and state values.
10. Click Next to move to the last Lookup Wizard step. Click Finish to complete the process.
11. A warning dialog box appears suggesting you save the design. Click Yes to save the table design and create the linkage between the two tables.
12. Type Employee's division in the Description column corresponding to the EmpDivisionID row.

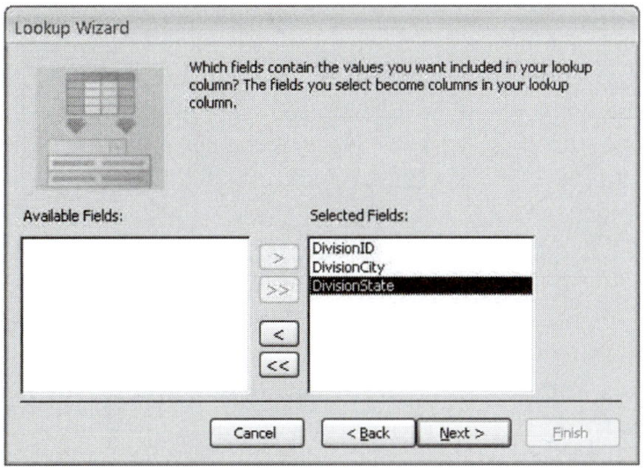

Fig. 3.5 Selecting all fields in the Lookup Wizard.

Microsoft product screen shot reprinted with permission from Microsoft Corporation.

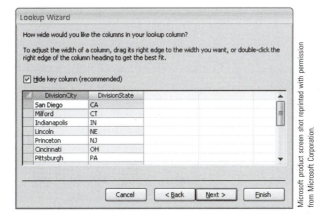

Fig. 3.6 Lookup columns that will display when the EmpDivisionID field is clicked.

Microsoft product screen shot reprinted with permission from Microsoft Corporation.

This completes the process of using the Lookup Wizard to define the EmpDivisionID lookup column. You will repeat this process to add the EmpTitleID column in the next exercise. This time, it should go a lot faster because you have done it once already.

EXERCISE 3.5: ADDING A LOOKUP COLUMN TO A TABLE

1. Click in the empty cell of the Field Name column just below the field name EmpDivisionID. Type EmpTitleID, press Tab, type L (the shortcut for Lookup Wizard), and press Enter. Access opens the Lookup Wizard.
2. Click Next because you want Access to look up values found in another table.
3. Ensure that the Tables radio button is selected (in the View panel). Click the entry Table: tblEmployeeTitle from the list of choices and click Next to continue.
4. Click the >> button (select all fields) to slide all the fields over to the Selected Fields panel and then click Next.
5. Let's sort the choices by title: Click the drop-down list arrow in the first list box, click Title, and then click Next.
6. Move the mouse to the right edge of the Title column header. When it becomes a double-headed arrow pointing left and right, double-click it to widen the displayed column. Click Finish to complete the process.

7. A warning dialog box appears suggesting you save the design. Click Yes to save the table design and create the linkage between the two tables.
8. Type Employee's title in the Description column.
9. Press Ctrl+S to save the design, right-click the *tblMyEmployees* table tab, and click Close to close (the "X" in the table design window's title bar) the table's Design view.

Deleting, Renaming, or Moving a Table Column
Deleting a Column

It is easy to remove unwanted columns from any table or to give one or more columns a new name. Though you don't need to delete table columns right now, you should learn how to do it. You can easily delete a column while viewing a table in either Datasheet view or Design view. To delete a table's column in Design view, right-click anywhere in the column you want to delete and then click Delete Rows in the pop-up menu. Any attribute rows that are below the deleted field are moved up to close the gap. Remember to click the Save button in the Quick Access Toolbar to post the changed table structure to your database. (You'll be prompted to do so if you attempt to close the altered table without saving it.) To delete a table column in Datasheet view, right-click the column's field selector and click Delete Column from the pop-up menu. In Datasheet view, any columns to the right of the deleted column move left to close the gap left by the deleted column.

Warning: If you delete a table column, then other objects that depend on that table column will not work. For example, if you delete EmpLName from the *tblMyEmployees* table and have already created a query that references EmpLName, then the query will prompt you to fill in a value for the missing field. In effect, it is "broken" and must be repaired.

Renaming a Column

You may decide that a column name no longer makes sense or is otherwise inappropriate. Renaming a column is straightforward. You can change a table column's name either in Datasheet view or Design view. In Datasheet view, simply double-click the column's selector, type a new name, and press Enter. The new name replaces the name originally assigned. Also, the renamed field's Caption property is deleted. (You will learn about field properties later in this chapter.) To rename a table column in Design view, first display the table in Design view. Next, double-click the Field Name cell (to easily select all the name text) that you want to change and type over the old name with its replacement. Finally, click Save in the Quick Access Toolbar to save the altered table design.

In previous versions of Access, if you renamed a table column, then you had to track down every object that referenced that field (queries, forms, and so on) and change the column name in those located objects also. That was a daunting task. Good news: Access 2007 automatically changes field names whenever you open an object that refers to the old name. In effect, Access does the legwork of changing names in other objects to match the change you made to a table column name. This Access 2007 feature is called *AutoCorrect*. There is a catch, however. You must make sure the feature is turned on. The next Try It shows you how.

TRY IT

Click the *Office* button, click the *Access Options* button, and click *Current Database* from the list on the left. *Ensure that Track name AutoCorrect info* and *Perform name AutoCorrect* check boxes are checked (see Figure 3.7). Then click *OK* to save any changes.

Fig. 3.7 Setting AutoCorrect options.

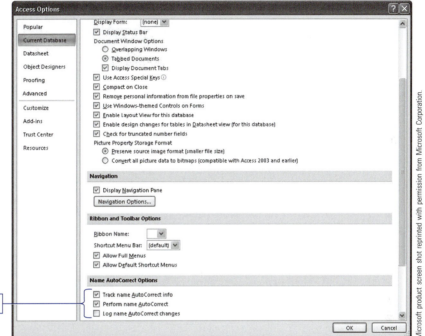

AutoCorrect options

Microsoft product screen shot reprinted with permission from Microsoft Corporation.

Moving a Column

Although the order of columns in a table has no importance whatsoever, you can rearrange table columns so they appear in a different order in Datasheet view to suit you. Just like other table structure alteration operations mentioned here, you can rearrange table columns either in Datasheet view or Design view. To move a column or a group of contiguous columns while in Datasheet view, you begin by selecting the column(s). Click the field selector of the column you want to move. To select adjacent columns, click a column field selector and move the mouse to adjacent columns without releasing the mouse. After selecting (indicated by darkened column names), release the mouse. Then, click and hold the mouse in the field selector again and drag the column(s) to their new location. Release the mouse button to "drop" the selected columns into their new locations. As usual, save the altered structure by pressing Ctrl+S or clicking Save in the Quick Access Toolbar. Moving a column *does not* affect any objects that depend on the table.

Establishing Intertable Referential Integrity

Access provides a way to enforce *referential integrity* whereby defined relationships between tables are maintained permanently and automatically. For example, referential integrity rules prevent you from adding a record to a related table if there is no associated record in the primary table. Additionally, the rules prevent deleting or changing records in a primary table that would result in orphan records in a related table. Suppose you want to enforce referential integrity between the employee table you created (*tblMyEmployees*) and the related employee title table (*tblEmployeeTitle*). Once you tell Access to enforce referential integrity rules between two tables, you cannot delete an employee title from the employee title table unless there are no related employees with that title in the employees table. If you think of the employee title table as the parent and the employees table as the child, then you cannot delete a title and leave an orphan child (an employee whose job title points to a now deleted entry). As you work more with Access, you will gain a deeper understanding of how referential integrity works to preserve a kind of "parent/child" relationship between tables falling under the integrity protection rules.

In the next exercise, you will do your work in the Relationships window, a window that displays linkages between tables for a given database. You define permanent linkages—primary key to foreign key relationships—to make forming multiple-table queries easier. You can also choose whether or not the Relationships window displays none, some, or all intertable relationships. To illustrate just how this works, you will establish referential integrity between the Employee table that we supply you (*tblEmployee*) and the division name and location table (*tblEmployeeDivision*). This will ensure that a division in the table *tblEmployeeDivision* cannot be deleted until all employees (*tblEmployee*) have been reassigned to a new division or removed completely.

EXERCISE 3.6: ESTABLISHING REFERENTIAL INTEGRITY

1. Click the Database Tools tab on the ribbon and then click the Relationships command located in the Show/Hide group. The Relationships tab opens, showing three tables and their relationships: *tblEmployeeDivision*, *tblMyEmployees*, *tblEmployeeTitle*. These relationships were created automatically when you used the Lookup Wizard twice earlier.
2. Click Show Table in the Relationships group to display the remaining table names. The Show Table dialog box opens.
3. Click the Tables tab in the Show Table dialog box, if necessary, to display only table names.
4. Double-click the tblEmployee table to add it to the Relationships window. You may want to drag the bottom border of *tblEmployee* to reveal all of its field names. Drag the right border, if needed, to reveal the longer field names (see Figure 3.8).
5. Click the Show Table Close button to close that dialog box.
6. Hide *tblMyEmployees* in the Relationships window by right-clicking anywhere in tblMyEmployees and clicking Hide Table in the pop-up menu. Click and drag the *tblEmployee* title bar to reposition the table roster between the two existing table rosters.
7. Click the DivisionID field in *tblEmployeeDivision* and drag and drop the field onto the EmpDivisionID field in *tblEmployee*.
8. Click the Enforce Referential Integrity check box to place a check mark in the check box (see Figure 3.9).
9. Click the Create button to establish referential integrity between the two tables (see Figure 3.10).
10. Right-click the Relationships tab, click Close in the pop-up menu, and click Yes when you are asked "Do you want to save changes to the layout of 'Relationships'?" This preserves the newly established relationship and the referential integrity constraint.

Fig. 3.8 **Show Table dialog box.**

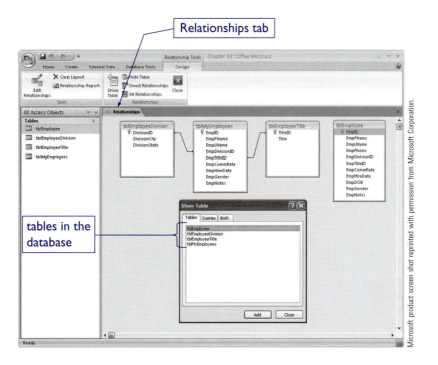

Fig. 3.9 **Linking related tables and enforcing referential integrity.**

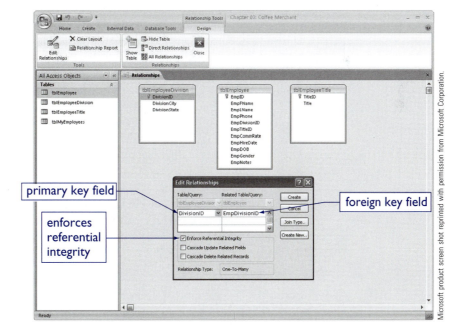

Figure 3.10 shows the Relationships window before you close it. On one end of the line connecting the two tables' field rosters is the number *1*, which indicates the primary key side of the relationship. On the other end of the line is the infinity symbol (∞), which indicates the foreign key side of the relationship. The infinity symbol means that several records can be related to a single record in the "parent" table.

Fig. 3.10 A join line connects two tables.

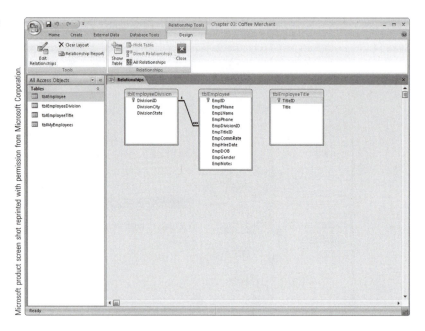

When you join two tables in the Relationships window as illustrated here, their Datasheet view is slightly different from the way it appears before the tables are joined. A new column called the *expand indicator* appears in the first column of each table that is explicitly linked to another table. The indicator displays either a plus sign (+) or minus sign (–). This indicates that there is a subdatasheet associated with a table and its records. A datasheet that is nested within another datasheet is called a *subdatasheet*. It appears whenever two tables are related to one another in a one-to-many relationship, such as the relationship between the employee division names table *tblEmployeeDivision* (the one side of the relationship) and the employee table, *tblEmployee*. When viewing a linked table in Datasheet view, you can click the expand indicator attached to any row to view any related records. The next exercise illustrates how to view related records in the *tblEmployee* and *tblEmployeeDivision* tables.

EXERCISE 3.7: DISPLAYING RELATED TABLES WITH THE EXPAND INDICATOR

1. Open the Chapter 3 database, if necessary.
2. Double-click tblEmployeeDivision in the Navigation Pane. The table opens in Datasheet view by default.
3. Click the expand indicator (+) of the first *tblEmployeeDivision* row, which corresponds to DivisionID 101.
4. If the Insert Subdatasheet dialog box opens, then click tblEmployee from the list of tables. Access fills in the master and child fields automatically from previously established relationships. Click OK.

   A portion of the Employee table opens, revealing which employees work in that division (see Figure 3.11). Notice that the expand indicator, normally a plus sign, changes to a minus sign. The minus sign indicates that the related table rows are open. Of course, if no rows are related to the row whose expand indicator you click, then an empty row appears.

Fig. 3.11 Opening a
subdatasheet of a
particular master row.

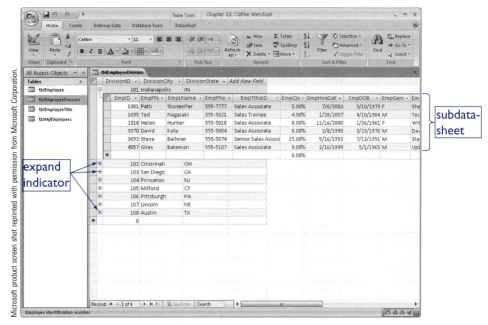

Not all rows in *tblEmployeeDivision* have a subdatasheet. For example, no employees
are currently working at the Milford, Connecticut facility. You can add rows to subdatasheets that are open by simply entering data in the open row at the end of the table—
next to the new row indicator. If you add a row to the *tblEmployee* table subdatasheet,
Access automatically fills in the foreign key field value for EmployeeDivisionID—the
value that corresponds to that group of related rows.

TRY IT

Click the expand indicator corresponding to Lincoln in *tblEmployeeDivision*. An
empty row appears. This indicates that no employee currently is assigned to that
location. Close the table tblEmployeeDivision.

Editing and Removing Intertable Relationships

You can remove or edit an existing relationship between pairs of tables by opening the
Relationships tab. For example, you can remove referential integrity checks between
tblEmployee and *tblEmployeeDivision* by opening the Relationships window, right-
clicking the line connecting the two tables, selecting Edit Relationship, and clearing
the Enforce Referential Integrity check box. This modifies the relationship between
the tables, but does not remove it. To remove a relationship, open the Relationships
window (choose Relationships from the Database Tools tab), click the line that connects the two tables, and then press the Delete key. Similarly, you can right-click the
line connecting the tables and select Delete from the pop-up menu that appears.
In either case, the connecting line disappears along with the explicit relationship
definition.

Deleting, Copying, Renaming, Hiding, and Showing Tables

It is easy to delete unwanted tables, copy them, rename them, hide them, or unhide them. All of these actions occur in the Navigation Pane, and the simplest way to invoke one of the table object changing actions is via the right mouse.

Deleting or Copying a Table

Delete a table, or any other object appearing in the Navigation Pane, by right-clicking it and selecting Delete from the pop-up menu. You cannot delete a table if it is open. So close the table's tab first and then delete it. Deleting a table can have serious and permanent consequences on any objects that depend on the table. So, be sure not to delete a table on which queries, forms, or reports depend. If you delete a table referenced by other objects, then those objects (queries, forms, etc.) will no longer work properly.

You can easily check on objects that depend on any table using the Navigation Pane and a feature new to Access 2007. The next Try It illustrates how.

TRY IT

Right-click the *Navigation Pane* menu at the top of the Navigation Pane, choose *Category* from the pop-up list, and click *Tables and Related Views*. Access rearranges objects in the Navigation Pane so that a table appears in each category followed by all objects that depend on that table. Just check the list for your table to see that there are no objects in its list. Click the Navigation Pane list arrow and then click Object Type to return to a Navigation Pane display of objects by type (Tables first followed by Queries, and so on).

You can copy an entire table—its structure or its structure and data. Right-click the table to be copied, click Copy, right-click a blank area of the Navigation Pane, and then click Paste. Next, fill in a new name (to replace the "Copy Of…" suggested default), and click OK. A faster alternative is the always available keyboard method of pressing Ctrl+C to copy followed by pressing Ctrl+V to paste. Additionally, you can copy a table by clicking it, holding down the Ctrl key, and dragging the table to the end of the list of table objects, and releasing the mouse.

Renaming a Table

Rename a table by right-clicking its name in the Navigation Pane and then selecting Rename from the pop-up menu. When AutoCorrect Options are on, renaming a table automatically renames the table anywhere it appears including in queries, forms, reports, and other record source properties. The only place where a table is not automatically renamed is in Visual Basic code. There, you'll have to manually change the renamed table's name in any code. This AutoCorrect option is very convenient and saves a lot of extra work whenever you decide to rename a table.

Hiding or Showing a Table

It's very simple to hide a table so most users don't know it exists. Right-click the table in the Navigation Pane, click Table Properties in the pop-up menu, click the Hidden check box, and click OK. The table either disappears entirely from the list of table objects, or its name is dimmed in the list. Which of these happens depends on certain Navigation

Pane settings. The next exercise will walk you through hiding and showing a table as well as changing the Navigation Pane attribute that displays (or disallows the display) of hidden objects.

Unhide a table or other object by following the same procedure, except you *clear* the Hidden check box to make the table reappear.

EXERCISE 3.8: HIDING A TABLE AND MAKING IT DISAPPEAR FROM THE NAVIGATION PANE

1. With Access open, close all open object window tabs.
2. Right-click tblMyEmployees in the Navigation Pane and click Hide in this Group in the pop-up list. The table is shown as a dim name.
3. Right-click the Navigation Pane menu at the top of the Navigation Pane, click Navigation Options, and click the Show Hidden Objects check box, if necessary, to clear it (see Figure 3.12). This prevents hidden objects from being shown.
4. Click OK to confirm the new Navigation Pane settings.

Fig. 3.12 Hiding objects by setting a Navigation Pane option.

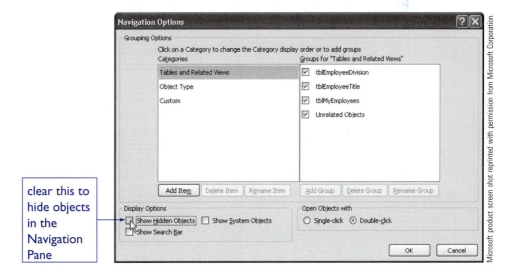

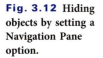

clear this to hide objects in the Navigation Pane

EXERCISE 3.9: SHOWING OBJECTS AS DIMMED IN THE NAVIGATION PANE AND SHOWING AN OBJECT

1. Set the Navigation Pane to show hidden objects as dimmed names: Right-click the Navigation Pane menu at the top of the Navigation Pane and click Navigation Options.
2. Click the Show Hidden Objects check box to place a check mark in it, and then click OK to reset this hidden object display directive. The table name *tblMyEmployees* reappears as a dimmed name in the list of tables.
3. Right-click tblMyEmployees and click Unhide in this Group in the pop-up menu.

Hiding and showing objects is not restricted to tables. You can use the same procedure to hide or show any database object including queries, reports, and forms.

Setting Field Properties

You can customize each field of a table by setting its specific properties. Each field has property settings that affect the way the field looks and behaves—in the table and in other classes of objects such as queries, forms, and reports. These property settings appear in the Field Properties panel that is visible when a table appears in Design view (see Figure 3.4). Once you set one or more properties for a particular field, Access enforces those properties wherever the field appears—including queries, forms, and reports.

The number and type of properties vary slightly depending on the field's data type. A numeric field, for instance, has a Decimal Places property, whereas a Text field does not. Similarly, a text field has a Field Size property, but a data type field does not. We will discuss a few of the most important properties here. You can learn about other field properties by pressing F1 to obtain online help.

Next, you will learn about several important properties. We present these in the same order as they appear from top to bottom in the Field Properties panel. After we explain key properties, we present exercises that show you how to set Field Properties values.

Field Size

The Field Size property allows you to specify the length of text and number fields. Text fields can be from 0 through 255 characters long. The default Field Size for text fields is 50. Number fields have sizes varying from a single-byte integer (Byte), to two integer sizes (Integer or Long Integer), and two floating point number sizes (Single or Double). The size of a text field limits how much information you can enter. Specifying a numeric field size restricts fields to a particular magnitude and to either integer numbers or real numbers (numbers containing decimal places). Data sizes that exceed the maximum length of any data in the column do not waste space. Access does not keep unused space in the database. For example, you can set the Field Size of a text field to 20 characters to limit how much a user can type. If the longest value in that text field is, in fact, only 12 characters, Access compresses the text column so it has no extra, unused spaces—eight spaces in this example.

Format

You can use the Format property to customize the way numbers, dates, times, and text appear when they are printed or displayed. For example, you can set the EmpCommRate (employees' commission rates) Format property to *Percent* and the Decimal Places property to 2 so that a value such as 0.057 displays 5.70% in the tables, queries, forms, or reports—wherever the field is referenced. The Format property uses different settings for different data types. Consult Access help for details about the several format choices.

Input Mask

The Input Mask property makes data entry easier and allows you to control the values that users can enter. For example, an Input Mask for a date field can indicate exactly what you expect the user to enter and prevent all keystrokes except digits: __/__/__. It is frequently easier to use the Input Mask Wizard to help you create an Input Mask.

Caption

The Caption property provides an alternative field name—an alias—that appears in various views. Field captions specify the heading for the field in a table's Datasheet view or a query's Datasheet view. When a field appears in a report or form, the table's caption appears as the field's label. The Caption property is a string expression that can contain up to 2,048 characters. If you do not specify the Caption property value, then the table's Field Name appears wherever the field is referenced.

Default Value

The Default Value property specifies a value that is automatically entered in a field when you create a new record. For example, if you are entering the names and addresses of members of your Chicago area club or organization, you can set the default value for the City field to Chicago. When anyone adds a new record to the table, "Chicago" automatically appears in the City field. You can either accept this value or enter the name of a different city. Set the Default Value property whenever you can identify a field whose contents are often a particular value. Access no longer sets the default value of a numeric field to zero—a long overdue enhancement.

Validation Rule and Validation Text

The validation rule allows you to limit the data that can be entered into a particular field. Used to eliminate some data entry errors, the validation rule is enforced in tables, queries that reference the table, forms, and reports. Useful for enforcing business rules, a validation rule ranges from simple to complex and always evaluates to true or false. For example, a validation rule in the EmpGender field

$$\text{In ("m", "f", "M", "F")}$$

rejects all data entries except the single character of *m* or *f* (either upper- or lowercase). The Validation Text line contains an optional message that appears whenever anyone attempts to enter a disallowed data value. For example, "Gender can be only m or f (lowercase or uppercase)" is a message that could accompany the validation rule shown above.

Required

The Required property set to *Yes* requires entering something in the corresponding field—it cannot be empty. Set to *No*, this field is not required and may be empty.

Allow Zero Length *(text data type)*

If set it to *Yes*, then you can specify a zero length string that appears blank. You enter a zero length string by typing two double-quotation marks in a row—without any character between them. Unlike a null value, an empty string can indicate "yes, I know there is no value for this field." For example, I know the company does not own a fax machine and therefore has no fax number. Leaving a field empty (null), on the other hand, indicates "I don't know whether or not the person or company has a fax number."

Indexed Property

The Indexed property has the value of Yes or No. When a field's Index property is Yes, Access performs a special operation on that field—called generating an index—to speed up searches on the field. Fields that have an Index property value of No do not have associated indexes. Although Access can search any field, search operations on indexed fields are much faster. Primary key fields are always indexed. You might want to index a LastName field of a table if you anticipate frequent searches by last name. In a small table, there is no noticeable difference between indexed and nonindexed field searches. In large tables—tables with 50,000 rows, for instance—the search times between indexed and nonindexed fields is significant.

Lookup Properties

Lookup properties appear when you click the Lookup tab in the Field Properties window. Figure 3.13 shows the Lookup properties for the EmpDivisionID column of your

Fig. 3.13 Lookup properties.

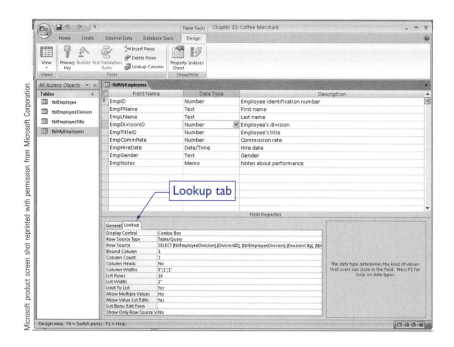

tblMyEmployees table. It has several properties because you created the column using the Lookup Wizard. Most other fields have none or only one Lookup property property—the Display Control. The Display Control property provides several control choices including text box, list box, combo box, and check box—depending on the data type of the field. It determines the type of control that appears in a Form displaying this particular field. Fields not created with the Lookup Wizard have only this field. In this example, the Row Source indicates the Structured Query Language (SQL) statement that the Lookup Wizard creates to populate the combo box for the EmpDivisionID field. (The Select SQL statement shown simply queries another table and retrieves values from it.)

Establishing Table-Level Data Validation

To illustrate how to set properties, you will set the field properties of EmpCommRate and EmpGender in your *tblMyEmployees* table. You will make several property changes to the commission rate field. The commission rate is a small number, so you will indicate that its field size is *Single* to accommodate small numbers with decimal places. Set the format so that the commission rate displays in percentage format with two decimal places. For example, the value 0.0895 displays as 8.95% in Datasheet view. You will change the Caption property so that the commission rate column displays the heading "Rate" instead of the default and awkward heading "EmpCommRate," the column's field name. New employees and management personnel earn no commission, so you want to set the default value for the commission field to zero (0) percent. Lastly, you will establish a valid range of commission rates so that no one can mistakenly enter an unreasonable commission rate such as 45%. A Validation Rule will validate all newly entered commission rates, and an appropriate Validation Text message will display when the commission rate is invalid.

The EmpGender field ought to have a validation rule that permits lowercase or uppercase versions of *m* or *f*, only. Changing the Caption property to display "Gender" makes the column label more intuitive.

EXERCISE 3.10: SETTING FIELD PROPERTIES FOR THE EMPLOYEE COMMISSION FIELD

1. Ensure that the Chapter 3 database is open and close all tabs. Right-click tblMyEmployees and click Design View in the pop-up menu to open the table in Design view.
2. Click anywhere in the EmpCommRate row and then press F6 (a shortcut) to move to the Field Size property in the Field Properties panel.
3. Click the Field Size drop-down list arrow and click Single.
4. Click the Format property, then click its drop-down list arrow, and click Percent.
5. Click the Decimal Places property, drag the mouse to select the current entry, and type 2 to designate two decimal places.
6. Click the Caption property and type Rate. Observe the comment in the right portion of the Field Properties panel. It has helpful information about the selected property.
7. Click the Default Value property and type 0.
8. Click the Validation Rule property and type between 0 and 0.15 to specify the (inclusive) range of valid commission rates. Be sure the second value is 0.15, not 15. A value of 15 means 1500%! (*Note:* the expression >=0 And <=0.15 is identical to the preceding one.)
9. Press Tab to move to the Validation Text property. Notice that the word "between" in the Validation Rule property changes to "Between" to indicate Access recognizes that it is a reserved word.
10. In the Validation Text property text box, type Commission rates range from 0% to 15%. Figure 3.14 shows *tblMyEmployees* in Design view and the new properties you have set so far.
11. Click Save on the Quick Access Toolbar to preserve the new property changes.

(*Note:* if you make these changes to an already populated table, a dialog box opens and displays a warning indicating that data integrity rules have been changed and that existing data may not be valid. Click No to bypass the validity check for existing data. The warning occurs because you have established criteria for the commission rate field—criteria that were not in place when some records were entered. Access recognizes that existing commission data may fall outside the acceptable range.)

Fig. 3.14 Altered *EmpCommRate* properties.

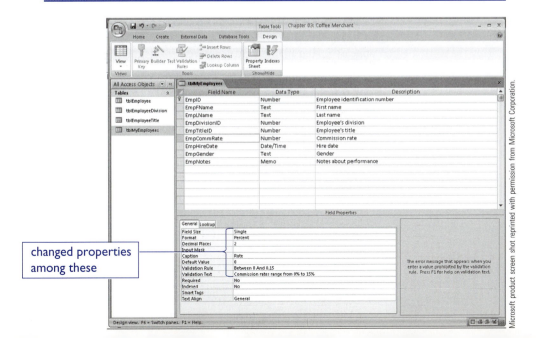

changed properties among these

EXERCISE 3.11: SETTING FIELD PROPERTIES FOR THE EMPGENDER FIELD

1. With *tblMyEmployees* still displayed in Design view, click anywhere in the EmpGender row and then press F6 to move to the Field Size property in the Field Properties panel.
2. Type 1 (the digit one) to limit the length of the gender entry to one character.
3. Press Tab twice to move to the Input Mask property and type >L, which changes any letter typed to uppercase. Be sure to type an uppercase letter l ("ell"). Otherwise you won't get the desired result.
4. Click the Caption property and type Gender.
5. Click the Validation Rule and type "F" or "M" to indicate the only allowed values. Notice that we don't worry about lowercase ("f" or "m") because the Input Mask property forces values to uppercase. The rule further restricts uppercase entries to the two values indicated.
6. Click the Validation Text and type Only F or M allowed in this field.
7. Click Save on the Quick Access Toolbar to save your changes. As before, if your table is populated, a warning message will appear indicating existing data may be invalid. If necessary, click Yes to save the changes.

You can specify more interesting Input Mask values for numeric and date/time fields. Some of the Input Mask property symbols require some explanation. For example, you could specify an Input Mask for a telephone number field as

$$000\backslash\text{-}0000;1;\_$$

to force any input telephone numbers conform to the style "555-1212"—three digits followed by a hyphen followed by four digits. Zeroes in the Input Mask mean that a digit is required in the given mask-digit position. A backslash indicates that the character that follows the backslash, a hyphen in this case, is a literal character and not an operator such as subtraction. The first semicolon ends the first part of the Input Mask. The value 1 between the semicolons indicates that the hyphen in any phone number that a user may enter will not be stored in the field—only the seven digits of the phone number. The second semicolon ends the second part of the Input Mask. Finally, the third part of the Input Mask, the underline character, specifies the character that Access displays for the location where an end user should type a character. In other words, an underline appears in the Phone field wherever no digits appear. The following Try It shows how selected properties and mask fields work.

TRY IT

Open *tblMyEmployees* in Datasheet view. Type *4567* in the EmpID column and press *Tab* to move to the next column. Type your first name in EmpFName, press *Tab*, type your last name in EmpLName. Press *Tab* and the select *Milford* from the drop-down list of cities. Press *Tab* and the select *Sales Manager* from the drop-down list of titles. Press *Tab* to move to the Rate column, type *55* and press *Tab*. What happens? Click *OK* to acknowledge the validation message and then type the valid commission rate, *12*. Press *Tab* twice to move to the Gender field and type *A* and press *Tab*. What happens? Again, your data validation caught this data entry error. Click *OK* to acknowledge the mistake and type your gender in lowercase. Press *Tab*. Notice that Access automatically changes the lowercase entry into uppercase. Move to a new row to post the new employee row to the table by clicking in the *EmpID* column of a new row. You may have noticed that the pencil icon in the record selector of the first row disappears. This indicates that the newly entered data has been saved in the database. Delete the new record: Click in any field in the row you just added, press the Delete command list arrow, and click *Delete Record*. The Delete Record command is found in the Records group of the Datasheet context tab. Click *Yes* when the dialog box appears to confirm the record-delete operation. Right-click the *tblMyEmployees* tab and click *Close* in the pop-up menu to close the Datasheet view window.

Be careful when you set both a field's Default and Validation Rule properties. They can come into conflict with each other if you aren't careful. For instance, suppose you set the default value of a field to 2 and subsequently type the validation rule *Between 3 And 25*. Clearly, the default value is not in the range of allowed values set forth by the Validation Rule property. That conflict can occur inadvertently when you skip the field and Access attempts to insert the default value, 2, into the field, thus violating the validation rule.

Establishing a Primary Key

A primary key is one or more fields of a table that uniquely defines each row. Tables must have a primary key if they are referenced by another table. For example, each customer must have a column such as CustomerID that uniquely identifies each customer. Otherwise, there is no reasonable way to associate, say, orders stored in their own table with the customers that ordered them. You recall that good database design dictates that separate facts are stored in separate tables. The ability to consolidate tables rests with their foreign key and primary key values. For instance, order rows in an order table are associated with the correct customers by matching a customer ID in the order table (a foreign key) with a like-valued customer ID in a customer table. Tables that don't have a primary key are stand alone and not related to other tables—a rare occurrence. Such tables constitute a flat file system.

Access is an example of a database system that does not *require* that a table be assigned a primary key. When you save a newly defined table without designating a foreign key, Access will display a dialog box stating, in part, "…Although a primary key isn't required, it's highly recommended…" and offers to insert a new, primary key column whose data type is AutoNumber.

Sometimes, primary keys consist of more than one column. Such a primary key can be called a *composite*, *compound*, or *complex primary key*. The Chapter 3 database does not have a need for a composite primary key as yet. However, there are common situations where they are useful. Consider the common example of employees and the customers they service. The primary key for an employee might be EmployeeID, and the primary key for the customer might be CustomerID. The EmployeeID uniquely identifies each employee (salesperson) so that their IDs can be recorded for each sale, and the CustomerID uniquely identifies each customer to whom that employee sold one or more items. This is an example of two tables that have a many-to-many relationship because any employee can provide customer service to many customers; similarly, any given customer may have been helped by several different employees. This is a very common situation. The best way to represent this relationship using a relational database system such as Access is to create a third table. This table—which may be called a *transition table* or a *bridge table*—has rows that contain a composite primary key. It consists of the primary key from the employee table and a related primary key from the customer table. Often, these two values, when used together, are unique. Whenever an employee can provide service to a customer multiple times in a day, however, this combination is not unique. Figure 3.15 shows the Relationships window of a small database like the one described here. It illustrates how two tables joined by including a third, bridge table. The bridge table's SalesAmount column is part of the bridge table's composite primary key because the combination of the CustomerID, EmployeeID, and sale amount *is* unique. That is, a given employee and customer pair can occur multiple times, but throwing in the sale amount into the primary key makes it unique. Of course, this bridge table then lets us list the customers served by a particular employee and vice versa—while preserving the relationship between customer and employee—as a unique key pair.

Fig. 3.15 Example bridge table joining two tables.

composite primary key consisting of primary keys from *tblEmployee* and *tblCustomer* (and *SalesAmount*)

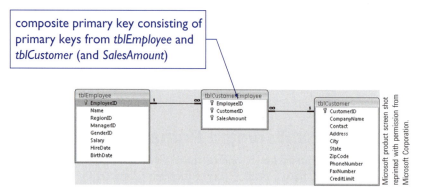

Microsoft product screen shot reprinted with permission from Microsoft Corporation.

Designating one or more columns as the primary key (or removing the primary key designation) is straightforward. Let's practice it.

EXERCISE 3.12: REMOVING THE PRIMARY KEY DESIGNATION FROM A COLUMN

1. Open the Chapter 3 database, if necessary, and close any open, tabbed database windows.
2. Right-click tblMyEmployees and click Design View in the pop-up menu.
3. Click anywhere in the EmpID row (Design view), and then click the Primary Key command in the Tools group of the Design contextual tab. Access removes the primary key symbol from EmpID's row selector.

EXERCISE 3.13: DESIGNATING TWO COLUMNS AS A TABLE'S COMPOSITE PRIMARY KEY

1. With the *tblMyEmployees* still open in Design view, click and drag through the row selectors for EmpFName and EmpLName to select both. A golden rectangle outlines both fields.
2. Click the Primary Key command in the Tools group of the Design contextual tab. Access places a small key in both row selectors (see Figure 3.16).
3. To reset EmpID as the single-column primary key, right-click any column in the EmpID row (including its row selector). Click Primary Key in the pop-up menu. (You can click the Primary Key command as before, but you may prefer this right-mouse alternative method.) Access removes the primary key indicators from the two rows previously set and places it in the row selector of EmpID.
4. Right-click the tblMyEmployees tab, click Close in the pop-up menu, and click Yes when asked if you want to save the changes to the table's design.

Fig. 3.16 Designating a composite primary key.

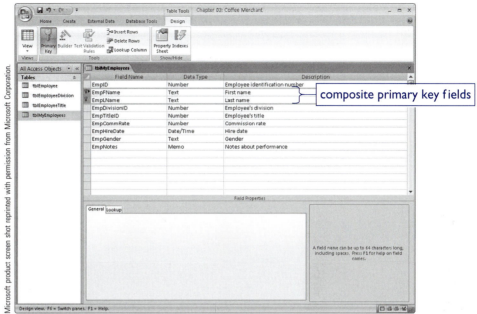

Examining and Setting Table Properties

Tables have their own set of distinct properties that you can examine and set. We will examine a small number of these properties. Table properties of interest to us include Subdatasheet Expanded, Description, Default View, Filter, Order By, Filter On Load, and Order By On Load. Briefly, these properties affect the associated table as a whole. Subdatasheet Expanded, a yes/no value, determines whether or not any many-side table appears expanded with each row. Description is simply commentary about the table, Default View is "Datasheet" by default, but you can choose PivotTable or PivotChart as the default view when you open the table. The Filter property specifies any automatically applied filter criteria that occur when you open the table in Datasheet view. The Order By table property allows you to specify a column by which the table is sorted whenever it is opened. The yes/no values for the Filter On Load and Order By On Load properties determine whether the table is filtered or sorted when opened in Datasheet view—based on the values of the related properties Filter and Order By. Let's experiment with these table properties by following the steps in the next exercise.

EXERCISE 3.14: SETTING TABLE PROPERTIES

1. With the Chapter 3 database open, close any open tabbed windows.
2. Right-click tblEmployeeDivision and click Design View in the pop-up menu.
3. Click the Property Sheet command in the Show/Hide group of the Design contextual tab. The table's property sheet appears.
4. Drag the left edge of the Property Sheet panel to the left to widen it so the Description (*Company division's location*) field's three words are visible.
5. Click the Order By property and type DivisionCity to automatically list the open table in city name order.
6. Ensure the Order By On Load value is Yes (see Figure 3.17).

7. Click the Datasheet View button in the Views group of the Design contextual tab. Click Yes when prompted to save the table. The datasheet opens in alphabetical order by city name (see Figure 3.18).

8. Undo the table property changes: Click the Design View button in the Datasheet contextual tab (*Views* group on the far left end of the ribbon).

9. Double-click the Order By property and press Del to erase its value. Click the Save button in the Quick Access Toolbar to save the change.

10. Click the Close button (X) on the Property Sheet title bar to close it, and then click the Datasheet View button to redisplay the *tblEmployeeDivision* table. Notice it is back to its original order—by primary key.

11. Close the table: Right-click the tblEmployeeDivision tab and click Close All.

Fig. 3.17 Setting table properties.

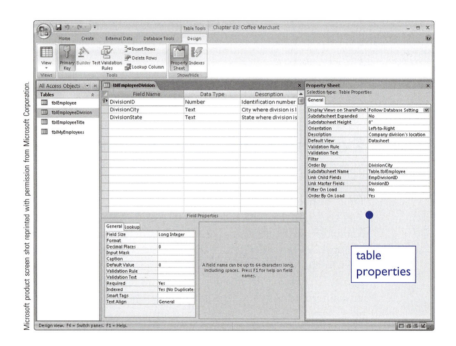

Microsoft product screen shot reprinted with permission from Microsoft Corporation.

Saving the Table Design

Throughout this chapter, you have been saving tables after you create or modify them. Access always prompts you whenever you make changes and then try to close an altered object without saving it. Bear in mind that the main time you have to save something in Access is whenever you change an object's design—create a new table, alter a table, create or alter a query, and so on. You *do not* have to save data that you enter into a table. Populated data changes are automatically saved by Access whenever you move up or down in a table—basically, anytime you move off the altered data row. So just remember the difference between these two save types: Access automatically saves any data that changes when you enter it into a table; you are responsible for saving any structural changes to objects including tables. Saving a changed table structure is simple. Just click the Save icon in the Quick Access Toolbar. Alternatively, you can click the Office button and then click Save in the Office menu.

Fig. 3.18 Sorting a table automatically.

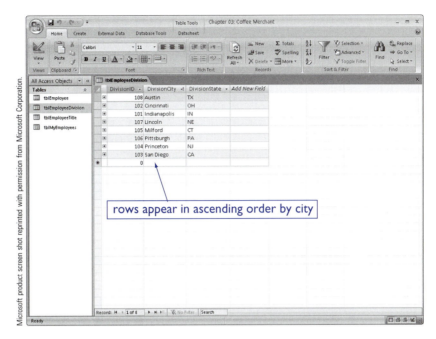

rows appear in ascending order by city

Printing Table Structure Information

Printing table structure information (its field names, data types, and so on) is a good way to document details about your tables. Once you have generated a hard copy output, you can keep it with the remainder of the system documentation. This is especially important documentation if others will be responsible for maintaining a database. The following Try It illustrates the simple procedure to produce a table structure information report.

TRY IT

Click the *Database Tools* tab, and then click the *Database Documenter* command in the Analyze group. Click the *Tables* tab in the Documenter dialog box; click the check box next to the *tblMyEmployees* table name to place a check mark in it, and click *OK*. A report appears in Print Preview view. Click the *Print* command in the Print group of the Print Preview contextual tab to open the standard Print dialog box. Fill out the Print dialog box (all pages or just selected pages, and so on). If you want to produce a report, then click *OK*. Otherwise, click *Cancel* to revoke the report production. Right click the *tblMyEmployees* tab and click *Close All* to close the table and the Print Preview window.

Populating a Table

When you ***populate a table***, you place data into a table whose structure already exists. Populating a table is straightforward. You can do that now. First, ensure that Ch03.mdb is open. Follow the steps in Exercise 3.15 to place some data into your customer table. You will use three different methods to move from one field to the next one: pressing Tab, clicking the next field, and pressing Enter. You can decide which method you prefer and use it to populate other tables.

EXERCISE 3.15: ENTERING DATA INTO A RECORD

1. Double-click tblMyEmployees table name in the Navigation Pane to open it in Datasheet view. (Double-clicking a table's name opens the table in Datasheet view by default.)
2. Type 1301 in the EmpID field.
3. Press Tab to move to the EmpFName cell and type Patti.
4. Click the empty cell below the column label EmpLName and type Stonesifer.
5. Press Enter to move to the next column, EmpDivisionID.
6. Click the list drop-down arrow and then click the Indianapolis row in the drop-down list, and press Tab to move to the EmpTitleID column.
7. Click the EmpTitleID column drop-down list arrow, click Sales Associate, and press Tab to move to the Rate column.
8. Type 5, and press Enter to set Patti's commission rate to 5% and move to the next column, EmpHireDate.
9. Click the Date Picker icon, click the Today button to set Patti's hire date to today's date, and press Enter to move to the Gender column.
10. Type W (for woman) and press Enter. A dialog box appears stating "Only F or M allowed in this field..." (see Figure 3.19). In Exercise 3.11 you set this field property (a constraint) to prevent anyone from typing disallowed data into this column. Also, notice that the Input Mask property you set in Exercise 3.11 automatically capitalizes the letter as you type it.
11. Click OK to close the dialog box. Press Backspace to erase the current entry and type F.
12. Press Enter to move to the last field, EmpNotes.
13. Type the following: She has worked hard her whole career. She embodies a true type A personality. (Include the second period in the field.) Press Enter to place the entered text into the EmpNotes column. Access moves to the second row of the *tblMyEmployees* table. It is currently empty.

Fig. 3.19 A validation rule in action.

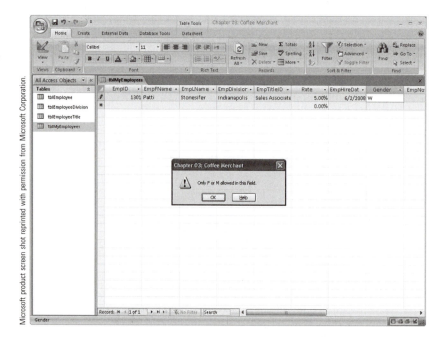

Did you notice the small pencil symbol in the row selector button of the table just before you pressed Enter in the previous step? A pencil symbol indicates that a record's contents have been changed but not yet saved in the table. You post changes to a table simply by moving to another table record. You will do that in a moment.

If you make a mistake anywhere in a row, simply use the arrow keys to move left or right in the field, or use the Backspace or Delete keys to delete information. Pressing a key inserts the letter into the field at the insertion point indicated by the cursor. To correct a value in a field to the left of the current field, press Shift+Tab repeatedly until the cursor arrives at the field to be changed. To display the blinking insertion point, simply press F2. Then you can use the arrow keys to move the insertion point within a field. Pressing Tab (move forward) or Shift+Tab (move backward) moves to another cell and selects its entire value.

Here's a handy tip to keep in mind as you enter data into any long text or memo field. You can press Shift+F2 to display the field in the Zoom box. Doing so allows you to see longer than usual data as you type it. The following Try It illustrates this.

TRY IT

With *tblMyEmployees* open in Datasheet view, click the *EmpNotes* cell corresponding to Patti Stonesifer's row. Press *Shift+F2* to open the Zoom box (see Figure 3.20). Click the mouse following the end of the text and type *What a great resource*. Click the *OK* button to close the Zoom box. Press *Enter* to move to the second data row and post the change.

Fig. 3.20 Opening the Zoom box.

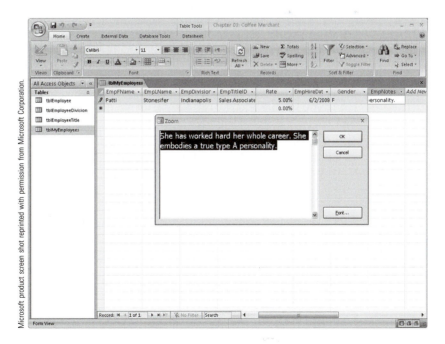

You won't need the *tblMyEmployees* table any longer. Your database has a fully populated employees table called *tblEmployee* and you will use that table for the remainder of this chapter. So, let's delete the table.

EXERCISE 3.16: DELETING A TABLE AND AUTOMATICALLY DELETING ITS RELATIONSHIPS

1. Ensure that *tblMyEmployees* is closed; then right-click the table name tblMyEmployees in the Navigation Pane and click Delete in the pop-up menu.
2. Click Yes to confirm your desire to delete the table.
3. Click Yes when the dialog box displays the warning message "You can't delete the table 'tblMyEmployees' until its relationships to other tables have been deleted." This simply indicates that there are foreign key and primary key relationships to the other tables named *tblEmployeeTitle* and *tblEmployeeDivision*.

Modifying a Table's Datasheet

Most of the modifications you have made to the *tblMyEmployees* table in this chapter have been to its *design*. Several of a table's Datasheet view characteristics can be altered, too. You might want to widen or narrow one or more of a table's columns to better see (and print) its data. Similarly, you might want to sort a table on one or more of its columns in ascending or descending values. In addition, you can hide columns you don't want to display in Datasheet view or reveal them. Formatting of columns including setting the font and font color is possible for a table in Datasheet view—similar to the way you can format Excel worksheets. Finally, new to Access 2007 is the ability to display aggregate statistics in a Total in a row below all the table rows. The sections that follow illustrate several Datasheet view display modifications.

Any change you make to a table's Datasheet view—hiding or freezing a column, altering its font or foreground color, and so on—is called a *layout change* (not a design change). If you attempt to close the table without saving it, Access asks you if you want to save changes to the table's layout. If you click Yes, then the formatting changes are preserved. However, doing so *does not* modify the table's design in any way. In other words, altering the Datasheet view merely changes the way the table is displayed. So, you can safely reply No to any layout changes without fear of upsetting some important design characteristic of the table. In essence, layout changes are merely cosmetic in nature.

Resizing and Rearranging Columns

Resizing columns of a table displayed in Datasheet view allows you to display columns in other than the default width. For example, the employee titles column, called EmpTitleID, is probably too narrow to see all the related titles—those pulled from the *tblEmployeeTitle* table. Similarly, you can economize on screen space by narrowing columns that are too wide, thus providing more printable column space. Similarly, you can move columns from their default, Design-view designated positions without actually affecting the underlying table design. For example, it might be better to display the employees hire date in the leftmost column; or, it might be desirable to move the primary key column, EmpID, to the far right so that name columns are leftmost in the Datasheet view.

EXERCISE 3.17: RESIZING AND REARRANGING TABLE COLUMNS IN DATASHEET VIEW

1. Right-click tblEmployee and click Open in the pop-up menu to open it in Datasheet view.
2. Move the mouse pointer to the column header line between EmpFName and EmpLName. When it changes to a left- and right-pointing arrow, double-click it to

    resize the column width to that of the widest data or label. EmpFName widens to accommodate the entire column name.

3. Similar to step 2, double-click the right edge of the EmpLName column name to widen it slightly.

4. Double-click the right edge in the EmpTitleID label to widen it. Now, the entire text string of the longest employee title is visible.

5. Move the mouse to the EmpFName column label. When it turns into a down-pointing arrow, click and drag the mouse through it and the EmpLName column so both columns are selected. You can tell they are selected because both columns turn light blue and they are surrounded by a golden rectangle. Release the mouse.

6. Click either the EmpFName column label or the EmpLName label and drag the two columns to the left—until the dark black vertical line is on the left side of the EmpID column. Release the mouse to complete the column-moving process. Now the first and last names are to the left of the primary key.

7. Right-click the tblEmployee tab, click Close, and click Yes when asked if you want to save changes to the *layout* of the table.

8. Double-click tblEmployee in the Navigation Pane to verify that the layout changes were saved.

If you are curious about whether you changed the *design* of *tblEmployee*, then run the next Try It to discover the answer.

TRY IT

Right-click *tblEmployee* in the Navigation Pane and click *Design View*. Notice that the EmpID column remains the leftmost column of the table's design—unlike the Datasheet view of *tblEmployee*. Right-click the *tblEmployee* tab and click *Close*.

Hiding and Freezing Columns

Sometimes you don't want to see or print all the columns in a table. But, you cannot simply delete a column you don't want to see in Datasheet view or else it will destroy important data and possibly break relationships established between tables. For instance, you might want to hide the EmpID, EmpPhone, and EmpNotes columns in Datasheet view for the time being. After all, you can always unhide them when needed. Hidden or not, columns are always available to other objects such as queries and reports. They are simply hidden in Datasheet view. Similarly, you might want to freeze the first name and last name columns so that scrolling to the right does not make those columns disappear off the left side of your screen. Such an action—to hold one a column in place for horizontal scrolling—is called *freezing* a column.

The next exercise shows you how to hide and freeze columns.

EXERCISE 3.18: HIDING COLUMNS

1. Double-click tblEmployee in the Navigation Pane to open the table in Datasheet view.

2. Drag the mouse through the EmpID and EmpPhone column labels to select both columns.

3. Right-click anywhere inside the selected columns and then click Hide Columns in the pop-up menu. Access hides the two columns. (You can display the table in Design view to affirm that the two columns exist but are not shown if you want.)
4. Leave *tblEmployee* open in Datasheet view.

Freezing columns is particularly handy when a table's columns in Datasheet view extend beyond the right edge of the screen. Freezing selected columns on the left side allows them to remain in place while you scroll to the right in the Datasheet.

EXERCISE 3.19: FREEZING COLUMNS

1. Drag the mouse through the EmpFName and EmpLName colums to select both columns.
2. Right-click anywhere inside the selected columns and then click Freeze Columns in the pop-up menu. Nothing appears to happen, but Access freezes those two columns in the leftmost position (see Figure 3.21).
3. Click anywhere outside the selected columns to deselect them.
4. Drag the horizontal scroll bar to the right to observe that the EmpDivisionID and columns to the right scroll out of view. The EmpFName and EmpLName columns remain fixed and visible on the left side of the Datasheet.

Fig. 3.21 Freezing columns in Datasheet view.

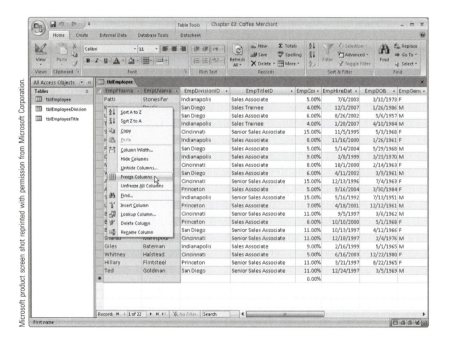

Unhiding and unfreezing columns is easy. Just remember that you right-click the column header—the labels at the tops of the table columns in Datasheet view.

EXERCISE 3.20: UNHIDING AND UNFREEZING COLUMNS

1. Right-click any column's header and then click Unhide Columns. *Tip:* If you don't see "Unhide Columns" in the pop-up menu, then you probably right-clicked inside a column's contents—one of its cells, not the header. Try again. Access displays an Unhide Columns dialog box indicating which columns are visible (check boxes contain check marks) and which are hidden (no check marks in the check boxes) (see Figure 3.22).
2. Click the EmpID and EmpPhone check boxes to place a check mark in them and click Close to close the dialog box.
3. Right-click any column's header and then click Unfreeze All Columns.

Fig. 3.22 Unhiding columns in Datasheet view.

hidden columns

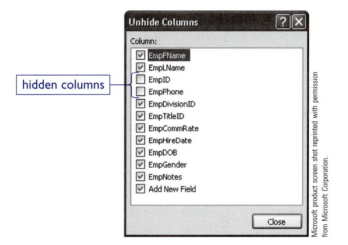

Microsoft product screen shot reprinted with permission from Microsoft Corporation.

All *tblEmployee* columns appear and the first name and last name columns are no longer frozen. Leave *tblEmployee* open in Datasheet view. When you close the Datasheet view, Access will ask you if you want to save changes to the layout. You can click Yes to preserve any layout changes (hiding, freezing, etc.) or click No to discard them. In this case, you reversed all changes so it doesn't matter which you choose on closing the Datasheet view.

Formatting the Datasheet

The Home tab of the ribbon displays a group of command buttons that allow you to format a table open in Datasheet view. The command buttons include options to change fonts, foreground colors, background colors, and text alignment. Any format changes affect only the active table displayed in Datasheet view, and they are saved when you save the table layout and appear when you close and then reopen the table in Datasheet view. You will experiment with a few of the formatting changes next.

EXERCISE 3.21: FORMATTING THE DATASHEET VIEW

1. Ensure that *tblEmployee* is open in Datasheet view.
2. Click the Home tab, if necessary.
3. Click the Font Color command list arrow in the Font group. Click the Dark Red color square (left column, bottom row). (*Hint:* Point to a color to display a color name.) The foreground color of all text in the table changes to the selected color.

4. Click the Fill/Back Color command list arrow in the Font group. Click the Yellow color square (last row, fourth column to the right). The background color of every other row of the table changes to the selected color. Notice that the selected foreground and background color squares appear in the Recent Colors panel of the drop-down colors (see Figure 3.23).

5. Click the Alternate Fill/Back Color command list arrow in the Font group. Click the Maroon 3 color square (fourth row from the top, sixth column to the right). The background color of alternative rows changes to the selected color. Wow! Those color choices are pretty wild.

6. Right-click the tblEmployee tab, click Close All, and click No when a dialog box appears asking if you want to save the layout changes.

Fig. 3.23 Formatting columns.

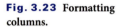

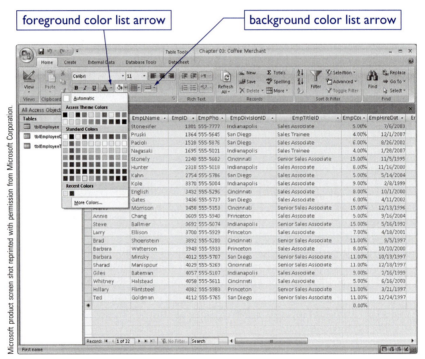

Displaying Column Totals

One very useful change introduced in Access 2007 is the Total row that optionally appears following the last row of a table or query displayed in Datasheet view. Clicking the Totals command found in the Records group on the Home tab toggles the Total row on and off. Click the Totals command once and the Total row appears below the empty row at the bottom of a table in Datasheet view. Click the command again and Access removes the Total row.

Cells in the Total row can be customized to display a variety of aggregate statistics for the column above the Total row cell including the average, count, maximum, minimum, standard deviation, sum, and variance for numeric columns. Average, count, maximum, and minimum are available for date-valued columns. Count is available for all data types including text and memo. Count calculates the number of the non-null entries in a column.

We will use the *tblEmployee* table to illustrate the Total row. However, a better use of the Total row might be in a query that displays summary results such as customers' invoice totals grouped by customer. In that case, a Total row serves the vital need of displaying the total of all unpaid invoices, for example. Here, we'll simply illustrate it using our *tblEmployee* table.

EXERCISE 3.22: **ADDING A TOTAL ROW**

1. Open *tblEmployee* in Datasheet view.
2. Click the Home tab, if necessary, and click the Totals button in the Records group. A new row appears below the last record. The word *Total* appears in the first column.
3. Click in the cell in the Total row below the EmpTitleID column, which displays employees' titles. Click the cell's drop-down arrow to display a list of aggregate functions. Only *None* and *Count* are available. (*None* removes any aggregate function from the selected cell.) Click Count Access displays 22—the number of nonempty values in that column.
4. Click in the cell in the Total row below the EmpCompRate column, which displays employees' commission rates. Click the cell's drop-down arrow to display a list of aggregate functions. Seven functions are available as well as *None*. Click Average. After a moment, Access displays the value 8.59%, which is the average commission of all employees.
5. Click in the Total row cell below EmpHireDate, click the cell's drop-down arrow, and click Minimum in the list of four aggregate function choices. Access displays the oldest ("minimum") hire date, 5/16/1992 (see Figure 3.24).
6. Right-click the tblEmployee tab, click Close, and click No when asked if you want to save the layout changes. There is no need to display the totals the next time you open *tblEmployee* in Datasheet view.

Fig. 3.24 Inserting column statistics in the Total row.

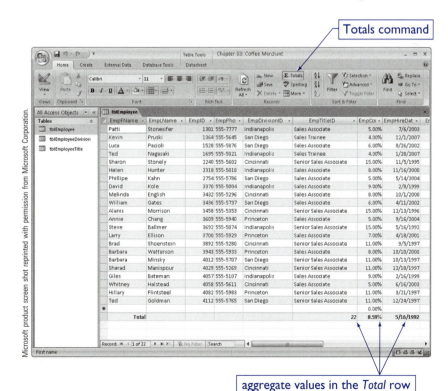

Printing Records

A table's records can be printed in a row and column format that resembles its Datasheet view. Unfortunately, there is little available control over page-layout details such as headers or footers, page numbering, titles, and so on. If you require high-quality printouts of table contents, then you have to design a report based on the table containing headers and footers, page numbers, repeating column headers, and other report-only features. Reports offer the best and most complete way to produce boardroom-quality printed results. If your needs are simple, then a simple printout of a table with default settings is fine in other situations. Best of all, simple printouts of tables are easy to produce. The following Try It exercises leads you through the process.

TRY IT

Close any open window tabs. Click the *tblEmployee* table name in the Navigation Pane. (No need to actually open it, though.) With *tblEmployee* highlighted, click the *Office* button, point to *Print* in the menu list, and click *Print Preview*. It is always preferable to preview the first page in a Print Preview display to ensure print settings are correct. The Print Preview contextual tab displays all the commands, including the Page Layout group. Click the *Landscape* button to reorient the printout. You probably notice not all employee columns appear on the page. Adjust margins to correct this problem: Click the *Margins* command, and click *Normal*. The only missing column in your preview probably is EmpNotes (see Figure 3.25). That's fine. Click the *Print* button in the Print group of the Print Preview contextual tab. Limit the printed page to just page 1: Click the *From*: text box and type *1*. Click *OK* to print the single page. Click the Close Print Preview button in the Close Preview group.

Fig. 3.25 Print preview of the employee table.

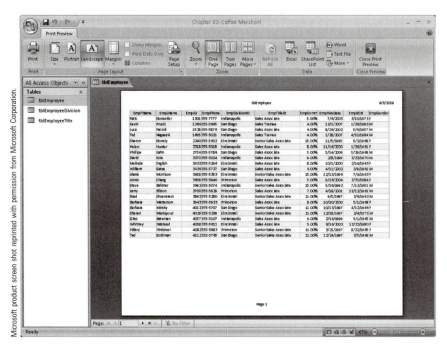

Review the printed results. At the top are the table's name (middle, top) and today's date. At the bottom of the page is the page number. If you have to turn in a printed page of any particular table, coax Access to print your name in the header. Use the following simple trick. First copy the table you want to print and paste it back into the Navigation Pane. Rename the copy with your first and last names. Select this copy to print. Now you can follow the procedure detailed above in the Try It exercise. Because Access prints the table name in the top of the page, printing the copy of the table named with your name causes *your* name to appear in the printed page's header.

Organizing Tables in the Navigation Pane

Located on the left edge of the screen, the Navigation Pane contains a list of all objects in the database, and it is the central location from which you display and edit all your database objects. It replaces the old Database window from earlier versions of Access. By default, the Navigation Pane appears when you open a database. As you have done multiple times, you can double-click an object in the Navigation Pane to open it, or you can drag an object name to the open window to open it. Right-click the object and choose Design View to edit the object.

On the right edge of the Navigation Pane is the Shutter Bar. To open or close it, you click the Shutter Bar Open/Close button (or toggle F11) in the Navigation Pane (see Figure 3.26) to reduce it to just its shutter bar whenever you need more screen real estate. The Navigation Pane is divided into two categories and groups. The categories appear at the top of the Navigation Pane and include *Tables and Related Views, Object Type, Created Date*, and *Modified Date*. Chapter 3 database objects have been displayed in the Tables and Related Views category throughout this chapter. Above the Object Type category is *Custom*. This category allows you to create your own named categories and group objects into them. Navigation Pane categories have their own groups. The Object Type category contains the familiar groups Tables, Queries, Forms, Reports, and All

Fig. 3.26 *Tables and Related Views* **category and related groups.**

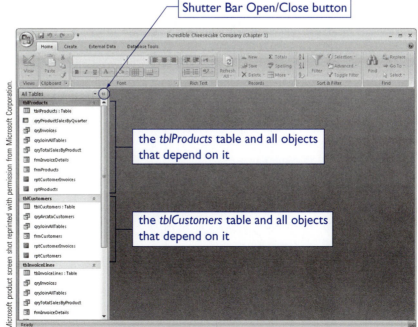

Access Objects. Other categories have other groups. The Tables and Related Views category organizes objects by table name, with related objects under those table groups. This is very handy, for example, when you want to which forms and queries depend on a particular table. Figure 3.26 shows an example of this category and resulting groups in the Navigation Pane. The database example we use in Figure 3.26 is the Chapter 1 database because it contains a larger variety and number of objects than the Chapter 3 database. The Object Type category is what you have seen so far in Chapter 3—tables grouped together followed by all queries, then forms, and so on. The Object Type category, which you have been using all along, groups objects by type. The groups available in this category include All Access Objects (the default), and the individual filter-by-group object types of Tables, Queries, Forms, Reports, Macros, or Modules. You display only tables, for example, by selecting Tables from the available groups. Figure 3.27 shows the Navigation Pane prior to selecting Queries as the filtering group. Once clicked, Queries only will appear in the Navigation Pane. If needed, you can display objects in created date or modified date category order.

Fig. 3.27 Preparing to display the Queries group of the Object Type category.

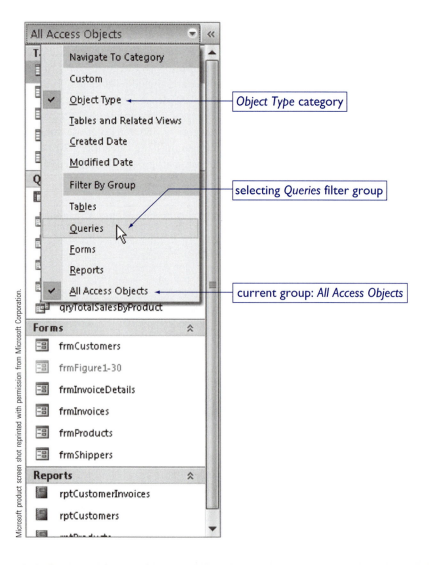

Microsoft product screen shot reprinted with permission from Microsoft Corporation.

Hiding and Revealing Object Names

You can hide some or all of the groups in a category. Recall from earlier in this chapter that you can right-click any object in a group and then click the command *Hide in this Group* from the pop-up menu. Normally this causes the object to appear dim in the group. Remember also, that you can cause any hidden group to disappear from the list of objects. The two Try It exercises that follow lead you through this process in two steps. The first Try It dims the object, preparing it to be hidden. The second Try It makes the dimmed object name disappear from the list of objects in the Navigation Pane.

TRY IT

Dim a table object in the Navigation Pane: With the Chapter 3 database open and all tabbed windows closed, right-click *tblEmployeeTitle* in the Navigation Pane. Click Hide in this Group. Select another table to confirm that *tblEmployeeTitle* is dimmed: Click *tblEmployee* in the Navigation Pane. Unless you have set the Navigation Pane option, the table name is dimmed but visible in the Navigation Pane list.

TRY IT

Make the table name disappear: Right-click the Navigation Pane menu located at the top of the Navigation Pane and click the *Navigation Options* command in the pop-up list. The Navigation Options dialog box opens. Clear the *Show Hidden Objects* check box by clicking it, if necessary, to erase its check mark. Click *OK*. Notice that the hidden table, *tblEmployeeTitle*, no longer appears in the Tables group. Re-execute these two Try It exercises to reverse what you just did and make *tblEmployeeTitle* reappear. First, check the Show Hidden Objects check box in this Try It. Then repeat the first Try It above this one (clicking *Unhide in this Group*, instead).

Creating New Categories

Whenever you create a new database without using one of the available templates, Microsoft Access 2007 automatically creates a custom category. The custom category displays one group that contains all the database objects. You can rename the custom category, create your own new custom groups, and add objects to those groups. To help you put categories and their groups in perspective, consider that all the figures shown in this chapter, so far, display the Navigation Pane with the *Object Type* category and the *All Access Objects* group of that category. Other groups belonging to the Object Type category are Tables, Queries, Forms, Reports, and so on. You can close selected groups and leave others open—close all groups except Tables, for example, in the Object Type category.

If you produce various types of reports for salespersons and other reports for managers, then you could organize your database by creating a *Company Reports* category and then create groups in that category called *Salesperson Reports* and *Managerial Reports*, for instance. Within the Salesperson Reports group are all the reports that pertain to salespersons; similarly, in the Managerial Reports group are only management reports.

This is a very handy organizing principle that avoids the object clutter problem of too many objects that previous versions of Access had. To make sense of categories and groups, we'll have you create both and then populate them with shortcuts to appropriate objects. You use the Navigation Options dialog box to create and manage custom categories and their groups. Custom categories and their groups replace *switchboards* from earlier versions of Access, and Access limits you to a maximum of 10 custom categories. Let's create a category and a couple of groups to understand how this works.

EXERCISE 3.23: CREATING A CUSTOM CATEGORY

1. Open the Chapter 3 database, if necessary, right-click the menu at the top of the Navigation Pane, and then click Navigation Options. The Navigation Options dialog box appears.
2. In the Navigation Options dialog box in the Categories list, click Add Item. A new category appears in the list (see Figure 3.28).
3. Type Managers to replace the suggested and highlighted *Custom Category 1* and press Enter. The new category appears in the Categories list. Notice that the caption for the groups changes to include the new category name. It displays *Groups for "Managers"* in the heading. Access creates, by default, a group named *Unassigned Objects*. Keep the Navigation Options dialog box open for the next exercise.

Fig. 3.28 Creating a custom category.

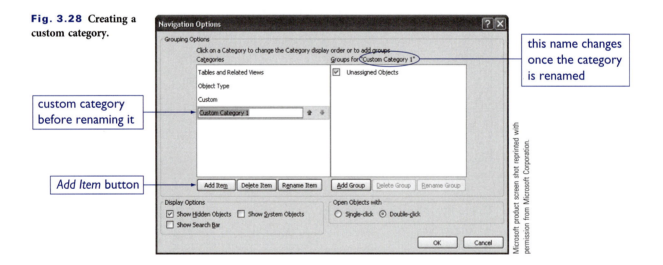

custom category before renaming it

Add Item button

this name changes once the category is renamed

Microsoft product screen shot reprinted with permission from Microsoft Corporation.

After you create a custom group, you can populate it with as many custom groups as you need. To do so, keep the Navigation Options dialog box open for the exercise that follows.

EXERCISE 3.24: CREATING CUSTOM GROUPS

1. Under the Groups for "Managers" panel on the right side of the Navigation Options dialog box, click Add Group. The group name *Custom Group 1* appears.
2. Create a name for the new group: Type Employee Data Entry Form, and press Enter.

3. Click Add Group again, type Employee Title Form, and press Enter to create a second custom group. Access displays the new group names in the Groups for Managers panel.
4. Click OK to close the Navigation Options dialog box.

Notice that the Navigation Pane does not display either the new category you created or the custom groups within the category. You must select the custom category for it to appear along with the newly created groups. In the next section, you will make the category visible and add a table into the custom groups you created.

Organizing Tables into Custom Categories

A handy way to customize your database objects within the Navigation Pane is to place them into one or more custom categories. You create a custom category either by renaming the *Custom* category (available by default) or by creating a new category that you can name virtually anything you want—as you did above. It is best to keep the number of custom categories and groups each contains to the minimum needed to make it easier to find objects within the database. Any custom categories and groups are local to the database in which you create them. In other words, you cannot transfer custom categories or groups to other databases—though you can recreate them in other databases. Once you create custom groups within any custom categories, then you place in the groups *shortcuts* to database objects—not the objects themselves. Suppose you create a custom group called *Managerial* and a custom group in that category called *CEOreports*. You reference a report by placing a shortcut to the report into the CEOreports group—much like you create shortcuts on your Windows desktop which represent actual programs stored in folders on your disk. Access allows you to create multiple shortcuts to a database objects—each shortcut in a different group. This is particularly handy when a report or form is useful to two or more different user groups represented by two Navigation Pane groups in a category. Whenever you view any of the custom categories and their groups in the Navigation Pane, you always see the shortcuts to the objects. You can easily identify shortcuts by the small arrow next to the icon in the lower left.

EXERCISE 3.25: ADDING OBJECTS TO A CUSTOM GROUP

1. Click the menu at the top of the Navigation Pane and click Managers, the new category you created in the previous exercises.
2. Widen the Navigation Pane to show the custom group names by its right edge to the right.
3. In the *Unassigned Objects* group, click tblEmployee and drag it into the Employee Data Entry Form group name. A shortcut icon to *tblEmployee* appears in the Employee Data Entry Form group.
4. Here's another way to put an object shortcut into a custom group: right-click tblEmployeeTitle in the Unassigned Objects group, point to Add to group in the pop-up menu, and click Employee Title Form in the cascade menu (see Figure 3.29). Access places a shortcut in the group Employee Title Form. Notice that the Unassigned Objects group contains only one object—*tblEmployeeDivision*—because it has not been placed in any custom group.

Fig. 3.29 Adding object shortcuts to custom groups.

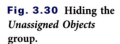

two custom groups

shortcut to the *tblEmployee* table

Optionally, you can hide the *Unassigned Objects* group so your end users aren't confused by objects and categories they won't use. You have done this with standard groups in a previous exercise. Just to refresh your memory, let's hide the *Unassigned Objects* group.

EXERCISE 3.26: HIDING THE *UNASSIGNED OBJECTS* GROUP

1. Right-click the menu at the top of the Navigation Pane and click Navigation Options in the pop-up menu.
2. Click the Managers group name in the Categories pane.
3. In the Groups for "Managers" pane, clear the Unassigned Objects check box (see Figure 3.30).
4. Clear the Show Hidden Objects check box so that hidden groups do not appear.
5. Click OK to complete this procedure and close the Navigation Options dialog box.

Fig. 3.30 Hiding the *Unassigned Objects* group.

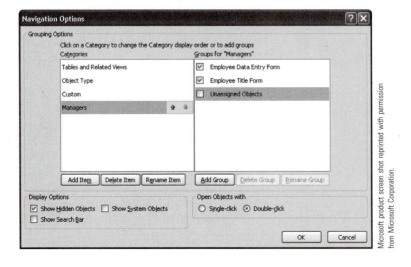

You can see the *Managers* category name appearing at the top of the Navigation Pane. Below it are the two custom groups you created called *tblEmployee* and *tblEmployeeTitle*. We realize that the group names are not descriptive of the objects they contain. They merely illustrate how you can create groups of your own names.

How do you redisplay the "standard" Navigation Pane with object types and their standard group names? That's easy. Just click the Navigation Pane menu and click the *Object Type* category name.

TRY IT
Click the Navigation Pane menu and click *Object Type* category name. The Access Navigation Pane displays the Tables group of the All Access Objects category.

Cleaning up your categories and groups is also important. Sometimes, you need to remove groups or entire categories. We show that in one final Navigation Pane exercise.

EXERCISE 3.27: DELETING CUSTOM CATEGORIES AND THEIR GROUPS

1. Right-click the menu at the top of the Navigation Pane and click Navigation Options in the pop-up menu. The Navigation Options dialog box opens.
2. Click Managers in the Categories panel, and then click the Delete Item button.
3. Click OK to confirm deletion of the category and all the groups it contains. Access removes the custom category *Managers* and deletes the groups and shortcuts it contains.
4. Click OK to close the Navigation Options dialog box.

Confirm that the Managers group has been removed, if you want, by clicking the Navigation Pane menu. Notice that there is no Managers category—only *Custom*, *Object Type*, on down to *Modified Date* appear as categories.

Separating Tables from Other Database Objects

When you are developing an application for a client server environment, you will find it convenient to separate an application's tables from its queries, forms, reports, and other database objects. Doing so allows you to store tables in one database and other related objects in another database. You can then create queries, forms, reports, macros, and modules based on linked tables. A linked table is stored in a file outside the open database from which Microsoft Access can access table records. You can perform almost all the normal database operations on linked tables that you can on tables stored in the same database. However, you cannot alter a linked table's structure in the database where the link is. This is not a big inconvenience, because you can always alter any table's structure by opening the database where it is stored. Then, you make any required changes in the database that links to the tables-only database to complete the changes.

Why would you bother to separate tables—the only database objects storing data—from other database objects? The most important reason is to provide application development independence. As a developer, you can continue to improve and develop the queries, forms, and reports embedded in your developer version of the databases. Then, when you are ready to update a client's application, you simply replace the client's database objects with the newest queries, forms, reports, macros, and modules from your developer's database—leaving the client's *tables* untouched. This way, your client's ever-changing tables are not affected, and the client can continue processing using the database. This method allows you to transparently update software without affecting the client's day-to-day operations that depend on the database application. Figure 3.31 shows a graphical representation of the table/object separation we recommend for developing client database applications. It uses the Chapter 1 database as an example, and the database labeled "Developer" contains links to the tables in the database called "Client." Both the Developer and the Client database contain queries, forms, and so on. The Developer database contains the latest versions of these other objects. When it's time to update the client's application objects including queries, forms, and reports, then the developer simply imports them into the Client database from the Developer database. The Client's tables are unchanged. The only skill you haven't practiced yet to create this

Fig. 3.31 Separating tables from other database objects.

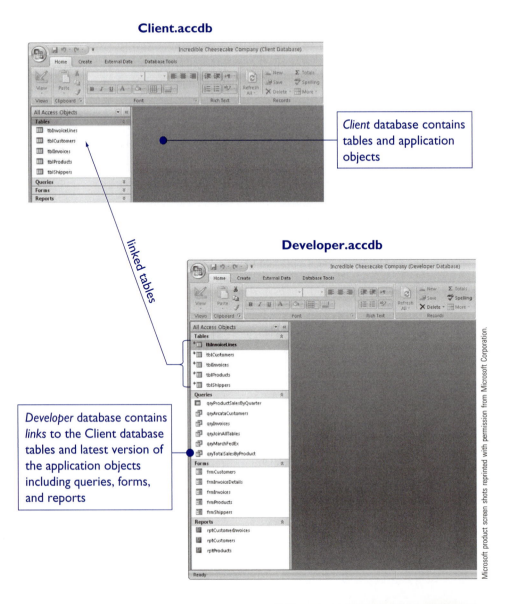

table/application separation is creating links to tables in another database. You will do that in the next section.

Linking to External Access Tables

Linking tables in one database to those actually stored in another has several advantages including those mentioned above. It also has some disadvantages. Linked tables are ideal for multiple users who share a single database across a network. Each user has a database with *links* to tables in a central database. Thus, each user always has the most current view of all corporate data in the database. As mentioned above, developers are free to modify application objects without disturbing the actual corporate table data. Linking to tables instead of storing a copy of them reduces the size of most databases, facilitating transporting databases to other computers. A distinct disadvantage of linked tables is that linked tables cannot be altered in Design view. However, this is also a blessing because it prevents unauthorized or novice users from altering a table's designs—a sometimes dangerous capability in the hands of the inexperienced.

The next exercise briefly describes how to create links to tables from another database. For this exercise, you will not use your Chapter 3 database that you have used throughout this chapter.

EXERCISE 3.28: LINKING TO TABLES IN ANOTHER ACCESS DATABASE

1. If the Chapter 3 database is open, click the Office button and then click Close Database to close it. The database closes but Access remains open.
2. With the *Getting Started with Microsoft Office Access* screen displayed, click the More hyperlink in the Open Recent Database panel on the right.
3. Using the Look in list box, navigate to the folder containing your Chapter 3 databases. Locate the database Developer.
4. Click Developer to select it and then click Open to open the database. The Navigation Pane shows Queries, Forms, and Reports objects. The database contains no tables right now.
5. Click the External Data tab, and click the Access button in the Import group. The Get External Data dialog box appears.
6. Click the Browse button, navigate to the folder containing the database called Client, click the Client database name in the File Open dialog box, and click Open. The Get External Data dialog box reappears (see Figure 3.32).
7. Click the Link to the data source by creating a linked table radio button, and then click OK. The Link Tables dialog box appears (see Figure 3.33).
8. Click Select All to select all tables in the list, and then click OK. The Navigation Pane Tables group appears automatically and the linked table names appear in the Tables group. Notice the small arrow to the left of each table name. This is the indicator that the tables are linked to those in another database and not stored herein.
9. Open a linked table to ensure that the table linkage process worked properly: Double-click tblInvoiceLines in the Tables group to open it in Datasheet view. The table opens and displays the first of 6149 rows.

As we mentioned earlier, you cannot modify the design of a table from a database that links to the table. (You can add data, update data, or delete rows, however.) Just to cement this concept in your mind, do the following Try It.

Fig. 3.32 *Get External Data* **dialog box.**

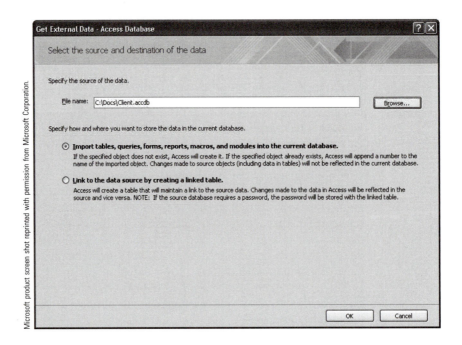

Microsoft product screen shot reprinted with permission from Microsoft Corporation.

Fig. 3.33 *Link Tables* **dialog box.**

Microsoft product screen shot reprinted with permission from Microsoft Corporation.

TRY IT

With the *tblInvoiceLines* table open in Datasheet view, right-click the *tblInvoice-Lines* tab, and click *Design View* in the pop-up menu. A warning dialog box opens explaining that you cannot modify the design of the *tblInvoiceLines* table because you are linked to it (see Figure 3.34). Click *No* to close the dialog box without attempting to alter the table's design.

Fig. 3.34 Linked table design warning dialog box.

Microsoft product screen shot reprinted with permission from Microsoft Corporation.

You are done with Access for now. Close the Access and the open database simultaneously by executing the following steps.

EXERCISE 3.29: CLOSING ACCESS

1. Click the Office button.
2. Click the Exit Access button in the Office menu. Access closes.

Summary

This chapter described how to use Access to design, populate, and display tables. You learned how to create tables from templates and from scratch. In Design view you created columns, set column data types, and defined lookup columns that display meaningful values from other tables and store foreign keys. You learned how to move, rename, and delete table columns; relational database management systems permit these column manipulations ever after a table is populated.

Once you created tables, you entered data into them and observed the effect of columns' validation rules in restricting what you can type into columns. You set limits on the type and size of information that one can enter into columns. To set inter-table relationships, you learned how to establish referential integrity between tables by linking one table's primary key to a related table's foreign key. We have stressed the importance of specifying primary keys when designing tables. You learned that tables hold all of the data in a database system.

Datasheet views of tables are subject to modification. You can rearrange a table's columns in Datasheet view without affecting the table's underlying design. Font, text size, color, and other text field display characteristics are available on the Datasheet contextual tab along with basic data type changing commands. Datasheet view of numeric fields provides even more formatting choices including currency, percent, comma, and increase or decrease decimal places. Of course, the formatting changes are cosmetic and do not affect the accuracy of the underlying data. New to Access 2007 are column totals. Available on the Home tab, the Totals command adds a summary row to the Datasheet view of any table. You can specify several column aggregate functions including Sum, Average, Count (for text fields also), Maximum, Minimum, and so on.

The Navigation Pane, new to Access 2007, provides an incredible number of object organizing facilities. Custom Navigation Pane categories and groups can be defined to hold shortcuts to all your database objects. You can hide categories, groups, and individual objects within groups. By setting a Navigation Pane option, you can choose to either display hidden objects in a dimmed font, or you can hide them altogether. The Navigation Pane replaces the Access Database window from earlier versions.

Finally, you learned the advantages of separating tables from other objects when developing database applications for clients. By separating tables from other objects, you can link to real tables while leaving them undisturbed and building queries, forms, and reports in the development system. You link tables through the Import group of the External Data tab. You can choose to link to a variety of data types, but this chapter illustrated only linking to other Access databases.

Questions and Problems for Review

Multiple-Choice Questions

1. Data is posted to a table the moment you
   a. type new data into the appropriate empty field.
   b. type data over the existing data in a field.
   c. move to another table record.
   d. none of the above

2. The expand indicator is used to
   a. open the Field Properties panel.
   b. expand a field when editing so all the data is visible.
   c. enlarge the current window.
   d. display any records related to the current row.
3. Remove table columns by doing what?
   a. Highlighting the column in Datasheet view and pressing the Delete key.
   b. Right-clicking the column heading and clicking Delete Column.
   c. Deleting the row corresponding to the data column in Design view.
   d. All of the above.
4. To link two tables, forming a relationship between them, you
   a. open the Relationships window and drag one table's primary key field to the other table's foreign key field.
   b. must always use a lookup field, because manually linking two tables otherwise is impossible.
   c. must first display both tables in Design view.
   d. None of the above is correct.
5. This field property allows you to control what values users can enter in Datasheet view.
   a. Caption.
   b. Default Value.
   c. Indexed.
   d. Input Mask.
6. Setting this table field property for text fields to "Yes" allows users to enter a special value that indicates "yes, I know the value but there is no value for this field." That field is called what?
   a. Required.
   b. Indexed.
   c. Allow Zero Length.
   d. Caption.
7. Taking this action allows you to keep selected table columns always in view when you scroll to the right in a table with many columns (Datasheet view).
   a. Tiling columns.
   b. Cascading columns.
   c. Resizing columns.
   d. Freezing columns.
8. This special Datasheet view row can display the number of nonempty values in a column of text.
   a. Column aggregate value row.
   b. Total row.
   c. Relationships row.
   d. Count row.
9. This replaces the Database window in older Access versions.
   a. Datasheet contextual tab.
   b. Relationships tab.
   c. Navigation tab.
   d. Navigation Pane.
10. You can create these as alternatives to "Object Type."
    a. Custom Navigation Pane.
    b. Custom groups.
    c. Custom categories.
    d. All of the above.

Discussion Questions

1. Discuss the advantage(s) of providing a data validity check in the Validation Rule field property. What might happen if you omitted validation rules from text fields, and how could that affect the integrity of your database tables?

2. Explain why referential integrity is so important when dealing with a database, such as The Coffee Merchant's, involving several related tables. Give a scenario in which the lack of referential integrity could cause problems. Be specific.

3. Discuss the problem with storing an employee's age in the *tblMyEmployees* table. In other words, why could you not simply add a column called EmpAge to replace EmpDOB in a table?

4. What role do a table's column properties play in a database management system? Discuss the following properties: Input Mask, Default Value, Validation Text, and Required.

5. What advantages do custom categories and custom groups provide in creating an accounting application?

Practice Exercises

1. Using the Navigation Pane, copy the table *tblEmployeeDivision* (right-click the table name) and then paste it (right-click the Navigation Pane) as your last name followed by your first name (for example, *SmithJoe*). Next, modify this new table's design by adding the following columns: Population (Number) and WebPage (hyperlink). Save the table design. Populate these new columns for the cities of Indianapolis, Cincinnati, San Diego, Princeton, and Milford with values you find by using Internet search engines. Set the Format property of the Population field to display commas and no decimal places. Switch to Datasheet view and add a Total row and display the average population. Resize columns as needed to display their widest values completely. Print the Datasheet view of this table.

2. Create a new table called *tblEmployeeMaritalStatus*. Create the following named columns and data types in this order: MaritalID (AutoNumber, primary key), MaritalStatus (text, maximum length 16 characters, Input Mask is ">L<aaaaaaaaaaaaaaa" without the double quotation marks, the greater than symbol, uppercase L, the less than symbol, and 15 occurrences of lowercase *a*). Populate the table with the following text values in this order: *Single, Married, Divorced, Widowed, Separated,* and *Domestic Partner* and then print the table's records. Close the table and then modify the *tblEmployee* table by adding a column called EmpMaritalStatus between the EmpLName and EmpPhone fields—so it is the new fourth column. Make it a lookup field referring the *tblEmployeeMaritalStatus* for its lookup values. Have the lookup field display only the text portion of the marital status, not its primary key; leave the list unsorted. Fill in the marital status field as follows (with *tblEmployee* in EmpID order): *Married* for the first 15 records; *Single* for the next three records, and *Divorced* for the remaining records. Print the first page (only) of the *tblEmployee* table (in portrait orientation).

3. Create a new table called *tblInventory* and populate it with coffee and tea products. Create the following columns with the following constraints for *tblInventory*:

COLUMN NAME	TYPE	LENGTH OR VALIDATION RULE	OTHER
InventoryID	AutoNumber		Primary key
Beverage	Text	One character; only "t" or "c" allowed	Force lowercase with input mask
ItemName	Text	30 characters	
UnitPrice	Currency	Valid value range: $3 through $45	
UnitsOnHand	Number	Only values from 0 through 5,000	Format: Standard; Decimal Places: 0
Caffeinated	Yes/No		

Be sure to include, for each column in Design view, some commentary in the Description column. After you create the table design, populate it with the following:

c	Jamaican Blue Mountain	$45.00	4,290	Yes
c	Kona Extra Fancy	$18.00	2,740	Yes
c	Kenya AA	$8.10	4,240	Yes
t	Jasmine	$9.50	71	Yes
t	Assam Fancy 2nd Flush	$3.00	315	No

Adjust all columns to print as wide as necessary for the widest column value (or column label) but no wider (Datasheet view). Print the populated table in Landscape orientation. Switch to Design view and highlight the Beverage column definition. Press Shift+PrtScr to capture the computer screen to the Clipboard, open a word processor, paste in the screen shot, and print it to create a hard copy of the table's design.

4.   Separate the tables from other objects—objects that you have not yet created but will—by creating a separate database containing links to the Chapter 3 database. Do the following tasks. Create a new database called Ch03LinkedTables and save it on your disk. Close the default table that Access creates to eliminate it. Create links to the three tables called *tblEmployee*, *tblEmployeeDivision*, and *tblEmployeeTitle* found in the Chapter 3 database, Ch03.accdb. Rename the three linked tables to *Employee*, *Division*, and *Title*, respectively. Create a Navigation Pane custom category called *My Category* (rename the Custom Group 1) and then create three groups called *Employees Only*, *Divisions Only*, and *Titles Only* (with a space between the two words in each group name and the category name). Place a shortcut to Employee in the Employees Only group, to Divisions in the Divisions Only group, and to Titles in the Titles Only group. After you create the shortcuts, go back and do not display the Unrelated Objects group and delete, if necessary, the Custom category. Display the My Category category in the Navigation Pane. Change the Application Title to your name followed by "Linked Tables" (without the double quotation marks). (Hint: Click the Office button, click Access Options, and click Current Database.) If your name were Alice Honeycutt, for example, then the application title would be *Alice Honeycutt Linked Tables*. Open the linked table Title in Datasheet view. To place a digital screen shot on the Clipboard, press Shift+PrtScr (press and hold the Shift key, tap the PrtScr key, and then release the Shift key). Launch a word processing program, paste the Clipboard contents into the document, and print the document.

5.   Create a new table called *tblShippers* that contains information about shipping companies that The Coffee Merchant uses to ship coffee to its customers. The table should contain the following columns (in this order): ShipID (primary key, AutoNumber), ShipName (text), ShipWeb (hyperlink; see trick at end of this problem to shorten the URL), ShipPhone (text, use Input Mask Wizard), ShipCity (text), ShipState (text, two characters, force all capital letters), and ShipStatement (attachment). Set the Caption of every column to the name of the column without the "Ship" prefix (e.g., "Phone" for the ShipPhone column). Populate the table with data about the following three express shippers (use Internet search engines to get data): DHL Express, FedEx, and UPS. Provide reasonable data integrity controls for the columns to limit the length and content where obvious. Populate the table with data you obtain from the Web. For the ShipStatement attachment field, see if you can find each shipper's mission statement, import it into a Word document, and then attach the Word document in the ShipStatement field. Display the table in Datasheet view, optimize the columns' widths to display as much as possible (except for hyperlink), and print the table in landscape orientation. (Right-click the hyperlink for a shipper, point to Hyperlink in the pop-up list, click Edit Hyperlink, and type an abbreviation such as DHL in the Text to display. Click OK to close the dialog box. The hyperlink displays in its shorter form.)

Problems

1. Create a new database called Problem1.accdb and then import (*not* link) from the Client.accdb database the *tblInvoices* and *tblCustomers* tables. Rename the imported tables to Invoices and Customers, respectively. Delete the relationship line between the two tables. (*Hint*: Reread the section called *Editing and Removing Intertable Relationships*.) Change the data type of the Invoices table column, called CompanyID, to a lookup field. It obtains its values from the Customers table columns CustomerID and CustomerName but displays only CustomerName sorted in ascending order in the lookup field. In Datasheet view sort the table in ascending order by ShipCost, filter on the CompanyName column so only companies whose names begins with "Ha" display. In the Total row display the total shipping cost and the average tax. Ensure all columns are wide enough to display their contents, and print the filtered, sorted, and totaled Datasheet view.

2. Create a new database called Problem2.accdb. In that database create a time card recorded table called *Time-Card* containing the following columns: EventID (primary key, Autonumber), EmployeeID (lookup field), MonthEnded (Date), and RegHours (Number), OverHours (Number). The EventID is self explanatory. EmployeeID is a lookup field that references the *tblCustomers* table. Import it from the Client.accdb database, and rename it MyEmployees. Rename the MyEmployees columns CustomerID to EmpID and Customer-Name to EmpName. Delete the four address columns (Street, City, State, and Zip) from the *MyEmployees* table. Use the EmpID and EmpName columns as your lookup columns for the EmployeeID column in the *TimeCard* table. Sort the lookup field by EmpName. The columns RegHours and OverHours are both hours worked each month, so limit RegHours to the range 0 to 180 (it is a *Required* field value). Limit OverHours to the values from 0 to 40 (it is *not* a required field—it can be empty). Set the Validation Text property of the two hours fields to the same string as their Validation Rules (copy/paste!). Set the Caption property of the columns to *Event*, *Employee*, *Month Ended* (with a space), *Regular Hours*, and *Overtime Hours*, respectively. Populate *TimeCard* with rows for any four distinct employees as follows:

EVENT	EMPLOYEE	MONTH ENDED	REGULAR HOURS	OVERTIME HOURS
1	David's Place	5/31/2009	180	
2	Jimmy's	5/31/2009	180	20
3	Texaco	6/30/2009	100	
4	Moondoogies	6/30/2009	180	40

Insert a Total row and sum the two hours columns in the table's Datasheet view. Resize the columns, as needed, so all values and column labels are fully visible. Print the TimeCard rows. Open *TimeCard* in Design view, click the RegHours field name, and press Shift+PrtScrn to capture the screen to the Clipboard. Open Word, paste in the screen shot, and print the document. (Press Ctrl+V to paste the Clipboard contents into Word.)

3. (We give you a little more help with this problem, because it involves skills we did not explicitly describe in this chapter.) Create a new database called Problem3.accdb. Using the Excel command on the Import group of the External Data tab, import the file called 108thCongress.xlsx into your database. Here are condensed instructions on importing this "foreign data:" Click External Data, click Excel in the Import group, and click the first radio button in the Get External Data dialog box ("Import the source data into a new…"). Click the Browse button to locate and select 108thCongress. Click Open. Back in the Get External Data dialog box, click OK. Click Next, click the First Row Contains Column Headings check box (place a check mark in it), and click the Finish button. Close the dialog box. Open the table 108thCongress in Datasheet view. Create a PivotTable from the table by selecting PivotTable View in the Views group of the Home tab. Drag and drop the *State* field onto the *Drop Row Fields Here* area. Drag and drop the *Party* field onto the *Drop Column Fields Here* area. Drag and drop the *HouseSenate* field onto the *Drop Filter Fields Here* area. Drag and drop the *LastName* field onto the *Drop Totals or Detail Fields Here* area. Click the HouseSenate drop-down arrow and clear all check boxes except Senate to display the 12 senators' names. Click the State drop-down arrow and clear all state abbreviations except states NC, ND, NE, NH, NJ, and NM. Print the pivot table. Close and save the layout view.

4. (We give you a little more help with this problem, because it involves skills we did not explicitly describe in this chapter.) Create a new database called Problem4.accdb and then import (*not* link) the *tblInvoice-Lines* table from the Client.accdb database. Create a new category called *Order Totals* and create a custom group within it called *Order Details*. Open the custom category Order Totals in the Navigation Pane. Rename the imported table, *tblInvoiceLines*, to *MyInvoiceLines*, and then place a shortcut to *MyInvoiceLines* in the Order Details custom group. Rename the shortcut, *not* the table, to *OrderTotalsPivotTable*. Open *OrderTotalsPivotTable* in Datasheet view. Next, open it in PivotTable view. Drag the ProductID field to the Row Fields area of the pivot table. Drag/drop the Quantity field to the Detail Fields area of the pivot table. Click the Quantity pivot table column header, click the AutoCalc button, and click Sum in the pop-up menu. Click the Hide Details button in the Show/Hide group of the Design contextual tab. Click the Sum of Quantity (new label) column header in the pivot table, click the Descending button in the Filter & Sort group. Click any individual cell under the Sum of Quantity header and then click Show Top/Bottom, point to Show Only the Top, and click 10 (not 10%). The top ten product IDs by their quantities appear in descending order. Print and close the pivot table. Save the layout changes.

5. Create a copy of the table *tblEmployee* found in your Chapter 3 database. Rename it *FemalesByDivision* and display the newly copied table in Datasheet view. Accomplish the following *without* resorting to any type of query and without deleting any table columns. (*Hint*: You can rearrange things in the Datasheet view any way needed.) Change the Caption property of some of the columns (it should be obvious which columns get which caption) to *First Name*, *Last Name*, *Division*, *Title*, *Comm. Rate*, and *Gender*. Sort the rows into ascending order by Division and then by Last Name within each division. Furthermore, display only the columns corresponding to first and last names, division, job title, commission rate, and gender (the columns are not necessarily in that order). In addition to all of the preceding, the layout of *FemalesByDivision* should show only females whose commission rate is greater than or equal to 6%. Add a row to display the average commission rate of this filtered and sorted set of rows. Print the table rows as displayed. Close the table and save the layout.

CHAPTER 4

Creating and Using Queries

This chapter extends the knowledge that you gained so far with detailed information about Microsoft Access queries. You will learn about creating queries, writing expressions in queries, sorting and filtering query results, and aggregating information using queries. Exercises throughout this chapter emphasize Microsoft Access techniques critical to building accounting information systems. Like previous chapters, this chapter is application-oriented and contains many hands-on exercises within the chapter. In this chapter you will learn how to:

- Create *select* and *action* queries.

- Review queries in Design, Layout, and SQL views.

- Join tables and establish referential integrity checks between them.

- Use the Query Wizard.

- Work in Layout View.

- Group and summarize data with queries.

- Create parameter queries.

- Create queries involving a single table.

- Create queries for tables having many-to-many relationships.

- Create queries involving multiple tables, derived column values, and expressions.

- Create queries with an outer join relationship to reveal hidden information.

- Build and run PivotTable and PivotChart queries.

- Work in SQL View to create SQL queries.

- Create and run action queries to alter data.

We continue using The Coffee Merchant's tables as the backdrop application in this chapter. The complete set of The Coffee Merchant tables is available for your use in this chapter. We will be creating various queries to answer accounting questions with one or more of these tables—perhaps not all of them, however. Unlike Chapter 3, you will spend very little time creating tables except for the action query to create a table and a frequency bins table used for frequency analysis. Download and save the database for this chapter called *Ch04.accdb*. Like all digital objects referenced in this textbook, this chapter's database is stored at its South-Western, Cengage Learning companion Web site, www.cengage.com/accounting/perry.

Introduction to Queries

A database's ability to retrieve a subset of one or more tables' rows and columns lies at the heart of its information retrieval ability. Managers seeking information about employees can retrieve rows and columns from an employee table, but information gathering would be limited if retrieval was restricted to a single table. Without the ability to specify particular rows and without the ability to select information from multiple, related tables, a database's retrieval capabilities would be no better than those of a flat file system. For example, suppose someone has to display an entire customer table in an attempt to locate customers from Idaho, or all the rows of inventory items to locate those supplied by manufacturers from California or Oregon. Manually scanning a list for candidate table rows satisfying those criteria would be time-consuming, frustrating, and error-prone. Queries provide the answer because you can build queries to return the requested row subset—customers in Idaho or manufacturer in either California or Oregon—by writing a simple query based on one or more tables that store the required information. Access provides an intuitive interface called *Query By Example* (QBE) in which you construct a query. The QBE interface allows you to specify what table columns you want to be returned, which columns sort the resulting rows, and any criteria that filter or limit the returned rows.

Types of Queries

There are two general types of queries you can use. They are called selection queries and action queries. *Selection queries* allow you to retrieve and display data from one or more tables or queries without changing any tables' contents. *Action queries* allow you to change, insert, create, or delete sets of data in your database—in other words, change tables' contents in some way. This chapter will provide you with plenty of examples of both types of queries, but the chapter's emphasis is on selection queries.

Selection queries pose questions to the database. Unlike tables, which hold information, queries instruct the database system to actively search specified tables and return answers to the questions. For instance, you can use a query to return a list of all employees in the San Diego branch office in order by department and last name within department. A query can be used to list all invoices that are over 30 days past due. Although you can accomplish a lot with datasheets—including sorting, updating, filtering, and printing—you will quickly find that manually manipulating a table's Datasheet view is restrictive and time-consuming. Queries are the answer. Selection queries provide you with a convenient way to filter, sort, and manipulate data. Furthermore, you can store the query so that you can repeat the operations on one or more tables. For instance, you can create a query to examine an airline reservation system's database and return the names of passengers on TWA Flight 711 from Memphis to Los Angeles. By creating a query to perform the actions of searching the flight data, extracting passengers' names for a particular flight, and sorting them in ascending order by name, you automate the multistep information retrieval process. When you run the stored query next week, the same query (a stored definition) returns a completely new result. The result is called a *dynaset*, which is a temporary table. Called a *closed set*, relational database queries search through tables and then they produce a table-structured result.

Action queries modify the contents of one or more database tables in some way. Update queries, one of the action query types, modifies one or more columns' values based on some criteria limiting which rows are subject to change. Other action queries include Make Table query, a Delete query, and an Append query. The Make Table query creates a new table from the structure and contents of an existing table or tables. A Delete query deletes rows from a table based on some selection or filtering criteria. The Append query copies selected rows from one table and places them in another table. An Update query is the best choice when you want to increase by 10% the retail price of each coffee product in your inventory. With a potential of hundreds of price changes, making such a change in a table manually (one item at a time) is time-consuming and error-prone.

Views

You can work with queries in five different views. Each view has a unique purpose. The query views are: Datasheet view, PivotTable view, PivotChart view, SQL view, and Design view. When you create a query or modify it, you work on it in Design view. A query's Design specifies the columns in a result, whether column(s) are sorted, criteria, and whether or not unique values appear. Design view appears as the QBE interface with a table pane and a criteria pane (see Figure 4.1). A query's results—the rows of columns it returns—appear in its Datasheet view. Queries shown in Datasheet view are identical in form to tables in Datasheet view. That's why Access queries and tables can provide data to other objects such as forms and reports—because they both provide table-formatted results. Less often used but still important are PivotTable view and PivotChart

Fig. 4.1 Five views of the same query.

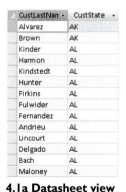

4.1a Datasheet view

SELECT CustLastName, CustState
FROM tblCustomer
ORDER BY CustState;

4.1b SQL view

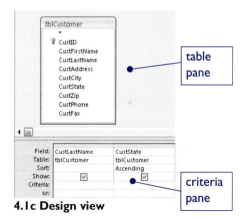

table pane

criteria pane

4.1c Design view

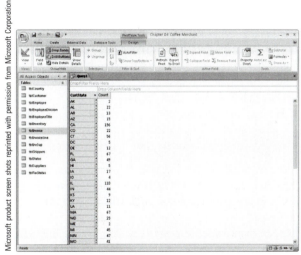

4.1d PivotTable view

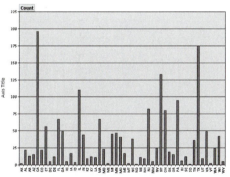

4.1e PivotChart view

view. These two views display aggregate information about two or more columns in a query in either table form or chart form. For example, a pivot table view of a customer table could show the number of customers (count) by state or the total value of all purchases by product (Y-axis) and by state (X-axis). Pivot charts chart the results of pivot tables. The SQL view is probably the least-used query view. It displays the query you likely created in Design view as a SQL (usually pronounced "sequel") statement. SQL is the universal language of relational database management systems. Any display of a table or query result, for example, results in a SQL statement being sent to Access. The resulting dynaset is produced in response to executing the underlying SQL statement. Figure 4.1 shows these five views of the same query—customers sorted by state name. The pivot table and pivot chart views show the tally of each customer by state. The query's Datasheet view appears in Figure 4.1a, SQL view in 4.1b, its original design in 4.1c, and the two pivot versions in 4.1d and 4.1e.

Creating a Basic Select Query

Queries provide powerful sorting, filtering, and table-joining features that allow you to display selected rows, columns, and values from one, two, or more related tables and display the results in order by one or more columns. Perhaps the most important feature of queries is their ability to join tables together. Using query tools, you can link tables together by specifying the related column(s) in two table pairs. Using the easy to use QBE (Query By Example) interface, you optionally set filtering criteria, grouping expressions, and sort columns. Any of the sorting, filtering, or grouping specifications are independently available or in concert. For example, you can specify a criterion value for a particular query column to eliminate unwanted data; selecting "Ascending" or "Descending" for one or more columns in a query cause the results to appear in sorted order by the columns you select to do so. You can specify one table in a query, or create an arbitrarily complex query joining dozens of tables. Joined tables must be linked on related fields. This usually means selecting the primary key of one table and matching it with a foreign key of a related table.

An example of a simple two-table query is one that lists the names and addresses of all customers whose invoices are more than 30 days past due. Only two tables are sufficient to answer that question: *tblCustomer* and *tblInvoice*. The first table, *tblCustomer*, contains the name and address fields, and the related table *tblInvoice* contains the InvoiceDate column that holds the date when the customer was invoiced. The two tables are related by their primary and foreign keys. The primary key in *tblCustomer* is CustID, and the related foreign key in *tblInvoice* is CustomerID. Notice the subtlety: primary key and foreign key values must match in order to combine rows from two related tables, but the key field *names* need not be spelled the same! The query's selection criteria limit retrieved rows to those whose InvoiceDate value is more than 30 days ago.

Building queries is not difficult. Here is an overview of the steps. This chapter provides you with a lot of practice using these steps to build queries to retrieve information from table data. There are a couple of ways to create a query, but here is a typical list of steps:

- *Click the Create tab and click Query Design in the Other group of the Create tab.*
- *Add the table to be included in the query from the Show Table dialog box that appears.*
- *Place the fields you want returned in the dynaset into the Field row of the QBE grid.*
- *Enter optional selection criteria so that Access returns only rows that match the criteria.*

- *Open the query in Datasheet view to see the query's results.*
- *Enter optional sorting requirements under any columns that appear in the Field row.*
- *Click the Datasheet View button to check your progress and review the results.*
- *Click the Design View button, if necessary, to revise the query to achieve the results you want.*
- *Run the query and optionally print the results.*
- *Save the query if you want to rerun it later.*

When you build queries involving more than one table, you follow the same basic steps outlined above except that you select additional tables for the query design. You cannot select arbitrary tables to form a query. Selected tables must be related to one another. You can either indicate the relation of one table to another as you design the query, or you can establish a more permanent relationship between tables in the Relationships window.

Before continuing, examine all the table relationships already established for your Chapter 4 database. Figure 4.2 shows the tables in your Chapter 4 database and the relationship between each pair. Take a moment to study the figure.

Fig. 4.2 Relationships among tables.

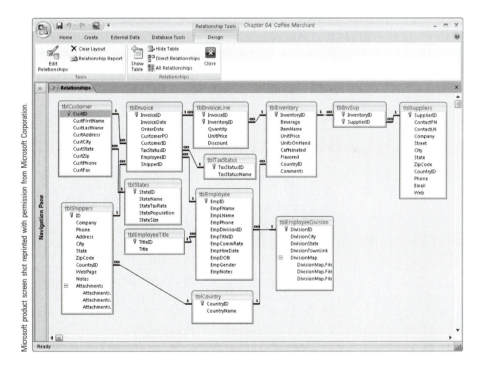

Microsoft product screen shot reprinted with permission from Microsoft Corporation.

Observe that tables appearing in the Relationships window that are related to one another have a line connecting the primary key of one table to a foreign key of a related table. For all tables in Ch04.accdb, the relationships are one-to-many (1-M). For example, *tblCustomer* (upper-left corner of Figure 4.2) is on the "one side" of a one-to-many relationship with *tblInvoice*. That means that for each customer record in the Customer table, there may be zero, one, or several related customer invoice records. The line connecting the tables indicates the "one" side of the relationship with the digit 1 above the line next to the primary key. Similarly, Access displays the symbol for infinity (∞) next to the table's foreign key to indicate the "many" side of the relationship. Of course, any given table may be related simultaneously to several other tables in the database. For example, *tblEmployee* has established relationships with three other tables, including *tblEmployeeDivision, tblEmployeeTitle,* and *tblInvoice.* You must explicitly establish any relationships between tables yourself. There are two ways to do this: You can create a relationship in the Relationships window where relationships persist when you create new queries, or you can create the relationship each time you create a query. Unless the name of a primary key in one table is spelled the same as the foreign key of another, Access will not automatically forge relationships between pairs of tables.

We introduce queries by starting with a single-table query—a query whose data is retrieved from one table. Then, you will build more complex queries involving some rows and some columns of a single table. Finally, you will build queries that draw data from many related tables.

Retrieving Selected Rows from a Table

A query is the best way to extract a select group of records from a large table. A one-table query is easy to construct, and it reduces the list you look at to a manageable size. We illustrate a one-table query with the *tblInventory* table. It contains several important product descriptors including the beverage type (the allowed values are only *c* or *t*, which stand for coffee and tea) and whether or not the coffee or tea is flavored (check boxes indicating yes or no). Other descriptors include the country of origin (a lookup table pointing to the *tblCountry* table and returning a country name using the CountryID column), and lively comments about the particular coffee bean or tea leaf. Figure 4.3 shows some of the rows of the inventory table. Only selected columns appear, and the results are sorted in descending order by the Beverage field and then by the name within matching Beverage values—all by using the QBE grid.

Fig. 4.3 Some rows of the *tblInventory* table.

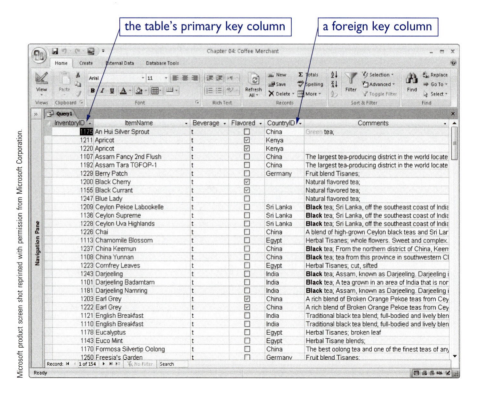

It is helpful to know which companies the supply chain manager can contact to order more products (UnitsOnHand field) for those near-zero or less-than-zero (backordered)

quantities. Fortunately, there is a related table that holds additional information related to items in inventory—the names and addresses of all suppliers supplying the inventory item. The relationship between the inventory and the suppliers who can send those inventory items is called many-to-many (M–M). Relational databases cannot deal with M–M relationships well, so this problem is solved by creating a second, intermediate table that forms the bridge between the two tables that otherwise have a many-to-many relationship. The intermediate table reduces the relationships to one-to-many to the inventory table on one side and the suppliers table on the other. It is formed by taking the primary keys from each of the tables and inserting them into the new, bridge table. Figure 4.2 (upper-right corner) shows this bridge table. It is called *tblInvSup* and provides the two one-to-many relationships linking *tblInventory* and *tblSuppliers*.

Next, you will create a simple query to locate and display all unflavored coffees whose beans are described as "hard bean" in the inventory description field, *Comments*. (Hard bean coffees are grown at higher altitudes than others and generally yield a better coffee.)

EXERCISE 4.1: CREATING A ONE-TABLE QUERY

1. Click the Create tab and click Query Design in the group called *Other*. (It is often easier to create queries without the Query Wizard.)
2. Double-click the tblInventory table name from the list presented in the Show Table dialog box, and click the Close button. If the Show Table dialog box does not appear, click the Design contextual tab and then click Show Table in the Query Setup group.
3. Drag the fields InventoryID, ItemName, Comments, Beverage, and Flavored from the *tblInventory* field roster found in the Table pane to the first through fifth cells in the Field row of the QBE grid in the Criteria pane.
4. Clear the Show check boxes under Beverage and Flavored in the QBE grid, because you do not want to display these fields in the result—they are in the query so we can use them to specify criteria.
5. Type the following three selection criteria in the Criteria row for the specified columns:
   - under the Comments column, type Like "*hard bean*" (including the quotation marks and asterisks at both ends of the string),
   - under the BeverageType column, type "c" (with the quotation marks),
   - and under the Flavored column, type no (letter case does not matter, but do not place quotation marks around this criterion or any other Yes/No criterion).
6. Select Datasheet View from the View menu to see the query results (dynaset).
7. To view the results better, widen the ItemName and Comments columns. Start with ItemName by double-clicking the dividing line on the column name's right side. Then drag the line at the right edge of the Comments column label to fill most of the remaining space. Remember you can click the Navigation Pane shutter Open/Close button to close (and alternately open) the Navigation Pane thereby creating more space to view the results.

Your dynaset should look like the one shown in Figure 4.4. We have saved this query as *qryHardBeanCoffee* in your Chapter 4 database, so you need not save yours. Simply close the query you just created.

What if you wanted to see all inventory items that were either not flavored or are coffees? We would place one criterion on one Criteria row and the other criterion on the "or" row below the previous criteria. (This type of query is a classic OR question.)

Fig. 4.4 One-table
query and dynaset.

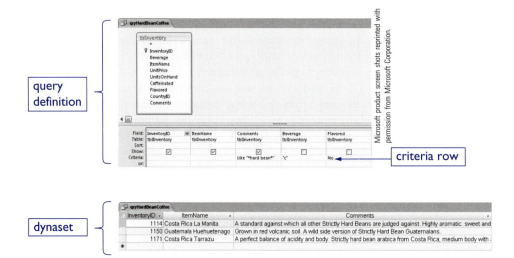

Figure 4.5 shows the OR query and part of the result. As indicated in the status line, the query returned many rows—all unflavored beverages (tea or coffee) and all coffees (flavored or not).

Fig. 4.5 Query with
multiple, independent
criteria.

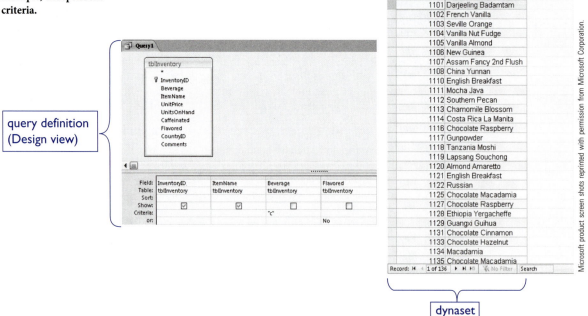

Working with a Dynaset

Access returns query results in a dynaset. Similar to a table in behavior and structure, a dynaset is only temporary. It is replaced every time you rerun the query. For most queries, you can alter information displayed by the dynaset while in Datasheet view simply by typing in new information. The new information replaces the appropriate row and column of the underlying table. Thus, most dynasets present live, updateable views of underlying table data. Some dynasets are not updateable, and Access will warn you when you attempt to update data through one of the nonupdateable dynasets. Most of the dynasets presented in this textbook are updateable.

You can alter the appearance of the dynaset so that the rows are arranged differently, the columns are displayed in a different order, or the columns are formatted in a special way. The next section illustrates how easy it is to make changes to the dynaset.

Producing Sorted Query Results

Suppose you want to rearrange dynaset rows so they are displayed in a more useful form. For instance, the list of coffees and teas shown in Figure 4.3 would be easier to use if it appeared in name order. Sorting dynasets is easy. Normally, Access displays dynaset records in ascending order on the table's primary key, if it has one, whether or not the primary key is displayed in the dynaset. Creating a query to sort data in other ways is particularly useful. For example, a list of employees in order by their last and first names is handy when you want to look up an employee's name from a printed list. In the case of the Coffee Merchant, suppose you want to list all flavored teas in stock in order by their names. First, you would construct a one-table query based on the *tblInventory* table. In the QBE Field row, you might include the fields InventoryID, ItemName, Flavored, and Beverage. Only IventoryID and ItemName would have their Show check boxes marked. Flavored and Beverage would contain the criteria values *Yes* and *t*, respectively, in the same criteria row to retrieve only flavored teas (both criteria must be met). How about the sorting part of it? Follow along in the Try It that follows to find out.

TRY IT

Open in Design view the query *qryFlavoredTea*, which selects flavored teas and displays them in a dynaset. To sort the dynaset results by ItemName, click the Sort cell under the ItemName column—the attribute by which you want the rows sorted—and click *Ascending* from the drop-down list. Select *Datasheet View* from the View menu to see the dynaset. Widen the ItemName column by double-clicking the dividing line on the column label's right edge. Notice that the rows are in ItemName order beginning with *Apricot* and ending with *Vanilla with Vanilla Bean*. You probably notice that Apricot appears twice as does Earl Grey and Orange Spice. That is because these three flavored teas come in two subdesignations —caffeinated and noncaffeinated. Therefore, there are two separate choices. This can be "fixed," but it is a bit too complex so early in this chapter. Close the query, but do not save changes to it when prompted.

You can specify a sort order for more than one column. Access sorts by the leftmost field first, followed by the next sort field to the right, and so on. Therefore, you should arrange the columns you want to sort, relative to each other, from left to right in the QBE grid. Note that the sort columns do not have to be the first group of columns in the QBE grid. You can sort by fields whose Show check box is cleared and thus does not appear, though the reasons may seem obscure at this point. We will explain later why this may be necessary.

Altering the Order and Size of Columns

You can alter the order of the dynaset columns. The dynaset columns' order is established by the query. For instance, the first field whose Show box is checked in the QBE grid is the first column in the dynaset, but you can alter the dynaset's column order either by altering the query's design or by altering the dynaset's column ordering after Access displays the dynaset. The former method is the best way.

To rearrange query columns, display the query in Design view and move the mouse pointer to the column selector of the field to be moved. (The column selector is the area just above the field name.) When the mouse pointer is on the column selector, it turns to a down-pointing arrow. Click the column. The entire column is darkened, indicating you have selected it. (Be careful not to move the mouse.) Release the mouse but keep it poised over the column selector. Next, click and drag the highlighted column to its new location. A rectangle appears below the pointer, indicating you are about to move the column, and a vertical bar appears as you drag the column, indicating where the column would reside if you were to release the mouse. Release the mouse when the column is in its new location. Columns to the right of the vertical bar move to the right, making room for the new column to be dropped in place.

You can enlarge individual columns by moving to the column selector area of a column and hover the mouse over the right side of the column selector. When the mouse changes from a down-pointing arrow to a double-headed arrow, click and drag the right edge to the right to enlarge the column, or drag it to the left to shrink the column. We mentioned earlier that you can double-click the two-headed mouse pointer to adjust the column width to the widest entry (or column label).

You can change both column order and column size in the dynaset—after Access executes a query. When the query results appear, you can move columns or change their size following the procedures outlined in the preceding paragraphs. You can right-click any column name (not a value in the column), then click Column Width in the pop-up menu. The Column Width dialog box appears (see Figure 4.6). Click the Best Fit button to size the column so it is just wide enough for the widest entry. You can also size multiple columns at once. Drag the mouse across all the column selectors to select multiple contiguous columns. Move the mouse to the right column line of any one of the selected columns. When it changes to a double-headed arrow, double-click the pointer to optimize the column width for all selected columns.

Fig. 4.6 Column Width dialog box.

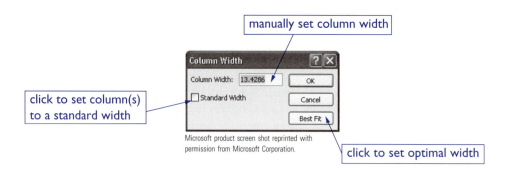

manually set column width

click to set column(s) to a standard width

click to set optimal width

Microsoft product screen shot reprinted with permission from Microsoft Corporation.

Altering Column Display Properties

Like other dynaset characteristics, column display formats can also be changed. First, display the query in Design view. Then, move the mouse to the Field row in the QBE grid of the column whose format you want to change. When you right-click a column, a pop-up menu displays several choices. Click the Properties selection to open the column's Property Sheet. You can experiment with changing characteristics such as format. For instance, try changing the format of the InventoryID dynaset column so that the data is displayed in Currency format. After you are done experimenting, there is no need to save the altered query.

Saving a Query and Printing Dynasets

Saving a Query

You should save queries that you anticipate using again. You will find your preferred way to do so. One simple way is to right-click the tab showing the object's actual or default name and then click Save. Save is also available on the Quick Access Toolbar. If you saved your query earlier, then Access saves it under its original name, replacing the older copy with the new one. If you want to save the query design under a different name, then click the Office button, point to Save As on the drop-down menu, and click Save Object As in the cascade menu. Type in the new query name and click OK to save it under its new name.

Printing Dynasets

Printing query results simply means that you print the dynaset retrieved by the query and displayed in the Datasheet view. You need not have the query open to display its dynaset. On the other hand, you might want to preview the results and decide whether or not to print all the pages it might span. In either case, click the query name in the Navigation Pane, click the Office button, point to Print in the drop-down Office menu, and click Print. When the Print dialog box appears, make any adjustments to the page range, and then click OK. However, we strongly suggest you click Print Preview from the Print cascade menu, instead of Print, to first check the layout and look of the dynaset before committing to printing it. Note that you do not have any control over the page headers or footers of a printed dynaset. Printing tables and dynasets provide a quick and dirty output without any of the fancy features available in Access reports.

Creating Queries with Query Wizards

Using the help of Query Wizards to create a query provides access to three other types of queries that are otherwise difficult to create manually. The three other types of Query Wizards, besides the "Simple Query Wizard," are the Crosstab, Find Duplicates, and Find Unmatched Query. These choices appear when you click the Query Wizard button in the Other group of the Create tab—just to the left of the Query Design button we used previously. We'll look at two of these wizards briefly, using exercises to illustrate how easy it is to create and run these queries with the wizard's help. The fundamental steps are simply:

- *Click the Create tab and click Query Wizard.*
- *Choose the wizard you wish to use from the choice of four listed (see above).*
- *Click OK and then follow the prompts and steps the wizard uses to build the query.*

We begin by building a Crosstab query.

Creating Crosstab Queries

A *crosstab query* is a special summary query that pours through large amounts of data and correlates values between two or more sets of field values. Similar in form and function to an Excel pivot table, an Access crosstab query provides a summary result in a handy spreadsheet format. A crosstab can calculate a sum, average, count, and other aggregate statistics grouped in two types of information—one down the left side of the datasheet and one across the top. The cell at the junction of each row and column displays the results of the query's calculation. For example, suppose you have a sales table that captures sales of cars, recreation vehicles, and boats by year, by quarter, and by region of the country. Raw data is just that—not very informative. Producing a crosstab query summarizing sales by quarter and product will likely reveal seasonal patterns, if they exist. The next exercise shows how to create a crosstab query of a sales journal. Though this particular table is not related to the other tables in The Coffee Merchant database, it illustrates how you could apply the same techniques to analyze The Coffee Merchant sales to discern patterns.

EXERCISE 4.2: USING THE QUERY WIZARD TO CREATE A CROSSTAB QUERY

1. Click the Create tab, click Query Wizard, click the Crosstab Query Wizard, and click OK. Access launches the Crosstab Query Wizard.
2. Click the table you want to use, tblAnExampleCrosstab. (If you see only queries, then click the Tables radio button in the View panel to display only tables.) Click Next.
3. In the Available Fields list, click Quarter—the field whose unique entries are to appear in as row headings—and click > to add the field to the Selected Fields list. Click Next to go to the next step. (Click Back if you want to make a change to a previous step.)
4. Click ProductCategory, the field whose unique values you want to appear as column headings, and then click Next.
5. Click SaleAmount in the Fields list, the value that you want to summarize, click Count in the Functions list to simply count the number of sales rather than sum them. Your Crosstab Query Wizard dialog box should match Figure 4.7. Click Next to proceed.
6. Drag through the suggested query name at the top of the dialog box, type MyCrosstabQuery, and click Finish.
7. Close the dynaset by right-clicking the query's display tab and clicking Close All.

Fig. 4.7 Defining a crosstab query.

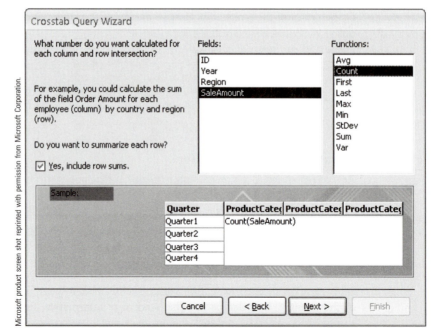

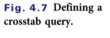

The dynaset created by the query shows counts of the number of sales and a breakout by product type. Notice that the Boat category has low sales counts in both the first and fourth quarters—as does the category RV (see Figure 4.8).

Fig. 4.8 Crosstab query showing sales counts by quarter and product.

Quarter	Total Of Sale	Boat	Car	RV
1	620	128	348	144
2	888	237	360	291
3	988	321	338	329
4	749	130	347	272

Creating Find Duplicates Queries

Duplicate table rows can sometimes creep into tables, so the Find Duplicates query is available to locate them for you. While you can create this type of query manually—just like you can the crosstab query—it is much simpler to let the wizard do it for you. Here, we won't ask you to actually launch the wizard, but we will step you through it. You click Create, click Query Wizard, and click the Find Duplicates Query Wizard, and click OK to launch it. Click the table you want to check for duplicate rows and then check the fields you want to check for duplicates. The key here is to include enough fields to identify true duplicate rows, not just duplicate values. For example, if you specify to check the inventory table (*tblInventory*) for duplicates and specify to check only the ItemName field, nearly every inventory row will be flagged as a duplicate. This is because almost all coffees in the inventory are available in both decaffeinated and caffeinated versions. Therefore, select most columns of a row—except of course the primary key—to see if there are duplicate rows based on the columns you select. If you create a Find Duplicates query specifying the Customer table and only the State field to check for duplicates, then the query returns the state abbreviation and the number of customers in each state (see Figure 4.9).

Fig. 4.9 Results of a Find Duplicates query.

Find duplicates for tblCustomer

CustState Field	NumberOfD
AK	2
AL	22
AR	13
AZ	15
CA	196
CO	22
CT	56
DC	5
DE	12
FL	67

Designing and Using a Parameter Query

So far you have examined and created queries with selection criteria directly in the criteria panel of the query design grid. However, you can create a special type of query that allows you to specify selection criteria when you *run* the query. Known as a *parameter query*, it prompts you to enter the selection criteria just before running the query. The main advantage of a parameter query over conventional queries is versatility. For example, you could create and run a query that lists all customers who live in Minnesota. Using the query as the basis of a report, Access could create a form letter that you mail to all Minnesota residents. When the northwest sales region decides to run a similar promotion, it can revise the Minnesota query, substituting "Oregon" for "Minnesota" in the criteria row to extract those residents. Imagine creating 50 such queries simply to generate a listing for each state. Creating those queries would be time-consuming, and your database would be filled with 50 copies of a query whose basic forms are identical except for the criteria each contains. A parameter query reduces the number of queries from 50 to 1 by using the state name as the "parameter."

You can create a single parameter query to replace all of the 50 individual queries. The only action required by a user running the query is to type the state name or abbreviation when prompted by Access. One query does the work of many. You can extend the use of parameter queries to an unlimited number of other accounting applications. A parameter query provides a perfect way to extract a group of invoices for varying time periods. Simply create a parameter query with two parameters—the beginning and ending dates for the billing period—and anyone can retrieve invoices from the date ranges a user enters when the query begins execution. Further, you can imagine a simple search engine query that retrieves a sales tax rate from a table when a user types the state name or state abbreviation. Simply enter the state name, and the query returns the sales tax rate for that state.

The best way to understand parameter queries is to build and run one. You will create a parameter query that displays a list of customers for any state that the user wishes. When anyone runs the query, he or she is prompted to enter a two-character state abbreviation. The query then retrieves addresses for customers in that state and displays them in the dynaset.

EXERCISE 4.3: CREATING A PARAMETER QUERY

1. Open the Chapter 4 database, if needed. Then, click the Create tab, click Query Design, double-click tblCustomer in the Show Table dialog box listing available tables and queries to add its field roster to the query, and click the Close button in the Show Table dialog box.
2. Double-click the following fields found in the field roster in this order: CustFirstName, CustLastName, CustAddress, CustCity, CustState, and CustZip. Access places each field in the Fields row of the QBE grid, left to right, in the same order as they are clicked.
3. Type [Enter a two-character state abbreviation:] into the first Criteria row below the CustState column. This sequence of characters, enclosed in beginning and ending brackets, provides the literal prompt text that the user sees and defines the parameter. (*Hint*: Press Shift+F2 to open a Zoom dialog box to see the entire criteria easier. Click OK when you are done to close the Zoom box.)
4. Click the View button in the Results group of the Design contextual tab. An Enter Parameter Value dialog box appears.
5. Type NE (either upper- or lowercase is fine) in the Enter Parameter Value dialog box. This indicates you want to display addresses for Nebraska customers (see Figure 4.10). Recall that the capitalization of search strings doesn't matter. Uppercase "NE" will match table entries such as "Ne" or "nE."
6. Click OK in the Enter Parameter Value dialog box to run the query. If you constructed the query correctly, Access will display a list of 11 customers—all from Nebraska (see Figure 4.11).

7. Select the Save icon in the Quick Access Toolbar, type the name MyParameterQuery; and click OK to save the newly named query.
8. Right-click the query tab and click Close from the pop-up menu to close the dynaset.
9. Try a new parameter: Double-click MyParameterQuery in the Queries group. When the Enter Parameter Value dialog box appears, type MT and press Enter to run the query to display any Montana customers. There are two customers who live in Montana.
10. Right-click the query's tab and click Close All from the pop-up.

Fig. 4.10 A parameter query design and run-time prompt.

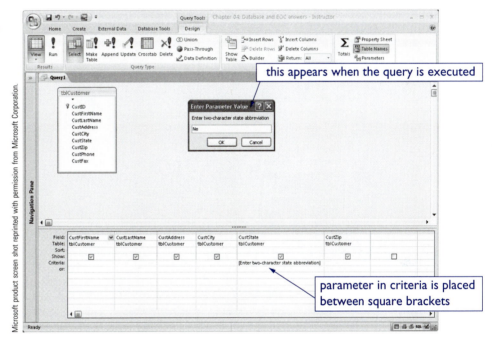

this appears when the query is executed

parameter in criteria is placed between square brackets

Microsoft product screen shot reprinted with permission from Microsoft Corporation.

Fig. 4.11 A parameter query dynaset.

Microsoft product screen shot reprinted with permission from Microsoft Corporation.

CustFirstNar ▾	CustLastNan ▾	CustAddress ▾	CustCity ▾	CustState ▾
Jeffrey	Gilbert	2120 South 72n	Omaha	NE
Richard	Frahm	1440 M Street	Lincoln	NE
Jose	Bicudo	4205 South 96T	Omaha	NE
Elizabeth	Jones	1700 Farnam St	Omaha	NE
Dominic	Crews	1440 M Street	Lincoln	NE
Doug	Mouzin	10901 Malcolm	Omaha	NE
Rafael	Nafikov	12100 West Cei	Omaha	NE
Michelle	Garcia	2407 West 24Tl	Kearney	NE
Joshua	Hushon	One Internatio	Omaha	NE
Giovanni	Deluca	P.O. Box 358	Valley	NE
Marit	Arana	One First Natic	Omaha	NE

Setting Query Properties

All queries have built-in properties that control the way the query appears and the way it creates the dynaset. You can review and change any query's properties by opening the query in Design view and then clicking the Property Sheet (or pressing Alt+Enter). Access displays the query's current properties in the Property Sheet window like the one shown in Figure 4.12.

Fig. 4.12 A query's properties.

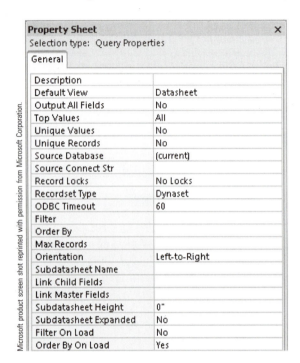

Several of the query properties control the appearance of the query. Others control the volume and orientation of the dynaset. For instance the Top Values property controls whether all the rows appear or only the specified top N percent or N records. The Orientation specifies whether the columns in the design appear left to right (the default) or reversed—right to left. The following is a brief explanation of other query properties.

Default View

The choices are Datasheet, PivotTable, and PivotChart. Datasheet is the default, but you'll find that a pivot table query, once closed, displays in Datasheet view when reopened. If you want the pivot table to be the default view when the query name is double-clicked, then set this default view property.

Output All Fields

Set to No, Access displays only the fields you specify in the query design grid Field row. Otherwise, Access displays all columns from the underlying table or query in the dynaset—regardless of the design grid.

Top Values

This value determines the number or percentage of rows that appear from highest to lowest or vice versa. The value 5 means the top (or bottom) 5 rows. The value 5% means the top 5% (perhaps 50 rows in a 1,000-row table, for example). To be effective, the query must specify sorting on one or more fields. Otherwise, the top/bottom row counts or percentages are completely meaningless. The default, All, displays all rows—subject to criteria filtering of course.

Unique Values

The default of No means that possibly duplicate column values can appear in the dynaset. Set to Yes, multiple occurrences of a value are suppressed. For example, if you created a query to display only the ItemName from the *tblInventory* table, sorted alphabetically, then several duplicate values would appear in the dynaset. Most products have both caffeinated and decaffeinated choices. Brazil Bourbon Santos appears twice in such a list. By setting the Unique Values property of the query to Yes produces nonduplicated names—just a list of all product names. Try it yourself.

Unique Rows

The default is No and means multiple column dynaset results could appear to be duplicates when, in fact, they are unique in fields not shown in the dynaset. Set to Yes, then any entire rows that are duplicates are not displayed. Individual unique column values still can occur.

Filter

The Filter property value provides a way to define a filter for the data that does not appear in the QBE grid. For example, if you set a filter in the Datasheet view of a query or table (right-click a column value and then select any of the suggested filters in its pop-up menu), then the filter is stored in the Filter property. The filter can be toggled on and off in the Sort & Filter group of the Home tab. Click Advanced in the Sort & Filter group of the Home tab and then click Clear All Filters to erase the value in the Filter property.

Order By

Type the field names of any columns in the query, separated by commas, to define the Datasheet view sort order. Setting any sort orders in the query or table's Datasheet view causes the sort specified to be stored in the Order By property.

Orientation

This property determines whether the fields are listed left to right (the default) like they are in the query design or reversed—right to left.

Working with Multiple-Table Queries

The Coffee Merchant database contains a number of tables that are in so-called normal form in order to avoid problems such as data redundancy and data inconsistency that occur when unnormalized tables are used. Data appear in several related tables, and the database must connect related tables to retrieve information that is found in multiple tables. When you connect related tables, you are *joining* them. You join related tables by indicating which columns are common to the table pairs. In Access, you can join tables by displaying table structures in the Relationships window and dragging the primary key from one table and dropping it on the foreign key of the related table. This is repeated for all table-pair relationships. For instance, you could join the *tblCustomer* and *tblInvoice* tables on the CustID column from the *tblCustomer* table and the CustomerID field found in the *tblInvoice* table. These columns that determine when rows of one table are related to those of another are not named the same, but they could be. It is often convenient to name columns that relate two tables with the same name; it helps document the primary key and foreign key pairs and facilitates joining tables.

Linking two or more tables is straightforward. You connect a table's primary key to another's foreign key to explicitly indicate how tables are linked. In many cases, Access can automatically determine how tables are linked when tables to be linked (*joined* is the preferred term) have identically named fields or they have been joined permanently via the Relationships window. If Microsoft Access does not automatically create join lines for you, you can join tables manually. On the other hand, if Microsoft forges an incorrect join of two tables, then you can easily break the link and create the correct one.

You can join tables permanently by forging the links in the Relationships window, or you can create temporary relationships between tables within a query. The latter affects only the query in which the tables are joined, not other queries containing references to the tables. You join tables manually in a query and by adding all the related tables to the query with the Show Table dialog box. Then, you can create a join line between each table pair by selecting the primary key field in one table and dragging it to the equivalent foreign key field in the other table. You create permanent relationships that Access remembers for any objects that reference the joined tables in the Relationships window. Simply click Database Tools and then click Relationships in the Show/Hide group. Once you join tables in the Relationships window, you never need to do so inside individual queries. Access remembers table-to-table relationships that you create in the Relationships window until you explicitly delete them.

Understanding Table Relationships

It is rare that you would encounter one or more tables that are not related to at least one other table. If there were such a table in a database system, you'd have to wonder why it is there in the first place. Normally, every table in a database system is related to at least one other table. An exception would be known as a flat file. An example of a flat file is a single-table database with information about the Incredible Cheesecake Company you first saw in Chapter 1. There, the tables were in normal form. Figure 4.13 shows a portion of a single-table version of the data. Notice all the duplication in the column values—places

Fig. 4.13 A single-table database.

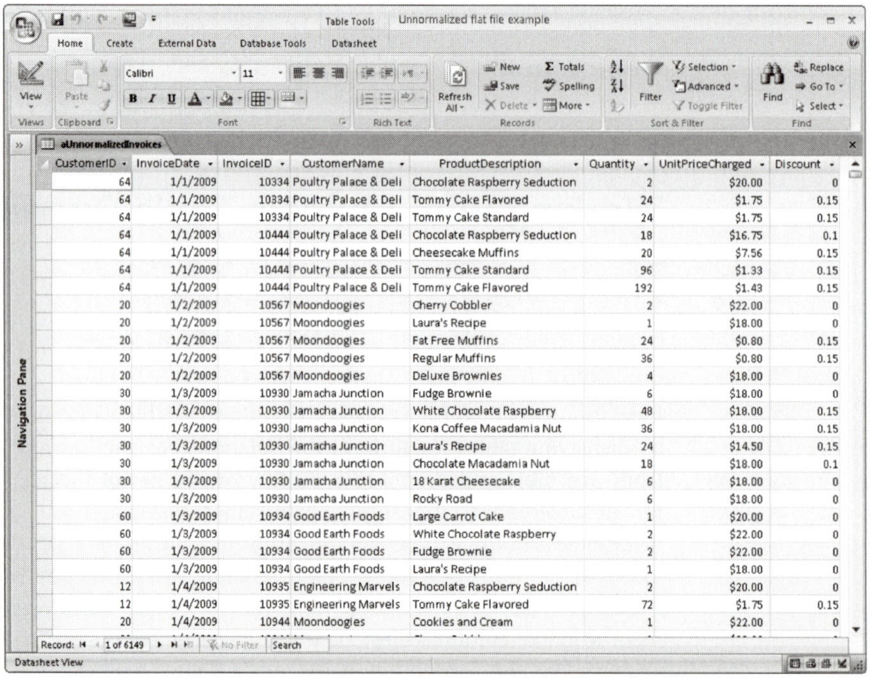

CustomerID	InvoiceDate	InvoiceID	CustomerName	ProductDescription	Quantity	UnitPriceCharged	Discount
64	1/1/2009	10334	Poultry Palace & Deli	Chocolate Raspberry Seduction	2	$20.00	0
64	1/1/2009	10334	Poultry Palace & Deli	Tommy Cake Flavored	24	$1.75	0.15
64	1/1/2009	10334	Poultry Palace & Deli	Tommy Cake Standard	24	$1.75	0.15
64	1/1/2009	10444	Poultry Palace & Deli	Chocolate Raspberry Seduction	18	$16.75	0.1
64	1/1/2009	10444	Poultry Palace & Deli	Cheesecake Muffins	20	$7.56	0.15
64	1/1/2009	10444	Poultry Palace & Deli	Tommy Cake Standard	96	$1.33	0.15
64	1/1/2009	10444	Poultry Palace & Deli	Tommy Cake Flavored	192	$1.43	0.15
20	1/2/2009	10567	Moondoogies	Cherry Cobbler	2	$22.00	0
20	1/2/2009	10567	Moondoogies	Laura's Recipe	1	$18.00	0
20	1/2/2009	10567	Moondoogies	Fat Free Muffins	24	$0.80	0.15
20	1/2/2009	10567	Moondoogies	Regular Muffins	36	$0.80	0.15
20	1/2/2009	10567	Moondoogies	Deluxe Brownies	4	$18.00	0
30	1/3/2009	10930	Jamacha Junction	Fudge Brownie	6	$18.00	0
30	1/3/2009	10930	Jamacha Junction	White Chocolate Raspberry	48	$18.00	0.15
30	1/3/2009	10930	Jamacha Junction	Kona Coffee Macadamia Nut	36	$18.00	0.15
30	1/3/2009	10930	Jamacha Junction	Laura's Recipe	24	$14.50	0.15
30	1/3/2009	10930	Jamacha Junction	Chocolate Macadamia Nut	18	$18.00	0.1
30	1/3/2009	10930	Jamacha Junction	18 Karat Cheesecake	6	$18.00	0
30	1/3/2009	10930	Jamacha Junction	Rocky Road	6	$18.00	0
60	1/3/2009	10934	Good Earth Foods	Large Carrot Cake	1	$20.00	0
60	1/3/2009	10934	Good Earth Foods	White Chocolate Raspberry	2	$22.00	0
60	1/3/2009	10934	Good Earth Foods	Fudge Brownie	2	$22.00	0
60	1/3/2009	10934	Good Earth Foods	Laura's Recipe	1	$18.00	0
12	1/4/2009	10935	Engineering Marvels	Chocolate Raspberry Seduction	2	$20.00	0
12	1/4/2009	10935	Engineering Marvels	Tommy Cake Flavored	72	$1.75	0.15
20	1/4/2009	10944	Moondoogies	Cookies and Cream	1	$22.00	0

where data entry errors are likely to occur. This flat file is unnormalized because each row likely contains information about products, customers, and invoices mixed in one table. It would be very difficult, for instance, to list the company's products. Similarly, it is possible to "lose" a customer when the invoice is paid and one or more rows of an invoice deleted —because customer information can be lost. So, that reinforces that rarely is there an unrelated table in a production system and if there is, it is probably in bad shape!

Tables are related to each other in three possible ways. They are: One-to-one, one-to-many, and many-to-many. While the one-to-many is the most common type of relationship found in relational database systems, one-to-one and many-to-many occur also.

Understanding One-to-One Relationships

A one-to-one (1–1) relationship exists between tables when for every record in one table, either none or at most one record in another table is related to it. These types of relationships are uncommon in relational database management systems. In fact, one-to-one tables violate normalization rules. However, circumstances sometimes favor splitting a table of many columns into two or more tables with fewer columns—thus the one-to-one relationship. This partitioning often occurs to provide extra security or "need to know" protection. For example, some employee information such as birth date, name, and address may be considered public. On the other hand, more sensitive information such as wage information, dependents, insurance, and health insurance elections should be placed in a separate table even though it normally would be in the same table as other employee information. The relationship between a table containing so-called public employee information and one containing private information is one-to-one. Similarly, if the number of columns in an Access table exceeds 255 columns, then you are forced to split the table into two tables related one-to-one.

Understanding One-to-Many Relationships

The most common relationship is one-to-many (1–M). In a one-to-one relationship, one row of one table, called the parent table, can be related to zero, one, or more rows in another table, called the child table. On the other hand, each row or record in the child table is related to *exactly* one row in the parent table. The situation should never have a row in the child table that is not related to a single row in the parent. If so, then an error has occurred to cause the orphan row. For example, in the customer/invoice one-to-many relationship, one row in the customer table may be related to zero (no outstanding invoices), one, or several invoice rows. In the latter case, one customer has placed several orders and there are several outstanding invoices. However, an invoice should never be found for which there is no customer row. If this were true, the company would have an invoice with no way to attach it to a customer. It would represent lost revenue due to the orphan transaction. Other one-to-many relationship examples include employees and sales transactions, people and health care visits, and teacher and student.

Dealing with Many-to-Many Relationships

The relationship between the *tblInvoice* and *tblInventory* tables is many-to-many (M–M). That is, any particular invoice can contain several items drawn from inventory, and any particular inventory item may be found in any number of invoices. Whenever an M–M relationship exists between two tables, you must create a relationship table. Minimally, the relationship table contains primary keys from both the *tblInvoice* and *tblInventory* tables for every item on a particular invoice and all invoices.

There are as many rows in the relationship table as there are invoice line items for all invoices. Invoice lines are stored in the *tblInvoiceLine* table. Access matches the invoice number with the InvoiceID attribute of *tblInvoiceLine* to retrieve all the items of a particular invoice. InvoiceID is the primary key of the *tblInvoice* table, whereas the attribute InventoryID in *tblInvoiceLine* is the primary key in *tblInventory*. Thus, InventoryID in *tblInvoiceLine* is a foreign key. The other attributes in the relationship table are Quantity, UnitPrice, and Discount. Quantity is the amount invoiced for a particular item on a given invoice line. UnitPrice is the price charged for this item. It can differ from the Price column stored in the *tblInventory* table. The Discount field holds the percentage discount for a line item on a particular invoice. Discounts vary from customer to customer and from one time of the year to another. The two *tblInvoiceLine* table attributes, InvoiceID and InventoryID, form a composite primary key, because they are both required to form a primary key for the relationship table called *tblInvoiceLine*.

If you encounter other tables having a many-to-many relationship, which cannot be handled easily by a relational database management system (RDBMS), the remedy is simple. Create a relationship table containing a composite primary key that is formed from the primary keys of the two tables having the M–M relationship—just as we have done with the *tblInvoiceLine* table. Once a relationship table is in place, then both of the original tables have a 1–M relationship with the relationship table. In other words, the relationship table provides the "glue" connecting two tables in a one-to-many relationship.

Using Expressions in a Query

There are times when you will want to see calculated results from Access derived by a query. For example, you may want to display a person's age given a date of birth field in a table. Perhaps you want to know the total value of each item held in inventory, which is the product of number of units on hand and price per unit for each item. You know not to include a table column that can be calculated or derived from other columns in the table. This would violate normalization rules and, more importantly, lead to inaccurate or out-of-date data. For instance, good database design and normalization rules prohibit inclusion of a column of extended prices in any of The Coffee Merchant's invoice tables. Because the extended price is calculated from the fields Quantity, UnitPrice, and Discount in the table *tblInvoiceLine*, an extended price should not be stored in the table. Why? Suppose the extended price is stored in *tblInvoiceLine* along with Quantity, UnitPrice, and Discount. What if someone discovers a mistake in the Quantity or UnitPrice values in one or more invoices? Changing either renders the extended price value inaccurate. Database experts would say that the database is inconsistent.

That leads us to this question: How do you produce the extended price and other useful calculated results? One answer is that you include any calculations in a query. Access allows you to write expressions that sum, average, and count values as well as write expressions that involve the arithmetic operators, fields, summary operators, numeric constants, and comparison operators. The arithmetic operators are the familiar ones: addition ($+$), subtraction ($-$), multiplication ($*$), and division ($/$). There are three comparison operators that can form six combinations of comparisons in expressions that evaluate to true or false. The six combinations, in no particular order, are $<$, $<=$, $>$, $>=$, $<>$, and $=$ and you refer to them as less than, less than or equal, greater than, greater than or equal, not equal, and equal. You reference table fields by enclosing their names in brackets. This is not required for fields that do not contain a blank in their name, but it is a good and consistent way to always refer to a field. It has the added benefit that a field name you write inside square brackets is changed to its corresponding capitalized version in the underlying table if you spell it correctly. To compute a result and display it in a query, you simply write an expression in its own Field row cell of the QBE grid of the query design window.

You define a calculated field by providing Access two things: the name of the calculated field and the expression that computes the resulting value. The name, often called a field alias, precedes the expression in the QBE grid. It is followed by a colon and then the expression. If you omit the calculated field's name, access supplies an artificial one starting with *expr1* and numbering sequentially. An example of this two-part syntax for calculated fields is:

Fieldname: expression

where *Fieldname* is the arbitrary name you choose for the field and *expression* is an arbitrarily complex combination of table field names, operators, and Access functions. For example, you could create a calculated field for a 20% discount of the retail price of a product with this phrase:

SalePrice: [RetailPrice]*0.80

SalePrice is newly defined column name in the query result and RetailPrice is a field from one of the tables included in the query. The value 0.80 is a constant. Every row in the dynaset will display this value, so if there are 120 rows in the dynaset, then the expression is recalculated for each of the 120 unique sale price values. Calculated expressions have one disadvantage. You cannot edit the value of the calculated expression in a dynaset, unlike other nonexpression columns displayed by a query.

Using Operators

Let's write an expression to see exactly how to perform calculations in a query using query fields and display them in a dynaset. In the next exercise, you will write a query to join the *tblInvoiceLine* and *tblInventory* tables and display invoice line items for invoices in the database. It displays the extended price, among other columns, using the following formula:

ExtendedPrice: [Quantity]*[UnitPrice]*(1–[Discount])

The columns are placed into the query and the expression is an extra column whose contents you write in an empty Field row cell. Consider the calculation: if someone is being invoiced for 20 pounds of a particular coffee priced at $10.00 per pound and has received a 5% discount, then the extended price would be the following when you substitute values for the field names:

ExtendedPrice: 20*10*(1–0.05)

The inventory table, *tblInventory*, contains a price field, UnitPrice, for each inventory item. However, customers may or may not be charged that *suggested* price. The actual price charged is stored in UnitPrice in the *tblInvoiceLine* table, and may vary from one customer to another. Because the field name UnitPrice occurs in both the *tblInvoiceLine* and *tblInventory* tables, you have to qualify the field name by preceding it with the table name. For example, you can write the fully qualified field reference, preceded by its containing table, like this:

[tblInvoiceLine].[UnitPrice]

That way, there is no possible confusion about which field is being referenced—the one from the *tblInvoiceLine* table in this case.

Next, you will write the query containing an expression in two phases. In the first phase, you'll include fields found in both tables. In the second phase, you will write the expression involving fields and operators.

EXERCISE 4.4: WRITING A BASIC QUERY

1. Click Create, click Query Design, add the *tblInventory* and *tblInvoiceLine* tables to the table panel of the query design by double-clicking their names, and close the Show Table dialog box.
2. Drag the fields InvoiceID, InventoryID, Quantity, UnitPrice, and Discount from the *tblInvoiceLine* table to the first five Field row cells in the QBE grid (in the order listed).
3. Double-click ItemName in the *tblInventory* field roster to add it to the right-most Field row cell.
4. Click in the Sort cell beneath the InvoiceID column in the QBE grid, click the drop-down list arrow, and select Ascending. This will sort the invoices in ascending order by invoice number.
5. Click Save in the Quick Access Toolbar, and type MyExtendedPrice in the Save As dialog box, and click OK to save the query design.
6. Click the View button in the Results group of the Design contextual tab to review the dynaset. Notice that the ItemName column is not wide enough to display the full item name. That's remedied in the next exercise.
7. Right-click (for a different way to change views) the MyExtendedPrice tab and click Design View in the pop-up menu.

Having saved the query, you can complete the query by writing the expression to calculate the extended price.

Using the Expression Builder

The Expression Builder is built into Access and helps you create expressions. It is a tool you can start just about anywhere you need an expression including table field properties, field expressions in designing queries, and in forms and reports. It offers easy access to the names of fields and controls in your database. In addition, it makes all of the Access built-in functions available in convenient groups of related functions. Using the Expression Builder, you can create an expression from scratch, or you can choose from the hundreds of custom expressions for displaying the date, page numbers, and so on. You use the Expression Builder next to select fields from an existing query to write an expression displaying information calculated from existing table fields in the *tblInvoiceLine* table.

EXERCISE 4.5: WRITING AN EXPRESSION TO COMPUTE EXTENDED PRICE

1. With the query MyExtendedPrice open in Design view, right-click the first empty Field row (drag the horizontal scroll box, if needed).
2. Click Build in pop-up menu. The Expression Builder opens.
3. If necessary click MyExtendedPrice in the leftmost of the three Expression Builder panels. Fields in the developing query appear in the middle panel.
4. Double-click Quantity in the middle panel and click * in the row of operators above the three panels.
5. Because the UnitPrice field occurs in at least two tables, we have to specify which table contains the UnitPrice we want (*tblInvoiceLine*, in this case): Double-click the expand button (a plus sign) to the left of the Tables group in the leftmost panel of the Expression Builder. All database table names appear.
6. Drag the vertical scroll box until *tblInvoiceLine* appears, and then click tblInvoiceLine. Its fields appear in the middle panel. Among them is UnitPrice—

the actual price charged in the invoice. Double-click UnitPrice in the middle panel to place its fully qualified name in the developing expression. Access adds "[tblInvoiceLine]![UnitPrice]" to the expression. The exclamation point separates the table name from the column name.

7. Drag the scroll box back to the top so you can see MyExtendedPrice at the top of the list of objects in the left panel. Click MyExtendedPrice.

8. Click * in the row of operators, type (1-, double-click Discount in the middle panel, and type) (a right parenthesis) to complete the expression. The expression you are building should match the one in Figure 4.14.

9. Tap the Home key to move the insertion point to the left end of the expression and type ExtendedPrice: (one word followed by a colon) to assign the calculated column a name.

10. Click OK to close the Expression Builder dialog box and place the completed expression in the Field row cell.

11. Right-click the MyextendedPrice tab and click Datasheet View from the pop-up menu. The dynaset displays the new ExtendedPrice column. Drag the right edge of the ExtendedPrice column to widen it (see Figure 4.15).

Fig. 4.14 Creating an expression using the Expression Builder.

Microsoft product screen shot reprinted with permission from Microsoft Corporation.

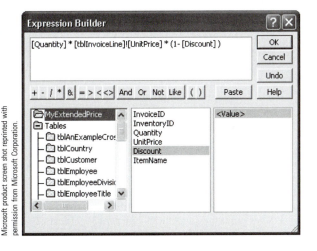

Fig. 4.15 Extended prices showing many decimal places.

Microsoft product screen shot reprinted with permission from Microsoft Corporation.

InvoiceID	InventoryID	Quantity	UnitPrice	Discount	ItemName	ExtendedPrice
214010	1195	17	$3.90	0%	Vienna	66.3
214010	1209	14	$6.20	15%	Ceylon Pekoe	73.7799994826317
214010	1237	17	$10.90	5%	China Keemun	176.034999861941
214010	1192	17	$13.30	10%	Assam Tara TGF	203.489999663085
214010	1184	18	$6.90	5%	Rose Potpourri	117.989999907464
214011	1211	10	$14.70	15%	Apricot	124.949999123812
214011	1104	19	$5.30	5%	Vanilla Nut Fuc	95.6649999249726
214011	1137	15	$7.00	15%	Chocolate Bran	89.2499993741512
214011	1197	2	$7.10	0%	Espresso Roast	14.2
214011	1133	8	$7.90	0%	Chocolate Haze	63.2
214012	1249	2	$11.90	0%	Nicaraguan Ma	23.8
214012	1203	12	$8.10	15%	Earl Grey	82.6199994206429
214012	1189	14	$5.30	15%	Vanilla Nut Cre	63.0699995577335
214012	1129	5	$8.40	0%	Guangxi Guihu	42

ExtendedPrice displays several decimal places

Access displays the extended prices with many decimal places of precision. That won't do for our customers. So, let's find a way to round the results to two decimal places—currency format where all decimal places to the right of the second one are all zero. Microsoft Access, like Excel, provides hundreds of built-in functions you can use in expressions.

Introduction to Access Built-In Functions

Access functions are very handy because they provide a rich variety of ways to manipulate numbers, dates, and text in ways that would be difficult to do with simple mathematical and text operators. An Access built-in function takes in data you supply, called arguments, performs some transformation or calculation on the input data, and returns a result. Functions can perform complex calculations, and they include dozens of individual functions grouped into fourteen groups. Some of these groups have familiar names such as *Date/Time*, *Financial*, and *Math*, while other group names such as *Inspection* or *Domain Aggregate* are less familiar. Exploring all or even many of these functions would quickly bore you. We will cover several frequently used functions and those important to accounting information systems work.

Using Math Functions

The next exercise gently introduces you to a math function whose use is familiar to you. It is the round function. Rounding the ExtendedPrice values to two decimal places makes them more tractable and yields better results—especially when the extended price values are tallied.

EXERCISE 4.6: USING AN ACCESS BUILT-IN FUNCTION

1. With the query MyExtendedPrice open in Design view, right-click the ExtendedPrice field cell and click Build to open the Expression Builder.
2. Double-click the + (the expand symbol) to the left of *Functions* in the leftmost panel. Click Built-In Functions in the left panel, click Math in the middle panel, and then click Round in the right panel.
3. Click the Help button to read about the Round function. After you read briefly about the Round function, click the close button (X) in the help title bar. Instead of pasting the function in, you will simply type it. It's much easier when editing an expression to type a familiar function with arguments then to paste it. Pasting it puts the function in the wrong place in the expression unless you begin the expression with a function and then work your way left to right filling in the function's arguments.
4. In the text box at the top of the Expression Builder, click just after the colon that follows the column name to move the insertion point. Type round(and then move the insertion point to the right end of the expression—following the right parenthesis following the Discount field by clicking that position.
5. Type ,2) (comma, 2, and a right parenthesis) to complete this function. Your completed expression, with the extended price nested as the first argument of the Round function, should match Figure 4.16.
6. Click OK to close the Expression Builder and confirm completion of the expression.
7. Right-click the MyExtendedPrice tab and click Datasheet View to display the dynaset.

Fig. 4.16 Rounded extended price values.

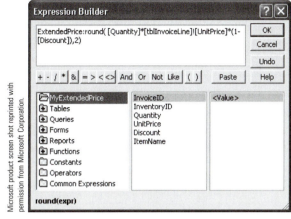

If all went well, then the first row's extended price displays 66.3 while the second one displays 73.78. Check your results to ensure they match these two check values. Notice that rounding to two decimal places does not necessarily display two complete decimal places. The value 66.3 merely indicates that the second decimal place is zero. You can *format* the results to look more acceptable.

There are several helpful math functions including Abs, Fix, Rnd, Val, and Format. *Abs* returns the absolute value of its single argument. *Fix* extracts the integer portion of its argument, lopping off any fractional parts. *Rnd* generates a random number between zero and one—useful in generating test accounting data. *Val* converts a string, containing a leading number, into a number you can use for calculation. *Format* turns a number into a formatted string. For example, the expression

Format(123.456,Currency)

returns the answer $123.46. To learn more about math functions on your own, click F1 to invoke help, type functions in the search text box, and click Functions (arranged by category). Scroll the help list down until you find Math, and click any of the listed function hyperlinks. Extensive help is available in the Access application and you should explore it on your own. It builds character!

EXERCISE 4.7: FORMATTING QUERY COLUMNS

1. Right-click the MyExtendedPrice tab and click Design View to display the query's design.
2. Click the ExtendedPrice Field cell in the QBE grid and click Property Sheet in the Show/Hide group of the Design contextual tab. (You can also press Alt+Enter, which is a faster way to display the Property Sheet.)
3. Click the Format text box (the empty text box to the right of the Format property name), click the list box arrow, and then click Currency from the drop-down list. Doing this formats the calculated expression to display the result rounded to two decimal places and includes a currency symbol and any necessary commas.
4. Click the Format dialog box Close button to close the dialog box.
5. Right-click the MyExtendedPrice tab and click Datasheet View to display the query's dynaset. Hooray! The extended price looks good.
6. Close the query and save it.

Dealing with Null Fields Referenced in Expressions

When you do calculations and use math functions, trouble can arise when one or more table fields, used in expressions, contain no value. When a field is empty, you say that it contains null. Null values involved in calculations return an empty value, not a zero. For example, if one or more of the UnitPrice fields of a particular invoice is empty—contains null—then the resulting ExtendedPrice calculation will also be empty. It may be better to display a zero in an expression that references a null value. You can experiment with this by following this Try It exercise.

TRY IT

Open in Datasheet view the query *MyExtendedPrice*. Drag through the UnitPrice value *3.90* in the first row—the row that corresponds to InvoiceID 214010 and the InventoryID value of 1195. Press the *Delete* key to replace the value with a null value. Bear in mind that most queries allow you to update data in the underlying table. You are about to change the UnitPrice field value in one of the rows of the *tblInvoiceLine* table—the price charged a particular customer for the item. Update the row by clicking anywhere in the second row. Now observe the ExtendedPrice cell in the first row. It is empty also. Click the *Undo* button in the Quick Access Toolbar to restore UnitPrice value to its original value. The ExtendedPrice value reappears as 66.30.

The oddly named Nz function delivers a zero result whenever its first argument value is null. Its form is

$$\text{Nz(expression, value if null)}$$

The first argument, expression, is the value you want to check for null. If it is, in fact, null, then the second argument, *value if null*, is returned as a result. Otherwise, the first-argument expression is calculated and returned. We won't ask you to make this change to your MyExtendedPrice query, but the following is a modification to that expression that yields a zero value if the expression results in a null value due to an omitted UnitPrice:

ExtendedPrice: Nz(Round([Quantity]*[tblInvoiceLine]![UnitPrice]*(1-[Discount]),2),0)

In other words, place the entire expression inside the Nz function as the *first* argument and type a comma, a zero, and a right parenthesis at the right end.

Using Date Functions

Date functions include the ever-popular function Date() that displays the current date and is useful in conjunction with dates stored in an invoice to compute days past due (e.g., Date()-InvoiceDate). Besides using functions in Field cells of a query, they can be used in a query's criteria row to filter the results. For example, placing the expression <Date()-60 in the criteria cell beneath the InvoiceDate in a query based on the table *tblInvoice* would display invoices over 60 days past due. Date logic is particularly powerful when you use it with the DatePart built-in function. The DatePart function has the form:

$$\text{DatePart(``interval'',expression)}$$

where *interval* can be any of those strings shown in Figure 4.17 and *expression*, the second argument, is the date-valued constant or field from a table or other query.

Fig. 4.17 Selected
DatePart function
arguments.

Format Argument	Description	Example for March 15, 2009
"yyyy"	Year in four-digit format	2009
"q"	Quarter (1 to 4)	1
"m"	Month (1 – 12)	3
"y"	Day of the year (1-365)	74
"d"	Day (1-31)	15
"w"	Day of week (1-7)	1
"ww"	Week of the year (1-52)	12

The DateDiff function is particularly useful in accounting applications because it returns the interval, or difference, between two dates. DateDiff can compute 30- 60- or 90-days past due values. Its form is

DateDiff("interval", date1, date2)

where *interval* is a quoted string whose possible values are those shown in Figure 4.17, date1 is a date value constant or field name, and date2 is a date value constant or field name. The second argument, date1, is usually the "older" date and date2 is the more recent date. The interval is returned in the units you specify (years, quarters, months, weeks, etc.). For example, the following returns the number of whole weeks between the order date and the invoice date:

DateDiff("w",OrderDate,InvoiceDate)

Similarly, the following computes the number of days past due, based on today's date, for each invoice in the table *tblInvoice*. The built-in function Date() has no arguments and returns today's date and time as follows:

DateDiff("d",InvoiceDate,date())

An exercise will help you understand how these functions work. Let's join the *tblInvoice* and *tblInvoiceLines* tables and then display calculated values of selected rows. You will use criteria to filter the rows so only selected ones appear in the dynaset.

EXERCISE 4.8: USING THE DATEDIFF FUNCTION

1. Click the Create tab, click Query Design, double-click tblInvoice and double-click tblInvoiceLine in the Show Table dialog box. Click the Close button to close the Show Table dialog box. The two table rosters appear in the table pane of the query design.
2. Double-click the following fields in the table rosters to add them, left to right, to the Field row of the QBE grid: CustomerID, OrderDate, and InvoiceDate.
3. Click in the empty Field cell just to the right of the InvoiceDate cell of the QBE grid and type the expression you typed before for extended price. This time, however, you do *not* have to qualify the UnitPrice field because it is the only so-named field in the two table rosters. Use the Expression Builder, or press Shift+F2, to open up a larger text box to type this:

ExtendedPrice: Round([Quantity]*[UnitPrice]*(1-[Discount]),2)

4. Right-click the next empty Field cell, the fifth one from the left, and click Zoom to open the Zoom box. Type the following expression to calculate and display the number of days between the order date and the invoice date:

OrderToInvoice: DateDiff("d",[OrderDate],[InvoiceDate])

Figure 4.18 shows the Zoom box (with a slightly larger font) with the completed expression.

5. Click OK to close the Zoom box.
6. Click in the Sort cell beneath the OrderToInvoice expression column in the QBE grid, click the drop-down list arrow, and select Descending. This will sort the invoices in large to small order by elapsed days.
7. Save the query: Click the Save icon in the Quick Access Toolbar, type MyDateDifference in the Query Name text box, and click OK to save the newly named query.
8. Look at the dynaset: Right-click the MyDateDifference tab and click Datasheet View from the pop-up menu. The dynaset shows the invoice lines sorted in descending order by elapsed days between the order date and the invoice date (see Figure 4.19).
9. Close the dynaset: Right-click the MyDateDifference tab and click Close All from the pop-up menu.

Fig. 4.18 Calculating the elapsed days between two dates.

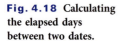

Microsoft product screen shot reprinted with permission from Microsoft Corporation.

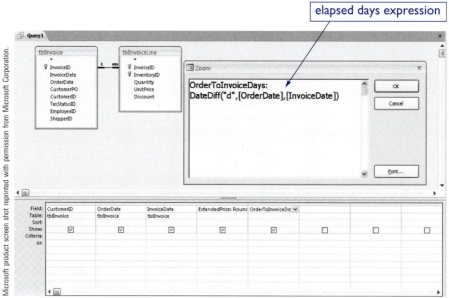

Using Criteria in Queries

At the heart of any query is its collection of criteria that filter the dynaset results by allowing only rows whose column values match the established criteria. Criteria are placed in one or more rows below the column in the QBE grid to which they apply. Criteria can be simple constants, such as "F" to filter employee rows by gender equal to female, or they can be arbitrarily complex expressions whose result is the same data type as the column under which they are found. All query criteria have the same form. They consist of one or more operands that can be *literal values* (self-defining strings, numeric constants, or dates), identifiers such as table column names or Access functions, and mathematical and logical operators (+, −, /, *, And, Or, Not, and so on). Nearly all criteria formulas

Fig. 4.19 Elapsed days dynaset.

elapsed days between order date and invoice date in descending order

CustomerID	OrderDate	InvoiceDate	ExtendedPri	OrderToInvc
34972	3/14/2009	4/12/2009	90.8	29
30596	9/28/2008	10/27/2008	79.9	29
30596	9/28/2008	10/27/2008	13.6	29
30596	9/28/2008	10/27/2008	84.8	29
31634	1/9/2009	2/7/2009	7	29
31634	1/9/2009	2/7/2009	64.09	29
31634	1/9/2009	2/7/2009	82.62	29
31634	1/9/2009	2/7/2009	85.68	29
31634	1/9/2009	2/7/2009	16	29
31634	1/9/2009	2/7/2009	30.6	29
32851	9/23/2008	10/22/2008	101.15	29
32851	9/23/2008	10/22/2008	79.73	29
32483	1/13/2009	2/11/2009	59.5	29
34972	3/14/2009	4/12/2009	45.05	29
31865	12/27/2008	1/25/2009	168.3	29
34972	3/14/2009	4/12/2009	95.76	29
34972	3/14/2009	4/12/2009	59.5	29
32851	9/23/2008	10/22/2008	104.5	29
32851	9/23/2008	10/22/2008	88	29
32851	9/23/2008	10/22/2008	68	29
31598	9/22/2008	10/21/2008	81.6	29
31598	9/22/2008	10/21/2008	69.3	29
31598	9/22/2008	10/21/2008	48.6	29
32483	1/13/2009	2/11/2009	87.55	29
32483	1/13/2009	2/11/2009	107.1	29
32483	1/13/2009	2/11/2009	100.89	29

MyDateDifference

that result in true or false when applied to each record in a table or combination of linked tables. A query's dynaset displays only records for which the criteria result in true.

Literal operands in criteria can be text. If so, then they must be enclosed in double quotation marks. If you omit the quotation marks, Access normally supplies them automatically (except in a few, odd cases). Literal operands can be numeric values such as 67.79 or 43227. No delimiters are used to surround numeric literal operands. Dates, another type of literal operand, are surrounded by pound signs. For example, #12/14/2009# is the way you would write this constant date criteria. True, False, and Null are special literal operands. The first two are obvious, but Null perhaps is not. Null appearing as criteria means that the field under which it appears must be empty to appear in the dynaset. You might want to know what employee records have no recorded date of birth, for example. Or you might want to know what invoices don't have any value in the InvoiceID column.

An identifier is a field name from the query's underlying table(s)—the table(s) on which the query draws its results. Whenever you use identifiers anywhere in the criteria —as part of a larger expression for example—always surround the identifier name with brackets. For example, use >[OnHand] to determine if the column is greater than the

OnHand field value for the record. Omitting the brackets as in >OnHand will confuse Access or result in an incorrect result.

Queries containing conditions are very useful. A condition provides a way for you to specify a range of values, or minimum and maximum values, for a field. For example, suppose the coffee buyer is ordering more coffee and tea from the ranches around the world. One of the important questions that the buyer must answer is which products are back-ordered. In The Coffee Merchant system of tables, a product is back-ordered when the OnHand field in *tblInventory* is negative. To make intelligent product-buying decisions, the buyer needs to know the product identification number, product name, and back-order volume column values. From that listing, he or she can order the correct quantity and types of products from the various suppliers.

To answer the buyer's question, we must construct a query involving the *tblInventory* table. We will use a special operator called a ***comparison operator*** to create the selection criterion in a new query. A comparison operator is a special symbol that compares one value to another. The comparison operators are shown in Figure 4.20.

Fig. 4.20 Comparison operators.

Operator	Meaning
<	Less than
<=	Less than or equal to
>	Greater than
>=	Greater than or equal to
=	Equal to
<>	Not equal to
Between	Test for a range of values where two extreme values are separated by the And operator
In	Test for "equal to" any member in a list
Like	Test a text or memo field to match a pattern string

EXERCISE 4.9: CREATING A QUERY THAT USES A COMPARISON OPERATOR TO FILTER ROWS

1. Click the Create tab, click Query Design, and double-click tblInventory in the Show Table dialog box. Click the Show Table dialog box Close button.
2. Double-click the following fields in the table roster to add them, left to right, to the Field row of the QBE grid: InventoryID, ItemName, and UnitsOnHand.
3. Click the Sort row beneath the UnitsOnHand column, click the list arrow, and click Descending.
4. Click in the topmost Criteria row beneath the UnitsOnHand column and type <0 (the less than symbol followed by zero).
5. Click View in the Results group of the Design contextual tab to display the dynaset. Move the mouse to the line between the ItemName and UnitsOnHand column names. When it becomes a double-headed arrow, double-click it to widen the ItemName column to the optimal width. Figure 4.21 shows both the query design and the resulting dynaset. Your screen may be arranged differently, but the dynaset should show the same rows as the figure.
6. After observing the result, right-click the datasheet tab and click Close All. Click No when asked if you want to save changes to the query.

Fig. 4.21 Filtering rows with a comparison operator.

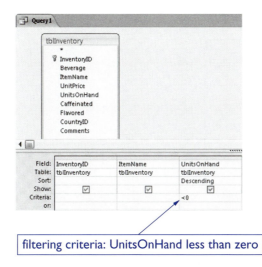

filtering criteria: UnitsOnHand less than zero

A *wildcard* character allows you to find information when you are unsure of the complete spelling of an alphanumeric field. Used with the *Like* operator (see Figure 4.20), the wildcard characters define positions that can contain any single character or zero or more characters in a text string match pattern. Figure 4.22 shows the three wildcard characters available in Access. Here's an example of how you can use them. Suppose you want to check The Coffee Merchant's stock for any beverages whose name contains the word *chocolate*—for example, *Dutch Chocolate*. You are interested in how much is available, if any. You can use the * (asterisk) wildcard character and the partial word *choc* to return any beverages whose Name field contains *choc* anywhere within it.

Fig. 4.22 Wildcard characters.

Wildcard Character	Meaning	Example Pattern Matches
?	Any single character	*b?lk* matches balk or bulk
*	Zero or more characters	*or* matches door, floor, and matador
		*or** matches ordinary, order, and organize
		or matches bored, category, and fluoride
#	Any single digit	*6#4* matches 604, 644, and 664

The query described above involves a single table, *tblInventory*. The key filtering criterion is the expression **choc** which contains asterisk wildcards on both ends of the partial string. Place this criterion in the Criteria row just below the *Name* column in the QBE grid. (After you type the preceding expression, Access automatically surrounds it with double quotation marks and precedes the entire phrase with *Like*.) The asterisk preceding *choc* indicates that any word, phrase, or character string can appear before the word—or none at all. Similarly, the asterisk following *choc* indicates that any characters

Fig. 4.23 Query
using a wildcard in
its criteria.

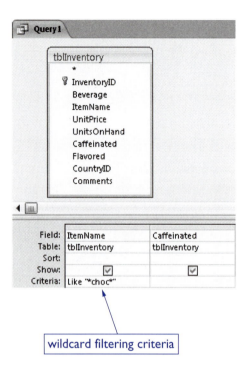

wildcard filtering criteria

Microsoft product screen shots reprinted with permission from Microsoft Corporation.

may follow the word—or none at all. That is, the search criterion requests any rows in which the partial word *choc* appears anywhere within the name. Figure 4.23 shows a query and the resulting dynaset.

Some other useful operators helpful in forming selection criteria are called ***logical operators***. Logical operators provide a way of bonding two comparison or wildcard criteria. There are several logical operators, but the ones used most often are AND, OR, and NOT. Using the AND operator, you can specify a condition in which two criteria must be true simultaneously. For example, suppose you want to examine the invoices issued during the first week in November 2008. A temporary employee was used to process the invoices that week, and you heard that some invoices were handled incorrectly. You can use the AND operator to bound the range of invoice dates you want to inspect. Specifically, you write the criterion expression

$$>= \#11/1/2008\# \text{ And } <= \#11/7/2008\#$$

in the Criteria row below InvoiceDate in the QBE grid. This selection criterion states a range of acceptable invoice dates. The range encompasses dates that are greater than or equal to November 1, 2008 *and* (simultaneously) less than or equal to November 7, 2008. Note: The # characters always surround dates so that Access doesn't confuse dates with arithmetic expressions. Thus, the criterion limits rows from the Invoice table to invoices issued during the first week. An equivalent and simpler way of writing the preceding criterion using the *Between* comparison operator is

Between #11/1/2008# And #11/7/2008#

Any dates between or matching the two dates satisfy the criteria.

Grouping and Summarizing Data

So far, all the queries in this book have generated information for individual, selected records. If the invoice table has 500 rows, then a query on that table displays a dynaset with 500 rows when no filtering criteria are used. Often, summary information is just as important in making management decisions. Summary information can reveal situations that are not obvious from examining detailed data. Examples are queries that

- *Count the number of invoices 60 days past due.*
- *Display an invoice total for each individual customer.*
- *Calculate total sales by product name.*
- *Total the value of order by customers in one or more states.*
- *Display the customer having the largest order total during a selected time period.*

The ability to sum, average, count, and so on are called information aggregation, and a special form of an Access query, called a **totals query**, provides the ability to group and summarize information. Access provides several operations that provide information aggregation and filtering for data groups or an entire table. Figure 4.24 lists all of the aggregate operations along with a brief description of what each one does. Of the listed operations, the most useful to accountants are the functions Avg, Count, Max, Min, and Sum.

Fig. 4.24 Aggregate operations for totals queries.

Name	Operation or Function	Description
Avg	Function	Computes a field's average value (ignores null fields).
Count	Function	Counts the number of non-null (empty) items in a field.
Expression	Operation	Returns a custom result based on an expression in a calculated column.
First	Operation	Returns the first value in the field.
Group By	Operation	Groups records according to unique values in a specified field.
Last	Operation	Returns the last value in the field.
Max	Function	Computes largest value in a field.
Min	Function	Computes smallest non-null value in a field.
Sum	Function	Computes the total of all items in a field.
StDev	Function	Computes the standard deviation of non-null values in a field.
Var	Function	Determines the variance of non-null values in a field.
Where	Operation	Filters rows based on criteria *before* grouping and calculating totals.

Sometimes you will want statistics for all rows of a table or joined set of tables. At other times, however, you will need summary statistics on smaller groups of records. For instance, it may be revealing to know the total number of pounds of each type of coffee and tea ordered each month—sorted high to low. This would disclose the more popular choices. Or, the accounts receivable department might be interested in a statistic such as the average elapsed days, by customer, between the time invoices are sent and their corresponding payments are received. When Access summarizes information for several sets of rows, that calculation involves grouping. *Grouping* information simply means forming groups of rows that share some common characteristic such as having identical values for a client name, customer identification number, invoice number, or other attribute stored in a table column.

The summary functions are often used in queries (but they can also be used in forms and reports). Before you can work with aggregate functions in a query, you must add the Total row to the QBE grid. The Total row appears when you click the Totals button in the Show/Hide group of the Design contextual tab. Recall that the Design contextual tab appears automatically when you display a query in Design view. The *Total* row cells each contain a list of the aggregate operations shown in Figure 4.24.

After you click the Totals toolbar button to add the Totals row to the QBE Design view grid, you can compute an average of a numeric field in a query. When the row appears, you type *Avg* in the Total row beneath the field whose values you want to average. Then, run the query. You can compute multiple summary statistics on a particular field as long as you include multiple copies of the field name in the QBE grid Field row.

In the next exercise, you will try out a summary function and learn how to meld two character fields into one field by concatenating them. You will join together three tables so that you can compute and display the total sales grouped by salespersons' names. In other words, you want to know how much each salesperson sold. The three tables involved in the query are *tblEmployee*, *tblInvoice*, and *tblInvoiceLine*. The fields required to form the query summarizing sales are all found in just two tables—*tblEmployee* and *tblInvoiceLine*. However, the relationship between *tblEmployee* and *tblInvoiceLine* is many-to-many. Because Access cannot link many-to-many tables together directly, the *tblInvoice* table serves as a "bridge" table that restructures the M–M relationship into two 1–M relationships.

Whenever you want to combine multiple text fields from a table into a single query field, you simply write an expression containing two or more fields separated by the symbol for ampersand, &. Suppose you want to produce an employee telephone book showing each employee's last name, a comma, a blank, and first name. The following expression provides the required single text field:

Name: [LastName] & ", " & [FirstName]

The ampersand adds one string onto another. In this case, the expression is "adding" three text strings together, back to back. This is a handy tool to keep in mind whenever you need to combine disparate fields from a table into a single field in a query, report, form, or Web page.

EXERCISE 4.10: USING AGGREGATE OPERATIONS IN A QUERY

1. Click the Create tab and click Query Design in the *Other* group.
2. Double-click tblEmployee, tblInvoice, and tblInvoiceLine to add those tables to the Tables panel of the query's design, and then close the Show Table dialog box. Drag the bottom edge of the table rosters if needed to reveal all their fields.
3. Click Totals in the Show/Hide group of the Design contextual tab to insert the Total row into the QBE grid.
4. In the first cell in the Field row enter the following expression, which combines the two name fields together, separated by a blank. Be sure to place a space between the two quotation marks.

Name: [EmpFName] & " " & [EmpLName]

(You can place a blank on either side of the two ampersand symbols, but you don't have to. Access will do that automatically after you move to another cell in the QBE grid.)

5. Click the Show box in the first column so that a check mark appears in it. This causes the employee name you created with the preceding expression to display when you run the query.

6. In the second cell in the Field row enter the following expression to compute and display sales totals, including any discount applied for each customer.

Sales: Round([Quantity]*[UnitPrice]*(1–[Discount]),2)

You may want to press Shift+F2 to produce a larger view of the cell in the Zoom dialog box. The larger display makes it easier to see the whole expression. When you are finished writing the expression in the Zoom dialog box, click OK to close the Zoom dialog box. Click the Show box in the second column so that a check mark appears in it.

7. Click in the QBE grid Total row beneath the second cell—the expression you just typed—and click the list box arrow. Then, click Sum from the drop-down.

8. Click in the QBE grid Sort row beneath the second cell, click the list box arrow, and click Descending from the drop-down list. You want to see the sales summary sorted from highest sales total to lowest.

9. Set the format of the second cell to Currency: Right-click the Field row cell containing the expression, click Properties, and then click Currency from the drop-down list in the Format box of the Field Properties dialog box.

10. Close the Property Sheet dialog box, and click the View button in the Results group of the Design contextual tab to see the results. Figure 4.25 shows both the query design and its dynaset.

11. Click Save in the Quick Access Toolbar and then type MyTotalSales to name the new query. Click OK to save the query. Do not close the query yet.

Fig. 4.25 Sorted sales totals for each employee.

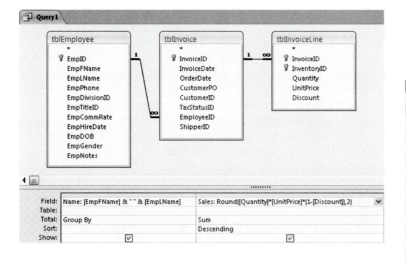

The dynaset calculates total sales for 19 salespersons. Close the query and then reopen it in Design view in preparation for a little experiment. Notice that Access has changed the expression in the summed column to

Sales: Sum(Round([Quantity]*[UnitPrice]*(1–[Discount]),2))

and placed the word *Expression* in the Total column. Can Microsoft Access compute the grand total of all invoices that are in the database? Yes. As a matter of fact, you can make a simple change to the query you created in the preceding exercise to yield the grand total.

TRY IT

Display the previous query in Design view. Move the mouse pointer just above the Field row of the Name field (an expression) in the QBE grid. When the pointer changes to a solid down-pointing arrow, click the mouse to select the entire Name column. Press the *Delete* key to delete that column. Click *View* in the Results group of the Design contextual tab to see the grand total of all invoices in the database. Your altered query should display a single row with the value of $176,728.07—the current total of all invoices. Right-click the *MyTotalSales* tab and click *Close All* to close the window and any others that are open. Click *No* when the dialog box displays a message asking if you want to save the query's design, because you want to preserve the original query you created above.

Remember the following when using aggregate (summary) functions. Place the aggregate function in the field you want to summarize (beneath an expression in our previous example). Rename a summary column when desired by typing the new name, a colon, a space, and then the alias (name).

Creating and Using an Outer Join Query

When you join two tables, you may find that one or more rows in one table do not have matching rows in the other table. Revealing rows that don't match can be important. For example, a sales manager might want to know if there are any salespersons who have sold nothing during a particular period. There are other examples of hidden information in your databases. In your Chapter 4 database, for example, you cannot glean which cities have no employees simply by performing a standard join of the *tblEmployee* and *tblEmployeeDivision* tables on matching primary and foreign keys. Instead, you produce this kind of information by using a query that joins tables with an *outer join*, which lists all rows from one table and only matching rows from another table.

The next exercise shows you how to create an outer join. It uses as its starting point the query you created in Exercise 4.10 called MyTotalSales. You will modify the join properties for both of the existing joins to form an outer join. (Each of the query's two joins is called an *inner join*.) The new query, when completed, will reveal the names of people who sold products and those who didn't sell anything.

EXERCISE 4.11: CREATING AN OUTER JOIN QUERY

1. Create a copy of MyTotalSales and then rename it by doing this: Click MyTotalSales in the list of queries in the Navigation Pane, press Ctrl+C, press Ctrl+V, type MyOuterJoin in the Paste As dialog box to name the cloned query, and click OK.
2. Right-click MyOuterJoin and click Design View.

3. Double-click the join line between the field lists of *tblEmployee* and *tblInvoice* in the upper part of the Query window to open the Join Properties dialog box.

4. Select the second option in the dialog box (see Figure 4.26), and click OK. You should now see an arrow on the join line pointing from the *tblEmployee* field list to the *tblInvoice* field list, indicating you have asked for an outer join with all records from *tblEmployee* regardless of whether or not corresponding records are found in *tblInvoice*.

5. Repeat steps 3 and 4 for the join line between the field lists of *tblInvoice* and *tblInvoiceLine*.

6. Display the query in Datasheet view, and scroll the display, if needed, so you can see dynaset rows 20 through 22. Notice that the Sales column is empty for Melinda English, Giles Bateman, and Brad Shoenstein. That means that they have no records in the *tblInvoiceLine* table and therefore no sales for the period.

   In the next step, you will tell Access to display only the rows whose total sales values are empty.

7. Display the query in Design view, move to the criteria row beneath the Sales (summed sales) column, and type Is Null into the Criteria cell. Display the query in Datasheet view. It displays only those employees who did not report sales for the period. Figure 4.27 shows both the query design and its dynaset.

8. Save and close the query.

Fig. 4.26 Creating an outer join.

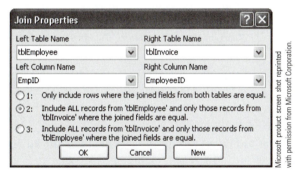

Microsoft product screen shot reprinted with permission from Microsoft Corporation.

Fig. 4.27 Using *Is Null* to display rows with empty fields.

Microsoft product screen shot reprinted with permission from Microsoft Corporation.

Building Pivot Table Queries

Access provides a powerful data analysis tool called a *PivotTable*. It enables you to review vast amounts of data in a condensed, profile-slice view. With it you can summarize data from one or more tables or queries in a tabular format. A PivotTable can display the total sales by region and by salesperson, with the regions running down a column and the different salesperson running across the top of the table. In this section, we provide an overview of PivotTables and why they are useful.

What Is a Pivot Table?

Pivot tables provide a higher level of complex data analysis. In comparison, a query that summarizes and groups information about salespersons, for example, provides one dimension of data analysis—an average or tally by salesperson. More frequently, managers want to review more complex relationships looking for patterns: What patterns do the sales by salespersons and by region display, where the summary is over two dimensions or variables: distinct salespersons and distinct customer sales regions? To provide these types of summaries, you can use an aggregate function to total sales by salesperson. However, what about sales by salespersons over 10 regions or even 50 regions? That would require many separate aggregate queries. A pivot table is the answer to providing "X by Y" aggregation—across two or more dimensions. Figure 4.28 shows an example of invoice information sliced two ways simultaneously: by region and by quarter within region. Notice that the first quarter listed is "Qtr4." It occurs *before* "Qtr1" and "Qtr2" because the Qtr4 values are from 2008 and the first and second quarters follow in 2009. Although totals appear, you can drill down to the details.

Fig. 4.28 Example pivot table.

qryPivotOne					
Drop Filter Fields Here					
	DivisionCity ▾				
	Cincinnati	Indianapolis	Princeton	San Diego	Grand Total
Quarters ▾	Total Sales	Total Sales	Total Sales	Total Sales	Total Sales
⊞ Qtr4	17,279.57	22,532.72	19,999.82	26,272.75	86,084.86
⊞ Qtr1	17,401.30	16,847.32	16,548.88	25,723.34	76,520.84
⊞ Qtr2	2,102.54	2,273.12	5,277.42	4,469.29	14,122.37
Grand Total	36,783.41	41,653.16	41,826.12	56,465.38	176,728.07

Microsoft product screen shot reprinted with permission from Microsoft Corporation.

Pivot Table Terminology

There are terms associated with pivot tables that you should be familiar with. A *field* is a category of data such as a region or time period (quarter 1, etc.) that is derived from a column in the source table or database. An *item* is a subcategory, or member, of a field. Items represent the unique entries from the field in the source data. For example, the item Qtr4 in Figure 4.28 represents all rows of data in the source list for which the InvoiceDate column falls within the fourth quarter. A *data field* provides the data values summarized by the pivot table. Usually a data field contains numbers, which are combined with the Sum summary function. A data field can also contain text, in which case the PivotTable report uses the Count summary function. A *row field* has a limited number of distinct date, text, or numeric values. The column labeled *Quarters* in Figure 4.28 is the row field. A *column field* also has a limited number of distinct date, text, or numeric values. It appears as the column headings of a pivot table. In Figure 4.28, DivisionCity is the column field listing distinct cities in which employees work. A *filter field*, also having distinct values, allows you to limit the data that is summarized in a pivot table by applying group criteria prior to summarizing. For instance, you could filter by sales representative so only some of the sales by particular sales representatives appear in the pivot table. Figure 4.28 does not have any filter. Finally, the *layout* of a pivot table is the design or arrangement of the items in a pivot table. Pivot tables in access are one of the available query views along with Datasheet view, PivotChart view, SQL view, and Design view.

Creating One- and Two-Dimensional Pivot Tables

The easiest pivot table to create is a combines a row field or a column field with summarized data. This type of pivot table extracts unique values from the row or column field—a column from a query. Pivot tables are based on queries, not tables. So, the first step in creating a pivot table is to design a query. In creating the query, ensure that at least one of the fields contains data that Access can group—data that has distinct, limited values.

Creating a One-Dimensional Pivot Table

You begin by creating a query and then build a pivot table from that query. Let's design a pivot table that displays total sales by employee sales region. While you could just as easily create a totals query (click the Totals to add a Total row and then summarize), a pivot table provides richer tools. You can collapse and expand detail, for example. Or, you can move summary rows up to columns and vice versa. Neither of the preceding is easily done with a simple query with a Total row. To prepare, make sure your Chapter 4 database is open. Close any open document windows (tabbed windows to the right of the Navigation Pane). Then, follow these steps to first build a query that will be the basis of a pivot table.

EXERCISE 4.12: CREATING A QUERY USED TO BUILD A PIVOT TABLE

1. Click the Create tab and click Query Design in the *Other* group.
2. Double-click the following table names to add them to the Tables panel of the query's design: tblEmployeeDivision, tblEmployee, tblInvoice, and tblInvoiceLine. Close the Show Table dialog box. Drag the bottom edge of the table rosters if needed to reveal all their fields.
3. In the Tables panel, double-click DivisionCity (*tblEmployeeDivision*) to add it to the first Field row cell.
4. Right-click the Field cell to the right of DivisionCity in the QBE grid and click Build from the pop-up menu. The Expression Builder dialog box appears.
5. Type the following expression in the Expression Builder text box, making use of tables and symbol buttons as you feel the need:

   Sales: Round([Quantity]*[UnitPrice]*(1–[Discount]),2)

   Of course, if you use fields from the Table list in the Expression Builder rather than type the field names, each field name will be preceded by its corresponding table name. That's okay.
6. Check that you have typed the Sales expression correctly by switching to Datasheet view. If the expression is correct, then Indianapolis should be the first series of rows to appear. Check that the first Sales value is 54.06 and that there are 2192 rows in the result.
7. Click the Save button in the Quick Access Toolbar, type the name MyPivotQuery in the Save As text box, and click OK.

The MyPivotQuery serves as the basis of the pivot table you are about to build. By saving the query, you can come back later and add fields to the query to provide more information to any pivot tables that depend on it. Next, you use the query to create a pivot table—known in Access as a PivotTable query.

EXERCISE 4.13: CREATING A PIVOT TABLE FROM A QUERY

1. Right-click the MyPivotTable tab and click PivotTable View in the pop-up menu. An empty pivot table opens with a PivotTable Field List dialog box displayed somewhere on the screen. (If there is no PivotTable Field List dialog box, then click the Field List button in the Show/Hide group of the Design contextual tab.)
2. Click the DivisionCity field in the PivotTable Field List. In the drop-down list at the bottom of the PivotTable Field list, click Row Area and then click the Add To button. Access adds the field to the pivot table's row area and displays the five regions in alphabetical order.
3. Click the Sales field in the PivotTable Field List dialog box and drag it to the *Drop Totals or Detail Fields Here* area of the pivot table. Access displays a long list of individual values to the right of each city (see Figure 4.29).
4. Click the value 65.1 at the top of the Sales column to select it, click the AutoCalc button in Tools group of the Design contextual tab, and click Sum to total sales by city. Totals appear at the bottom of each city in the Sales column of the pivot table.
5. Right-click the Sales button (gray) that appears in the heading of the Sales column and then click Hide Details in the pop-up menu. (Alternatively, you can click the Hide Details button in the Show/Hide group.) Access displays total sales by city in a concise, easily understood format (see Figure 4.30).
6. Click Save in the Quick Access Toolbar to save this alternative view of the original query you created previously. Notice that you do not have to supply a new query name. Both the original query design and its pivot table view are saved in the same query.
7. Right-click the MyPivotQuery tab and click Close All to close the query and any other open windows.

Fig. 4.29 Pivot table showing sales detail by employee city.

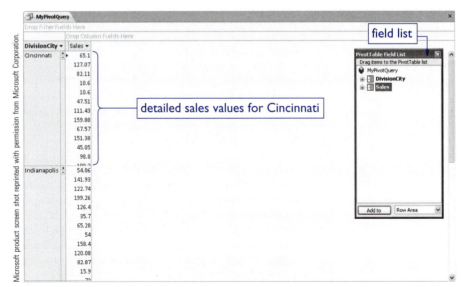

Creating a Two-Dimensional Pivot Table

A two-dimensional pivot table is one that displays two variables—either in the same row, the same column, or one in the row and one in the column—and a summary value or values. Here, you will modify the previous MyPivotQuery to add the InvoiceDate column from the *tblInvoice* table and then summarize by date *and* employee city. Let's preserve the original query and clone a duplicate.

Fig. 4.30 Sales summarized in a pivot table.

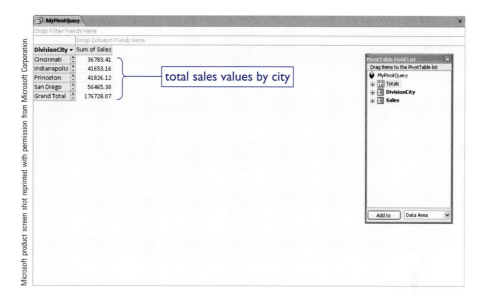

EXERCISE 4.14: CREATING A TWO-DIMENSIONAL PIVOT TABLE

1. Right-click the MyPivotTable in the Navigation Pane, click Copy in the pop-up menu, right-click the MyPivotQuery entry again, click Paste, type MyPivotQueryTwo, and click OK to create a copy of the query.
2. Right-click MyPivotQueryTwo and click Design View.
3. Double-click InvoiceDate in the *tblInvoice* field roster to add it to the third Field cell column in the query design.
4. Right-click the MyPivotQueryTwo tab and click PivotTable View in the pop-up menu to redisplay the pivot table design.
5. Click the Field List button, if necessary, to display the available pivot table fields. Notice that three new columns are available: InvoiceDate, InvoiceDate By Week, and InvoiceDate By Month.
6. Click the InvoiceDate By Month expand button in the PivotTable Field List dialog box to reveal additional choices. Other choices include Years, Quarters, Months, and so on.
7. Click Quarters. In the drop-down list at the bottom of the PivotTable Field list, click the list box arrow, click Row Area and then click the Add To button. Access places quarterly summary data to the right of each city.
8. Click the DivisionCity gray row field button in the pivot table. Then, drag and drop it onto the *Drop Column Fields Here* area of the pivot table. Access places DivisionCity as the column field (see Figure 4.31).

There is a lot more to pivot tables than what you have done here, and you can do a lot more with them. Unfortunately, this text is not the place to learn more details about pivot tables. We introduce them here hoping that you will experiment with additional features on your own.

Working in SQL View

Whenever you create a query in Access, behind the scenes Access is actually creating a Structured Query Language (SQL) statement. Usually pronounced *SEE-kwul*, a SQL

Fig. 4.31 Two-dimensional pivot table.

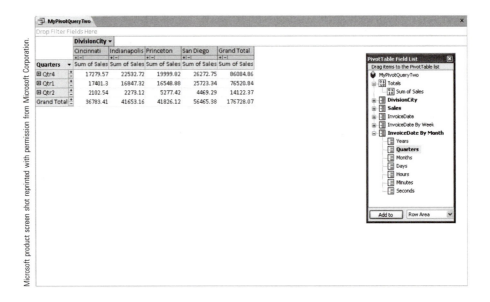

statement is the universal language used by all RDBMSs to communicate commands to the database system. A standard recognized worldwide, SQL provides statements to retrieve, update, delete, and add records to tables. Additionally, there are hundreds of other statements in the SQL language to perform all the required actions such as table creation. An example of a SQL statement that displays a few columns from the *tblCustomer* table and return them sorted in descending order on the CustLastName column is this:

> SELECT CustID, CustFirstName, CustLastName
>
> FROM tblCustomer
>
> ORDER BY CustLastName DESC;

Fortunately, you need not know SQL to create most any query returning information from one or more tables. However, there are times when it is difficult or impossible to use the Access QBE environment to write the required query. Frequently it is handy to use the results of one query in a second query. The only way to do that is to create a query directly in SQL. Occasionally, you can use the QBE grid to answer these types of queries, but more frequently, such queries require SQL. For example, suppose you want to list all employees who sold more than the average total sales of all employees. That type of query requires that Access first calculate the total average sales by all employees. Then that value is used as criteria for a second query. Using SQL, you can return the result in one query.

Select Statement Syntax

The purpose of this section is not to make you proficient in SQL. Rather, it is to make you aware that you can, if necessary, write relatively simple SQL statements via the QBE interface to answer more difficult questions that require the results of one query to be fed into an outer, containing query. Therefore, we will introduce you to just a few of the SQL SELECT statements that allow you to do "fancier" data retrieval. The SELECT statement creates a dynaset based on one or more tables, fields of those tables, criteria to filter which rows are selected, and clauses that direct sorting the dynaset before it is returned. The basic syntax of the SELECT statement is this:

SELECT [ALL | DISTINCT | TOP n] *select-list*

FROM *table-name*

WHERE *criteria*

ORDER BY *field-list*;

The word SELECT indicates the SQL command request retrieval. The keywords in brackets represent options and indicate that all, unique, or the first n rows only are requested. The select list is a comma-separated list of columns to return. You can substitute asterisk (*) to return *all* columns. The WHERE clause lists all criteria (e.g., Gender = "M"). Finally, the ORDER BY clause lists, left to right, the columns that are used to sort the dynaset. The most important is the leftmost column. Subsequent columns in the comma-separated list are so-called tie breakers at each level.

Self-Join Queries with SQL

A self-join is a query that joins a table to a copy of itself. In a standard Access QBE query, you add a second copy of the table to the QBE grid Table panel and then return columns from the original table and its copy. For example, an employee table often has a field (but not our *tblEmployee* table) that indicates the employee's manager (e.g., ManagerID). The manager indicator is a foreign key pointing to the primary key of the same table. A self-join query such as the following would list each employee and the name of his or her manager:

SELECT w.FirstName, w.LastName, m.FirstName, m.LastName

FROM Employee w INNER JOIN Employee m ON w.ManagerID = m.EmployeeID;

Such a query produces the desired result, returning workers' (*w* alias) names along with managers' (*m* alias) names. We will not ask you to formulate such a query in SQL.

Using a Subquery to Find Customers Without Invoices

You can use a SQL statement as criteria for a column within the QBE grid interface that you are familiar with. Suppose you want to list the first and last names of customers who have no outstanding invoices. You could do this in two steps by first finding which customers *do* have invoices by selecting the CustomerID from the *tblInvoice* table. That list of primary keys indicates customers with outstanding invoices. If you run that list of numbers—foreign keys to the *tblCustomer* table—against the CustID column in the *tblCustomer* table and ignore the "hits" and, instead, return the customer IDs that *are not* in the list of invoice ID values, you'll have customers who don't have invoices. You can use a similar technique to determine which salespersons, if any, do not have any current customers. Let's try this simple query making use of SQL and also the standard QBE interface.

EXERCISE 4.15: FORMULATING CRITERIA USING A SQL STATEMENT

1. Click the Create tab and click Query Design in the *Other* group.
2. Double-click tblCustomer to add it to the Tables panel of the query's design. Close the Show Table dialog box. Drag the bottom edge of the table roster, if needed, to reveal all its fields.
3. In the Tables panel, double-click the following fields, in the order specified, to add them to the Field row cells: CustFirstName, CustLastName, CustID, CustLastName, and CustFirstName. Notice that you are adding *two* copies of the CustFirstName and CustLastName fields.
4. Click in the Criteria cell directly below the CustID column. Press Shift+F2 to open the Zoom dialog box.
5. Type the following and then click OK to close the Zoom box when you are done:

Not In (Select CustomerID From tblInvoice)

6. Click the Show box in the rightmost three columns (CustID, CustLastName, and CustFirstName) to clear their check marks. The last three columns of the five do not appear in the result. Check marks should appear only in the first two columns. (The duplicates of the last and first names provide sort columns that are not displayed.)
7. Click the Sort row beneath the rightmost CustLastName column, type Asc, and press Enter. Click the Sort row beneath the rightmost CustFirstName column, type Asc, and press Enter. Access will sort the dynaset in ascending order by customers' last names and then by ascending order on first names when last names match (see Figure 4.32).
8. Click the Run button in the Results group of the Design contextual tab to run the query.
9. Click the Save button in the Quick Access Toolbar, type MySQLQuery, and click OK to save the query. (Leave the query open for a Try It exercise that follows.)

Fig. 4.32 A query with a SELECT statement as criteria.

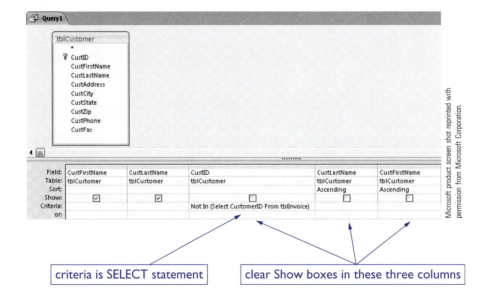

criteria is SELECT statement   clear Show boxes in these three columns

You'll probably observe a noticeable delay (4 or 5 seconds) before the dynaset appears. That delay is due to the extra time it takes to run the query in the criteria and then compare every customer ID value against the returned list of IDs. If your query worked correctly, the customer name in the list should be *Ole Aaes*, and there should be 1358 customers in the dynaset. That is, 1358 customers of the 1789 *do not* have outstanding invoices.

The Try It exercise that follows illustrates how to review the SQL statement that Access generated for the preceding query. It is instructive to review what statement is sent to the Access database to generate and return the dynaset.

TRY IT

With the MySQLQuery query open in either Design view or Datasheet view, right-click the *MySQLQuery* tab and then click *SQL View* in the pop-up menu. Access displays the SQL statement that retrieves the dynaset shown in Figure 4.32. Access tends to use a lot of extra, unneeded parentheses, but using them makes the precedence of operations unmistakable. Right-click the *MySQLQuery* tab and then click *Close* to close the query.

Finding Employees with Longer than Average Tenure

Finding employees who have worked for The Coffee Merchant longer than the average of all employees is another example where using a SQL statement can make finding the correct answer easier. Think about the problem in two pieces. First, how would you write an Access query to calculate the average length of time all employees have worked at The Coffee Merchant? You would do so with a Totals query that has an expression in the Field row that computes the elapsed time between today's date and each employee's hire date. Then, you would select the *Avg* function in the Total row beneath the elapsed hire time expression to compute the average length of service, or *tenure*. Once you have that value, then the second step is to select all employees from the *tblEmployee* table whose length of service is greater than the preceding average service length for all employees.

Using a technique that is similar to the previous SQL example, you can construct a *single* query to deliver the dynaset. When executing the query, Access computes the average length of service then compares it against the computed average length of service for the current employee row. If the current employee row's computed length of service value exceeds the compute average, then the selected columns from the employee row appear in the dynaset. The process of computing the overall average length of service and comparing against an employee row's computed length of service is repeated over and over until Access has processed all employee rows. Thus, you get an idea that this can be a computationally time-consuming process. Let's write this query completely in SQL. You will measure length of service in days but display it in weeks, though any sufficiently granular interval would work equally well (except *years*).

EXERCISE 4.16: FINDING ABOVE AVERAGE LENGTH OF SERVICE AMONG EMPLOYEES

1. Click the Create tab and click Query Design in the *Other* group.
2. Click the Show Table dialog box Close button. Access displays SQL in the View button in the Results group of the Design contextual tab.
3. Click SQL in the Results group of the Design contextual tab. A large text box—your SQL palette—opens. It is in this panel you will write the single SQL SELECT statement to deliver the payload.
4. Type the following SQL statement. Be very careful and double check it against what is written here before you click the Run button. The statement you are to type is the following one. Write it on the same number of lines as shown here, pressing Enter each time to move to a new line.

   SELECT EmpFName, EmpLName, DateDiff("w",EmpHireDate,Now()) AS Weeks
   FROM tblEmployee
   WHERE Now()-EmpHireDate >
           (SELECT AVG(Now()-EmpHireDate) FROM tblEmployee)
   ORDER BY 3 DESC;

5. Click the Run button (the red exclamation point) in the Results group of the Design contextual tab to see the results (see Figure 4.33). (Your values in the Weeks column will vary depending on today's date—the date when you run the query.) If Access indicates any type of mistake, then click OK to close the error text box, check your SQL statement against what is above. Make any corrections and run it again. The results show the 10 employees who have worked at The Coffee Merchant longer than the overall average.
6. Click the Save button on the Quick Access Toolbar, type MySQLQuery2, and click OK to save it. Close the query.

Fig. 4.33 Dynaset produced from a user-written SQL statement.

EmpFName	EmpLName	Weeks
Steve	Ballmer	846
Sharon	Stonely	665
Alanis	Morrison	608
Hillary	Flintsteel	594
Brad	Shoenstein	570
Barbara	Minsky	564
Sharad	Manispour	555
Ted	Goldman	554
David	Kole	495
Giles	Bateman	494
*		

Microsoft product screen shot reprinted with permission from Microsoft Corporation.

Although it is unlikely that you will need to resort to SQL to manually create queries, sometimes it is instructive to know that you can and how it works.

Creating and Running Action Queries

Besides selection queries, Access provides other types of queries known collectively as *action queries*. Action queries provide a powerful means to make changes to a database's tables. Action queries can create a new table, remove records from an existing table, update one or more fields of an existing table, and add new records to an existing table. Action queries resemble selection queries such as those discussed in the previous section. The major difference is that they *alter* the database in some way, not merely display results from the database. Action queries include Make Table, Update, Delete, Append, and Crosstab.

With a *Make Table* query, you can retrieve a subset of rows from one or more tables and save the dynaset as a table. Perhaps you want to concentrate on the smaller table or you want to export the smaller table to Excel to analyze it further. *Update* queries allow you to change existing database information. You can create or run an update query to increase all programmers' hourly pay rates by 8%, for instance. A *Delete* query selects and removes records from one or more tables. You could run a delete query to purge records of clients who have not contacted your office in over two years. With an *Append* query, you can add new records to an existing table. Finally, a *Crosstab* query summarizes and combines data from more than one source to present a compact, spreadsheet-like result. We present a concise description of how to create and run four of these action query types next.

Make Table Query

You can create a new table from existing tables by using a Make Table query. Suppose you want to create a new table from the *tblCustomers* table that contains only customers from Rhode Island. You can create a Make Table query in one step, but it is better to make a select query, check the dynaset to ensure it is what you expect, turn the select query into a Make Table query, and run the Make Table query. The Try It that follows leads you through the process.

TRY IT

Click the *Create* tab, click *Query Design*, and double-click *tblCustomer* to add that table roster to the Tables panel of the QBE grid. Close the Show Table dialog box. Double-click the following field names to add them to the Field row of the QBE grid: *CustFirstName*, *CustLastName*, *CustAddress*, *CustCity*, *CustState*, and *CustZip*. Click the criteria cell below the CustState column in the QBE grid, type *RI*, and press *Enter*. (Access surrounds the text filter with quotation marks.) Check your results by clicking the View button in the Results group. Six customer rows appear. Click the View button again to return to Design view. Click the Make Table button in the Query Type group, type the new table name *MyRhodeIslandCustomers*, and click *OK*. Click *Save* in the Quick Access Toolbar and type *qmakRiCustomers* to name the query. (The prefix *qmak* indicates the query is a Make Table query.) Now you can run the query to create a new table: In Design view, click *Run* in the Results group (see Figure 4.34). If a warning dialog box indicates "You are about to paste 6 row(s) into a new table," click *Yes* to approve creating the new table. Close the query and then examine the new table MyRhodeIslandCustomers.

After you run the Make Table query, a new table appears among those listed in the Tables group of the Navigation Pane. You can delete the table (you may want to save the query, however) by right-clicking the table name (only when the table is closed, however), and clicking Delete in the pop-up menu.

Update Query

Update queries allow you to make changes to many records in a table in one operation. You can update one field, or you can simultaneously update several fields. Update queries alter individual table fields, replacing them with new values. For instance, suppose you want to make a mid-year adjustment to female employees' commission rates.

Fig. 4.34 Running a Make Table query.

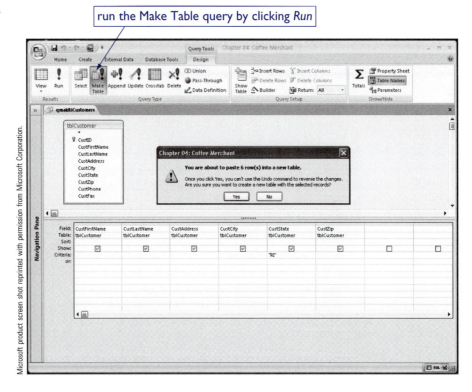

run the Make Table query by clicking *Run*

You've decided that they should receive a 1% raise across the board. (Their male counterparts will have to wait an additional six months to qualify for a raise.) An Update query facilitates changes to the table containing employees' commission rates. Of course, our table is small, but this is an example of the kind of database change that would be laborious if it were done manually, one record at a time. The following activity leads you through making an Update query. In order to not disturb the existing *tblEmployee* table contents, we suggest, in the activity, that you first clone the table and then practice the update on the *copy* of the employee table.

TRY IT

Make a copy of the *tblEmployee* table and call it *MyEmployees*: right-click *tblEmployee*, click *Copy*, right-click the Navigation Pane, click *Paste*, type *MyEmployees*, and click *OK*. Click the *Create* tab, click *Query Design*, and double-click *MyEmployees* to add the table roster to the Tables panel of the QBE grid. Close the Show Table dialog box. Double-click the field names *EmpCommRate* and *EmpGender* to add them to the Field row of the QBE grid. (EmpCommRate will be updated, but EmpGender restricts updated rows to female employees.) In the Criteria row, type "*F*" below the EmpGender column. In the Criteria row, type *<=0.14* below the EmpCommRate column so the update does not violate the table's commission rate validation rule (between zero and 15%). Before proceeding, view the affected records to ensure your selection criteria are in good shape by clicking the *View* button in the Results group. Ten records appear in the datasheet. Switch back to Design view and continue. Click *Update* in the Query Type group. Notice that the QBE grid changes with the addition of a new "Update To" row. In the *Update To* row beneath the EmpCommRate column, type the expression

[EmpCommRate]+0.01 (be sure to enclose EmpCommRate in square brackets). Figure 4.35 shows the design of the completed update query prior to execution. Run the query to update the EmpCommRate field by clicking the *Run* button in the Results group. Click the *Yes* button when the warning dialog box appears indicating "You are about to update 10 row(s)." Close the query and save it under the name *MyUpdateQuery*.

Fig. 4.35 Running an Update query.

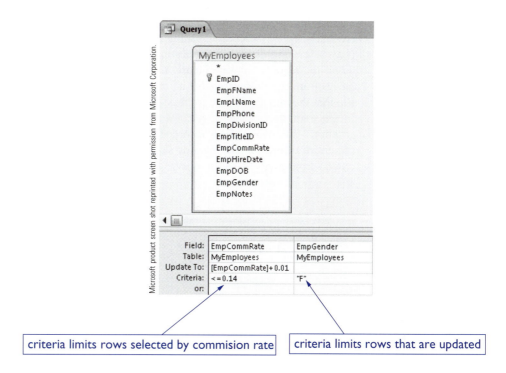

criteria limits rows selected by commision rate   criteria limits rows that are updated

Microsoft product screen shot reprinted with permission from Microsoft Corporation.

If you open the *MyEmployees* table, you'll see that Patti Stonesipher's commission rate has been updated from 5% to 6%. Other female employees' commission rates are 1% higher except Alanis Morrison and Sharon Stonely. These latter two already had a maximum allowed commission rate of 15%. Sorry, ladies!

Beware: Access cannot reverse an update operation when you click Undo. You can undo some update operations by formulating a new Update query to restore updated values, but many update operations are irreversible. For instance, suppose you want to update the location field of an employee's work address to "New York" for all employees whose city is currently Indianapolis. This will move all Indianapolis employees to New York. However, you cannot easily reverse the change if other employees already are listed as living in New York. It is not a matter of changing the DivisionCity field of New York back to Indianapolis, because some are New Yorkers who were never located in Indianapolis in the first place! Always select Datasheet View before running an Update query to check the scope of your changes.

Delete Query

A Delete query is used to delete records from tables. It is not used to delete entire tables. To delete an entire table, you can right-click the table's name in the Navigation Pane and then click Delete from the pop-up menu. Access removes the entire table—structure and data—from the database.

Deleting records is a much more subtle activity, and you must take care to not delete the wrong records. Once deleted, records cannot be retrieved into a table. Suppose, for instance, that you want to remove from the *tblInvoice* table all invoices (and their related *tblInvoiceLines* rows) for any invoices prior to January 1, 2009. A Delete query with the proper selection criteria will do the trick. First, create a Selection query, and then examine its Datasheet view to ensure that proper records appear in the dynaset. Next, change the query's design to a Delete query and run it.

Once you have properly defined a Delete query, simply run it to delete the targeted records. Because *tblInvoice* rows and *tblInvoiceLines* are related and you set "enforce referential integrity" when establishing the relationship between the two tables, Access displays a warning dialog box indicating there are key violations and asks if you want to delete the records anyway. Figure 4.36 shows an example of the Delete query that removes from the *tblInvoice* table all records whose invoice date is prior to 1/1/2009. Notice that the only fields that are needed in the QBE grid are those being used for criteria. In this example, only the InvoiceDate field is required, because that is the sole selection criterion—the invoice dates recorded for the transactions. Of course, Access will delete the entire record for any records satisfying the deletion criteria. *Warning*: if you omit criteria from a table's Delete query, all rows are deleted. Only the structure will remain after such an operation.

Fig. 4.36 A Delete query design.

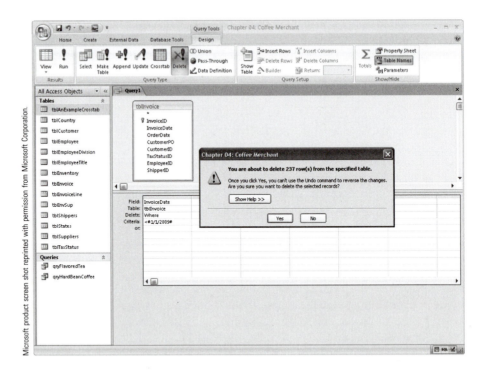

Microsoft product screen shot reprinted with permission from Microsoft Corporation.

Append Query

An Append query adds records from a table or query to the end of another table. For instance, you could use an Append query to create a comprehensive employee table containing all employees in all divisions of a multidivision company. The table *tblEmployee*, for instance, might represent only one division of a larger company coffee conglomerate. By creating an Append query, you can add other divisions' employee records to the *tblEmployee* table.

To create an Append query, simply create a Selection query including fields from the source tables that are in the target (destination) table and any fields that are used as criteria. In the Criteria row of the query, establish the conditions that are used to select records from the other table to append to the current table (for instance, only Division 1 and Division 2 employees). View the potential new records by clicking the Datasheet View button. Then, switch back to Design view and select Append from the Query Type group to turn the Selection query into an Append query. When prompted for the target table name by the Append dialog box, enter the target table's name or select it from the Table Name drop-down list. Click OK to complete the query definition. Figure 4.37 shows an example in which a fictitious division's employee records are to be appended to the *tblEmployee* table.

Fig. 4.37 An Append query design.

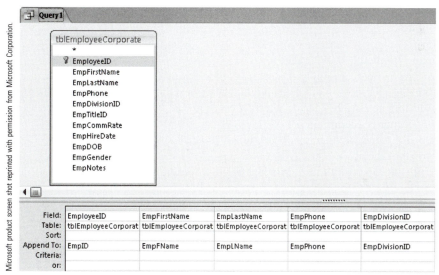

Summary

This chapter has described how to create and run Access queries. Access Select queries retrieve data from one or more tables to produce combined results that display related data fields as well as calculated results derived from table columns. You learned to create queries using wizards and manually. You know how to write and save queries that involve both single and multiple tables coupled using both equijoin and outer join connections. Queries can contain expressions comprised of comparison operators, arithmetic operators, example elements, and wildcard characters. Using queries, you can focus on the data elements important to you. You learned about the one-to-one, one-to-many, and many-to-many relationships that tables can have. You learned about parameter queries, how to create expressions using operators and the Expression Builder, how to incorporate math and other Access built-in functions in expressions, and how to build pivot tables. Occasionally, you need to write queries in their native SQL language. You learned how use a SQL statement in a QBE grid criterion, and you created a query entirely from SQL. Access also support action queries including the Make Table query, Update query, Delete query, and Append query. Unlike select queries, action queries all modify table contents in some way.

Review Questions

Multiple-Choice Questions

1. What are the key differences between action queries and select queries?
   a. Action queries allow you to change data, whereas select queries allow you to view data from multiple tables or queries.
   b. Selection queries allow you to select and change data, whereas action queries allow you to only look at data.
   c. Action queries allow you to retrieve and display data from multiple tables, whereas select queries allow you to select, create, and delete data.
   d. All of the above.

2. There are five views available for queries. The four views are (in no particular order)
   a. Design, Parameter, Datasheet, Pivot, and SQL.
   b. Datasheet, PivotTable, PivotChart, Design, and SQL.
   c. PivotTable, PivotChart, SQL, Parameter, and Design.
   d. None of the above.

3. No relational database, including Access, can deal with this type of inter-table relationship directly.
   a. one-to-one
   b. one-to-many
   c. many-to-many
   d. Access and other relational databases *can* deal with all of the preceding relationships.

4. To build a query in Design view, minimally you need to do what?
   a. Add the tables to be included in the query and drag the fields to be returned to the QEB.
   b. Enter your selection criteria.
   c. Open the query in Datasheet view to see the results.
   d. Do all of the above.

5. What field property allows you to control what value appears in a field if the user doesn't enter it?
   a. caption
   b. default value
   c. indexed
   d. input mask

6. What type of query correlates values between two or more sets of field values?
   a. crosstab
   b. parameter
   c. sql
   d. update

7. When writing expressions to perform calculations in queries, table fields are referenced by enclosing the field name in
   a. parenthesis ().
   b. brackets [].
   c. quotes "".
   d. pound signs ##.

8. Using an _____ will list all rows from one table and only matching rows from another table.
   a. inter join
   b. intra join
   c. outer join
   d. in line join

9. What clause in the SQL statement filters (provides the criteria) rows, limiting the dynaset to those that satisfy the filter?
   a. SELECT.
   b. FROM.
   c. WHERE.
   d. ORDER BY.

10. What is the advantage of using a parameter query over conventional queries?
    a. It is more versatile.
    b. Selection criteria is specified when the query is run.
    c. It provides varied results based on criteria entered.
    d. All of the above.

Discussion Questions

1. Discuss the problem with storing an extended price (an invoice item quantity multiplied by an item's wholesale or retail price) in the *tblInvoiceLine* table. Why could you not simply add a column called ExtendedPrice to the *tblInvoiceLine* table?

2. Discuss the advantages of an outer join query. Give an example, different from the one used in the textbook, of using an outer join to display information from two tables related in a query with an outer join. What role does the expression "Is Null" serve in outer join queries?

3. Suppose a table *tblStudents* contains the first and last names of students and that *tblClassRosters* contains the list of students enrolled in each class in the university. Discuss the relationship between *tblStudents* and *tblClassRosters*. Is it 1–1, 1–M (or vice versa), or M–M? Are there any problems representing the relationship of these two tables to one another?

4. What is the main advantage of an Access pivot table query when compared to a crosstab query?

5. Discuss how you would formulate a query to return the name and address of anyone from Idaho who has ordered anything in the last six months. For this question, assume there is an additional table called *tblOrders* with these fields: OrderID, CustID, OrderDate, TaxStatus, EmpID, and CustPO. They contain just what you think (left to right): a primary key, the related customer making the order, the order date, retail or wholesale indicator, the ID of the employee taking the order, and the customer's purchase order number.

Practice Exercises

1. Create a query that lists all inventory items on hand (*not* out of stock) whose price is greater than $9.99. Make sure the dynaset includes InventoryID, ItemName, UnitPrice, and UnitsOnHand. Sort the results in descending order by UnitPrice. Ensure that the ItemName column is wide enough to display each item name. Print the dynaset and then write your name at the top.

2. Create a query to count the number of invoices for each customer. Display the customer's first name, last name, and count of their orders in descending order by the count and ascending order by last name among matching count values. Display in the dynaset the top 15 customers by count. Assign new column aliases (Caption property) as follows: *First Name*, *Last Name*, and *Invoice Count*. Ensure the dynaset columns are wide enough to display the column names and data. Print the dynaset and write your name at the top.

3. Create a query joining tables, *tblCountry* and *tblInventory*. Display the table columns ItemName, Beverage, CountryName, and Comments. Include only Brazil and Colombia in the result. Sort by CountryName in descending order. Assign the column aliases of *Product*, *Item Type*, and *Country* to the first three columns. Ensure the Product, Item Type, and Country columns are wide enough to display the widest of their results. Widen the Comment column, but only to about 35 characters. Print the dynaset.

4. List all products that are out of stock (UnitsOnHand) *or* have more than 4000 items in stock. (This is a "too little or too much" query.) In the dynaset display InventoryID, ItemName, and UnitsOnHand. Add column aliases as follows: *Item Number*, *Product*, *Qty In Stock*. Sort the dynaset in ascending order by the UnitsOnHand value. Optimize column widths so everything—labels and data—is visible. Print the dynaset results and write your name at the top.

5. Modify the Try It exercise that generated a new table of Rhode Island customers by changing it into a parameter query. Change the CustState criteria to allow the user to run the make table query, type in any state abbreviation, and generate a new table of that state's customers. Of course, the new table will replace the contents of the old one, and a warning dialog box will appear asking if it is okay to replace the table. Print the new table you created.

Problems

1. Create and run a query that displays all employees from the employee table who have the title *Senior Sales Associate*. This requires that you join related tables and select columns from all them but display only some of the columns. In the dynaset display each qualifying employee's last name, gender, city, and state where they work (arrange columns left to right in this way). Sort the dynaset in ascending order by state and then by last name within each state group. Assign aliases to the column as follows: *Name*, *Gender*, *Work City*, and *Work State*. Optimize the dynaset column widths. Print the resulting dynaset and write your name on the output.

2. You want to examine the invoices issued in November 2008 in order by date. You are interested only in general information. To answer this question, form a query that joins at Coffee Merchant tables. (See Figure 4.2 to decide which tables you need in the query.) Display the customers' first and last names, invoice dates, and invoice numbers (InvoiceID) for invoices issued during the month of November 2008. Sort the dynaset in ascending order by invoice date and then by customer last name among the matching invoice dates. Change the caption of CustFirstName and CustLastName to *First Name* and *Last Name*, respectively. Ensure columns are sufficiently wide for all results and column labels. Print all pages and write your name on all pages.

3. Write a query that displays the seven most densely populated states in the United States. Use criteria to eliminate the District of Columbia from the dynaset. Include in the dynaset the full state name, the abbreviated state name, and the density—a calculated field (people per square mile). Assign the column alias *Density* to the population density column. Format the Density column so that it displays figures with commas and two decimal places. Sort the dynaset in descending order by Density. (*Hint*: The table *tblStates* contains state names, populations, and area (in square miles) of each state. Open the Property Sheet and then click in the Tables area of the query design to locate and set the Top Values property.) Print the dynaset and write your name on it.

4. Create and run a query that produces invoice information from the following Coffee Merchant's tables: *tblCustomer*, *tblEmployee*, *tblInvoice*, *tblInvoiceLine*, and *tblInventory*. Display the following columns: InvoiceID, InventoryID, Quantity, UnitPrice (from the tblInvoiceLine table), Discount, InvoiceDate, OrderDate, CustID, and EmpLName. Write the expression for extended price shown in this chapter so many times (remember to use the Round function too) and rename the expression column to *Extended Price*. Format the Extended Price column to display the Currency format with two decimal places. Sort the dynaset in descending order by Extended Price. Using the Property Sheet, set up the query properties so that only the first 35 rows appear (Top Values). (Thirty six rows appear because there is a tie value in the Extended Price column.) Use Page Setup to print in landscape instead of the default, portrait. Adjust the margins so that all columns appear on a given page. You may have to narrow some output columns or set the Margins to the Narrow choice in the Page Layout group. *Beware*: The output is very long, so **print only the first three pages**. Write your name on all three pages.

5. The boss has decided to split the table *tblInventory* into one for teas and one for coffees, dropping the "beverage" field in the process. Write two Make Table queries to split the table, making a coffee-only table called *tblCoffee* and a tea-only table called *tblTea*. Run the Make Table queries, and then print the two tables.

6. Create and print a pivot table query. It summarizes employee invoice shipments by carrier by counting shipments by employee/carrier pairs. Form a query that joins *tblEmployee*, *tblInvoice*, and *tblShippers*. Include the fields EmpLName, Company (*tblShippers*), and InvoiceID, which is the field you will ask Access to count. In PivotTable View, place EmpLName on the Row Field area, place Company on the Column Fields area, and place InvoiceID in the Detail area. Ensure that counts appear in the data field, not sums. Eliminate details so only counts appear in the pivot table. Finally, display results only for DHL Express and FedEx in the Column area. Print the pivot table.

CHAPTER 5

Creating and Using Forms

CHAPTER OBJECTIVES

This chapter extends your Access knowledge by providing detailed information about Microsoft Access forms. You will learn about the advantages of using forms and about defining and using accounting forms. Throughout this chapter, exercises emphasize Microsoft Access techniques critical to building accounting information systems. Like the chapters before it, this chapter is application-oriented and contains very little theory. Exercises actively engage you in using the theory you learned earlier to create typical accounting forms and reports. In particular, you will learn how to:

- **Put forms to work in a variety of accounting applications.**

- **Create a form with formatted fields and aesthetic enhancements.**

- **Add controls including a label, text box, and drop-down list box to a form.**

- **Build forms and associated subforms from queries and tables.**

We continue using The Coffee Merchant's database system as this chapter's backdrop application. The database for this chapter contains the objects you need to do all the exercises in this chapter. It is found on this book's companion Web site and is called Ch05.accdb. Go to the book's South-Western, Cengage Learning Web site, www.cengage.com/accounting/perry, for all the book's database files.

Putting Forms to Work

Forms display information from one or more tables in an easily understood, attractive format on a computer screen. Unlike the Datasheet view of a table, a Form window can show one row of a table at a time. Another advantage of a form over a Datasheet view of a table is that you can design a database form to resemble any of a company's paper forms. When database forms match paper forms, the computer forms are almost always intuitive and familiar to those using them. Because the computer forms look familiar, they are not intimidating to new computer users. Forms are the primary interface between users and database applications. As far as your users know, forms are the application—not the tables and other objects that are behind the scenes. Forms can be used to store information and pass it from one form to another or from one phase of your application to the next.

Forms can have a plain but functional design, or they can be elaborate, with drop-down lists, built-in help, attractive field designs, graphics, and buttons that activate predefined activities when users click them. Forms, like queries, do not store any information. They simply display information retrieved from one or more tables. Data exhibited in a form can be retrieved from a single table or from multiple tables joined on a common key field. Forms can also display data directly from a query of arbitrary complexity. Any of the queries we created in Chapter 4 could be the basis of a form.

Forms provide a convenient way to control application flow and organize your database application. Using command buttons on a form, you can create macros or code (VBA) that automate all major database procedures. When a user clicks one of the buttons, it activates a procedure such as producing a report or displaying invoices. Forms can contain code that runs when a specific event occurs. For example, you can easily create code, stored with one of your forms, that performs a specific action when someone clicks a button, opens a form, or moves to a particular text box on a form.

Forms are a particularly attractive and effective way to maintain complete control over the data users enter into a database. For example, you could create a form for entering new information into an invoice table. The new form contains a feature that can prevent a user from entering an already-assigned invoice ID number or entering an unreasonable value for a unit cost field. You can provide these types of data consistency checks as part of the logic of a form. Such checks are far more versatile and robust than the elementary table property checks. Figure 5.1 shows an example of an inventory input form.

Forms are by far the most widely used interface for entering, editing, and checking database information. You can use forms to add, change, or delete information from one or several tables at once. Forms allow you to lock selected table fields to prevent their alteration. Other options allow forms to fill in values with default and calculated values based on other entries the user makes.

Creating forms that display the progress of a database application is an effective way to communicate with the user. During a particularly lengthy database update process, for example, you can display a form that contains a progress chart indicating how far along the update operation is. Forms are one way to display informative messages such as warnings or error conditions in various parts of the database. Although forms are designed primarily for viewing on a screen, you can print them. An invoice form can serve the dual role of input and output. Data entry personnel can use a form to enter invoice information, and accounts receivable personnel can use the same form to generate individual invoices to mail to customers. The differences between the input form and the printed form may be slight. An input form may have different headers and footers—one for the customers and one for the company's data entry personnel.

Fig. 5.1 Example data entry form.

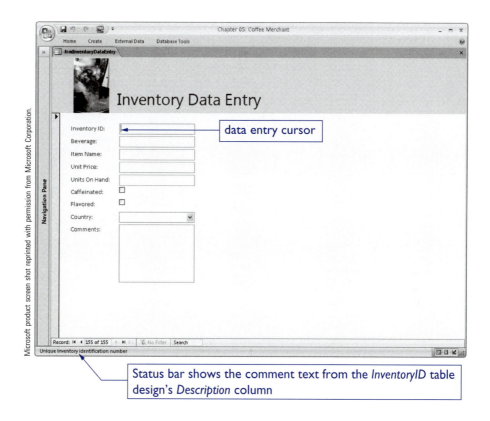

Viewing Form Types

You can create several different types of forms either manually or by using the Form Wizard. Normally, the Form Wizard is your best choice for creating most forms—at least until you become comfortable with creating forms.

A form can contain several sections, or subdivisions. These include the Page Header and Page Footer sections, Form Header and Form Footer sections, the Detail section, and any number of Group Header and Group Footer sections. Headers or footers for each section are independent of each other. That is, a Page Header may appear in a form without its corresponding Page Footer. Similarly, a form may contain a Group Header listing the department to which a list of employees belongs but no Group Footer. As you have probably guessed, Page Headers and Footers occur at the beginning and ending of each page, respectively. Likewise, a Form Header appears at the top of each form, and a Form Footer appears at the bottom of each form—regardless of whether a form is displayed or printed. The Detail section contains information from the database and labels to identify individual items. Typically, information in the Detail section is variable, because the information there is obtained from queries and tables in the database. Figure 5.2 shows an example of a form containing Header, Detail, and Footer sections. Unless you view a multipage printout of forms, it is difficult to distinguish a form's Page Header from a Form Header.

A form type that is particularly useful for browsing through several records at once is a ***multiple items form***. A multiple items form displays several records simultaneously on one form. The form resembles a spreadsheet, because labels appear at the top of each field and row selectors appear on the left side of each record. Figure 5.2 is an example of a multiple items form showing all of the fields of several employee records. To view

Fig. 5.2 Example form with Page Header, Detail, and Page Footer sections.

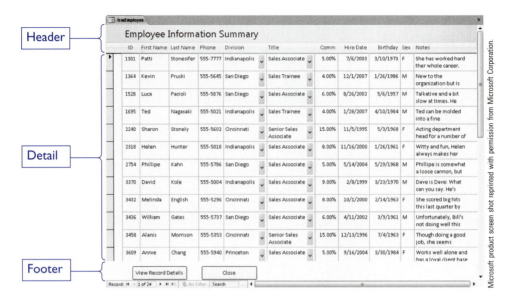

the remaining records, you click the scroll bar on the right side of the form or you can click the record number box and navigation buttons in the lower left portion of the form.

Periodically in a database application it is helpful to have a window that remains the topmost window on the Windows desktop. Known as a *modal dialog box*, it is really a form. It might display an opening statement the first time you open a database file, or a modal dialog box might provide users with information about the person who developed the database application. Unlike most windows, a modal dialog box remains the topmost window, regardless of which other windows you activate on your desktop. This is especially useful to ensure that the database user reads the important information found in the modal dialog box (form). Modal dialog boxes always contain a button—usually labeled OK—that, when clicked, closes the dialog box. Unlike other access forms, a modal dialog box requires a response before the user can continue working on any other part of the application. Figure 5.3 shows an example of a modal dialog box.

Fig. 5.3 A modal dialog box example displaying developer contact information.

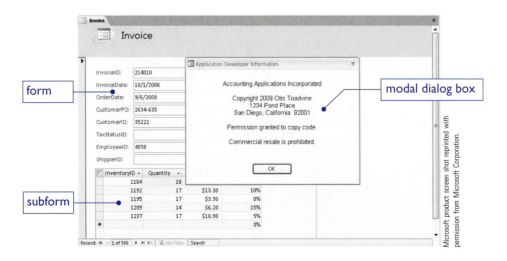

A *split form* has two sections with the top half displaying a standard form and the bottom half displaying a datasheet. Both display the same data. A split form provides the combined advantages of a datasheet—navigation speed, for example—with the advantages of a form—including a nicer and more intuitive design. Clicking in the datasheet portion of the split form displays the corresponding row in the form above the datasheet. A change made in one of the two sections appears simultaneously in the other. Figure 5.4 shows an example split form displaying information from the customer table, *tblCustomer*.

Fig. 5.4 Example split form.

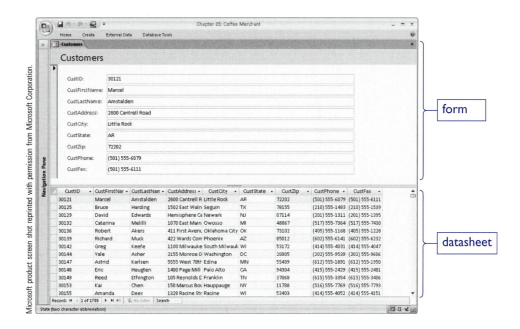

Another ubiquitous form you'll encounter is a form and its related subform. A *subform* is especially useful when you want to display information on the "many" side of a one-to-many relationship. For example, a subform is a perfect way to display invoice lines that make up a larger form that is the entire invoice. An invoice's main form displays customer information, while a subform displays details about the line items. You will see several examples of this form/subform relationship in this chapter—particularly when you create invoice forms by following this chapter's exercises. Figure 5.5 shows a form and subform example.

We begin our exploration of forms and their utility by creating a rather simple form from a single table. Then we will create a form whose data is derived from multiple related tables. The last form will be created from a query.

Building a Form

Creating forms is greatly simplified in Access 2007. As in earlier versions, you can create a form from scratch using Design view tools, or you can use a wizard. If you have simpler needs and you don't want to spend the time tweaking and fiddling in Design view, Access 2007 provides a streamlined form design layout called Layout view. Layout view eliminates a lot of the Design view alignment and object movement required in earlier versions. You will see just how handy Layout view is when you create a form.

Fig. 5.5 Example
form and subform.

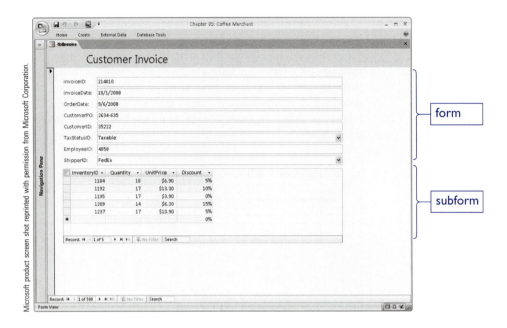

Building a Standard Form

We begin by building a form based on a single table very quickly. A form provides a much more intuitive interface in which to review, update, and create records. Let's build a form based on the table *tblCustomer*.

EXERCISE 5.1: CREATING A ONE-TABLE FORM

1. Click tblCustomer in the Tables group of the Navigation Pane to highlight the table name.
2. Click the Create tab and click MoreForms in the Forms group and then click Form Wizard. The first of a few Form Wizard dialog boxes appears.
3. The available fields in the *tblCustomer* table appear in the *Available Fields* panel. Click the >> button to send all available table fields to the *Selected Fields* panel (see Figure 5.6).
4. Click the Finish button to complete the automated building process, because you don't need to make any other adjustments in subsequent Form Wizard steps for now. Access displays the newly created form containing the first table record (see Figure 5.7).
5. Right-click the tblCustomer form tab and click Close in the pop-up menu to close the form.

Notice that the first row of the *tblCustomer* table appears with each of its fields named the same way as the column names. The form navigation buttons appear along the bottom. The navigation buttons move from one customer record to another. The *current record* indicator that appears between the previous and next buttons among the record navigation buttons indicates both the current record and the total records in the table—1789 in this case.

Fig. 5.6 Creating a form using the Form Wizard.

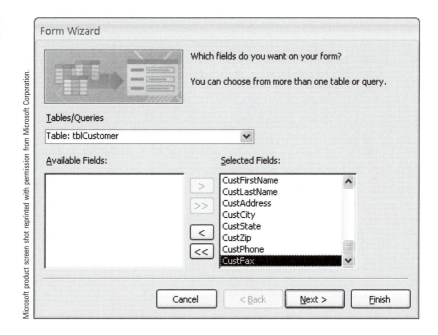

Fig. 5.7 Completed customer form.

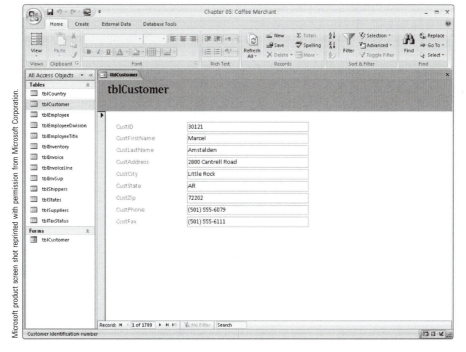

Notice that Access automatically saves the form under the same name as the table: *tblCustomer*. You can rename it easily by doing the Try It exercise that follows.

TRY IT

Right-click *tblCustomer* in the Forms group and click *Rename* in the pop-up menu. Then, type *MyCustomer1* and press *Enter* to change the form's name in the Navigation Pane.

One of the easy ways to create a form to enter or examine data in a table is by using the Form Wizard. However, your form is limited to what the wizard creates. You can subsequently alter the default form to suit your needs, making it more attractive and functional by adding graphic elements, rearranging fields, modifying field labels, and so on.

One of the fundamental operations you will use in the Form design window is moving and sizing fields and other form objects. When you select an object in Design view or the new Layout view, the object appears within a golden rectangle. In Design view, the selected object has a sizing handle on its right end that allows you to reduce or enlarge the object. To enlarge the object, drag its sizing handle to the right; reduce it by dragging the sizing handle to the left. In Layout view, the surrounded object does not have a sizing handle. However, you can change the object's height or width by pointing the mouse at any golden border. Once the mouse pointer becomes a double-headed arrow, drag it away from the object's center to enlarge it or toward the center to make it smaller in the dimension dragged. For example, hovering over the right end of the object and dragging to the left makes the object narrower. We suggest you resize any object or objects in Layout view, because record values appear in the fields and you can tell when a field will be too small or too large for typical, real field values. In Design view, you cannot tell whether a resized field is not sized well.

You can resize several objects by clicking the object, hovering the mouse over the top edge of the selected object until it becomes a down-pointing arrow, and then clicking the mouse to select the column of objects—either labels or data fields. Once selected, you can resize them and dragging the edge of the group (up, down, left, or right). Next, you will modify the default form you created above by changing its title found in the form's header.

EXERCISE 5.2: ALTERING A FORM'S TITLE AND CHANGING ITS FIELD LABELS

1. Right-click MyCustomer1 in the Navigation Pane and click Layout View in the pop-up menu. The form appears in Layout view. Notice the Select All button in the upper-left corner of the form near the CustID label. Clicking it selects all form objects: labels and data fields.
2. Click on the label tblCustomer in the header area above the form. A golden rectangle surrounds the label.
3. Click inside the tblCustomer header to create a vertical insertion style mouse pointer. Click and drag the entire label to select it, type Customers, and press Enter to complete the title change.
4. Next, you will change the field labels slightly from their field names to more readable names: Click the CustID label twice to create a vertical bar insertion style cursor. Drag the mouse through the entire label to highlight it, then type ID and press Enter to complete the change.
5. Click the label CustFirstName, click CustFirstName again to establish an insertion cursor inside the label, drag through the entire label, type First Name, and press Enter.
6. Repeat step 5 to change label for *CustLastName* to *Last Name*.
7. Repeat step 5 to drop the prefix "Cust" from the remaining six labels. Your finished form should resemble the one shown in Figure 5.8 (shown in Form view).
8. Save and then close the altered customer form.

Fig. 5.8 Altered customer form.

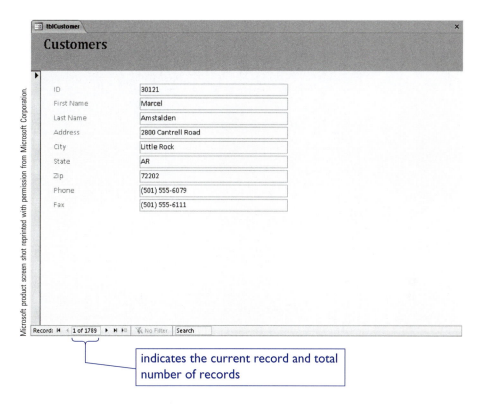

indicates the current record and total number of records

Building a Split Form

Split forms let you rapidly navigate the records in a table as well as view a record's data in an intuitive form. Use the datasheet portion of a split form to scroll through records. Use the form to modify or view a record once you locate it in the datasheet. Let's create a split form and use it to experience how handy it is.

EXERCISE 5.3: CREATING A SPLIT FORM AND NAVIGATING THROUGH ITS RECORDS

1. In the Navigation Pane, click the table name tblEmployee in the Tables group to highlight it.
2. Click the Create tab and then click Split Form in the Forms group. Access quickly creates a split form, in Layout view, with a form in the upper pane and a datasheet in the lower pane.
3. Right-click the tblEmployee tab of the newly displayed split form, and then click Form View in the pop-up menu to change to that view (see Figure 5.9).
4. In the Datasheet pane, click the EmpID field containing 4012 and corresponding to Barbara Minsky's record. (You will have to drag the vertical scroll bar down to locate that record.) The Form pane displays the newly selected record also.
5. Right-click the tblEmployee tab, click Save in the pop-up menu, type MySplitForm in the Form Name text box, and click OK to name and save the split form.
6. Right-click the MySplitForm tab (naming the form changes the tab name too) and click Close All in the pop-up menu to close the new form and any other open objects.

Fig. 5.9 A split form.

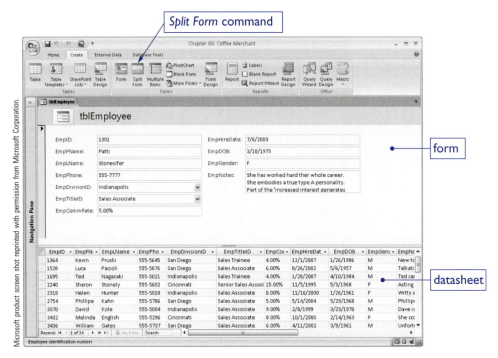

Normally, you would modify the split form by changing the field labels and altering the form header from *tblEmployee*. The important point is that the Split Form Wizard creates the starting point for a form that you can modify to suit your needs. The rudimentary split form saves you a lot of work that would be required if you decided to create it from scratch with Design view.

Building a Multiple Items Form

A multiple items form is another hybrid of a form and a datasheet. The form has a tabular layout similar to a datasheet with multiple rows displayed on the form instead of only one. The field headings appear along the top of the form. Unlike a datasheet, a multiple items form can display up to three lines of data for each record. Create one using the Multiple Items Form wizard next.

EXERCISE 5.4: CREATING A MULTIPLE ITEMS FORM AND NAVIGATING THROUGH ITS RECORDS

1. In the Navigation Pane, click the table name tblStates in the Tables group to highlight it.
2. Click the Create tab and then click Multiple Items in the Forms group. Access quickly creates a multiple items form and displays it in Layout view.
3. Click the header text tblStates to select the object and then click again to display the edit cursor within the label. Drag through the tbl prefix and press Delete to remove it. Click outside the label to deselect the object.
4. Click the column label StateID, click it again to display the edit cursor, and place a space between *State* and *ID*.

5. Repeat Step 5, placing spaces between the words in the column labels *StateName, StateTaxRate, StatePopulation,* and *StateSize.*
6. Click Form View in the Views group of the Home tab to display the form in Form view (see Figure 5.10).
7. Right-click the tblStates tab, click Save in the pop-up menu, type MyMultipleItemsForm in the Form Name text box, and click OK to name and save the form.
8. Right-click the MyMultipleItemsForm tab and click Close in the pop-up menu to close the form.

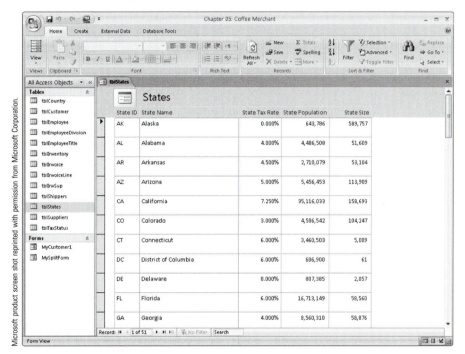

Fig. 5.10 A multiple items form.

Microsoft product screen shot reprinted with permission from Microsoft Corporation.

In addition to the three form types discussed above, you can create a blank form, a pivot table, or choose to create an empty form in Design view for a particular table. We do suggest you avoid these form types until you become more comfortable with Access generally and form building specifically. Let the wizards give you a head start and then modify the default forms they produce.

Guidelines for Good Form Design

The people who will be using the forms you create should be uppermost in your mind as you design the forms. Here are some guidelines to remember to help you do that.

- *Make forms robust and bulletproof. Use list boxes, radio buttons, and other controls to simplify the choices available to form users and to reduce the errors.*
- *Keep keyboard users in mind. Many people prefer using the keyboard and limit the use of the mouse to form selection. Keeping one's hands on the keyboard can be more*

efficient when filling out a form and navigating through it. Switching back and forth between a mouse and the keyboard can slow the data entry process.

- *Keep the form colors to a minimum. This probably doesn't require much explanation. Too many colors can confuse and distract users.*
- *Group controls into logical units. Forms have families of related controls such as the group consisting of name and address. Another group on an invoice is the vendor information. Another group is the collection of invoice line items. Keep controls in the same family grouped together, and alter the tab order so that pressing the tab key visits all members of one group before going to the next one.*
- *Identify controls and include help. Make the meaning of a field clear as well as its format. For example, it is frustrating to try to determine what format the date should be. Is it "MM/DD/YYYY" or is it "YYYY/MM/DD" (European). Identify the field, for example, as the* Invoice Date *or the* Purchase Date *and then include the format in an automatically generated tool tip (e.g., "enter mm/dd/yyyy").*
- *Make forms similar to their paper-form counterparts when necessary. Access form fields, form layout, and design that is consistent with previously used paper forms make the electronic versions instantly intuitive to new users. They are familiar with the paper version, therefore the electronic version, they reason, must be the same or similar.*

If you remember the preceding simple guidelines as you design forms, you'll find the people that use your forms will be less likely to call the help desk with form questions, and the form users will be happier with your form designs.

Creating Basic Forms Using the Form Wizard

Using the Form Wizard is usually the best choice to create a form. The Form Wizard is slightly better than the Form, Split Form, or Multiple Items choices on the Forms group of the Create tab because you have more control over the content and placement of controls on the form. Still, the Form Wizard may not produce the exact look and feel of a form that you wanted. Later, you can choose to modify the Form Wizard-created form by altering it in Design view. Creating a form using the Form Wizard is a popular choice, so let's see how that works.

EXERCISE 5.5: USING THE FORM WIZARD TO CREATE A BASIC FORM

1. Click the Create tab, click the More Forms list box in the Forms group, and click Form Wizard. The first Form Wizard dialog box appears.
2. Click the Tables/Queries list box arrow and then click Table: tblInventory from the list to select that table and its fields as the basis of your developing form.
3. Click the double greater than button (>>) to move all fields from the *Available Fields* list to the *Selected Fields* list. Only the fields you move to the Selected Fields list are included in the form.
4. Click the Next button to move to the next step. Leave the suggested *Columnar* radio button selected. Click Next to move to the style dialog box. Click Foundry form the style list, and then click Next to move to the last step. Click the What title do you want for your form? text box twice to select its entire text, *tblInventory*, and then type MyInventory to modify the form's title and its object name.
5. Click the Finish button to complete the form-building process. Access completes and then displays the form in Form view (see Figure 5.11).

Fig. 5.11 A form created by the Form Wizard.

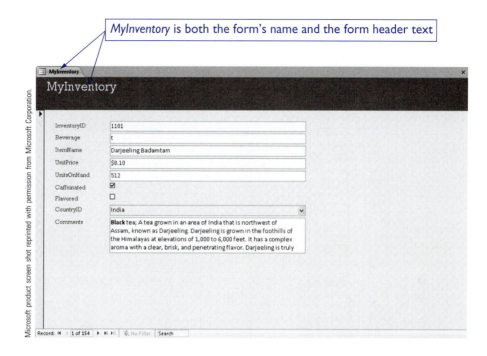

MyInventory is both the form's name and the form header text

Creating a Form from Scratch in Design View

The Form Wizard is a terrific tool for creating a default form for any table you select. However, the Form Wizard isn't always the best choice when you want to create an Access form that matches an existing paper form—a form with which people in a company are familiar. Using an Access form that closely matches an organization's paper form makes filling out the Access form intuitive and immediately makes users comfortable with the electronic form. If you seek the greatest flexibility in creating a form, then creating a form in Design view is the best choice. Recognize that one disadvantage of creating a form in Design view is that it can be tedious and time-consuming. Among its biggest advantages, Design view provides you with complete control over the type, position, and behavior of every form control. Simultaneously, you have to specify each and every control and its behavior. To illustrate the process, you will create a form from scratch—starting with a blank form in Design view—and add table fields as required.

EXERCISE 5.6: CREATING A BLANK FORM IN DESIGN VIEW

1. Click the Create tab, click Blank Form in the Forms group, click the View list box in the Views group of the Format contextual tab, and click Design View. A blank form opens with a Field List pane open on the right side of the screen. (If the Field List pane is not open, then press Alt+F8.)
2. To display or hide a background grid on the empty form, click the Arrange contextual tab and then click the Grid command in the Show/Hide group (see Figure 5.12). The Grid command is a toggle, so click it, if necessary, to display the form's grid.

With an empty form, you must next tell Access which table and fields to choose to populate the form. You do that by placing table fields on the empty form. Access automatically binds the controls on the form to the appropriate database fields. A form field

Fig. 5.12 A blank
form with its grid
displayed.

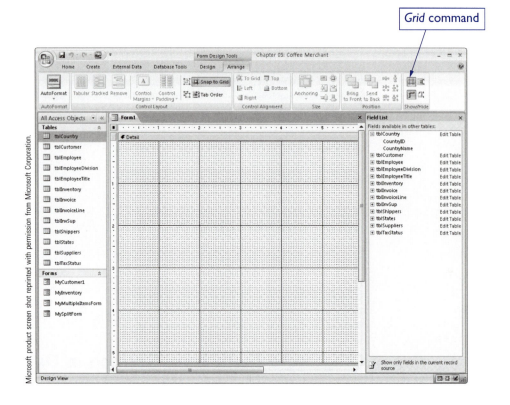

that displays a field from a table or a query is called ***bound control***. The other two types
of form controls are unbound controls and calculated controls. An ***unbound control*** is
independent of any database field. Examples are a form's title or a field label. An unbound control remains constant regardless of the record being displayed. A ***calculated
control*** uses an expression to derive its data. Expressions include combinations of fields,
operators (addition, subtraction, etc.), control names, functions, and constants. For example, a control to calculate sales tax based on another form control holding the purchase total is a common example of a calculated control.

Next, you will populate the empty form with bound controls from one of the existing
Coffee Merchant tables. Placing the controls on an empty form is a matter of selecting
the field and then double-clicking it to place it in a default location.

EXERCISE 5.7: PLACING BOUND CONTROLS ON A FORM

1. With the blank form open in Design view, click the + expansion indicator next to
   the *tblShippers* name in the Field List panel to display the tables field names.
2. Double-click the following fields, in turn, to place them on the blank form: ID,
   Company, Address, City, State, and ZipCode. Access places these controls on the
   blank form, binding them to their corresponding *tblShippers* table fields. Access
   arranges the label and text box pairs in a vertical arrangement.
3. Click the Add Existing Fields command in the Tools group of the Design
   contextual tab to close the Field List pane. (You also can click the X in the Field
   List pane title bar to close it.)

Adding a Title to a Form

A title, new to Access 2007, provides users with a quick reference as to the form's use. Appearing in the form's header, a title is easy to add: You simply click Title in the Controls group of the Design contextual tab to place a title in the form's header. You do that next.

EXERCISE 5.8: ADDING A TITLE TO A FORM

1. With the form still open in Design view, click the Title button in the Controls group of the Design contextual tab. Access opens up the form header band and places a default title ("Form1") in it.
2. With the default title text highlighted, type Preferred Shippers and then press Enter to alter the title.

The title appearing in the Form Header portion of the form identifies the data as that of The Coffee Merchant's preferred shippers. Some of the fields from the *tblShippers* table are absent from this form, so it is not a form you can use to update the shippers information. The last step to finish this small form is to add a corporate logo to the form.

Adding a Logo to a Form

Adding a logo to a form identifies the form as that of the company to which it belongs and adds visual appeal. Different logos can be used on distinct forms depending on each form's use. In this small example, we add a simple picture of a coffee bag as the logo for this preferred shipper form.

EXERCISE 5.9: ADDING A LOGO TO A FORM

1. With the form still open in Design view, click the Logo button in the Controls group of the Design contextual tab. Access opens an Insert Picture dialog box allowing you to navigate to the folder containing the logo.
2. Using the Look in list box, navigate to the folder containing the Chapter 5 database, click CoffeeBag (CoffeeBag.jpg if you have the extensions displayed on your computer), and click OK. Access inserts the picture into an image control (an unbound control) in the form header (see Figure 5.13).

With these changes made, it is time to save the form and name it properly. A well-named form makes its use more obvious to end users.

EXERCISE 5.10: SAVING AND NAMING A NEW FORM

1. Right-click the form's tab (probably named "Form1"), click Save in the pop-up list, and type MyShipperForm, and click OK to save and name the new form. The new form's name appears in the Navigation Pane under the Forms group.
2. Right-click the MyShipperForm tab and click Close All to close this form and any other objects that may be open.

Fig. 5.13 Form with
bound controls, title,
and logo (Design view).

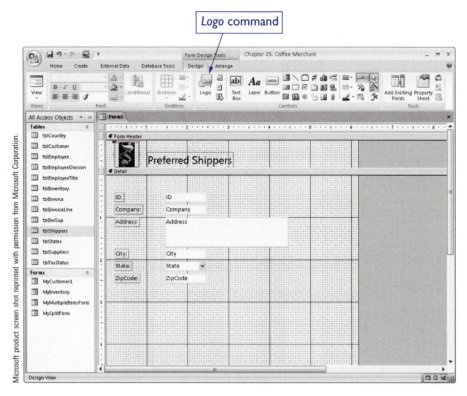

After creating a form from scratch or even modifying it slightly, you should display the form in Form view so you can check its design. Looking at a form from a user's perspective can reveal design mistakes, if any.

EXERCISE 5.11: OPENING THE FORM IN FORM VIEW AND THEN LAYOUT VIEW TO ALTER IT

1. Double-click MyShipperForm in the Navigation Pane to open it in Form view. Click the Next record navigation button repeatedly to view all four supplier records. Notice that the Company field is too short to display the complete names for records 3 and 4. Let's correct this.
2. Right-click the MyShipperForm window tab and then click Layout View in the pop-up menu. Using the record navigation buttons at the bottom of the form, go to record 4, USPS: United States Postal Service. Click the Company bound control—the one displaying the company name, move the mouse to the right edge of the golden rectangle until the mouse becomes a double-headed arrow. Click and drag the mouse to the right until the entire company name is visible (see Figure 5.14).
3. Save and close the form.

This is the first hint you have that the Layout view is especially helpful when you want to ensure that the bound data will display properly in the controls. This is neither easy nor convenient in Design view.

Fig. 5.14 Resizing a control in Layout view.

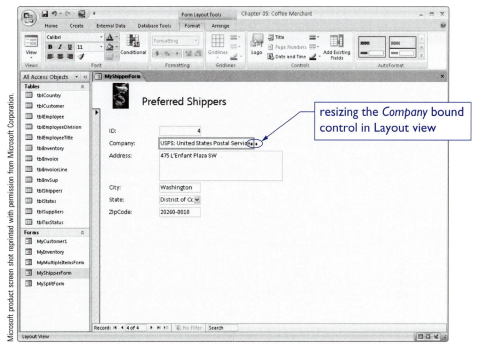

Navigating a Form

You can navigate from control to control on a form in several different ways. In addition, you have experienced briefly navigating from one record to the next. There are several ways to navigate within fields on a form. Pressing the Enter key stores any data you have typed or updated and moves to the next field. (In programming, this is often called moving the *focus*.) Pressing the Tab is another way to move from one field to another in a form. Holding down the Shift key and pressing the Tab key moves in reverse order in the form.

The order in which the fields and buttons get the focus when you press Tab is called the form's ***tab order***. Occasionally, the form's tab order is not what you expected and controls receive the focus in seemingly random order when you repeatedly press the Tab key. The tab order of the form you just created is fine, because the order is initially determined by the order in which the controls are placed on the form. However, the tab order can become unacceptable if you move controls around on the form. It is simple in Access to rearrange the tab order to your satisfaction. Let's modify the previous form to illustrate this concept.

EXERCISE 5.12: MODIFYING THE TAB ORDER OF A FORM'S CONTROLS

1. Right-click MyShipperForm in the Navigation Pane and click Design View to display it in Design view.
2. Click the ID text box control so it is surrounded by a golden rectangle. Notice the label associated with the text box has a move handle (large square) and is selected also.

3. Drag the Form Footer band down to make more space in the Detail area: Move the mouse to the Form Footer band. When it becomes a double-headed arrow, click and drag it down about one-quarter inch.

4. Move the mouse over the selected ID text box. When it becomes a four-headed arrow, drag the control down below the ZipCode text box, aligning the two text boxes as best as possible. Release the mouse to finalize the position of the ID label and text box.

5. Click View in the Views group of the Design contextual tab to display the form in Form view. Notice that the focus is placed on the newly moved ID control, not on the first control corresponding to the Company name.

6. Display the form in Design view. Click the Arrange contextual tab, and then click Tab Order in the Control Layout group. The Tab Order dialog box, which allows you to easily alter the controls' tab orders, appears (see Figure 5.15).

7. Click Auto Order to reorder the Tab Orders to match the form layout—top to bottom—and click OK to close the dialog box.

8. Right-click the MyShipperForm tab and click Form View. Notice the form's focus begins in the Company text box. Press Tab repeatedly to review the tab order, and then close and save the design changes to the form.

Fig. 5.15 Tab Order dialog box.

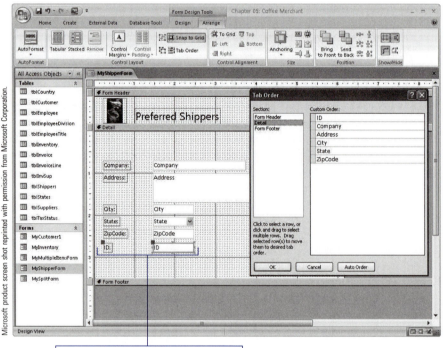

Microsoft product screen shot reprinted with permission from Microsoft Corporation.

repositioned ID text box and label

Printing a Form

Normally, forms are not printed. However, printing one page of a form is a good way to keep track of all the forms you have developed for any accounting system. Printing a form is a straightforward task. First, open the form you want to print in Form view. Optionally, you can use the form navigation buttons to display a particular record, or you can simply print the first record that appears in a form. In either case, click the Office button, point to Print in the Office menu, and then click Print. When the Print dialog box opens, click the Selected Record(s) option button so that Access prints only one form (see Figure 5.16). Click OK to start the print process. If your form is wider than can be accommodated by the current print setup, you will receive a warning similar to the one shown in Figure 5.17. In that case, click the Cancel button to close the warning dialog box and click Page Setup in the File menu. Next, click the Page tab and click the Landscape option button. That should fix the print problem.

Fig. 5.16 Preparing to print a single form.

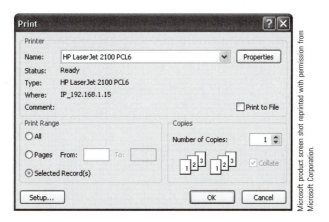

Fig. 5.17 Print width warning dialog box.

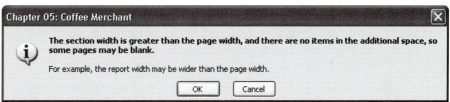

You can print properties, permissions, and design information for database objects, including your forms' designs. Printing the design characteristics of your database objects helps you document your database's design and the accounting application you develop. To print this design information, click the Database Tools tab and then click Database Documenter in the Analyze group. Then, check the objects for which you want printed definition information, being sure to review all database object tabs such as Tables, Queries, and so on for objects of interest. Finally, click OK to create the report and display it in a new Object Definition tab. If you decide to print the report, simply click Print in the Print group of the Print Preview contextual tab. If not, click Close Print Preview in the Close Preview group button to discard the report.

TRY IT

Close any open tabs. Click *Database Tools* and then click *Database Documenter* in the Analyze group. Click the *Forms* tab of the Documenter dialog box, and click the check box to the left of the form *MyShipperForm*. Click *OK*. Access takes a second or two to construct a report and display it on the Object Definition tab. Examine the report. Click the mouse to zoom in, or manipulate the Zoom scroller at the bottom-right side of the form to zoom in or out. Click *Close Print Preview* in the Close Preview group button to discard the report after you are done.

When you want to see a comprehensive list of information from one or more tables, then printing forms is not adequate. Instead, you need a report. Reports and how to produce them are described next.

Modifying a Form in Layout View

One difficulty with creating and modifying a form in Design view is that you cannot see the data as you design the form and position and size the controls. Access 2007 has solved that problem by introducing Layout view. Layout view is a cross between Design view and Form view because it allows you to manipulate the controls on a form and simultaneously see the bound control data to ensure that the form controls are sufficiently large to display the data. Seeing a live view of the data in controls and being able to modify the controls' properties in the same view reduces form design time. The Field List pane that appears in Layout view allows you to add a new field from an existing table or a related table simply by dragging a field from the Field List onto the form. Layout view provides stacked and tabular layouts. Stacked layout and tabular layout group controls in forms or reports so that you can manipulate them as one unit. This allows you to easily rearrange bound controls and their labels together, columns, rows, or even entire layouts. You will use this feature to revise a form you created earlier.

When viewing a form in Layout view, Access' ribbon displays the Format and Arrange contextual tabs that enable you to modify fonts, change foreground and background colors, change text alignment, and so on. This is yet another advantage of Layout view over Design view when modifying a form or report. We'll illustrate modifying a form in Layout view by reusing one of the forms you have already created. First, you will change the form's default view before modifying it.

Modifying a Form's Default View

The split form you created previously in this chapter (MySplitForm) displays employee information. Make a copy of that form and rename it so you can work on a copy rather than the original one. One of the properties of a form is its default view. The *default view* is its appearance when you double-click its name in the Navigation Pane or open it by right-clicking the form and selecting Open from the pop-up menu. A form's default view can be any of the following: Single Form, Continuous Forms, Datasheet, PivotTable, PivotChart, or Split Form.

EXERCISE 5.13: CHANGING THE DEFAULT VIEW OF A FORM

1. Create a copy of the form named MySplitForm: Right-click MySplitForm in the Navigation Pane, click Copy in the pop-up menu, right-click anywhere in the Navigation Pane, click Paste in the pop-up menu, type MyEmployeeForm in the Paste As dialog box, and click OK. Access creates a copy of MySplitForm and places it in the Forms group.
2. Right-click MyEmployeeForm in the Navigation Pane, click Design View in the pop-up menu, and click Property Sheet in the Tools group of the Design contextual tab, if necessary, to display the Property Sheet.
3. Click the Selection type list box and click Form to display the form's properties.
4. Click the Form tab of the Property Sheet, if needed, click the Default View property list arrow (the second property from the top), and click Single Form to select this form's default view (see Figure 5.18).
5. Click View in the Views group of the Design contextual tab to check that the form displays in Form view by default.

Fig. 5.18 Changing a
form's default view.

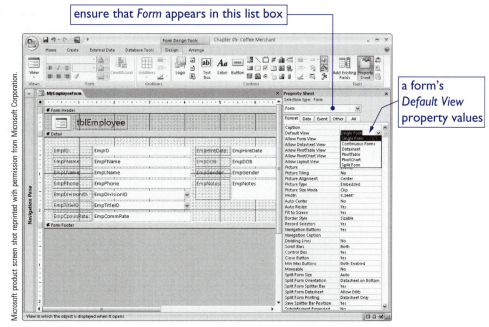

Microsoft product screen shot reprinted with permission from Microsoft Corporation.

Now that the form's default view is changed to a single form, you can experiment with modifying a form's controls in Layout view for the single form. First, you will modify each of the labels using a few different techniques. To modify an unbound control such as labels that identify bound controls, you display the form in either Design view or Layout view and proceed to change the labels. Here, you will use Layout view.

EXERCISE 5.14: MODIFYING LABELS IN LAYOUT VIEW

1. Right-click MyEmployeeForm in the Navigation Pane and click Layout View in the pop-up menu to display it in Layout view.
2. Click the Form Header text tblEmployee to select the control. (When you select a control in Layout view, a golden rectangle surrounds it.) Using the mouse, drag through the entire text and type Employees to change it. Press Enter to finalize the change.
3. Click the label EmpID label to select it. Double-click EmpID to select the text inside the label control and type Employee ID to replace the text.
4. Try a different technique to alter an unbound control: Ensure the Property Sheet is open (press F4 to toggle it open if needed) and click the EmpFName label control on the form. Click the Format tab in the Property Sheet pane, click the text in the Caption property, and select all of it (double-click the existing text, for example). Type First Name and press Enter to change the text.
5. Change the remaining labels as outlined in Figure 5.19 using either of the techniques in steps 2 or 3.
6. After completing the previous step, press F4 to close the Property Sheet pane and click Save on the Quick Access Toolbar to save the form's changes.

As you see, a label control almost always accompanies a bound control that displays a table field. The label control's Caption property is the text that appears in the label. Changing the Caption property value causes the text in the control to take on the changed value.

Fig. 5.19 Modifying
label control contents.

Existing Label Text	New Label Text
EmpLName	Last Name
EmpPhone	Phone
EmpDivisionID	Division
EmpTitleID	Title
EmpCommRate	Commission Rate
EmpHireDate	Hire Date
EmpDOB	Birth Date
EmpGender	Gender
EmpNotes	Notes

Applying Conditional Formatting to a Control

You can format any control to customize it in a large number of ways by using the buttons and list choices available in the Design tab. The commands in the Font group of the Design contextual tab, for example, set and change the alignment of text, its display characteristics including font, font size, bold, Italic, and underline. The Conditional formatting command allows you to apply a font, font color, and other display characteristics dynamically, based on the value displayed in the control. For instance, you can set the conditional formatting of a bound text box displaying employees' commission rates to display a red foreground font color if the value is between zero and 7% (inclusive) or a black foreground color if it is greater than 7%. Controls in the right-third of the Controls group format controls line thickness, line type, line color, and control default properties. Let's experiment with formats on the employee form. In the next exercise, you will format the commission rate value—the bound control, not the label—to display commission rates in two different foreground colors as described above. You can apply any number of separate conditions to a control by clicking the Conditional Formatting dialog box's Add button. Just make sure there are no overlapping conditions.

EXERCISE 5.15: APPLYING CONDITIONAL FORMATTING

1. If the form is not in Layout view, then right-click MyEmployeeForm in the Navigation Pane and click Layout View in the pop-up menu.
2. Click the Commission Rate bound control. Click Conditional in the Font group of the Format contextual tab.
3. Click the condition list box arrow and select between; press Tab, type 0, press Tab, type 0.07, click the font color list arrow, and select a red font color (seventh row, second column from the left, for example).
4. Press the Add button, click the condition list box arrow and select greater than; press Tab, type 0.07, click the font color list arrow, and select the black font color (see Figure 5.20).
5. Click OK to close the Conditional Formatting dialog box.
6. Scroll through the first six employee records using the form navigation buttons and note the font color change in the commission rate control.
7. Click Save on the Quick Access Toolbar to save the modified form.

Fig. 5.20 Applying **conditional formatting** to a bound control.

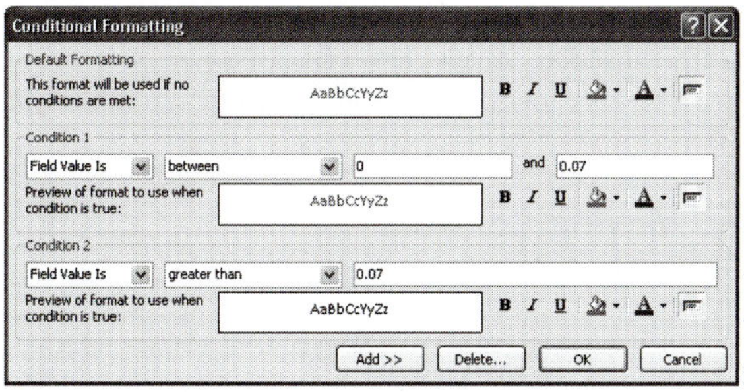

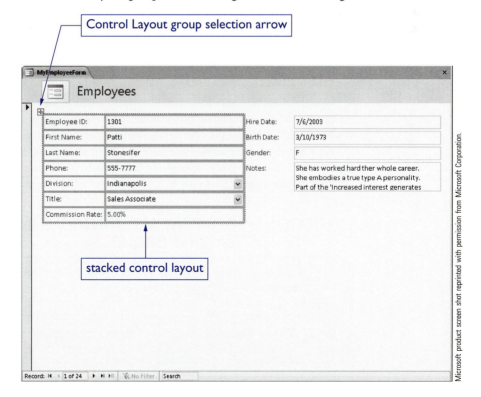

Understanding Control Layouts

Control layouts align your form controls both horizontally and vertically to provide it with a good appearance. A control layout resembles a table, and the controls it contains can be moved and resized as a single unit with one movement of the mouse. There are two types of control layouts: tabular and stacked. A ***tabular control layout*** aligns controls in rows and columns similar to a spreadsheet. Across the top are labels. A ***stacked control layout*** arranges controls in a vertical group with a label to the left of each control—like your MyEmployeeForm form. There can be multiple control layouts of both types on a form. In the MyEmployeeForm, for example, there are two stacked control layouts—one for the seven controls on the left side of the form and one for the four controls on the right side.

You can rearrange the location of controls in a control layout by dragging it to the location you want. A horizontal or vertical line appears indicating where the control will be placed as you drag the control. Occasionally, you may want to remove a control from a control layout—so you can resize it independently of other controls for example. To remove a control from its control layout, select the control and then click Remove in the Control Layout group of the Arrange contextual tab. Figure 5.21 shows one of the

Fig. 5.21 Selecting a control layout.

two control layouts highlighted. You can highlight an entire Control Layout group by clicking the four-headed arrow that appears when you click any of the controls of a group. Control layouts are a handy tool for form modifications.

Sizing and Moving Controls

Typical form modifications include resizing bound controls by using their sizing handles. When you select a control, Access displays a frame around the label and bound control pair and highlights the selected control with a golden rectangle. Place the mouse over any edge. When it changes to a double-headed arrow, you can change the size of the control by dragging away from or toward the center of the control. All controls in the Control Layout group resize together. If you want to resize an individual control, then you must first remove it from its control layout and then resize it. However, one great advantage of grouping (new to Access 2007) is that you can resize and move many controls at once. To move a control, simply click within the control and move it to its new location. Similarly, you can move all controls in a particular control layout by selecting the entire layout and then clicking and dragging within the control layout to reposition it. Next, you will move one of the two stacked layout groups in the MyEmployeeForm and merge the two groups.

EXERCISE 5.16: MOVING A STACKED LAYOUT AND MERGING IT WITH ANOTHER GROUP

1. Ensure that MyEmployeeForm is in Layout view.
2. Click the Birth Date bound control (not the label).
3. Click the Layout Group selector for that group of four controls—it is the four-headed arrow at the upper-left corner of the stacked layout—and drag it to the left. A line appears in the leftmost group indicating the location of the inserted group if the mouse were released.
4. Drag the group down until the indicator line appears between Last Name and Phone. Release the mouse to drop the group in the middle of the left control group. Access joins the two groups into one stacked control group.

Now the form has only one stacked layout consisting of 11 bound controls and a like number of labels identifying them. Next, let's resize the controls as one. Later, you'll resize individual controls that are taken out of the Stacked Layout group.

Most of the bound controls are far wider than needed for the data they display. The lone exception is the Notes bound control, which contains a lot of text and probably should be even wider and deeper to display the entire notes for the average record.

EXERCISE 5.17: RESIZING ALL CONTROLS IN A STACKED LAYOUT GROUP

1. With MyEmployeeForm in Layout view, click any bound control (e.g., EmployeeID).
2. Move the mouse to the right edge of the golden selection rectangle. When the mouse turns to a double-headed arrow, click and drag it to the left to shorten all bound controls simultaneously. Release the mouse when the bound control for Title (showing Sales Associate for the first record) is wide enough to display the value but no wider—about half the width of the controls prior to shortening them.

If you want to resize a control or move a control independently of its Layout group, then you must remove it from its Layout group before resizing or moving it. The Notes bound control could be larger to display more of the sometimes lengthy text it contains. First you will remove the label and bound control pair from the Layout group. Then you will resize it.

EXERCISE 5.18: RESIZING AN INDIVIDUAL CONTROL

1. Click the Notes bound control to select it, click the Arrange contextual tab, and click Remove from the Control Layout group. Access liberates the bound control pair from the Stacked Layout group, moving it to the right and shifting other controls up to fill the void (see Figure 5.22).
2. Click the Notes bound control (not the label "Notes:") to deselect its label.
3. Click and drag the right edge of the control (the mouse is a double-headed arrow) to the right to lengthen it. Click and drag the bottom edge of the control to make it deeper. When the bottom edge is approximately aligned horizontally with the bottom of the Commission Rate control, release the mouse.
4. With the Notes bound control still selected, click Stacked in the Control Layout group to place the Notes in its own Stacked Layout group. Your modified form should be similar to the one shown in Figure 5.23.
5. Save the modified form under a new name: Click the Office button, hover over Save As, and click Save Object As in the pop-up menu. Type MyEmployeeForm2 in the highlighted text box, and click OK.
6. Close the form: Right-click the MyEmployeeForm2 tab and click Close All in the pop-up menu.

Fig. 5.22 Removing a control from a Layout group.

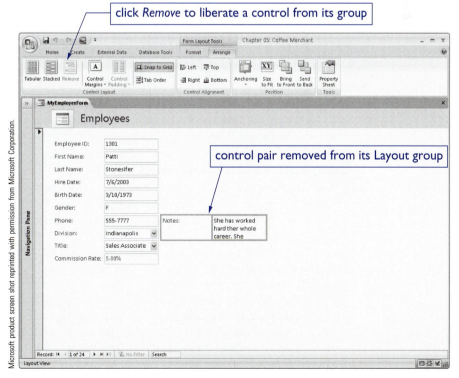

Fig. 5.23 Modified form.

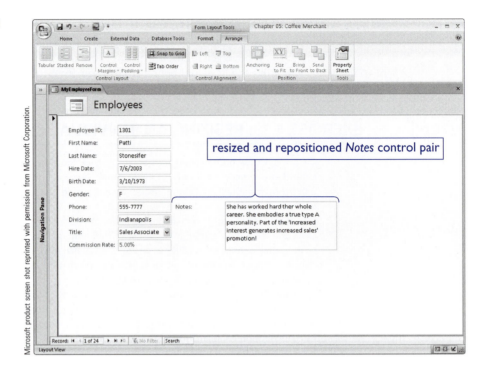

Enforcing Data Integrity and Consistency with Forms

Tables that contain data errors can cause business decisions based on those tables to be misguided or, at worst, disastrous. The types of errors that can creep in include data values that fall outside the allowable or reasonable range such as a credit limit that is a power of ten too large or an item price that is negative. Another type of error is data that is of the wrong type such as a numeric value entered into a text field—a so-called wrong data type. Many errors can be highlighted by data validation controls built into tables themselves, such as validation rules in place on a table field. Table field properties such as Input Masks can ensure that data is in a particular format or capitalized a certain way. Forms provide another way to ensure that the data anyone enters into a table or tables is accurate and valid.

Using Data Validation to Avoid Errors

Access' data validation features catch data entry errors and provide messages that assist in identifying the error and correcting it. Establishing data validation means creating rules that specify the kind of data and value ranges of data that can be entered. Optional pop-up messages can appear to display information about the data problem.

Just like the table fields that they display, form controls have validation rules and validation text. By setting the Validation Rule property of a form's control, you provide protection and dictate what values are allowed to pass through that control (or not) and into the table field to which the control is bound. The associated Validation Text property displays a message when one attempts to enter data that violates the validation rule. That, too, can be set for the control corresponding to a table field to be protected.

What is the difference between setting data validation rules through the Validation Text of a table field versus setting it in the control of a form that is bound to a table field? Setting data validation in a table field's property affects *all* objects which are bound to that field—all forms and queries that refer to a table field with validation rules set at the table level are, in turn, bound by those rules. That is, rules in the table are enforced for a form field bound to that table field. Of lesser impact are any data validation rules established in a form bound to a table. For example, suppose you do not set up a data validation rule for the UnitPrice field in the *tblInventory* table that allows values between 5 and 70 only. Any form field that is bound to the UnitPrice table column must obey that table field rule. However, if a validation rule is not in place on a table field, then any form field validation rule is enforced only by the form. Other form controls that reference the UnitPrice table column do not have the validation rule. So, table validation rules are global, whereas form field validation rules are local to the form.

Let's establish validation rules on the *tblInventory* table by setting them in the form you created earlier referencing MyInventory. The rules you'll establish on the MyInventory form will govern UnitsOnHand values and UnitPrice values. Specifically, let's limit the UnitsOnHand to values less than or equal to 8000. Negative values of inventory are allowed, because they signify when items are backordered and the extent of the shortfall. The second limit will be that unit prices for inventory must be between $2.00 and $500.00. (Kopi Luwak, an unusual and exotic coffee can sell for hundreds of dollars per pound.) The following exercise adds these data validation rules to the controls on the form bound to the UnitsOnHand and UnitPrice table columns in *tblInventory*. In the process, we'll clean up the labels on the form identifying bound controls.

EXERCISE 5.19: SETTING DATA INTEGRITY RULES IN FORM CONTROLS

1. Open MyInventory in Layout view. Save the form under a new name before making further changes: Click the Office button, point to Save As, click Save Object As, type MyInventory2, and click OK.
2. Click the UnitPrice bound control—the text box, not the label, and press F4, if necessary, to display the Property Sheet. Ensure that the drop down list box at the top of the Property Sheet displays *UnitPrice*, which names the control whose properties appear in the Property Sheet dialog box.
3. Click the Data tab, if necessary, and click inside the Validation Rule property. If the property already contains an expression, then select all the text to replace it. Type between 2 and 500 and press Enter. Access will capitalize the first letter of the word *between* and the word *and*, signifying it recognizes the expression as correctly formed.
4. Click the Validation Text property and type the following: Value must be between 2 and 500, inclusive. Press Enter.
5. Click the object selector list box arrow at the top of the Property Sheet and select UnitsOnHand from the list. Click the Validation Rule property. Type <= 8000 and press Enter.
6. Click the Validation Text property and type Value must be less than 8001. Press Enter.
7. Change the labels *InventoryID*, *ItemName*, *UnitPrice*, *UnitsOnHand*, and *CountryID* to these labels: Inventory ID, Item Name, Unit Price, Units On Hand, and Country. In other words, in Layout view, click each label control and then click it again to enter edit mode. Place a space between words, press Enter, and change the next label. Drop the "ID" from the label CountryID.
8. Click the Title control in the Form Header and then click it again. Then, edit the title to simply Inventory.

9. Make all the bound controls about half their current length by moving the mouse to the right edge of any selected bound control. Then, when the mouse pointer turns to a double-headed arrow, drag the edge to the left.
10. Save and then close the MyInventory2 form.

Inserting Controls to Limit Choices: Buttons and List Boxes

Another effective way to ensure data integrity is to limit user choices on data input. Another rule that reduces errors is to reduce or eliminate typing altogether. Whenever people must type even short entries, they can often introduce mistakes. Using controls other than text boxes—which Access creates and binds to table fields when creating forms—are a tool to reduce or eliminate mistakes. If you have a yes/no text box field, it is better to use a check box to eliminate the large number of possible ways to spell (and misspell) *yes* and *no*. For database fields that have just a few possible choices such as company-approved shippers, then a list box is a better choice than a text box for the form to display. You can type a small number of choices such as DHL, FedEx, USPS, and UPS as the choices rather that allowing all the variations that data entry people might type (e.g., *Federal Express, Inc.* or *United Parcel Service*). For entries such as customer names or sales representatives in which there could be dozens, hundreds, or even thousands of choices, then a combo box or list box that gets its values from a table of values is the answer to avoiding the drudgery of typing long text strings.

In this next exercise, you will replace the check box control corresponding to the Caffeinated field with option buttons and replace the Beverage text box bound control with a list box control. Adding list boxes and option buttons is done in Design view, *not* Layout view.

First, you open MyInventory2 and save it under a new name so that each of the forms you create is preserved for each exercise.

EXERCISE 5.20: REPLACING A TEXT BOX CONTROL WITH A LIST BOX

1. Right-click the form name MyInventory2 found in the Forms group in the Navigation Pane and then click Design View in the pop-up menu. Click the Office button, point to Save As, click Save Object As, type MyInventory3, and click OK.
2. Make sure *Use Control Wizards* (a wand with stars) is selected. It is in the upper-right corner of the Controls group. If it is not selected, click it to activate it. Click the List Box control in the Controls group. (If you move the mouse over the controls, a tool tip will appear displaying the control's name.)
3. Move the mouse down to an empty area to the right of the Beverage control and click the mouse to launch the List Box Wizard. Click the I will type in the values that I want radio button and click Next.
4. Type 2 in the Number of columns text box, click the Col1 text box below it, type c, press Tab, type Coffee, and press Tab to move to the second row.
5. Type t in the Col1 text box of the second row. Press Tab to move to Col2 and type Tea.
6. Make Col1 invisible by moving the mouse to the dividing line between values column headers *Col1* and *Col2* (see Figure 5.24). When it turns to a double-headed

arrow, drag to the left until Col1 is invisible. The text in Col1 is stored in the table. The text in Col2 merely appears on the form.

7. Click Next. Ensure that Col1 is highlighted and click Next.
8. Click the Store that value in this field radio button, click the list arrow to its right, and click Beverage. This choice tells Access which field in the table stores the list box value selected by the form user. Click Next to go to the last step.
9. Type Beverage in the text box to create the label that appears next to the list box, and click Finish to complete the list box creation process.
10. Switch to Layout view. Drag the bottom edge of the list box up toward the top edge to until only one beverage choice appears in the list.

Fig. 5.24 Creating list box values.

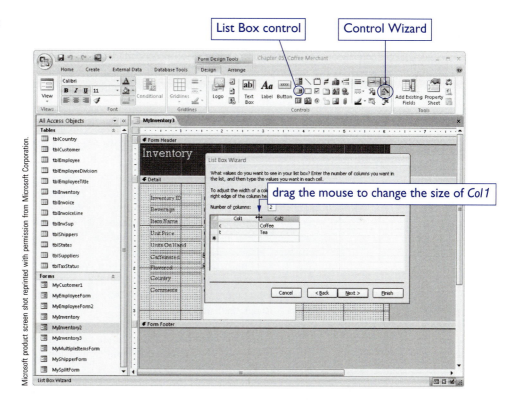

Microsoft product screen shot reprinted with permission from Microsoft Corporation.

TRY IT

Right-click the form's tab and click *Form View*. Scroll through the first four or five records and observe the text box value for Beverage and the list box value. They should correspond. That is, for every *c* in the Beverage text box, the list box should automatically display *Coffee*. The same is true for *t* and *Tea*. Display the form in Design view for further work.

To tidy up the form, you remove the old beverage text box control and slide in the new list box control in its place in the tacked layout. It is very easy to do this in Access 2007, as you will see by doing Exercise 5.21.

EXERCISE 5.21: DELETING THE OLD CONTROL AND MOVING IN THE NEW LIST BOX

1. Display the form in Design view for further work. In Design view, select the text box (original) corresponding to Beverage and press the Delete key to remove the original label/textbox control pair.
2. Click the new list box control and drag it into the Stacked Control group. When the golden horizontal line appears between the Inventory ID and the Item Name controls, release the mouse. The new list control aligns with existing controls.
3. Click the Save button in the Quick Access Toolbar to save the changes.

Another useful form control is an option button, also known as a radio button. It provides a list of mutually exclusive choices. Clicking one of the radio buttons in a grouping of them automatically stores numeric values you assign in the database. The advantage of radio buttons over typing numbers or text should be obvious: The user selects one of a limited number of choices and Access stores one from a list of uniform values in the bound field of the table. This eliminates the possibility of spelling variations or erroneous values corrupting a database. Exercise 5.22 illustrates how to replace a check box with radio button choices.

EXERCISE 5.22: INSERTING OPTION BUTTONS TO REPRESENT VALUE CHOICES

1. Display MyInventory3 in Design view. Ensure the *Use Control Wizards* button is highlighted, click the Option Group button, click an empty place on the form to the right of the Caffeinated control to release the control and launch the wizard.
2. Type Caffeinated in the first row of the Label Names text box, click the second row, type Decaffeinated, and click Next.
3. Click the No, I don't want a default radio button and click Next.
4. Type -1 (negative one represents true—a check mark in a check box) in the Values column of the first row, press the Down Arrow key, type 0 (zero represents false— a cleared check box), and click Next.
5. Click the Store the value in this field radio button, click the list box arrow to its right, and click Caffeinated. Caffeinated is the field in which the radio button value will be stored and from which the radio button for the corresponding choice "lights up." Click Next.
6. Click Next again to accept the choices for radio button style. Type Caffeinated? in the text box to establish the label that appears just above the two radio buttons, and click Finish.
7. Next, remove the old Caffeinated check box field and label: Click the old Caffeinated label or check box and press Delete to remove the pair. Access removes them and moves the controls below it up to fill the gap.
8. Click the Save button in the Quick Access Toolbar to save the changes.
9. Switch to Form view to review the changes to your form (see Figure 5.25). Use the navigation button to view the first dozen records. Notice the radio button change as you scroll through the records. Those changes reflect whether or not the beverage is caffeinated.

Fig. 5.25 Radio button controls representing two choices.

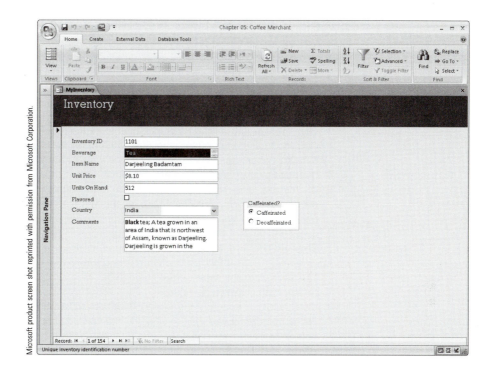

Microsoft product screen shot reprinted with permission from Microsoft Corporation.

Creating a Behind-the-Form Query

As you scrolled through the records using the inventory form, you probably noticed that the rows display in seemingly random order. In fact, rows appear in the form in primary key order—based on the value of the InventoryID field. This is not the best choice. It would be better to display the inventory in some more organized order—by beverage type and then alphabetically within beverage type for example. That way, coffees would appear first in the list followed by teas. Coffees would appear subsorted by item name as would teas. One way to accomplish this is to create a query containing all the inventory fields and specifying sorting in ascending order first by the Beverage column and then by ItemName column. Then, you could modify the form to get its data from the new query rather than directly from the table *tblInventory*. A "safer" and more elegant solution is to modify the form to use a behind-the-form query. A behind-the-form query is one that is transparent to the database, does not appear in the Queries group, and that can be used only by the form to which it is attached. This approach is safer, as mentioned above, because it prevents anyone modifying a query in the Queries group that affects this form. That is, hidden forms cannot be accidentally modified and therefore not inadvertently affect database forms or other objects that depend on them.

Let's make one final modification to the MyInventory3 form so that it automatically delivers records in sorted order, regardless of the order in which they appear in the table. You will do that by changing the form's Record Source to a query. The next exercise shows you how.

EXERCISE 5.23: CREATING A BEHIND-THE-FORM QUERY TO SORT ROWS

1. Display MyInventory3 in Design view. Press F4, if necessary, to display the Property Sheet pane.
2. Ensure that the form is selected: Click the list box arrow at the top of the Property Sheet and click Form.
3. Click the Data tab on the Property Sheet, click the Record Source property, then click the triple-dotted button (the Build button) on the right side of the property. Click Yes when asked if you want to create a query based on the table.
4. Double-click the * (asterisk) in the table field roster to place it in the first Field cell.
5. Double-click Beverage in the field roster and double-click ItemName to place Beverage and then ItemName in the second and third Field cells, respectively.
6. Clear the Show check boxes corresponding to Beverage and ItemName in the query grid so they do not display twice.
7. Click the Sort cell in the Beverage column, click its list arrow, and then select Ascending. Repeat this for the ItemName column. This will cause Access to sort the rows from the table in Beverage order first and then in ItemName order (within distinct Beverage values).
8. Click the Close button in the Close group of the Design contextual tab, and click Yes when asked if you want to save the change and update the query. The Record Source property, associated with the form, is changed into a SQL statement that selects all fields from the table *tblInventory* and then sorts them. Figure 5.26 shows the Property Sheet enlarged so the entire SELECT statement is visible.
9. Click Save in the Quick Access Toolbar to save the changed form.
10. Close the Property Sheet. Click View in the Views group to display the form in Form view. Scroll through the first half-dozen records to verify that coffee products display in name order (beginning with Almond Amaretto).

Fig. 5.26 Changed *Record Source* property, a SQL statement, to sort rows.

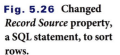

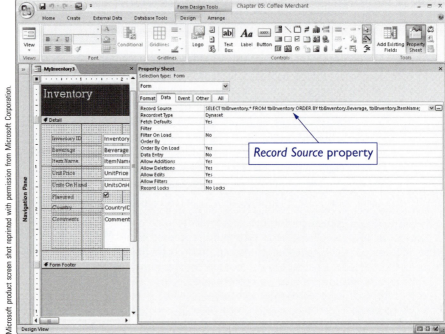

Microsoft product screen shot reprinted with permission from Microsoft Corporation.

Creating a Multitable Form and Subform

Most forms you build are for the purpose of data entry and often display data from a single table. However, there are many times when you need to enter or display data from more than one table. Information about invoices and their details are a good example. That is an example of a form that retrieves and stores data into more than one table. A single invoice form can display data from, say, the *tblInvoice* table and the *tblInvoiceLine*—two related tables. The form would contain data such as invoice date, customer number, and employee number retrieved from *tblInvoice*. Invoice details such as the individual items invoiced appear in the *tblInvoiceLine* table and include invoice ID, quantity ordered, unit price, and discount.

When you create a form based on one table having a one-to-many relationship to another table (such as *tblInvoice* and *tblInvoiceLine)*, Access creates a corresponding form and a subform. You have the most control over which tables appear in a form and subforms that appear by using the Form Wizard. Using the Form Wizard, you can specify the tables, fields, record groupings, and sorting that occurs before the data appears in the form and its subforms. On the other hand, you can create a quite nice fundamental form and subform by selecting the "parent" table (the one-side table in a 1–M relationship) and simply clicking Form on the Create tab. The form displays data from the parent table in the top and the related record(s) from the many side of the relationship in a subform.

The invoice form that you will build in this section is actually two forms: a main form and a subform. The main form displays one record from the *tblInvoice* table. Simultaneously, the subform displays any related records that are line items in the invoice. Information on the subform includes inventory number, quantity ordered, unit price, and discount. Extended price, which is the formula quantity*price*(1-discount) is *not* found in *tblInvoiceLine*. If you want to include a calculated field in a form, then you must first create a query containing the calculation and then build the form or subform on that query rather than on a table. We'll also discuss how to create this more useful version of the invoice form.

Creating a Multiple-Table Form

Creating a form and subform from related tables is straightforward. Let's create a basic form the fastest way possible and then later modify it.

EXERCISE 5.24: CREATING A FORM AND RELATED SUBFORM

1. Click tblInvoice in the Tables group to highlight it.
2. Click the Create tab and then click Form in the Forms group. Access quickly builds a standard form and subform and displays the first *tblInvoice* and related invoice line details (see Figure 5.27).
3. Click Save in the Quick Access Toolbar, type MyInvoiceForm1, and click OK to save the new form. Access saves the new form in the Forms group of the Navigation Pane and changes the form tab to MyInvoiceForm.

Examine your new form. Notice that there are two sets of navigation buttons. The navigation buttons nearest the bottom of the form move through the invoices whereas the navigation buttons above them move through the individual invoice lines.

Microsoft product screen shot reprinted with permission from Microsoft Corporation.

Fig. 5.27 A form and subform.

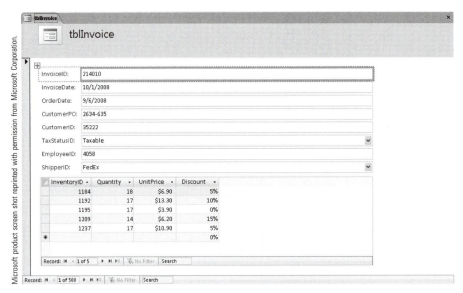

Of course, there is more work to do to the form to improve it. For example, all the unbound controls that label the data fields should be altered (e.g., change "OrderDate" to two words, and so on). However, you know how to do that and can do so at another time. A more important change we should make is to incorporate into the subform the name of the item invoiced and its extended price. Because the extended price is not a field in any table, we will have to create a query containing the calculation.

Creating a Subform From a Query

A query is needed to combine fields from the *tblInvoiceLine* and *tblInventory* tables. The one field needed from the inventory table is ItemName. The query also contains the expression you have seen multiple times before in this text:

$$\text{Round}([\text{Quantity}]*[\text{tblInvoiceLine}]![\text{UnitPrice}]*(1-[\text{Discount}]),2)$$

The round function enfolds the familiar extended price expression. The "[tblInvoiceLine]![UnitPrice]" specifies the UnitPrice value in the table *tblInvoiceLine*—not the same-named field in *tblInventory*.

Let's build the requisite query and then create a new form and subform that reference *tblInvoice* together with the query you are about to create. Because you know the details of creating queries by now, the steps that follow are less explicit than usual. If you are rusty on creating a query, then review Chapter 4 (*Creating and Using Queries*).

EXERCISE 5.25: CREATING A QUERY FOR USE BY A SUBFORM

1. Create a new query joining *tblInvoiceLine* and *tblInventory*.
2. In Design view, place the following fields in the Field row in the order listed: InvoiceID, ItemName, Quantity, UnitPrice, and Discount.
3. Click Save in the Quick Access Toolbar, type MyInvoiceSubformQuery, and click OK. Saving the query now allows the names of the fields in the developing query to appear if you choose the Builder to write the expression in the next step.
4. In field cell in column six of the query grid, create the following expression (be careful about the number and placement of parentheses):

   ExtPrice: Round([Quantity]*[tblInvoiceLine]![UnitPrice]*(1–[Discount]),2)

5. Click Save in the Quick Access Toolbar. Close the query. Right-click the query's tab and click Close.

Next, you will use the Form Wizard to create a form from *tblInvoice* and MyInvoice-SubformQuery, joining the two objects on their common linking field InvoiceID.

EXERCISE 5.26: CREATING A FORM AND RELATED SUBFORM

1. Click More Forms in the Forms group of the Create tab. Click Form Wizard.
2. Click the Tables/Queries list box arrow, and click Table: tblInvoice in the list.
3. Click >> (select all) button to place all Available Fields into the Selected Fields list.
4. Click the Tables/Queries list box arrow, and click Query: MyInvoiceSubformQuery from the list.
5. Move the fields ItemName, Quantity, UnitPrice, Discount, and ExtPrice over to the Selected Fields list. (Click ItemName then click > five times.) Do not include the InvoiceID field listed in the query's Available Fields list.
6. Click Next. Click by tblInvoice in the *How do you want to view your data?* list box to ensure the proper grouping (see Figure 5.28).
7. Click Next, click Next again, click the Access 2007 style, and click Next.
8. Double-click the Form text box below the question *What titles do you want for your forms?* Type MyInvoiceForm2 to name the form in the Navigation Pane. Select all the text in the Subform name text box and type MyInvoiceSubform2 to name the affiliated subform. Click the Finish button. Access creates the form/subform pair and displays them in Form view (see Figure 5.29).

Fig. 5.28 Form and subform hierarchy.

ensure *by tblInvoice* is highlighted

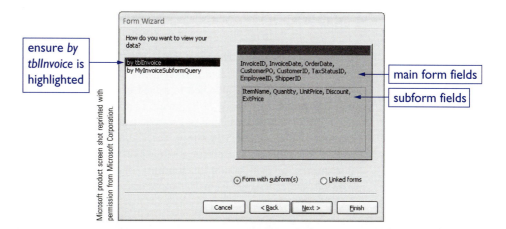

main form fields

subform fields

Microsoft product screen shot reprinted with permission from Microsoft Corporation.

Fig. 5.29 Invoice form and subform.

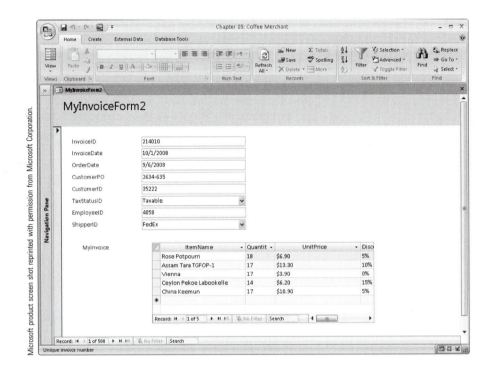

The form and subform have a few flaws, but they contain the essential data. You can scroll through the form to view each customer's invoice and related invoice line details using the navigation bar at the bottom of the form. Though the form needs some clean up, resist doing so now. It is a problem at the end of the chapter!

Creating Special Purpose Forms

Access forms are useful for purposes besides displaying and changing data. You can create useful business forms that perform calculations containing only unbound controls whose values are derived from mathematical expressions. An example is the mortgage calculation form that you will explore in this section. Another type of form that is not tied to any databases' fields is a switchboard. The form consists of buttons that open other forms comprising the database applications. This type of form is described in this section also.

Creating a Mortgage Calculation Form

A mortgage calculation form demonstrates that Access forms need not have bound controls—controls that are attached to a field of a table or query. Though this application is one that you might more easily create in Excel, we include it here to demonstrate the flexibility of Access and how to create calculated controls referencing other controls on the same form. Figure 5.30 shows the completed form with an example monthly payment. The values shown on the form are text boxes that the user fills in with the exception of the bolded values for monthly payment and total interest paid. Those two controls are calculated from the input values supplied by the four assumptions: loan amount, payment frequency, term, and interest rate. This form is a bit advanced, so we filled in all the formulas and event procedures except the expression to calculate the monthly payment text box. You will create a simple version of that form, test the altered form, and save it.

Fig. 5.30 Completed mortgage computations form.

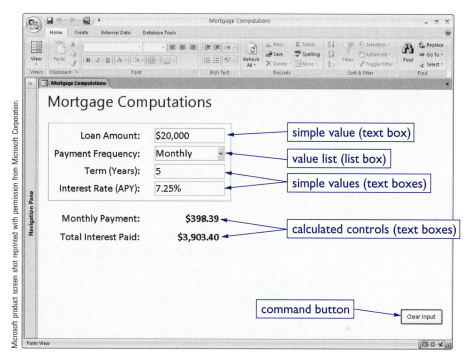

The incomplete Mortgage Computations form is hidden in your Chapter 5 student database. It is simple enough to reveal it, because you have done that in a previous chapter. We unhide the starter form in the next exercise.

EXERCISE 5.27: UNHIDING THE MORTGAGE COMPUTATIONS FORM

1. Right-click the Navigation Pane title bar and click Navigation Options in the pop-up menu. The Navigation Options dialog box appears.
2. Click the Show Hidden Objects check box to place a check mark in it, and click OK. The dimmed form name *Mortgage Computations* appears at the top of the forms group.
3. Right-click Mortgage Computations in the Navigation Pane and click Unhide in this Group in the pop-up menu to make the name bold—just like the other form group objects.

Now that the form is visible, you can modify it by adding the missing expression in the monthly payment control. Before doing so, double-click Mortgage Computations to open it in Form view.

TRY IT

Open Mortgage Computations in Form view. Navigate through the form: Click the *Clear Input* button to clear any results already in the text boxes. Press *Tab* repeatedly to visit each of the unbound controls corresponding to the four input values. Notice that "Monthly" automatically appears in the Payment Frequency control. It is the default value. Click the Loan Amount text box, type *20000*, press *Tab*, type *M*, press *Tab*, type *5* in the Term text box, press *Tab*, and type *7.25* in the Interest Rate text box. Press *Tab* once more. Nothing appears in Monthly Payment or Total Interest Paid text boxes.

In the preceding Try It exercise, you experienced a form that displayed no results. The reason nothing appears in the Monthly Payment text box is that it is a simple text box and not (yet) a calculated control. The Total Interest Paid text box *does* contain an expression whose value will appear when the payment calculation is completed. Next, you will create an expression for the Monthly Payment text box (more correctly known as the "periodic payment" text box because it computes payments for different periods including once annually, monthly, weekly, or daily).

EXERCISE 5.28: INSERTING AN EXPRESSION IN A TEXT BOX'S CONTROL SOURCE PROPERTY

1. Right-click the Mortgage Computations tab, click Design View, and click the text box to the right of the label "Payment." It displays *Unbound* indicating it is a text box that does not get its value from a database field or an expression.
2. Press F4, if necessary, to open the Property Sheet. Make sure that *PeriodicPayment* (one word) appears in the list box at its top.
3. Click the Data tab, if necessary, click the Control Source property, and press Shift+F2 to open the Zoom box.
4. Type the following expression in the text box:

   =Round(Pmt([InterestRate]/[FrequencyPerYear],[FrequencyPerYear]*[Duration],[LoanAmount])*-1,2)

   There are *no* blanks in the expression, and it is written as one, continuous line; the Zoom box may force a soft return in the expression and wrap parts of it to a new line.
5. Click OK to save the expression and close the Zoom box. Press F4 to close the Property Sheet.
6. Display the form in Form view. If *#Error* appears in the Payment text box, simply ignore it.
7. Type the values you see in Figure 5.30 in the corresponding text boxes, pressing Tab to move between them.
8. Press Tab after filling the value for Interest Rate so Access calculates the payment values. Your form values should match those in Figure 5.30—the Monthly Payment value should be $398.39. If not, recheck your payment formula by repeating steps 1 through 4 above.
9. Click the Clear Input button and try other values including the choice "Weekly" for the Payment Frequency. Notice that the label changes to *Weekly Payment*.
10. Click the Office Button, click Save As in the menu, type MyMortgage to replace the form's name, and click OK to save the altered form under a new name. If you simply save the form without changing its name, that's okay too.
11. Right-click the form's tab and click Close All to close it and any other open objects.

There are improvements that you could make to the calculated control you just created. One is to surround the entire expression in an IIF (Immediate IF) function that tests the four unbound controls to ensure they have values before calculating a periodic payment. However, that is beyond the scope of this book! We mention it just in case you want to turn this into a business application you use regularly.

Building a Switchboard

Although you probably feel quite comfortable working with tables, queries, and forms by now, the same is not true for everyone—especially those who will be using your database application. In addition, you might want to prevent users from opening the Forms group or the Tables group in the Navigation Pane and launching forms or opening tables randomly. An alternative way for users to access your database application is through a switchboard. A *switchboard* is an Access form that has no underlying database and that allows you to facilitate navigation or perform tasks within your database application. Normally, a switchboard contains only buttons that the user can click to open other database application forms allowing, for example, updating customer records, producing accounting reports, and so on. In other words, a switchboard's purpose is to lead the user to other forms.

To create a switchboard quickly, use the Switchboard Manager that is located in the Database Tools group on the Database Tools tab. The first time you click this button in a given database, Access informs you that it cannot find an existing switchboard. The message asks if it should create one. Simply click *Yes* to continue with construction of the switchboard.

Once you create the initial switchboard, you can customize it in any number of ways. Once created, a switchboard should open automatically when the database application opens. If you decide to eliminate a switchboard, then it is easy to delete it. Let's build a switchboard that opens selected forms you have built in this chapter. When a user clicks one of the switchboard buttons, then it launches an employee form, inventory form, invoice form, or mortgage form.

EXERCISE 5.29: CREATING A SWITCHBOARD

1. Click the Database Tools tab and click Switchboard Manager in the Database Tools group. A warning dialog box appears indicating that Access could not "... find a valid switchboard in this database." Click Yes to create one.
2. Click Edit to modify the default switchboard. Drag through the text *Main Switchboard* to select it and type Coffee Merchant, its new name.
3. Click New to create a new menu command. The Edit Switchboard Item window appears. You supply two pieces of information in the Edit Switchboard Item dialog box: The text of the menu command and the actual command that Access should perform when the button you are creating is clicked.
4. Type Display Customers in the Text text box, press Tab, click the Command list box arrow, click Open Form in Edit Mode from the list of choices, press Tab to move to the Form text box, click the Form list arrow, and click MyCustomer1 from the list of form choices (see Figure 5.31). The Open command tells Access to open the form MyCustomer1 and allow display and editing of data that appears in the form.
5. Click OK to finalize the first command on the switchboard. Access places the "Display Customers" command in the *Items on this Switchboard* list.
6. Repeat steps 3 through 5 above three more times using the information in Figure 5.32 showing the text, command, and form for each of the three new

menu items. Your completed *Edit Switchboard Page* dialog box should match Figure 5.33.

7. Click Close on the Edit Switchboard Page dialog box. Click Close on the Switchboard Manager dialog box to save the completed switchboard.

8. Double-click Switchboard in the Forms group to display the completed switchboard form (see Figure 5.34).

Fig. 5.31 Creating a switchboard command.

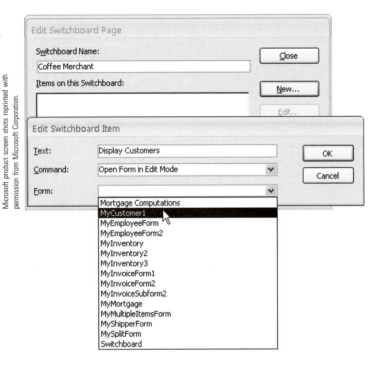

Fig. 5.32 Text, command, and form name for step 6 of Exercise 5.29.

Command Text	Command	Form
Display Employees	Open Form in Edit Mode	MyEmployeeForm2
Display Inventory	Open Form in Edit Mode	MyInventory3
Exit	Exit Application	

Fig. 5.33 Completed *Edit Switchboard Page* dialog box.

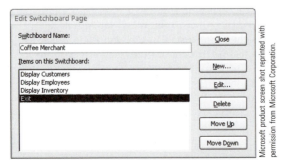

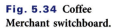

Fig. 5.34 Coffee
Merchant switchboard.

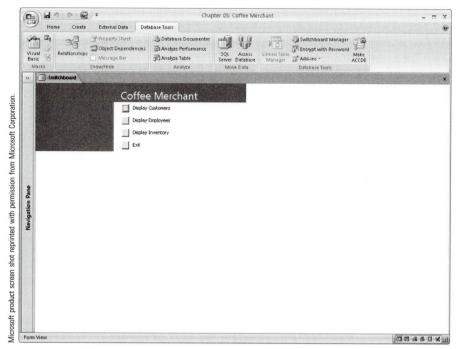

Microsoft product screen shot reprinted with permission from Microsoft Corporation.

TRY IT

Double-click *Switchboard* in the Forms group of the Navigation Pane. The switchboard opens. Click the *Display Customers* button to open that form. Click the *Switchboard* tab to redisplay that form and then click the *Display Inventory* button. Notice the three tabs open: Switchboard, tblCustomer, and MyInventory. Right-click the *Switchboard* tab and click *Close All* to close all open objects.

If you click the Exit button on the switchboard, Access closes. It is handy to be able to close Access from the menu. Resist clicking it for now. We want to do just a little more work on the Chapter 5 database before quitting.

Examine the new objects that building the switchboard created. In the Tables group is *Switchboard Items*. Open that table and you will see, in order from top to bottom of the switchboard menu items, the title text and each of the button's item text, command (coded as a number), and form names. In other words, the switchboard form is populated with the rows from the Switchboard Items table. This facilitates editing the switchboard form because adding commands means simply adding rows to the Switchboard Items table. Conversely, removing command buttons from the switchboard form results in removing one or more corresponding rows from the associated Switchboard Items table. Be sure not to hand edit that table because incorrectly doing so could ruin the switchboard form's menus.

Designating a Startup Form

Because the switchboard is really the access portal to the rest of your database, you might as well make it the form that displays automatically when anyone opens up the database.

That way, users don't have to struggle to locate the switchboard—even if they are fortunate enough to know there is such a thing as a switchboard. The last exercise shows you how to make the switchboard open up automatically.

EXERCISE 5.30: MAKING THE SWITCHBOARD THE STARTUP FORM

1. Click the Office button and click the Access Options button at the bottom, right side of the Office menu. The Access Options dialog box opens.
2. Click Current Database in the list on the left. The settings for the current database appear.
3. Under the heading *Application Options* at the top of the dialog box, look for the Display Form list box. Click the Display Form list box arrow and click the selection Switchboard (in this case) to designate that form as the auto-launch form (see Figure 5.35).
4. Click OK to close the Access Options dialog box. A dialog box appears indicating that you must close the database for the option to take effect. Click OK to close the informative dialog box.

Fig. 5.35 Selecting the database's startup form.

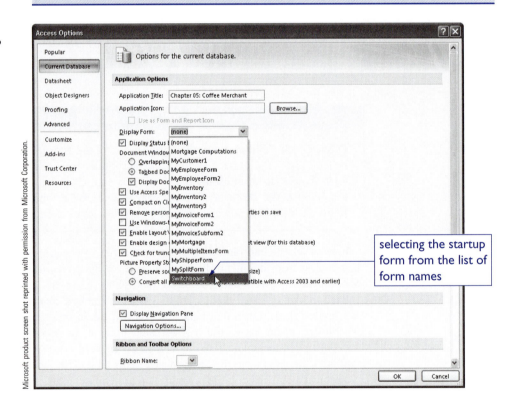

If you want to be really particular about preventing users from looking at database objects, you can hide the Navigation Pane and instruct users to always use the switchboard for all their work. Of course, the application built in this chapter needs reports and other objects to be complete. Once all reports and forms are in place, you can edit the switchboard to include the new command buttons to launch the newly added reports and forms. Our final Try It exercise closes the database and reopens it to ensure that the switchboard form automatically opens.

TRY IT

Try out your new switchboard startup form. Close the database: Click the *Office* button and click *Close Database*. Click the database name in the Open Recent Database list—it should be at the top of the list. The switchboard form will display automatically!

You have completed all the work in the body of this chapter. Close the Chapter 5 database by clicking the Office button and clicking the Exit Access button.

Summary

This chapter has described using Access to create and modify forms. Forms display information from one or more database tables, and forms provide a friendlier, more intuitive interface between the form user and the database. A standard Access form displays one table row per form. A split form displays table fields in a standard form in the upper half and a datasheet view of the table in the lower half. Split forms synchronize any changes in either view of the data. A multiple items form displays data in rows and columns, with the field names from the underlying table appearing at the top of each column.

The Form Wizard speeds form creation. Multiple tables can be displayed on one form by selecting data sources, one at a time, from the list of available tables and queries. You can modify forms in Layout view or Design view. Each has its advantages. Layout view facilitates moving columns and groups as one unit quickly and easily. Design view allows you to add Windows controls such as check boxes, list boxes, and radio buttons to a form. Every detail of a control's properties is available in Design view through the property sheet. Access the property sheet in Design view by pressing F4.

Enforce data integrity by establishing range and reasonableness rules for the control that displays a table field. For example, set the Validation Rule property of a bound field to enforce rules about what data entry is acceptable for that field. Option buttons and list boxes provide a natural way to limit user choices to those in the set of radio buttons or the drop-down list choices.

Forms can have embedded subforms. Subforms are a handy way to display the records of a many-side table in a one-to-many relationship. Create a form and subform by selecting the one-side table in a 1–M relationship and then click Form on the Create tab.

Forms can have no relationship to any underlying table. A form can contain only unbound text boxes and calculated controls to implement an application whose calculated controls derive their value from other text boxes contained on the form. The mortgage calculation form is a good demonstration of this type of form. It consists of dependent text box values whose control names are referenced by the expressions you write as the control source for calculated controls.

A switchboard is a special form containing buttons that open other application forms. Switchboards provide an interface for users who are not familiar with Access. By clicking a button on the switchboard, another form appears that allows users to edit or review table data. Another switchboard button might display a report or an invoice. Access will automatically open any form that is designated as the "Display Form" in the Current Database selection of Access options accessible through the Office button. A form that automatically opens when the database opens is its startup form.

Questions and Problems for Review

Multiple-Choice Questions

1. Which type of form requires a response before the user can continue working?
   a. continuous form
   b. subform
   c. multiple-page form
   d. modal form

2. The active field on a form into which you can type or press the spacebar is called
   a. the hub.
   b. the focus.
   c. the domain.
   d. the center.
3. When using Form Wizard, clicking the >> button will
   a. move all fields from Available to Selected fields.
   b. move only the highlight field from Available to Selected fields.
   c. move all fields from Selected to Available fields.
   d. move only the highlighted field from Selected to Available fields.
4. Which type of control has an expression as its data source?
   a. Bound.
   b. Unbound.
   c. Calculated.
   d. Processed.
5. What view do you use to move controls on a form or subform?
   a. Datasheet.
   b. Design.
   c. Form.
   d. Properties.
6. The text that appears in a label control is its _____ property.
   a. Name
   b. Caption
   c. Form
   d. Default View
7. This type of form has two sections: A form and a datasheet. What type of form is it?
   a. Multiple Items.
   b. Pivot Table.
   c. Modal Dialog.
   d. Split.
8. The _____ layout form groups controls into an arrangement similar to a paper form with labels to the left of each field. The grouping facilitates manipulation of many controls at once.
   a. tabular
   b. stacked
   c. modal
   d. grouped
9. You use _____ to catch any form data entry errors and provide informative error messages.
   a. radio buttons
   b. check boxes
   c. table properties
   d. data validation
10. This form provides controls to open other forms.
   a. Switchboard.
   b. Default.
   c. Layout.
   d. Modal.

Discussion Questions

1. Discuss the advantage(s) of providing a list box or a combo box in a form. How does it help a user? What possible disadvantages are present when using a list box control?

2. What are the advantages of using a form to view or update data in a table? Are there any disadvantages to using a form rather than viewing the table directly?

3. Explain why you might want to use a form to search a database. Can you change values in underlying tables through a form? Explain.

4. Explain, or speculate, when it is best to use a query as the basis of a form and when it is better to use a Form Wizard and select multiple, related tables.

5. Discuss when and why one might use a switchboard in a database. In other words, what might give rise to using one, what advantages might accrue, and when is a switchboard not particularly useful.

Practice Exercises

1. Create a default form that displays all the information from the table *tblSuppliers*. Change the title to *Coffee Merchant Preferred Shippers*. In Design view, delete the subform. Add a label control to the form header containing your name. Save the form as MyPracticeExercise1. Resize all controls and the page so it prints in Portrait orientation. Print the first page. (There will be more than one form on the printed page.)

2. Open the MyInventory form you created in Exercise 5.5. Navigate to the last inventory record and determine the next available InventoryID. (Just add one to the highest current InventoryID value.) Add a new record for a coffee whose name is "Zimbabwe Special" and whose cost is $8.50. Enter an on-hand amount of 500. This coffee is caffeinated but not flavored. Its country of origin is obvious. Insert the comment "Delicate, fruity aroma; medium body; high level of acidity; moderately sweet flavor." Close the form. Next, go to *tblInventory* and sort by the table on the InventoryID column in descending order. Print page 1 (so your new item shows at the top of the list). Write your name at the top of the printed page.

3. Create a form that uses *tblEmployee* as the main form and *tblInvoice* as the subform. Shorten the main form bound controls to about one-half their current lengths. Change main form labels to real words instead of their concatenated meanings. Begin by removing "Emp" from the labels (e.g., "ID" instead of "EmpID," "Phone" instead of "EmpPhone," and so on). Ensure that all modified labels completely display; if not, widen the labels to accommodate the longest one (probably *Commission Rate:*) Change the title to *Employees and Their Invoices*, remove the logo placeholder, and add a label in the Form Header containing your name. Use a form filter (Sort & Filter group on the Home tab) to locate the main form and subform for employee Luca Pacioli. Print the form and subform in landscape orientation.

4. Create a split form based on the table *tblSuppliers*. Change the title to "Suppliers" and remove the logo placeholder. Add your name as a label to the Form Header. Save the altered form as MyPracticeExercise4. In Form view, scroll to the 14th record. Click the Shutter Bar Open/Close Button to close the Navigation Pane. Capture the form to the Clipboard by pressing Shift+PrtScrn. Open a new PowerPoint presentation, right-click the blank slide area, and click Paste in the pop-up menu to paste the captured form onto the PowerPoint slide. Print the single-slide presentation.

5. Click Form Design on the Forms group of the Create tab to open an empty form. Then, add all the fields from the *tblStates* table to the form. Add your name as a label to the Form Header. In Form view, click the StateName bound control. Using a text filter, display only states whose name begins with the letter *o* (e.g., Ohio). Save the form as MyPracticeExercise 5. Print the single page filter set of forms.

Problems

1. Create a form that resembles the Inventory Data Entry form shown in Figure 5.1 First, select *tblInventory* in the Tables group. Then, click Form in the Forms group of the Create tab. Make the following modifications to the default form. Change the Title to *Inventory*. Resize the control that contains the label so that it is long enough to contain the text but no longer. Change all the labels to correct English (e.g., "Inventory ID" instead of "InventoryID," and so on). Change the label "CountryID" to "Country."Add a label to the Form Header that contains your first and last names and place it on the right side of the Form Header. Change the font size of your name to 14 point. Use the picture of the coffee bag as the form logo. (The graphic, called CoffeeBag.jpg, is included in your Chapter 5 student data.) Resize the bound controls to

about one-half their default lengths so the bound controls match Figure 5.1 (approximately). (*Hint*: Do this in Layout view.) In Design view, ensure the form is not wider than the page width. If it is, move things around and narrow the form so it prints in portrait orientation. Finally, use the Filter command (Form view) to locate any coffee produced in Papua New Guinea. Print the form showing Papua New Guinea coffee. Save the form as MyProblem1.

2. Create a Multiple Items form displaying data from the table *tblStates*. Add a calculated control that computes and displays the population density. (Population density is the population divided by the land area and is measured, in this case, in people per square mile.) Move the calculated control's label into the form header above the control and change it to "Density." Format the calculated control Fixed with two decimal places. Change any unbound controls (labels) such as "StateName" to "State Name" so that no label contains two or more words back to back. Use the Text Align property to set all bound controls (text boxes showing database values) so that their values display in the left side of their respective text boxes. (This is not the same as using the Format menu Align command.) Change the Title to "State Densities" and place an unbound control with your first and last name in the Form header, right side. Remove the logo, and then slide the title to the left so its left edge is above the left edge of the State ID column. Print the first page of the Multiple Items form. Save the form as MyProblem2.

3. Modify the form and subform you created in Exercise 5.26 (MyInvoiceForm2 and MyInvoiceSubform2). Incorporate the changes below and then print one page of the form to show the changes: Change the title ("MyInvoiceForm2") to "Invoices" in the Form Header. Change the labels so that they are proper English words ("Invoice Date" instead of "InvoiceDate," and so on). In Design view, insert a label in the Form header with your name. Select the MyInvoice subform label, click Remove in the Arrange contextual tab, click the MyInvoice label (if needed) and press Delete to remove the label. In Layout view, slide the subform to the left so its left edge aligns (approximately) with the labels in the main form. Resize the right edge so that the other subform fields are visible in the subform. Resize the subform fields to a smaller, optimal width. Switch to Design view. Then, format the ExtPrice column to currency and change its caption to "Extended Price." Right-align all subform fields *except* the Item Name fields. (*Hint*: Look for the Text Align property on the Format tab.) Change the labels in the subform columns to proper English words ("Item Name" instead of "ItemName," "Extended Price" instead of "ExtPrice," and so on). While in Design view, insert a page break immediately below the bottom of the subform. (This ensures only one form/subform appears on each printed page.) Save the changes to the form and subform. Switch to Form view. Print the form corresponding to the first invoice record. (Choose the *Pages* radio button in the Print dialog box. Then type 1 in the *From* and *To* text boxes.)

4. You are to finish a partially complete future value computation form that calculates the future value of an initial investment. The form is found in the database called Ch05Problem4 among the Chapter 5 files. Open that database and open, in Design view, the form called *FutureValue*. It has the required text box controls already in place and properly formatted. Users type in four values: An amount to invest, an annual interest rate, the number of payments per year (1, 12, or 52), and the number of years the amount is invested (from 1 to 30). After filling in the last value, pressing Enter will cause the Future Value text box to compute and display the future value of that investment. You are to make the following changes to the form:

   - Write the formula for future value in the last text box, named txtFV. That formula has the following general form:

     =FV(PeriodicIntRate, NumbPayments, PeriodicPayment, PresentValue,1)

     where PeriodicIntRate is the annual interest rate divided by the number of payments per year; NumbPayments is the number of years times the frequency per year; PeriodicPayment is zero (you are not paying each period); and PresentValue is the initial investment.

   - The input text boxes are named (top to bottom) txtPMT, txtPV, txtAPY, txtNPER, and txtYears. These are the four variables used in the FV function.

- In Design view, add the following Validation rules (and corresponding Validation text) to the four input values: txtPV must be greater than zero, txtAPY (periodic interest) must be between 1% and 10%; txtNPER (payments per year) must be 1, 12, or 52; txtYears (time period) must be between 1 and 30 years.
- Add your name as a label in the Form header.
- Do a test calculation with $10,000 for initial investment, 6% annual interest rate, 1 payment per year, and 5 years invested. The result should be $13,382.26. Print the form with these values set.

You can click the Clear Input Values button to clear the four input values to try other combinations.

5. Use the Form Wizard to create a tabular layout form to display some columns of the *tblInventory* table. Once the Form Wizard has built the initial form, create a behind-the-form parameter query so that rows appear in a particular order and are filtered by data that the user supplies at run time. Details about the form's layout and the query are as follows. In step 1 of the Form Wizard, select the first seven fields to display: InventoryID, Beverage, ItemName, UnitPrice, UnitsOnHand, Caffeinated, and Flavored. In step 2, select the Tabular option button. In step 3, select the Access 2007 style. In the last step, replace *tblInventory* with the name MyProblem5Form. After the form appears, switch to Layout view. Change the title to Inventory. Change all column-top labels to their English word equivalents, inserting spaces where needed. Modify the columns' widths so all labels at the top of the columns appear. (*Hint:* Select the label and double-click the right edge.) Switch to Design view. Add a label to the Form header that contains your name. Display the Property Sheet for the form ("Form" appears in the Property Sheet list box at the top). Using the Record Source property's build button, create a query that sorts the seven-column result in ascending order by the UnitsOnHand field. (Be sure to include the exact same seven columns as appear in the original form and no more.) In the criteria for UnitsOnHand, enter a criterion that will display all inventory items whose UnitsOnHand value is less than or equal to the value entered at form display time by the user. In other words, create a parameter query with a bracketed criterion that states "Enter maximum value for UnitsOnHand" (remember the square brackets). Remember to use the appropriate relational operator (<, =, >, >=, <=, or <>) preceding the parameter phrase. Close and save the query. In Design view, ensure the report is narrow enough to display on one page by dragging the right edge of the dotted background as far left as you can. Save the form. Display the form in Form view, enter the value 5 when prompted for the maximum value, and press Enter to see the result. Print the form in landscape orientation.

CHAPTER **6**

Creating and Using Reports

CHAPTER OBJECTIVES

This chapter extends your Access knowledge by providing detailed information about Microsoft Access reports. You will learn about the advantages of using reports and about defining and using accounting reports. Throughout this chapter, exercises emphasize Microsoft Access techniques critical to building accounting information systems. Like the chapters before it, this chapter is application-oriented. Exercises actively engage you in using the theory you learned earlier to create typical accounting and other reports. In particular, you will learn how to:

- Build a report quickly from a selected table.

- Modify a report in Layout view.

- Create a report using the Report Wizard.

- Understand guidelines for good report design.

- Create a report from scratch with the Design View.

- Create a multitable report.

- Publish a report on paper, as a PDF, and in XPS format.

- Create mailing labels.

We continue using The Coffee Merchant's database system as this chapter's backdrop application. The database for this chapter contains the objects you need to do all the exercises in this chapter. It is found on this book's companion Web site. Go to the book's South-Western, Cengage Learning Web site, www.cengage.com/accounting/perry, for all the book's database files.

Creating a Basic Report Quickly

Creating a report from a single table is probably the simplest and fastest way to create a report based on the selected table. Reports are most often printed, though you can review them and display them on the computer. A report's primary purpose is as a printed document. Suppose, for instance, that you want a hard copy of all the customers on record. A quick, basic report will do in this example. Your first choice for a quick report is to use the Report command found in the Reports group on the Create tab. Similar to the simple form you created in Chapter 5 by clicking Form, these reports take just seconds to build. Let's build one now.

EXERCISE 6.1: CREATING A ONE-TABLE REPORT

1. Click tblCustomer in the Tables group of the Navigation Pane to highlight the table name.
2. Click the Create tab and then click Report in the Reports group. Access creates a report quickly and effortlessly and then displays it in Layout view (see Figure 6.1). (The Group, Sort & Total pane may not appear on your screen.)

Fig. 6.1 Customer report in Layout view.

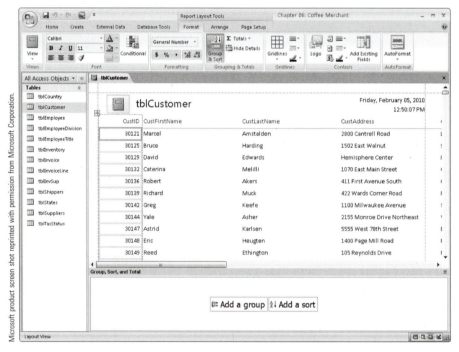

Reports, like forms, have four views. They are Report view, Print Preview view, Layout view, and Design view. Layout view, the default view displayed when you create a report, is new to Access 2007 and makes modifying a report quite easy—much easier than using Design view to make report modifications, for example. Notice that the name of the table from which the report is generated appears in the report header (*tblReport*) and that the current date and time also appear in the report header. Page break lines appear as dashed vertical and horizontal lines in Layout view. It is evident that there are more columns in the report than can be accommodated completely on a page. Before making modifications to the report, it is a good idea to name and save it.

Saving a report places it in the list of objects appearing in the Navigation Pane. Continuing with the report you created above, let's save the report.

EXERCISE 6.2: SAVING A NEW REPORT

1. Click Save in the Quick Access Toolbar.
2. Type MyCustomerReport in the Report Name text box and click OK. Access saves the table and displays its name in the Reports group of the Navigation Pane.

The indicator *Layout View* appears in the lower-left corner of the Access window to indicate that the report appears in Layout view. Another indication is the appearance of the golden rectangle around any selected data or column name in the report. In the report shown in Figure 6.1, the golden rectangle highlights CustID 30121 in the first row of the report. In addition, all data values appearing in the CustID report column are highlighted in a lighter yellow; the report column label has a dashed line around it, and a four-headed arrow appears in the upper-left corner of the column header. That four-headed arrow hints that you can click and drag it to move the column elsewhere in the report. We show you that next. First, let's close the report.

EXERCISE 6.3: CLOSING A REPORT

1. Right-click the MyCustomerReport tab.
2. Click Close in the pop-up menu. Access closes the report and the report window.
3. Ensure that the Navigation Pane displays all objects by clicking the Navigation Pane list box at its top and clicking Object Type.

Modifying a Report in Layout View

One of the great advantages of displaying a report in Layout view is that you can see the data from the report's record source and simultaneously modify the design of the report. This allows you to immediately see the effect of narrowing a report column for example or judge the effectiveness of moving a column to another location in a report. Although Report view displays the data on the report, you cannot modify the report's structure in that view. Design view has the opposite problem: you can modify a report's structure in a large number of ways, but you cannot see the effect changes have on displayed data in that view. You must switch to either Report view, Print Preview view, or Layout view to see the changes. In other words, Layout view is the best choice when altering the structure of a report. The quick report you created earlier needs some changes to be an effective report.

Adding a Logo and a Title

A report's logo and title appear at the top of the entire report in Layout view. In Design view, they are in a report band called the Report Header. By adding a logo to the Report Header, you enhance the visual appeal of the report. A meaningful title quickly provides anyone reviewing the report an idea of the contents of the report. A logo might be the company's logo, or it might be supplied by one of the departments that the report addresses. Access provides Logo and Title commands in the Controls group on the Format contextual tab in Layout view or in the Design contextual tab in Design view. The Logo command inserts any selected image into the Report Header section and the image dimensions to fit within the logo's size. Let's add a logo and modify the report's title while displaying it in Layout view.

EXERCISE 6.4: ADDING A LOGO AND MODIFYING A REPORT'S TITLE IN LAYOUT VIEW

1. Right-click MyCustomerReport in the Navigation Pane and then click Layout View from the pop-up menu to open the report in Layout view.
2. Click Logo in the Controls group of the Format contextual tab, navigate to the folder containing your Chapter 6 database and other objects, click CoffeeRoasted, and click OK. Access inserts the logo into the report.
3. Click the Title command in the Controls group of the Format contextual tab to select all the text in the title, *tblCustomer* appearing at the top of the report.
4. Type Customers by State and press Enter to complete the title (see Figure 6.2).

Fig. 6.2 Report with logo and new title.

Microsoft product screen shot reprinted with permission from Microsoft Corporation.

Deleting, Moving, and Resizing Columns

Whenever you want to delete, move, or resize report columns, the best choice is to do so in Layout view. In that view, each column and its column-top label acts as a unit because both are in the same control layout. To delete an unneeded column, click the column label or the data within the column and press the Delete key. Moving a column is a matter of simply hovering over the column, ensuring the pointer is a four-headed arrow, dragging the column to its new location, and releasing the mouse. Resize a column by moving the mouse to one of the column's edges. When it becomes a double-headed arrow, click and drag the column's edge toward its center to narrow the column or drag it away from its center to widen it.

The default report still needs more work. Let's assume that the only report columns we need are the customer name and address information. The customer ID, for instance, need not be in the report, and we don't need to display the phone or fax information. Once we prune unneeded columns, then we can modify columns sizes and locations.

EXERCISE 6.5: DELETING UNNEEDED COLUMNS

1. Click the light-blue column label *CustID* and press Del to delete that column from the report.
2. Drag the horizontal scroll bar to the right to reveal other report columns. Click anywhere in the CustPhone column and press Del. Click a data value in the CustFax column and press Del. Access removes both columns.

Moving columns is simple. Click and drag any value in the column and then drag the column to the right. Release the mouse when the vertical bar appears in the location where you want to move the column.

EXERCISE 6.6: MOVING A COLUMN

1. Click Amstalden in the CustLastName column to highlight all data values in the column (still in Layout view).
2. Drag the column to the left until the vertical golden line is to the left of the CustFirstName column. Release the mouse to place the CustLastName column.

Remember: If you make a mistake, simply click the Undo button in the Quick Access Toolbar to reverse the last change. You can click the Undo button to reverse any number of changes.

You notice that not all columns appear on the report page. Columns that don't fit are placed on a subsequent page. You can correct this in several ways. You can narrow each column in Layout view to the smallest value in which all data values still appear. Another way is to display the report in landscape orientation. That may be enough to allow all report columns to appear. Another change is to reduce the margins. The first modification to try is making the report columns narrower starting with the CustLastName column.

EXERCISE 6.7: RESIZING COLUMNS

1. Click CustLastName, the label above the customers' last names. Access surrounds the label with a golden rectangle and places dashed lines around the data that are part of the Control Layout group.
2. Move the mouse to the right edge of the golden rectangle surrounding the label. When the mouse becomes a double-headed arrow, double-click the mouse. Access narrows the column so that it is just wide enough to display the column label.
3. Repeat Step 2 for the CustFirstName column.
4. To resize the remaining labels, click each column label in turn and then drag the right border of the golden rectangle to the left. Each column has different width requirements. Ensure that the columns are wide enough to display city names,

> state names, and the zip codes. This should allow all columns to appear on one portrait-oriented page (see Figure 6.3).
> 5. Click Save on the Quick Access Toolbar to preserve all the changes you have made so far.

Fig. 6.3 Resized report columns in Layout view.

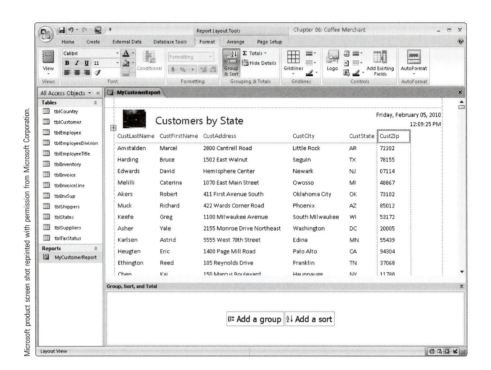

Modifying Column Titles

Access chooses the names of the source record fields for its report column titles. Often the column titles need to be altered. This is the case with the customer report. Changing the column titles follows the same steps you used to change control labels in forms. Namely, you click a column title once to select it and click it again to edit its contents. Alternatively, you can double-click a title to edit it.

EXERCISE 6.8: CHANGING COLUMN TITLES

1. With the MyCustomerReport open in Layout view, double-click CustLastName. Drag the cursor through the entire label to select it, type Last Name (with a space), and press Enter to complete the modification.
2. Repeat Step 1, changing the labels (left to right) to First Name, Address, City, State, and Zipcode. Press Enter after each change.
3. Review the report: Right-click the MyCustomerReport tab and then click Print Preview. Figure 6.4 shows the report's new column labels in Print Preview view.
4. Save the changes: Right-click the MyCustomerReport tab and click Save.

Fig. 6.4 Customer report with new column labels.

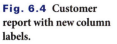

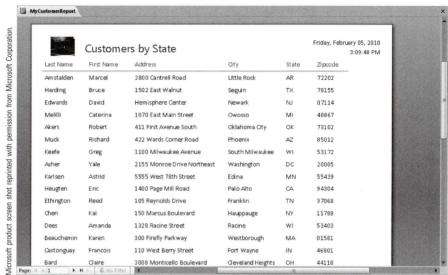

The customer report is quite long. You can preview all of its pages by reviewing it in Print Preview layout and using the navigation buttons to display successive pages or go to the last page.

TRY IT

In Print Preview view, click the *Next Page* navigation button located near the bottom of the window. Access displays the contents of the second print page. Click the *Last Page* button. Notice that the Current Page between the two sets of navigation buttons displays the number of the last page. (This number may vary depending on your default page margins.) Right-click the *MyCustomerReport* tab and click *Layout View* in the pop-up menu.

The customer report is in random order. Reports are more useful if they show information organized into useful groups in an order that helps those reviewing the report. A report whose rows appear in order by the customers' unique ID is of very little value.

Sorting and Grouping

Although the customer report retrieves and displays information in record ID order, you can use Access tools to sort and group that data. Doing so means that the report is far more useful because data appears in an order and organized in a way that makes sense. For example, you might want to sort the customer report in last name order. That facilitates locating customer Conroy much easier. Unsorted rows mean that you have to perform a very long search of the report to locate a particular person. It may be helpful to sort the report in order by city within state. Finding customers in Cincinnati, Ohio, becomes easy when sorted in that way. When producing mass mailings, it makes sense to sort the customer report in zip code order prior to producing mailing labels to save postage.

Access allows you to group records. A **_group_** is a set of related records. Accounting invoices grouped by customer name or ID makes sense. Grouping sounds like sorting. Sorting and Grouping are different. Grouping provides the advantage that Access creates two new report sections called a group header and group footer. The **_group header_** appears in a report before the new group of records appears. You use a group header to identify the group. The **_group footer_** appears below all members of the group—prior to the first record in a new group. You can display summary information about the group in the footer. For example, suppose you group the customer records by state. Because state abbreviations appear in place of full state names, all of the records for Alaska customers (AK) appear at the top of the report followed by Alabama (AL) because the default sorting of groups is ascending order. At the end of the report are customers from Wyoming (WY). In the group header for each state is the state name. The group footer can contain the count of the customers in each state, or it can contain any other statistic that summarized the records in the group. If you group invoices by invoice ID, for example, then the group footer for each invoice could contain the sum of the extended prices of each item in the invoice.

Modifying the customers report to contain groups and sorting will make this topic clear to you. In the next exercise, you will render the customer report more useful by grouping the customers into states and then sorting them by city and then last name within city. That way, it will be easy to locate a list of customers living in Lincoln, Nebraska, for example.

Note: In order to use the group and sort options, the Group, Sort, and Total pane must be open. You open that pane by clicking the Group & Sort button in the Grouping & Totals group of the Format tab while the report is in Layout view. If you are viewing the report in Design view, then the Group & Sort button is found in the Grouping & Totals group on the Design contextual tab that appears below the Report Design Tools.

EXERCISE 6.9: ADDING A GROUP TO THE CUSTOMER REPORT

1. With the MyCustomerReport open in Layout view, ensure that the Group, Sort, and Total pane is open.
2. Click Add a group in the Group, Sort, and Total pane. A pop-up list appears. It contains the names of the fields you can choose to group the report—including fields not in the current report.
3. Click CustState in the pop-up list. Access adds CustState *Group On* list to the Group, Sort, and Total pane. Access creates groups based on the state abbreviation in sorted order by state abbreviation.

The Group On list is the orange-colored ribbon that appears in the Group, Sort, and Total pane. Click More in the Group On list to display options. Group options include ascending (the default) sorting of groups, descending sort order, creating totals on any numeric field you want, choosing whether or not to show a group header or group footer, and choosing whether or not to ensure group members are kept together on a page.

Sorting within groups helps locate records within larger groups. For our customer report, you will sort by city within state. Although you might be tempted to subgroup states by city names instead of sorting by city, that creates the overhead of an additional header and footer for each city with a state. That is probably not necessary for this report. Sorting by city will suffice.

EXERCISE 6.10: **SORTING WITHIN A GROUP**

1. Click Add a sort beneath the CustState Group On list in the Group, Sort, and Total pane. A list of available fields appears in a pop-up list.
2. Click CustCity to sort by city within each group.
3. Click the Group & Sort button in the Grouping & Totals group of the Format contextual tab to close the Group, Sort, and Total pane.
4. Using the vertical scroll bar, scroll down to Alabama. Customers in Birmingham are followed by the cities of Dothan, Eufaula, Gadsden, Huntsville, Mobile, and so on—in ascending order by city (see Figure 6.5).
5. Click Save in the Quick Access Toolbar to save all of your report changes.

Fig. 6.5 Grouping and sorting customer records.

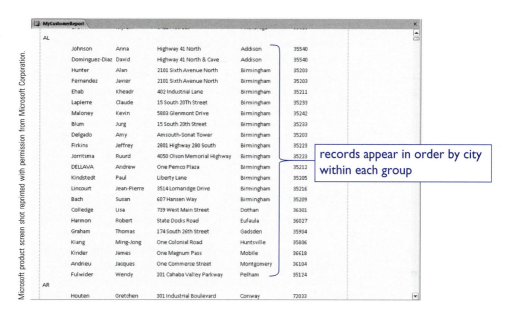

Microsoft product screen shot reprinted with permission from Microsoft Corporation.

Formatting Reports

You can format a report's controls by applying one of the predefined AutoFormat layouts, which are located in the AutoFormat group on the Format contextual tab. If none of the existing AutoFormats suit your requirements, then you can customize them. Customization choices for the AutoFormats include creating a new AutoFormat based on the displayed form, modifying an AutoFormat with values from the form, or deleting one or more of the AutoFormats. Finally, if you create your own AutoFormat, you can format controls manually and then save the result as the division standard report format, for example. You can experiment with AutoFormat by clicking several and finding one that works well for any given report. Bear in mind that some report AutoFormats may be unsuitable when they are printed on a monochrome laser printer. For example, an AutoFormat with a dark title background color may obscure the title or logo. Choose carefully and then preview each prior to finalizing your choice.

Formatting individual controls is straightforward. First, select the control and then use the buttons and lists in the Font group of the Format tab in either Design view or Layout view. For example, click the Bold, Italic, or Underline buttons to apply those formats to the selected control(s). Similarly, change the foreground color by clicking the Font color button list and selecting a color. Change the background color of a control by clicking the Fill/Back color button. Of course, you can modify the font and change styles from Calibri to Times New Roman, for example. Any formatting changes you make to a control apply to all the bound values displayed in that control.

Applying Conditional Formatting to a Control

You can fine tune formatting so that a control displays one or another characteristic depending on its value. A format that automatically applies to a control based on the particular value condition of the data displayed in the control is called *conditional formatting*. (We introduced conditional formatting in Chapter 5.) Conditional formatting might include bold typeface for values above some defined threshold, or a red font color could indicate values indicating subpar performance. How you format a control using conditional formatting partially depends on the medium used to display the results. As mentioned above, if you plan on printing a report on a black-and-white laser printer output, then color-based conditional will not display well. On the other hand, restrained use of color in conditional formats nicely highlights exceptional values on a color printer. The Customers by State report you created contains customer name and address information. Because it does not contain any numeric values, that report does not lend itself to conditional formatting. Reports containing numeric values such as invoice amounts, larger than normal quantities, or unusual quantity on hand values are better candidates for conditional formatting. We will illustrate conditional formatting with an example in another section of this chapter.

Previewing a Report

In addition to Layout view, Access provides two additional ways to preview your report prior to printing it: Print Preview view and Report view. *Print Preview view* displays the report the way it will appear with the actual fonts, shading, lines, and so on. Print Preview view is a static view and disallows changing anything in the report, but it shows how pages will break when printed. It is always best to click the Print Preview button to review your report before actually printing. Clicking the Last Page button in the report navigation button set shows you how many pages the report contains.

Report view is more flexible than Print Preview view because it allows you to dynamically filter the data and drill down to print only the information you need. Data in Report view looks similar to that shown in Layout view, but you cannot make report design changes of any kind in Report view. In Report view, you can select report text and copy it to the clipboard. To select entire rows, click and drag in the margin next to the rows that you want to select and then click Copy in the Home tab Clipboard group. You can apply filters directly to your report without leaving Report view. For example, if you want to see only those report rows containing *Springfield* in the City column—customers who live in Springfield in any state—then you can select an "exact" filter to display only those rows matching that filter criterion. The next exercise illustrates Report view filtering.

EXERCISE 6.11: FILTERING ROWS IN REPORT VIEW

1. Right-click the MyCustomerReport tab and click Report View in the pop-up menu to display the report in that view.
2. Right-click any city name in the City column (*Anchorage*, for example).

3. Point to Text Filters and then click Equals in the submenu (see Figure 6.6). A Custom Filter dialog box appears in which you type the string by which you want to filter the column.

4. Type Springfield in the Custom filter dialog box and click OK. Access displays only rows in which the city name matches Springfield (see Figure 6.7).

5. Toggle the report filter off: Click Toggle Filter in the Sort & Filter group of the Home tab. The entire report appears, unfiltered.

6. Right-click the MyCustomerReport tab and click Report View in the pop-up menu.

7. Remove the column filter entirely: Right-click a city name in the City column and click Clear filter from CustCity. Access permanently removes the column filter and displays all report rows again.

8. Right-click the MyCustomerReport tab and click Close All in the pop-up menu to close the report and any other open window. Click Yes when asked if you want to save changes to the design of the report.

Fig. 6.6 Filtering records in Report view.

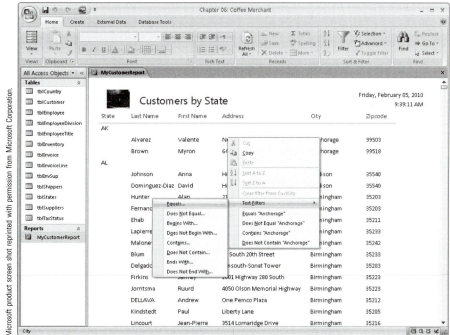

Building a Report Using the Report Wizard

Access' Report Wizard is the fastest and easiest way to create a report. The Report Wizard resembles the other wizards in Office products. It displays a series of dialog boxes in which you make decisions. You get a fair amount of control over the design of the report, and you control what database columns are included in the report. The best way to understand this is to build a simple, one-table report using the Report Wizard. To use the Report Wizard, you click a table from the Navigation Pane, click Report Wizard in the Reports group of the Create tab, and step through the dialog boxes making your decision.

Using the Report Wizard dialog boxes is intuitive. It just takes a bit of practice. The first dialog box displays the fields of the selected table in an Available Fields list. You

Fig. 6.7 **Filtered report.**

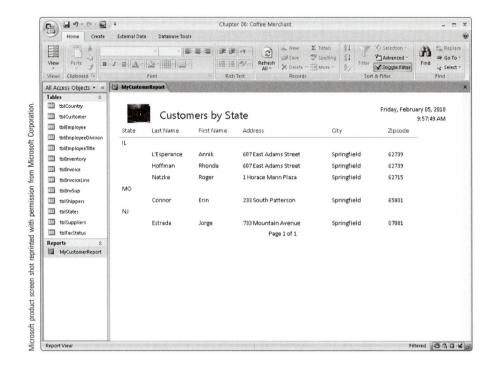

begin by clicking the > button to add a field from the Available Fields to the Selected Fields list. (Only the fields in the Selected Fields list appear in the report.) You can click the double greater than symbol (>>) to move *all* fields in the Available Fields list to the Selected Fields list. In either case, clicking Next moves to the next dialog box. It requests you to identify any grouping fields, which organize the report by the field you choose. If you choose State, for example, then the report displays detail rows grouped and sorted by state name. The state name, itself, appears in a group header once, instead of being repeated with each row. You can designate many grouping levels, but usually one or two do the job. You can choose to not group records at all, or use the suggested grouping that Access chooses. Pressing Next moves to the third Report Wizard dialog box where you can choose to sort the detail records on up to four fields and, importantly, select summary options in which you designate aggregate statistics on selected fields such as average salary by state or number of employees in a division. These Summary Options are just that—options. The next dialog box has option buttons for the report layout and orientation. Layout options include stepped, block, and outline. Orientation choices are obvious: portrait or landscape. A check box allows Access to squeeze the margins and fonts so that all fields appear on one page. The next dialog box contains a list of Auto-Report templates from which you can choose. Click the template you want to use and then click Next. The final dialog box lets you modify the name of the stored report. The report name also appears in the report title. Therefore, we suggest you think of a descriptive report title and use it. After Access creates the report, you can rename it to a shorter name in the Navigation Pane. Two option buttons provide the choice of previewing the report right away or displaying the report in Design view immediately after building it. You click Finish to complete the report building process. Access builds the report to your specifications and displays it in a tabbed window.

During any of the dialog box steps prior to clicking Finish, you can also click Back and go back one or more steps and change your choices in previous dialog boxes. It is not until you click Finish that the report is written "in stone" and cannot be altered within the Report Wizard. If you decide to abandon the report creation process altogether, then you can click the Cancel button in any step of the Report Wizard. Of course, you can modify any aspect of the report in Layout or Design views once the Report Wizard has completed its work. Let's build a simple report based on the related tables *tblEmployee*, *tblEmployeeDivision*, and *tblEmployeeTitle*. The Report Wizard makes pulling information from these three tables easy.

EXERCISE 6.12: CREATING A REPORT WITH THE REPORT WIZARD

1. Click the tblEmployee tab in the Navigation Pane to select that table.
2. Click the Create tab and click Report Wizard in the Reports group. The first Report Wizard dialog box appears with the fields in the *tblEmployee* table in the Available Fields list. (Trouble? Look in the Tables/Queries list box to ensure that *Table: tblEmployee* appears. If not, then click the list arrow and click Table: tblEmployee in the list.)
3. Click EmpFName in the Available Fields list and click the > button to place that field in the Selected Fields list.
4. Repeat Step 3 for EmpLName, EmpCommRate, EmpHireDate, EmpDOB, and EmpGender. (*Hint:* You can click the > key without first selecting a field if the next field immediately follows one you just placed in the Selected Fields list. Access automatically highlights the next field name in the Available Fields list. Check to be sure before clicking the > key.)
5. Click the Tables/Queries list box arrow and then click Table: tblEmployeeDivision in the list of available tables and queries.
6. Double-click DivisionCity in the Available Fields list to send it over to the Selected Fields list.
7. Click the Tables/Queries list box arrow and then click Table: tblEmployeeTitle, and double-click Title in the Available Fields list to send it over to the Selected Fields list (see Figure 6.8). Click Next to go to the next dialog box in the sequence.
8. Group by the division in which the employees work by clicking by tblEmployeeDivision in the left panel. Access displays a representation of the grouping field, removing it from the detail line (see Figure 6.9). Click Next. Access requests any other grouping fields.
9. Click Next because no further grouping fields are needed in this report.
10. Click the list box arrow in the sort-order field 1 and click EmpLName. Click the list box arrow in sort-order field 2 and click EmpFName. This causes Access to sort detail rows in last name order and then first name order for any ties among matching last names.
11. Click the Summary Options button and then click the Avg check box for the only numeric field listed and in the report, EmpCommRate (see Figure 6.10). Click OK to close the Summary Options dialog box, and click Next to go to the next Report Wizard dialog box.
12. Ensure that the *Adjust the field width so all fields fit on a page* check box contains a check mark, and then click Next.
13. Click Access 2007 in the list of templates. You may have to use the scroll bar to scroll to the top of the list of choices, which are in alphabetical order. Click Next to go to the last step.
14. Double-click the title text box at the top of the dialog box and type Employees by Division. Click Finish. The Report Wizard closes and Access displays the completed report in Print Preview view (see Figure 6.11).
15. Right-click the report tab and click Close All. Right-click Employees by Division in the Navigation Pane, click Rename, type MyEmployeeReport, and press Enter to rename the stored report.

Fig. 6.8 Selecting
fields for a report.

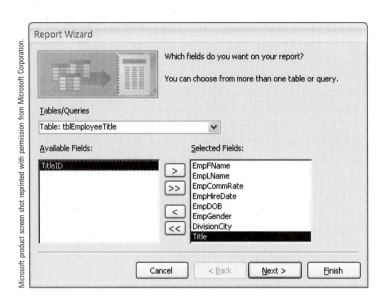

Fig. 6.9 Specifying a
grouping field.

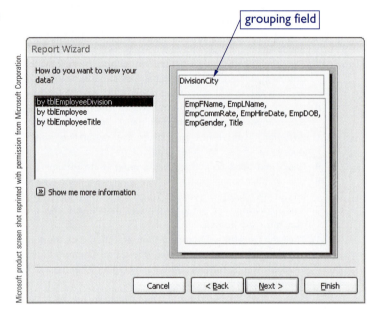

The report is not perfect, and we need to do some adjustments to make the report better. The Title column is truncated, for example. All in all, Access has done a lot of the difficult work of creating report and group headers and footers as well as group aggregate information such as average commission rate.

Fig. 6.10 Setting summary options.

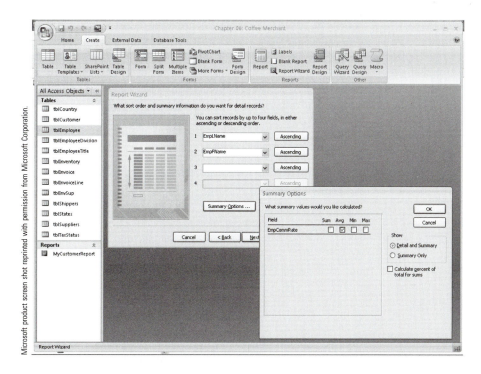

Microsoft product screen shot reprinted with permission from Microsoft Corporation.

Fig. 6.11 Completed employee report.

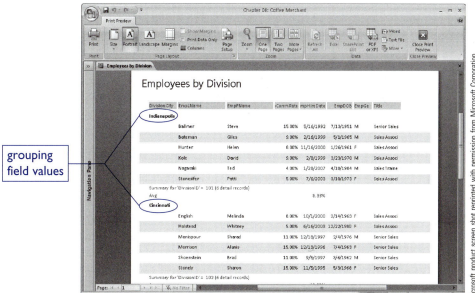

grouping field values

Microsoft product screen shot reprinted with permission from Microsoft Corporation.

A Few Guidelines for Good Report Design

Much has been written about creating attractive, easily understood, and useful reports. In the previous chapter we listed a few guidelines for good form design. Similarly, there are some considerations you should keep in mind as you create your reports—report guidelines. Before considering these guidelines, it is most important always to consider who will be reading the reports and for what purpose. Design the report so that readers can find information easily and quickly. For example, creating a report of employees by division along with their telephone numbers may be great for division managers wanting a concise list of those who work for them along with essential employee details. However, such a report would not be useful as a telephone book reference because one would have to know what division an employee works in to locate their telephone number. If the report receives wide readership such as most employees in the company, then be sure to adhere to any corporate standards and design rules (e.g., the company logo on the top of every page, a company confidential notification at the bottom of each page, and so on). The following guidelines are useful no matter who your audience is.

Use Existing Paper Reports When Needed

Access reports that are destined to replace older paper reports are more acceptable and easier to understand if they resemble the older, legacy reports they are about to replace. Departing wildly from existing report designs can confuse and alienate your would-be readership. This does not preclude making improvements to old paper reports. Part of the utility of digital reports is that their design can be changed easily. The point is to not stray too far from the original with the first iteration of an Access report. Over time, you can improve and change reports in small increments.

Use Page Numbers, Dates, and Times

Multipage reports should always have page numbers. In addition, page headers identifying changes in the content they head up are a handy reference. Page headers and footers provide useful road signs that help keep readers oriented as to where they are and the relevance of each page. Dates and times appearing unobtrusively in a page header or footer indicate the timeliness of the report information. There is nothing worse than pouring over a report for an hour or two and then discovering it is last month's report because there was no date or time anywhere on the report.

Ensure Field Order Makes Sense

The left-to-right order and the top-down order of information should mimic that of any legacy report that you are replacing with the Access report. Address information should appear in order by street, city, state, country, and postal code—no other order. Invoice reports showing invoice detail should be headed by purchaser and vendor information. Detail information follows lower in the same report.

Sorting and Grouping Are Always Welcome

Report information whose data appears in rows and columns in no particular order is about as worthless as can be. Consider a customer listing in which the customer information appears in CustomerID order. How absurd! Instead, the report should display customers in some meaningful order—sorted by name or grouped by state and then city within state and then by last name. A daily report for express shipment drivers delivering packages to customers should be in street order to minimize travel route time. In this latter case, package recipients sorted by last name would be of little value. Grouping information together by one or more common fields means related information is found close together. That makes finding everyone who bought a particular product, for example, easy to identify when the report groups purchases by product name.

Keep it Simple

Reports that contain information in an organized, easy-to-read format are best. What you should avoid is overdesigning a report to the point where it contains a lot of color effects, too many visual distractions, and other special effects. Just because you *can* include some special whiz bang feature does not mean it is a good idea. We have all seen word processed documents with too many different fonts, too much color, too many changes in emphasis, or all of the preceding. Avoid this in reports too. Keep to just a couple fonts, use bolding sparingly, and keep it simple. When in doubt, it is best to follow the "less is more" rule.

Creating a Report from Scratch in Design View

In this chapter, you have created a report using Report command. You probably agree that it is a fast and efficient way to create a report. You have also created reports by using the Report Wizard. The Report Wizard gives you more control over which tables are included in the report and control over the template used to create the report. When your report needs require a high degree of customization, not available with either of the preceding two report generation methods, then you can turn to creating a report from scratch—a blank report drawing pad—and control every aspect of the design and appearance of every individual control and visual element in your report. Designing a report this way begins by selecting the Report Design button in the Reports group of the Create tab. The cost of having all this flexibility and design control is that the report creation process will take more time. The advantage is complete control over the report and its design. While we do not advocate always creating from scratch, it is useful to know how to do so. Later, when you have to modify a report created with the Report Wizard, for instance, you can display the report in Design view and make both small and large changes to it. These skills you can learn by creating a report from scratch in Design view. Report view gives you unlimited control over the placement of controls, their individual properties and behaviors, their position, and formatting details throughout the report.

Creating a Blank Report and Adding Fields

To begin creating a report in Design view you have two choices: In the Reports group of the Create command you can (1) Click Blank Report button and then click Design View in the View group on the Format contextual tab or (2) Click Report Design. Either way, you end up in the same place. The report you will create, bit by bit, displays the product inventory grouped by the country in which it is produced. Groups of products will be sorted by product name, and the average units on hand will appear at the bottom of each group. First, create a new, blank report in Design view by doing the following exercise.

EXERCISE 6.13: OPENING A NEW, BLANK REPORT IN DESIGN VIEW AND ADDING FIELDS

1. Click the Create tab and then click Report Design in the Reports group. Access creates a blank report in Design view and displays a list of tables and the fields they contain.
2. If the Field List panel is not open, click the Add Existing Fields button in the Tools group of the Design contextual tab.
3. Click the Expand button (+) to the left of the *tblInventory* table name to display the field names.
4. Double-click the following field names in *tblInventory* to add them to the report: Beverage, ItemName, UnitPrice, UnitsOnHand, Caffeinated, and Flavored. Access adds the selected fields to the report.

Selecting Fields from Related Tables

The *tblInventory* table is related to several other tables, but *tblCountry* is particularly important in the report you are creating. It contains the name of the country that exports the inventory item. Notice that once you pick a table to add to the report, it opens another panel in the Field List labeled *Fields available in related tables*. Access knows those tables carry a relationship to *tblInventory* because of the relationships initially defined in the Relationships window—the primary key to foreign key relationships between table pairs. To add fields to a report, simply select one or more of the fields in the related tables to the report. Access will do the rest by adding to the report only fields you select in rows whose primary and foreign key fields match.

EXERCISE 6.14: ADDING A RELATED FIELD FROM ANOTHER TABLE TO A REPORT

1. Click the Expand button (+) to the left of the *tblCountry* table name in the *Fields available in related tables* panel to display its field names.
2. Double-click CountryName to add that field to the report. Access adds *tblCountry* to the Fields List panel labeled *Fields available for this view*.
3. The newly added field CountryName should still be highlighted and may not be in the correct position. Move the mouse over the CountryName text box (white background). When the mouse becomes a four-headed arrow, click and drag the field and its associated label to a position above Beverage text box and label (see Figure 6.12).
4. Click the Add Existing Fields button in the Tools group of the Design tab to close the Field List panel.

Fig. 6.12 Creating a report in Design view.

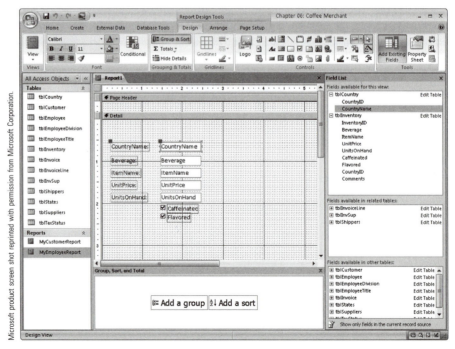

Creating a Tabular Control Layout

The labels and database fields that appear in the report are both called controls. The labels to the left of the text boxes are called *unbound controls* because they do not vary from one database record to the next—they are fixed. The controls that are associated with changing database field values are called *bound controls* because each control is bound to, or displays, a single database field. A third type of control is called a *calculated control* and can contain an expression that computes a value based on controls in the report. We will add calculated controls to the report a little later in this chapter.

With the bound and unbound controls in place (the unbound controls require further modification so they are more familiar English words), we can organize the controls into a single control layout for easier manipulation.

EXERCISE 6.15: CREATING A TABULAR CONTROL LAYOUT FROM INDEPENDENT CONTROLS

1. In the report design window, click and drag the mouse around all controls on the report. Before you release the mouse, a dashed line appears around all the controls.
2. Release the mouse to select all the report controls—both unbound and bound. If you skipped one or two controls, hold down the Shift key and click any missing controls to add them to the selected controls. Remember to click both the bound and unbound controls.
3. Click the Arrange tab and then click Tabular in the Control Layout group. The controls snap into two rows with the unbound controls in the Page header and the bound controls in the Detail report section.
4. A lot of changes have been made. Save the new report: Click Save in the Quick Access Toolbar, type MyInventoryReport in the Save As text box, and click OK. Access names and saves the report.
5. Click in a blank area of the Detail report section and drag the mouse around all of the bound controls.
6. Move over the upper edge of any selected bound control. When the mouse becomes a four-headed arrow, drag up toward the Detail band until the controls touch the band. Release the mouse. This reduces the space between detail database record lines in the report (see Figure 6.13).

Grouping and Sorting

Grouping report rows is an invaluable tool when you have a large volume of information in a report. Using report grouping and sorting options, you can arrange data into smaller, related groups and then carry out calculations on each group. Consider the inventory report you have been developing. There are several natural ways to group the inventory rows depending on how you use the report. Access can group items by beverage type (coffee or tea), by vendor supplying each item (though we do not include that information here), or by country of origin. Grouping by country of origin provides a picture of the areas of the world from which The Coffee Merchant gets its coffee and tea products. Recall that you have learned how to group information in a query. That type of group provides aggregate information but no details about the data that comprise each group, and you can perform calculations (expressions) on each individual group. Grouping in a report provides detail information that is followed by summary information about the group. Report grouping rather than grouping in a query supplying data to a report is

Fig. 6.13 Forming controls into a Tabular control layout.

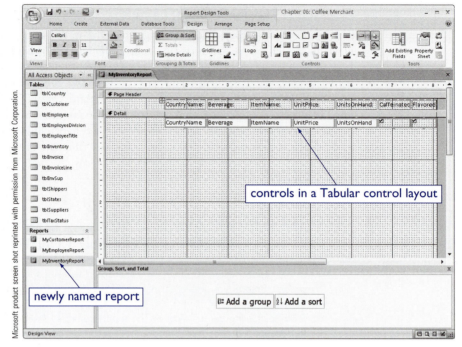

superior whenever you want to see both details and summary information. You can include multiple grouping levels to expose trends that may not be obvious in the ungrouped report results.

Grouping and sorting options are available in the group pane appearing in Design view or Layout view. It is labeled "Group, Sort, and Total" at the top of the pane. If it does not appear, simply click the *Group & Sort* button in the Grouping & Totals group of the Design tab in Design view. (In Layout view, click the *Group & Sort* button on the Format contextual tab.)

Let's modify the report MyInventoryReport to display inventory items grouped by country of origin and sorted in each individual group by item name. Then, we'll add computations in the group footer to display counts and averages.

EXERCISE 6.16: GROUPING AND SORTING REPORT LINES

1. Open MyInventoryReport in Design view, if necessary.
2. If the Group, Sort, and Total pane does not appear at the bottom of the report's design, click Group & Sort in the Grouping & Totals group of the Design contextual tab.
3. In the Group, Sort, and Total pane, click Add a group and click CountryName in the field list pop-up menu. Access adds a list to the Group, Sort, and Total pane (see Figure 6.14). You can sort the groups into ascending or descending order by choosing from the sort order list. The default is ascending order and appears as *with A on top* in the sort order list.
4. Click More in the Group on list to display properties for the grouping field, and then click the *without a footer section* list arrow (see Figure 6.15) and click with a footer section to add a group footer section to the report.
5. In the Group, Sort, and Total pane, click Add a sort and click ItemName in the field list pop-up menu. This will sort the items in each group into ascending alphabetical order by the ItemName field.

6. Reduce the space between detail lines: Scroll down the report until you locate the CountryName Footer section. Point to the top of that named bar. When the mouse becomes a double-headed arrow, drag it to a point just below the Detail line section. In fact, you can drag the footer midway into the Detail fields and the footer will snap back to immediately below the fields.

Fig. 6.14 Adding a *Group on* list to the Group, Sort, and Total pane.

Smart Tag warning about report width

a *Group on* list

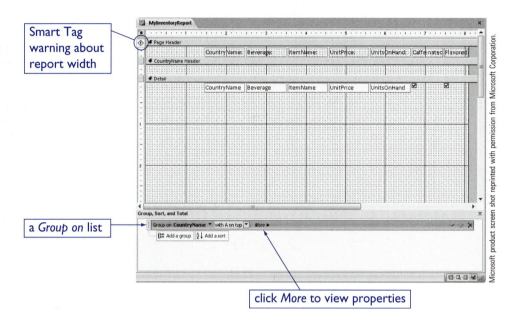

click *More* to view properties

Fig. 6.15 Adding a group footer.

Microsoft product screen shot reprinted with permission from Microsoft Corporation.

It is likely that there is a Smart Tag in the upper-left corner of the report design indicating that the report's width is greater than the page width. You can rearrange fields to reduce the width. The next exercise shows you how. More importantly, it also illustrates how to rearrange fields to conserve space. Before you can move one of the fields to a new position, you will have to remove it from the control group containing it.

EXERCISE 6.17: MOVING A FIELD TO THE GROUP HEADER

1. Click the CountryName field in the Detail group, click the Arrange contextual tab (one of three Report Design Tools contextual tabs), and click Remove in the Control Layout group. Access removes CountryName and its label in the Page Header section from the Control Layout group.
2. With CountryName still selected in the Detail section, press Ctrl+X, click the CountryName Header band, and press Ctrl+V. Those keyboard shortcuts cut and paste the control to its new location in the group header.

3. Click Beverage in the Detail section to display the Control Layout move handle (a four-headed arrow), and then click the Control Layout move handle and drag the labels and their fields to the right to reveal the CountryName label in the Page Header.
4. Click CountryName in the Page Header (a column label, not a bound control) and press the Delete key to delete the label.
5. Click Beverage in the Detail section, click and drag the Control Layout move handle to the left so that the Beverage field is near the right edge of the CountryName field in the group header. Figure 6.16 shows the approximate position. (We turned off the grid temporarily so that the Control Layout move handle is easier to see.)

Fig. 6.16
Repositioning a control layout.

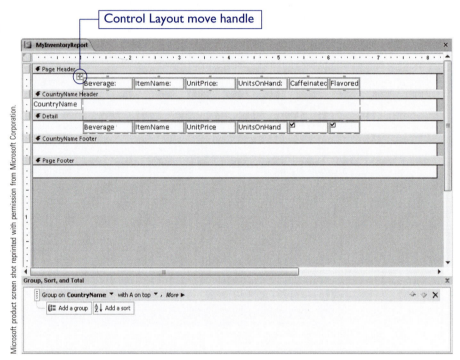

Microsoft product screen shot reprinted with permission from Microsoft Corporation.

A report's fields sometimes are positioned such that they overlap the physical limits of the page. This is probably the case with your MyInventoryReport as it is designed now. Notice that the grid lines extend beyond the eight-inch mark on the ruler (Design view). If your ruler does not appear at the top of the Design view page, then click Grid in the Show/Hide group of the Arrange contextual tab. The remedy for a too-wide report, once fields and labels are within page boundaries, is to move the right edge of the grid so that it is within the page boundaries. This Try It exercise shows you how.

TRY IT

In Design view, point to the right edge of the grid background. When the mouse pointer changes to a double-headed arrow pointing left and right, click and drag the grid's right edge to the left until it is positioned at the seven-inch mark on the ruler.

Adding Calculations to a Report

Often reports merely display data such as the inventory records. However, analysts may need more than a list of the inventory. They might want to know the average inventory levels for each group of products or the number of items in each group, which inventory items are most plentiful or which need to be replenished. Answering these questions with a report requires that the report contain one or more calculations. Calculations are expressions that are not stored in any underlying table. Instead, calculations get their value as the report is produced from the values in an entire report or a subset of it such as each of the report's groups. The easiest way to produce calculations is to use the Group, Sort, and Total pane. Alternatively, you can manually add text boxes and write expressions in their Control Source properties. Use the Totals list in the Group, Sort, and Total pane to create calculations quickly. The next exercise shows you how.

EXERCISE 6.18: ADDING CALCULATIONS TO THE GROUP FOOTER

1. In the Group, Sort, and Total pane, click More in the *Group on* list, if necessary, to display Group on options.
2. Click the Totals list box arrow (it probably displays *with no totals* to the left of the list arrow).
3. Click the Total On list box arrow, click UnitsOnHand from the list, click the Type list box arrow, click Average, and click the Show in group footer check box (see Figure 6.17). These actions display the average units on hand in the CountryName footer.
4. Click anywhere in the report design to close the Total On list. Access creates an expression to calculate the average units on hand and places it in the CountryName footer.
5. Click the Totals list box arrow again, click the Total On list box arrow, click Beverage from the list, and click the Show in group footer check box. Because Beverage is not a numeric field, Access automatically displays "Count Values" in the Type list box—exactly what we need.
6. Click anywhere in the report design to close the Total On list. Access creates an expression to count the number of items in each group and places it in the CountryName footer.
7. Click the Save button in the Quick Access Toolbar to save all the report's changes.

Fig. 6.17 Selecting a field, its aggregate function, and its placement.

Microsoft product screen shot reprinted with permission from Microsoft Corporation.

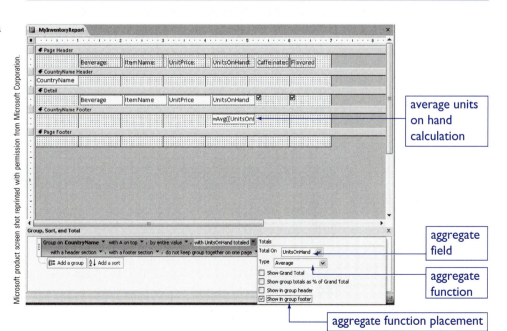

average units on hand calculation

aggregate field

aggregate function

aggregate function placement

It is handy to preview the report before going on. It is difficult to see how the report looks in Design view.

TRY IT

Right-click the *MyInventoryReport* tab and click *Print Preview* in the pop-up menu. Access displays the report the way it will look if you were to print it. Notice that average value for the units on hand contains far too many places to the right of the decimal place. A little formatting tweak can fix that. Right-click the *MyInventoryReport* tab and click *Design View* in the pop-up menu.

Adding Page Breaks Before Sections

A report containing groups and aggregate group information may be easier to read if you start each group or section on a new page. Although you can manually add a page break control, Access can add automatically insert page breaks by modifying a section's property called *Force New Page*. That property, one of many, is found by opening the Property Sheet while the report is displayed in Design view.

EXERCISE 6.19: ADDING A SECTION PAGE BREAK

1. With MyInventoryReport displayed in Design view, click the CountryName Header band to highlight it. The section band turns black indicating you have selected it.
2. Click the Property Sheet button in the Tools group of the Design contextual tab.
3. Click the Format tab. Click the Force New Page property, click the list arrow on the right of its value, and click Before Section (see Figure 6.18).
4. Close the property sheet and click Save in the Quick Access Toolbar to save all the changes you have made since you last saved the report.

With the Force New Page property set to "Before Section," Access will go to a new page each time a new group heading is printed. Therefore, each country's products will begin on a new page. Review the report you have created in Print Preview to ensure it is correct and on track so far.

TRY IT

Right-click the *MyInventoryReport* tab and click *Print Preview* in the pop-up menu. Access displays the report the way it will look if you were to print it. The first page displays three entries for Brazil. Click the *Next Page* navigation button to review the report's second page. You see the 15 entries for China. Right-click the *MyInventoryReport* tab and click *Design View* in the pop-up menu.

Fig. 6.18 Setting the Force New Page property.

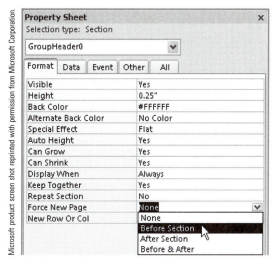

In Design view the labels for each column appear in the Page Header. Because each group now appears on a new page, the page header conveniently appears above the first row of each group. Previously, the columns for various groups did not have column headers directly above the group columns because many of the groups did not appear on a new page. An alternative way to place headers to appear above each group is to move the labels from the Page Header section to the CountryName Group Header section.

Modifying Report Properties

Every report you create in Access has hundreds of properties you can set. You can set report-wide properties such as its page footer and header, its default view, and its caption (the text that appears in the report's tab). In fact, every object on the report has its own set of properties you can set. Although you will likely not be faced with setting many of the available properties, the report's controls will look better if we set just a few properties so that values such as the average units on hand display in a more readable format. Setting report object controls is the same regardless of whether it is a report header, group header, or an individual bound control: Display the report in Design view, click the object, open the property sheet, and modify one or more selected properties. In the next exercise, you will set one report property to open the report in Print Preview by default and modify the display properties of the average units on hand summary statistic found in the group footer.

EXERCISE 6.20: MODIFYING REPORT PROPERTIES

1. With MyInventoryReport displayed in Design view, click Property Sheet in the Tools group of the Design contextual tab, if necessary, to open the property sheet.
2. Click the list box arrow in the Selection type list box located at the top of the property sheet. Click Report. (You may have to scroll the list. It is in alphabetical order.)
3. Click the Format tab, if necessary, click the Default View property, click its list box arrow, and click Print Preview. From now on, the report will open in Print Preview by default.

4. Click the list box arrow in the Selection type list box located at the top of the property sheet. Click AccessTotalUnitsOnHand, and click the Format tab, if necessary.
5. Click the Format property, click its list box arrow, and click Standard. The Standard format selection displays numbers with commas where required.
6. Click the Decimal Places property value and type 0 for the property value, if necessary.
7. Click Save in the Quick Access Toolbar, right-click the MyInventoryReport tab, and click Close All in the pop-up menu.
8. Double-click MyInventoryReport in the Navigation Pane. Notice that the report opens in Print Preview by default. Also notice that the value of average units on hand is nicely formatted. (You may have to increase the zoom level to see report details.)
9. Redisplay the report in Design view: Right-click MyInventoryReport tab and click Design View.

There are several properties available in the property sheet for any controls. You can experiment changing some of them. We suggest you save the report before experimenting with properties in case you want to revert to the original report format.

Applying Conditional Formatting to a Control

The formatting you applied to the average units on hand control is static formatting. That is, the formatting remains fixed unless you manually change it. Next, you will apply conditional formatting to a control. You have learned about this term in the Forms chapter. To reiterate, conditional formatting is applied when the value of a control meets a particular specification or value. For example, you could set a conditional format to display dates in bold when they are more than 60 days past due. Or, a control could display in a different color to draw attention to it when the value is abnormal or unusual. In the MyInventoryReport, it would be helpful to highlight inventory in-stock levels (units on hand) that are below a predefined reorder value. Conditional formatting for inventory levels that are unusually low might be set to bolded, Italic, or both for example. It would likely make a procurement person notice the unusually formatted values. He or she could then take action to correct the inventory shortfall situation. Experimenting with conditional formatting for report values will make this concept clear to you.

To apply conditional formatting to an object, you can click Conditional in the Font group of the Design contextual tab. Another way to open the Conditional Formatting dialog box is a technique we show you in the next exercise.

EXERCISE 6.21: APPLYING CONDITIONAL FORMATTING TO A REPORT CONTROL

1. Right-click UnitsOnHand in the Detail report band and click Conditional Formatting. If you mistakenly right-click the UnitsOnHand *label* in the Page Header, just press Esc and start again with the bound control in the Detail section of the report. The Conditional Formatting dialog box appears.
2. Click the relational condition appearing in the second text box and click less than in the list of values.
3. Click in the third Condition 1 text box and type 123.
4. Click the Bold button and click the Underline button (see Figure 6.19). You could add other conditions as needed by clicking the Add button. This is enough for now.
5. Click OK to commit the conditional formatting changes.

6. Click Save on the Quick Access Toolbar.
7. Preview the report by right-clicking MyInventoryReport and clicking Print Preview. Notice the bolded and underlined units on hand values. They are all less than 123. Close the report.

Fig. 6.19 Setting a conditional format.

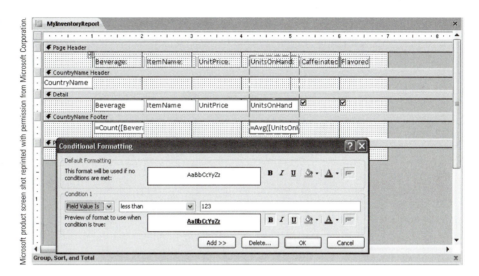

Microsoft product screen shot reprinted with permission from Microsoft Corporation.

Fine-Tuning the Report

More fine-tuning is required before the report is complete. Several of the column labels require modification to convert them to proper English words (e.g., *UnitsOnHand* should be changed to *Units On Hand*). The inventory item names are obscured because their fields are not wide enough in most cases. Some columns such as *Beverage* are wider than they need to be. It is easiest and best to make these types of changes to the report while it is displayed in Layout view. It is not necessary to do so now, but you could switch to that view, click the ItemName column label, and drag it to the right to widen it. Changing column names is simple, too. This is left as an exercise to the student. When you are done, remember to save the report.

Creating a Multitable Report Based on a Query

Although more firms are using electronic data interchange every day, many insist on receiving an invoice printed on paper. The Access report facility provides all the needed tools to build a nicely formatted invoice. Because one of the columns in the invoice is an extended price field (quantity times unit price minus any discount), the first step in generating an invoice report is to build a query that will gather the information we have stored about the sales transactions stored in *tblCustomer*, *tblEmployee*, *tblInventory*, *tblInvoice*, and *tblInvoiceLine*. We omit other related tables such as *tblShippers* and *tblTaxStatus* to simplify the invoice report.

Examining a Query Supplying Report Data

You will participate in building the invoice report, and we will help. You are familiar with all of the steps needed to build the invoice report except for a few. We will explain these carefully in individual exercise steps. We begin by examining the query—one that you have not seen before—that joins five tables to assemble all the fields needed to produce an invoice. Using a query for the basis of a report is a good choice because it includes an expression to compute the extended price.

Figure 6.20 shows the query that produces the fields needed for each invoice. The Query By Example (QBE) grid columns are narrow so that you can see several of the Field row entries, though most fields are out of view. The query shown is the foundation of the invoice report you will build, and it supplies all data fields to the report. To save some time, we have created the query for you. It is hidden in the Navigation Pane and is named qryInvoiceReport, so you will have to unhide it before you can open it. The Try It exercise below refreshes your memory on how to reveal hidden Navigation Pane objects.

Fig. 6.20 Query to select fields for an invoice report.

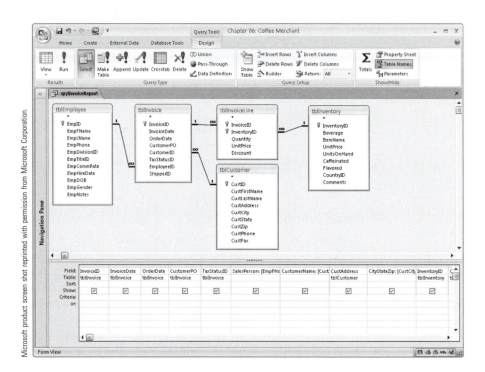

Microsoft product screen shot reprinted with permission from Microsoft Corporation.

TRY IT

Right-click *All Access Objects* at the top of the Navigation Pane, click *Navigation Options*, click the *Show Hidden Objects* check box to place a check mark in it, and click *OK* to close the Navigation Options dialog box. The hidden query appears as a dimmed name. You can open an object "hidden in this group" the same way you do an unhidden one: double-click it or right-click it and click the view you desire from the pop-up list.

Open the query qryInvoiceReport in Design view. Observe how the tables are joined. The *tblCustomer* and *tblInvoice* tables are joined by column CustomerID. Similarly, *tblInvoice* is joined to *tblInvoiceLine* by column InvoiceID found in both tables. Other joined tables are *tblInvoice* to *tblEmployee* on the column EmployeeID, and *tblInvoiceLine* to *tblInventory* by column InventoryID. Thus, the five tables are joined by four sets of primary key to foreign key pairs. Scroll to the rightmost field in the query. The last field contains the calculation for extended price. It is as follows:

Extended: Round([tblInvoiceLine]![Quantity]*[tblInvoiceLine]![UnitPrice]*
(1-[tblInvoiceLine]![Discount]),2)

The sixth field from the left in qryInvoiceReport concatenates the salespersons' first and last names together (with a space between) using the expression

SalesPerson: [EmpFName] & " " & [EmpLName]

Ampersands connect the first name, a literal blank character (between double quotation marks) and last name together in one string that is assigned the alias *SalesPerson*, A field's alias is the optional string that precedes a colon and the expression. An alias, if it is included, always occurs first in a field—to the left of any expression. There are additional table fields that appear in the query as concatenated strings. Examine the field CustomerName and the field CustStateZip. Both of these fields, named with the aliases listed above, consist of several table fields joined together by the string concatenation operator ampersand (&). If you have trouble reviewing a long field expression, press Shift +F2 to open the Zoom dialog box. It is a large textbox similar to Notepad that displays an arbitrarily long string within it. Close the query after you have finished examining it. Figure 6.21 shows a typical invoice that you can produce with Access. The report produces one customer invoice per page and is ready to be mailed to customers.

Fig. 6.21 First page of the invoice report.

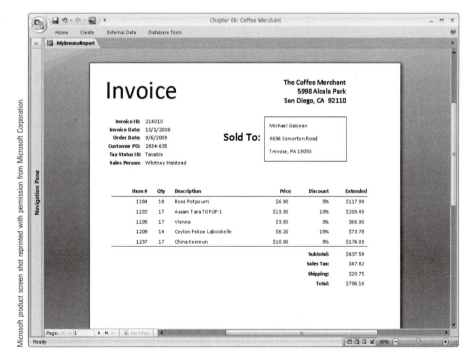

To close and hide the query, reverse the actions in the Try It above: Right-click the Navigation Pane's title bar, click Navigation Options, click Show Hidden Objects to clear that check box, and click OK to close the Navigation Options dialog box. Notice that the query is hidden and the Queries group name disappears because there are no other queries in this database.

You will create the invoice report in a series of drafts. You begin by creating the first draft. Following that, further modifications to the report result in better and better drafts until you arrive at a good quality final draft. (However, nothing is really "final." There will likely be further improvements that you will want to make if you keep this report and put it to use.) Here is a brief outline of the steps needed to create the invoice report from the qryInvoiceReport query:

- *Create a blank report and then open the report's properties and add qryInvoiceReport as the report's Record Source property.*
- *Create an InvoiceID group header and footer.*
- *Open up the* available fields *panel and move selected report fields into the InvoiceID group header.*
- *Rearrange detail rows so that they form a Tabular control layout.*
- *Add text box objects to the InvoiceID Footer and write Record Source expressions that calculate the invoice subtotal, sales tax (if any), shipping, and invoice total for each invoice.*
- *Resize report fields as needed.*

After completing each draft of the invoice report, be sure to save your report design. So you can have a separate copy of each draft, we will suggest you save each draft under a slightly different name. That way, you can revert to a previous version if the newest one you create is a total mess, and you have an audit trail of your drafts you can show your instructor.

Creating the First Draft of an Invoice Report

When you want to arrange fields in a particular way and have complete control over their placement and properties, creating a report from scratch is sometimes the best approach. We do that here to minimize work. Alternatively, you could create a report using the Report Wizard, but experimenting with creating the invoice report both with and without the Report Wizard has shown us that the best choice is to not use the Report Wizard. If you were to use the Report Wizard for this report, it would be fine. But you would end up doing a lot of cutting and pasting of controls to rearrange them in the proper location. Using a blank slate is sometimes better therefore. You have a lot of control right from the start.

EXERCISE 6.22: CREATING A REPORT BASED ON A QUERY

1. Click the Create tab and click Report Design in the Reports group.
2. Click the Property Sheet button in the Tools group of the Design contextual tab, ensure that the Report object is selected in the list box at the top of the properties pane, click the Data tab, click the Record Source property, click the list box arrow at the property's right end, and click qryInvoiceReport at the top of the selection of the query and several tables. This establishes the source of the report's data to be the named query.
3. Click the Property Sheet button to close the Property Sheet pane.
4. Click Group & Sort in the Grouping & Totals group of the Design contextual tab, if necessary, to open the Group, Sort, and Total pane.
5. Click Add a group, click InvoiceID, click More in the Group On list, click the *without a footer section* list arrow, and click with a footer section to add a group footer.
6. Scroll down the design and drag the InvoiceID footer band up until it is about two inches (see left ruler) below the Detail band (see Figure 6.22).

Fig. 6.22 Empty report with group header and footer.

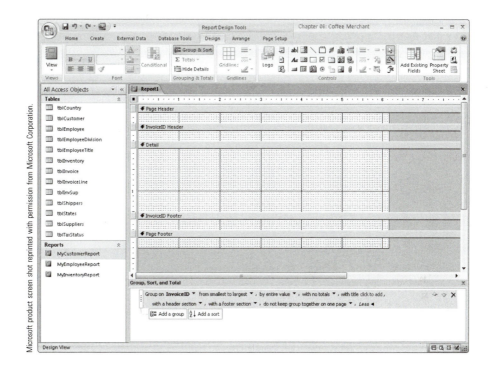

Manually Adding Fields

With the empty report canvas displayed in Design view, you can place the report fields it the Detail band and labels associated with them in the InvoiceID header—along with customer and company information. Access lets you select from any of the available database tables, but you will select fields from the query developed specifically for this invoice report and that is the data source—qryInvoiceReport. At first, the placement of bound and unbound controls may seem disorganized. But later steps will organize them into a cohesive and understandable arrangement. It takes just a few steps in Access 2007. Execute the next exercise to place query fields onto the report surface.

EXERCISE 6.23: ADDING FIELDS TO THE INVOICEID HEADER

1. Click Add Existing Fields in the Tools group of the Design contextual tab to display a list of available fields. If the Fields available for this view panel shows several tables and their fields, then click the Show only fields in the current record source link at the bottom of the Field List pane to display only qryInvoiceReport field names.
2. Drag the Detail header down to open up about 2 inches of space in the InvoiceID Header area. In the Field List pane, click InvoiceID, hold down the Shift key, and click CityStateZip. Access highlights nine fields in the Field List pane: InvoiceID, InvoiceDate, OrderDate, CustomerPO, TaxStatusID, SalesPerson, CustomerName, CustAddress, and CityStateZip.
3. Click inside the selected Field List field names, drag them to the left side of the InvoiceID Header area, and release the mouse to drop the fields in the InvoiceID Header (see Figure 6.23).

Fig. 6.23 Adding fields to a report from the Field List pane.

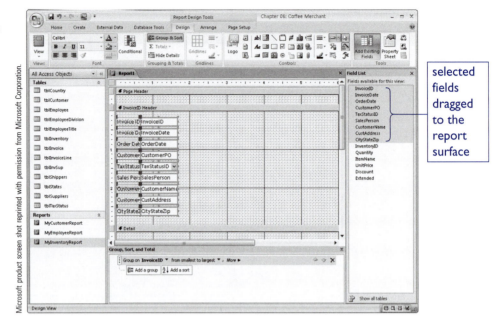

selected fields dragged to the report surface

Next, add database fields to the Detail section of the report. These are the fields that display one or more invoice lines associated with each invoice. That is, if a particular invoice, identified by its InvoiceID field, consists of ten detail items that are on the invoice, these lines appear in the detail area. Fields in the Detail section—bound controls—include InventoryID, Quantity, ItemName, UnitPrice, Discount, and the expression Extended. You add those detail lines next.

EXERCISE 6.24: ADDING FIELDS TO THE DETAIL BAND

1. To make the controls easier to see, click the Arrange tab and then click the Grid button in the Show/Hide group to hide the grid. Turn it on or off as you prefer. We have turned it off for these steps so the controls are easier for you to see in the figures.
2. In the Field List pane, click InventoryID, hold down the Shift key, and click Extended. Access highlights six fields.
3. Click inside these newly selected Field List field names, drag them to the Detail band, and release the mouse to drop the fields. Access places the bound controls and their associated labels (unbound controls) in a stacked arrangement in the Detail band. Press Alt+F8 (a shortcut alternative) to close the Field List pane.
4. With the newly moved Detail band items still selected, click the Arrange contextual tab and click Tabular in the Control Layout group. Access rearranges the labels and bound controls into two rows, places the column labels in the Page Header band, and leaves the database bound controls in the Detail band.
5. Click in any blank area to deselect the highlighted controls and then drag through the controls in the Page Header to select all six of them.
6. Click Remove in the Control Layout group of the Arrange contextual tab to disassociate the labels from the bound controls. (This facilitates moving the labels independently of the bound controls.)
7. Right-click the mouse inside any of the selected label controls in the Page Header you just highlighted and click Cut in the pop-up menu.

8. Click the InvoiceID header band, itself, to darken it, right-click any blank area in the InvoiceID Header section, and click Paste from the pop-up menu. The label controls reappear inside the InvoiceID Header section.
9. Click and drag the selected labels so they appear just above the Detail band.
10. With the labels still selected, hold down Shift, drag through all the bound controls in the Detail section, release Shift, and click Tabular in the Control Layout group of the Arrange contextual tab. This re-associates the labels and their bound controls in a tabular layout and ensures that they act as one group. You will find this helpful later when you widen or narrow selected columns. Click a blank area of the report to deselect the controls in the new control layout.
11. Click the InventoryID bound control in the Detail band and drag it up to just below the Detail band. All of the bound controls move together as a group and appear immediately below their labels.
12. Save the first draft of the report: Click Save in the Quick Access Toolbar, type MyInvoiceReportVer1 in the Report Name text box, and click OK. Access saves the report and its new name appears in the Navigation Pane (see Figure 6.24).

Fig. 6.24 Rearranging Detail band fields.

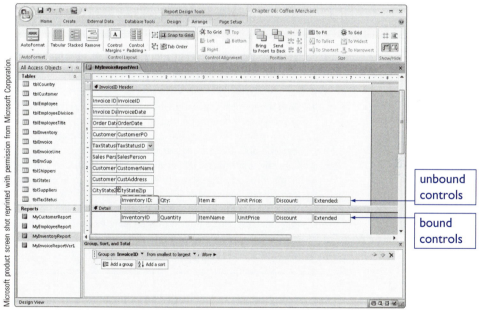

Rearranging and Reorganizing Fields

The size of the Detail band dictates spacing between the rows of the invoice detail lines. Let's adjust the Detail band items—the invoice lines—so that there is minimal space in between lines.

EXERCISE 6.25: ARRANGING FIELDS IN THE DETAIL BAND AND MINIMIZING ITS VERTICAL HEIGHT

1. Select all six controls in the Detail band by clicking the mouse to the left of the leftmost control and dragging to the right past the end of the rightmost control and then releasing the mouse.

2. Move the mouse inside any of the selected Detail band bound controls. When the mouse becomes a four-headed arrow, drag up toward the bottom of the Detail band so that the tops of the controls touch the Detail band.
3. Minimize the vertical length of the Detail band by moving the mouse to the InvoiceID Footer. When the mouse becomes a double-headed arrow, drag the InvoiceID Footer band up until it is just below the Detail band controls. (*Hint:* You can drag the band into the middle of the bound controls in the Detail band. Access adjusts the band so that it is immediately below the bottom of the bound controls.)
4. Right-click the MyInvoiceReportVer1 tab and click Layout View to review your design work. The detail lines should be close together and headed by their respective column labels.
5. Right-click the MyInvoiceReportVer1 tab and click Design View to continue your work in Design view.

Next, rearrange the fields in the InvoiceID header. You do this by dragging the mouse through the label/bound control pairs including CustomerName, CustAddress, and CityStateZip and them clicking and dragging the six controls up and to the right. Do that on your own. The labels (not the bound controls) associated with the customer address are unneeded, so you will delete them next.

EXERCISE 6.26: DELETING LABELS ASSOCIATED WITH BOUND CONTROLS

1. With the invoice in Design view, click the Property Sheet button in the Tools band of the Design contextual tab to open it. It is best to see the name of any control you are deleting to ensure it is not a bound control. The Property Sheet reveals the type and name of any selected control.
2. Click the label to the left of the CustomerName bound control. The selection type in the Property Sheet pane should display "Label" with a control name of the form *Labelx*, where "x" is a number (e.g., *Label8*).
3. Press the Delete key to delete the label. If you mistakenly delete a bound control, then click the Undo button in the Quick Access Toolbar to reverse that action.
4. Repeat Steps 2 and 3 for the labels CustAddress and CityStateZip.
5. Close the Property Sheet.

Rearranging labels and controls on a form or a report is easier in Layout view. In some of the next steps and other steps in this text, you are asked to shift-click controls. When you *shift-click* controls, you press and hold the Shift key while you click more than one control. This action groups the controls—selects them all—so you can perform some task on all controls at once.

EXERCISE 6.27: REARRANGING OTHER INVOICEID CONTROLS

1. Right-click the tab MyInvoiceReportVer1 and click Layout View.
2. Shift-click the six bound controls to the right of the labels Invoice ID, Invoice Date, Order Date, Customer PO, TaxStatusID, and Sales Person.
3. Click inside any selected control, drag the grouped bound controls to the right about one inch, and release the mouse.

4. Move the mouse to the right edge of any of the selected bound controls. When it becomes a double-headed arrow, drag to the right to lengthen the controls until they are about 50% wider than originally.
5. Shift-click the customer bound controls and repeat Step 4 to lengthen the controls so all the address information is visible. This is one of the reasons that Layout view is so helpful. You can manipulate controls and simultaneously observe data values as you do so.
6. Click the TaxStatusID label (not the bound control), click it again to display a vertical edit cursor, and edit the label to Tax Status ID by inserting two blank spaces. Then, click outside the control to deselect it.

Remember: To alter labels, click once the label you wish to change to select the entire label. Then, click the label a second time (do not double-click the label). A vertical I-beam (insertion point) cursor appears in the label so you can add and delete characters. If you find the activity of slowly clicking twice difficult, you can use an alternate technique: Double-click the label to bring up its property sheet. Then click the property sheet's Format tab, and type in the Caption property text box the corrected label. You can close the property sheet or leave it open. Leaving it open makes it simpler to change other labels' Caption properties.

Saving a Report Under a New Name

If you want to save the stages of change you have made to the invoice report, then you must save the changes since you last saved the report by using a new name. You simply click the Office button and follow steps to save it under a new name.

EXERCISE 6.28: SAVING A REPORT WITH A NEW NAME

1. Click the Office button, point to Save As in the Office menu, and click Save Object As.
2. Type MyInvoiceReportVer2 in the Save As text box, and click OK. Access saves the modified report under the new name, and that name appears in the Navigation Pane. Notice that the name on the report tab changes also.

Adding Calculated Controls

Comparing the report to Figure 6.21 showing the model invoice format we are building, you see that the invoice lacks values for subtotal, sales tax, shipping, and total. Those are calculated controls and you add them to a report displayed in Design view. *Calculated controls* are controls containing expressions referencing bound data controls, constants, and Access functions. The expressions calculate in real time as the report is generated, and calculated controls consist of text boxes containing expressions you type in their Control Source property. Text boxes are one type of several controls found in the Controls "toolbox" of the Controls group of the Design view contextual tab, Design. We add the required calculated controls in the next section.

Writing an expression involving arithmetic operators, numeric or character constants, table field names, and report objects creates a calculated control and tells Access exactly how to compute and display the result—similar in form to an Excel expression. For example, the query *qryInvoiceReport*, which supplies information to the report, contains several expressions. One of them contains the product of the Quantity, UnitPrice, and Discount fields. The expression is encased in the Round built-in function, which rounds the results to two decimal places. The expression is:

$$\text{Round}([\text{tblInvoiceLine}]![\text{Quantity}]*[\text{tblInvoiceLine}]![\text{UnitPrice}]*$$
$$(1-[\text{tblInvoiceLine}]![\text{Discount}]),2)$$

You can create calculated controls, or expressions, in forms and reports. For example, Subtotal, Sales Tax, Shipping, and Total in Figure 6.21 are calculated fields. They are not values stored in tables, because that would violate normalization rules and quickly lead to inconsistent data. Because the four mentioned fields are calculated, their values change with each invoice, printed or otherwise. The Report Wizard can automatically create Subtotal report field in the InvoiceID Footer if you click the Summary Options button and then check the Sum check box beneath the Extended column. However, we did not opt for that. Instead, you will create the missing Subtotal calculated control. It computes the sum of the extended price fields for each invoice. Later, you create other calculated controls including Sales Tax, Shipping, and Total.

The expressions found in controls' Control Source properties will reference the subtotal report control you create to sum the extended prices. In the next exercise you create that control, and you will rename it *ctlSubtotal*. The name prefix *ctl* helps you remember that the source of a value is a report control. Assigning objects names such as *ctlSubtotal* or *ctlSalesTax* accomplishes two important things. First, the names document the meaning of the fields you create on a design document (report or form). Second, names are mnemonic and easy to remember when you construct other calculated expressions.

The next exercise steps through creating the *ctlSubtotal* calculated control. It appears just below the Extended column in the InvoiceID Footer. It cannot appear in the Detail band because Access has to first retrieve and display all invoice lines in one invoice before any aggregate statistics are available for them. Therefore, the group footer is an ideal place for subtotals and other calculations on a group of related records in a report. But first, you need to create more room in the InvoiceID Footer so that it can accommodate the additional field (and more, later).

EXERCISE 6.29: CREATING THE SUBTOTAL CALCULATED CONTROL

1. Close any open reports or other objects if necessary.
2. Right-click MyInvoiceReportVer2 in the Navigation Pane; click Design View in the pop-up menu.
3. Move the mouse to the bottom edge of the InvoiceID footer. When the pointer changes to a double-headed arrow, drag the bottom edge of the InvoiceID Footer down so that it is approximately two inches high. This provides space for calculated controls you'll add next.
4. Click the Design contextual tab, if necessary. Click Group & Sort in the Grouping & Totals group to close the Group, Sort, and Total pane. That frees up some needed screen real estate.
5. Click Text Box in the Controls group. The tool displays "ab|" and appears in the top row of the Controls group (see Figure 6.25). (Hover the mouse pointer over a tool for a moment, and a ToolTip displaying *Text Box* will appear.)

6. Move the crosshair cursor to a position in the InvoiceID Footer immediately below the Extended bound control in the Detail band. Click the mouse to place a label and empty text box in the InvoiceID Footer (see Figure 6.25).

7. Click Property Sheet in the Tools group of the Design contextual, if necessary, to display the new control's property sheet.

8. Change the control's name: Click the Property Sheet Other tab, click in the Name property to highlight its assigned value, and type ctlSubtotal to rename the control.

9. Click the Format tab in the Property Sheet pane, click the Format property, click the property list box arrow, and click Currency from the list (see Figure 6.26).

10. Click the Data tab in the property sheet.

11. Click anywhere inside the Control Source text box, and then click the Build button that appears at the right side of the Control Source property. (The Build button has three dots, called an ellipsis.) The Expression Builder dialog box opens.

12. In the Expression Builder box, type =SUM([Extended]) and then click OK to close the dialog box. Be sure to use parentheses surrounding the field name that is, itself, contained with square brackets.

13. Click, twice, the label control to the left of the calculated control, type Subtotal: and press Enter.

14. Click the label to reselect it. (Click only once this time.)

15. Click the Format tab, click the Text Align property, click its list box arrow to display a list of choices, and click Right. Click outside the label to deselect it.

16. Close the Property Sheet.

Fig. 6.25 Placing a text box in a group footer.

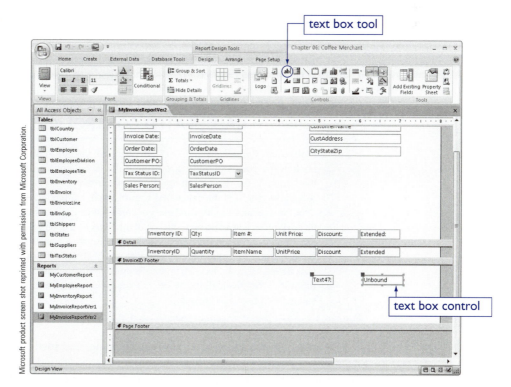

Fig. 6.26 Formatting a control.

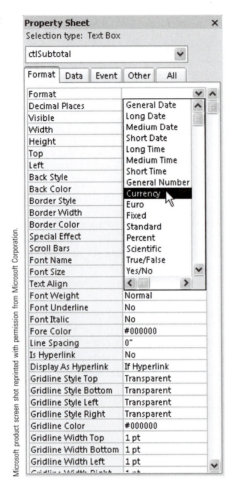

Microsoft product screen shot reprinted with permission from Microsoft Corporation.

You probably want to see if your newly added control works properly and displays property. The next small exercise makes final tweaks to the control and its label.

EXERCISE 6.30: MAKING SMALL CHANGES TO A CALCULATED CONTROL AND ITS LABEL

1. Right-click MyInvoiceReportVer2 tab and click Layout View.
2. Look at the placement and size of both the calculated control and its label. Adjust the length of the label by dragging its left border.
3. Adjust the length of the calculated control, itself, so that it does not overlap the label.
4. Click the calculated control and use your arrow keys to make small movements to adjust its position so it lines up with the last of the Extended price values—176.03 in this case. Your total value should display $637.59, matching the value shown in Figure 6.27.
5. Save the modified report under a new name: Click the Office button, point to Save As, click Save Object As, type MyInvoiceReportVer3 in the Save As text box, and click OK.
6. Right-click MyInvoiceReportVer3 tab (its new name) and click Close All. Access saves the report and closes it.

The procedure for adding the sales tax, shipping, and total controls is similar to the steps above. We leave adding those steps as an exercise found at the end of the chapter. Review the previous two exercises before starting the end-of-chapter exercise.

Fig. 6.27 Report with completed calculated control.

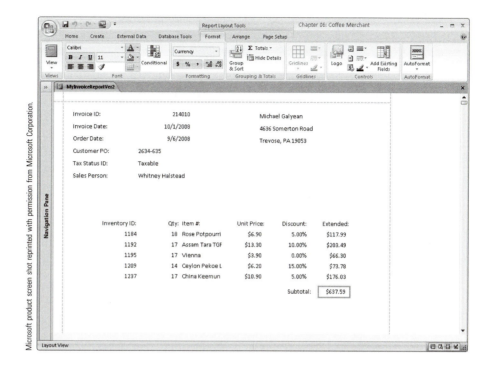

Adding Labels and Graphics

The sample report shown in Figure 6.21 contains two labels, a few simple graphics, and a page break (that is transparent). The labels include the word *Invoice* and the other one displays *Coffee Merchant* followed by the company address. The graphics are the two horizontal lines before and after the detail lines and the rectangle surrounding the customer's name and address. Adding both labels and graphics can dress up the invoice without going overboard. Begin by adding labels to the Page header.

EXERCISE 6.31: ADDING LABELS TO THE PAGE HEADER

1. Right-click MyInvoiceReportVer2 in the Navigation Pane tab and click Design View.
2. Increase the vertical height of the Page Header area by dragging the InvoiceID Header band down about one inch.
3. Click the Label control in the Controls group of the Design contextual tab. Click in the upper left corner of the Page Header area to locate the label. Then, type Invoice and press Enter. The label control contains *Invoice* and the control is still selected.
4. Click the Font Size list box in the Font group, type 48 and press Enter. If the label seems to disappear, then the mouse to the label's lower-right sizing handle. When it turns to a double-headed arrow pointing from the upper-left to the lower-right, double-click the mouse to enlarge the label container.
5. Repeat Step 3, placing the label in the upper-right corner of the Page Header area. Type the following multiline label text. *Important:* Press Ctrl+Enter to move to a new line within the label.

   The Coffee Merchant
   5998 Alcala Park
   San Diego, CA 92110

6. Press Enter to select the label box, then click Align Text Right button in the Font group. Click the Font Size list box, type 14, and press Enter to finalize your settings. Resize the label box by dragging its sizing handles so that the text resembles the company label shown in Figure 6.21. See Figure 6.28 showing the label placement in Design view.

Fig. 6.28 Placement of report labels.

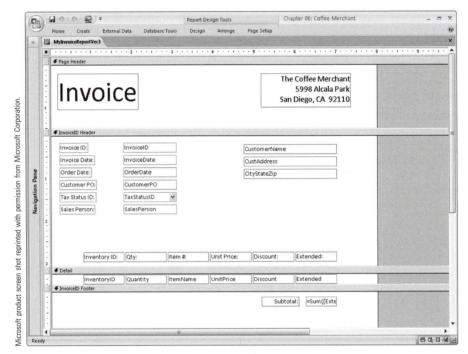

The only graphics in the invoice shown in Figure 6.21 are two lines and a rectangle. These are easy to add. In order for the a line to appear before the first detail fields, it must be placed in the header immediately below the column labels (Item #, Qty, and so on) and just above the Detail band itself. Similarly, you place the line appearing below the last of the detail items (see Figure 6.21) just below the InvoiceID Footer band before the subtotal calculated control.

EXERCISE 6.32: ADDING LINES AND A RECTANGLE

1. Click and drag the top edge of the Detail header band down enough to accommodate a thin line between it and the labels in the InvoiceID Header.
2. Click the Line button in the Controls group of the Design contextual tab (the report is in Design view still).
3. Press and hold the Shift key and click and drag the mouse from the left side of the Detail band, but just above it, to the right—just past the label *Extended*. Release the mouse and the Shift key. (Holding the Shift key while dragging the line control ensures that the line remains horizontal.)
4. Repeat Step 3 for the InvoiceID Footer, placing the line just below the InvoiceID Footer but above the subtotal label and calculated control.

5. With the line still selected, press the Up arrow key, if necessary, to nudge the line right up against the lower edge of the InvoiceID Footer. If you nudge it into the Detail area, just use the Down arrow key to move it back down.

6. Click Rectangle in the Controls group. Don't click the Option Group, which has a small label at the top of the rectangle. Surround the customer information in the InvoiceID Header by clicking above and to the left of the customer information and dragging down and to the right. Release the mouse when the rectangle encloses all the customer information.

7. Notice that the rectangle hides the fields. Right-click within the rectangle, point to Position in the pop-up menu, and click Send to Back. Alternatively, you can click Fill/Back Color in the pop-up menu and click Transparent in the pop-up color palette (see Figure 6.29).

8. Click the Office button, point to Save As, click Save Object As, type MyInvoiceReportVer4 in the Save As text box, and click OK.

Fig. 6.29 Making a rectangle transparent.

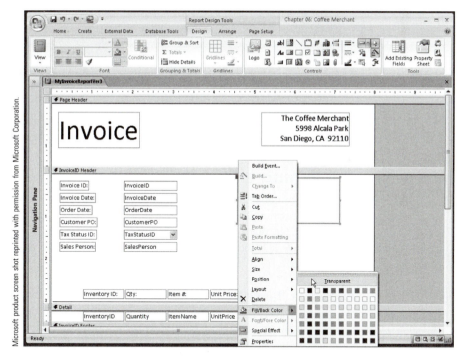

Microsoft product screen shot reprinted with permission from Microsoft Corporation.

Review the graphics and two labels. Print preview provides the best way to see the newly added graphics and labels.

TRY IT

Right-click the *MyInvoiceReportVer4* tab and click *Print Preview*. Access displays the invoice report so you can note how it will look when printed (see Figure 6.30). Close the report by right-clicking its tab and clicking *Close* or *Close All*.

Notice that the report shows more than one invoice on a page. Each customer invoice should be on a separate page to facilitate mailing it. We leave that and some other report

Fig. 6.30 Preview of the partially complete invoice report.

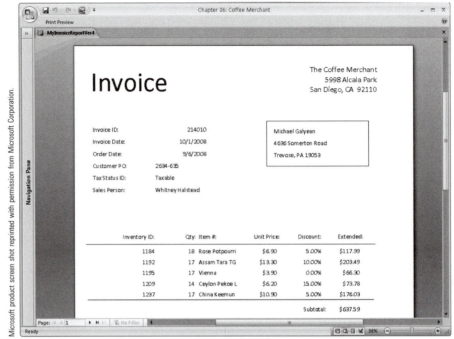

adjustments and additions as an end-of-chapter exercise. If you want to finish the invoice so it looks like Figure 6.21, then complete Practice Exercise 3 at the end of the chapter.

Publishing a Report

Access accommodates report readers' needs to view a report distributed on the Internet as well as providing the usual hard-copy options. You can publish a report to e-mail and send it over the Internet, publish a report on paper, export a report to Microsoft Office Word, or save it in PDF or XPS format. We explore each of these alternative publishing methods next.

Printing a Paper Report

Creating a printed copy of a report is a typical choice. For example, a printed report is required when you need to discuss product development with a group of gathered management leaders and want to reference data found in the report. Printing a report is straightforward. The steps are:

- *Click the Office button, point to Print in the Office menu, and click Print Preview to check settings.*
- *In the Page Layout group, set the orientation, margins, columns, and so on.*
- *Click the Print button in the Print group of the Print Preview tab.*
- *Select a printer from the list.*
- *In the Print Range frame, click the All radio button to print all pages or click the Pages radio button and type the* From: *and* To: *page number values, and click OK.*

You can print the report without first previewing it, but we suggest you preview it to ensure that the data fits on a page. In Print preview, be sure to click the Last Page button to see how many pages are in the report. It can be a nasty surprise to start printing 500 pages when you thought the report was only 5 pages long!

Exporting a Report to Word

If you are sending an electronic copy of a report to someone who does not have Microsoft Access 2007, then you can export the report in Rich Text Format (rtf) format. An rtf report can be opened in a variety of products including just about any version of Microsoft Word. The next exercise produces an rtf-format report from the MyEmployeeReport you created earlier in this chapter.

EXERCISE 6.33: PRODUCING AN RTF-FORMAT REPORT

1. Right-click MyEmployeeReport in the Reports group of the Navigation Pane and click Layout View in the pop-up menu.
2. Click the External Data tab and click Word in the Export group.
3. Click the Browse button, if needed, to navigate to the folder where you want to save the rtf-format report. Type MyRtfReport in the File name list box. Click Save to save the report in the file named *MyRtfReport.rtf*. Access returns to the Export RTF file dialog box.
4. Click OK.
5. When the *Save Export Steps* step appears after the wizard has converted the report, click Close. Alternatively, if you click the Save Export Steps check box, then you can repeat the report generation process another time without using the wizard.
6. Close the report by right-clicking the Employees by Division tab and clicking Close in the pop-up menu.

Access creates a report in rtf-format and saves it in the designated folder on your computer. You open the rtf-format report outside Access. The Try It exercise that follows show you how to open the rtf report in Word.

TRY IT

Minimize Access. Launch Windows Explorer, navigate to the folder containing the report *MyEmployeeReport.rtf*. Double-click the file name *MyEmployeeReport.rtf*. Word launches, converts the rtf-format into Word format, and displays the report in Print Layout view (see Figure 6.31). Close Word. Close Windows Explorer.

Producing a PDF- or XPS-Format Report

You cannot assume that the person(s) to whom you are sending a report have Access, Word, or any Microsoft products for that matter. To be universally usable, a report must be in a format that anyone can open—in some format that is easily rendered. One such format is the widely accepted Portable Document Format (or PDF). A second choice, though less universally accepted, is XPS. PDF-format files preserve all the fidelity of the software that created them. And, PDF files can be opened and displayed with the free product Acrobat Reader widely available on the Internet. XPS-format files are the Microsoft file sharing standard that, like PDF format, preserves report formatting and layout. To render an XPS document, you need Internet Explorer 7 or higher. Because PDF is the widely accepted standard for high fidelity documents, we suggest you produce that format whenever you have to share documents with others. You can count on PDF documents to preserve every nuance of the Access reports from which they are derived. And almost everyone has Acrobat Reader installed on their computers.

Fig. 6.31 Opening an rtf-format report in Word 2007.

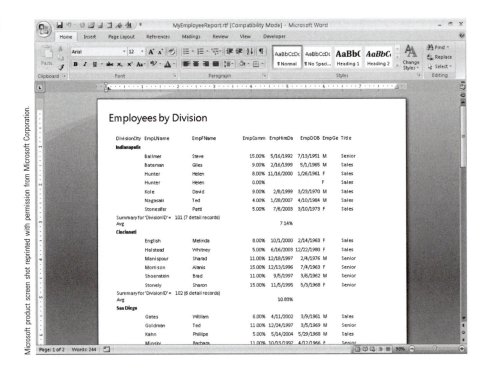

Before you can produce either a PDF or an XPS format report, you must install an add-in from Microsoft. You can determine if you need the add-in or not by opening a report, clicking the Office button, pointing to Save As, and observing if *PDF or XPS* appears near the top of the Save As menu—just below the *Save Object As* choice. If it does not, then *Find add-ins for other file formats* appears in its place. If so, then you need to install the add-in to produce PDF- or XPS-format results from Access reports. Close Access before installing the add-in. Figure 6.32 shows the Microsoft.com Web page that appears prior to downloading the required add-ins.

Assuming your installation of Access has the requisite add-ins, let's produce a PDF-format report. If your installation does not have the add-ins, then either install them or skip this next exercise.

EXERCISE 6.34: PRODUCING A PDF-FORMAT REPORT

1. Double-click MyInvoiceReportVer4 in the Navigation Pane to open it in Report View.
2. Click the Office button, point to Save As, and click PDF or XPS.
3. Navigate to the folder where you want to save the report. Type MyPdfReport in the File name list box.
4. If necessary, click the Save as type list box arrow and select PDF.
5. Click the Standard (publishing online and printing) radio button.
6. Click the Options button, click the Pages radio button, and ensure that the *From:* and *To:* spin controls have 1 in them to publish only one page. Click OK to set these page generation options.
7. Click Publish. Access exports the PDF format file to the designated folder. Access exports the report in PDF format. It reappears in Acrobat Reader.
8. Close Acrobat Reader and close the Access report.

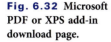

Fig. 6.32 Microsoft PDF or XPS add-in download page.

Publishing to E-mail

When you have to get a report across the office or across the country, you can e-mail it. A summary of the steps to send an Access report via e-mail are these:

- *Click the report in the Navigation Pane that you want to e-mail.*
- *Click the Office button, click E-mail in the Office menu, and select one of the available formats in the* Send Object As *dialog box that appears. The choices are HTML, PDF Format, Rich Text Format, Snapshot Format, Text Files, and XPS Format. Click OK to convert the report into the selected format.*
- *The Snapshot Format is a format that enables the recipient to view the report without having Microsoft Access. Microsoft supplies Snapshot Viewer program online. The link to download the program is: http://support.microsoft.com/kb/175274.*
- *Microsoft may display a dialog box with other options for selected format choices you make. If so, make appropriate choices.*
- *After Access converts the report into the selected format, it activates your e-mail program. The converted report is an e-mail attachment. You can include a message if you wish before sending the e-mail message to its destination.*
- *Finally, send the message.*

Of course, you can create a PDF of XPS file on your computer and then manually attach it to an e-mail message. Either way, the recipient receives an electronic copy of the report that can be easily opened.

Creating Mailing Labels

Besides the variety of reports you have seen so far, Access provides additional specialized reports to produce mailing labels. Mailing labels are particularly useful when you need to send out mailers, reminders, invitations, and so on, to customers, suppliers, and others whose addresses you have stored in Access. For instance, you might want to do a mailing campaign to existing customers in a particular city or state to entice them to purchase goods with special discount coupons. PivotChart reports are well-suited for summarizing complex data.

Access provides a Label Wizard that guides you through the process of creating labels for the major label brands and all the products each produces. You simply supply the data source—a table or query—that supplies the data to the Data Wizard. If you specify a table as the data source, then the wizard allows you to select the fields you want in the label and their location. In addition, you can specify sort criteria to produce labels in a particular order. For example, you might want to sort address labels in order by zip code then by last name within matching zip codes. Sorting in zip code order can save postage costs by allowing you to bundle similar zip codes together and using bulk mail. However, you cannot filter the data using the Label Wizard. For example, the Label Wizard has no step that asks if you want to produce labels for selected addresses in a particular state or a particular city. If you want the ability to limit the labels to a subset of a table, then you have two choices: (1) Build a query that includes the fields to appear on the label and the filtering criteria, or (2) build the label report with the Label Wizard and then modify the query behind the report to include filtering. Either way accomplishes your goal, but the second choice is slightly more complex.

The next exercise uses the Label Wizard to create mailing labels for *all* customers using the data found in the table *tblCustomer*. A subsequent exercise shows you how to modify the query behind the report to filter the data by state.

EXERCISE 6.35: PRODUCING MAILING LABELS

1. In the Navigation Pane, click the table tblCustomer to highlight it. (You do not need to open the table.)
2. Click the Create tab and click Labels in the Reports group. Access launches the Label Wizard.
3. Click Avery in the Filter by manufacturer list box, if necessary, and locate and click 5660 in the Product number list. That particular label is 3-across by 10 rows or 30 labels per page (see Figure 6.33).
4. Click Next. The Label Wizard prompts you for font information.
5. Click Next to display the layout of the label. Available fields appear in the left panel and the developing label structure appears on the right.
6. Double-click CustFirstName, press Spacebar, double-click CustLastName and press Enter to build the first line of the label.
7. Double-click CustAddress, press Enter, double-click CustCity, type a comma and a space, double-click CustState, press Spacebar twice, and double-click CustZip. Your prototype label should match the one shown in Figure 6.34.
8. Click Next to display sort options. Click Next to go to the next step.
9. Type MyCustomerLabels to name the report. Click Finish to complete the report. (Click OK if a dialog box appears indicating the horizontal space is insufficient.) Access displays the labels in Print Preview. Leave the report open for the next and final exercise to add behind-the-scene filtering.

While the label report is fine as produced for Avery 5660 labels, it includes all customers. You can supply filtering criteria by switching to the report's Design view and modifying the report's Record Source property.

Fig. 6.33 Selecting a
label by manufacturer
and number.

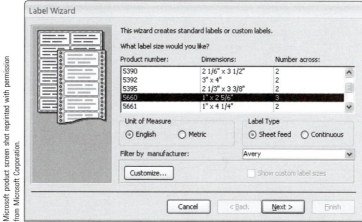

Microsoft product screen shot reprinted with permission from Microsoft Corporation.

Fig. 6.34 Prototype
label.

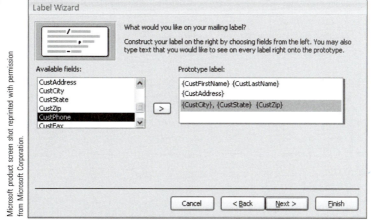

Microsoft product screen shot reprinted with permission from Microsoft Corporation.

EXERCISE 6.36: FILTERING LABELS WITH A QUERY BEHIND THE REPORT

1. Right-click the MyCustomerLabels tab, click Design View, and press Alt+Enter to open the Property Sheet.
2. Click the Data tab in the Property Sheet pane, click the build button (…) in the Record Source property value, and click Yes when a dialog box appears asking if you want to invoke the query builder on a table.
3. Double-click the asterisk (*) in the *tblCustomer* roster list to place all fields from the table into the query. Double-click CustState to place that field in the second Field row of the query grid.
4. Click the Show check box beneath the CustState column to clear it. Type the following in the Criteria cell beneath the CustState column: [Type a state abbreviation] and press Enter. (Be sure to include the initial and terminal brackets. Without them, the query will work incorrectly.) This allows the user to specify the state filter as the report is produced—in "real time."
5. Double-click CustZip to place that field in the third Field row of the query grid. Click the Show check box beneath the CustZip column to clear it. Click the Sort cell below CustZip and click Ascending.
6. Click Close in the Close group of the Design contextual tab to close the query. Click Yes when the dialog box appears asking if you want to save changes to the SQL statement.

7. Click Save in the Quick Access Toolbar to save the modified label report design.
8. Right-click the MyCustomerLabels tab and select Print Preview. If a dialog box appears indicating some data may not be displayed, click OK to dismiss it.
9. An Enter Parameter dialog box appears asking you to *Type a state abbreviation*. This is the run-time filter that limits the labels to the state abbreviation you type. Type pa (for Pennsylvania) and click OK. Access displays the labels, sorted by zip code, for the state of Pennsylvania in Print Preview view. See Figure 6.35, which shows the labels with the Navigation Pane reduced and the ribbon minimized.
10. Close the report: Right-click the report tab and click Close All.
11. Close Access.

Fig. 6.35 **Print Preview view of Pennsylvania customer labels.**

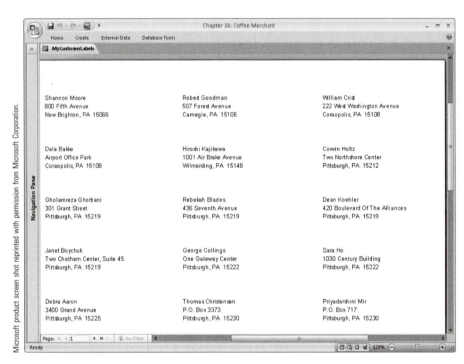

Building labels is that easy! If you ever want to remove the state filter restriction from the report, simply open it in Design view and delete the criteria from beneath the query grid cell CustState and resave the query and the report design.

Summary

You have gained a lot of knowledge about Access reports in this chapter. You created a report in Layout view, added a logo and report title, and added sorting and grouping to aggregate information in the report. By applying conditional formatting to a report field, Access highlighted values in a field that are different or unusual. Using the Report Wizard speeds creating reports but also has the disadvantage of less control over the content and design of reports. Keep in mind the guidelines for good report design including using existing reports as a template for electronic reports, ensuring the order and placement of report fields is understandable, and using sorting and grouping. In short, keep the report simple to use and easily understandable.

Creating a report from scratch in Design view is more difficult, but it affords you the most flexibility and widest possible range of control over a report's design, layout, and control placement. Adding calculations to a report is best done in Design view. Calculated controls are text boxes whose Control Source property contains an expression that calculates and displays a result based on other control values found in a report. Often, calculated controls are placed in footers including group footers, page footers, or report footers. Multitable reports exploit the natural relationships between related tables such as customers and invoices or employees and sales. Reports can also be created from queries. When values must be calculated from other fields, you can create a query that includes the required calculation and then create a report based on the query. Report publishing options include printing a paper report, exporting the report to an rtf format that Microsoft Word can open and render, producing PDF- or XPS-format reports, or creating mailing labels for all of the standard label brands such as Avery labels.

Questions and Problems for Review

Multiple-Choice Questions

1. Which section of a report is required?
   a. Report Header.
   b. Report Footer.
   c. Page Header.
   d. Detail.
2. Reports have four views. They are Report, Print Preview, Design, and what?
   a. Report Preview.
   b. Layout.
   c. Export.
   d. Word.
3. If you need to move, resize, or delete one or more columns in a report, then the best view to accomplish this is
   a. Design.
   b. Layout.
   c. Print Preview.
   d. Report.
4. What is the name of the report band that appears immediately after the Detail band and that can hold summary information about the detail lines above it?
   a. Report footer.
   b. Detail footer.
   c. Group footer.
   d. Page footer.
5. What do you apply to a report control when its display characteristics depend on its value?
   a. Formatting.
   b. Immediate formatting.
   c. Dynamic formatting.
   d. Conditional formatting.
6. Report controls that display database fields are called what?
   a. Bound controls.
   b. Calculated controls.
   c. Unbound controls.
   d. Field controls.
7. Grouping labels and other report controls so that they can be moved as a group in Layout view, for example, is called what?
   a. Layout columns.
   b. Control layout.
   c. Controlled layout.
   d. Tabular layout.

8. You add calculated values, expressions, to a report by including what from the available Controls in Design view?
    a. Label control.
    b. Option group control.
    c. Expression control.
    d. Text box control.
9. If you want to add an expression to the Detail band of a report, the best way is to base the report on what?
    a. A table containing an expression.
    b. Another report containing an expression.
    c. A query containing the expression.
    d. None of the preceding is correct.
10. The best way to send a report to another person so that it can be viewed is in what format?
    a. XPS.
    b. Access Database.
    c. PDF.
    d. Microsoft Word.

Discussion Questions

1. Explain, or speculate, when it is best to use a query as the basis of a report and when it is better to use a Report Wizard and select multiple, related tables.
2. Discuss why Layout view, new to Access 2007, is advantageous in modifying reports.
3. Discuss the advantages of using the Report Wizard to create a report.
4. Discuss conditional formatting and what capabilities it provides. Differentiate it from standard formatting.
5. Discuss, briefly, the options to share, electronically, an Access report with other users.

Practice Exercises

1. Create a simple report using the Report Wizard that lists suppliers from the table *tblSuppliers*. Include only the following fields in the report: Company, Street, City, State, ZipCode, and CountryID. Group the report by CountryID. Sort the detail lines by Company. Change the page orientation to landscape, ensure all columns appear on one page, and count the number of suppliers from each group (country). Save the report as MySuppliersReport. Change the report title to "Suppliers" and add your name in the Report Header section as a label. Remove the date from the Page Footer. Resize the columns (Layout view) as needed so they are optimal—wide enough but not too wide. Bold the column titles. Print the short report.
2. Create a report named MyInventoryOnHand with the title "Inventory On Hand" appearing on each page. The report is based on two tables that you specify when you use the Report Wizard. Include these fields from *tblInventory*: Beverage, ItemName, UnitPrice, and UnitsOnHand. Include CountryName from *tblCountry*. Group the rows by CountryName. Sort the rows within each group by ItemName. Sum the units on hand for each group (CountryName). Modify the labels so that they include spaces (e.g., Item-Name becomes Item Name). Remove the group footer text string beginning with "Summary for" and remove the text "Sum." Adjust the sum of units on hand so it aligns with the detail column values it sums. Remove everything appearing in the Page Footer and the Report Footer. Enter your name as a label control in the Report Header. Place it on the right side. Ensure all the columns fit in portrait orientation. Remove all fields from the Report Footer. Print only the first page of the report.
3. Clean up and print the report MyEmployeeReport you created as an exercise in the chapter body. In particular, modify the column names to these, left to right: *Division, First Name, Last Name, Commission Rate, Hire Date, DOB, Gender,* and *Title.* Adjust the column widths (narrow the commission rate column, employee first and last name columns and widen the title column). Add label and text boxes showing minimum and maximum commission rates for each division (group). Eliminate the text string beginning "Summary for 'DivisionID'..." and add your name, using a label control, in the Report Header on the right

side. Delete all controls in the Page footer and reduce its size to zero. Ensure all columns fit in the portrait orientation. Print all pages of the employee report.

4. Create a report based on a query hidden behind the report. The report contains all the fields from the table *tblStates*: StateID, StateName, StateTaxRate, StatePopulation, and StateSize. In addition, the report displays Density in the rightmost position. Make sure the query is "behind the report." That is, create a report the standard way. Then, then modify the report's Record Source (call the Query Builder) by adding the Density expression in the query and saving the modified query. The Density expression has the column alias "Density:" which computes the number of people per square mile. (StateSize is the area of the state in square miles.) Enter sort criteria in the Sort cell below the Density function so records appear in the report in descending density order. Save the query and add the new Density calculated field to the report. (*Hint*: Click Add Existing Fields in the Controls group of the Format contextual tab in Layout view.) Format the Density report field to "Standard" and zero decimal places. Remove the word "State" from each column label and ensure that they include spaces between words. Ensure that all columns fit on one page. Modify the report title to "Population Density" and move it into the Page Header above the column labels so it appears on both pages. Place your name in the Page Header by using a label control. Remove any space on the Report Header. Remove everything that appears in the Page Footer and the Report Footer. Remove the date and time from the Report Header. Print the two-page state report.

5. Produce a report grouped by employee title. The two tables involved are *tblEmployeeTitle* and *tblEmployee*. Select only the fields Title, EmpFName, and EmpLName. Display the Group, Sort, and Total pane and group by Title (not the TitleID), sort beneath that group by last name, and add a control to count the employees in each title category. Remove everything from the Page Footer, move the title to the Page Header, add your name in the Page Header, and change the title to "Employees by Title." Change the employee column labels to "First Name" and "Last Name" and bold all three column labels. Place a horizontal line between the column labels and the data columns and place a line following each group but before the next group begins. Print the one-page report.

Problems

1. Use the Report Wizard to build a report that displays products and their suppliers. The report is referenced whenever supplies run low. Then, the procurement officer selects a supplier from whom he can order a particular product. For example, which of the suppliers sells us, at wholesale, Kenya AA coffee beans? Which supplier has Kona coffee available for sale? The report shows product names and the suppliers who sell them, grouped by product name. Start by using the Report Wizard and include ItemName from *tblInventory* as the grouping field. Detail lines display the *tblSupplier* fields of Company and State (in that order left to right). After the Report Wizard is done, switch to Layout view and change the Group, Sort, and Total pane to group on ItemName (InventoryID is the initial grouping). Then, add a sort to sort by State. Filter the state column to eliminate blank state names (foreign countries). (Hint: Locate a blank state name, right-click in Layout view, and select the appropriate filter.) Place the label "Suppliers by Product" and your name in the Page Header. Clear the Report Header and reduce its height to zero. Remove the Report Footer and Page Footer. Ensure the grouping and detail fields are sufficiently wide to display the data in portrait orientation. Print the first two report pages.

2. Create a report that lists employees' first and last names and the total sales based on invoice extended prices. Begin by creating and saving a query. Review the Relationships window to see the three tables required and the primary and foreign keys that link them. The query should contain the employee first and last name fields; it should also contain an expression for extended price that you have seen several times in this chapter. The values for extended price expression include fields available in the *tblInvoiceLine* table, *not* the *tblInventory* table. The query should be a Totals query that sums the extended price field for each employee. Once you get the query right, save it as MyEmployeeInvoiceSales. Produce a report based on MyEmployeeInvoiceSales that displays sales in decreasing value of extended price totals by employee. Format it attractively (modify the column labels at least), remove the date and time from the Report Header, change the report title to "Total Invoices Per Employee," place your name in the Report Header, remove

all fields from the Page Footer and the Report Footer, save the report under any name you choose, and export the report to a PDF-format file. Print the PDF file.

3. Modify the invoice report you created in this chapter whose latest version is named MyInvoiceReportVer4. Right-align the labels on the left side of the report, left-align the bound control contents corresponding to those labels, and ensure the invoice ID through Sales Person are equally spaced vertically and aligned with one another. Add calculated controls for sales tax, shipping, and total. Name the controls ctlSalesTax, ctlShipping, and ctlTotal, respectively. The ctlSalesTax expression should use the IIF function to return 0 (zero) if Tax Status ID is "Tax Exempt" or the tax of 7.5% of the subtotal (ctlSubtotal). Shipping is the 25 cents times the total quantity found in the Qty column. (Hint: Use *Sum([Quantity])* in the expression.) Total is the sum of subtotal, sales tax, and shipping. In addition, add a page break control just below the calculated control *Total* to force each invoice onto a new page. Align the four calculated controls and rearrange objects as needed to match, as closely as possible, the example in Figure 6.21. Include your name in the Page Header between the words *Invoice* and *Coffee Merchant*. Print only page four—the invoice for Helen Miller. *Caution*: be careful when you print. There are 500 pages in this report!

4. You want to mail out a large number of flyers to all your current customers. Use the Access Label Wizard to create a report. The report is a set of Avery labels. Create a new report based on the table *tblCustomer*. Select Label Wizard from the list of report types. Then, make the following choices: Click "English Unit of Measure" and select Avery 5160 labels. Place the following fields on your mailing labels: CustFirstName, CustLastName, CustAddress, CustCity, CustState, and CustZip. Arrange the fields on the label with the customer first and last name on line 1, street address on line 2, and city, state, and zip code on line 3. Place a comma between the city and state. Ensure there is at least one blank following the comma and between state and zip code. Sort the mailing labels by state and then by city within state. Open up the report in Design view and place you name in the Page Header using a label control in the Controls group. Name your report PR4MyCustomerLabels and save it. Print only the first page of the report. Be careful in making your Print dialog box choices—the report is almost 60 pages long.

5. This is a difficult problem. It resembles problem 2 above, except you are to list the employees who *do not* have any invoices. Create a report that lists employees' first and last names for those employees who do not have any invoices currently in the table *tblInvoice* table. Begin by creating a report displaying EmpLName, EmpFName, and InvoiceID. Then, modify the report's Record Source property to a query that uses a left outer join. Review *Creating and Using an Outer Join Query* in Chapter 4. Save the behind-the-report query. In Layout view, delete the InvoiceID column. Change the title of the report to "Employees with No Invoices" and add your name in the Report Header. Format it attractively (modify the column labels at least). Remove all fields from the Page Footer and the Report Footer, save the report under any name you choose. Print the small, one-page report.

CHAPTER **7**

Introduction to Data Modeling for Accounting Information Systems

CHAPTER OBJECTIVES

This chapter explains the basic concepts of designing accounting information systems (AISs) using a relational database such as Microsoft Access. Unlike the previous chapters, which focus on the technical aspects of using Microsoft Access, this chapter introduces you to the steps you need to complete *before* you begin building your AIS in Microsoft Access. Exercises throughout the chapter emphasize the steps in the AIS database design process critical to building accounting information systems. Although the content of the chapter is conceptual, this chapter contains several hands-on exercises. In this chapter you will learn how to:

- **Create a value system model of an enterprise.**
- **Create a value chain model of an enterprise.**
- **Create business process models of an enterprise.**
- **Create a Microsoft Access database based on business process models.**

In this chapter and subsequent chapters we will design and implement an AIS for Pipefitters Supply Company.

Introduction to Data Modeling

The method we use in this book to design accounting information systems is based on the view that an enterprise's economic activity is a series of exchange events. This view is consistent with the theory of economic exchange. An economic exchange consists of a "give" event and a "take" event. Every give event has a related take event. For example, when a business purchases inventory, they "give" cash and "take" inventory. William McCarthy identified a set of events common to business enterprises, which became the foundation of the REA (resources, events, agents) enterprise ontology, which he introduced over 25 years ago. An ontology defines what exists; the REA enterprise ontology defines the business and economic events that exist in business enterprises; the resources and agents involved in these events; and the relationships between events, resources, and agents. Moreover, REA modeling is designed in such a way that the resulting model can be easily translated into a relational database.

REA modeling is a top-down approach to database design. You first start with a high-level overview of the business enterprise, the *value system*, by identifying the enterprise's external partners and the resource flows between the business and its external partners. Even at this macro view of a business, you are able to identify all of the resources that flow into and out of the business as well as its external agents.

This step is followed by focusing on the enterprise itself and identifying the essential business processes that make up its *value chain*. The five essential business processes are financing, acquisition/payment, human resources, conversion, and sales/collection. Moreover, you also identify the key economic exchange events within each business process and the resource flows from one process to another.

After creating a value chain model of the business, the next step is to create models of the individual *business processes* such as the acquisition/payment process. At this more detailed level of modeling, you form the main set of tables for your Access database. This is the most detailed level at which a common set of items has been identified for business enterprises. Moreover, business process models contain sufficient detail to build basic AIS in Microsoft Access.

To make the system more complete, you should look at each event in the business process and identify the individual tasks involved accomplishing each event. These task-level models are often illustrated with document flow charts. Flowcharts may reveal additional information that needs to be included in the AIS. However, in this book, we will stop our data modeling at the business process level as it is sufficient to implement a very basic AIS in Access.

In the following sections, we will guide you to create a value system, value chain, and business process model for Pipefitters Supply Company, which purchases pipes and pipe fittings from manufacturers and sells them to end-users like contractors and construction companies. This part of their business is typical of merchandising companies. In addition to selling pipes and fittings to its customers, Pipefitters also assembles pipes and fittings into a set of standard assemblies for its customers. You will learn more about Pipefitters' operations below as you use the information presented to create your data models. You will use the business process model to create an Access database for part of Pipefitters' business operations. In subsequent chapters, you will design and implement a complete rudimentary accounting information system for Pipefitters Supply Company, input transactions, and derive financial data that you will use to create financial statements.

Creating a Value System Model of an Enterprise

Pipefitters Supply Company was started as a corporation by two friends, Arthur Kamedes and Paul Van Cleave. They used their own money to start Pipefitters about

40 years ago. Since then, they have financed their growth by borrowing money from banks and by reinvesting profits in their business. Although they are the only two share-holders, they may consider financing future growth by issuing stock to outside investors. Pipefitters employs 50 people.

EXERCISE 7.1: CREATING THE VALUE SYSTEM MODEL

Based on what you have learned so far about Pipefitters Supply Company, you can draw a value system model of Pipefitters. In a value system, the entity (Pipefitters) is shown as a large oval in the middle of the page with the name of the company inside the oval. Each type of external partner, such as creditors (e.g., the bank) is represented by a rect-angle with the name of the external partner inside the rectangle. A common convention to make the value system easier to read is to place the partners from which a business acquires its inputs on the left side of the enterprise and partners to whom a business gives its outputs on the right side of the business. Finally, draw the flow lines as one-way arrows between the business and each external partner. Therefore, a business will have an inflow arrow and outflow arrow to each external partner. Do not forget to label the arrows with the type(s) of resources flowing into or out of the business. The value system for Pipefitters is illustrated in Figure 7.1. Be sure to try to draw the value system yourself before looking at the solution.

Fig. 7.1 Value system.

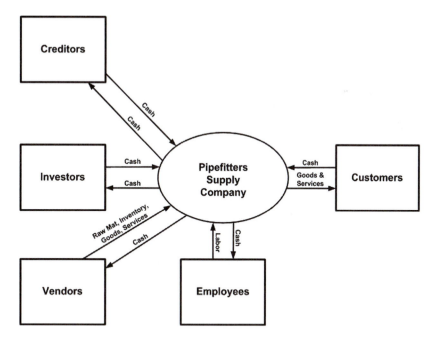

The value system in Figure 7.1 for Pipefitters Supply Company is typical for most types of businesses. The flow lines between the business and the external partners indicate the resource flows that result from exchanges between the enterprise and its partners. One line represents an inflow of resources that an enterprise *gets* from the external partner and the other line is the outflow of resources an enterprise *gives* to the partner:

- An enterprise gets *cash from creditors as loans and* gives *cash in the form of principle and interest payments.*
- An enterprise gets *cash from owners/investors as capital contributions and* gives *cash in the form of dividends and/or stock redemptions.*

- *An enterprise* gets *goods like inventory and services like advertising from vendors and* gives *cash to pay for them.*
- *An enterprise* gets *labor from employees and* gives *cash to pay them.*
- *An enterprise* gets *cash from customers and* gives *inventory and/or services to them.*

Because the value system only looks at external exchanges of resources, employees at this level of detail are viewed only as external partners because a business negotiates with employees to *get* labor from them and the business *gives* cash in the form of wages to the employees. Also, remember that a particular enterprise may not have all of the external partners listed in Figure 7.1. Additionally, you may determine that there are other external partners relevant for a particular enterprise such as labor unions.

Even at this broad level, you have already identified many of the resources and external partners that we will likely need to track in our accounting system. We now turn our attention to what happens within the business; the resource flows between the business processes that make up an enterprise's value chain.

Creating a Value Chain Model of an Enterprise

The *value chain model* shows how resources exchanged with its external partners, called *external agents*, are used within the enterprise. The value chain contains the core business processes necessary to provide goods and services to its customers. Identifying the main business process provides the framework for your AIS. In a value chain model, each business process is represented by a large circle. The *economic increment* (get event) and *economic decrement* (give event) events are drawn as rectangles and the *duality relationship* connecting them is drawn as a diamond. Dualities are the relationships that connect give and get events. A "+" sign is placed next to the economic increment event and a "−" sign is placed next to the economic decrement event. The name of the business process is also included within the circle, usually at the top. Figure 7.2 shows the acquisition/payment (also called the acquisition) process. Note that it is not necessary to include the word *duality* in the relationship diamond because it is the only type of relationship in a value chain model.

Fig. 7.2 Acquisition/ payment process for a value chain model.

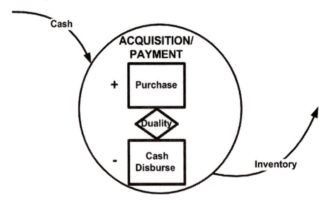

After all of the business processes for an enterprise have been identified and drawn, it is time to add the resource flows from one business process to another. The economic decrement event uses the resource that flows into that business process. In the acquisition/payment process, the economic decrement event is a cash disbursement. The *cash disbursement* event uses cash from the financing process to pay for goods and services acquired in the acquisition/payment process.

The economic increment event is the activity that causes a resource to flow into a business. In the acquisition process, the purchase event causes an inflow of a resource such as inventory, fixed assets, utilities, or services. We focus our attention on the acquisition of inventory to simplify the AIS database you will design and implement in this textbook. The resource that increases in a business process is the resource that will be transferred to another business process. For the acquisition/payment process, raw materials inventory is transferred to the conversion process; merchandise inventory (inventory acquired that is ready to sell to customers) is transferred directly to the sales/collection process (also called the sales process) for sale to customers.

EXERCISE 7.2: CREATING THE VALUE CHAIN MODEL

You have all of the information you need about each of Pipefitters Supply Company's business processes, other than the conversion process, to complete a value chain model for Pipefitters. The resource exchanges depicted in Pipefitters' Value System model (see Figure 7.1) are the result of the pairs of economic events in each of Pipefitters' business processes. One way to think about a Value Chain model is as a way to link external partners and their related resource exchanges with the lifecycle of a new business. This lifecycle is sometimes referred to as the *business entrepreneur's script* because this set of activities is common to most new business ventures:

1. Get money to start the business.
   * From which external partner(s) do you acquire capital?
2. Acquire property, plant, and equipment, inventory, services, etc., to start the business.
   * From which external partner(s) do you acquire goods and services?
3. Acquire labor to help convert raw materials into finished goods.
   * From which external partner(s) do you acquire labor?
4. Convert raw materials into finished goods.
   * Resource transfers related to converting raw materials into finished goods do NOT directly involve any external partners.
   * We will not discuss the conversion process in this textbook. However, for purposes of this exercise assume that assembling pipes and fittings into standard assemblies involves primarily the use of raw materials (pipes and fittings) and labor. Although machinery and tools are likely also used in the conversion process we will assume that the use of machinery and tools is not sufficiently significant to track by individual assembly or production run of assemblies.
5. Sell inventory—finished goods in a manufacturing business or merchandise inventory in a merchandising company.
   * To which external partner(s) do you sell merchandise?
6. Repay partners from which you acquired capital.
   * From which external partner(s) did you acquire capital that need to be paid?

Notice that the business entrepreneur's script on which the Value Chain model is based parallels the organization of the statement of cash flows:

* *The financing section of the statement of cash flows is made up of events in Item 1, get money to start the business. Also note that Item 6, repay money, also a financing activity, is the other side of the financing process duality relationship.*
  * *Get money (cash receipt) is the economic increment event, and*
  * *Repay money, (cash disbursement) is the economic decrement event.*
* *The investing activities section of the statement of cash flows, part of the activities in Item 2, is made up of purchases [and payments for] property, plant, and equipment.*

- *The operating activities section of the statement of cash flows contains non-long-term purchases of goods and services from Item 2, labor acquisitions [and payments] comprising Item 3, and Item 5, selling inventory [and collecting cash].*
- *Note that Item 4, the conversion process, does not appear on the statement of cash flows because it does NOT directly involve resource exchanges with external partners.*

Be sure to attempt to draw the value chain for Pipefitters Supply Company before looking at the solution given in Figure 7.3.

Fig. 7.3 Value chain.

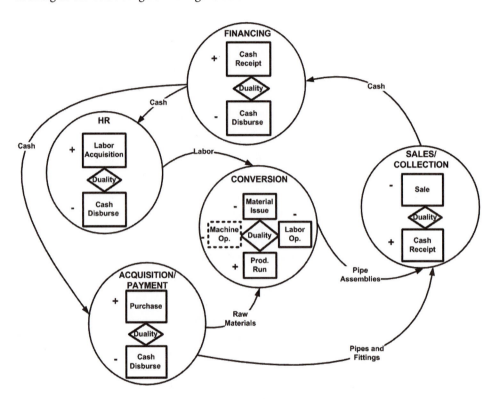

Although the closed loop of the value chain represents the continuous nature of a business, a business cycle begins with the acquisition of cash from the financing process. Part of the cash acquired from cash receipt events—economic increments—is used by the acquisition process to acquire inventory. Cash disbursement events (economic decrements) in the acquisition process use cash to pay for resources.

Cash from the financing process is also used to acquire labor in the Human Resources process. Again, cash receipt is the economic increment in the financing process where cash is acquired. The cash acquired from financing flows into the Human Resources (HR) process. The HR process uses the cash in cash disbursement events (economic decrements) to pay for acquired labor.

Next, raw materials inventory (pipes and fittings) acquired in the acquisition process and labor acquired in the HR process flow into the conversion process to produce finished goods inventory. The acquisition of raw materials in purchase events are economic increments. The conversion process uses raw materials in material issue events, which are economic decrement events. Similarly, labor acquired in labor acquisition events (economic increments) in the HR process is used by the conversion process in labor operation events (economic decrements).

The economic decrement events raw material issues and labor operations are paired with Production Run (or batch, the economic increment event that produces finished goods). The production run is where all the material issues and labor operations (and machine operations for some enterprises) come together in this economic increment event to produce the finished product. In managerial accounting you gathered much of this information in the work-in-process (WIP) account. The finished goods are then used by the sales/collection process to sell to customers. A sale event occurs when an enterprise gives merchandise to a customer, which is why it is the economic decrement that uses finished goods. Additionally, goods used in sale events of merchandising companies come from economic increment events in the acquisition process—purchases.

Finally, cash acquired from the sales/collection process is used by the financing process to repay loans, pay dividends, redeem stock, etc. *Cash receipt* is the economic increment in the sales/collection process where cash is acquired, and the decrement event in the financing process that uses the cash is cash disbursement.

Creating a Business Process Model of an Enterprise

In the next four chapters you will create business process models and implement them using Access for the following business processes: sales/collection, acquisition/payment, human resources, and financing. In the final chapter, you will integrate all four business processes into a single accounting information system. We will use the acquisition/payment process in this section to illustrate the basics of creating a business process model and then use the business process model to create an Access database.

At this point in your data modeling of Pipefitters Supply Company, you already identified the economic exchange events in the acquisition/payment process (purchase and cash disbursement) and the resources connected with each event in the process (inventory and cash, respectively) from the Value Chain model. Also, you already identified the external agent involved in these events from the Value System model (vendor). At the business process level, you now focus on the details of the process, including identifying the internal agent(s) (employees) involved with each event. Also, you need to identify the attributes to capture in your system for each event, including which attribute(s) will serve as the primary key for each event, resource, and agent represented by a table in your database AIS. Additionally, you will identify the business rules governing the relationships between events, resources, and agents in your system.

Creating Events, Resources, and Agents and the Relationships Between Them

The first step in creating a business process model for the acquisition process for Pipefitters Supply Company is to identify the events, resources, and agents and the relationships between them. To do this you need more information about Pipefitters Supply Company, which purchases pipes and fittings from a variety of vendors, both wholesalers and manufacturers. All vendors must be approved before a purchase order can be placed with a particular vendor. Only employees classified as purchase agents have the authority to place purchase orders. Pipefitters tracks inventory by item number rather than by tracking each individual piece of inventory. Pipefitters will have one record for each part it carries in its inventory. This is similar to the way a supermarket would keep track of 12 oz. cans of Hormel Spam Lite—you wouldn't expect a grocery store to create an individual record for each can of Spam Lite it receives. When merchandise arrives at the receiving dock, only one receiving clerk counts the inventory items and records which items were received and enters their quantities on a receiving report. Pipefitters usually pays in full for all of its inventory receipts from a particular vendor with a single check at the end of the month.[1] However, it sometimes pays early to take advantage of purchase discounts. Also, Pipefitters may make partial payments over two or more months for large purchases. Checks are written by an employee from the accounting department.

Pipefitters uses a single table to store all employee data. Employee type—such as purchasing agent, materials handler, accountant—is kept in a separate table such that each employee has only one employee type.

A good place to start in creating your business process model of Pipefitters' acquisition process is to start with the economic events: purchase and cash disbursement. From the Value Chain model, you learned that the relationship between an economic increment (purchase) and economic decrement event (cash disbursement) is a *duality* relationship. In this text, we will draw business process models to look similar to the relationship view in Access. Figure 7.4 shows how to draw the duality relationship for Pipefitters Supply Company. Each entity—event, resource, and agent—is represented by a rectangle with the title in the upper portion and the attributes are listed in the lower portion. Relationships are represented by lines connecting entities, and the lines are labeled with relationship names. In a database all tables must have unique names, so each entity in the model has its own name. Also, each relationship is given a unique name because many-to-many relationships, as well as some other relationships, are implemented by creating relationship tables.

Fig. 7.4 Acquisition/ payment process duality.

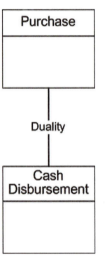

Each event is connected to the resource being exchanged. The relationship between a resource and an economic increment is an *inflow* and the relationship between a resource and an economic decrement event is an *outflow*. Someone within the business is responsible for each event so there will be an *internal participation* relationship between the event and the responsible *internal agent*. Events also involve an *external agent*, such as a vendor or customer, so the relationship between an event and an external agent is an *external participation*.

One additional relationship you need to model for the acquisition process for Pipefitters Supply Company is the relationship between *employees* and *employee type*. We call this relationship a *typification* because employees have an *is a kind of* relationship with employee type. That is, Sidney, an accountant, is a kind of employee type called accountant.

---

[1]Pipefitters' payment terms described here differ from the payment terms described for the acquisition/ payment process in Chapter 9 to illustrate a different set of business rules.

EXERCISE 7.3: CREATING THE BUSINESS PROCESS MODEL— EVENTS, RESOURCES, AGENTS, AND RELATIONSHIPS

You have all of the information you need to draw the entities and relationships for Pipe-fitters Supply Company. One event mentioned in the description of Pipefitters' acquisition process is Purchase Order. Do NOT include Purchase Order in your model as we will discuss these kinds of events when we discuss the details of each business process in subsequent chapters. Be sure to try drawing the acquisition process before looking at the solution in Figure 7.5.

Fig. 7.5 Acquisition/payment process with entities and relationships.

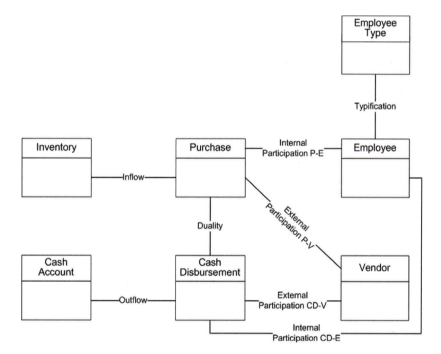

Notice in Figure 7.5 that the economic events are in the middle of the business process model with the resources on the left and the agents on the right. This Resources-Events-Agents orientation of the model makes it easy to read due to consistent placement of the entities. Also, this orientation tends to reduce the number of relationship lines that cross each other. Also note the relationship names for the internal and external participations become unique by simply adding the initials of the entities connected by the relationship to the end of the relationship name.

Adding Relationship Cardinalities to the Business Process Model

Recall from Chapter 2 that the three fundamental relationship types are one-to-one (1–1), one-to-many (1–M), and many-to-many (M–M). We will refer to the 1s and Ms as *cardinalities*, a relational database term. Now that you have established the entities in the acquisition process—events, resources, and agents—as well as the relationships between them, you next need to determine the cardinalities for each relationship. These cardinalities are the way that business rules are expressed in a relational database. For example, recall that the business rules regarding the duality relationship between purchase and cash disbursement are as follows:

1.   Pipefitters usually pays for all of its inventory receipts (purchase events) from a particular vendor in full with a single check at the end of the month.
2.   However, it sometimes pays early to take advantage of purchase discounts.
3.   Also, Pipefitters may make partial payments over two or more months for large purchases.

Item 1 indicates that a particular cash disbursement (writing a check to pay for inventory) may be for many purchases. Although Item 2 indicates that a cash disbursement may be for only one purchase, the AIS must allow for a cash disbursement to participate with "many" purchases. Therefore, the cardinality on the purchase side of the purchase–cash disbursement relationship as shown in Figure 7.6 must be "M." Also, note that you read "across" the relationship—cash disbursement can be associated with more than one (many) purchase.

Fig. 7.6 Acquisition/ payment process duality relationship with one cardinality.

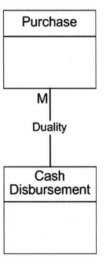

Item 3 indicates that a single purchase may be associated with many cash disbursements. This cardinality is shown as an "M" on the cash disbursement side of the purchase–cash disbursement relationship. These business rules result in a many-to-many relationship for the duality purchase–cash disbursement.

EXERCISE 7.4: CREATING THE BUSINESS PROCESS MODEL— ADDING CARDINALITIES TO RELATIONSHIPS

In this exercise, you will add cardinalities to the relationships depicted in Figure 7.5 of Pipefitters' acquisition process. To do so, you need to reread the description of Pipefitters' acquisition process at the beginning of this section to determine the business rules. If a business rule is not explicitly stated in the information, then apply what you believe to be normal business practices to determine the cardinalities.

When determining the appropriate cardinality for a given relationship, ask yourself the following question, "Over time, can an instance of A participate with more than one instance of B?" If the answer is yes, then the cardinality is "M." If not, then the cardinality is "1," indicating that an instance of A can be associated with at most one instance of B. Be sure to fill in all of the cardinalities before looking at the solution in Figure 7.7.

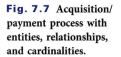

Fig. 7.7 Acquisition/ payment process with entities, relationships, and cardinalities.

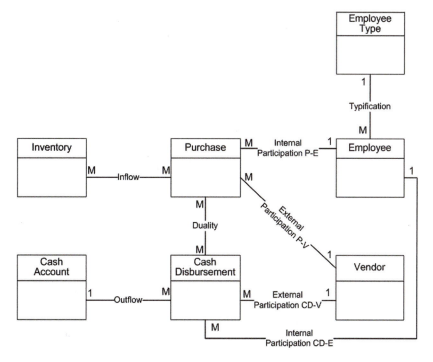

Figure 7.7 shows a many-to-many outflow relationship between inventory and purchase. These cardinalities can be derived from the following information about Pipefitters:

Pipefitters tracks inventory by item number rather than by tracking each individual piece of inventory. Pipefitters will have one record for each part it carries in its inventory.... When merchandise arrives at the receiving dock, only one receiving clerk counts the inventory items and records which items were received and enters their quantities on a receiving report.

From this information you learn that a purchase can be for various quantities of many different inventory items, indicating that the cardinality on the inventory side of the inflow relationship is "M." Also, since the inventory table tracks parts by inventory item number (one record for each inventory item number), each inventory item may be associated with many purchases; the cardinality on the purchase side of the inflow relationship will also be "M."

One of the cardinalities in the internal participation P-E relationship can be determined from this piece of information about Pipefitters' acquisition process:

When merchandise arrives at the receiving dock, a single receiving clerk counts the inventory items and records which items were received and enters their quantities on a receiving report.

This information tells us that a purchase involves a single employee. Therefore, the cardinality on the employee side of this relationship is "1." Although there is no information about the maximum number of purchases for which a certain employee can be involved, logic tells us that a receiving clerk will likely be involved with many purchases. Therefore, the cardinality on the purchase side of the relationship is "M."

Although the information about Pipefitters does not specify business rules concerning the external participation between purchase and vendor, you can ask yourself the cardinality question about each side of the relationship, "Over time, can a particular purchase involve more than one vendor?" Clearly the answer is "no," so the cardinality on the vendor side of external participation P-V is "1." The second question is, "Over time, can a particular vendor participate in more than one purchase?" Since the answer to this question is "yes," the cardinality on the purchase side of the relationship is "M."

Now, let's look at the typification relationship between employee and employee type. The information clearly describes the cardinality on the employee type side of the typification relationship:

> *Employee type—such as purchasing agent, materials handler, accountant—is kept in a separate table such that each employee has only one employee type.*

Therefore, the cardinality on the employee type side of the relationship is "1." As for the employee side of the typification relationship, ask the question, "Over time, can a particular employee type have more than one employee?" Yes. Therefore, the Cardinality is "M."

The same logic applied to internal and external participation relationships with purchase also apply to the participation relationships with the cash disbursement event.

Finally, the outflow relationship between the cash account and cash disbursement needs to be resolved by answering the cardinality question with logic due to the absence of an explicit description of this relationship. First, "Over time, can a particular cash account be associated with more than one cash disbursement?" Yes, because Pipefitters likely writes many checks over time from a single checking account. Therefore, the cardinality on the cash disbursement side of outflow is "M." Second, "Over time, can a particular cash disbursement come from more than one cash account?" The answer is "no" because checks are drawn from a single account. Thus, the cardinality on the cash account side of outflow is "1."

Adding Attributes to the Business Process Model

The information you were given about Pipefitters Supply Company was sufficient to create the basic structure of the acquisition/payment business process: entities (events, resources, agents), relationships, and the cardinalities. All that is missing from this business process model are the attributes—the pieces of information of which Pipefitters Supply Company actually tracks in its AIS. The attributes include the primary key for each entity and the other attributes. Although the attributes for Pipefitters were not presented with the other information about the acquisition process, all information for a system implementation would be gathered at the same time. Oftentimes, the attributes that a company wants to track affect the entities and relationships that appear in a business process model.

EXERCISE 7.5: CREATING THE BUSINESS PROCESS MODEL— ADDING ATTRIBUTES

The list of attributes presented in Figure 7.8 is an abbreviated set of attributes that we will use later in the book when we create Pipefitters' complete acquisition/payment process. From this list, identify the primary key and other attributes for each table. Start by drawing the acquisition/payment process model in Figure 7.7. Place the attributes in the bottom portion of each entity. Identify the primary key for each table by placing "(P)" next to each one.

Fig. 7.8 Attributes
for the acquisition/
payment process.

Attribute Name
Account Description
Bank Account #
Bank Name
Cash Acct ID #
Cash Disbursement Date
Check #
Date Received
Description
Employee ID #
Employee Name
Employee Type ID #
Employee Type Name
Inventory ID#
Receiving Report #
Vendor ID #
Vendor Invoice #
Vendor Name

The solution for this exercise is provided in Figure 7.9. Each of the entities in Figure 7.9 will become tables in the Pipefitters' database AIS.

Fig. 7.9 Acquisition/
payment process with
attributes.

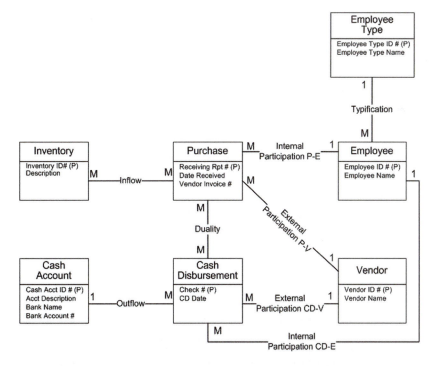

The primary key for each table is an identification number, the number on a prenumbered document, or a standardized number. For example, the Cash Account ID # is NOT the actual bank account number. Using the actual account number on company documents, especially on documents that are sent to vendors or customers would create a huge internal control weakness. Imagine if the employee ID # entered on documents was the employee Social Security number! That is why a number with no intrinsic meaning is often used as a primary key. Other numbers, such as check # or Receiving Report #, can be used as a primary key because such documents are prenumbered, ensuring that the primary key is a unique identifier. Finally, some numbers that are standardized like SKU numbers (bar code numbers) can be used as a primary key because they are known to be unique.

Converting a Business Process Model to a Logical Database

With the addition of the primary keys and other attributes to the Pipefitters' acquisition business process model, your data model is complete. However, before you can implement Pipefitters' acquisition process in Access, you need to convert the business process model to a *logical model*. Since Access is a relational database, the logical model shows how the data needs to be represented to implement it in a relational database. This conversion entails creating the relationships by posting foreign keys and creating relationship tables.

For Pipefitters' acquisition process, you will follow the rules for creating relationships based on cardinalities. There are sometimes other considerations involved in deciding whether to use a foreign key or a relationship table to link entity tables together, but we will focus only on the cardinalities in this example. Other concerns are addressed in subsequent chapters.

Keep these three general rules in mind when creating relationships:

1. For 1–M relationships, post the primary key from the "1" side of the relationship into the table on the "M" side of the relationship. The primary key from the "1" side becomes a foreign key in the table on the "M" side.

2. Always create a relationship table for M–M relationships. The primary key for the relationship table is created by combining the primary keys from each of the tables involved in the relationship. This is called a *composite* primary key (sometimes referred to as a concatenated or compound primary key).

3. For 1–1 relationships, post either primary key into the other table, but do NOT post both keys. Before posting a foreign key, be sure that you have a need for keeping the data in two separate tables instead of combining the two tables into a single table.

EXERCISE 7.6: CREATING THE BUSINESS PROCESS MODEL— ADDING FOREIGN KEYS AND RELATIONSHIP TABLES

Apply the first two rules for creating relationships to the solution to Exercise 7.5 (see Figure 7.9). The third rule does not apply to Pipefitters' acquisition process because there are no 1–1 relationships. Add foreign keys to the appropriate tables and place the primary keys for relationship tables directly under the relationships that become tables.

The solution is presented in Figure 7.10. The back side of the arrows in Figure 7.10 shows the tables from which the foreign keys originate and the front of the arrows shows the tables in which they are posted. The arrows always come from the "1" side of the relationship and go to the "M" side of the relationship.

Figure 7.10 also shows rectangles around the many-to-many relationships. The rectangles indicate that M–M relationships become tables just like the rectangles representing entities become tables in a database.

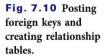

Fig. 7.10 Posting
foreign keys and
creating relationship
tables.

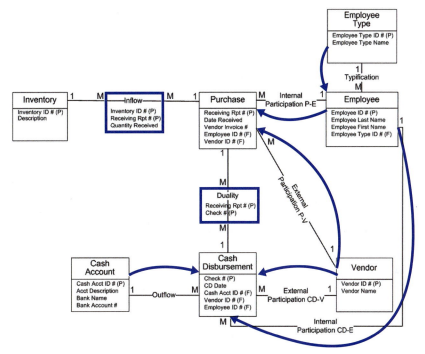

Creating the Access Database

Figure 7.10 shows a list of all tables, complete with foreign keys and relationship tables, that you will put into your Access database. When you start with a blank database, it is helpful to create a **_data dictionary_** before creating the tables. The data dictionary shown in Figure 7.11 lists all detailed information about each attribute in each table, including the type of attribute, its size, and whether it is a primary key, foreign key, or non-key attribute. The data dictionary serves two purposes. First, it helps you keep track of all the attributes and tables that you need to include in your database. Second, it provides documentation to aid developers in making changes to the database, and also provides information for auditors.

Fig. 7.11 Data
dictionary.

Attribute Name	Table	P, F, or *	Related Table for Foreign Keys and Relationship Primary Keys	Properties	Caption	Begins with	Field size
CashAccountID	CashAccount	P		Text	Account #	301	3
AccountDescription	CashAccount	*		Text	Description		255
BankName	CashAccount	*		Text	Bank		50
BankAccountNumber	CashAccount	*		Text	Bank Account #		50
CheckNumber	CashDisbursement	P		Text	Check #	10001	5
CashDisbursementDate	CashDisbursement	*		short date	Date	input mask	
CashAccountID	CashDisbursement	F	Cash Account	Text	Cash Account	301	3
EmployeeID	CashDisbursement	F	Employee	Text	Employee #	101	3
VendorID	CashDisbursement	F	Vendor	Text	Vendor #	10001	5
ReceivingReportID	Duality-CashReceiptCashDisbursement	P	Purchase	Text	Employee Type #	100001	6
CheckNumber	Duality-CashReceiptCashDisbursement	P	CashDisbursement	Text	Employee Type Name	10001	5
EmployeeID	Employee	P		Text	Employee #	101	3
EmployeeLastName	Employee	*		Text	Last Name		30
EmployeeFirstName	Employee	*		Text	First Name		30
EmployeeTypeID	Employee	F	EmployeeType	Text	Type	10	2
EmployeeTypeID	EmployeeType	P		Text	Employee Type #	10	2
EmplyeeTypeName	EmployeeType	P		Text	Employee Type Name		50
ReceivingReportID	Inflow-InventoryPurchase	P	Purchase	Text	Receiving Report #	100001	6
InventoryItemID	Inflow-InventoryPurchase	P	Inventory	Text	Item #	101	3
InventoryReceiptQuantity	Inflow-InventoryPurchase	*		Integer	Quantity		
InventoryItemID	Inventory	P		Text	Item #	101	3
InventoryDescription	Inventory	*		Text	Description		50
ReceivingReportID	Purchase	P		Text	Receiving Report #	100001	6
ReceivingReportDate	Purchase	*		short date	Date Received	input mask	
ReceivingReportVendorInvoiceNumber	Purchase	*		Text	Vendor Invoice #		20
EmployeeID	Purchase	F	Employee	Text	Employee #	101	3
VendorID	Purchase	F	Vendor	Text	Vendor #	10001	5
VendorID	Vendor	P		Text	Vendor #	1001	4
VendorName	Vendor	*		Text	Name		25

EXERCISE 7.7: CREATING AN ACCESS DATABASE BY IMPORTING DATA FROM AN EXCEL WORKBOOK

Open the Excel file, Ch07 data for tables.xlsx and print a copy of the first worksheet entitled Data Dictionary. To print the entire data dictionary on a single sheet of paper, select Landscape from the Orientation on the Page Layout tab, and select 1 page for both Width and Height in the Scale to Fit group on the Page Layout ribbon (see Figure 7.12). The worksheets that follow the data dictionary contain the data for each of Pipefitters Supply Company's acquisition/payment process tables. Close the Excel file.

1. Launch Access and create a new database by double-clicking the Blank Database icon (see Figure 7.13). Name your database Ch07AcquisitionProcess by typing in the name in the File Name text box. You can click on the file folder icon if you want to save the database in a location other than the default location shown. Then, click the Create button (see Figure 7.14).

2. To import the tables from the *Ch07 data for tables.xlsx* file, click the Excel in the Import group on the External Data tab. Be sure that the radio button for Import the source data into a new table in the current database is selected (see Figure 7.15). Then click the Browse button to open the Open File dialog box, change the directory if necessary, click the Excel file, and then click Open (see Figure 7.16). When the dialog box closes, click OK. This starts the Import Spreadsheet Wizard.

3. In the Import Spreadsheet Wizard, make sure that the radio button for the Show Worksheets option is selected. Then, select tblCashAccount from the list of worksheets contained in the Excel file (see Figure 7.17) When you click Next be sure to select the check box for First Row Contains Column Headings. Checking this box tells the wizard to use the first row as field names (field and attribute can be used interchangeably).

4. When you go to the next window, you will see the following field options: Field Name, Data Type, and Indexed. The Data Type for each attribute is listed in the data dictionary table. For CashAccountID the Data Type is Text. For single primary keys the value for Index should be set to Yes (No Duplicates). For composite primary keys (*tblDuality-PurchaseCashDisburse* and *tblInflow-InventoryPurchase*), the index should be set to Yes (Duplicates OK). When you finish selecting values for CashAccountID, select the next attribute by clicking its name (see Figure 7.18). When you finish the last attribute in the table, click Next.

5. The next window to appear is to select the primary key for the table (see Figure 7.19). Click the radio button for Choose my own primary key. The primary keys for all tables are listed in the data dictionary. For *tblCashAccount* select CashAccountID. Then click Next.

6. The final window that appears is to name the table (see Figure 7.20). The name that appears in the Import to Table: text box is the worksheet name. Since the worksheets' names are the actual table names to be used in the database, *tblCashAccount* should appear in the text box. If something else appears in the text box, change the name to *tblCashAccount*. Then click on the Finish button to complete the process. If given the option, do *not* save the import steps as the Save Import Steps option creates a set of steps to import the exact same table, *tblCashAccount*, you just created. After you have completed this step, your database should look like Figure 7.21.

7. Repeat this process for the remaining eight tables.
   - Refer to the data dictionary for each attribute's properties.
   - Don't forget to set the Index for foreign keys to Yes (Duplicates OK).
   - In Step 6 for *tblDuality-PurchaseCashDisburse* and *tblInflow-InventoryPurchase*, select the radio button for No primary key because the Import Spreadsheet Wizard cannot accommodate composite primary keys. You will have to set composite primary keys afterward in the Design view for each table.

Fig. 7.12 Page
Layout ribbon in Excel.

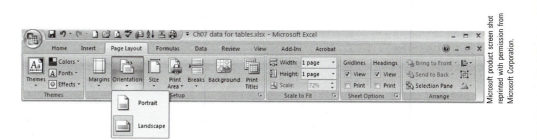

Fig. 7.13 Getting
Started window.

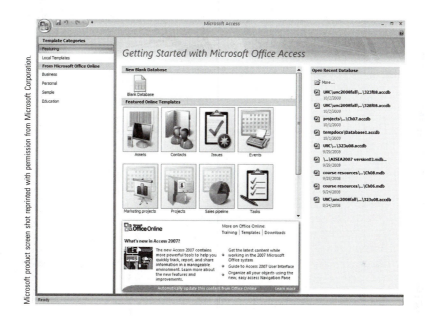

Fig. 7.14 Saving new
database.

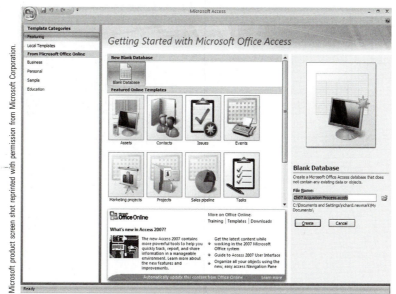

Fig. 7.15 Get
External Data window.

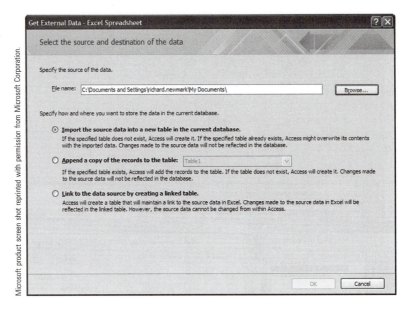

Fig. 7.16 File Open
dialog box.

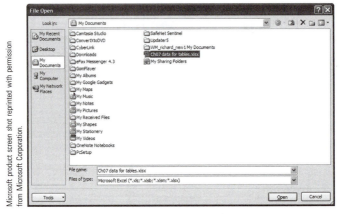

Fig. 7.17 Import
Spreadsheet Wizard for
tblCashAccount.

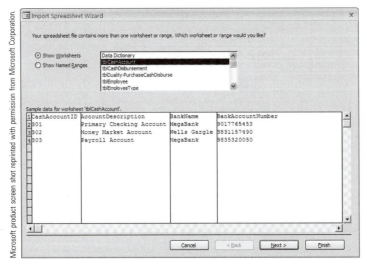

Fig. 7.18 Field options.

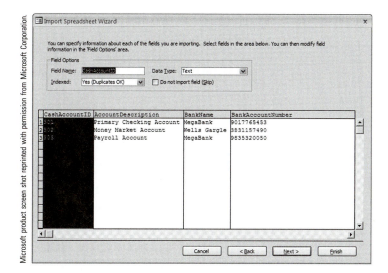

Fig. 7.19 Selecting the primary key for imported tables.

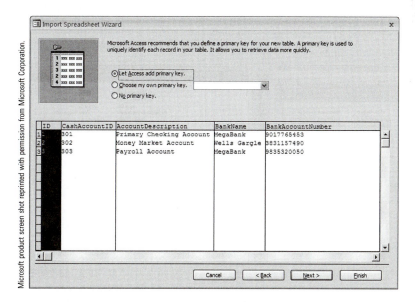

Fig. 7.20 Table Name dialog box.

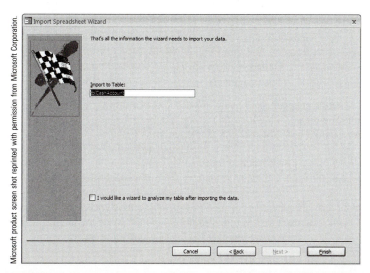

Fig. 7.21 Database
after importing
tblCashAccount.

Microsoft product screen shot reprinted with permission from Microsoft Corporation.

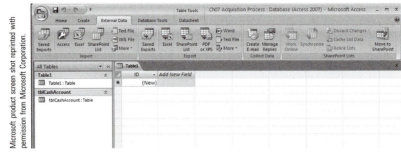

Now that you have created all of the tables for the database, all that is left to do is to create the relationships between the tables by linking the tables together.

EXERCISE 7.8: LINKING TABLES IN AN ACCESS DATABASE

1. Launch Access and open the *Ch07.accdb* Access database. This database includes all of the property settings and captions from the data dictionary as well as the data imported from the Excel database.

2. Click the Database Tools tab, open the Relationship window by clicking Relationships in the Show/Hide group. You should see all nine tables in the relationship window (see Figure 7.22). Be sure that the tables are set up like the data model in Figure 7.10. This will make it easier to keep track of all of the links you need to create.

3. Looking at Figure 7.10, you will drag the primary key from the table at the back of each arrow onto the foreign key in the table the arrow points to. Also, for each relationship table, you will drag the primary key from the tables connected by the relationship table into the relationship table.

4. Drag CashAccountID from *tblCashAccount* onto CashAccountID in *tblCashDisbursement*. When you do, you will see the Edit Relationships dialog box with the table you dragged "from" on the left and the table you dragged "to" on the right. Check the box for Enforce Referential Integrity and the box for Cascade Update Related Fields (see Figure 7.23).

   a. Enforcing referential integrity ensures that the only cash account numbers that can be entered for each cash disbursement are cash accounts that have already been entered in *tblCashAccount*.

   b. Also, if Pipefitters Supply Company decided to change the value of CashAccountID for one or more bank accounts (perhaps somebody made a typo when entering a new bank account), selecting Cascade Update Related Fields will automatically update all related records. However, Pipefitters should have controls in place so that only certain employees can change primary keys because such a change wipes out the original data.

   c. **NEVER** select Cascade Delete Related Records because it will allow you to delete the primary record (the "1" side of a relationship) even if it is involved in one or more relationships. Moreover, this option will delete all related records in other tables. Thus, if this option is chosen the potential to accidentally or purposely wipe out many records with a single deletion exists. For example, deleting an employee from the database will wipe out all transactions involving that employee.

5. Repeat Step 4 for all of the foreign keys and relationship tables in Figure 7.10. The result should look like the relationship window depicted in Figure 7.24.

Fig. 7.22 Relationship window.

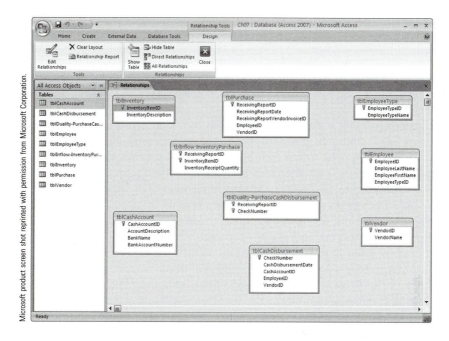

Fig. 7.23 Edit Relationships dialog box.

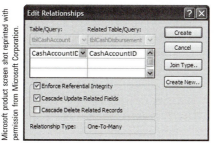

Fig. 7.24 Database tables with foreign keys, relationship tables, and relationships.

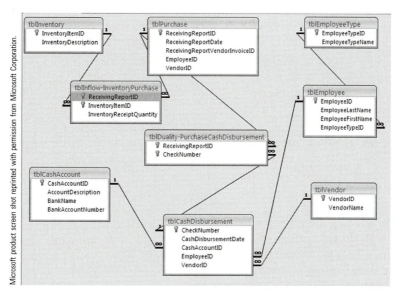

Summary

This chapter described how to create models of an accounting information system and use them to implement an Access database. The data modeling method discussed in this chapter is based on the REA (resources, events, and agents) enterprise ontology. It is a top-down process that focuses on economic exchanges. The Value System is the top-level model in which you depicted the resource exchanges between Pipefitters Supply Company and its outside partners.

You then learned to create a Value Chain model. It shows the resource flows between core business processes within an enterprise. The business processes we focused on are financing, acquisition/payment, human resources, conversion, and sales/collection. Within each business process you included the economic increment events used to obtain resources and the economic decrement events that use resources.

You then drilled down to the business process level, where you expanded the duality relationship depicted within each business process in the value chain model. In addition to modeling the economic increment and decrement events, you added the resources and agents involved in the events, and the relationships between them. These entities—events, resources, and agents—become the main tables in your Access database. Moreover, you incorporated business rules in your model with cardinalities.

To complete your business process model in sufficient detail to convert it into an Access database you identified primary keys for each entity, and determined where various attributes belong. You then learned how to post the foreign keys and create relationship tables based on the cardinalities, which enabled you to implement the business process model in Access.

Finally, you created tables in Access by importing data from an Excel file to create the database tables. Once the tables were created, you then incorporated additional business rules by enforcing referential integrity in the relationships you created in Access between tables.

Questions and Problems for Review

Multiple-Choice Questions

1. The value system model shows which of the following?
   a. Resource flows between business processes.
   b. Internal agents.
   c. External agents.
   d. Both b and c are correct.

2. Resource flows are shown in a _____ model.
   a. value system.
   b. value chain.
   c. business process.
   d. All of the above are correct.

3. Which business process does not have any external agents?
   a. Acquisition/payment.
   b. Conversion.
   c. Financing.
   d. Human resources.

4. All of the following business processes are included in a value chain model except the
   a. support process.
   b. conversion process.
   c. financing process.
   d. acquisition/payment process.

5. Which of the following about the duality relationship is NOT true?
   a. It connects give events with get events.
   b. It connects inflows to outflows.
   c. It is based on the theory of economic exchange.
   d. It may be represented with a relationship table.

6. The resource acquired in the human resources process is
    a. labor.
    b. employee.
    c. cash.
    d. inventory.
7. Business rules, such as paying for all purchases from a vendor during the month with a single check, are represented in an AIS by
    a. resources.
    b. relationships.
    c. participation cardinalities.
    d. attributes.
8. Which of the following would make the best primary key?
    a. Social Security number for *tblEmployee*.
    b. Receiving report number for *tblPurchase*.
    c. Bank account number for *tblCashAccount*.
    d. Date/time for *tblCashDisbursement*.
9. A data dictionary_____?
    a. lists the primary keys for each table in a database.
    b. lists the values of each primary key in a database.
    c. lists the participation cardinalities for each relationship in a database.
    d. is automatically populated in Access when you enter new fields in a table.
10. If Pipefitters Supply Company wants to ensure that purchases are for inventory items that are already in their database, it should use which relationship property?
    a. Cascade Update Related Fields.
    b. Cascade Delete Related Records.
    c. An outer join.
    d. Enforce Referential Integrity.

Discussion Questions

1. Examine Pipefitters Supply Company's value system in Figure 7.1. What other external partners may Pipefitters include in its value system? What resources may be exchanged?
2. The Value Chain model for a particular enterprise depends on the activities it performs as well as the information it wishes to gather in its AIS. Which business process would every for-profit enterprise have in its Value Chain model? Explain.
3. Assume that all cash disbursements are made by Arthur Kamedes, one of Pipefitters Supply Company's owners. What impact does this have on Pipefitters' acquisition/payment business process model?
4. How would the business process model in Figure 7.10 change if Pipefitters sometimes used two or three materials handlers (employees) to record a shipment, and in which table would you record the amount of time each materials handler spent on each inventory receipt?
5. What attribute needs to be added to the database to compute the cost of merchandise received without storing computed amounts in the database?

Practice Exercises

The Practice Exercises illustrate some of the benefits of using a relational database AIS by having you derive some non-accounting information from the database. Refer to Chapter 4 if you need help creating the queries.

1. Create a query to list all employees alphabetically first by employee type name, and second by employee last name, and third by employee first name. Name your query PE1-qryEmployeeByType.
2. Create a query to show a count of employees by EmployeeTypeName. The names should be in alphabetical order. Name your query PE2-qryCountOfEmployeeType.

3. Create a query that finds the earliest date a payment was made for each purchase. Only include purchases that have at least one cash disbursement associated with it. Sort your results in ascending order by ReceivingReportID. Name your query PE3-qryEarliestPaymentForPurchase.

4. For each purchase that has at least one related cash disbursement (see Practice Exercise 3), create a query to compute the number of days between the purchase date and the first payment for that purchase. Sort your query by purchase. Name your query PE4-qryDaysToPayForPurchases.

5. Create a query to summarize your results from Practice Exercise 4. Your query should show the minimum, maximum, and average number of days it takes Pipefitters to make a payment on its purchases. Name your query PE5-qryMinMaxAvgDaysToPay.

Problems

The following problems explore Big R General Merchandise Store's business processes For Problems 1 through 4, draw a business process model like the one in Figure 7.7. Include the events, resources, and agents (internal and external) in the business process as well as the relationships and cardinalities. State any assumptions you needed to make.

1. Big R acquires some of its capital by borrowing money from banks. One of its three owner/employees immediately deposits cash received from a loan into only one cash account. All loans are received in exactly one cash receipt. Short-term loans are term loans; they are repaid in full with exactly one payment on the maturity date of the loan. Installment loans are used for longer-term loans. These require monthly payments throughout the duration of the loan. Loan repayments are made by an accounts payable clerk from one of its checking accounts. Create Big R's financing business process model.

2. Big R purchases merchandise from many different vendors. Purchases are for varying quantities of one or more different items. When a purchase is received, one or more materials handlers unpacks the shipment and records the items received. All shipments are paid in full within 30 days from one of its checking accounts by an accounts payable clerk. Sometimes, one check will be used to pay for several purchases. Create Big R's acquisition/payment business process model.

3. Big R has 20 employees on its payroll. Employees may perform many different duties so their time is recorded by type of work (e.g., sales, materials handling, accounts receivable, accounts payable). Treat work type as a resource (like inventory). Employees record the amount of time spent on each type of work daily. This is stored in the work-performed table. Each employee is paid on Fridays with only one check. Cash disbursements for payroll are made by one of the three owners from the payroll account. Each payroll check is for many work-performed events. Create Big R's human resources business process model.

4. Big R sells all sorts of merchandise to businesses and to retail customers. Each sale may be for varying quantities of one or more different items. Sales to large customers may involve two or three salespeople. Sales to small businesses and individuals need only one salesperson. Some customers pay their bill in full while others make installment payments for up to six months. All funds from a cash receipt are deposited into only one cash account. Create Big R's sales/collection business process model.

5. Combine all four business process models into a single, unified model. Events, resources, agents, and relationships should only appear in the model once. For example, the acquisition/payment process and HR process both have a cash disbursement, a cash account, and an outflow relationship linking the two entities. Show each entity and the relationship only once. Use a large sheet of paper if drawing the model by hand. You can also use the drawing tools in Microsoft Excel or use a drawing application such as Microsoft Visio.

CHAPTER 8

Sales/Collection Process

CHAPTER OBJECTIVES

Sales/collection activities include accepting orders from customers, shipping merchandise to customers (the sale event), and collecting cash from customers. Information about these events are recorded for decision making, financial reporting, and maintaining records of the resources involved in these events (merchandise inventory and cash) as well as the agents involved (customers and employees). In this chapter, you will learn how to use Microsoft Access to design tables, queries, and forms that can help you:

- Create a model of the sales/collection business process.
- Create a Microsoft Access database based on the business process model.
- Create controls to enforce business rules.
- Create and maintain customer records.
- Create and maintain finished goods inventory records.
- Record sale orders.
- Record sale/shipment information.
- Print invoices.
- Record payments received from customers.
- Produce information for financial statements.
- Produce information for internal purposes.

Introduction

This chapter describes the sales/collection business process of an accounting information system. We illustrate many of these components of this process using example data for the Pipefitters Supply Company. As mentioned in Chapter 7, we will focus only on the merchandising activities of the firm. The sales/collection process (also referred to as the sales process or the revenue process) includes activities related to the sale of goods or services. These activities include everything from sales calls and other marketing activities all the way through collecting cash from customers. Whether firms are manufacturers, merchandisers, or service businesses, their sales processes are similar. For example, manufacturing and merchandising firms sell products to customers; service firms perform services for customers. In all cases, customers place orders for a product or service they are purchasing. Then, the selling firm ships the product or performs the service. Customers, pursuant to the terms of the sale, pay the amount due in one or more payments before, during, and/or after the sale.

We urge you to download to your computer, or other storage device, the Access database from the book's Companion Web site. The unzipped database is named *Ch08.accdb*. It contains all the objects that you will need to follow the illustrations in this chapter as well as to complete the end-of-chapter exercises and problems. It provides a place for you to store all your Chapter 8 database work.

Pipefitters Supply Company's Sales/ Collection Business Process

Pipefitters Supply Company accepts orders over the telephone and via fax, e-mail and regular mail. When an order arrives, one of the salespersons enters it as a sale order. The sale order includes the customer's name and a list of the inventory items that the customer wishes to purchase. This inventory list includes the quantity of each inventory item and the actual sale price of each item on the sale order. The actual sale price may differ from the item list price that is stored for that item in the inventory table if the item is on sale or Pipefitters decides to offer a quantity discount for a particularly large quantity ordered. Pipefitters sends a confirmed sale order back to the customer for the customer's records.

When the order is ready to ship, a materials handler uses the sale order information to pick the ordered merchandise from the warehouse, pack it in boxes, and load it on a delivery truck. When the goods are loaded on the truck, Pipefitters records the sale and prints an invoice as Pipefitters always ships goods *FOB shipping point*. FOB shipping point means that title changes hands when the goods leave the seller's premises, and Generally Accepted Accounting Principles (GAAP) states that a sale is generally recorded when title changes hands.

Sometimes, some of the inventory items a customer has ordered are not in stock. In those cases, Pipefitters will ship partial orders. Customers are expected to pay their invoices within 30 days. Most customers pay on time with only one payment. However, some customers arrange to make partial payments over two or more months. To make our database more manageable, we will assume that each customer payment is for only one invoice. Payments received are always deposited into only one bank account, usually the operating account.

Duality of Economic Events

EXERCISE 8.1: MODELING THE DUALITY RELATIONSHIP FOR PIPEFITTERS SUPPLY COMPANY'S SALES/ COLLECTION PROCESS

1. Based on the narrative for Pipefitters' sales/collection process, draw the entities and relationship involved in the duality as it was illustrated in Chapter 7.
2. Identify the economic increment event (the event wherein Pipefitters receives something) with a "+" sign.
3. Identify the economic decrement event (the event wherein Pipefitters gives something) with a "−" sign.
4. Add the cardinalities to your drawing.

Figure 8.1 shows the duality for the sales/collection process. Sale is the economic decrement event; merchandise is shipped to the customer. Cash receipt is the economic increment event. Note that the two events do not need to occur at the same time. When merchandise is sold before cash is received, as is often the case in business-to-business transactions, the company will have accounts receivable. Unlike a double-entry bookkeeping system, we do NOT record accounts receivable. Instead, we can derive accounts receivable by taking the sum of all sales and subtracting the sum of all cash receipts related to sales. You will use queries to derive accounts receivable and other financial information later in the chapter.

Fig. 8.1 Pipefitters Supply Company sales/ collection duality.

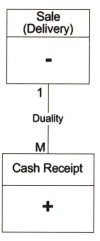

Since Pipefitters allows some customers to make partial payments, a sale can have many cash receipts associated with it. Therefore, the cash receipt side of the relationship is "M." Since a cash receipt pertains to only one invoice, the sale side of the relationship is "1."

Basic Sales/Collection Data Model

In the following exercise you will add resources and agents to each event to the duality relationship. Economic increment events have an *inflow* relationship with a resource and economic decrement events have an *outflow* relationship with a resource. Events generally participate with at least one internal agent—an *internal participation* relationship. Events usually participate with only one external agent in an *external participation* relationship. The resulting data model forms the core of most sales/collection business processes.

EXERCISE 8.2: ADDING RESOURCES AND AGENTS TO THE SALES/COLLECTION DUALITY RELATIONSHIP

1. Add to your model the resource and agents for the sale event and their relationships with sale.
2. Add cardinalities to the relationships with sale.
3. Add to your model the resource and agents for the cash receipt event and their relationships with cash receipt.
4. Add cardinalities to the relationships with cash receipt.

Sale Event

The data model in Figure 8.2 shows that a sale results in an outflow of inventory to the customer (external agent), and that an employee (internal agent) also participates in the relationship. The one-to-many relationship between customer and sale are typical cardinalities between events and external agents; the relationship indicates that a particular customer can participate in many sales and that a sale has at most one customer.

Fig. 8.2 Pipefitters Supply Company sales/ collection duality with resources and agents.

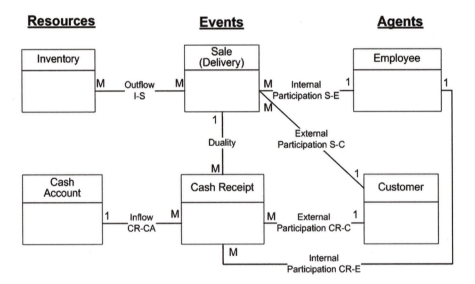

Likewise, the one-to-many relationship between employee and sale indicates that a specific employee may participate in many sales and that a sale participates with only one employee. However, there may be some companies that use two or more employees to prepare merchandise for delivery. If two or more employees were to participate in the delivery, then the internal participation relationship would be many-to-many.

The outflow relationship between sale and inventory is many-to-many because a particular inventory item number (e.g., item 1001: brass, 4-foot, .25-inch diameter pipes) can be involved in many sales, and a sale can have many different item numbers (e.g., item 1001, 1008, and 1019). The quantity of each item ordered does not affect the cardinalities; for example, ordering 65 of item 1001 is still considered one item.

Cash Receipt Event

Figure 8.2 shows that a cash receipt results in an inflow of cash from the customer (external agent), and that an employee (internal agent) also participates in the relationship. Like the sale event, both participation events are one-to-many. Even if the customer transfers funds directly into Pipefitters' bank account using an electronic funds transfer, the cash receipt will still require an employee because the participation denotes *responsibility* for proper execution and recording of the event, even if the employee did not physically collect and record the cash receipt as one would do when receiving a check from a customer.

The resource, cash account, is used because we track information about cash accounts (e.g., operating account, payroll account, petty cash account), including the date and amount of inflows and outflows. The one-to-many cardinalities indicate that a cash account may have inflows from many cash receipt events and that any particular cash receipt will be deposited into only one cash account.

Sale Order Event

In Exercise 8.3 you are going to add the sale order event to your data model of Pipefitters' sales/collection process. A sale order is neither an economic increment event nor an economic decrement event. Instead, a sale order is a ***commitment*** event, committing Pipefitters to provide the specified merchandise at a specified price to be delivered at a particular location at a specified time. The sale order also commits the customer to pay for the merchandise according to the terms specified in the sale order.

When Pipefitters accepts a sale order, it reserves inventory for delivery to the customer: a ***reservation*** relationship between sale order and inventory. Also, since customers place sale orders with salespeople, sale order is related to both a customer and an employee. Finally, Pipefitters fulfills a sale order by shipping ordered merchandise to the customer, so the relationship between a sale order and sale (delivery) is a ***fulfillment*** relationship. After adding the sale order and related components to the model, you will be ready to convert the model to tables that you will create in Access.

EXERCISE 8.3: ADDING THE SALE ORDER EVENT TO PIPEFITTERS SUPPLY COMPANY'S SALES/COLLECTION DATA MODEL

1. Add sale order to the sales/collection data model in Figure 8.2 and the appropriate relationships.
2. Add the cardinalities to the relationships.

Figure 8.3 shows the complete sales/collection data model for Pipefitters Supply Company. The fulfillment relationship between sale order and sale is one-to-many because a sale order will have more than one sale (delivery) when Pipefitters makes a partial shipment due to a stockout. The reservation relationship between sale order and inventory has the same many-to-many relationship as the actual outflow of inventory because a sale order can be for many different items, and an item can be ordered many times. Also like the sale event, the cardinalities for the participation relationships with sale

Fig. 8.3 Pipefitters Supply Company sales/ collection process with all resources, events, and agents.

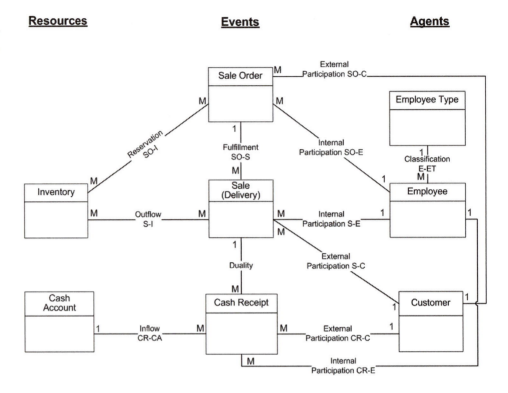

order (sale order–customer; sale order–employee) are one-to-many because sale orders have only one customer and one employee, and customers and employees can participate with many sale orders over time.

One additional entity has been added to the model in Figure 8.3—employee type. Employee type is added so that Pipefitters can ensure that only salespeople make sales, materials handlers handle shipments, and only accountants handle cash receipts.

Completing the Sales/Collection Model

Now that all of the entities (resources, events, and agents), relationships, and cardinalities have been identified, primary keys must be chosen for each entity, and relationships must be made by using foreign keys (posting the primary key on the "1" side of a one-to-many relationship into the table on the "M" side) and relationship tables (using composite primary keys for many-to-many relationships).

EXERCISE 8.4: MAKING RELATIONSHIPS WITH FOREIGN KEYS AND RELATIONSHIP TABLES

1. Using the primary keys provided for Pipefitters' data model in Figure 8.4, create foreign keys for the one-to-many relationships.
2. Add relationship tables and composite primary keys for the many-to-many relationships.

If your foreign keys and relationship tables do not match those in Figure 8.5, review the "Relational Database Management Systems" section in Chapter 2.

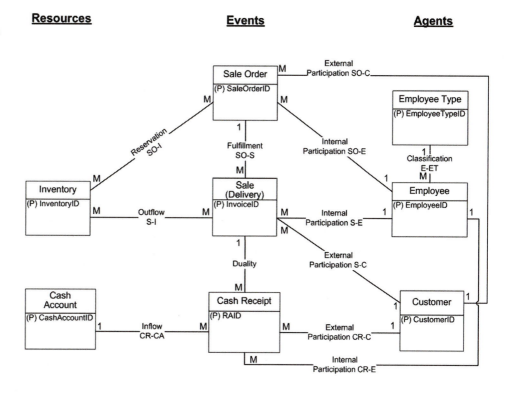

Fig. 8.4 Sales/collection process with primary keys.

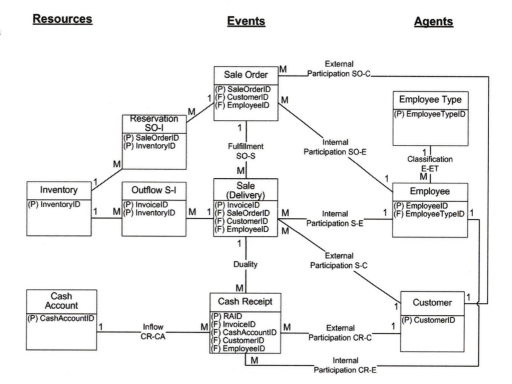

Fig. 8.5 Sales/collection process with primary keys, foreign keys, and relationship tables.

In addition to handling orders, invoices, and incoming payments, the sales/collection process portion of an accounting system must maintain a permanent record of customer information and provide tools for updating and revising that customer information. Users must also be able to perform update and maintenance tasks on finished goods inventory information. As you learned in Chapter 2, a key feature of database accounting systems is their ability to store much more information about each transaction than a traditional double-entry system. To take full advantage of this feature, users must be able to access the sales/collection process information stored in the system to provide financial and non-financial data for internal decision makers as well as provide data for external financial reporting.

Customer Information

Customers are the lifeblood of any business; therefore, accounting system database tables must include many details about each customer. At a minimum, firms want to know where their customers are located, what they have purchased, and when they purchased it. Businesses also want to track when their customers pay and the amounts of individual payments. Some businesses do not record information about their customers' identities. For example, businesses such as retail stores, fast-food restaurants, and amusement parks seldom record individual customers' names and addresses. Customers of these businesses pay cash and would not tolerate the time it would take to record their identities. Increasingly, these types of firms are developing ways to obtain information about their customers' identities. Many stores now use customer loyalty cards that give customers discounts on merchandise and other incentives. The cost of the discounts and incentives is the price firms are willing to pay to obtain detailed customer information. Even businesses without customer loyalty cards often keep careful records of customer traffic by day, hour, and location.

Customer information appears on many documents that businesses create and use. Invoices, shipping documents, and end-of-month account statements require customer names and addresses. For example, the marketing department might want a list of customers that includes the name and telephone number of customer contact persons or a set of mailing labels for a particular group of customers. To ensure that customer information is consistent wherever it is used, many firms keep all customer information in one database table. Any document or report that includes customer information obtains it from that table. If, for example, a customer moves to a new location, the customer's address needs to be changed only once. A relational database accounting system stores customer information in a Customer table.

The Customer Table

The first table in the sales/collection process we will describe is the Customer table. The Customer table provides a central location for storing all information about each customer. This makes adding, deleting, displaying, or changing customer information easy and efficient. The Customer table needs a primary key field that uniquely identifies each row in the table and exists for every row.

To ensure that each CustomerID is unique, many firms assign a sequential number to each new customer. A sequential number scheme gives each new customer a number that is one greater than the largest customer number that currently exists. In Exercise 8.5, you will begin creating a Customer table called *tblCustomer*. In this exercise, you will begin by opening a new table and you will create its primary key field, CustomerID. Pipefitters uses a five-digit sequential numbering scheme for its customer numbers, starting with 10001, which can accommodate up to 89,999 customers (10001 through 99999).

EXERCISE 8.5: CREATING *TBLCUSTOMER*

1. Start Microsoft Access, and click the Blank Database icon in the center panel of the screen. In the File Name box, type the name you want to give your database, click the folder icon next to the File Name box if you want to change the folder in which you want to save your Pipefitters Sales/Collection database, and then click Create.
2. Select Table1 from the Navigation Pane, and click the Design View command that appears in the Home tab. Access asks you to name the table.
3. Type tblCustomer in the Save As dialog box and then click OK to save the newly named table. Access displays the table, as yet undefined, in Design view.
4. Type the name of *tblCustomer's* first field, CustomerID, and press Tab. When you press Tab, the first row in the Data Type column changes into a combo box, and the Field Properties list appears in the bottom pane of the Table window.
5. Notice, by default, that the first row has a small key in the record selector column. The key indicates that the field CustomerID is the table's primary key. You can set the primary key manually or change it to a different column. CustomerID is, in fact, our table's primary key column, so we will leave it as is. Also note that the Indexed property sets itself to Yes (No Duplicates).
6. Since you will not be using the CustomerID field in any calculations, set its data type to Text. The Data Type combo box contains Text as its default selection for all fields other than the initial field named ID.
7. Press Tab to accept the Text default selection. You can use the Description column to store a description of the CustomerID field, if you wish. The Description column is a built-in documentation tool that is especially useful for storing explanations of complex or potentially confusing fields.
8. Press F6 to switch to the Field Properties pane. The cursor will highlight the default Field Size value of 255. Type 5 in the Field Size column to replace the default selection.
9. Press the Tab key three times, and type Customer # (including the space) as the field's Caption property. This Caption property setting will cause *Customer #*, rather than the field's name, *CustomerID*, to appear as the default text for form and report controls that reference the field. Creating a useful Caption property setting can be a real time saver when you are building reports and forms that use table fields. The panel on the right side of the Field Properties pane provides detailed instructions for each step in the property-setting process. Figure 8.6 shows the new Customer table with the CustomerID primary key field and the caption setting in Design view.
10. Use Figure 8.7 to add the remaining nine attributes to *tblCustomer*.

Adding Controls to the Customer Table

Field properties are an excellent way to implement *preventive* internal controls—controls that preclude erroneous data from entering the accounting system. The other two main categories of internal controls are (1) *detective* controls, which find errors after they have occurred but before the error causes damage, such as bank reconciliations, and (2) *corrective* controls, which are designed to recover from damage caused by errors such as using backup files to restore data that was accidentally deleted.

Input Mask vs. Validation Rule

Input masks and validation rules are two ways to control the values that users enter. Input masks are especially useful when values have a specific format like phone numbers, dates, and state abbreviations. For example, an input mask for a phone number provides the parentheses and dash so the user only needs to enter the actual numbers,

Fig. 8.6 The
CustomerID field in
tblCustomer.

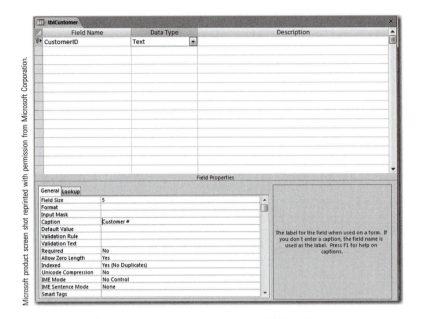

Microsoft product screen shot reprinted with permission from Microsoft Corporation.

Fig. 8.7 Attributes
for *tblCustomer.*

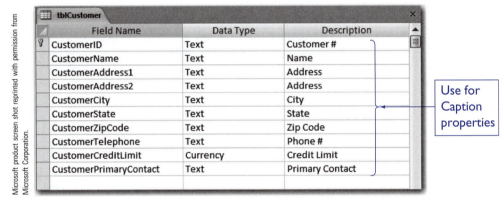

Microsoft product screen shot reprinted with permission from Microsoft Corporation.

which speeds up data entry and prevents input errors. Additionally, input masks can be set to only allow certain types of characters (e.g., numbers only, text only) and specify whether the characters are required or optional.

Input Mask property settings include three parts; each part is separated by a semicolon. The first part contains the template, which may include required and/or optional placeholders. The template may also include one or more *literals*—characters preceded by a backslash—which tells Access to recognize the next character as itself. The second part of the setting, between the first and second semicolon, tells Access whether or not to store literals along with the characters input in the field. The third part of the setting is the character used as a placeholder that will appear in field controls on data entry forms.

The Validation Rule property also limits the values that a user can enter for a table field. Like the input mask, validation rules can be used to specify the types of valid characters and the number of required characters. However, the validation rule can specify a range of valid entries. For example, a validation rule can specify that a customer's credit limit must be between $0 and $50,000.

Input masks alone are a sufficient control when the values for a field must have a specific format and length, but have no restriction on the values of the characters, such as the five-digit primary key, CustomerID in *tblCustomer.* Although a validation rule can also provide the same control, the input mask is preferable in this case because invalid characters cannot be entered at all, whereas a validation rule allows the invalid characters to be input only to be rejected when the user moves to the next field or record.

However, a validation rule for CustomerID would be superior to an input mask if CustomerID had to be within a specified range (e.g., between 30001 and 49999) because the validation rule can specify that five digits are required *and* that the value of the entry must be within the specified range.

Finally, using both an input mask and validation rule is appropriate when a specific format must be followed, such as using two upper-case letters for state abbreviations, and not allowing customers to use a delivery address in either Alaska (AK) or Hawaii (HI). In this case, an input mask will make sure that only two characters are used (and the input mask will convert lower-case letters to upper-case letters as you will see in the next exercise) and the validation rule can specify that AK and HI are invalid entries.

TRY IT

The following exercise will use a number of different characters in the Input Mask properties of the fields in *tblCustomer*. To see a complete list of characters that you can use in customizing Input Mask properties, consult the Microsoft Access online help feature. With all tables closed, select the help icon and type *input mask*. Click the Search button; click *Control data entry formats with input masks*. This help topic includes a complete list of available characters and examples of how they are used. Click the Close button to close the Microsoft Access Help dialog box.

EXERCISE 8.6: SETTING INPUT MASK AND VALIDATION PROPERTIES FOR *TBLCUSTOMER*

1. Open your *tblCustomer* in Design view and click CustomerID.
2. Press F6 to switch to the Field Properties pane, and then press Tab twice or click the Input Mask property box.
3. Type the expression 00000;0 in the Input Mask box to prevent a user from entering anything other than exactly five digits in the CustomerID field.
4. Click the Datasheet view icon. Try typing in letters or symbols; the input mask will not allow you to enter them. Now type 1234 and try to tab to the next field. Access generates an error message to let you know that the value you typed is inappropriate for the input mask specified for this field. Press ESC twice to delete the new record.
5. Return to Design View by clicking the Design view icon on the ribbon.
6. Click CustomerCreditLimit. Then click the Validation Rule property box. Type <=50000 to set the maximum customer credit limit to $50,000. This validation rule enforces Pipefitters' business rule of granting customers no more than $50,000 of credit.
7. Tab once or click the Validation Text property box. Type Invalid entry. The maximum customer credit limit is $50,000. The text you enter as a field's Validation Text property will appear in an error message dialog box whenever a user attempts to enter a CustomerCreditLimit value that violates the Validation Rule. Return to Datasheet View. Type 65000 in the CustomerCreditLimit field and Tab to the next field. What happened? Could you achieve the same control with an input mask?
8. Press ESC twice to delete the new record and return to Design View. You will now create an input mask to ensure that state abbreviations are in the correct

format use a validation rule to enforce Pipefitters' business rule of only shipping products within the continental United States (disallow entering AK for Alaska and HI for Hawaii).

9. Click CustomerState. Then click the Input Mask property box. Type >LL in the Input Mask property box. The > symbol converts lowercase letters to uppercase letters. For example, if a user enters the letters *oh*, the input mask converts them to *OH*. The LL placeholders *in* the expression limit the entry to *two* letters.

10. Move your cursor either with the tab key or mouse to the Validation Rule property box. Type not ("AK" or "HI") in the Validation Rule property box. This rule disallows entering either AK or HI for CustomerState. The parentheses are necessary to apply the "not" to everything within the parentheses.

11. Click the Validation Text property box. Type Invalid entry. Customer addresses must be within the continental United States in the Validation Text property box. Your control for CustomerState is now complete.

TRY IT

The Input Mask Wizard contains preset input masks for many commonly used fields (see Figure 8.8). Use the Input Mask Wizard to create an input mask for CustomerZipCode. To open the Input Mask Wizard, click the Input Mask field property and click the Builder button. The extended portion of the zip code input mask (the last four digits) is optional (9 is the symbol for an optional digit) because many people do not know or do not use their zip code extension. Now use the Input Mask Wizard to create an input mask for CustomerTelephone. Do you think that area code should be optional as indicated by 999 in the input mask? What if the company's home area code changes?

Fig. 8.8 Input Mask Wizard.

Microsoft product screen shot reprinted with permission from Microsoft Corporation.

Required Field Property

Although input masks and validation rules control values input into the accounting system, the Required field property ensures that all necessary data is entered into the accounting system. This is accomplished simply by setting the Required field property value to Yes. When set to Yes, a user must enter all required fields before the record is accepted as a valid record. Setting the Required field property to No is appropriate for either optional data or if that particular field will be completed *after* the initial data is entered. In *tblCustomer*, are there any fields that are optional?

The Allow Zero Length field property seems like it should always be set to No when Required is set to Yes. However, a zero-length field is an empty text string created by typing two double-quotation marks in a row—without any characters between them. Therefore, the Allow Zero Length field property value depends on whether or not an empty string is a valid value for that particular field. Additionally, the Validation Rule property setting will override the Allow Zero Length property. Finally, *note* that setting the Required property to Yes for a primary key field does not alter the database's behavior; setting Required for a primary key to Yes is perfectly acceptable.

EXERCISE 8.7: SETTING THE REQUIRED FIELD PROPERTY FOR *TBLCUSTOMER*

Take a look at the attributes in *tblCustomer*. Which fields would you require to be completed when a new customer is added to the database? Are any fields optional and therefore *not* required?

1. Open *tblCustomer* in Design view and set the Required field property for all attributes.
2. Is a null string (zero-length) a valid entry for any fields in *tblCustomer*? If so, set Allow Zero Length to Yes. Otherwise, set it to No.

Indexed Field Property

Since the CustomerID field is the primary key of *tblCustomer*, Access requires a unique value to be entered for each record before saving it. That is why Access automatically set the Indexed property for CustomerID to Yes (No Duplicates) in Exercise 8.5. The "(No Duplicates)" setting portion of setting the Indexed property to Yes (No Duplicates) ensures that each customer's identification number is unique, thus, preventing errors caused by two customers having the same CustomerID.

The "Yes" portion of the setting causes Access to generate a special operation on that field—generating an index—to speed up searches on that field. That is why indexing is set to Yes for primary keys—because queries and other searches are often based on primary keys. Since foreign keys are also the basis of searches, foreign keys should be indexed, too. However, the index property for foreign keys should be set to Yes (Duplicates OK) because foreign keys are *not* unique. You can also index non-key fields. For example, bulk mailings need to be sorted by zip code. So, Pipefitters should index CustomerZipCode if they frequently send mass mailings to their customers.

EXERCISE 8.8: SETTING THE INDEXED FIELD PROPERTY FOR *TBLCUSTOMER*

Take a look at the attributes in *tblCustomer*. Are there any foreign keys? Will Pipefitters likely use any other attributes for frequent searches?

1. Open *tblCustomer* in Design view and set the appropriate indexed field property for all attributes.
2. *tblCustomer* is now complete.

The Customer Information Form

You can enter customer information in *tblCustomer* while it is open in Datasheet view. However, the number and size of the fields in the table makes this a difficult task. Depending on your screen resolution, only six or seven of the table's ten fields will be displayed in the Datasheet view window. Entering customer information in Datasheet view requires that you scroll back and forth to enter all ten field values for each record. In this section, you will learn how to create a form for *tblCustomer* that will make entering, changing, and deleting customer information much easier.

EXERCISE 8.9: CREATING THE CUSTOMER DATA ENTRY FORM

You can create a form for *tblCustomer* by using the AutoForm tool.

1. Click tblCustomer in the Navigation Pane. Then, click the Create tab and click Forms in the Form group.
2. Click the X in the upper-right-hand corner of the *tblCustomer* tab to close the form.
3. When the Save As dialog box appears, change the form name to frmCustomer. Use the prefix **frm** for forms to easily distinguish between the customer table (*tbl*) and the customer data entry form.

AutoForm examines the selected table and creates a form that accommodates many of the table's field characteristics. AutoForm is quick, easy to run, and often creates a usable form. Even when it does not create an ideal form, it creates a form that you can edit to meet your specific needs. The results of the AutoForm action appear in Figure 8.9. If you cannot see the entire form, you can close the Navigation Pane to enlarge the form by clicking << at the top of the Navigation Pane. Note that the form shown in the figure is bound to the version of *tblCustomer* with 52 customer records that is included on the Companion Web site. Your form will not show any data unless you have entered or copied data into your Customer table object.

Fig. 8.9 AutoForm-generated Customer Data Entry form.

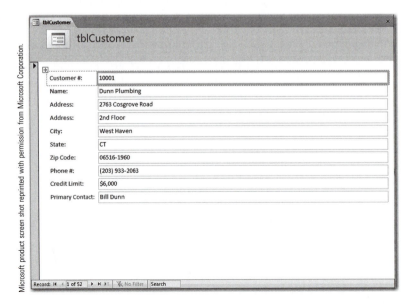

Although AutoForm created a usable form, you can improve the appearance of the form and enhance its usefulness. You will learn how to do this in the next exercise. As you follow these instructions, remember that you should try to develop your own sense of what makes a form useful. Your forms do not need to look exactly like the forms we show in this book.

EXERCISE 8.10: IMPROVING THE FORMATTING OF THE CUSTOMER DATA ENTRY FORM

1. Double-click frmCustomer in the Navigation Pane to open it up in Form view. This is the view you use to enter data in the form. Close the Navigation Pane if you cannot see the entire form.

2. Microsoft added Layout view to Access 2007. This view is ideal to make cosmetic changes to forms. To enter Layout view while the new form is displayed, click the bottom of View in the Views group (on the Home tab) and click Layout View (see Figure 8.10).

3. To make all the data entry fields narrower, click the CustomerName data field, move the pointer to the right edge of the box, and then click and drag the edge to the left until you reach the desired width—the amount of space you think the largest entry will use. Did you notice that all of the data fields moved together when you dragged the box?

4. To allow each field to move independently, press Ctrl+A to select all objects, click the Arrange tab, and click Remove in the Control Layout group. Return to the Format tab.

5. Now let's adjust other fields. Go ahead and switch to Form view to enter a customer record so you can see how much space you need for each field. Click the bottom of View in the Views group (on the Home tab) and click Form View (see Figure 8.10).

6. Return to Layout view. Adjust the fields that will always have the same number of characters—CustomerID, CustomerState, CustomerZipCode, and CustomerTelephone.

7. What is the maximum customer credit limit? You entered this amount as part of this field's validation rule in Exercise 8.6. Adjust the field width to accommodate the maximum credit limit.

8. Adjust the labels. Note that AutoForm automatically added colons at the end of each label. These are the same labels you entered when creating *tblCustomer*. These labels will also appear in queries and reports rather than the actual field names. Select all label controls by holding down the Shift key as you click each control. Click Align Right Text in the Font group to right-justify the label controls.

9. Click Bold in the Font group to format labels as bold text.

10. Finally, change the form title. Double-click the title tblCustomer. Change it to Customer Information. Click the Form icon next to the title and delete it with the Delete key. Click and drag the title box to the left to align the title.

11. Save your changes and close the form. If you forget to save your changes before closing the form, Access provides a control by asking you if you want to save your changes before it closes the form.

You can make additional adjustments to the form's look to satisfy your own sense of aesthetics. Figure 8.11 shows a finished version of the Customer Information form.

Fig. 8.10 Layout
View command button.

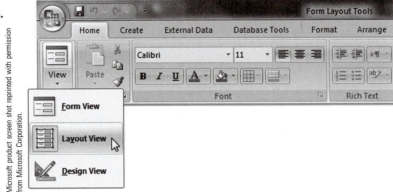

Fig. 8.11 Finished
Customer Information
form in Form view.

TRY IT

Open *frmCustomer* in Layout view. Right-click *frmCustomer* in the Navigation
Pane and click *Layout View* in the pop-up menu. The form appears in Layout
view. You can also change from one view to another by right-clicking on the
form in the Navigation Pane.

Maintaining Customer Records

Now that you have created a Customer table to store customer information and a form
that makes using that table easy, you can efficiently and effectively maintain customer
records. First, you will want to create records for new customers. Second, you will occasionally delete customer records you no longer need. Third, you will need to update the
table as customers move, get new telephone numbers, and change other information that
you have entered in *tblCustomer*.

You will want to keep your file of customer information current. Remember, one advantage of using a relational database model for an accounting system is that you need to
add, delete, or change information in only one place. For customer information, *tblCustomer* is that place.

To use *frmCustomer* to add customers to *tblCustomer*, open the form by double-clicking it. To enter customer information, just begin typing. Press Enter after typing the information into each control field. Notice how the Input Mask and Validation Rule properties that you set for *tblCustomer* help you avoid data entry errors in the CustomerID, CustomerState, CustomerZipCode, and CustomerTelephone fields.

After entering all of the information for a customer, press Enter to go to the next record. After you have entered a number of customers, you can move backward and forward through the table using the PgUp and PgDn keys or the navigation buttons at the bottom of the form.

Deleting records from *tblCustomer* is a dangerously easy operation. Open the Customer Information form by clicking the Forms tab in the Database window and double-clicking frmCustomer. To delete a record, move to that record by using the navigation buttons at the bottom of the form; then select the entire record by clicking the Record Selector. Press the Delete key to delete the record (if you are using the database supplied on the Companion Web site, it will not permit you to delete customer records because of integrity constraints that we have built into that database). Microsoft Access gives you a warning message that asks you to confirm the deletion. The deletion is *not* reversible, because Access does not store table records in a buffer when it deletes them. You can also delete a record by moving to that record and clicking Delete Record from the Delete menu in the Record group on the Home tab (see Figure 8.12).

Fig. 8.12 Deleting a record.

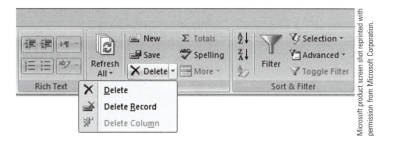

You can delete individual fields in a record using the Delete key while you are in Form view. Individual field deletions are reversible by pressing Esc before you move to another field. After you move to another field, you can reverse all field deletions in the current record by selecting Edit, then Undo Current Field/Record from the menu, or pressing Esc. If you want to reverse changes you have made to a field and changes to other fields in the record, press Esc twice. All other deletions are permanent.

Deleting records in accounting databases is an action you will always want to consider carefully. Data in accounting tables is usually related to data in other tables. For example, if you examine a record in a Sale Order table, it will contain a customer number. The only place you will find that customer's name and address is in the related Customer table. If someone deletes that customer's record in the Customer table, you might never find out who the customer was! Fortunately, you will be instructed to add integrity constraints to prevent such an occurrence.

Keeping existing customer records current to reflect address changes, new telephone numbers, and other changes is an easy and straightforward task using *frmCustomer*. Open the Customer Information form by clicking the Forms tab in the Database window and double-clicking *frmCustomer*. Use the navigation buttons at the bottom of the form to move to the customer record that you want to change. The Input Mask and Validation Rule property settings for *tblCustomer* will limit any changes you make to field contents, just as though you were entering data for the first time.

TRY IT

When you use the navigation buttons to advance from one record to another in the Customer Information form, you will notice that the records are not in alphabetical order. Unless you know a customer's CustomerID, it will be difficult to find a particular customer in the form. You can sort the form alphabetically by CustomerName by right-clicking on the *Name field* and then clicking *Sort A to Z*. The form is now sorted by CustomerName.

Inventory Information

Customer information is very important to any business, but potential customers will become actual customers only if a firm has something to sell to them. *Inventory* is a generic term for what firms sell to their customers. Broadly defined, inventory may include products, services, or both. For example, a hardware store sells products, an accounting firm sells services, and an auto repair shop sells both products and services.

In this sales/collection process discussion of inventory, we are interested only in the goods or services available for sale to customers. You will learn how to track the acquisition of inventory in Chapter 9. Firms need information about the inventory they have for sale in the sales/collection process because they must track which inventory items they sell, at what price they are sold, when they are sold, and to whom they are sold.

To ensure that inventory information is consistent throughout the enterprise, firms try to keep all inventory information in one database table. Any document, report, or transaction that needs inventory information obtains it from that one inventory table.

The Inventory Table

The sales/collection process requires an inventory table that contains at least two fields. The first field should be the primary key—a number or code that uniquely identifies the product or service. For products, this field might contain an item number, catalog number, UPC (universal product code), or SKU (stock-keeping unit) number. For services, this field might contain a labor code, task code, or service number. The second field should contain a description of the product or service.

Sometimes companies classify inventory by category or type. In that case, the database will have an inventory type table containing a minimum of a primary key and description. The inventory table will then contain a field for the foreign key—inventory type. Some firms use an additional field to store inventory selling prices in the inventory table. If a firm has fixed selling prices for each inventory item, it can store those selling prices in the inventory table. Firms that sell the same product or service at different prices to different customers must store selling prices in a sale–inventory relationship table. Firms that offer discounts from the list price to certain customers or classes of customers can store the list price in an inventory table and store the discount percentage in their Customer table.

One problem that firms face when they store their inventory prices in the inventory table occurs when they change their prices. For example, if a firm recalculates and prints an invoice from last year with this year's prices, it will obtain an incorrect result. The solution used in this chapter is to store the actual selling price in a sale–inventory relationship table. This solution also allows a firm to change the actual sale price to reflect a one-time discount if goods are slightly damaged or if the item is the demonstration item.

Moreover, if the list price stored in the inventory table is usually the actual selling price, then it can be used as the default value in the sale–inventory table.

Pipefitters Supply Company is a plumbing supply business that sells pipes and related fittings. Each item (pipes and fittings) has three characteristics: composition, type, and diameter. Figure 8.13 shows the values and codes Pipefitters uses for its inventory. Each characteristic will be a separate field in the inventory table. Additionally, the inventory table will have a primary key and the inventory list price as shown in Figure 8.14.

Fig. 8.13 Inventory items.

Composition	Code	Type	Code	Diameter (Inches)	Code
Brass	B	4-foot pipe	4	0.25	025
Copper	C	8-foot pipe	8	0.50	050
		Cap fitting	C	1.00	100
		Elbow	L	2.00	200
		T-connector	T	3.00	300
				4.00	400

Fig. 8.14 Populated inventory table in Datasheet view.

Microsoft product screen shot reprinted with permission from Microsoft Corporation.

tblInventory				
Inventory #	Composition	Type	Diameter	List Price
1001	B	4	025	$21.95
1002	B	4	050	$26.49
1003	B	4	100	$34.79
1004	B	4	200	$43.69
1005	B	4	300	$55.29
1006	B	4	400	$65.19
1007	B	8	025	$40.95
1008	B	8	050	$50.95
1009	B	8	100	$62.39
1010	B	8	200	$80.39
1011	B	8	300	$99.47
1012	B	8	400	$119.97
1013	B	C	025	$5.25
1014	B	C	050	$8.69
1015	B	C	100	$13.29
1016	B	C	200	$21.47
1017	B	C	300	$29.97
1018	B	C	400	$42.95
1019	B	L	025	$5.29
1020	B	L	050	$7.47
1021	B	L	100	$10.45
1022	B	L	200	$14.59
1023	B	L	300	$19.79
1024	B	L	400	$24.95
1025	B	T	025	$7.95
1026	B	T	050	$9.97

Record: 1 of 60   No Filter   Search

Using separate fields for each part of the inventory description, rather than storing the entire description in one field, makes it easier to create effective input validity checks. Using separate fields also lets users search, query, and generate reports from the table more easily. In the following exercises, you will learn how to create an inventory table and related inventory type tables for the Pipefitters' data and use another method to help ensure that only valid data is input into the system.

EXERCISE 8.11: CREATING THE INVENTORY TABLE

1. Click the Create tab, click Table found in the Tables group, and click the Design View command that appears in the Datasheet context tab. Access asks you to name the table.
2. Type tblInventory in the Save As dialog box, and then click OK to save the newly named table. Access displays the table, as yet undefined, in Design view.
3. To create the primary key, type InventoryID in the first row of the Field Name column. Notice the *key* symbol in the first row, indicating that Access makes the first field the primary key by default. Set the Data Type set to Text.
4. Press F6 to move the cursor to the Field Properties pane of the Table window, set the Field Size to 4, and then Tab twice to move the cursor to the Input Mask property line.
5. Type 0000;;_ in the Input Mask property box. The input mask requires four digits, and the underscore character is the placeholder.
6. Tab once and set the Caption property to Inventory #.
7. Tab to the Required property box and set to Yes.
8. Tab once and set Allow Zero Length to No.
9. Tab once and set Indexed to Yes (No Duplicates).
10. Press F6 to get back to Field Names and Data Types.
11. Follow Steps 3 through 10 for the remaining four fields using the information provided in Figure 8.15.
12. Enter at least two inventory records.

Fig. 8.15 Field names and properties for *tblInventory*.

Field Name	InventoryComposition	InventoryType	InventoryDiameter	InventoryListPrice
Data Type	Text	Text	Text	Currency
Field Size	1	2	3	n/a
Format or Decimal Places	None	None	None	2
Input Mask	>L;;_	>Aa;;_	000;;_	None
Caption	Composition	Type	Diameter	List Price
Required	Yes	Yes	Yes	Yes
Allow Zero Length	No	No	No	n/a
Indexed	Yes (Duplicates OK)	Yes (Duplicates OK)	Yes (Duplicates OK)	No

Assuming that the first record in the table will have a primary key value of 1001, how many different inventory items can be stored in the inventory table?

In *tblCustomer*, you used validation rules to filter valid data from invalid data. You can do the same thing in *tblInventory*. For example, you can create the following validation rule for InventoryComposition: = "B" or "C". What happens if Pipefitters starts carrying PVC pipes and fittings? Only employees with permission to make changes to the database structure would be able to change the validation rule. Therefore, in the next two exercises you will validate the data by creating a table to store all of the categories of InventoryComposition and link *tblInventory* to *tblInventoryComposition*. You will also create category tables (sometimes referred to as type or typification tables) for InventoryType and InventoryDiameter and link them to *tblInventory*.

EXERCISE 8.12: CREATING CATEGORY (TYPE) TABLES

1. Click the Create tab, click Table in the Tables group, and click the Design View command that appears in the Datasheet context tab. Access asks you to name the table.
2. Type tblInventoryComposition in the Save As dialog box and then click OK to save the newly named table. Access displays the table, as yet undefined, in Design view.
3. To create the primary key, type InventoryComposition in the first row of the Field Name column. Note the *key* symbol in the first row, indicating that Access makes the first field the primary key by default. Set the Data Type set to Text.
4. Press F6 to move the cursor to the Field Properties pane of the table window. Enter the same properties for InventoryComposition as in Figure 8.15, except you need to set Indexed to Yes (No Duplicates) because primary keys must be unique.
5. After entering the field properties for InventoryComposition, press F6 to return to the Field Names pane of the table window.
6. Enter CompositionDescription in second row of the Field Name column. Leave the Data Type set to Text.
7. Press F6 to the Field Properties pane. Set the following field properties:Field Size— 25; Caption— Description; Required—Yes; Allow Zero Length—No; Indexed—No.
8. Click Datasheet in the Views group to switch to Datasheet view so you can enter data. Be sure to Click Yes in the Save Table dialog box to save your work.
9. Enter the data from Figure 8.13 for InventoryComposition (Code column) and CompositionDescription (Composition column).
10. Create *tblInventoryType* and *tblInventoryDiameter* by repeating Steps 1 through 9. Be sure to change the field names and sizes in the instructions to the appropriate values for each table. Also, make the description field size large enough to accommodate what you think the longest description could be (see Figure 8.13 for descriptions of the current field values).

TRY IT

Enter a new record in *tblInventory*. Try entering values for InventoryComposition, InventoryType, and InventoryDiameter that are *not* listed in your category tables. Also enter an InventoryListPrice. Notice that you can enter any value as long as it is permitted by the input masks for those fields. This occurs because the category tables are not yet linked to the inventory table. We will do this in Exercise 8.13.

EXERCISE 8.13: LINKING CATEGORY TABLES TO *TBLINVENTORY*

1. Open your *Ch08.accdb* database if it is not already open. If it is open, close all Access objects.
2. In the Database Tools tab, click Relationships in the Show/Hide group. Your Relationships window should be empty like in Figure 8.16.
3. Select all tables except *tblCustomer*. To do this, click Show Table in the Relationships group (on the Design tab), press Ctrl and click each table except *tblCustomer*, click Add, and then click Close.
4. Link *tblInventoryComposition* by dragging its primary key, InventoryComposition, right on top of InventoryComposition in *tblInventory*. You should now see the Edit Relationships dialog box like the one in Figure 8.17. Underneath Table/Query

you see *tblInventoryComposition* (the name of the table you dragged from) and *tblInventory*, which is the table you want to create a relationship with. Under each table name, you see the attributes you are using to link the two tables. It is good practice to always drag from the primary table which contains the primary key (the one side of the relationship) to the related table containing the foreign key (the many side of the relationship). Notice that the relationship type at the bottom of the dialog box is One-to-Many. Access knows this because of the way you set the Index property for the attributes.

5. In the Edit Relationships dialog box, check Enforce Referential Integrity. Enforcing referential integrity only allows the user to enter values in the foreign key field of the related table (InventoryComposition in *tblInventory*) that already exist in the primary key of the primary table (InventoryComposition in *tblInventoryComposition*).

6. In the Edit Relationships dialog box, also check Cascade Update Related Fields. When this box is checked, a change to a value in the primary key field will automatically cause the value in the related foreign key field to be updated.

7. Click Create in the dialog box. The dialog box closes and you now see a One-to-Many relationship between *tblInventoryComposition* and *tblInventory*.

8. Repeat Steps 1 through 7 with *tblInventoryType* and *tblInventoryDiameter*. Your Relationships tab should now look like Figure 8.18.

Fig. 8.16 Relation-
ships tab without
tables.

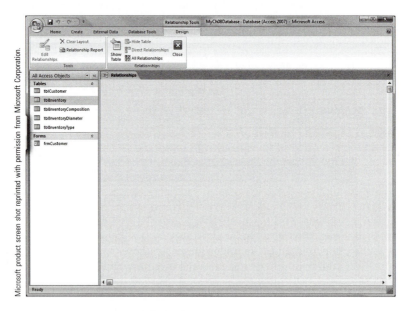

Microsoft product screen shot reprinted with permission from Microsoft Corporation.

Fig. 8.17 Edit
Relationships dialog
box.

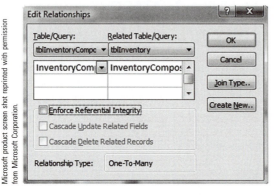

Microsoft product screen shot reprinted with permission from Microsoft Corporation.

Fig. 8.18 Relationships tab after completing Exercise 8.13.

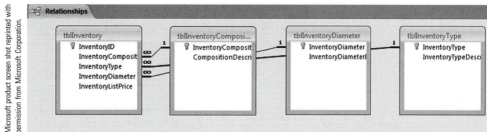

TRY IT

Enter a new record in *tblInventory*. Try entering a value for InventoryComposition that is *not* listed in *tblInventoryComposition*. When you move to the next field it appears that referential integrity is *not* being enforced. However, when you try to write the record to the database by either moving to another record or closing the table, referential integrity is enforced and you receive the following message, "You cannot add or change a record because a related record is required in table '*tblInventoryComposition*.'"

The link you created between *tblInventoryComposition* and *tblInventory* creates several controls. First, enforcing referential integrity acts as a control by limiting entries in the InventoryComposition field of *tblInventory* to "B" and "C", the values you entered in the category table *tblInventoryComposition*. Second, Access will automatically update the inventory composition code in *tblInventory* for changes to primary key values in *tblInventoryComposition*.

TRY IT

Enter a new record in *tblInventory*. Enter in the InventoryComposition field. Remember that you must fill in all fields because you set the Required property field to Yes for all fields in the table. Leave *tblInventory* open. Now open *tblInventoryComposition* and change the B in the Composition field to *R*. Then *Tab* twice to get to the next record. Now click the *tblInventory* tab. The B in your new record is now an R. Undo this change by going back to *tblInventoryComposition* and changing the R back to *B*. Close both tables.

A third control created by enforcing referential integrity is that you cannot delete a record from *tblInventoryComposition* if there is a related record in *tblInventory*. That is, you cannot delete the *Brass* record in *tblInventoryComposition* as long as Pipefitters has any *Brass* inventory items. There is a fourth control you imposed by *not* checking Cascade Delete Related Records. If this box were checked, deleting the *Brass* record from *tblInventoryComposition* would automatically delete *all* Brass inventory items from *tblInventory*! Moreover, this operation is irreversible; you cannot use the *undo* button to bring back the deleted records.

The Inventory Form

Although you can enter data directly into *tblInventory* more easily than you could enter data into *tblCustomer*, you can make data entry and update tasks easier and less error-prone by creating a Data Entry form for *tblInventory*. In our example firm, we restricted the range of values for inventory composition, type, and diameter. Although this is somewhat unrealistic for our example firm, it allows us to illustrate some form design techniques that you will find useful in many different accounting applications.

In Exercise 8.14 you will create an Inventory Data Entry form. Pipefitters' employees can use this form to enter new inventory items into their accounting system. Since *tblInventory* has only five small fields, you do not need to use a columnar form layout to fit the fields into view on the form. You can display a number of records at one time by using a tabular form layout.

EXERCISE 8.14: CREATING THE INVENTORY DATA ENTRY FORM

1. Click tblInventory in the Tables group of the Navigation Pane to highlight the table name.
2. Click the Create tab and click MoreForms in the Forms group, and then click Form Wizard. The first of a few Form Wizard dialog boxes appears.
3. The available fields in *tblInventory* appear in the *Available Fields* panel. Click the >> button to send all available table fields to the *Selected Fields* panel (see Figure 8.19).
4. Click the Next button to get to the Layout dialog box. Click Tabular to create a form that displays many records at one time with each record displayed in a single row.
5. Click the Next button twice to enter a form name. Type frmInventory in the text box.
6. Click the Finish button, which closes the dialog box and opens *frmInventory* in Form view. It should look like Figure 8.20.

Unlike AutoForm, Form Wizard lets you determine which fields will appear in the form, even if they are from multiple tables or queries. This is particularly helpful when creating a form with a subform as we will do later in this chapter. Form Wizard also allows you to select the layout of the form (tabular in this case) as well as the style. The next two exercises will help you become more familiar with the features available in both Layout view and Design view. Exercise 8.15 focuses on appearance whereas

Fig. 8.19 Form Wizard dialog box.

Microsoft product screen shot reprinted with permission from Microsoft Corporation.

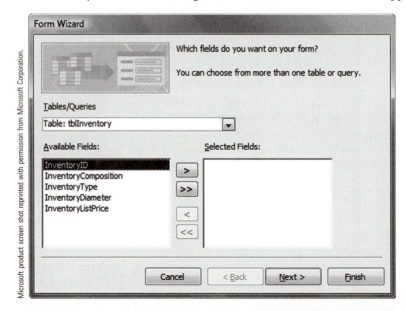

functionality is addressed in Exercise 8.16 through the use of combo boxes. For Exercise 8.15, use Figure 8.21 as a guide while you work through the steps of this exercise. Figure 8.21 is populated with the same data from the *Ch08.accdb* database found on the Companion Web site.

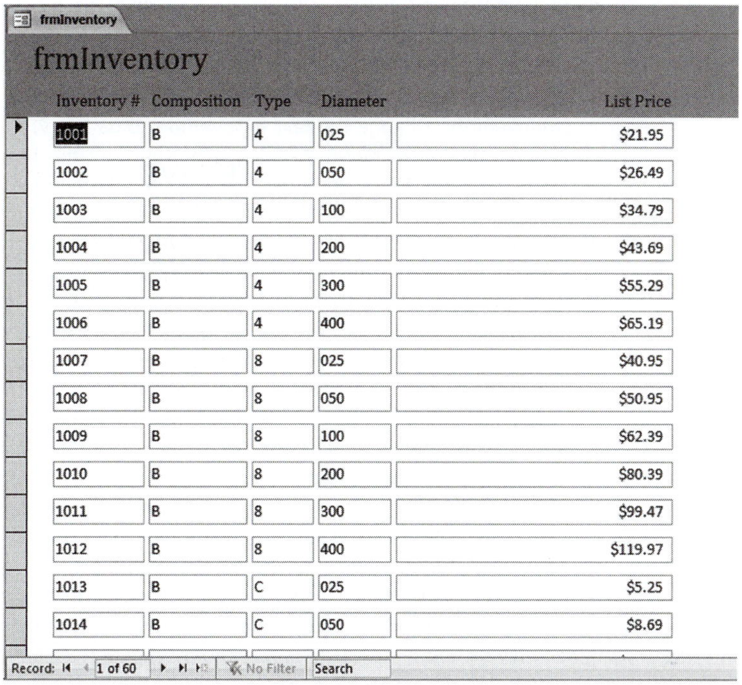

Fig. 8.20 Inventory Data Entry form created with Form Wizard.

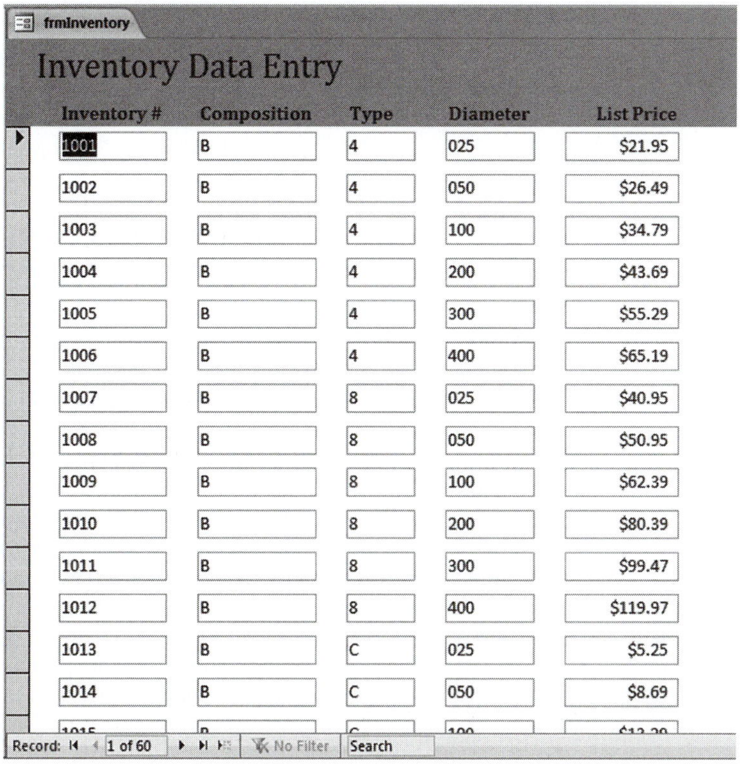

Fig. 8.21 Improved Inventory Data Entry form.

Microsoft product screen shot reprinted with permission from Microsoft Corporation.

EXERCISE 8.15: IMPROVING THE APPEARANCE OF THE INVENTORY DATA ENTRY FORM

1. Open your form in Layout view. Right-click frmInventory in the Navigation Pane and click Layout View in the pop-up menu.
2. Make the ListPrice control box narrower. Click the ListPrice text box. Place your cursor on the right edge of the box. Drag the right side of the box to the left until the width better fits the data.
3. Change the title text and resize the title textbox. Double-click the form title text frmInventory. Change the text to Inventory Data Entry. Click the right side of the text box and hold down the mouse button until the box outline changes color. Then, drag the right side of the text box until the entire title fits on one line. Now click and drag the bottom side of the box until the title fits just inside the box.
4. Bold the five label controls. Select the five label controls; press and hold the Shift key and then click each label control. Click the Bold button in the Font group. The Font group appears on both the Format ribbon and the Home tab.
5. Increase the horizontal spacing between the fields. Change to Design view by right-clicking frmInventory in the Navigation Pane and then clicking Design View. Select the five text boxes; click to the right of the InventoryListPrice text box and drag your cursor to the left, creating a narrow rectangle that touches all five text boxes. Your rectangle will select all objects that the rectangle touches. Click the Arrange tab. Click the Control Padding menu in the Control Layout group and select Wide. Notice that there is more space between text boxes as well as below them. See how the form looks by going back to Form view.
6. To reduce the space between rows of data, return to Design view and press Ctrl +A to select all objects. Now, go to the Arrange ribbon and click Remove in the Control Layout group. This allows each object to be adjusted independently. The labels and text boxes are no longer treated as a single table object. Move the cursor to the top of the Form Footer bar so the cursor turns into a resizer ↕. Click and drag the Form Footer up to the bottom of the field control boxes.
7. Check your form in Form view.

EXERCISE 8.16: ADDING THE INVENTORY COMPOSITION COMBO BOX TO THE INVENTORY DATA ENTRY FORM.

1. Open frmInventory in Design view. Remove the text box controls for the three fields you will replace with combo boxes. While holding down the Shift key, click the InventoryComposition, InventoryType, and InventoryDiameter text boxes. Then, press Delete. Now you can use the Combo Box Wizard to create new controls.
2. On the Design ribbon (it should be visible), click the Combo Box button in the Controls group (see Figure 8.22). Move the cursor into the Detail section of the form just below the Composition label (the cursor will become a cross with a combo box icon when you move it over the Detail section); then double-click to start the Combo Box Wizard. Use Figure 8.23 to guide you through the Combo Box Wizard.
3. In the first dialog box click the first option button with the caption *I want the combo box to look up the values in a table or query;* then click the Next button.

4. The next dialog box asks *Which table or query should provide the values for your combo box?* Select tblInventoryComposition; then click the Next button.

5. In this dialog box, click on the field CompositionDescription and then click > to select it. This field will be what you see when you click on the down arrow in the combo box. Click the Next button.

6. Sort order is what you will set in this dialog box. Ascending order is the default option. You are only creating the combo box so you can choose the inventory composition based on a description to avoid having to memorize all of the codes. Select CompositionDescription as the field Access will use to sort the values in the combo box. Click the Next button.

7. This dialog box allows you to adjust the size of the column displayed, though there is no need to do so in this case. Also, leave the *Hide key column (recommended)* check box checked because viewing the inventory composition code will not help the user select the correct composition. Click the Next button.

8. Click the second radio button with the caption *Store that value in this field*; then, click the combo box arrow button and select the InventoryComposition field. This step stores the inventory composition code in the InventoryComposition field of *tblInventory*. Click the Next button to open the last dialog box (not shown in Figure 8.23), and click the Finish button. The Wizard creates a combo box control according to your specifications and places it on the Inventory form.

9. Change the name of the combo box by clicking on the Property Sheet button in the Tools group. Click the Other tab and type cboInventoryComposition as the value for the Name property (see Figure 8.24), and press Enter.

10. Delete the label for the combo box you just created. Click the label control box which may be difficult to see because it will overlap the InventoryID text box. Press the Delete key.

11. To test the new control, click the View menu button in the Views group. Then, click the InventoryComposition combo box arrow button to display the two choices—Brass and Copper. Return to Design view by clicking the down arrow on the View menu and clicking Design View. Your new combo box control should still be selected. Select the combo box label (and only the label) by clicking and dragging through it. You may want to click the label's handle in its upper-left corner and drag it away from other controls if it is overlaying them. Press the Delete key. You can then adjust the position of the combo box control to match the text box control it replaced by clicking and dragging the combo box to your desired location.

12. Adjust the size of the combo box to be the same as the *Composition* label. Press and hold the Shift key while you click both the combo box and the Composition label box. Now click the Arrange tab. Match the width of the combo box to the width of the label. Since the combo box is slightly wider than the label, click the Size to Narrowest button in the Size group. If you needed to match the height of the combo box to another field, you would click on both the combo box and the other box and then click the Size to Tallest or Size to Shortest button (see Figure 8.25).

Fig. 8.22 Design ribbon.

combo box button   Page break

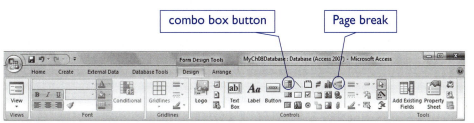

Fig. 8.23 Combo
Box Wizard.

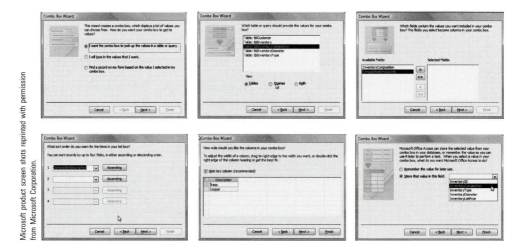

Microsoft product screen shots reprinted with permission from Microsoft Corporation.

Fig. 8.24 Property
Sheet.

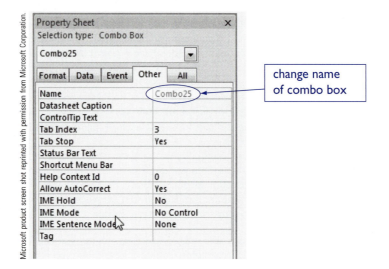

Microsoft product screen shot reprinted with permission from Microsoft Corporation.

change name
of combo box

Fig. 8.25 *Size to* and
Alignment buttons.

Alignment buttons

"size to" buttons

Microsoft product screen shot reprinted with permission from Microsoft Corporation.

EXERCISE 8.17: ADDING OTHER COMBO BOXES AND COMPLETING THE INVENTORY DATA ENTRY FORM

1. Repeat Steps 3 through 13 from Exercise 8.16 for InventoryType and InventoryDiameter.
2. Make the InventoryType label in the header as wide as the InventoryType combo box by using the *Fit to Widest* button on the Arrange tab. Do the same for InventoryDiameter. Also do this for ListPrice (not a combo box).

3. Move the labels in the header for InventoryDiameter and ListPrice to allow a reasonable amount of space between them. Click the Arrange tab. Make an equal amount of space between each label; press and hold the Shift key while clicking on each of the five labels. Then click the Make Horizontal Spacing Equal button in the Position group.

4. Align each field box with its label. These instructions are based on the Design view in Figure 8.26. Start with ListPrice. Press and hold the Shift key while clicking both the list price text box and label. Then click the Right button in the Control Alignment group. Perform the same steps with InventoryDiameter and InventoryType.

5. Align all of the text boxes and combo boxes vertically. Press and hold the Shift key while clicking each box. Then, click the Top button in the Control Alignment group. Click and drag the Form Footer up to the bottom of the text and combo boxes to complete the formatting.

6. Click the Design tab and then click the View button (Form icon visible) to test the form in Form view. Now tab through an existing record. Notice that the cursor skips around instead of moving to each successive field.

7. Click the View button (Layout icon visible) to fix the tab order in Layout view. Click the Arrange tab. Click the InventoryComposition combo box and then click the Property Sheet button in the Tools group. Now click the Tab Order button in the Control Layout group. Click the Auto Order button to correct the tab order. Then click OK. You can also change the order manually by clicking and dragging each item in the Custom Order list to its desired location. Return to Design view to test the tab order.

Fig. 8.26 Unfinished Inventory Data Entry form in Design view.

Microsoft product screen shot reprinted with permission from Microsoft Corporation.

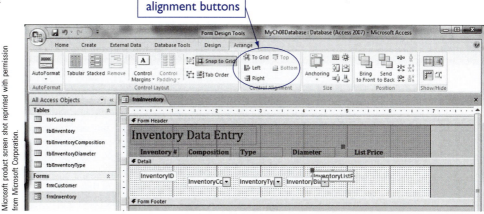

Sale Orders

When customers decide to buy products or services, they communicate this desire by sending a purchase order form, sending a letter, making a phone call, telling a salesperson, or filling out an online order form. Each of these actions is a type of *purchase order*. Firms receiving the purchase order often record it in its own records as a *sale order*.

Whether the order arrives as printed paper in the mail, a verbal order over the telephone, or a Web-based order, all sale orders contain common components—identifying when the sale order occurred, which customer placed the order, and which inventory item(s) the customer wishes to purchase.

Review the data model in Figure 8.5 to determine the tables, including relationship tables, and foreign keys that Pipefitters Supply Company will need to record each sale order. At this point, do not worry about the fulfillment relationship between sale order and sale. You will create the fulfillment relationship when you build the sale table by adding SaleOrderID as a foreign key in the sale table and linking the tables in the Relationship window.

Adding Employees to the Database

The model in Figure 8.5 shows that Pipefitters Supply records the salesperson responsible for each sale order. Tracking sale orders by salesperson can be used for control purposes as well as for evaluation. One obvious control based on this information is the ability to determine the salesperson responsible for sale order errors. A less obvious control facilitated by this data is to look for fraudulent sale orders by querying the database to determine if the delivery address of the customer is the same as any of the salespersons' addresses. Additionally, Pipefitters can use this information to evaluate salespeople by querying the database to determine how many sales they are making by quantity of sale orders and by total dollar amount of sales.

The sales/collection process model in Figure 8.5 shows that the salespersons are represented in the sale order table by their employee identification number (EmployeeID attribute). This foreign key links the sale order table to the employee table because EmployeeID is the primary key of the employee table. You will use the *tblEmployee* and *tblEmployeeType* in the Chapter 8 database on the Companion Web site so that you can add employee-related controls to both the sale order table and the sale order form. You will create the employee table and related forms in Chapter 10, the human resources process chapter.

EXERCISE 8.18: COPYING EMPLOYEE TABLES TO YOUR DATABASE

1. Open your Chapter 8 database if it is not yet open.
2. Start a new instance of Access by opening Access from the Windows Start menu. Open the *Ch08.accdb* database. Right click tblEmployee and click Copy.
3. Switch to your Chapter 8 database. You can use the keyboard shortcut Alt+Tab to switch to the next window until you get to your Chapter 8 database.
4. Right-click the Navigation Pane, click Paste. When the Paste Table As dialog box appears, select Structure and Data and click OK. The *tblEmployee* and its data from *Ch08.accdb* is now in your Chapter 8 database.
5. Repeat steps 2 through 4 for *tblEmployeeType*.

The Sale Order Table

Since each sale order comes from only one customer and a sale order needs a customer to exist, you can build the customer-sale order link into the sale order table. CustomerID, the primary key in *tblCustomer*, will become a foreign key in *tblSaleOrder*. Likewise, the employee-sale order link will be accomplished by posting the primary key of *tblEmployee*, EmployeeID, as a foreign key in *tblSaleOrder*. Of course, the sale order table will need its own primary key and a field for the date of the sale order.

Since customers often send purchase order forms to indicate what items they want to buy, you will include a field to store customers' purchase order numbers. Storing the customer purchase order number with the sale order data provides the documentation necessary for auditors and others to easily verify the authenticity and accuracy of sale orders.

Pipefitters also stores the total price of the items on the customer order. Although the total sale price of all items ordered can be computed by summing the price times the quantity of each item ordered, Pipefitters stores the total as a control. If the price or quantity of an item ordered is changed either accidentally or purposely after the order was placed, then the sum of the price times the quantity of the individual items will not equal the sale order total. A periodic query to compare these two amounts for all sale orders will reveal possible errors and/or irregularities. Therefore, *tblSaleOrder* will have six fields: a primary key, a date, a foreign key link to *tblCustomer*, a foreign key link to *tblEmployee*, a total sale order amount, and a record of the customer's purchase order number. Exercise 8.19 shows you how to create *tblSaleOrder*.

EXERCISE 8.19: CREATING THE SALE ORDER TABLE

1. Create a new table. Click the Create tab, and click Table Design in the Tables group.
2. Create the primary key. Type SaleOrderID in first Field Name box, and then click Primary Key in the Tools group. Leave the Data Type as text. Notice that Access automatically switched to the design ribbon because you are working in *Design* view.
3. Press F6 to move to the Field Properties section of the window, and change the Field Size to 6. This setting will allow Pipefitters to enter 899,999 sale orders if they use a starting number of 100001.
4. Set the SaleOrderID field's Input Mask property to 000000;;_ and its Caption property to Sale Order #. Set the Required property to Yes and the Allow Zero Length property to No. Notice that Access automatically set the Indexed property to Yes (No Duplicates) when you made SaleOrderID the primary key.
5. Type EmployeeID in the next Field Name box and leave the Data Type set to Text. Set the Field Size to 3, the Input Mask to 000;;_, and the Caption property to Employee #. This field is the foreign key link to *tblEmployee*. Set the Required property to Yes, the Allow Zero Length property to No, and the Indexed property to Yes (Duplicates OK).
6. Next, create the sale order date field by entering a Field Name of SaleOrderDate and a Data Type of Date/Time. Set its Format property to Short Date and its Input Mask property to 99/99/0000. Set its Caption property to Date.
7. Pipefitters enters sale orders as they are received so the default value for SaleOrderDate should be set to the current date. This control minimizes data entry errors for the date. Enter Date () for the Default Value property. Also set the Required property to Yes.
8. Type CustomerID in the next Field Name box and leave the Data Type set to Text. Set the Field Size to 5, the Input Mask to 00000;;_, and the Caption property to Customer #. This field is the foreign key link to *tblCustomer*. Although the field's name in this table need not match its name in *tblCustomer*, it is a good idea to use the same name. We follow this convention throughout the textbook. More importantly, the Data Types of these two fields must be compatible. The easiest way to ensure Data Type compatibility is to make the data type and field size match exactly. The primary key in *tblCustomer* is CustomerID, a Text field with a Field Size of 5. Set the Required property to Yes, the Allow Zero Length property to No, and the Indexed property to Yes (Duplicates OK).
9. Enter CustomerPO as the next Field Name, leave its Data Type set to Text, and set its Field Size property to 15. Set the Caption property to Customer PO #. This field must allow any combination of numbers, letters, and symbols that

customers might decide to use in identifying their purchase orders. Since you cannot anticipate the characteristics of this field, you cannot build any data entry internal controls into the table for this field. Leave the Required property set to Yes and the Allow Zero Length property to No. Even though some sale orders may not have customer purchase order numbers, Pipefitters salespeople enter "None" to indicate that no related customer purchase order exists.

10. The last field name to enter is SaleOrderAmount. Set the Data Type to Currency. Set the Decimal Places property to 2. This ensures that all sale order amounts will be displayed as dollars and cents. Set the Caption property to Amount.

11. Since it does not make sense to have a negative sale order amount, you will add a validation rule to prevent negative amounts. In the Validation Rule property type >=0. This rule allows for a $0.00 total because Pipefitters may, on rare occasion, need to send a customer a part for free to resolve a customer complaint. For the related Validation Text property enter something like Sale order amount must be non-negative. Finally, set the Required property to Yes.

12. Close and save the table as tblSaleOrder.

TRY IT

Create the link between *tblSaleOrder* and *tblCustomer* and the link between *tblSaleOrder* and *tblEmployee*. Use Exercise 8.13 as a guide. Be sure to check the boxes Enforce Referential Integrity and Cascade Update Related Fields.

This completes the basic design of *tblSaleOrder*. The table that appears in Datasheet view in Figure 8.27 is included as *tblSaleOrder* in the *Ch08.accdb* database on the Companion Web site.

Fig. 8.27 *tblSale-Order* in Datasheet view.

Sale Order #	Employee #	Date	Customer #	Customer PO #	Amount
100001	112	1/14/2010	10001	101-PR-753979	$1,941.51
100002	107	1/16/2010	10003	26754	$4,419.30
100003	109	1/16/2010	10007	BP-8666789	$781.00
100004	111	1/17/2010	10005	276-555438	$825.76
100005	115	1/17/2010	10010	985553	$2,322.50
100006	116	1/18/2010	10005	276-555497	$631.20
100007	102	1/18/2010	10006	DD-78725-NC3	$4,519.80
100008	107	1/18/2010	10001	101-PR-754007	$641.55
100009	110	1/19/2010	10002	8779465QW	$739.40
100010	142	1/20/2010	10004	B-462-121894	$1,442.30
100011	123	1/20/2010	10024	8675309	$1,116.25
100012	123	1/22/2010	10035	ACR-1501	$708.75
100013	123	1/22/2010	10016	Q-54-2743	$583.20
100014	115	1/23/2010	10017	97613	$1,358.60
100015	115	1/23/2010	10029	PBR-6905	$825.05
100016	111	1/24/2010	10031	HZ-37-PZR	$476.00
100017	111	1/24/2010	10048	5790-808	$303.90
100018	102	1/25/2010	10050	212-35P	$736.07
100019	118	1/26/2010	10046	84-PB-634	$580.15
100020	119	1/26/2010	10012	2112-3	$606.65
100021	118	1/26/2010	10048	5790-812	$173.78
100022	110	1/28/2010	10037	GH-3731	$3,082.80
100023	102	1/28/2010	10022	K-100267	$362.25
100024	103	1/28/2010	10021	59-66532	$1,792.45
100025	123	1/30/2010	10033	NCC-10006	$479.70

Record: 1 of 100   No Filter   Search

The Sale Order table identifies when an order was received; records which customer placed the order, which employee recorded the order, the total amount of the order; and assigns the sale order a unique identifying number as its primary key. You can enter only part of the sale order information in this table because *tblSaleOrder* does not store information about which inventory items customers order. This would require *tblSaleOrder* to have repeating fields—a violation of the normalization rules you learned in Chapter 2. To store this additional information, the sales/collection data model in Figure 8.5 includes a relationship table, *tblReservation-SaleOrderInventory* to link *tblSaleOrder* and *tblInventory*.

The Sale Order-Inventory Table

The Sale Order-Inventory table records the many-to-many reservation relationship between *tblSaleOrder* and *tblInventory*. Therefore, *tblReservation-SaleOrderInventory* will store four fields:

1. The primary key of *tblSaleOrder*.
2. The primary key of *tblInventory*.
3. The quantity of each inventory item that appears on each sale order.
4. The price of each inventory item that appears on each sale order.

The primary keys from *tblSaleOrder* and *tblInventory* will combine to form the composite primary key in *tblReservation-SaleOrderInventory*. In Microsoft Access, you create a composite primary key by creating two separate fields—one for each entity table's primary key and then designating both fields as primary keys. If you are using the Microsoft Access help screens, you may notice that Microsoft uses the term *junction table*, instead of relationship table, in its online help and other documentation. Before you begin the next exercise, close any open tables or forms.

EXERCISE 8.20: CREATING THE *TBLRESERVATION-SALEORDERINVENTORY* RELATIONSHIP TABLE

1. Create a new table. Click the Create tab, and click Table Design in the Tables group.
2. Enter a Field Name of SaleOrderID and leave its Data Type set to Text.
3. Press F6, and change the Field Size property to 6.
4. Set the Input Mask property to 000000;;_
5. Set the Caption property to Sale Order #, the Required property to Yes, and the Indexed property to Yes (Duplicates OK). The Indexed property setting must allow duplicates because a field that is part of a composite primary key may contain duplicate values, though the combination of *both* primary keys *will* be unique. Remember that composite primary keys, like foreign keys, must always match exactly the primary key in the original table on both Type and Size. These matched fields allow the database to store values simultaneously in the SaleOrderID fields in this table and in *tblSaleOrder*. The other half of the composite primary key is the primary key of *tblInventory*, InventoryID.
6. In the second Field Name row, enter InventoryID and leave its Data Type set to Text. Press F6, and change the Field Size property to 4. Set the Input Mask property to 0000;;_, the Caption property to Item #, the Required property to Yes, and the Indexed property to Yes (Duplicates OK).
7. While pressing the Ctrl key, click the record selectors for SaleOrderID and for InventoryID.

8. With both fields selected, click Primary Key in the Tools group. The primary key symbol should appear in the record selectors of both fields, as shown in Figure 8.28.

9. The next field in *tblReservation-SaleOrderInventory* will store the quantity of each inventory item a customer orders on a particular sale order. Enter a Field Name of QuantityOrdered, and set its Data Type to Number. Set the Field Size property to Long Integer, the Decimal Places property to 0, the Caption property to Quantity, and the Required property to Yes. The integer property setting assumes that Pipefitters Supply Company does not accept orders for fractional units. The long integer property setting will allow the company to record a quantity of up to 2 billion units for any one inventory item on any one sale order.

10. The last field in *tblReservation-SaleOrderInventory* will store the price that the customer agrees to pay for each inventory item on each sale order. To create this field, enter Field Name of SOPrice, set its Data Type to Currency, leave its Field Size property set to Currency, set its Decimal Places property to 2, set its Caption property to Price, and set the Required property to Yes.

11. Close and save the table as tblReservation-SaleOrderInventory.

Fig. 8.28 Creating a composite primary key for *tblReservation-SaleOrderInventory.*

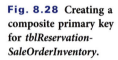

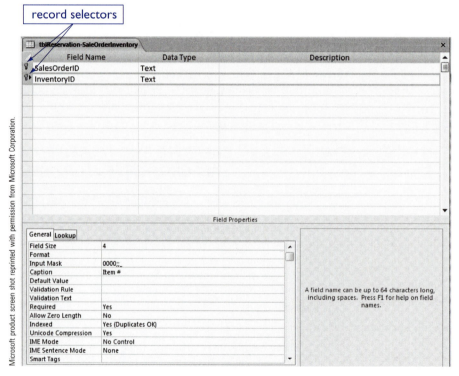

This completes the basic design of *tblReservation-SaleOrderInventory*. A version of this table that includes data for the Pipefitters Supply Company is included in the *Ch08.accdb* database on the Companion Web site.

You learned how to create *tblCustomer*, *tblInventory* (and the related inventory category tables), *tblSaleOrder*, and *tblReservation-SaleOrderInventory*. You previously established the relationships between *tblInventory* and the three inventory category tables. Now you are ready to finish creating all of the relationships between these tables as specified in Figure 8.5. Exercise 8.21 will show you how to size and move tables in the relationship window to make your database model easier to read. If you have entered your own data in the tables, you must make sure that the data in key fields are compatible before you begin the exercise. For example, if you entered any new sale orders in *tblSaleOrder*, the exact values for CustomerID must exist in the CustomerID field in *tblCustomer*. Similarly, any values you entered in the SaleOrderID or InventoryID fields in *tblReservation-SaleOrderInventory* must exist in the corresponding fields of *tblSaleOrder* and *tblInventory*, respectively. If corresponding values do not exist in these fields where the Required property is set to Yes, Access will not permit you to establish referential integrity on those links.

The Sale Order Entry Form

The sale order entry task requires a more complex form than either the tasks of customer information entry or inventory information entry required. To enter all of the information contained in customers' sale orders, your database needs the following links:

- *tblSaleOrder* to *tblCustomer*—to obtain information such as the customer's name and address.
- *tblSaleOrder* to *tblEmployee*—to obtain the employee's name who takes the sale order.
- *tblSaleOrder* to *tblReservation-SaleOrderInventory*—to obtain a list of the inventory item numbers, quantities, and prices for each item on each sale order.
- *tblReservationSaleOrderInventory* to *tblInventory*, and from *tblInventory* to the inventory category tables—to obtain a description for each item on each sale order.
  - You already created the links from *tblInventory* to the inventory category tables in Exercise 8.13.

Creating Relationships with the Sale Order Table

A sale order entry form that meets these objectives will use all of the above tables. The form must read from *tblCustomer*, *tblEmployee*, *tblInventory*, *tblInventoryComposition*, *tblInventoryDiameter*, and *tblInventoryType*, and write to *tblSaleOrder* and *tblReservation-SaleOrderInventory*. Since this form will read data from *tblCustomer* and *tblInventory*, you must have data entered in these tables. The *Ch08.accdb* database on the Companion Web site includes populated versions of these tables. You can copy all of the individual records from the *Ch08.mdb* and paste them into your database tables. Just open *Ch08.accdb* in a new instance of Access and then copy all of the records from the *Ch08.accdb* table and paste them into your table. This procedure will save you the time and trouble of entering large amounts of data into tables and will help speed you along to the exercises that follow.

EXERCISE 8.21: CREATING RELATIONSHIPS FOR ALL TABLES RELATED TO THE SALE ORDER EVENT

1. Close all open tables and forms.
2. In the Database Tools tab, click Relationships in the Show/Hide group. Your Relationships window should look like how you left it at the end of Exercise 8.13 (see Figure 8.18).
3. Minimize the Navigation Pane by clicking the << at the top-right corner of the pane. This gives you more room for your database model, which will make it easier to read.

4. Resize the tables to show the complete table name and all attributes. Move your cursor to the bottom right-hand corner of tblInventory so that the mouse pointer turns into a *resizer*. Click to *grab* the corner and drag it up and to the right until the table is as small as it can be while displaying the entire table name and all attributes. Repeat this process with the other three tables.

5. Move the tables to be consistent with the REA (resources, events, and agents) model format: resource tables on the left, event tables in the middle, and agent tables on the right. Since all four tables are related to inventory, which is a resource, move them to the left side of the Relationships window. Move tables one at a time by grabbing them on the title bar and dragging them so the end product looks like Figure 8.29.

6. Click Show Table in the Relationships group (on the Design tab), and press Ctrl and click all tables other than the four inventory-related tables already visible. Click Add and then click Close.

7. Resize and move the newly added tables to look like the Relationship window in Figure 8.30. Notice that the relationship table is placed between the resources and events columns.

8. Create your links the same way you did in Exercise 8.13. Drag from the primary key to the matching foreign key or from the primary key to the matching part of a composite primary key.

9. When the Edit Relationships dialog box appears (see Figure 8.17) make sure that the correct attributes appear in the tables you dragged from and to. The relationship type at the bottom of the dialog box should always be One-to-Many. Check Enforce Referential Integrity and Cascade Update Related Fields. Finally, click Create in the dialog box. When you are finished, your Relationship window should look like the one in Figure 8.31.

10. Click the X button in the Relationships group to close the Relationships window, click the Yes button in the dialog box to save your changes, then click >> on the Navigation Pane to restore it.

Fig. 8.29 Relationship window after sizing and moving inventory-related tables.

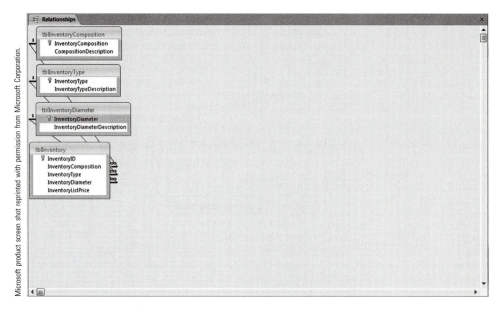

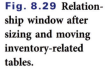
Microsoft product screen shot reprinted with permission from Microsoft Corporation.

Fig. 8.30 Sale order-related tables arranged in REA format.

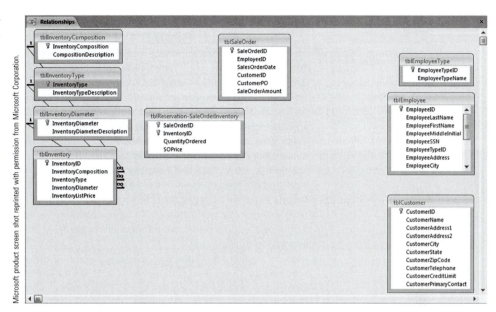

Microsoft product screen shot reprinted with permission from Microsoft Corporation.

Fig. 8.31 Relationship window with all sale order-related tables.

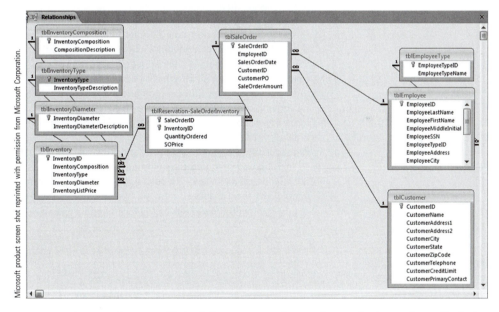

Microsoft product screen shot reprinted with permission from Microsoft Corporation.

Now that you have established the necessary foreign key and relationship table links, you can create a Sale Order Entry form. First, you will create two queries before creating the form instead of making changes to the queries "behind" the form that Access creates as its source for form data. Creating the queries up front makes it easier to correct mistakes in the query. Also, if you have multiple forms that use the same query, you need to create the query only once.

Creating a Query for Customer Data Used in the Sale Order Form

The sale order form requires customer address information. Although this information is included in *tblCustomer*, the city, state, and zip code information are stored separately. To make the sale order form look like a paper form, CustomerCity, CustomerState, and CustomerZipCode need to be combined to look like a standard address, such as "Greeley, Colorado 80639-0131." In Exercise 8.22 you will create a query containing customer information that also *concatenates* these three fields to form a new field, CityStateZip.

EXERCISE 8.22: CREATING *QRYCUSTOMERINFO* FOR THE SALE ORDER ENTRY FORM

1. To create a new query in Design view, click the Create tab and click Query Design in the Other group.
2. The only table you need for this query is *tblCustomer*. Double-click the tblCustomer table name from the list presented in the Show Table dialog box, and click the Close button. Double-clicking the table selects and adds it to the Table Pane so you do not need to click the Add button.
3. Select all of the fields in the tblCustomer Field Roster by clicking on CustomerID to highlight it. Now press and hold the Shift+Down Arrow until all of the fields are highlighted. Then, drag all of the fields from the tblCustomer Field Roster to the Criteria Pane.
4. Save the query as qryCustomerInfo before creating the address. Saving the query first allows you to select the address attributes from the query when using the Expression Builder.
5. Click on the first row of the next available column of the Criteria Pane and click on Builder in the Query Setup group. You should see the Expression Builder dialog box.
6. Build the following expression: CityStateZip: [CustomerCity] &", " & [CustomerState] &" " & [CustomerZipCode]. Instead of typing the attributes with the brackets (e.g., [CustomerCity]), you can just double-click on them in Expression Builder. Notice that when you add [CustomerCity] after typing CityStateZip: Expression Builder adds <<Expr>> to your expression. Just delete it by double-clicking to highlight <<Expr>> and pressing the Delete key. Click the OK button when you are finished (see Figure 8.32).
7. Delete CustomerCity, CustomerState, and CustomerZipCode by highlighting those three columns of the Criteria Pane and pressing the Delete key. Highlight columns by moving your cursor just above the Field row of CustomerCity so the cursor turns into a down arrow and click the column; press and hold Shift+Right Arrow until all three fields are highlighted.
8. Highlight the CityStateZip column and move it to the right of CustomerAddress2 by clicking and dragging the column.
9. Save your query. View the resulting dynaset by clicking on either View (you should see the Datasheet icon) or Run in the Results group. Figure 8.33 shows the dynaset with the data from *Ch08.accdb*. Close qryCustomerInfo.

Fig. 8.32 Expression Builder.

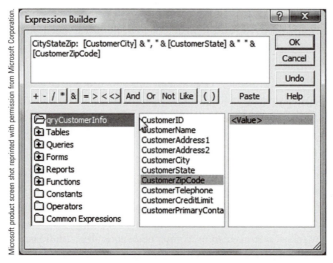

Fig. 8.33 *qry-CustomerInfo* dynaset.

Customer #	Name	Address	Address	CityStateZip	Phone #	Credit Limit	Prima
10001	Dunn Plumbing	2763 Cosgrove Road	2nd Floor	West Haven, CT 06516-1960	(203) 933-2063	$6,000	Bill Dunn
10002	Ace Construction Co.	3788 Spring Grove Aven		Cincinnati, OH 45217-0830	(513) 451-4264	$9,000	Roger "Ace
10003	Bryant Boiler Repair	357 East Wentworth Dri	#207	Chicago, IL 60629-1597	(312) 447-3198	$15,000	William Br
10004	Bucknell Air Conditioning	3198 Storm Lake Road		Lewisburg, PA 17837-3285	(717) 938-4761	$6,000	Michelle V
10005	Cole & Co.	720 Conover Court	Building #4	Fargo, ND 58105-2930	(701) 565-3099	$8,000	Patricia Sp
10006	Burch Builders' Supply	21887 Larwood Rd.		Reno, NV 89557-0014	(702) 784-1866	$18,000	Cynthia Str
10007	Lin Plumbing Repair, Inc.	1297 Lambert Lane		New Orleans, LA 70148-2793	(504) 288-5869	$12,000	Jong-Dae L
10008	Mattison Maintenance Co.	7743 Van Meter Place		Bozeman, MT 59717-2020	(406) 994-2086	$5,000	Matt Stami
10009	Central Plumbing Supply	709 Baker St.		Baltimore, MD 21210-2993	(301) 233-8672	$20,000	Tom Miche
10010	Entero Construction	615 Lewis Ave.	Suite 103	Louisville, KY 40292-7319	(502) 585-7755	$6,000	Howard Ba
10011	Nalco Plumbing	5719 20th Street		Washington, PA 15301-1309	(412) 502-9616	$10,000	Phil Napie
10012	Cotts Mechanical	3839 Logan Avenue		Santa Barbara, CA 93105-9557	(805) 691-2302	$9,000	Bob Cotts
10013	Helix Electric	7740 Blystone Lane		Sonora, CA 95370-8141	(209) 546-3051	$2,000	John Dunn
10014	Cadigan Construction	8789 Fresno Street		Mount Carmel, IL 62863-9619	(618) 701-3286	$5,000	Dan Cadiga
10015	Stimpson Construction	3173 Fore Street		York, PA 17403-3511	(717) 107-1442	$2,000	William Sti
10016	S&G Mechanical	9099 Orange Avenue	3rd Floor	Hoboken, NJ 07030-5007	(201) 486-8283	$3,000	Sean Youn
10017	Tukes Plumbing	8933 Home Street		Jersey City, NJ 07304-7569	(201) 425-8949	$5,000	Doug McKe
10018	Brown Engineering	9201 30th Street		Sonoma, CA 95476-9884	(707) 541-7688	$10,000	Curtis Brov
10019	Campbell Heating and Air	7317 Kirk Street		Susanville, CA 96130-5996	(916) 793-9798	$2,000	Tara Camp
10020	Blackburn & Co.	7414 Grant Avenue		Gibbsboro, NJ 08026-1066	(609) 922-6815	$5,000	Lucas Black
10021	Southshore Inc.	2017 Allen Road		Lyndhurst, NJ 07071-7147	(201) 992-5857	$20,000	Shari Limsl
10022	Totherow Constuction	8139 Patterson Avenue		Taft, CA 93268-2815	(805) 957-8358	$6,000	Bill Tother
10023	Aho Electrical Services	2570 Harkle Road		Marlboro, NJ 07746-8648	(908) 137-6974	$5,000	Alan Aho
10024	Thompson Plumbing Repa	6743 Cahill Road		Spring Mills, PA 16875-6375	(814) 222-4791	$10,000	Chris Thon
10025	R & J Builders	2965 Station Circle		Marshall, IL 62441-6665	(217) 652-7182	$4,000	John Prew

Record: 1 of 52   No Filter   Search

Creating a Query for Sale Order Line Items

Individual line items on a sale order include the item number, a description of the item ordered, the quantity ordered, the sale price per item, and the line item extension (sale price × quantity). Therefore, sale order line items use information from the following tables: *tblReservation-SaleOrderInventory*, *tblInventory*, *tblInventoryComposition*, *tblInventoryType*, and *tblInventoryDiameter*. Additionally, you will add two new fields. One field, SaleOrderLineExtension, will contain the sale price × quantity ordered expression. The other field, FullDescription, will concatenate the descriptions of each item's composition, type, and diameter.

EXERCISE 8.23: CREATING *QRYSALEORDERLINEITEM* FOR THE SALE ORDER ENTRY FORM

1. Create a new query in Design view. Click the Create tab and click Query Design in the Other group.
2. Select the following tables in the Show Table dialog box by double-clicking them: tblReservation-SaleOrderInventory, tblInventory, tblInventoryComposition, tblInventoryType, and tblInventoryDiameter. Click the Close button (see Figure 8.34).
3. Drag the following items from the field rosters in the Table Pane to the Criteria Pane:
   • InventoryID from *tblReservation-SaleOrderInventory*.
   • InventoryDiameterDescription from *tblInventoryDiameter*.
   • CompositionDescription from *tblInventoryComposition*.
   • InventoryTypeDescription from tblInventoryType.
   • QuantityOrdered and SOPrice, respectively, from *tblReservation-SaleOrderInventory*.
   • InventoryListPrice from *tblInventory*.
   • SaleOrderID from *tblReservation-SaleOrderInventory*. Although this attribute will not appear in the sale order form it is necessary to link sale order line items to their related sale orders.
4. Save the query as qrySaleOrderLineItem before creating SaleOrderLineExtension.
5. Create the SaleOrderLineExtension expression. Scroll right in the Criteria Pane, select the first open Field column and click on Builder in the Query Setup group to open up the Expression Builder dialog box.
6. Enter the following expression by typing and selecting fields from the query: SaleOrderLineExtension: [QuantityOrdered] * [SOPrice].

7. On the Criteria Pane, move SaleOrderLineExtension to the right of InventoryListPrice.
8. Click PropertySheet in the Show/Hide group. Type Extension in the Caption property field. Close the Property Sheet.
9. Create the following expression using the Expression Builder in the same way you created CityStateZip in Step 6 of Exercise 8.22: FullDescription: [InventoryDiameterDescription] & " " & [CompositionDescription] & " " & [InventoryTypeDescription].
10. Delete the following columns from the Criteria Pane because they are now part of the expression you created: InventoryDiameterDescription, InventoryCompositionDescription, and InventoryTypeDescription.
11. Move FullDescription to the right of InventoryID.
12. Click PropertySheet in the Show/Hide group. Type Description in the Caption property field. Close the Property Sheet (see Figure 8.35).
13. Save your query. View the resulting dynaset by clicking on either View (you should see the Datasheet icon) or Run in the Results group. Figure 8.36 shows the dynaset with the data from *Ch08.accdb*. Close qrySaleOrderLineItem.

Fig. 8.34 Table Pane for *qrySale-OrderLineItem.*

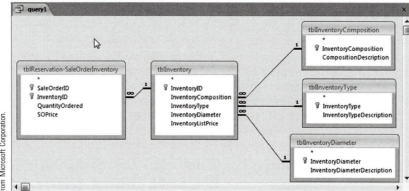

Microsoft product screen shot reprinted with permission from Microsoft Corporation.

Fig. 8.35 Property Sheet in query Design view.

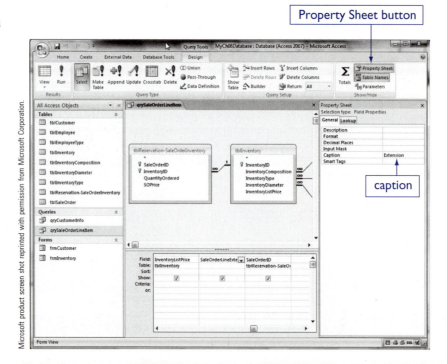

Microsoft product screen shot reprinted with permission from Microsoft Corporation.

Fig. 8.36 *qrySale-OrderLineItem* dynaset.

Item #	Description	Quantity	Price	List Price	Extension	Sale Order #
1001	0.25-inch Brass 4-foot pipe	20	$21.95	$21.95	$439.00	100003
1001	0.25-inch Brass 4-foot pipe	15	$21.95	$21.95	$329.25	100014
1001	0.25-inch Brass 4-foot pipe	15	$21.95	$21.95	$329.25	100019
1001	0.25-inch Brass 4-foot pipe	12	$21.95	$21.95	$263.40	100025
1001	0.25-inch Brass 4-foot pipe	5	$21.95	$21.95	$109.75	100031
1001	0.25-inch Brass 4-foot pipe	15	$21.95	$21.95	$329.25	100049
1001	0.25-inch Brass 4-foot pipe	45	$21.95	$21.95	$987.75	100053
1001	0.25-inch Brass 4-foot pipe	15	$21.95	$21.95	$329.25	100059
1001	0.25-inch Brass 4-foot pipe	30	$21.95	$21.95	$658.50	100079
1001	0.25-inch Brass 4-foot pipe	25	$21.95	$21.95	$548.75	100087
1002	0.50-inch Brass 4-foot pipe	20	$26.49	$26.49	$529.80	100011
1002	0.50-inch Brass 4-foot pipe	20	$26.49	$26.49	$529.80	100033
1002	0.50-inch Brass 4-foot pipe	35	$26.49	$26.49	$927.15	100052
1002	0.50-inch Brass 4-foot pipe	30	$26.49	$26.49	$794.70	100060
1002	0.50-inch Brass 4-foot pipe	30	$26.49	$26.49	$794.70	100067
1002	0.50-inch Brass 4-foot pipe	35	$26.49	$26.49	$927.15	100088
1002	0.50-inch Brass 4-foot pipe	5	$26.49	$26.49	$132.45	100093
1002	0.50-inch Brass 4-foot pipe	15	$26.49	$26.49	$397.35	100099
1003	1.00-inch Brass 4-foot pipe	10	$34.79	$34.79	$347.90	100008
1003	1.00-inch Brass 4-foot pipe	40	$34.79	$34.79	$1,391.60	100043
1003	1.00-inch Brass 4-foot pipe	10	$34.79	$34.79	$347.90	100060
1003	1.00-inch Brass 4-foot pipe	20	$34.79	$34.79	$695.80	100075
1003	1.00-inch Brass 4-foot pipe	10	$34.79	$34.79	$347.90	100083
1004	2.00-inch Brass 4-foot pipe	10	$43.69	$43.69	$436.90	100011
1004	2.00-inch Brass 4-foot pipe	10	$43.69	$43.69	$436.90	100032

Record: 1 of 300 No Filter Search

Using Form Wizard to Build the Sale Order Entry Form

The Sale Order Entry form is a complex form as it actually contains a form based on *tblSaleOrder* and *qryCustomerInfo* and a subform based on *qrySaleOrderLineItem*. Creating such a form from scratch is a time-consuming task. Therefore, you will use Form Wizard in the next exercise to create a Sale Order Entry form that will need only minor adjustments to become a user-friendly form.

EXERCISE 8.24: CREATING THE SALE ORDER ENTRY FORM

1. Click tblSaleOrder in the Navigation Pane. Click More Forms in the Forms group of the Create tab. Click Form Wizard.
2. You should see tblSaleOrder in the Tables/Queries list box. If not, click the list box arrow, and click Table: tblSaleOrder in the list. Click >> (select all) button to place all Available Fields into the Selected Fields list.
3. Click the Tables/Queries list box arrow, and click Query: qryCustomerInfo from the list.
4. Move all of the fields except CustomerID over to the Selected Fields List. Click CustomerName and then click > seven times. Do not include the CustomerID field listed in the query's Available Fields list.
5. Click the Tables/Queries list box arrow, and click Query: qrySaleOrderLineItem from the list. Move all of the fields except SaleOrderID over to the Selected Fields List. This time, click >> button to place all Available Fields into the Selected Fields list. The last field, qrySaleOrderLineItem.SaleOrderID, should be highlighted. This is the SaleOrderID field from qrySaleOrderLineItem (Access attaches the table/query name to a field when two fields in the *Selected Items list* have the same name). Click the < button to remove qrySaleOrderLineItem.SaleOrderID from the Selected Fields (see Figure 8.37).
6. Click Next. Click by tblSaleOrder in the *How do you want to view your data?* list box (if it is not already selected) to ensure the proper grouping (see Figure 8.37). Notice that the Form with Subform(s) radio button is already selected.

7. Click Next. Click Tabular in the *What layout would you like for your subform?* Radio button.
8. Click Next. Click the Office style if it is not already selected, and click Next.
9. Double-click the Form text box below the question *What titles do you want for your forms?* Type frmSaleOrder to name the form in the Navigation Pane. Select all the text in the Subform name text box and type fsubSaleOrder to name the affiliated subform. Click the Finish button. Access creates the form/subform pair and displays them in Form view (see Figure 8.38). Notice that we use *frm* to identify forms and *fsub* to identify subforms, and the name after the prefix for both form and subform is the same.

Fig. 8.37 Form Wizard dialog boxes.

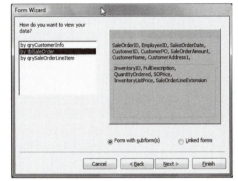

Fig. 8.38 *frmSale-Order* created by Form Wizard.

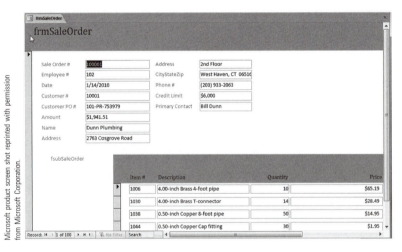

Although this Wizard-generated form is certainly usable and includes many basic controls needed to enter, delete, and modify sale order information, you can probably see some ways to improve it. The next two exercises show you how to make improvements that will make the form and subform more effective and easier to use. You might identify other improvements or alternative ways of making the improvements we suggest. We encourage you to experiment, since form design is as much an art as a science. Just remember that you are designing a form for an input clerk to use many hours each day, so avoid bright colors and other design features that might irritate the user.

EXERCISE 8.25: IMPROVING THE LOOK OF THE SALE ORDER ENTRY FORM

1. Open frmSaleOrder in Design view. Remove the layout applied to the form's controls. Press Ctrl+A to select all objects. Now, go to the Arrange ribbon and click Remove in the Control Layout group. Remove the layout applied to the subform's controls by clicking a control within the subform, pressing Ctrl+A, and clicking Remove on the Arrange ribbon.
2. Change the Form Header to Sale Order Entry, and resize both the text box and header.
3. Delete the labels for CustomerName, CustomerAddress1, CustomerAddress2, CityStateZip, and CustomerTelephone.
4. Delete the fsubSaleOrder label on the Subform object.
5. Bold and right-justify the remaining labels in frmSaleOrder.
6. Bold the labels in fsubSaleOrder. You may find it easier to make changes to the subform by closing frmSaleOrder and opening fsubSaleOrder. To see how your changes look in the form, close fsubSaleOrder and open frmSaleOrder.
7. Resize and align the fields in the form and subform so the form looks like Figure 8.39. This is similar to what you did in Exercise 8.15. Some tasks may be easier to accomplish in Layout view and others may be easier in Design view.

Fig. 8.39 Partially improved sale order form in Form view and Design view.

Microsoft product screen shots reprinted with permission from Microsoft Corporation.

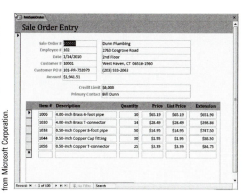

EXERCISE 8.26: CHANGING CONTROL PROPERTIES TO PREVENT USERS FROM CHANGING REFERENCE DATA

Some fields on the sale order form are reference items and should not be changed in this form, like the customer's name and address and the inventory description. In the next exercise you will change the field properties to prevent reference data from being changed in this form.

1. Open frmSaleOrder in design view. Click Property Sheet in the Tools group.
2. Click the empty Detail space just above the CustomerName control box and drag down to select CustomerName, CustomerAddress1, CustomerAddress2, CityStateZip, and CustomerTelephone.
3. Format these fields to blend in with the background. Click the Format tab on the Property Sheet if it is not already visible. Change the Back Style and Border Style properties to Transparent.
4. Lock the controls to prevent users from changing customer data in the sale order entry form. Click the Data tab on the Property Sheet. Change the Enabled property to No and the Locked property to Yes.

5. Remove the tab stop to prevent users from moving the cursor to fields that cannot be changed. Click the Other tab on the Property Sheet. Change the Tab Stop property to No (see Figure 8.40).
6. Repeat Steps 2 through 5 in the subform for FullDescription, InventoryListPrice, and SaleOrderExtension. Your sale order entry form should now look like Figure 8.41.
7. Save both frmSaleOrder and fsubSaleOrder.

Fig. 8.40 Property Sheet tabs.

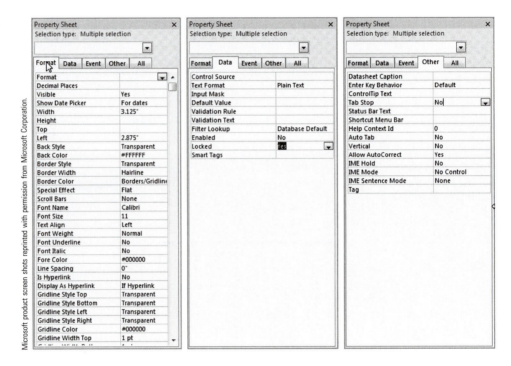

Fig. 8.41 Sale Order Entry form in Form view after completing Exercise 8.27.

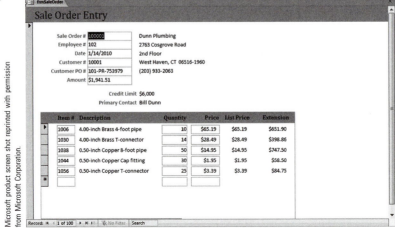

You may notice that the form does not scroll through the sale orders in numeric order. The Form Wizard did not include a sorting rule in the query it built behind *frmSaleOrder*. Also, the tab order is not correct. Fortunately, these problems are easy to fix.

EXERCISE 8.27: CHANGING THE SORT ORDER AND *TAB ORDER IN FRMSALEORDER*

1. Open frmSaleOrder in Design view.
2. Click Property Sheet in the Tools group to open the Property Sheet if it is not already open.
3. Select Form from the combo box above the Property Sheet tabs if Form is not already selected.
4. Click the Properties sheet's Data tab, and then click the Record Source property's Build button to open the Query Builder window for the query behind the form.
5. Select or type Ascending in the SaleOrderID field's Sort cell in the Criteria Pane.
6. Click Close in the Close group to close the Query Builder. Click the Yes button in the dialog box to save your changes.
7. Click the Arrange tab. Click Tab Order in the Control Layout group to open the Tab Order window. Click Detail in the Section column if it is not already selected. In the Custom Order column, click and drag fsubSaleOrder to right under SaleOrderAmount.
8. Click the OK button. Switch to Form view. Notice that the tab stops are in correctly, moving sequentially through the top part of the form and then to the subform.
9. Go to the next record. Notice that the records are now sorted by sale order number. Save your changes to the form.

When examining the form, you might ask yourself the following questions. How can the salesperson avoid mistyping his or her employee ID? How can Pipefitters help ensure that only salespeople take sale orders? In the next two exercises you will add a combo box that displays an alphabetical list of Pipefitters' salespeople so the user needs to select only his or her name from the list.

EXERCISE 8.28: CREATING A QUERY FOR THE SALESPERSON COMBO BOX

1. Create a new query in Design view. Click the Create tab and click Query Design in the Other group.
2. The only table you need for this query is *tblEmployee*. Double-click tblEmployee from the list presented in the Show Table dialog box, and click the Close button.
3. Double-click the following fields in the order listed to move them to the Criteria Pane: EmployeeID, EmployeeLastName, EmployeeFirstName, EmployeeMiddleInitial, EmployeeTypeID.
4. Limit the employee list to salespeople. In the Criteria cell for EmployeeType type "30" and press Enter.
5. Save the query as qrySalesperson. View the resulting dynaset by clicking on View or Run on the Design Ribbon. Notice that the results are sorted by EmployeeID, even though you want your combo box to be sorted alphabetically. This is fine because the sort order of the combo box can be determined when you create it, without regard to the sort order of the underlying table or query. Close the query.

EXERCISE 8.29: REPLACING THE EMPLOYEE ID CONTROL WITH A SALESPERSON COMBO BOX

1. Open frmSaleOrder in Design view. Remove the EmployeeID control box and its label by clicking the control box and pressing the Delete key.
2. Click the Combo Box button in the Controls group. Move the cursor to the empty space where the EmployeeID control was located; then, double-click to start the Combo Box Wizard.
3. In the first dialog box click the first option button with the caption *I want the combo box to look up the values in a table or query;* then, click the Next button.
4. The next dialog box asks *Which table or query should provide the values for your combo box?* Click the Queries radio button, and double-click *qrySalesperson*.
5. Double-click the following fields in the Available Fields list to move them to the Selected Fields list: EmployeeID, EmployeeLastName, EmployeeFirstName, EmployeeMiddleInitial. Click the Next button.
6. Sort in ascending order first by EmployeeLastName, second by EmployeeFirstName, third by EmployeeMiddleInitial. Click the Next button.
7. Adjust the column size for Employee # and MI to fit the current data because its size is fixed. Leave the Last Name and First Name columns as is to allow for longer names. Click the Next button.
8. Click EmployeeID from the Available Fields list because you want to store this value in *tblSaleOrder*. Click the Next button.
9. Click the second radio button with the caption *Store that value in this field;* then, click the combo box arrow button, and select the EmployeeID field. This step stores the Employee ID in the EmployeeID field of *tblSaleOrder.* Click the Next button to open the last dialog box.
10. Enter Salesperson as the control's label, and then click the Finish button. The Wizard creates a combo box control according to your specifications and places it on the sale order form.
11. Change the name of the combo box from the default name Combo## (where ## is a number generated by Access), by clicking on the Property Sheet button in the Tools group. Click the Other tab and type cboSalesperson as the value for the Name property and press Enter.
12. Change the tab order. Click the Arrange tab. Click Tab Order in the Control Layout group to open the Tab Order window. Click Detail in the Section column if it is not already selected. In the Custom Order column click and drag cboSalesperson to right under SaleOrderID. Click the OK button.
13. Make the format and size of the combo box and its label consistent with the other input controls. Figure 8.42 shows the completed sale order form.
14. Test the new control in Design view. Notice that the salespeople are sorted alphabetically in ascending order. Save the form and close it.

After creating the employee combo box, you may think of other control-related questions. How can the salesperson remember Dunn Plumbing's customer number (and avoid making a typo even if he or she does remember it)? How can the salesperson remember all inventory item IDs, and how can typos be prevented? Does the sale order total equal the sum of the extensions, and can this process be automated? We will address some of these control issues in the end-of-chapter problems and others will be discussed in Chapters 9 through Chapter 12.

Fig. 8.42 Sale Order Entry form with combo box.

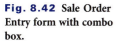

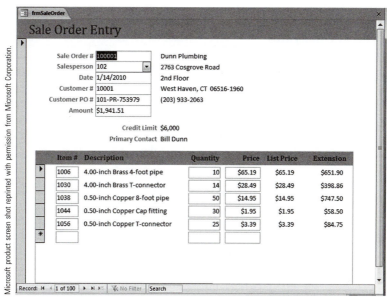

Recording Sales

Companies like Pipefitters Supply Company that sell products and services to other businesses typically sell merchandise with credit terms such as *n/30* (pay the net amount within 30 days). Often, sale orders must be approved by the credit department before the goods are shipped. Since a sale is considered complete when title changes hands, companies record sales in their accounting systems for the goods actually shipped at the time they are shipped, even if the shipment is only for part of the goods ordered. Therefore, one of Pipefitters' materials handlers enters the invoice information when preparing goods for shipment. When the merchandise is ready for shipment, the system creates an invoice and shipping documents in paper and/or electronic form. Shipping documents, such as bills of lading or packing slips, vary greatly in appearance and design. However, they always contain a subset of the information that appears on the invoice.

In this section, we will show you how to create an invoice form for internal use and how to modify the invoice form to generate paper documents for customers. Also, you can easily modify this invoice to create shipping documents that suit a particular application. Invoice data is generated in the sales/collection process. To capture sale data your database will use the same tables you used to record sale orders except *tblReservation-SaleOrderInventory*, plus you will create *tblSale* and the *tblOutflow-SaleInventory* relationship table as shown in Figure 8.5.

The Sale Table

The sale table stores information similar to the sale order table. Figure 8.43 shows the similarities between the fields of the two tables. The main difference is that the primary key from *tblSaleOrder* is posted as a foreign key in *tblSale*. This link allows Pipefitters to determine which sale orders have been filled, and for the unfilled and partially filled orders, which inventory items still need to be delivered.

Fig. 8.43 Comparison of fields for *tblSaleOrder* and *tblSale*.

Table Name	*tblSaleOrder*	*tblSale*
Primary Key	SaleOrderID	SaleID
Date	SaleOrderDate	ShippingDate
Amount	SaleOrderAmount	SaleAmount
Other Attribute	CustomerPO	n/a
Customer (FK)	CustomerID	CustomerID
Employee (FK)	EmployeeID	EmployeeID
Other (FK)	n/a	SaleOrderID

EXERCISE 8.30: CREATING THE SALE TABLE

1. Right-click tblSaleOrder in the Navigation Pane. Click Copy. Right-click anywhere in the Navigation Pane. Click Paste. In the Paste Table As dialog box type tblSale in the name box, click the Structure Only radio button, and then click OK.
2. Open tblSale in Design view.
3. Copy SaleOrderID. Right-click the Primary Key field of SaleOrderID. Move your cursor to the first empty row, right-click and then click Paste to create a copy of SaleOrderID. Notice that the copy of SaleOrderID is *not* a primary key. Change the Indexed property to Yes (Duplicates OK)
4. Make the following changes to the FieldNames and Captions. Do NOT delete fields:
   - Change SaleOrderID (the primary key) to InvoiceID.
     - Change the caption of InvoiceID from Sale Order # to Invoice #.
   - Change SaleOrderDate to ShippingDate.
   - Change SaleOrderAmount to SaleAmount.
5. Delete CustomerPO. Right-click on CustomerPO, click Delete Rows.
6. Move a Field Row by clicking the Record Selector next to the Field Name. Then click and drag it to its desired place. Move EmployeeID and SaleOrderID so your Fields are in the same order as the table in Figure 8.44.

Fig. 8.44 *tblSale* Field list.

Field Name	Data Type
InvoiceID	Text
ShippingDate	Date/Time
CustomerID	Text
SaleOrderID	Text
EmployeeID	Text
SaleAmount	Currency

The Sale-Inventory Table

The Sale-Inventory table records the many-to-many outflow relationship between *tblSale* and *tblInventory*. These are the goods actually shipped to customers. Therefore, *tblOutflow-SaleInventory* will store four fields:

1. The primary key of *tblSale*.
2. The primary key of *tblInventory*.
3. The quantity of each inventory item that appears on each sale invoice.
4. The price of each inventory item that appears on each sale invoice.

The primary keys from *tblSale* and *tblInventory* will combine to form the composite primary key in *tblOutflow-SaleInventory*. Before you begin the next exercise, close any open tables or forms.

EXERCISE 8.31: CREATING THE *TBLOUTFLOW-SALEINVENTORY* RELATIONSHIP TABLE

1. Right-click tblReservation-SaleOrderInventory in the Navigation Pane. Click Copy. Right-click anywhere in the Navigation Pane. Click Paste. In the Paste Table As dialog box type tblOutflow-SaleInventory in the name box, click the Structure Only radio button, and click OK.
2. Open tblOutflow-SaleInventory in Design view.
3. Make the following changes to the FieldNames and Captions. Do NOT delete fields:
   • Change SaleOrderID (the primary key) to InvoiceID.
     • Change the caption of Invoice ID from Sale Order # to Invoice #.
   • Change QuantityOrdered to QuantitySold.
   • Change SOPrice to InvoicePrice.
4. Save and close the table.

The Sale Entry Form

The Sale Entry form closely resembles the Sale Order Entry form that you created earlier in this chapter. The Sale Order Entry form lets Pipefitters Supply Company enter the items that its customers order. The Sale Entry form lets Pipefitters enter the items it actually shipped to its customers. If Pipefitters were certain that it would have all inventory items in stock at all times, it could generate invoices directly from information in the Sale Order table. Unfortunately, this assumption is unrealistic for most companies.

Creating Relationships with the Sale Table

In Exercise 8.32 you will add the relationships with *tblSale* necessary to build the Sale Entry form. Before you create these relationships, copy the data from *tblSale* and *tblOutflow-SaleInventory* in the *Ch08.accdb* database into *tblSale* and *tblOutflow-SaleInventory* in your database.

EXERCISE 8.32: CREATING RELATIONSHIPS RELATED TO THE SALE EVENT

1. Close all open tables and forms.
2. On the Database Tools tab, and click Relationships in the Show/Hide group. Your Relationships window should look like how you left it at the end of Exercise 8.21 (see Figure 8.31).
3. Minimize the Navigation Pane by clicking the << at the top-right corner of the pane.
4. Click Show Table in the Relationships group (on the Design tab), and double-click tblSale and tblOutflow-SaleInventory. Then click Close.
5. Create your links the same way you did in Exercise 8.21. Drag from the primary key to the matching foreign key or from the primary key to the matching part of a composite primary key.

6. When the Edit Relationships dialog box appears make sure that the correct attributes appear in the tables you dragged from and to. The relationship type at the bottom of the dialog box should always be One-to-Many. Check Enforce Referential Integrity and Cascade Update Related Fields. Finally, click Create in the dialog box.
7. Resize and move the newly added tables to look like the Relationship window in Figure 8.45. You may also refer back to Figure 8.5 which lists the primary and foreign keys in each table.
8. Close the Relationships window and click the Yes button in the dialog box to save your changes, then click >> on the Navigation Pane to restore it.

Fig. 8.45 Relationships window after adding sale event.

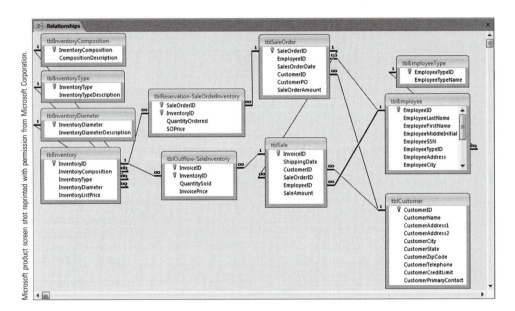

Microsoft product screen shot reprinted with permission from Microsoft Corporation.

Now that you have established the necessary foreign key and relationship table links, you can create a Sale Entry form. Although the Sale Entry form is similar to the Sale Order Entry form, it will be easier to create a new form from scratch because the changes required to alter the Sale Order Entry form are much more complex than was necessary to change *tblSaleOrder* into *tblSale*. Since you already created a Customer Information query for the Sale Order Entry form, you need to create a query only for sale line items.

Creating a Query for Sale Line Items

The only difference between the query for sale order line items and the query for sale line items is that *tblReservation-SaleOrderInventory* and its fields are replaced with *tblOutflow-SaleInventory* and its fields.

EXERCISE 8.33: CREATING *QRYSALELINEITEM* FOR THE SALE ENTRY FORM

1. Right-click qrySaleOrderLineItem in the Navigation Pane. Click Copy. Right-click anywhere in the Navigation Pane. Click Paste. In the Paste Table As dialog box type qrySaleLineItem in the name box, then click OK.

2. Open qrySaleLineItem in Design view.
3. Click Show Table in the Query Setup group, double-click tblOutflow-SaleInventory, and click the Close button. You may need to move and resize *tblOutflow-SaleInventory* in the Table Pane to make it easy to work with.
4. Change the table reference for InventoryID. On the Criteria Pane, click the Table cell for InventoryID and change it to tblOutflow-SaleInventory.
5. Change the table reference for QuantityOrdered to tblOutflow-SaleInventory. Change the Field from QuantityOrdered to QuantitySold.
6. Change the table reference for SOPrice to tblOutflow-SaleInventory. Change the Field from SOPrice to InvoicePrice.
7. Change the table reference for SaleOrderID to tblOutflow-SaleInventory. Change the Field from SaleOrderID to InvoiceID. Save your changes.
8. Click the SaleOrderLineExtension on the Criteria Pane, click Builder in the Query Setup group. In Expression Builder change the original expression to InvoiceLineExtension: [QuantitySold]*[InvoicePrice]. Click OK.
9. Delete tblSaleOrderLineItem from the Table Pane. Save your changes.
10. Check your query. Click Run in the Results group. The dynaset should look like Figure 8.46. Close the query.

Fig. 8.46 *qrySale-LineItem* dynaset.

Microsoft product screen shot reprinted with permission from Microsoft Corporation.

Item #	Description	Quantity	Price	List Price	Extension	Invoice #
1001	0.25-inch Brass 4-foot pipe	20	$21.95	$21.95	$439.00	100003
1001	0.25-inch Brass 4-foot pipe	15	$21.95	$21.95	$329.25	100019
1001	0.25-inch Brass 4-foot pipe	15	$21.95	$21.95	$329.25	100021
1001	0.25-inch Brass 4-foot pipe	12	$21.95	$21.95	$263.40	100026
1001	0.25-inch Brass 4-foot pipe	5	$21.95	$21.95	$109.75	100031
1001	0.25-inch Brass 4-foot pipe	15	$21.95	$21.95	$329.25	100052
1001	0.25-inch Brass 4-foot pipe	45	$21.95	$21.95	$987.75	100054
1001	0.25-inch Brass 4-foot pipe	15	$21.95	$21.95	$329.25	100063
1001	0.25-inch Brass 4-foot pipe	30	$21.95	$21.95	$658.50	100080
1001	0.25-inch Brass 4-foot pipe	25	$21.95	$21.95	$548.75	100090
1002	0.50-inch Brass 4-foot pipe	20	$26.49	$26.49	$529.80	100011
1002	0.50-inch Brass 4-foot pipe	20	$26.49	$26.49	$529.80	100036
1002	0.50-inch Brass 4-foot pipe	35	$26.49	$26.49	$927.15	100053
1002	0.50-inch Brass 4-foot pipe	30	$26.49	$26.49	$794.70	100062
1002	0.50-inch Brass 4-foot pipe	30	$26.49	$26.49	$794.70	100069
1003	1.00-inch Brass 4-foot pipe	10	$34.79	$34.79	$347.90	100010
1003	1.00-inch Brass 4-foot pipe	40	$34.79	$34.79	$1,391.60	100046
1003	1.00-inch Brass 4-foot pipe	10	$34.79	$34.79	$347.90	100062
1003	1.00-inch Brass 4-foot pipe	20	$34.79	$34.79	$695.80	100077
1003	1.00-inch Brass 4-foot pipe	10	$34.79	$34.79	$347.90	100086
1004	2.00-inch Brass 4-foot pipe	10	$43.69	$43.69	$436.90	100011
1004	2.00-inch Brass 4-foot pipe	10	$43.69	$43.69	$436.90	100033
1004	2.00-inch Brass 4-foot pipe	10	$43.69	$43.69	$436.90	100042
1004	2.00-inch Brass 4-foot pipe	12	$43.69	$43.69	$524.28	100065
1004	2.00-inch Brass 4-foot pipe	25	$43.69	$43.69	$1,092.25	100083

Record: 1 of 257

Using Form Wizard to Build the Sale Entry Form

Since the Sale Entry form is similar in complexity to the Sale Order Entry form, you will use Form Wizard to create it. The main form is based on *tblSale* and *qryCustomerInfo*, and the subform is based on *qrySaleLineItem*. In addition to the controls used in the Sale Order Entry form, you will add controls to this form that resolve the following questions: How can a salesperson remember so many customer numbers and avoid making typos, even if he or she remembers some of the numbers? How can a salesperson remember all inventory item IDs and how can typos be prevented?

EXERCISE 8.34: CREATING THE SALE ENTRY FORM

1. Click tblSale in the Navigation Pane. Click More Forms in the Forms group of the Create tab. Click Form Wizard.
2. Click Table: tblSale in the Tables/Queries list box. Click >> to move all Available Fields into the Selected Fields list.
3. Click the Tables/Queries list box arrow, and click Query: qryCustomerInfo from the list. Move all of the fields except CustomerID from the Available Fields list to the Selected Fields List.
4. Click the Tables/Queries list box arrow, and click Query: qrySaleLineItem from the list. Move all of the fields except InvoiceID over to the Selected Fields List. This time, click >> button to place all Available Fields into the Selected Fields list. The last field, qrySaleLineItem.InvoiceID, should be highlighted. This is the SaleID field from *qrySaleLineItem* (Access attaches the table/query name to a field when two fields in the *Selected Items* list have the same name). Click < button to remove qrySaleLineItem.InvoiceID from the Selected Fields.
5. Click Next. Click by tblSale in the *How do you want to view your data?* list box (if it is not already selected) to ensure the proper grouping. Notice that the Form with Subform(s) radio button is already selected.
6. Click Next. Click Tabular in the *What layout would you like for your subform?* radio button.
7. Click Next. Click the Office style if it is not already selected, and click Next.
8. Double-click the Form text box below the question *What titles do you want for your forms?* Type frmSale to name the form in the Navigation Pane. Select all the text in the Subform name text box, and type fsubSale to name the affiliated subform. Click the Finish button. The form created will look similar to the Sale Order form that the Form Wizard created (see Figure 8.38). Access creates the form/subform pair and displays them in Form view.
9. Use Exercises 8.25 through 8.28 to improve Sale Entry form. For the employee query, make a copy of qrySalesperson, change EmployeeTypeID criteria to "50", and rename the query, qryMaterialsHandler. Finally, name your combo box cboMaterialsHandler and use Materials Handler # for the combo box label. Expand the label box to accommodate the entire label. Your finished product will look similar to your Sale Entry form (see Figure 8.47).

Fig. 8.47 Completed Sale Entry form.

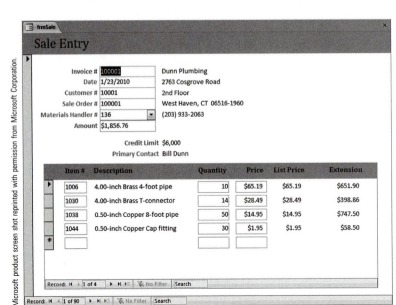

Microsoft product screen shot reprinted with permission from Microsoft Corporation.

Printing Invoices

The most common way to create paper documents in Access is to build a report. However, since the Sale Entry form we discussed in this chapter looks very similar to a printed invoice, you will modify *frmSale* and *fsubSale* to create a printable invoice. One characteristic of an invoice is to sum the line extensions at the bottom of the detail. To accomplish this you will create a query to sum the line extensions for the invoices you will be printing.

Also, to be able to use the summed values in your printable invoice form you need to store the values by invoice in a temporary table. Storing the line extension totals in a separate table allows you to add these totals to the query behind the form. Your query will therefore be a Make Table query. Finally, to avoid running a query for all sales in the database, which over time could be thousands, you will add parameters to limit the computations to only those invoices you print.

EXERCISE 8.35: CREATE *QRYSUMOFINVOICELINEEXTENSIONS*

1. Click the Create tab and click Query Design in the Other group.
2. Click the Queries tab, double-click qrySaleLineItem in the Show Table dialog box. Close the dialog box.
3. Double-click InvoiceID and InvoiceLineExtension, respectively from *qrySaleLineItem* in the Table Pane.
4. Click Totals (the summation sign) in the Show/Hide group. Since you want the sum of the line extensions for each invoice you print, leave the InvoiceID Total cell set to Group By. Change the Total cell for InvoiceLineExtension to Sum.
5. Open the Property Sheet. Click Property Sheet in the Show/Hide group. Type Total as the caption for the sum of the line extensions. Close the Property Sheet.
6. Click Run and you will see the totals for all the line items for each invoice. Return to Design view and save the query as qrySumOfSaleLineExtensionsByInvoice.
7. Convert your Select query (what you might call a regular query) to a Make Table query. Click Make Table in the Query Type group. In the Make Table dialog box type tblSumOfSaleLineExtensionsByInvoice. Click the Current Database radio button if it is not already selected. Click OK. The Make Table icon on the Design ribbon should be highlighted indicating that you now have a Make Table query.
8. The last thing to do is add parameters in the Criteria row of InvoiceID. Type Between [First Invoice] and [Last Invoice]. When you run the query you will be prompted to enter the first and last invoice numbers for the range of invoices you wish to print.
9. Save your query. Notice the Make Table query icon next to the query name in the Navigation Pane (see Figure 8.48). Also, *qrySumOfLineExtensionsByInvoice* is the first query in the list of queries because Access lists queries (and other objects) alphabetically by type. Close the query.
10. Run the query by double-clicking qrySumOfLineExtensionByInvoice to see the results of your query. Click Yes to the dialog box that says *You are about to run a make-table query that will modify data in your table.* Type 100008 in the first *Enter Parameter Value* dialog box. Click OK. Type 100023 in the second dialog box. Click OK.
11. Click Yes to the dialog box warning that you cannot undo pasting 16 rows into the table. The results are in the new table created, tblSumOfInvoiceLineExtensionsByInvoice. To view your results, double-click tblSumOfInvoiceLineExtensionsByInvoice.
12. Change the field name SumOfInvoiceLineExtension to Total by going into Design view and entering Total in the Caption property for SumOfInvoiceLineExtension.
13. Go to Datasheet view to view your change. Then close the table.

Fig. 8.48 Make Table
query added to
Navigation Pane.

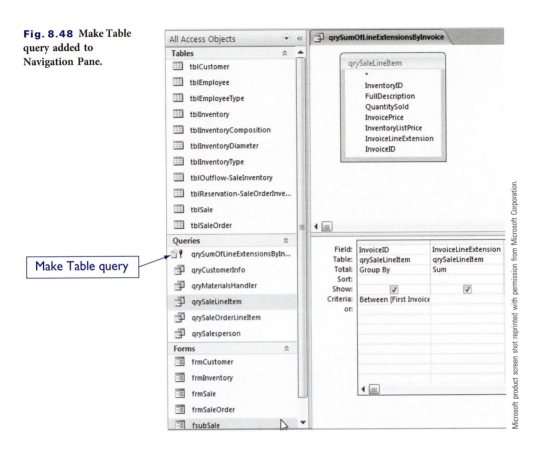

Now you are ready to make a copy of the Sale Entry form and convert into a print-able invoice. The finished product in Design view will look like Figure 8.49.

Fig. 8.49 Invoice for
printing in Design
view.

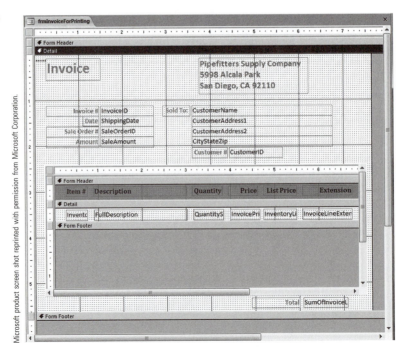

EXERCISE 8.36: CREATE A PRINTABLE INVOICE FORM

1. Click frmSale in the Navigation Pane. Press Ctrl+C to copy the table. Press Ctrl+V to paste it and name it frmSaleInvoiceForPrinting. Copy and rename fsubSale as fsubSaleInvoiceForPrinting.

2. Open frmSaleInvoiceForPrinting in Design view. Click the subform so the outline is highlighted. Press the Delete key to delete the subform. Click fsubSaleInvoiceForPrinting on the Navigation Pane. Drag it into the form.

3. Link fsubSaleInvoiceForPrinting to the main form. Click Property Sheet in the Tools group. Click the Data tab. Click the Link Master Fields property. Click ... to bring up the Subform Field Linker. Both the Master Fields and Child Fields should already be set to InvoiceID. Click OK. View the form in Form view and scroll through a few records to see that the form and subform are linked. Return to Design view.

4. Add a page break at the very top of the Detail section of the form. This causes Access to start each invoice on a new page. Click the Page Break icon in the Controls group. Move your cursor to the top-left of the Detail section and double-click to put the page break at the top of the section.

5. Delete the following controls so they do not appear in the invoice: EmployeeID, CustomerTelephone, CustomerCreditLimit, CustomerPrimaryContact, and the subform label.

6. Move the remaining controls, except the subform, to the positions shown in Figure 8.49. Be sure to decrease the width of the Customer # label to just fit the text.

7. Click and drag the Sale Entry title to the top of the Detail section. Change the title to Invoice. Use the same font and color as the form's labels and increase the size to 24 points and Bold the title.

8. Click and drag the Detail bar up to the top of the form to eliminate the header.

9. Copy and paste the Invoice title in the form's Detail section. This title will be for the company name and address. Change the font to 14 points. Move and resize the Title box to look like the one in Figure 8.49. Type the company name and address in Figure 8.49. Press Shift+Enter to move to a new line of text in the title box.

10. Copy the CustomerID label and paste the copy in the Detail section. Change the text to Sold To:. Resize the label box and move it into place (see Figure 8.49).

11. Change the Back Style and Border Style for all controls in the form and subform (including the border surrounding the subform) to Transparent.

12. Add the sum of the line extensions. Open the Property Sheet. Select Form from the combo box at the top of the Property sheet. Click the Data tab. Click ... in the Record Source property. Click Show Table in the Query Setup group. Add SumOfInvoiceLineExtensionByInvoice to the existing tables and queries. Double-click SumOfInvoiceLineExtension to add it to the Criteria Pane. Close the query and click the Yes button in the dialog box to save your changes to the query. Save the form.

13. Click Add Existing Fields in the Tools group. Click and drag SumOfInvoiceLine-Extension to the Detail section below the subform. Move the control and label to the position indicated in Figure 8.49. Bold the label. Change the Back Style and Border Style of the control to Transparent.

14. Save your changes. View the form in Form view. Click the Office button > Print > Print Preview to view how the printed invoices will look. Figure 8.50 shows an example of a printed invoice. Close the form when you are finished.

Fig. 8.50 Printed
Sale Invoice.

Invoice

Pipefitters Supply Company
5998 Alcala Park
San Diego, CA 92110

Invoice # 100008	Sold To: Cole & Co.
Date 1/28/2010	720 Conover Court
Sale Order # 100004	Building #4
Amount $825.76	Fargo, ND 58105-2930
	Customer # 10005

Item #	Description	Quantity	Price	List Price	Extension
1035	3.00-inch Copper 4-foot pipe	20	$18.25	$18.25	$365.00
1041	3.00-inch Copper 8-foot pipe	10	$38.59	$38.59	$385.90
1047	3.00-inch Copper Cap fitting	4	$4.19	$4.19	$16.76
1053	3.00-inch Copper Elbow	6	$5.29	$5.29	$31.74
1059	3.00-inch Copper T-connector	4	$6.59	$6.59	$26.36

	Total:	$825.76

Recording Cash Received From Customers

The ultimate objective of the sales/collection process is, of course, to receive customers' payments for the goods or services they have purchased. Firms need to record the amount and date of each incoming customer payment and to which sale the payment applies. In this section, you will learn how to construct a simple cash receipts table that tracks cash receipts by customer and invoice number. You can satisfy many business information needs with the basic customer payment tracking procedure described in this section.

Cash Account Information

The fungible nature of cash makes it a resource that requires many controls. One control we can build into the database is to show the cash account in which a cash receipt is deposited. In the next exercise, you will create a cash account that you will link to the cash receipts. You will then create a Cash Receipt Entry form.

EXERCISE 8.37: CREATE CASH ACCOUNT TABLE

1. Create a new table. Click the Create tab, and click Table Design in the Tables group.
2. Enter the Field Names, Data Types, and Properties for the four attributes of this table in Figure 8.51. AccountID is the Primary Key.
3. Name the table tblCashAccount.
4. Go to Datasheet view and enter the data in Figure 8.51 for Pipefitters' two bank accounts. Close the table.

Fig. 8.51 Field properties and data for *tblCashAccount*.

Field Name	CashAccountID	AccountDescription	BankName	DateAccountEstablished
Data Type	Text	Text	Text	Date/Time
Field Size	3	30	25	
Format				Short Date
Input Mask	000;;_			99/99/0000;;_
Caption	Account #	Description	Bank Name	Date Established
Required	Yes	Yes	Yes	Yes
Allow Zero Length	No	No	No	n/a
Indexed	Yes (No Duplicates)	No	No	No

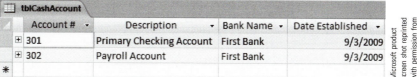

tblCashAccount				
Account #	Description	Bank Name	Date Established	
301	Primary Checking Account	First Bank	9/3/2009	
302	Payroll Account	First Bank	9/3/2009	

The Cash Receipt Table

The Cash Receipt table includes information about payments received from customers. The customer check number is not a good primary key because you cannot be certain that the number is unique. Most firms use a *remittance advice number* as the primary key for their Cash Receipt tables. You have probably seen remittance advices but might not have known what they were called. For example, the portion of a credit card statement that you tear off and return with your payment is a remittance advice. Businesses usually prepare remittance advices for, or assign remittance advice numbers to, every check they receive.

In addition to the remittance advice number primary key, you will want to include fields for the date that the check was received, the customer check number, the amount of the check, the invoice number to which it relates, the customer number, the bank account into which it was deposited, and the employee number of the employee who received the check. Figure 8.5 shows the foreign keys that link the cash receipt event to the related event (*tblSale*), resource (*tblCashAccount*), and agents (*tblEmployee* and *tblCustomer*). In this exercise you will build a Cash Receipts table for Pipefitters.

EXERCISE 8.38: BUILDING A CASH RECEIPT TABLE

1. Create a new table. Click the Create tab, and click Table Design in the Tables group.
2. Enter the Field Names, Data Types, and Properties for the first four fields of this table in Figure 8.52. RemittanceAdviceID is the Primary Key.

3. Name the table tblCashReceipt.
4. Enter the foreign keys. Since foreign keys are primary keys from other tables, the data types, input masks, and other properties have already been entered in other tables. The information for the foreign keys is summarized in the second table in Figure 8.52. Notice that the Indexed property for the foreign keys is set to Yes (Duplicates OK) because the same foreign key value may occur many times in this table.
5. Put the Fields in following order: RemittanceAdviceID, CashAccountID, CustomerID, EmployeeID, InvoiceID, CashReceiptAmount, CustomerCheckNum, CashReceiptDate

Fig. 8.52 Field Properties for *tblCashReceipt.*

Field Name	RemittanceAdviceID	CashReceiptDate	CashReceiptAmount	CustomerCheckNum
Data Type	Text	Date/Time	Currency	Text
Field Size (or Decimal Places)	6		2	15
Format		Short Date		
Input Mask	000000;;_	99/99/0000;;_		
Caption	RA #	Cash Receipt Date	Amount Received	Customer Check #
Default Value		Date ()		
Required	Yes	Yes	Yes	Yes
Allow Zero Length	No			No
Indexed	Yes (No Duplicates)	No	No	No

Primary Key and Attributes

Field Name	InvoiceID	CashAccountID	CustomerID	EmployeeID
Data Type	Text	Text	Text	Text
Field Size (or Decimal Places)	6	3	5	3
Format				
Input Mask	000000;;_	000;;_	00000;;_	000;;_
Caption	Invoice #	Cash Account #	Customer #	Employee #
Default Value				
Required	Yes	Yes	Yes	Yes
Allow Zero Length	No	No	No	No
Indexed	Yes (Duplicates OK)	Yes (Duplicates OK)	Yes (Duplicates OK)	Yes (Duplicates OK)

Foreign Keys

Creating Relationships with the Cash Receipt Table

In Exercise 8.39 you will add relationships with *tblCashReceipt* necessary to build the Cash Receipt Entry form. Before you create these relationships, copy the data from tblCashReceipt in the *Ch08.accdb* database into tblCashReceipt in your database.

EXERCISE 8.39: CREATING RELATIONSHIPS RELATED TO THE CASH RECEIPT EVENT

1. Close all open tables and forms.
2. In the Database Tools tab, click Relationships in the Show/Hide group. Your Relationships window should look like how you left it at the end of Exercise 8.32 (see Figure 8.45).

3. Minimize the Navigation Pane by clicking the << at the top-right corner of the pane.
4. Click Show Table in the Relationships group (on the Design tab), double-click tblCashAccount and tblCashReceipt. Then click Close.
5. Create your links the same way you did in Exercise 8.32. Drag from the primary key to the matching foreign key or from the primary key to the matching part of a composite primary key.
6. When the Edit Relationships dialog box appears make sure that the correct attributes appear in the tables you dragged from and to. The relationship type at the bottom of the dialog box should always be One-to-Many. Check Enforce Referential Integrity and Cascade Update Related Fields. Finally, click Create in the dialog box.
7. Resize and move the newly added tables to look like the Relationship window in Figure 8.53. You may also refer back to Figure 8.5, which lists the primary and foreign keys in each table.
8. Close the Relationships window and click the Yes button in the dialog box to save your changes, then click >> on the Navigation Pane to restore it.

Fig. 8.53 Sales/ collection Relationships window with Cash Receipt event included.

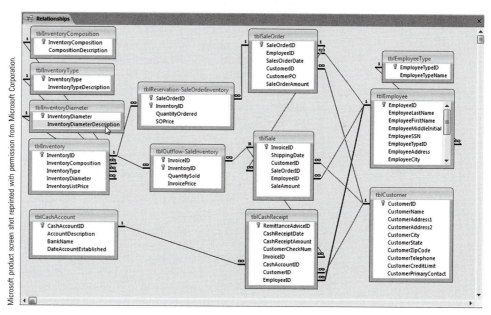

Microsoft product screen shot reprinted with permission from Microsoft Corporation.

The Cash Receipt Entry Form

When one of Pipefitters' accountants receives a customer's check, he or she should be able to compare the amount received for a particular invoice to the balance due on that sale. If the amount collected is less than the sale amount, the accountant should check to see if this customer is allowed to make partial payments. If the amount received is greater than the balance due, the accountant needs to find out why there is a difference. Additionally, it is helpful to see the customer's payment history for the invoice related to the current cash receipt. Therefore, you will build a query for your form that computes the current balance due by invoice. The balance due will be used in the Cash Receipt Entry form as a control. Because the balance due will not update until the Balance Due query is run again by closing and opening the form, you will add a button on the form to update the balance due.

EXERCISE 8.40: BUILDING A QUERY TO COMPUTE OUTSTANDING INVOICE BALANCES—SUM OF PRIOR CASH RECEIPTS

In this exercise you will build the first of two queries. The first query uses an *aggregate function* to sum the cash received for each invoice. The second query (Exercise 8.41) uses a *horizontal computation* to subtract the sum of the cash received from the invoice amount to arrive at the balance due. Two queries are needed because the aggregate function combines (sums in this case) many values in a single column (many records for a single field), which must be done before the horizontal computation uses these aggregated amounts to perform a computation with many fields across the same row. Therefore, a general database rule is to perform aggregate functions and horizontal computations in separate queries.

1. Click the Create tab and click Query Design in the Other group. Double-click tblCashReceipt in the Show Table dialog box. Close the dialog box.
2. Double-click InvoiceID and CashReceiptAmount, respectively from the tblCash-Receipt Field Roster.
3. Click Totals (the summation sign) in the Show/Hide group. Since you want the sum of the amounts received for each sale, leave the InvoiceID Total cell set to Group By. Change the Total cell for CashReceiptAmount to Sum.
4. Open the Property Sheet. Click Property Sheet in the Show/Hide group. Type Prior Receipts as the caption for the sum of cash receipts. Close the Property Sheet.
5. Save the query as qrySumOfCashReceiptsByInvoice.
6. Run the query. You should have 79 invoices with prior cash receipts. Close the query.

EXERCISE 8.41: BUILDING A QUERY TO COMPUTE OUTSTANDING INVOICE BALANCES—COMPUTE BALANCE DUE

1. Click the Create tab, and click Query Design in the Other group. Double-click tblSale in the Show Table dialog box, click the Queries tab, and then double-click qrySumOfCashReceiptsByInvoice. Close the dialog box.
2. Double-click the link between tblSale and qrySumOfCashReceiptsByInvoice. Click the second Radio Button in the Join Properties dialog box (see Figure 8.54). Click OK to close it. Notice the arrow pointing from the left table to the right table. This is known as a **left outer join**. We will discuss its significance shortly.
3. Double-click InvoiceID, SaleAmount, and CustomerID, respectively, from *tblSale* in the Table Pane; double-click SumOfCashReceiptAmount in *qrySumOfCashReceiptsByInvoice*.
4. Save your query as qryBalanceDueFromCustomer.
5. Click the first available field on the Criteria Pane. Click Builder in the Query Setup group. Enter BalanceDue: [SaleAmount]-Nz([SumOfCashReceiptAmount],0). In Step 2, you created an outer join so that all invoices from *tblSale* will be selected even if there is not a corresponding cash receipt, which regularly occurs for recent sales because customers have not yet made a payment. **Nz** is the **Null-to-zero** function. If there is not a corresponding cash receipt for a sale, the value for SumOfCashReceiptAmount will be **null** which prevents Access from computing the difference. The Nz function replaces the null value with the second argument in the function, which in this case is 0 so that the computation will have a valid result.

6. Open the Property Sheet. Click Property Sheet in the Show/Hide group. Type Balance Due as the Caption for your newly created field, BalanceDue.
7. Double-click ShippingDate from *tblSale* in the Table Pane. Change its Caption on the Property Sheet to Invoice Date.
8. Save your query. Run your query. Notice that there are 90 invoices—the first 79 with a zero balance (the same 79 invoices from *qrySumOfCashReceiptsByInvoice*) and the last 11 unpaid (no cash receipts associated with them). Close the query.

Fig. 8.54 Join
Properties dialog box.

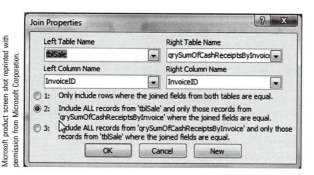

EXERCISE 8.42: CREATE THE CASH RECEIPT ENTRY FORM

The Cash Receipt Entry form uses the form/subform design. The top portion of the Cash Receipt Entry form will contain invoice-related data from *qryBalanceDueFromCustomer*. None of these fields will be editable because they are for reference only. The main form will also show customer information (i.e., name and address), which you will have to add after running Form Wizard because Form Wizard would add the customer information to the subform, which contains all of the fields from *tblCashReceipt*. The CustomerID and InvoiceID fields will be linked to the main form that will automatically populate these fields, ensuring that cash receipts are recorded for the correct customer and invoice. Using data from the sale table serves as a control because cash receipts can only be recorded for sales that exist in *tblSale*.

1. Click More Forms in the Forms group of the Create tab. Click Form Wizard.
2. Click Query: qryBalanceDueFromCustomer in the Tables/Queries combo box. Click >> to move all Available Fields into the Selected Fields list.
3. Click the Tables/Queries combo box arrow, and click Table: tblCashReceipt from the list. Click >> to move all Available Fields into the Selected Fields list.
4. Click Next. Click by qryBalanceDueFromCustomer in the *How do you want to view your data?* list box (if it is not already selected) to ensure the proper grouping.
5. Click Next. Click the Datasheet radio button in the *What layout would you like for your subform?* dialog box.
6. Click Next. Click the Office style if it is not already selected, and click Next.
7. Double-click the Form text box, type frmCashReceipt to name the form, tab to the Subform: text box and type fsubCashReceipt. Click the Finish button. Close the form.

EXERCISE 8.43: COMPLETING THE CASH RECEIPT ENTRY FORM

Make changes to the subform.

1. Open fsubCashReceipt in Design view. Change the CashReceiptAmount label to Amount, change the CashReceiptDate to Date, change the CashAccountID label to Cash Acct. #.

2. The values of CustomerID and InvoiceID will be set by the link between the subform and form. Make them unavailable as you did in Exercise 8.26.

3. Streamline the look of the subform. Select Form from the Property Sheet combo box. On the Format tab, change the Navigation Buttons property to No, and change the Scroll Bars property to Neither. Save your changes and close the subform.

4. Adjust the column widths of the subform datasheet. Change to Datasheet view. Click the Datasheet Selector (see Figure 8.55), click the More menu in the Records group on the Home ribbon, click Column Width, and click the Best Fit button to make both the column headers and data visible.

Add customer information to the form.

5. Open frmCashReceipt in Design view, open the Property Sheet. Select Form from the Property Sheet combo box, click the Data tab. Click the Query Builder button for the Record Source property. Click Show Table in the Query Setup group, add qryCustomerInfo to the Table Pane. Link qryCustomerInfo to tblSale by clicking and dragging CustomerID from qryCustomerInfo to tblSale.

6. Add the following fields to the Criteria Pane: CustomerName, CustomerAddress1, CustomerAddress2, CityStateZip, CustomerTelephone, and CustomerPrimaryContact. Close and save your changes to the query. The warning dialog box states, "The RecordSource or RowSource property contained the name of a query when you invoked the Query Builder, so the original query was modified." Open qryBalanceDueFromCustomer in Datasheet view. Notice that the query has been modified for the additional fields you just added. Since this change has no effect on computing BalanceDue, it is not a problem.

7. Copy the customer controls from frmSale. Open frmSale in Design view. Select the controls for the fields you just added to the form's Record Source query, and the Primary Contact label by pressing and holding the Shift key and clicking on the controls. Press Ctrl+C, return to frmCashReceipt, move the subform down an inch, click the Detail section, and then press Ctrl+V, left justify the Primary Contact label. Close frmSale.

8. Make all of the non-customer information controls in the form unavailable as you did in Exercise 8.26. If you select all six controls you can change the properties to all of the controls at the same time.

9. Link CustomerID from the subform to the form. Select fsubCashReceipt from the Property Sheet combo box, click the Data tab. Click the Builder button next to the Link Master Fields Property box to open the Subform Field Linker. Add CustomerID to the Master Fields column and to the same row of the Child Fields column (see Figure 8.56). Click OK.

10. Edit the form to look like the one in Figure 8.56. Ignore the command button on the form. You will add that in the next exercise.

11. Save the form. View your form in Form view. Notice that the correct Customer # and Invoice # populate the new Remittance Advice rows as you advance to succeeding records.

12. Open qryBalanceDueFromCustomer in Datasheet view. Notice that the customer information fields you added to the query behind form qryBalanceDueFromCustomer are now part of this query. This means that any changes you make to a query will affect forms and other database objects that use that query.

Fig. 8.55 *fsubCash-Receipt* in Datasheet view.

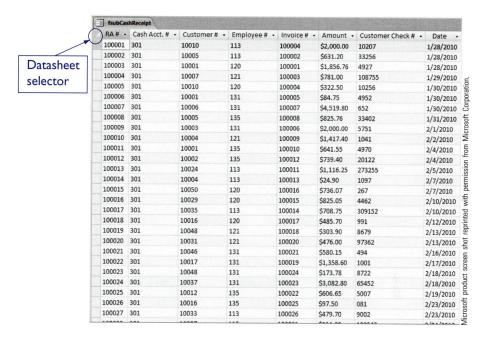

Fig. 8.56 Cash Receipt Entry form in Design view with Subform Field Linker open.

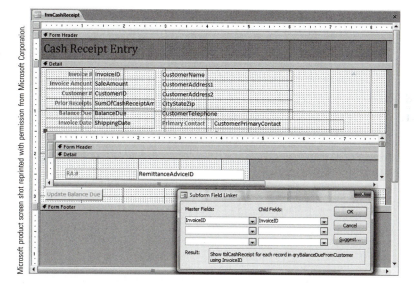

EXERCISE 8.44: USING A MACRO TO UPDATE THE BALANCE DUE IN THE CASH RECEIPT ENTRY FORM

Create the update macro.

1. From the Create tab click the Macro menu in the Other group, click Macro. In the first row of the Action column, select or type Requery, which will run the query of the object currently active—*frmCashReceipt*. Beware, this command will also return you to the first record of the form. Returning to the current record requires coding that is beyond the scope of this textbook.

2. Close the macro and name it mcrRerunQuery. Notice that we use **_mcr_** to denote macros.
3. Open frmCashReceipt in Design view. On the Design ribbon click Button in the Controls group. Move your cursor to the button location shown in Figure 8.56 and double-click to start the Command Button Wizard.
4. Click Miscellaneous in the Categories list, click Run Macro in the Actions list, and click Next.
5. Since you only have one macro to choose from, click Next. In the next screen click the Text Radio button and type Update Balance Due in the text box. Click Next.
6. Name your button cmdUpdateBalanceDue. Resize and move the button if necessary.
7. Save and close the form.
8. Double-click frmCashReceipt in the Navigation Pane.
9. Save and close the form.

TRY IT

Test the Update Balance Due button in *frmCashReceipt*. Double-click *frmCash-Receipt* in the Navigation Pane. Go to the last record. The Invoice Amount is $786.35 and there are no Prior Payments so the Balance Due is $786.35. Add a test record: RA # 999999, Cash Acct. # 301, Employee # 120, Amount $500, Customer Check # 7777, and Date 9/9/2010. Click the *Update Balance Due* button. Notice that the form returns to the first record. Go to the last record. Prior Payments is now $500.00 and Balance Due has been updated to its current balance of $286.35. Delete RA # 999999 by clicking on the *Record selector* and pressing the *Delete* key.

Deriving Financial Statement Information

You have now successfully created a working sales/collection business process in Access that allows you to enter all the information into the system related to sale orders, shipments (sales), and cash receipts. Now it is time to harness the power of your relational database to produce financial statement information. The two main financial statement items that only depend on the activities in the sales/collection process are Sales and Accounts Receivable.

We will use the following naming conventions for financial statement queries, which often require multiple queries to obtain the final result: *qryQueryGroupName#-QueryName*. For example, the first query for Accounts Receivable is to sum the Sales, so we will name it *qryAccRec1-SumOfCR*. This will make it easy for you to follow the steps in the textbook and also to review your work in your database.

Sales

Income statements show the revenues and expenses for a period of time. As such, income statement items, such as Sales, are reported for the period between the beginning of the period and the end of the period. Therefore, your query to derive Sales will contain a date constraint. Moreover, you will use parameters for the beginning date and ending date to allow users to change the time period without editing the query.

EXERCISE 8.45: CREATING A SALES QUERY

1. Click the Create tab and click Query Design in the Other group.
2. Double-click tblSale in the Show Table dialog box, Close the dialog box.
3. Double-click SaleAmount and ShippingDate, respectively from the tblSale Field Roster.
4. Click Totals in the Show/Hide group. Change the Total cell for SaleAmount to Sum.
5. Open the Property Sheet. Click Property Sheet in the Show/Hide group. Type Sales as the caption for the sum of sales. Close the Property Sheet.
6. Change the Total cell for ShippingDate to Where. In the Criteria cell type between [Beginning of Period Date] and [End of Period Date]. Sales will be summed between (and including) the dates specified by the user.
7. Save the query as qrySales1-Sales.
8. Check your query by running it. Click Run in the Results group. Use 2/1/2010 for the beginning of the period date and 2/28/2010 for the end of period date. Total sales for the period should be $44,861.86.

Accounts Receivable

Unlike Sales, there is no Accounts Receivable field in our database. Accounts Receivable is merely a timing difference between Sale events and the related Cash Receipt events. Therefore, Accounts Receivable can be determined by computing the sum of the sales and subtracting the sum of the cash receipts related to those sales. Since a horizontal computation (e.g., sum of sales—sum of cash receipts) cannot use the result of an aggregate function within the same query (e.g., sum of sales, sum of cash receipts), the computation of Accounts Receivable requires three queries: summing sales, summing cash receipts related to sales, and subtracting the total cash receipts from total sales.

What kind of date constraints do you need to compute balance sheet items like Accounts Receivable? Remember that a balance sheet reports the account balances of assets, liabilities, and equities at a specified point in time. You have to sum the sales and related cash receipts from the company's inception through the balance sheet date. Therefore, balance sheet queries only have an ending date constraint.

EXERCISE 8.46: USING QUERIES TO COMPUTE ACCOUNTS RECEIVABLE—SUM OF SALES AND SUM OF CASH RECEIPTS RELATED TO SALES

Create the first query by copying *qrySales* and modifying its date criteria.

1. Click qrySales1-Sales in the Navigation Pane, press Ctrl+C, press Ctrl+V, type qryAccRec1-SumOfSales in the Paste As dialog box to name the cloned query, and click OK.
2. Open qryAccRec1-SumOfSales in Design view. In the Criteria cell of ShippingDate replace the current expression with <=[End of Period Date].
3. Save your changes. Check your query. Click Run in the Results group. Use 2/28/2010 for the end of period date, which is the balance sheet date. Total sales for the date ended should be $67,301.90.Close the query.

Create the second query to sum cash receipts related to sales. Although you will not use any fields from *tblSale*, the ***inner join*** (the default join which includes rows where the joined fields from both tables are equal) between *tblSale* and *tblCashReceipt* ensures that only cash receipts related to sales are summed. Although it seems superfluous now to restrict cash receipts to those related to sales since the only cash receipts Pipefitters has in this chapter are from sales, it is necessary when you work with a complete accounting system that contains cash receipts from other events. You will work with a complete AIS in Chapter 12.

1. Click the Create tab and click Query Design in the Other group. Double-click tblSale and tblCashReceipt in the Show Table dialog box, Close the dialog box.
2. Double-click CashReceiptAmount and CashReceiptDate, respectively from the tblCashReceipt Field Roster.
3. Click Totals in the Show/Hide group.
4. Change the Total cell for CashReceiptAmount to Sum.
5. Open the Property Sheet. Click Property Sheet in the Show/Hide group. Type Cash Receipts as the caption for the sum of cash receipts. Close the Property Sheet.
6. Change the Total cell for CashReceiptDate to Where. In the Criteria cell type <= [End of Period Date].
7. Save the query as qryAccRec2-SumOfCR.
8. Check your query. Click Run in the Results group. Use 2/28/2010 for balance sheet date. Total cash receipts related to sales for the date ended should be $41,201.05.

EXERCISE 8.47: USING QUERIES TO COMPUTE ACCOUNTS RECEIVABLE

The third and final query uses the results of the first two queries to compute Accounts Receivable. It is similar to the second query in Exercise 8.41, except you will not use an outer join.

1. Click the Create tab and click Query Design in the Other group. In the Show Table dialog box click the Queries tab, double-click qryAccRec1-SumOfSales, and qryAccRec2-SumOfCR. Close the dialog box. The fields in these two queries are independent of one another and do not need to be joined. If they did need to be joined you would need to add a common field in each query to provide a way to join them.
2. Double-click SumOfSaleAmount from qryAccRec1-SumOfSales and SumOfCash-ReceiptAmount from qryAccRec2-SumOfCR.
3. Save your query as qryAccRec3-AccountsReceivable.
4. Click the first available field on the Criteria Pane. Click Builder in the Query Setup group. Enter AccountsReceivable: [SumOfSaleAmount]-Nz([SumOfCashReceiptAmount],0). If there are no cash receipts for the period covered by your query, the Nz function replaces the null value with the second argument in the function, 0, so that the computation will have a valid result.
5. Open the Property Sheet. Click Property Sheet in the Show/Hide group. Type Accounts Receivable as the Caption for your newly created field, AccountsReceivable.
6. Save your query.
7. Test the Nz function by running the query and using 1/27/2010 as the balance sheet date. Your result should be $14,615.31 (see Figure 8.57).
8. Now rerun your query using 2/28/2010 as the balance sheet date. Your result should be $26,100.85. Notice that sales and cash receipts in Figure 8.57 match the results from the individual queries.

Fig. 8.57
qryAccRec3-AccountsReceivable
dynasets.

Dynaset for 1/27/2010

Dynaset for 2/28/2010

Why did the End of Period Date dialog box appear in *qryAccRec3-AccountsReceivable*? Even though you did not use a date parameter in this query you used the results from queries that did use date parameters. If that is so, then why did only one End of Period Date dialog box appear? Since you used the exact same parameter name in both queries you only have one parameter, so the date you enter is used by both queries. This becomes even more critical when you create a complete income statement and balance sheet in Chapter 12 to ensure that all financial statement items are computed using the same dates.

Deriving Other Information Useful for Decision Making

Database accounting information systems include much information that is useful to non-accountants. Traditional accounting records contained only the date and dollar amount of each sale and cash receipt. A database accounting system contains much more information about each sale and cash receipt. The sales, sale order, inventory, and customer tables we describe in this chapter can be combined in many ways to provide useful information to the marketing and strategic management functions.

Accounts Receivable by Customer

In addition to computing Accounts Receivable in the aggregate for financial reporting purposes, firms also need to track Accounts Receivable by customer. This can be accomplished by making modifications to your existing Accounts Receivable queries.

EXERCISE 8.48: MODIFYING ACCOUNTS RECEIVABLE QUERIES TO GENERATE ACCOUNTS RECEIVABLE FOR INDIVIDUAL CUSTOMERS—PART 1

Create the first query by copying and modifying *qryAccRec1-SumOfSales*.

1. Click qryAccRec1-SumOfSales in the Navigation Pane, press Ctrl+C, press Ctrl+V, type qryARByCustomer1-SumOfSales in the Paste As dialog box to name the cloned query, and click OK.
2. Open qryARByCustomer1-SumOfSales in Design view. Click and drag CustomerID from the tblSale Field Roster into the first column of the Criteria Pane. You are using CustomerID to group sales by customer.
3. Save your changes. Check your query. Click Run in the Results group. Use 2/28/2010 for the balance sheet date. The totals are now listed by customer. You should have a total of 38 customers in your result. Close the query.

Create the second query by copying and modifying *qryAccRec2-SumOfCR*.

4. Click qryAccRec2-SumOfCR in the Navigation Pane, press Ctrl+C, press Ctrl+V, type qryARByCustomer2-SumOfCR in the Paste As dialog box to name the cloned query, and click OK.
5. Open qryARByCustomer2-SumOfCR in Design view. Click and drag CustomerID from the tblCashReceipt Field Roster into the first column of the Criteria Pane.
6. Save your changes. Check your query. Click Run in the Results group. Use 2/28/2010 for the balance sheet date. The totals are now listed by customer. You should have a total of 28 customers in your result. Close the query.

EXERCISE 8.49: MODIFYING ACCOUNTS RECEIVABLE QUERIES TO GENERATE ACCOUNTS RECEIVABLE FOR INDIVIDUAL CUSTOMERS—PART 2

Create the third and final query, which will be similar to *qryAccRec3-AccountsReceivable*. Since some customers in the database have no sales or cash receipts, and other customers have sales and no cash receipts, you will need outer joins like you did in Exercise 8.41.

1. Click the Create tab and click Query Design in the Other group. In the Show Table dialog box click the Queries tab, double-click qryCustomerInfo, qryARByCustomer1-SumOfSales, and qryARByCustomer2-SumOfCR. Close the dialog box.
2. Double-click the following fields: CustomerID and CustomerName from the qryCustomerInfo Field Roster, SumOfSaleAmount from the qryAccRec1-SumOfSales Field Roster, and SumOfCashReceiptAmount from the qryAccRec2-SumOfCR Field Roster.
3. Save your query as qryARByCustomer3-AccountsReceivable.
4. Click the first available field on the Criteria Pane. Click Builder in the Query Setup group. Enter AccountsReceivable: Nz([SumOfSaleAmount],0)-Nz([SumOfCashReceiptAmount],0). You need to add the Nz function to SumOfSaleAmount because you may have customers in the database that do not have any sales associated with them.
5. Open the Property Sheet. Click Property Sheet in the Show/Hide group. Type Accounts Receivable as the Caption for your newly created field, AccountsReceivable.
6. Save your query.
7. Click and drag CustomerID from the qryCustomerInfo Field Roster to CustomerID in the qryARByCustomer1-SumOfSales Field Roster to create a link between the two queries. Double-click the link to bring up the Join Properties dialog box. Select Radio Button 2 because you want all customers to appear in the results even if Pipefitters did not sell them anything. Click OK to close the dialog box. Your link should now be an arrow pointing to *qryCustomerInfo* to *qryARByCustomer1-SumOfSales*.
8. Repeat the previous step by clicking and dragging CustomerID from qryARByCustomer1-SumOfSales to qryARByCustomer2-SumOfCR. Your query in Design view should now look similar to Figure 8.58.
9. Save your changes. Check your query. Click Run in the Results group. Use 2/28/2010 for the balance sheet date. The dynaset is shown in Figure 8.59. Notice that there are now 52 customers listed because all customers in the database are included, even customers who did not purchase anything from Pipefitters on or before 2/28/2010. Close the query.

Fig. 8.58
qryARByCustomer3-AccountsReceivable in Design view.

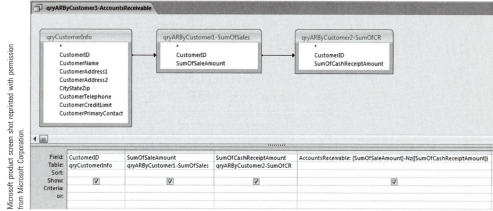

Fig. 8.59 Dynaset for *qryARBy Customer3-AccountsReceivable* on 2/28/2010.

Customer #	Name	Sales	Cash Receipts	Accounts Receivable
10001	Dunn Plumbing	$3,446.91	$3,446.91	$0.00
10002	Ace Construction Co.	$1,182.40	$739.40	$443.00
10003	Bryant Boiler Repair	$5,336.95	$4,419.30	$917.65
10004	Bucknell Air Conditioning	$2,668.55	$1,442.30	$1,226.25
10005	Cole & Co.	$1,684.81	$1,684.81	$0.00
10006	Burch Builders' Supply	$5,457.85	$4,519.80	$938.05
10007	Lin Plumbing Repair, Inc.	$1,115.80	$1,115.80	$0.00
10008	Mattison Maintenance Co.	$1,074.50		$1,074.50
10009	Central Plumbing Supply	$1,540.50	$1,540.50	$0.00
10010	Entero Construction	$2,322.50	$2,322.50	$0.00
10011	Nalco Plumbing	$810.45		$810.45
10012	Cotts Mechanical	$1,149.00	$606.65	$542.35
10013	Helix Electric	$496.50	$496.50	$0.00
10014	Cadigan Construction			
10015	Stimpson Construction			
10016	S&G Mechanical	$1,056.95	$583.20	$473.75
10017	Tukes Plumbing	$1,701.45	$1,358.60	$342.85
10018	Brown Engineering			
10019	Campbell Heating and Air	$1,487.10		$1,487.10
10020	Blackburn & Co.			
10021	Southshore Inc.	$2,458.25	$1,792.45	$665.80
10022	Totherow Constuction	$1,504.85	$362.25	$1,142.60
10023	Aho Electrical Services			
10024	Thompson Plumbing Repairs	$3,200.70	$1,116.25	$2,084.45
10025	R & J Builders			
10026	Knohaulff Maintenance	$1,269.50		$1,269.50

Record: 1 of 52   No Filter   Search

TRY IT

Run *qryARByCustomer3-AccountsReceivable* using 2/28/2010 as the end-of-period date. The query is currently sorted by Customer #. Try sorting the results based on different criteria. What other ways could you sort the query results that would be useful for Pipefitters' management team?

Open Sale Orders

Sale order information is vital to effectively managing a business. For example, comparing sale orders to inventory on hand helps firms know when to order new merchandise. Also, customer relations personnel, such as salespeople, should be able to quickly access the status of sale orders so they can respond to customer inquiries about their orders. In the following exercise, you will create a set of three queries to produce a list of items that customers have ordered but have not yet received.

EXERCISE 8.50: BUILDING A SET OF QUERIES TO PRODUCE A LIST OF OPEN SALE ORDER ITEMS—PART 1

Create the first query to produce a list of items ordered on or before a specific date.

1. Click the Create tab and click Query Design in the Other group.
2. Double-click tblSaleOrder and tblReservation-SaleOrderInventory in the Show Table dialog box. Close the dialog box.
3. Add attributes to the Criteria Pane. Double-click SaleOrderID from tblSaleOrder. Double-click InventoryID and QuantityOrdered, respectively, from tblReservation-SaleOrderInventory. Double-click SaleOrderDate from tblSaleOrder.
4. Enter <=[End of Period Date] in the Criteria cell for SaleOrderDate.
5. Click Property Sheet in the Show/Hide group. Type Date Ordered in the Caption property.
6. Click QuantityOrdered in the Criteria Pane and set the Caption property to Quantity Ordered.
7. Save your query as qryOpenSaleOrders1-ItemsOrdered.
8. Check your query. Click Run in the Results group. Use 2/28/2010 for the end of period date. You should see a list of 217 items ordered on or before 2/28/2010. Close the query.

EXERCISE 8.51: BUILDING A SET OF QUERIES TO PRODUCE A LIST OF OPEN SALE ORDER ITEMS—PART 2

Create the second query by copying and modifying *qryOpenSaleOrders1-ItemsOrdered*.

1. Click qryOpenSaleOrders1-ItemsOrdered in the Navigation Pane, press Ctrl+C, press Ctrl+V, type qryOpenSaleOrders2-ItemsShipped in the Paste As dialog box to name the cloned query, and click OK.
2. Open qryOpenSaleOrders2-ItemsShipped in Design view.
3. Click Show Table in the Query Setup group.
4. Double-click tblSale and tblOutflow-SaleInventory in the Show Table dialog box. Close the dialog box.
5. Change the Table property for SaleOrderID and SaleOrderDate to tblSale.
6. Change the Table property for InventoryID and QuantityOrdered to tblOutflow-SaleInventory.
7. Change the QuantityOrdered field to QuantitySold. Open the Property Sheet and change the Caption to Quantity Sold.
8. Change the SaleOrderDate field to ShippingDate and set the Caption to Shipping Date.
9. Click Totals in the Show/Hide group. Change the Total cell for QuantitySold to Sum so that the same inventory item from different shipments on the same order will be combined. Leave the Total property for ShippingDate set to Group By to display the shipping date in the query results.
10. Delete tblSaleOrder and tblReservation-SaleOrderInventory from the Table Pane in your query. Save your changes.
11. Check your query. Click Run in the Results group. Use 2/28/2010 for the end of period date. You should see a list of 181 items ordered on or before 2/28/2010. Close the query.

EXERCISE 8.52: BUILDING A SET OF QUERIES TO PRODUCE A LIST OF OPEN SALE ORDER ITEMS—PART 3

The third query will compute the unfilled quantity of each item ordered by subtracting QuantityShipped from QuantityOrdered. Additionally, you will use the Nz function and outer joins.

1. Click the Create tab and click Query Design in the Other group. In the Show Table dialog box click the Queries tab, double-click qryOpenSaleOrders1-ItemsOrdered, and qryOpenSaleOrders2-ItemsShipped. Close the dialog box.
2. Create two outer joins, one for SaleOrderID and the other one for InventoryID. Drag each attribute from qryOpenSaleOrders1-ItemsOrdered to qryOpenSaleOrders2-ItemsShipped. Click Radio Button 2 in the Join Properties dialog box for both links. The resulting join arrow should point toward *qryOpenSaleOrders2-ItemsShipped*.
3. Double-click all of the Fields from the qryOpenSaleOrders1-ItemsOrdered Field Roster to add them to the Criteria Pane.
4. Drag SumOfQuantitySold from the qryOpenSaleOrders2-ItemsShipped Field Roster to the Criteria Pane next to SumOfQuantityOrdred. Double-click ShippingDate to move it next to SaleOrderDate on the Criteria Pane.
5. Save your query as qryOpenSaleOrders3-OpenItems.
6. Click the first available Field on the Criteria Pane. Click Builder in the Query Setup group. Enter UnfilledQuantity: [QuantityOrdered]-Nz([SumOfQuantitySold],0).
7. Open the Property Sheet. Click Property Sheet in the Show/Hide group. Type Unfilled Quantity as the Caption for your newly created field, UnfilledQuantity.
8. Save your query.
9. Check your query. Click Run in the Results group. Use 2/28/2010 for the end-of-period date. You should see a list of 217 items ordered on or before 2/28/2010. Figure 8.60 shows the status of items ordered between 2/13/2010 and 2/19/2010. Notice that the unfilled quantity is 0 for items that have shipped.
10. Return to Design view. Type >0 as the Criteria for UnfilledQuantity. Rerun your query using 2/28/2010 again. Now, only the 36 open items are displayed. Save and close the query.

Fig. 8.60 *qryOpen-SaleOrders3-OpenItems* dynaset with filled items included.

Sale Order #	Item #	Quantity Ordered	Quantity Shipped	Unfilled Quantity	Date Ordered	Shipping Date
100052	1002	35	35	0	2/13/2010	2/23/2010
100052	1026	30	30	0	2/13/2010	2/23/2010
100053	1001	45	45	0	2/14/2010	2/23/2010
100053	1019	25	25	0	2/14/2010	2/23/2010
100053	1025	15	15	0	2/14/2010	2/23/2010
100054	1031	35		35	2/14/2010	
100054	1037	15		15	2/14/2010	
100054	1055	20		20	2/14/2010	
100055	1035	20	20	0	2/16/2010	2/25/2010
100055	1047	15	15	0	2/16/2010	2/25/2010
100056	1038	20	20	0	2/16/2010	2/25/2010
100056	1056	15	15	0	2/16/2010	2/25/2010
100057	1036	5	5	0	2/16/2010	2/25/2010
100057	1042	5	5	0	2/16/2010	2/25/2010
100057	1054	5	5	0	2/16/2010	2/25/2010
100058	1034	25	25	0	2/17/2010	2/25/2010
100058	1058	40	40	0	2/17/2010	2/25/2010
100059	1001	15	15	0	2/18/2010	2/28/2010
100059	1019	20	20	0	2/18/2010	2/28/2010
100059	1025	10	10	0	2/18/2010	2/28/2010
100060	1002	30	30	0	2/18/2010	2/26/2010
100060	1003	10	10	0	2/18/2010	2/26/2010
100060	1027	30		30	2/18/2010	
100061	1010	15	15	0	2/19/2010	2/28/2010
100061	1022	20	20	0	2/19/2010	2/28/2010
100062	1004	12	12	0	2/19/2010	2/28/2010
100062	1028	8	8	0	2/19/2010	2/28/2010
100063	1007	20		20	2/19/2010	
100063	1013	10		10	2/19/2010	
100063	1025	15		15	2/19/2010	

Record: 159 of 217   No Filter   Search

One of the end-of-chapter exercises requires you to compute average days to deliver ordered items. We included the order date and shipping date in the query so you can easily modify *qryOpenSaleOrders3-OpenItems* to complete this exercise.

Summary

This chapter described how to design and implement the sales/collection business process in Access. In the design phase, you identified the duality of economic events, added the sale order event, and identified and linked the resources and agents associated with the events. After that you added primary keys, foreign keys, and relationship tables. You also used the design phase to enforce business rules and add controls.

After designing the database, you implemented it in Access by building the tables and creating relationships between them. You added field-level controls such as input masks, validation rules, and required fields. You learned how to create type/category tables for inventory to make data input easier.

Once the tables and relationships were completed, you learned to create simple and complex queries to use in forms. You used Autoform to create a simple form and Form Wizard to create complex forms, including forms with subforms. You used combo boxes, form and field properties, a make-table query, and a simple macro to add additional controls to your forms.

Finally, you built queries from sales/collection data for external financial statements and for internal use. You learned how to use parameters in queries to produce Sales for an income statement and Accounts Receivable for a balance sheet. Additionally, you created complex queries to produce information for internal use: accounts receivable by customer and open sale order items.

Questions and Problems for Review

Multiple-Choice Questions

1. The sales/collection process includes all of the following except
   a. keeping customer information current.
   b. recording the cost of merchandise purchased.
   c. recording payments received from customers.
   d. summarizing sale information.
2. What event is captured by *tblSale*?
   a. Making sales calls to customers.
   b. Processing sale orders.
   c. Shipping goods to customers.
   d. Collecting cash from customers.
3. The Pipefitters Supply Company database described in this chapter uses Type/Category tables to enforce a business rule instead of using
   a. a Validation Rule property in *tblInventory*.
   b. an Input Mask property in *tblInventory*.
   c. a combo box control on the Purchase Order Data Entry form.
   d. referential integrity on the InventoryDiameter field.
4. The InventoryItemID field in *tblInventory* is a
   a. composite primary key.
   b. foreign key.
   c. primary key.
   d. relationship key.
5. How does the query for the combo box in the Sale Order Entry form limit the employee choices to salespersons only?
   a. The criteria for EmployeeType is set to "30".
   b. The table *tblEmployeeType* is included in the query's Table Pane.
   c. The EmployeeID field uses a parameter as its Criteria.
   d. EmployeeType in *tblEmployee* uses a validation rule.

6. Data entry form text box controls that are for reference only, like the customer's address on the Sale Order Entry form, should have their Locked and Tab Stop properties set as
    a. Locked = Yes, Tab Stop = Yes.
    b. Locked = Yes, Tab Stop = No.
    c. Locked = No, Tab Stop = Yes.
    d. Locked = No, Tab Stop = No.

7. Why does the query to compute balance due from customer by invoice, *qryBalanceDueFromCustomer*, use a left outer-join between *tblSale* and *qrySumOfCashReceiptsByInvoice*?
    a. We need to compute the balance due only for sales that have related cash receipts.
    b. Balance due needs to be computed for all customers, even if there are no sales for that customer.
    c. We need to compute balance due for each cash receipt, even if there is no related sale for a particular cash receipt.
    d. We need to compute the balance due for all sales, even if they do not have related cash receipts.

8. If customers could make partial payments for sales, and customers could also pay for all sales made during a particular month with a single check, the relationship between *tblSale* and *tblCashReceipt* would be represented by
    a. posting the primary key from *tblSale* into *tblCashReceipt*.
    b. enforcing referential integrity between *tblSale* and *tblCashReceipt*.
    c. posting the primary key from *tblCashReceipt* into *tblSale*.
    d. creating a relationship table.

9. Which Field property—validation rule or input mask—disallows data from being entered into a field *before* moving to the next field?
    a. Validation rule only.
    b. Input mask only.
    c. Both validation rule and input mask.
    d. Neither validation rule nor input mask.

10. Which tables would you need to provide a listing of open sale order items?
    a. *tblSaleOrder, tblReservation-SaleOrderInventory, tblSale,* and *tblOutflow-SaleInventory*.
    b. *tblReservation-SaleOrderInventory, tblSale,* and *tblOutflow-SaleInventor*.
    c. *tblCustomer, tblSaleOrder, tblSale,* and *tblInventory*.
    d. *tblCustomer, tblSaleOrder, tblReservation-SaleOrderInventory, tblSale, tblOutflow-SaleInventory,* and *tblInventory*.

Discussion Questions

1. The examples in this chapter assumed that Pipefitters Supply Company was doing business only in the United States. What changes would you make if Pipefitters had many customers from other countries?
2. Service businesses, such as real estate agents, law firms, and accounting firms, do not have inventory. What table would an accounting firm have instead of *tblInventory*?
3. Restaurants do not usually record customers' names and addresses or send out invoices. What tables and forms might you use in the accounting information system for a restaurant's sales/collection process?
4. How would you decide whether to enforce referential integrity for a foreign key link?
5. Discuss the problem with storing an extended price (quantity of item sold multiplied by the actual sales price) in the *tblOutflow-SaleInventory* table. Why could you not simply add a column called ExtendedPrice to the tblInvoiceLine table?

Practice Exercises

Note: Before attempting any of the following practice exercises, save a new copy *Ch08.accdb* from the Companion Web site to use for the Practice Exercises. Then, clear the copied database's Read-only file attribute. Begin the names of all Access objects you create in the Practice Exercises with PE#-. Replace # with the Practice Exercise number.

1. Create a query to compute the average days to deliver ordered items. You will need two queries, because you have to separate the horizontal computation to compute days to ship each item from the aggregate function to compute the average of the result of your horizontal computation. Start your first query by making a copy of *qryOpenSaleORders3-OpenItems* and renaming it PE1-1qryDaysToShipItems. Use it to compute days to ship items. Name the second query to compute the average days to ship items PE1-2qryAvgDaysToShipItems.

2. Change *frmCustomer* so that the CustomerState field will accept only legal state and U.S. territory abbreviations. Name your new form PE2-frmCustomer. Hint: You should consider adding another table to the sales/collection database to accomplish this task.

Note: Practice Exercises 3 and 4 will be used to create a report in Practice Exercise 5.

3. Create a query to sum both the quantity and price of items ordered for each salesperson during any period of time. (Hint: make period of time between two dates.) Show sales by customer with sales by product grouped under each customerEach row; your query should include the salesperson's employee #, item #, sum of quantity ordered, and sum of the sale order price. Name your query PE3-qrySumSalesBySPAndItem.

4. Create a second query that includes the information from *PE3-qrySumSalesBySPAndItem* and includes all salespersons, even if they did not make any sales for the period. (Hint: You can accomplish this with join properties. Also, *qrySalesperson* provides a list of all salespeople.) In this query, salespeople should be identified by name (Lastname, Firstname) instead of employee #. Name your query PE4-qrySumSalesBySPAndItem.

5. Use *PE4-qrySumSalesBySPAndItem* to create a report with the requirements listed below. Use Chapter 6 Exercises 8.22 through 8.30 and the related figures to guide you.
   - Use *PE4-qrySumSalesBySPAndItem* as the report's Record Source.
   - The report title should be Sales by Salesperson and Item # from mm/dd/yyyy to mm/dd/yyyy. Use a text box for each date. If you enter the exact date parameters you used in *PE3-qrySumSalesBySPAndItem*, the dates you enter when you run the report will be used in the query and also appear in your title.
   - Use two grouping levels. Group by EmployeeName and InventoryID.
   - The page number is in the EmployeeName Header.

Problems

Note: Before attempting any of the following Problems, save a new copy *Ch08.accdb* from the Companion Web site to use for the Problems. Then, clear the copied database's Read-only file attribute.

1. Green, Prakash, and Singh, LLP (GPS) is a law firm that has asked for your help in developing a billing and revenue collection database. The three partners, Sidney Green, Prem Prakash, and Rahul Singh, perform several types of legal services for corporations (the firm does not work for unincorporated individuals or partnerships), including general litigation, insurance defense, general corporate, and tax planning. Each partner has a different billing rate. The partners keep track of the time they work on cases by client and by type of services. They record time in six-minute (one-tenth of an hour) intervals. GPS sends bills to clients every Friday for the services rendered during the week ended on that Friday. Most clients pay at the end of each month, but some pay every week, and others run an unpaid balance from month to month and pay what they can when they are able. GPS does not apply cash receipts to specific invoices. List the events, resources, and agents (internal and external) that exist in the GPS sales/collection process. State any assumptions you needed to make.

2. Refer to the GPS case described in Problem 1, and create a diagram similar to that shown in Figure 8.2 for the GPS law firm. The diagram should show the entities you identified in Problem 1 along with the relationships between those entities and their cardinalities.

3. Refer to the GPS case described in Problem 1 and the work you did in Problem 2. Use Access to build the tables and create the relationships you have defined. You may copy the structure and data of *tblCustomer* and *tblCashReceipt* in the *Ch08.accdb* database and paste them in your database to save data entry time and

effort. Use the name *tblClient* instead of *tblCustomer* and change the field names so they begin with Client instead of Customer. For other tables, add only the attributes necessary to complete Problems 4 and 5. Populate the tables with a few sample records you create, and test the tables to make certain that the relationships operate to enforce referential integrity as appropriate.

4. Refer to the work you have done in the preceding three problems. Create data entry forms for the GPS sales/collection process that allow you to enter data into every table without opening the table itself. Use the forms in the *Ch08.accdb* database as guides. You are not required to add elaborate controls. Add combo boxes where appropriate and lock fields that populate automatically.

5. Refer to the work you have done in the preceding four problems. Create reports for the GPS sales database as follows using Practice Exercise 5 and the reports in Chapter 6 as guides:

   a. Create a weekly report that shows services provided by partner and then by client.
   b. Create a weekly report that shows cash receipts by client.
   c. Create a client list that shows the types of legal services that the firm has provided to each client.
   d. Create any additional specific reports your instructor might have assigned.

CHAPTER 9

Acquisition/Payment Process

CHAPTER OBJECTIVES

A company's acquisition/payment activities include placing orders with vendors, receiving merchandise (the purchase event), and paying vendors. Information about these events are recorded for decision making, financial reporting, and maintaining records of the resources involved in these events (merchandise inventory and cash) as well as the agents involved (vendors and employees). In this chapter, you will learn how to use Microsoft Access to design tables, queries, forms, and reports that can help you:

- **Create a model of the acquisition/payment business process.**
- **Create a Microsoft Access database based on the business process model.**
- **Create controls to enforce business rules.**
- **Create and maintain vendor records.**
- **Create and maintain finished goods inventory records.**
- **Record purchase orders.**
- **Record purchase/inventory receipt information.**
- **Record payments to vendors.**
- **Produce information for financial statements.**
- **Produce information for internal purposes.**

Introduction

This chapter describes the acquisition/payment business process of an accounting information system. We illustrate many of these components of this process using example data for the Pipefitters Supply Company. As mentioned in Chapter 7, we will only focus on the merchandising activities of the firm. The *acquisition/payment process* (also referred to as the acquisition process or the purchase process) includes activities related to the purchase of goods or services. Although acquiring employee labor is a type of acquisition, these activities are usually viewed as part of the human resources process because the data related to acquisition and payment for employee labor is very different than other acquisitions. Therefore, we will cover the human resources process in a separate chapter.

In manufacturing and merchandising firms, the main focus of the acquisition/payment process is ordering, receiving, and paying for inventory—raw materials and indirect materials for manufacturers, and merchandise inventory for merchandisers. Since materials acquisition is not a major concern for many service firms, the acquisition/payment process is somewhat less important to them than it is to manufacturing and merchandising firms. All businesses—even service firms—use their acquisition/payment process to acquire goods and services that support all business processes.

The acquisition/payment process described here is for organizations with separate departments. Smaller firms may only formalize parts of this process. The acquisition/payment process begins when a need arises to acquire goods or services. These requests may be for anything from raw materials for manufacturing to supplies for the human resources department. When this process is formalized, a *purchase requisition* is created either electronically or in hard copy. Sometimes, purchase requisitions are automatically generated by the enterprise's information system. In some manufacturing systems, purchase requisitions are automatically generated by the computer when materials inventory falls below a predetermined reorder point. For example, in a *materials requirement planning (MRP) system*, the computer can use the master schedule to generate timely materials requisitions without human intervention. In a *just-in-time (JIT) production control system*, materials requisitions are generated frequently—often daily or weekly. Regardless of how it is generated, a materials requisition is sent to the purchasing department.

Once approved, the purchasing department uses the purchase requisition information to prepare a *purchase order*. In many automated MRP and JIT systems, the computer generates the purchase order directly. To cope with unpredictable demand, purchasers often use daily sales reports, inventory reports, market research, and their intuitions to make inventory purchase decisions.

The purchasing department sends the purchase order information to a vendor. Vendors send back a formal approval of the purchase order. Purchase order information is then sent to the receiving department. Quantity information is often omitted to ensure that materials handlers accurately count the goods received. When shipments of ordered goods arrive, the receiving department completes a receiving report. Various controls are used to help the accounting department ensure that goods received are the goods actually ordered, and that payments to vendors are only for goods actually received.

The accounting department prepares payment authorization (a check is a paper payment authorization) and supporting information (such as the purchase order, receiving report, and vendor invoice) for goods actually received. This information is forwarded to the treasurer for payment. The treasurer makes the payment and clearly indicates on the supporting information that the goods received have been paid for.

We will create the acquisition/payment business process for Pipefitters Supply Company. We will use some of the tables and other objects you created in Chapter 8. Download the *Ch09.accdb* database on the book's companion Web site. It contains all the objects that you will need to follow the illustrations in this chapter as well as to complete the end-of-chapter exercises and problems. Also, download *Ch09.xlsx* from the Companion Web site, as it contains data for the new tables you will create in this chapter.

Pipefitters Supply Company's Acquisition/ Payment Business Process

Pipefitters Supply Company contacts vendors to place purchase orders. Each purchase order can include many inventory items. The purchase order includes the vendor's name and a list of inventory items Pipefitters wishes to purchase. This inventory list includes the quantity of each inventory item and the actual purchase price of each item on the purchase order. The actual purchase price often differs slightly from the item standard cost, which is stored for that item in the Inventory table because Pipefitters purchases inventory from many vendors. Pipefitters sometimes receive sale orders from customers who need the inventory delivered quickly. If the desired merchandise is out of stock, Pipefitters may purchase those items from vendors who charge more, provided the vendors can deliver the merchandise in time to meet its customers' needs.

When a shipment arrives at the receiving dock, a materials handler counts the inventory items and records which items were received and their quantities as an inventory receipt. The inventory receipt record also includes a notation of the purchase order on which the inventory items were ordered. Pipefitters usually purchases goods *FOB destination*. FOB destination means that title changes hands when the goods arrive at the purchaser's premises, and GAAP (Generally Accepted Accounting Principles) states that a purchase is generally recorded when title changes hands.

An accountant pays for inventory received by writing a check to the vendor usually within ten days of receiving the inventory. Although Pipefitters Supply Company usually pays for inventory receipts in full, it usually limits individual payments to $5,000. When it receives greater than $5,000 of merchandise in one shipment, it pays the first $5,000 within ten days of receipt and pays the balance ten days after that. To make our database more manageable, we will assume that Pipefitters does *not* pay for multiple invoices with only one check. Payments are usually made from the operating account.

Duality of Economic Events

The duality of economic events in the acquisition/payment process is a mirror image of the sales/collection duality of events. In the acquisition/payment process, inventory is associated with an economic increment event—purchase; and cash is associated with the economic decrement event—cash disbursement. These two events need not occur at the same time. The accounting term for the timing difference that occurs when merchandise is received before cash is paid is *accounts payable*. Like accounts receivable, accounts payable is derived, rather than recorded directly, by taking the sum of all purchases and subtracting the sum of all cash disbursements related to purchases. You will use queries to derive accounts payable and other financial information later in the chapter.

Since Pipefitters sometimes makes partial payments, a purchase may have many cash disbursements associated with it. Therefore, the cash disbursement side of the duality relationship is M. Since a cash disbursement pertains to only one inventory receipt, the purchase side of the relationship is 1.

Basic Acquisition/Payment Data Model

In the following exercise, you will draw a diagram of Pipefitters' basic acquisition/payment process: the duality events that make up the economic duality, and the resources and agents to which each event is linked. Economic increment events have an *inflow* relationship with a resource and economic decrement events have an *outflow* relationship with a resource. Events generally participate with at least one internal agent—an *internal participation* relationship. Events usually participate with only one external agent in an *external participation* relationship. The resulting data model forms the core of most acquisition/payment business processes.

EXERCISE 9.1: CREATING THE BASIC ACQUISITION/PAYMENT DATA MODEL

1. Draw the duality of economic events and the relationship between them, including the cardinalities.
2. Add the resource and agents for the purchase event and their relationships with purchase.
3. Add cardinalities to the relationships with purchase.
4. Add to your model the resource and agents for the cash disbursement event and their relationships with cash disbursement.
5. Add cardinalities to the relationships with cash disbursement.

Purchase Event

The data model in Figure 9.1 shows that a purchase results in an inflow from inventory to the external agent, vendor, and that an employee (internal agent) also participates in the relationship. The one-to-many relationship between vendor and purchase is a typical set of cardinalities between events and external agents; the relationship indicates that a particular vendor can participate in many purchases and that a purchase has, at most, one vendor.

Fig. 9.1 Pipefitters Supply Company acquisition/payment duality with resources and agents.

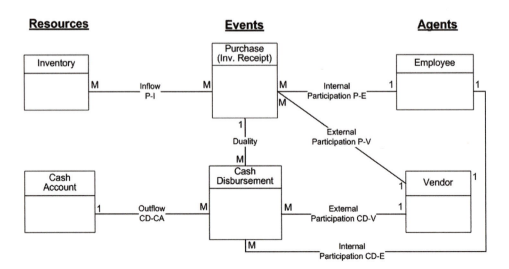

Likewise, the one-to-many relationship between employee and purchase indicates that a specific employee may participate in many purchases, and that a purchase involves only one employee.

The inflow relationship between purchase and inventory is many-to-many because a particular inventory item number (e.g., item 1001: brass, 4-foot, .25-inch diameter pipes) can be involved in many purchases, and a purchase can have many different item numbers (e.g., three of item 1001, two of item 1008, and one of item 1019).

Cash Disbursement Event

Figure 9.1 shows that a cash disbursement results in an outflow of cash to a vendor (external agent), and that an employee (internal agent) also participates in the event. Like the purchase event, both participations with cash disbursement are one-to-many. Also, the one-to-many cardinalities involving the cash account resource indicate that a cash account may participate in many cash disbursement events, and that any particular cash disbursement will come from only one cash account.

Compare the data models in Figure 9.1 and Figure 8.2. Notice the similarities and differences between the sales/collection process and the acquisition/payment process. As stated earlier, the main differences are the direction of the resource flows. Inventory flows in from a purchase and out from a sale, whereas cash flows out from a cash disbursement and in from a cash receipt. Also, the acquisition/payment process involves resource exchanges with vendors, whereas the resource exchanges in the sales/collection process are between the firm and customers.

Purchase Order Event

Pipefitters' acquisition/payment process begins by sending a purchase order to a vendor. Once approved by the vendor, this *commitment* event commits Pipefitters to pay for the specified merchandise it receives from the vendor in accordance to the terms in the purchase order. It also commits the vendor to provide the specified merchandise.

When Pipefitters places a purchase order it has a *reservation* to receive inventory from the vendor: a *reservation* relationship between purchase order and inventory. Also, since purchasing agents place purchase orders with vendors, the purchase order is related to both a vendor and an employee. Finally, a purchase order is *fulfilled* by receiving the ordered merchandise from the vendor, so the relationship between a purchase order and purchase (inventory receipt) is a *fulfillment* relationship. After adding the purchase order and related components to the model, you will be ready to convert the model to tables that you will create in Access.

EXERCISE 9.2: ADDING THE PURCHASE ORDER EVENT TO PIPEFITTERS SUPPLY COMPANY'S ACQUISITION/PAYMENT DATA MODEL

1. Add purchase order to the acquisition/payment data model in Figure 9.1 and the appropriate relationships.
2. Add the cardinalities to the relationships.

Figure 9.2 shows the complete acquisition/payment data model for Pipefitters Supply Company. The fulfillment relationship between purchase order and purchase is one-to-many because a purchase order may have more than one purchase (inventory receipt)

Fig. 9.2 Pipefitters Supply Company acquisition/payment process with all resources, events, and agents.

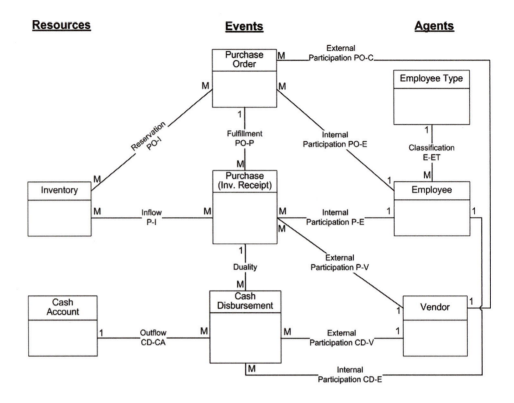

when a vendor makes a partial shipment due to a stockout. The reservation relationship between purchase order and inventory has the same many-to-many relationship as the actual inflow of inventory because a purchase order can be for many different items, and an item can be ordered many times. Also, like the purchase event, the cardinalities for the participation relationships with purchase order (purchase order – vendor; purchase order – employee) are one-to-many because purchase orders have only one vendor and one employee, and vendors and employees can participate with many purchase orders over time.

One additional entity has been added to the model in Figure 9.2—employee type. Employee type is added so that Pipefitters can ensure that only purchasing agents make purchases, materials handlers receive shipments, and only accountants make cash disbursements.

Completing the Acquisition/Payment Model

Primary keys must be chosen for each entity, and relationships are made by using foreign keys and relationship tables.

EXERCISE 9.3: MAKING RELATIONSHIPS WITH FOREIGN KEYS AND RELATIONSHIP TABLES

1. Using the primary keys provided for Pipefitters' data model in Figure 9.3, create foreign keys for the one-to-many relationships.
2. Add relationship tables and composite primary keys for the many-to-many relationships.

If your foreign keys and relationship tables do not match those in Figure 9.4, review the "Relational Database Management Systems" section in Chapter 2.

Fig. 9.3 Acquisition/payment process with primary keys.

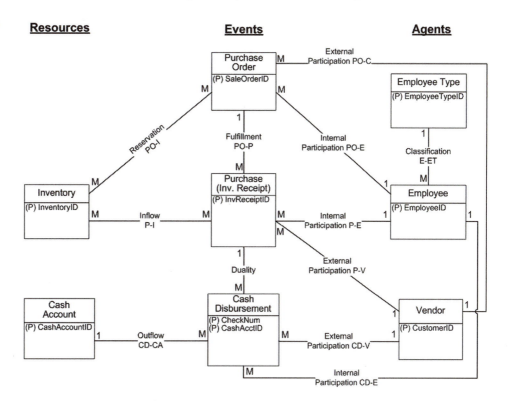

Fig. 9.4 Acquisition/payment process with primary keys, foreign keys, and relationship tables.

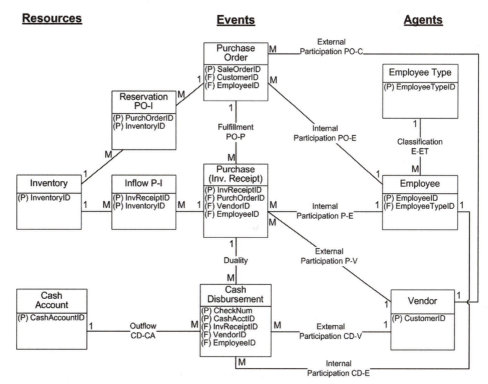

Like the sales/collection process described in Chapter 8, the acquisition/payment process portion of an accounting system maintains information about external agents (vendors) and resources (inventory and cash accounts).

Vendor Information

Firms need easy and quick access to information about their vendors. Purchasing agents need vendor names, addresses, and telephone numbers. They also need to know for which inventory items a particular vendor has been approved. Vendor information appears on many business documents such as purchase orders and checks. To ensure that vendor information is consistent wherever it is used, firms keep all vendor information in one table. Any document that needs vendor information obtains it from that one table. If, for example, a vendor moves to a new location, the vendor's address is changed only once. In a relational database accounting information system, vendor information resides in a vendor table.

The Vendor Table

Since Pipefitters sells merchandise to other businesses, the Vendor table is almost identical to the customer table. Figure 9.5 shows the two tables in Design view. There are two minor differences between the two tables other than the beginning of each Field Name. First, the Field Size of VendorID is only 4 digits instead of the 5 digits used for CustomerID because it is highly unlikely that Pipefitters will ever have more than 8,999 (1001 through 9999) vendors. The other difference is the absence of a credit limit field in the Vendor table.

Fig. 9.5 *tblVendor* and *tblCustomer* in Design view.

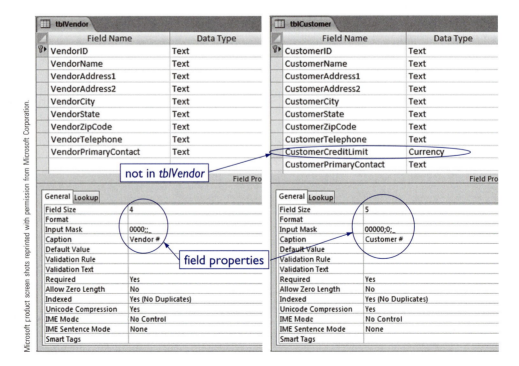

EXERCISE 9.4: CREATING *TBLVENDOR* FROM *TBLCUSTOMER*

1. Start Microsoft Access, Open the *Ch09.accdb* database you downloaded from the Companion Web site.
2. Right-click tblCustomer in the Chapter 8 Tables section of the Navigation Pane. Click Copy. Right-click anywhere in the Navigation Pane. Click Paste. In the Paste Table As dialog box type tblVendor in the name box, click the Structure Only radio button, and click OK.
3. Open tblVendor in Design view. It will be located in the Unassigned Objects section of the Navigation Pane.
4. Change the Primary Key name from CustomerID to VendorID. Change the Field Size, Input Mask, and Caption as shown in Figure 9.5.
5. Delete CustomerCreditLimit. Right-click on CustomerCreditLimit, and click Delete Rows. Change the Field Names of the remaining attributes (see Figure 9.5).
6. Save and close the table.

EXERCISE 9.5: IMPORTING DATA FROM AN EXCEL FILE INTO *TBLVENDOR*

1. Import the vendor data from *Ch09.xlsx*. Click Excel on the External Data ribbon. Click the Browse button to find the location where you stored *Ch09.xlsx*. Double-click Ch09.xlsx.
2. Click the Radio Button for the second option Append a copy of the records to the table; select tblVendor from the combo box. Click OK.
3. In the next dialog box, highlight the worksheet tblVendor if it is not already highlighted. Click Next twice.
4. In the last dialog box, tblVendor should already be entered in the *Import to Table:* textbox. Click Finish. Open tblVendor in Datasheet view to verify that all 14 records were imported into the database. Instead of using the import function, you could copy-and-paste the data from the Excel worksheet into *tblVendor*.

The Vendor Information Form

The Vendor Information form contains almost the same exact data as the Customer Information form you created in Chapter 8. Therefore, you will start with a copy of the Customer Information form and simply change the source of the data from *tblCustomer* to *tblVendor*.

EXERCISE 9.6: USING THE CUSTOMER INFORMATION FORM TO CREATE THE VENDOR INFORMATION FORM

1. Click frmCustomer in the Chapter 8 Forms section of the Navigation Pane. Then, press Ctrl+C, then Ctrl+V. In the Paste As dialog box, type frmVendor.
2. Open frmVendor in Design view. It will be located in the Unassigned Objects section of the Navigation Pane.
3. Click Property Sheet in the Tools group if the property sheet is not already open.
4. Select Form from the combo box at the top of the property sheet. On the Data tab, Change the Record Source to tblVendor.

5. Change CustomerID to VendorID. Click the CustomerID control. On the property sheet, change the Control Source to VendorID by clicking on the combo box arrow. Adjust the Input Mask to allow for only four digits by deleting a 0 in the first part of the Input Mask. Change the label to Vendor #.
6. Delete the CustomerCreditLimit control. Move the CustomerPrimaryContact control to where CustomerCreditLimit used to be.
7. Change the Control Source of the remaining fields to the appropriate fields from *tblVendor*. For example, change the source from CustomerName to VendorName.
8. Change the header to Vendor Information.
9. Save the form. View the form in Form view. It should look like Figure 9.6.

Fig. 9.6 Vendor Information form.

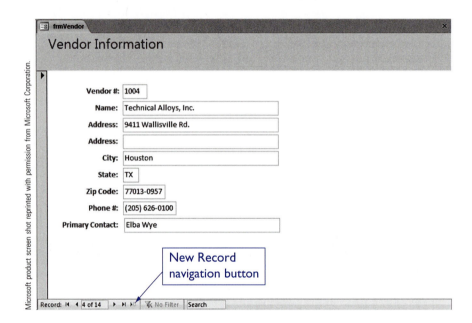

Microsoft product screen shot reprinted with permission from Microsoft Corporation.

Maintaining Vendor Records

You have now built a Vendor table to store vendor information and a Vendor Information form that makes it easy to enter and view data in that table. With the Vendor Information form, you can:

- *Create records for new vendors.*
- *Delete records for vendors that have become inactive or have gone out of business.*
- *Update Vendor table records as vendors move, get new telephone numbers, and change other items of information you have stored in the Vendor table.*

You will want to keep your file of vendor information current. A key advantage of the relational database model is that you add, delete, or change information in only one table. To use the Vendor Information form to add vendors to *tblVendor*, open *frmVendor*. As you enter values, notice how the Input Mask and Validation Rule properties you set in *tblVendor* limit the values you can enter in the VendorID, VendorState, VendorZipCode, and VendorTelephone controls. Try entering out-of-range values in these fields to test the internal controls you built into the table.

> ## TRY IT
>
> Deleting records from the Vendor table is easy. Open the Vendor Information form by double-clicking frmVendor in the Navigation Pane. To delete a record, move to that record using the navigation buttons at the bottom of the form, then click Delete in the Records group and click Delete Record. Access gives you a warning message that asks you to confirm the deletion. This deletion is not reversible. Delete the record for Vendor 1004. You can delete individual fields in a record using the Delete key in Form view. Individual field deletions are reversible by pressing the Esc key, even after you move to another field as long as you are still within the same record. Now add Vendor 1004 back to the database. Click the New Record navigation button. Enter the information from Figure 9.6.

Be careful when deleting records in accounting databases. Data in one accounting table is usually related to data in other tables. For example, if you examine a record in a purchase order table, it will contain a vendor number. The only place that vendor's name and address is stored is in the related Vendor table. If someone deletes that vendor's record in the Vendor table, you may never be able to identify the vendor.

Keeping existing vendor records current to reflect address changes, new telephone numbers, and other changes is straightforward. Use the navigation buttons at the bottom of the form to move to the vendor record that you want to change. You can move through the individual fields of the displayed record by using the Enter key or the Tab key. The Shift+Tab key moves backward through the record. The up and down arrow keys also move the cursor through the form. Any changes you make to field contents will be limited by the Input Mask and Validation Rule property settings for *tblVendor*.

> ## TRY IT
>
> When you use the navigation buttons to advance from one record to another in the Vendor Information form, you will notice that the records are not in alphabetical order. Unless you know a vendor's VendorID, it will be difficult to find a particular customer in the form. You can sort the form alphabetically by VendorName by right-clicking on the Name field, and then clicking Sort A to Z. The form is now sorted by VendorName.

Inventory Information

In Chapter 8, you created *tblInventory* to store information about merchandise inventory, and you also created a form to make it easy to add, change, and delete inventory data. In this chapter, you will track events related to the acquisition of inventory as part of the acquisition/payment process. As with the data model of the acquisition/payment process, the tables, queries, and forms you build for this business process will mirror the Access objects you created for the sales/collection process.

Firms use inventory records to provide inventory descriptions on purchase orders, receiving reports, and other documents in the acquisition/payment process. To ensure that materials inventory information is consistent wherever it is used, firms keep all inventory information in one location. Pipefitters keeps its inventory information in the Inventory table and its related type/category tables. Any document, report, or transaction that needs inventory information obtains it from the same place.

The Inventory Table

The *Ch09.accdb* database includes the Inventory table you created in Chapter 8. We also use this table for the acquisition/payment process because the inventory Pipefitters purchases is the same inventory it sells to customers. However, an additional field is necessary to facilitate events in the acquisition/payment process.

The original inventory table contains a list price field. Pipefitters' sales prices are based on its list prices. Likewise, Pipefitters needs a reference price to which it compares the actual purchase price. In managerial accounting this is often referred to as the ***standard cost***, which is the amount Pipefitters expects to pay for each inventory item. Purchasing agents can use standard cost information to guide them in choosing the best vendor for particular types of inventory. Additionally, management can use reports comparing standard costs to actual costs to evaluate its vendors and the effectiveness of its purchasing agents. Of course, standard costs become irrelevant unless they are updated periodically to reflect current market conditions.

EXERCISE 9.7: ADDING STANDARD COST TO THE INVENTORY TABLE

1. Open tblInventory in Design view. It will be located in the Unassigned Objects section of the Navigation Pane.
2. Click the Key Indicator column next to the InventoryListPrice Field Name. Press Ctrl+C, click the Record Selector in the first open Field row, and press Ctrl+V. Change the new Field Name to InventoryStdCost. Click the Record Selector for InventoryStdCost, and drag the row to just above the InventoryListPrice row.
3. In the Field Properties for InventoryStdCost, change the Caption to Std. Cost and change the Required property to No. This is necessary because you do not have any data in this field.
4. Switch to Datasheet view, and click Yes in the dialog box to save your changes.
5. Open the Ch09.xlsx file and click on the tblInventory worksheet. Copy the 60 StdCost cells and paste them in the Std. Cost column of your Access table.
6. Return to Design view. Change the Required property for StdCost back to Yes.
7. Save and close the table.

The Inventory Form

The materials inventory form you created in Chapter 8 helps users enter inventory records easily and accurately. The form also provides a convenient way for users to view, update, or delete existing inventory records. In Exercise 9.8 you will add the standard cost field to *frmInventory*. Even after adding a sixth field to *tblInventory*, the number and size of the fields are still sufficiently small so as to use a tabular form layout so you can easily display many records at one time.

EXERCISE 9.8: ADDING STANDARD COST TO THE INVENTORY DATA ENTRY FORM

1. Open frmInventory in Design view. It is located in the Unassigned Objects section of the Navigation Pane.

2. Make a copy of the InventoryListPrice control and label. Click the InventoryListPrice control, press and hold the Shift key and click the ListPrice label to select both objects. Press Ctrl+C, then Ctrl+V.

3. Move the *original* InventoryListPrice control and label to the right edge of the form. Select both items as you did in Step 2, and use your Right Arrow key to move both objects to the right.

4. Click the *new* ListPrice label twice (slower than a double-click), and change the text to Std. Cost.

5. Align the Std. Cost label with the other labels. Select both the Diameter label and the Std. Cost label. Click the Arrange tab, and click Align Top in the Control Alignment group. Repeat this alignment process with the *new* InventoryListPrice control and cboInventoryDiameter.

6. Make the horizontal spacing equal between all labels. Click on the blank space in the Form Header directly under the Inventory # label. Click and drag the box until it touches all of the labels (see Figure 9.7). Click Make Horizontal Spacing Equal in the Position group. Repeat this process for the controls in the Detail section of the form.

7. Remove the blank space below the labels by clicking and dragging the top of the Detail bar upward. Remove the blank space below the controls by clicking and dragging the top of the Form Footer bar upward.

8. Click the Design tab; click the *new* InventoryListPrice control. Click Property Sheet in the Tools group. On the Data tab, change the Record Source to InventoryStdCost.

9. Change CustomerID to VendorID. Click the CustomerID control. On the Other tab, change the Name to InventoryStdCost. Close the Property Sheet.

10. Click the Arrange tab. Click Tab Order in the Control Layout group. Notice that InventoryListPrice appears before InventoryStdCost in the Custom Order column. To correct the tab order, you can either click InventoryStdCost, then click and drag it up above InventoryListPrice, or you can click Auto Order. Click OK.

11. Return to Form view. The form should look like Figure 9.8. Press the Tab button several times. Notice that it moves from one field to the adjacent field, and from the last item in one record to the first item in the next record.

12. Save and close your form.

Fig. 9.7 Selecting multiple items in *frmInventory* to make horizontal spacing equal.

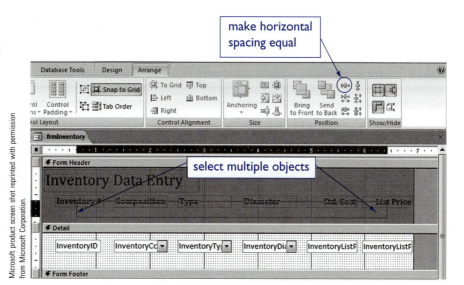

Fig. 9.8 Updated
Inventory Data Entry
form.

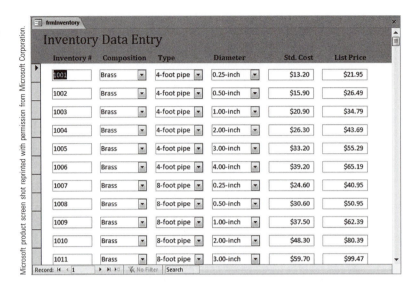

<table>
<tr><th colspan="2">TRY IT</th></tr>
</table>

The Combo Box Wizard writes a query that accesses *tblInventoryType* and inserts the five values from the Category field in that table. To examine this query, click the InventoryType combo box in Design view with the property sheet open, click the Data tab, select the Row Source property, and click its Build button. It is a simple query, but it does the job. Close the query and form.

Purchase Orders

Now that you have built tables and forms that a firm could use to enter and maintain records of vendors and inventory, you can build the system components that facilitate ordering inventory items from vendors. At Pipefitters Supply Company, purchasing agents are responsible for monitoring inventory levels. They must ensure that there is a sufficient supply inventory on hand to meet current demand without unnecessarily tying up capital by purchasing too much inventory. Once purchasing agents identify inventory to be purchased, they must

- *Identify vendors that provide these inventory items.*
- *Select a vendor.*
- *Send a purchase order to the chosen vendor.*

The form of purchase orders varies from firm to firm; however, all purchase orders must contain the following:

- *Order date.*
- *Vendor name and address.*
- *Identification of the inventory item(s) to be purchased.*
- *Quantities and prices of the inventory item(s) to be purchased.*

The purchase order also frequently contains shipping information, including an expected delivery date. The foreign key in the Purchase Order table in Figure 9.4 creates the participation relationship between the Vendor table and the Purchase Order table. This link enables you to identify vendors with specific purchase orders because, as the one-to-many cardinalities in Figure 9.4 indicate, each purchase order is placed with only one vendor. However, the reservation relationship connecting purchase orders to the specific inventory items listed on each purchase order requires a separate relationship table to model the many-to-many nature of that link.

Review the data model in Figure 9.4 to determine the tables, including relationship tables, and foreign keys that Pipefitters Supply Company will need to record each purchase order. At this point, do not worry about the fulfillment relationship between purchase order and purchase. You will create the fulfillment relationship when you build the purchase table by adding PurchaseOrderID as a foreign key in the purchase table.

The Employee Table

The model in Figure 9.4 shows that Pipefitters Supply records the purchasing agent responsible for each purchase order. This is similar to how Pipefitters records the salesperson responsible for each sale order. Purchasing agents are represented in the Purchase Order table by their employee identification number (EmployeeID attribute). This foreign key links the Purchase Order table to the employee table as EmployeeID is the primary key of the employee table. You will use the same *tblEmployee* and *tblEmployeeType* that you used in Chapter 8. It is contained in the *Ch09.accdb* database.

The Purchase Order Table

The Purchase Order table is similar to the sale order table you created in Chapter 8 because the two events they are modeling are similar. Like a sale order, a purchase order is a commitment event that leads to an economic event. Sale orders lead to sales (giving inventory to a customer is an economic decrement event) and purchase orders lead to purchases (getting inventory from a vendor is an economic increment event). Both order events are linked to only one external participant and, at Pipefitters Supply Company, only one employee. Also, both order events have a many-to-many relationship with the inventory resource.

One other similarity between the two tables is that Pipefitters stores the total price of the items ordered in both tables. Although the total price of all items ordered can be computed by summing the price times the quantity of each item ordered, Pipefitters stores the total as a control. As discussed in Chapter 8, Pipefitters should periodically run a query to compare the sum of the order line items to the total in the order table to reveal possible errors or irregularities.

Figure 9.9 shows the six fields for *tblPurchaseOrder*. Notice that *tblPurchaseOrder* has a second date field for the expected delivery date. Pipefitters can use this information to create a series of queries to determine expected inventory available for delivery customers on a certain date, rather than just relying on the computation of actual inventory on hand.

EXERCISE 9.9: CREATING THE PURCHASE ORDER TABLE

1. Create a new table. Click the Create tab, and click Table Design in the Tables group.
2. Create the primary key. Type PurchaseOrderID in first Field Name box and then click Primary Key in the Tools group.
3. Press F6 to move to the Field Properties section of the window. Enter the Field Properties for PurchaseOrderID listed in Figure 9.9.
4. Enter the remaining Data Types and Field Properties for the foreign keys EmployeeID and VendorID as listed in Figure 9.9.
5. Next, create the purchase order date field by entering a Field Name of PurchaseOrderDate. Enter the data type and Field Properties listed in Figure 9.9 other than the Default Value.

6. Pipefitters' accounting information system sends purchase orders to vendors as soon as the data is entered into the system. Therefore, the purchase order date is generally the current date. Therefore, you need to set the default value for PurchaseOrderDate to the current date by entering Date () for the Default Value property. This control minimizes data entry errors.
7. Save the table as tblPurchaseOrder.

Fig. 9.9 Fields for *tblPurchaseOrder.*

Field Name	PurchaseOrderID	EmployeeID	VendorID
Data Type	Text	Text	Text
Field Size	6	3	4
Format			
Input Mask	000000;;_	000;;_	0000;;_
Caption	Purchase Order #	Employee #	Vendor #
Default Value			
Required	Yes	Yes	Yes
Allow Zero Length	No	No	No
Indexed	Yes (No Duplicates)	Yes (DuplicatesOK)	Yes (DuplicatesOK)

Primary key and foreign keys

Field Name	PurchaseOrderDate	ExpectedDeliveryDate	PurchaseOrderAmount
Data Type	Date/Time	Date/Time	Currency
Decimal Places			2
Format	Short Date	Short Date	
Input Mask	99/99/0000;;_	99/99/0000;;_	
Caption	Date Ordered	Expected Delivery	Amount
Default Value	Date ()		
Validation Rule			>=0
Validation Text			Purchase order amount must be non-negative
Required	Yes	Yes	Yes
Allow Zero Length			
Indexed	No	No	No

Attributes

You now have a functioning Purchase Order table with some general controls built into it, ensuring that data entered is reasonable; ID numbers must have the correct number of digits, purchase order amounts are not negative, and the default purchase order date is the current date. What do you think is a reasonable restriction on the expected delivery date? Should the expected delivery be earlier than the purchase order date? Although we cannot write a *field-level* validation rule to compare the value of one field in a record to the value of another field in the same record, we can create a *table-level* validation rule to accomplish this task.

EXERCISE 9.10: CREATING A TABLE-LEVEL VALIDATION RULE FOR *EXPECTEDDELIVERYDATE*

1. Open tblPurchaseOrder in Design view if it is not already open. It will be located in the Unassigned Objects section of the Navigation Pane.
2. Click Property Sheet in the Show/Hide group to bring up the table-level properties (see Figure 9.10).
3. On the Property Sheet, click the Validation Rule Control box to activate the Expression Builder button. Click the Expression Builder button to open Expression Builder (see Figure 9.10).
4. Build the validation rule in Figure 9.10. Double-click ExpectedDeliveryDate in the list of fields in Expression Builder. Type >=, and double-click PurchaseOrderDate. Click OK to close Expression Builder.
5. Add the following to the Validation Text property, which will appear when a user enters an expected delivery date that is earlier than order date: Expected delivery date cannot be earlier than purchase order date.
6. Save and close the table.

Fig. 9.10 Creating a table-level validation rule.

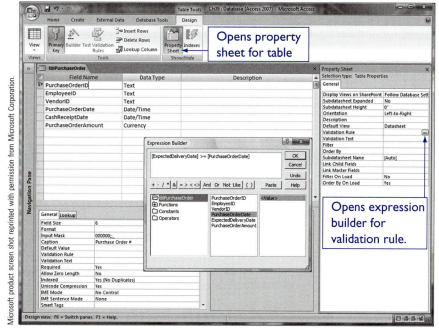

Microsoft product screen shot reprinted with permission from Microsoft Corporation.

EXERCISE 9.11: IMPORTING DATA FROM AN EXCEL FILE INTO *TBLPURCHASEORDER*

1. Import the purchase order data from *Ch09.xlsx*. Click Excel on the External Data ribbon. Click the Browse button to find the location where you stored *Ch09.xlsx*. Double-click *Ch09.xlsx*.
2. Click the Radio Button for the second option Append a copy of the records to the table:; select tblPurchaseOrder from the combo box. Click OK.
3. In the next dialog box, highlight the worksheet tblPurchaseOrder. Click Next twice.
4. In the last dialog box, tblPurchaseOrder should already be entered in the *Import to Table:* textbox. Click Finish. Open tblPurchaseOrder in datasheet view to verify that all 24 records were imported into the database.

This completes the basic design of *tblPurchaseOrder*. The table with the data imported from *Ch09.xlsx* appears in Datasheet view in Figure 9.11.

Fig. 9.11 *tblPurchaseOrder* in Datasheet view.

Purchase Or ▾	Employee # ▾	Vendor # ▾	Date Ordere ▾	Expected De ▾	Amount ▾	Add New Field
100001	106	1001	1/2/2010	1/7/2010	$3,812.75	
100002	114	1007	1/5/2010	1/15/2010	$2,108.25	
100003	114	1003	1/9/2010	1/16/2010	$8,569.50	
100004	150	1008	1/10/2010	1/15/2010	$4,700.50	
100005	130	1001	1/13/2010	1/20/2010	$2,196.05	
100006	150	1008	1/13/2010	1/17/2010	$3,973.00	
100007	132	1009	1/16/2010	1/23/2010	$426.00	
100008	132	1004	1/18/2010	1/24/2010	$317.00	
100009	133	1011	1/19/2010	1/27/2010	$9,298.75	
100010	106	1007	1/20/2010	1/28/2010	$6,298.75	
100011	106	1003	1/25/2010	2/1/2010	$1,855.75	
100012	132	1013	1/26/2010	2/1/2010	$2,254.70	
100013	150	1011	2/1/2010	2/9/2010	$3,587.25	
100014	114	1008	2/3/2010	2/8/2010	$3,985.00	
100015	114	1003	2/7/2010	2/10/2010	$3,462.75	
100016	133	1006	2/8/2010	2/15/2010	$1,754.75	
100017	130	1001	2/11/2010	2/20/2010	$5,283.65	
100018	130	1008	2/14/2010	2/21/2010	$5,889.00	
100019	114	1003	2/15/2010	2/24/2010	$1,608.75	
100020	114	1006	2/20/2010	3/1/2010	$155.15	
100021	114	1002	3/2/2010	3/10/2010	$2,520.00	
100022	103	1008	3/8/2010	3/15/2010	$270.00	
100023	150	1003	3/21/2010	3/26/2010	$1,860.35	
100024	150	1002	3/22/2010	3/28/2010	$1,674.50	
*				4/13/2009		

Record: ◄ ◄ 1 of 24 ► ►I ►⋇ ☒ No Filter | Search

TRY IT

Open *tblPurchaseOrder* and enter a new record. Enter 999999 for PurchaseOrderID, 999 for EmployeeID, and 9999 for VendorID. You are allowed to enter these values even though they do not exist in the related tables because you have not yet linked *tblPurchaseOrder* to its related tables and enforced referential integrity. Leave the default date in the PurchaseOrderDate field. In the ExpectedDeliveryDate field, enter the date one month earlier than PurchaseOrderDate. Tab to the PurchaseOrderAmount field and type 9999. Tab to the next record. Notice that a dialog box with your validation text appears when you try to go to the next record. After clicking OK, you can either delete the current record by pressing the Esc key or enter a valid date for ExpectedDeliveryDate. Delete the record and close the table.

The Purchase Order-Inventory Table

The Purchase Order-Inventory table is similar to the Sale Order-Inventory table in that they both record the many-to-many reservation relationship between a commitment event table and the resource table *tblInventory*. Therefore, *tblReservation-PurchaseOrderInventory* will have four fields similar to the fields stored in *tblReservation-SaleOrderInventory*:

1. The primary key of *tblPurchaseOrder*.
2. The primary key of *tblInventory*.

3. The quantity of each inventory item that appears on each purchase order.
4. The price of each inventory item that appears on each purchase order.

Additionally, *tblReservation-PurchaseOrderInventory* stores the vendor's part number for each item ordered because the same item may be ordered from more than one vendor, and vendors often use their own part numbers.

The primary keys from *tblPurchaseOrder* and *tblInventory* will combine to form the composite primary key in *tblReservation-PurchaseOrderInventory*. In Microsoft Access, you create a composite primary key by creating two separate fields, one for each entity table's primary key, and then designating both fields as primary keys. Before you begin the next exercise, close any open tables or forms.

EXERCISE 9.12: CREATING THE *TBLRESERVATION-PURCHASEORDERINVENTORY* RELATIONSHIP TABLE

1. Right-click tblReservation-SaleOrderInventory in the Chapter 8 Tables section of the Navigation Pane. Click Copy. Right-click anywhere in the Navigation Pane. Click Paste. In the Paste Table As dialog box type tblReservation-PurchaseOrderInventory in the name box, click the Structure Only radio button, then click OK.
2. Open tblReservation-PurchaseOrderInventory in Design view. It is located in the Unassigned Objects section of the Navigation Pane.
3. Change the first Field Name of the composite Primary Key from SaleOrderID to PurchaseOrderID. Change the Caption to Purchase Order #.
4. Change the fourth Field Name from SOPrice to POPrice.
5. Add the fifth attribute. The Field Name is VendorItemID. Leave the Data Type set to Text. Set the following Field Properties: Field Size 20, Caption Vendor Item #, Required Yes, Allow Zero Length No, and Indexed Yes (Duplicates OK). Indexed is set to Yes because Pipefitters will likely need to look up inventory items by the vendor item number.
6. Save and close the table.
7. Import the data for *tblReservation-PurchaseOrderInventory* from the *Ch09.xlsx* file. Follow the instructions for Exercise 9.11, substituting tblReservation-PurchaseOrderInventory for tblPurchaseOrder. After importing the data, open tblReservation-PurchaseOrderInventory in Datasheet view to verify that you imported all 181 records.

The Purchase Order Entry Form

The purchase order entry form is fairly complex. To enter purchase orders, you will create a form that links:

- tblPurchaseOrder *to* tblVendor, *to obtain information such as the vendor's name and address.*
- tblPurchaseOrder *to* tblEmployee *to obtain the employee's name who creates the purchase order.*
- tblPurchaseOrder *to* tblReservation-PurchaseOrderInventory, *to obtain a list of the inventory item numbers, quantities, prices, and vendor item numbers for each item on each purchase order.*

- tblReservationPurchaseOrderInventory *to* tblInventory, *and from* tblInventory *to the inventory category tables to obtain a description for each item on each purchase order. (Note that you already created the links from* tblInventory *to the inventory category tables in Chapter 8.)*

Creating Relationships with the Purchase Order Table

A purchase order entry form that meets these objectives will use all of the above tables. The form must read from *tblVendor, tblEmployee, tblInventory, tblInventoryComposition, tblInventoryDiameter,* and *tblInventoryType,* and write to *tblPurchaseOrder* and *tblReservation-PurchaseOrderInventory.* Since the form will read data from all of the above tables, you will need to have data in these tables to test the form's operation as you build it. The employee tables and inventory category/type tables in *Ch09.accdb* were already populated with data. If you have not already imported the data from *Ch09.xlsx* in the Chapter 9 exercises, you need to do so now before creating the Purchase Order Entry form.

EXERCISE 9.13: CREATING RELATIONSHIPS FOR TABLES RELATED TO THE PURCHASE ORDER EVENT

1. Close all open Access objects.
2. In the Database Tools tab, click Relationships in the Show/Hide group. Minimize the Navigation Pane by clicking the << at the top-right corner of the pane. This gives you more room for your database model, which will make it easier to read. Your Relationships window should look like Figure 9.12.
3. Add the following tables to the Relationships tab: tblPurchaseOrder, tblReservation-PurchaseOrderInventory, and tblVendor. To do this, click Show Table in the Relationships group, click tblPurchaseOrder, press Ctrl, and click the other two tables. Click Add, then click Close.
4. Resize your tables to show the entire table name and all of the attributes. Move the tables to be consistent with the REA model format: resource tables on the left, event tables in the middle, and agent tables on the right. Place relationship tables between the two tables they join.
5. Create links between tables. Drag from the primary key to the matching foreign key or from the primary key to the matching part of a composite primary key.
6. After you click and drag the primary key in one table (the *1* side of the relationship) to the foreign key or composite primary key in the other table (the *many* side of the relationship) the Edit Relationships dialog box appears. Make sure that the correct attributes appear in the tables you dragged from and to. The relationship type at the bottom of the dialog box should always be one-to-many. Check Enforce Referential Integrity and Cascade Update Related Fields. Finally, click Create in the dialog box. When you are finished, your Relationships window should look like the one in Figure 9.13.
7. Click the X button in the Relationships group to close the Relationships window, click the Yes button in the dialog box to save your changes, then click >> on the Navigation Pane to restore it.

Now that you have established the necessary foreign key and relationship table links, you can create a Purchase Order Entry form. Like other database objects you created in this chapter, you will learn how to reuse objects you created earlier to save time and effort. Additionally, you will create two queries—*qryVendorInfo* and *qryPurchaseOrder-LineItem.* Access will use data from these two queries and *tblPurchaseOrder* to populate the Purchase Order Entry form.

Fig. 9.12 Relationships window before adding purchase order-related tables created in Chapter 9.

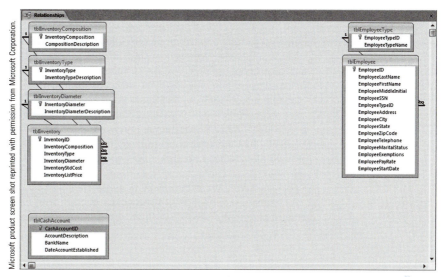

Fig. 9.13 Relationships window with all purchase order-related tables and relationships.

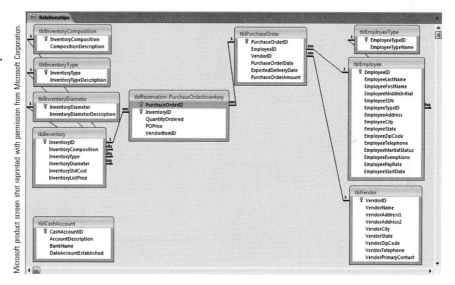

Creating a Query for Vendor Data Used in the Purchase Order Form

The primary purpose of this one-table Vendor Information query is to concatenate the city, state, and zip code fields to present a view of this information to users in a familiar format.

EXERCISE 9.14: CREATING *QRYVENDORINFO* FOR THE PURCHASE ORDER ENTRY FORM

1. Click the Create tab, and click Query Design in the Other group.
2. Double-click tblVendor from the list presented in the Show Table dialog box, and click the Close button.
3. Select all fields in the *tblVendor* field roster by clicking on VendorID to highlight it. Press and hold the Shift key. Press the Down Arrow key until all fields are highlighted. Then drag the fields to the Criteria Pane.
4. Save the query as qryVendorInfo before creating the address.

5. Click on the first row of the next available column of the Criteria Pane, and click Builder in the Query Setup group. You should see the Expression Builder dialog box.
6. Build the following expression: CityStateZip: [VendorCity] &", " & [VendorState] &" " & [VendorZipCode].
7. Delete VendorCity, VendorState, and VendorZipCode from the Criteria Pane. Highlight columns by moving your cursor just above the Field row of VendorCity. Click the column when the cursor turns into a down arrow, and then press the Delete key. Delete VendorState and VendorZipCode in the same manner.
8. Highlight the CityStateZip column, and move it to the right of VendorAddress2 by clicking the column when the cursor turns into a down arrow and then dragging the column.
9. Save your query. View the resulting dynaset by clicking on either View or Run in the Results group. Figure 9.14 shows the dynaset with the data from *Ch09.accdb* after importing the vendor information from *Ch09xlsx*. Close qryVendorInfo.

Fig. 9.14 *qryVendor-Info* dynaset.

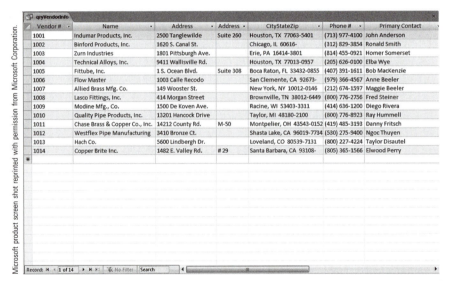

Microsoft product screen shot reprinted with permission from Microsoft Corporation.

Creating a Query for Purchase Order Line Items

Individual line items on purchase orders are similar to sale order line items. They both include the item number, a description of the item ordered, the quantity ordered, the purchase price per item, and the line item extension (purchase price × quantity). Additionally, purchase order line items also include the vendor item number because the vendor's inventory numbering system is usually different than the system used by the purchaser. Therefore, purchase order line items need information from the following tables: *tblReservation-PurchaseOrderInventory*, *tblInventory*, *tblInventoryComposition*, *tblInventoryType*, and *tblInventoryDiameter*. Additionally, you will create two additional fields: PurchaseOrderLineExtension, which will contain the purchase price × quantity ordered expression; and FullDescription, which will concatenate the descriptions of each item's composition, type, and diameter. Due to the complexity of this query and its similarity to *qrySaleOrderLineItem*, you will create *qryPurchaseOrderLineItem* by starting with a copy of *qrySaleOrderLineItem* and making changes to it.

EXERCISE 9.15: CREATING *QRYPURCHASEORDERLINEITEM* FOR THE PURCHASE ORDER ENTRY FORM

1. Click qrySaleOrderLineItem in the Chapter 8 Queries section in the Navigation Pane. Press Ctrl+C and then Ctrl+V. Type qryPurchaseOrderLineItem in the text box of the Paste Table As dialog box, and then click OK.
2. Open qryPurchaseOrderLineItem (in the Unassigned Objects section of the Navigation Pane) in Design view.
3. Click Show Table in the Query Setup group, double-click tblReservation-PurchaseOrderInventory, and click the Close button. Resize *tblReservation-PurchaseOrderInventory* to show the entire table name and all field names. Then move it on top of *tblReservation-SaleOrderInventory* to make it easier to work with.
4. On the Criteria Pane, change the Table for the fields InventoryID and QuantityOrdered to tblReservation-PurchaseOrderInventory.
5. Change the Table for SOPrice to tblReservation-PurchaseOrderInventory. Change the SOPrice Field to POPrice.
6. Change the Table for SaleOrderID to tblReservation-PurchaseOrderInventory. Change the SaleOrderID Field to PurchaseOrderID.
7. Change the InventoryListPrice Field to InventoryStdCost.
8. Click SaleOrderLineExtension, click Builder in the QuerySetup group. Change the expression from SaleOrderLineExtension: [QuantityOrdered] * [SOPrice] to PurchaseOrderLineExtension: [QuantityOrdered] * [POPrice].
9. Drag VendorItemID from the tblReservation-PurchaseOrderInventory field roster to the Criteria Pane onto the FullDescription column to place VendorItemID between InventoryID and FullDescription.
10. Click tblReservation-SaleOrderInventory; press the Delete key to remove the table from the query.
11. Save the query. Click Datasheet View in the Results group to view the dynaset created by running the query (see Figure 9.15). Open tblReservation-PurchaseOrderInventory in Datasheet view. Notice that both the query dynaset and table have 181 records. Click the Sort arrow in the Item # column of *tblReservation-PurchaseOrderInventory* to sort in ascending order. Compare the first four rows in the table to your dynaset for the query. They should match because the information for the query comes from *tblReservation-PurchaseOrderInventory*.
12. Close the query and table. Do not save the changes to the table.

Using the Sale Order Entry Form to Create the Purchase Order Entry Form

The Purchase Order Entry form is similar to the Sale Order Entry form. Its data is drawn from the sources: *tblPurchaseOrder* and *qryVendorInfo* for the main part of the form and a subform based on *qryPurchaseOrderLineItem*. Because these database objects are similar to the table and queries used to create the Sale Order Entry form, it will be easier to modify the existing Sale Order Entry form than to create the Purchase Order Entry form with the Form Wizard. Although modifying the queries and data sources used by a form can be tricky, it is a valuable skill to learn as it enables you to find and fix errors and make substantial modifications to existing forms.

Fig. 9.15 *qryPur-chaseOrderLineItem* dynaset.

Item #	Description	Quantity	Price	Std. Cost	Extension	Vendor Item #	Purchase Order #
1001	0.25-inch Brass 4-foot pipe	75	$13.20	$13.20	$990.00	B1009024	100001
1001	0.25-inch Brass 4-foot pipe	75	$13.00	$13.20	$975.00	102	100009
1001	0.25-inch Brass 4-foot pipe	20	$13.00	$13.20	$260.00	102	100013
1001	0.25-inch Brass 4-foot pipe	60	$13.20	$13.20	$792.00	B1009024	100017
1002	0.50-inch Brass 4-foot pipe	25	$15.95	$15.90	$398.75	B1009027	100001
1002	0.50-inch Brass 4-foot pipe	60	$16.00	$15.90	$960.00	105	100009
1002	0.50-inch Brass 4-foot pipe	65	$16.00	$15.90	$1,040.00	105	100013
1002	0.50-inch Brass 4-foot pipe	40	$15.95	$15.90	$638.00	B1009027	100017
1002	0.50-inch Brass 4-foot pipe	30	$16.00	$15.90	$480.00	24-050	100021
1003	1.00-inch Brass 4-foot pipe	15	$20.89	$20.90	$313.35	B1009085	100001
1003	1.00-inch Brass 4-foot pipe	50	$21.00	$20.90	$1,050.00	98	100009
1003	1.00-inch Brass 4-foot pipe	15	$21.00	$20.90	$315.00	98	100013
1003	1.00-inch Brass 4-foot pipe	35	$20.89	$20.90	$731.15	B1009085	100017
1004	2.00-inch Brass 4-foot pipe	15	$26.30	$26.30	$394.50	554820	100002
1004	2.00-inch Brass 4-foot pipe	25	$26.30	$26.30	$657.50	554820	100010
1004	2.00-inch Brass 4-foot pipe	15	$26.30	$26.30	$394.50	B-4ft-2in	100014
1004	2.00-inch Brass 4-foot pipe	30	$26.30	$26.30	$789.00	B-4ft-2in	100018
1005	3.00-inch Brass 4-foot pipe	15	$33.25	$33.20	$498.75	554830	100010
1005	3.00-inch Brass 4-foot pipe	30	$33.20	$33.20	$996.00	B-4ft-3in	100014
1005	3.00-inch Brass 4-foot pipe	40	$33.20	$33.20	$1,328.00	B-4ft-3in	100018
1006	4.00-inch Brass 4-foot pipe	35	$39.25	$39.20	$1,373.75	554840	100002
1006	4.00-inch Brass 4-foot pipe	10	$39.25	$39.20	$392.50	554840	100010
1006	4.00-inch Brass 4-foot pipe	10	$39.20	$39.20	$392.00	B-4ft-4in	100014
1007	0.25-inch Brass 8-foot pipe	25	$24.75	$24.60	$618.75	B1009101	100005
1007	0.25-inch Brass 8-foot pipe	60	$24.50	$24.60	$1,470.00	125	100009
1007	0.25-inch Brass 8-foot pipe	50	$24.50	$24.60	$1,225.00	125	100013
1007	0.25-inch Brass 8-foot pipe	20	$24.75	$24.60	$495.00	B1009101	100017

Record: 1 of 181 | No Filter | Search

Whenever you work with form-subform combinations in Access, you should start with the innermost subform and work out from that to the main form. First, you will modify *fsubSaleOrder* in Exercises 9.16 and 9.17. Then, you will modify *frmSaleOrder* in Exercises 9.18 and 9.19. After you have a functional Purchase Order Entry form, you will add additional controls in Exercises 9.20 through 9.26.

EXERCISE 9.16: CREATING *FSUBPURCHASEORDER* BY MODIFYING *FSUBSALEORDER*—PART 1

In this exercise you will change the subform's Record Source and the Control Source for all existing fields.

1. Click fsubSaleOrder in the Chapter 8 Forms section in the Navigation Pane. Press Ctrl+C and then Ctrl+V. Type fsubPurchaseOrder in the text box of the Paste Table As dialog box, then click OK.

2. Open fsubPurchaseOrder (in the Unassigned Objects section of the Navigation Pane) in Design view. Click Property Sheet in the Tools group. You can compensate for the decrease in the amount of subform visible by hiding the Navigation Pane.

3. Change the data source of the subform. Select Form from the combo box at the top of the Property Sheet if it is not already selected. Click the Data tab if it is not already selected. Click the combo box arrow in the Record Source property and select qryPurchaseOrderLineItem. Notice that you will have to scroll up to find *qryPurchaseOrderLineItem* and that only part of the name is visible.

4. Change the name that appears on the form's tab. Click the Format tab. Change the Caption to fsubPurchaseOrder.

Notice that the upper-left corner of SOPrice has a green triangle invalid control indicator just like the controls for InventoryListPrice and SaleLineItem. The green triangles appear in these control boxes because they are no longer connected to the form's data source as you changed it from *qrySaleOrderLineItem* to *qryPurchaseOrderLineItem*.

Why were there no green triangles on InventoryID, FullDescription, and Quantity Ordered?

5. Click the SOPrice control. Change the Control Source property from SOPrice to POPrice in the Data tab by either typing or selecting the item from the combo box. Click the Other tab. Change the Name to POPrice.
6. Click the InventoryListPrice control. Change the Control Source on the Data tab to InventoryStdCost. Change the Name on the Other tab to InventoryStdCost.
7. Change the List Price label to Std. Cost.
8. Click the SaleOrderLineExtention control. Change the Control Source on the Data tab to PurchaseOrderLineExtention. Change the Name on the Other tab to PurchaseOrderLineExtention.
9. Save your changes to *fsubPurchaseOrder*.

EXERCISE 9.17: CREATING *FSUBPURCHASEORDER* BY MODIFYING *FSUBSALEORDER*—PART 2

The Purchase Order Entry form's line items contain a field for the vendor's inventory item number, which is absent from the line items on the Sale Order Entry form. You will add this field to your subform in the next exercise.

1. Close the Property Sheet to increase your work space. Click and drag the right edge of the Detail section to the 8-inch mark because you need to add an additional field for VendorItemID. Select all labels other than Item # by pressing and holding the Ctrl key and clicking on each label. Press and hold the Right Arrow key (or press it repeatedly) to move the labels to the right edge of the Header portion of the form. Move the controls to the right edge of the Form Detail section in the same manner.
2. Add a control for VendorItemID. Press and hold the Shift key, and click the InventoryID control and its corresponding label. Press Ctrl+C and then Ctrl+V to make a copy of the control and label. Change the text in the Label box to Vendor Item #. Notice that the label box expands to fit the larger label.
3. Click the new InventoryID Control (the one you just created). Open the Property Sheet. Click the Data tab if it is not already selected. Change the Control Source to VendorItemID. Delete the Input Mask. Click the Other tab. Change the Name to VendorItemID.
4. Press and hold the Shift key, and click the Vendor Item # label so that both the Field control and label are selected. Click the Arrange tab. Click Size to Widest in the Size group.
5. Use the Top Control Alignment to align the VendorItemID Control with the FullDescription Control. Do the same with the related labels.
6. Change the text in the Item # label to Our Item #. Use the Size to Widest button in the Size group to make the size of the InventoryID Control as wide as the Our Item # label.
7. Click Tab Order in the Control Layout Group (on the Arrange ribbon). In the Tab Order dialog box, click the Auto Order button. Notice that the Field Names in the Custom Order list are in reordered from left to right on the form. Click OK.
8. Click and drag the Detail bar to remove the blank space below the field controls. Click and drag the Header bar to remove the blank space below the labels.
9. Close the Property Sheet. Press Ctrl+A to select all Field Controls and Labels. Click the Make Horizontal Spacing Equal button in the Position group.
10. Save your changes. View the form in Form view. It should look like Figure 9.16.

Fig. 9.16 *fsubPurchaseOrder* in Form view.

Our Item #		Vendor Item #	Description	Quantity	Price	Std. Cost	Extension
1001	▾	B1009024	0.25-inch Brass 4-foot pipe	75	$13.20	$13.20	$990.00
1001	▾	102	0.25-inch Brass 4-foot pipe	75	$13.00	$13.20	$975.00
1001	▾	102	0.25-inch Brass 4-foot pipe	20	$13.00	$13.20	$260.00
1001	▾	B1009024	0.25-inch Brass 4-foot pipe	60	$13.20	$13.20	$792.00
1002	▾	B1009027	0.50-inch Brass 4-foot pipe	25	$15.95	$15.90	$398.75
1002	▾	105	0.50-inch Brass 4-foot pipe	60	$16.00	$15.90	$960.00
1002	▾	105	0.50-inch Brass 4-foot pipe	65	$16.00	$15.90	$1,040.00
1002	▾	B1009027	0.50-inch Brass 4-foot pipe	40	$15.95	$15.90	$638.00
1002	▾	24-050	0.50-inch Brass 4-foot pipe	30	$16.00	$15.90	$480.00
1003	▾	B1009085	1.00-inch Brass 4-foot pipe	15	$20.89	$20.90	$313.35
1003	▾	98	1.00-inch Brass 4-foot pipe	50	$21.00	$20.90	$1,050.00
1003	▾	98	1.00-inch Brass 4-foot pipe	15	$21.00	$20.90	$315.00
1003	▾	B1009085	1.00-inch Brass 4-foot pipe	35	$20.89	$20.90	$731.15
1004	▾	554820	2.00-inch Brass 4-foot pipe	15	$26.30	$26.30	$394.50
1004	▾	554820	2.00-inch Brass 4-foot pipe	25	$26.30	$26.30	$657.50

Record: ◄ ◄ 1 of 184 ► ►I ►✱   ⅛ No Filter   Search

After completing Exercise 9.17, you likely realize that modifying *frmSaleOrder*, which draws its data from two queries and a table, will require more effort than modifying a subform with data from only one query. One of the interesting tasks you will perform in Exercise 9.18 is to modify a query that is behind the form.

EXERCISE 9.18: CREATING *FRMPURCHASEORDER* BY MODIFYING *FRMSALEORDER*—PART 1

In this exercise you will create *frmPurchaseOrder* by creating a copy of *frmSaleOrder* and changing titles and labels to properly identify *frmPurchaseOrder*. Additionally, you will change the Source Object of the subform to *fsubPurchaseOrder* and link it to *frmPurchaseOrder*.

1. Click frmSaleOrder in the Chapter 8 Forms section in the Navigation Pane. Press Ctrl+C and then Ctrl+V. Type frmPurchaseOrder in the text box of the Paste Table As dialog box, then click OK.
2. Open frmPurchaseOrder (in the Unassigned Objects section of the Navigation Pane) in Design view.
3. Click the title in the Header and change the title to Purchase Order Entry.
4. Change the name that appears on the form's tab. Click Property Sheet in the Tools group. Hide the Navigation Pane. Select Form from the combo box at the top of the Property Sheet. Click the Format tab if it is not already showing. Change the Caption to frmPurchaseOrder.
5. Change the data source of the subform. Select fsubSaleOrder (you have not yet changed the name to *fsubPurchaseOrder*) from the combo box at the top of the Property Sheet. Click the Data tab. Click the combo box arrow in the Source Object property and select fsubPurchaseOrder. Notice that *fsubPurchaseOrder* is immediately displayed in the subform box. Type PurchaseOrderID in both the Link Master Fields property and the Link Child Fields property. These properties link the subform to the form, which enables the form to display the correct Purchase Order Line Items for each Purchase Order.
6. Change the name of the subform in the Other tab (on the Property Sheet) to fsubPurchaseOrder.

EXERCISE 9.19: CREATING *FRMPURCHASEORDER* BY MODIFYING *FRMSALEORDER*—PART 2

In this exercise, you will create a new Record Source query behind the form and associate the Field Controls with data from the form's new Record Source.

1. Open frmPurchaseOrder in Design view if it is not already open. Change the form's data source. Select Form from the combo box at the top of the Property Sheet. Click the Data tab. Click the Builder button in the Record Source property. You should see a query window with frmPurchaseOrder : Query Builder on the tab.

2. Click on the qryCustomerInfo field roster in the Table Pane and press the Delete key. Delete the tblSaleOrder field roster the same way. Both the Table Pane and Criteria Pane should be empty.

3. Click Show Table in the Query Setup group. Double-click tblPurchaseOrder in the Table tab, and click the Query tab and double-click qryVendorInfo. Click the Close button.

4. Move and resize the tblPurchaseOrder and qryVendorInfo field rosters so you can see all field names, and leave some space between them to make it easy to see the link you will create.

5. Link *tblPurchaseOrder* to *qryVendorInfo* on their common field, VendorID. Click and drag the VendorID field from the qryVendorInfo field roster to the VendorID field in the tblPurchaseOrder field roster. You must create this link manually because Access does not automatically create links to/from queries.

6. Select all attributes in the *tblPurchaseOrder* field roster. Click PurchaseOrder, press and hold the Shift key, press the Down Arrow key repeatedly until all attributes are selected, and click and drag the attributes onto the Criteria Pane.

7. Add all attributes from the qryVendorInfo field roster except VendorID to the first available blank column in the Criteria Pane. You may need to use the Criteria Pane's Scroll Bar to make a blank column available.

8. Sort the form by PurchaseOrderID by selecting Ascending in the Sort cell of PurchaseOrderID.

9. Close the Query Builder. Click Yes in the Save Changes dialog box. Notice that all of the Field Controls have green triangle invalid control indicators because the source data they point to no longer exists in the form's Record Source—the query you just changed.

10. Change Field Controls and labels. Open the Property Sheet if it is not already open. Click the SaleOrderID control. Change the Control Source on the Data tab to PurchaseOrderID. Click the Other tab and change the Name to PurchaseOrderID. Click the Sale Order # label and change it to Purchase Order #. Repeat this process for all of the attributes listed in Figure 9.17.

11. Change the Input Mask (on the Property Sheet Data tab) for VendorID to 0000;;_. Delete Short Date from the Format property on the Format tab.

12. Change the Input Mask for PurchaseOrderDate to 99/99/0000;0;_. Set the Default Value to Date().

13. Change the Input Mask for ExpectedDeliveryDate to 99/99/0000;0;_.

14. Switch to Form view. Your form should look like Figure 9.18. Notice that the Primary Contact information is too low and that part of the subform is obscured from view without using the scroll bars. Return to Design view and move the Primary Contact control and label, and increase the height and width of the subform box. You will need to increase the width of the form to 8-1/2 inches. Figure 9.19 shows the completed form in Design view. Save your changes and close the form.

Fig. 9.17 Labels and Controls to change in *frmPurchaseOrder*.

Old Label	New Label	Old Record Source	New Record Source
Sale Order #	**Purchase Order #**	SaleOrderID	**PurchaseOrderID**
Salesperson	**Purchasing Agent**	n/a	**n/a**
Date	**Vendor #**	SaleOrderDate	**VendorID**
Customer #	**Order Date**	CustomerID	**PurchaseOrderDate**
Customer PO#	**Expected Delivery**	CustomerPO	**ExpectedDeliveryDate**
Amount	**Amount**	SaleOrderAmount	**PurchaseOrderAmount**
n/a	**n/a**	CustomerName	**VendorName**
n/a	**n/a**	CustomerAddress1	**VendorAddress1**
n/a	**n/a**	CustomerAddress2	**VendorAddress2**
n/a	**n/a**	CustomerTelephone	**VendorTelephone**
Credit Limit	**DELETE**	CustomerCreditLimit	**DELETE**
Primary Contact	**Primary Contact**	CustomerPrimaryContact	**VendorPrimaryContact**

Fig. 9.18 Purchase Order Entry form in Form view before final adjustments in Exercise 9.19.

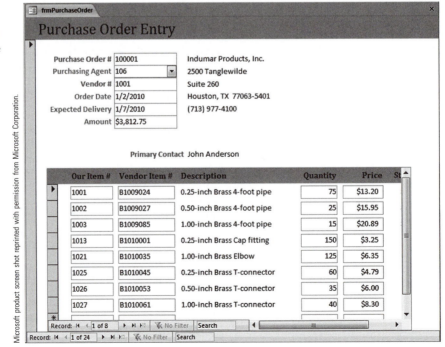

Fig. 9.19 Purchase Order Entry form in Design view after completing Exercise 9.19.

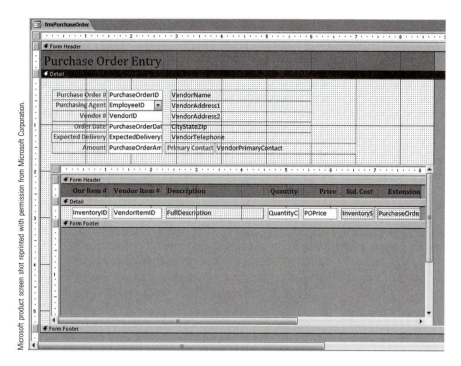

Microsoft product screen shot reprinted with permission from Microsoft Corporation.

The form you created is not quite yet functional. The Record Source for the Employee-ID combo box is *qrySalesperson*, which limits the employee choices to salespersons. You will modify *qrySalesperson* in the next exercise to create a purchasing agents query from which the combo box will derive its data.

EXERCISE 9.20: CHANGING THE *EMPLOYEEID* COMBO BOX

1. Click qrySalesperson in the Chapter 8 Queries section in the Navigation Pane. Press Ctrl+C and then Ctrl+V. Type qryPurchasingAgent in the text box of the Paste Table As dialog box, then click OK.
2. Open qryPurchasingAgent (in the Unassigned Objects section of the Navigation Pane) in Design view.
3. Change the Criteria for EmployeeTypeID to "60", which is the EmployeeTypeID for purchasing agents. View the query in Datasheet view to verify that all employees in the Dynaset are of Type 60. Save and close the query.
4. Open frmPurchaseOrder in Design view if it is not already open. Open the Property Sheet. Click the EmployeeID combo box. On the Data tab of the Property Sheet, change the Row Source to qryPurchasingAgent. Change the Name property on the Other tab to cboPurchasingAgent.
5. Switch to Form view. Notice that the Column Heads are not visible (see top of Figure 9.20). To make them visible, return to Design view. Click the Format tab and change the Column Heads property to Yes. Switch again to Form view. The Column Heads should now appear as they do in the bottom part of Figure 9.20.
6. Save and close the form.

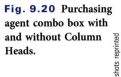

Fig. 9.20 Purchasing agent combo box with and without Column Heads.

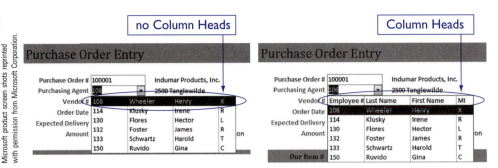

Microsoft product screen shots reprinted with permission from Microsoft Corporation.

EXERCISE 9.21: CREATING THE QUERY FOR AN INVENTORY LOOKUP COMBO BOX

1. Click qryPurchaseOrderLineItem in the Unassigned Objects section in the Navigation Pane. Press Ctrl+C and then Ctrl+V. Type qryPOInventoryItemLookup in the text box of the Paste Table As dialog box, and then click OK.

2. Open qryPOInventoryItemLookup (in the Unassigned Objects section of the Navigation Pane) in Design view.

3. Click tblReservation-PurchaseOrderInventory in the Tables Pane and delete it by pressing the Delete key. Notice that all fields referring to the Reservation table were also deleted. Delete PurchaseOrderLineExtension by clicking its column and pressing the Delete key.

View the query in Datasheet view. Notice that the inventory items are sorted by InventoryID. The only other option to sort this field is alphabetically in either ascending or descending order, which would sort items by size, then by composition, and then by type. If the purchasing agents later told you that they needed inventory sorted differently you would have to reconstruct the FullDescription expression to change the sort order. Therefore, to add more design flexibility, you will make a separate field for each category/type description.

4. Return to Design view. Delete the FullDescription field. If you cannot see all of the tables and their fields, either move the tables in the Table Pane or click and drag the separator between the Table Pane and Criteria Pane to enlarge the Table Pane.

5. Assume that Pipefitters would like the inventory sorted by Composition/Diameter/ Type. Drag CompositionDescription, InventoryDiameterDescription, and InventoryTypeDescription from their respective tables to the first, second, and third columns in the Criteria Pane, respectively. Select Ascending as the Sort property for all three fields.

6. Click and drag InventoryID from tblInventory to the first column of the Criteria Pane. InventoryID must be included in the query even though you will not see it in the combo box because InventoryID is the value you will store in *tblReservation-PurchaseOrderInventory*.

7. Switch to Datasheet view. Std. Cost is listed first because we made changes to an existing query. Click the Std. Cost Column Head to select the whole column. Click and drag the column to the right of the Type column. Also, notice that the items are no longer sorted by InventoryID because you changed the sort order to make it easier for Pipefitters' purchasing agents to find the inventory (see Figure 9.21).

0. Save and close the query.

Fig. 9.21 Inventory combo box in Form view.

Inventory #	Description	Description	Type	Std. Cost
1001	Brass	0.25-inch	4-foot pipe	$13.20
1007	Brass	0.25-inch	8-foot pipe	$24.60
1013	Brass	0.25-inch	Cap fitting	$3.20
1019	Brass	0.25-inch	Elbow	$3.20
1025	Brass	0.25-inch	T-connector	$4.80
1002	Brass	0.50-inch	4-foot pipe	$15.90
1008	Brass	0.50-inch	8-foot pipe	$30.60
1014	Brass	0.50-inch	Cap fitting	$5.30
1020	Brass	0.50-inch	Elbow	$4.50
1026	Brass	0.50-inch	T-connector	$6.00
1003	Brass	1.00-inch	4-foot pipe	$20.90
1009	Brass	1.00-inch	8-foot pipe	$37.50
1015	Brass	1.00-inch	Cap fitting	$8.00
1021	Brass	1.00-inch	Elbow	$6.30
1027	Brass	1.00-inch	T-connector	$8.30

EXERCISE 9.22: CREATING THE INVENTORY LOOKUP COMBO BOX

1. Open fsubPurchaseOrder in Design view. Click the InventoryID control and press the Delete key.
2. Create the Inventory Lookup combo box. Click Combo Box in the Controls group, and double-click in the Detail section of the subform where the InventoryID Control Box used to be.
   - In the first dialog box click the Next button to select the first option, *I want the combo box to lookup the values in a table or query*.
   - In the second dialog box, click the Queries radio button, and double-click Query: qryPOInventoryItemLookup to select the query and advance to the next dialog box.
   - Click >> to select all fields. Click the Next button.
   - Click the Next button because you already created your sort order in the query.
   - Click the Next button to accept the default size of the columns.
   - Click the Next button because InventoryID is already selected as the value to be stored in *tblReservation-PurchaseOrderInventory*.
   - Click the *Store that value in this field:* radio button, select InventoryID from the combo box. Click the Next button.
   - Click the Finish button to create the combo box.
3. Delete the label for the combo box you just created. Click the label control box, which may be difficult to see because it will overlap the InventoryID text box. Press the Delete key.
4. Move the combo box and its column head to the left edge of the subform.
5. Open the Property Sheet. Click the combo box. Change the Name property of the combo box on the Other tab to cboPOInventoryLookup. Change the Column Heads property on the Format tab to Yes.
6. Use Tab Order in the Control Layout on the Arrange ribbon to Auto Order the tabs on the subform. Click OK to accept the new tab order and close the form.
7. Check your new combo box (see Figure 9.20) and the tab order by switching to Form view. When you are done, save and close the subform.

The Purchase Order Entry form should also have a combo box as a control to help ensure that the correct VendorID is entered. Since creating a VendorID combo box is similar to other combo boxes you created, we will leave this task for you as an end-of-chapter exercise.

The Purchase Order Entry form already has many controls built into it, including the controls built into the tables (e.g., input masks, required fields, validation rules), database-level controls like enforcing referential integrity, and form level controls like disabling reference data and using combo boxes. In the next series of exercises you will create a Make-table query, an Update query, a macro, and a button, all to update the total amount of the purchase order.

EXERCISE 9.23: CREATING A MAKE-TABLE QUERY TO SUM PURCHASE ORDER LINE EXTENSIONS BY *PURCHASEORDERID*

This query is similar to the Make-table query you built in Chapter 8 to sum the Sale Line Extensions by sale invoice. Therefore, we will use that query as our starting point.

1. Click qrySumOfLineExtensionsByInvoice in the Chapter 8 Queries section in the Navigation Pane. Press Ctrl+C and then Ctrl+V. Type qrySumOfPOLineExtensionsByPO in the text box of the Paste Table As dialog box, then click OK.

2. Open qrySumOfPOLineExtensionsByPO (in the Unassigned Objects section of the Navigation Pane) in Design view by right-clicking on the query to bring up the shortcut menu.

3. Click Show Table in the Query Setup group, click the Queries tab, and double-click qryPurchaseOrderLineItem. Close the dialog box. Resize the query box to see all of the field names.

4. Double-click PurchaseOrderID and PurchaseOrderLineExtension, respectively, from *qryPurchaseOrderLineItem* in the Table Pane.

5. Change the Total cell for PurchaseOrderLineExtension to Sum.

6. Add a parameter in the Criteria row of PurchaseOrderID. Type [PO #]. When you run the query you will be prompted to enter the PurchaseOrderID of the Purchase Order amount you wish to update. Without the parameter, Access will recompute the sum of the line extensions for all purchase orders, which will take an increasingly long time to compute as more and more Purchase Orders are entered into the system.

7. Click the qrySumOfLineExtensionsByInvoice field roster in the Table Pane and press the Delete key to remove the query from the Table Pane and its two related fields in the Criteria Pane.

8. Open the property sheet. Click Property Sheet in the Show/Hide group. Click an empty area in the Table Pane to bring up the Query Properties in the Property Sheet.

9. Change the Destination Table property to tblSumOfPOLineExtensionsByPO. The query result will now be stored in a temporary table, *tblSumOfPOLineExtensionsByPO*. Each time this query is run, a new version of the table will be created. The old data will be lost. Close the property sheet and save your changes.

10. Click Run and type 100001 in the Enter Parameter Value dialog box. Notice the dialog box warning that you are about to paste one row into a new table, which cannot be undone. Click Yes and close the query. Verify the result by double-clicking tblSumOfPOLineExtensionsByPO, the table you just created, in the Unassigned Objects section of the Navigation Pane. Close the table when you are done. Double-click qrySumOfPOLineExtensionsByPO to run the query again. A dialog box warns that you are about to run a make-table query that will modify data in your table. Click Yes and you will receive another warning that the existing version of the table will be deleted before running the query. Click Yes and enter the Purchase Order number containing the Purchase Order Total you wish to update, and click OK. You will receive the warning that you are about to irreversibly paste one row into a new table. Click Yes. Close the query and open tblSumOfPOLineExtensionsByPO to verify the results. Close the table when you are done.

11. Open tblSumOfPOLineExtensionsByPO in Datasheet view to verify that the query results were transferred to the table (see Figure 9.22). Close the table.

Fig. 9.22 *qrySumOf-POLineExtensionsByPO* and *tblSumOfPOLine-ExtensionsByPO* in Datasheet view. For PO # 100001.

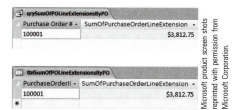

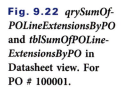

Now you need to transfer the total purchase order amount from *tblSumOfPOLineExtensionsByPO* to *tblPurchaseOrder*. This requires an Update query.

EXERCISE 9.24: CREATING AN UPDATE QUERY TO TRANSFER THE SUM OF PURCHASE ORDER LINE EXTENSIONS TO *TBLPURCHASEORDER*

1. Click the Create tab and click Query Design in the Other group.
2. In the Show Table dialog box double-click tblPurchaseOrder. Double-click tblSumOfPOLineExtensionsByPO. Close the dialog box. Resize the field rosters to show the entire table name and all field names.
3. Click Update Query in the Query Type group. You will see an Update To row appear in the Criteria Pane. The field and table in the first two rows of the Criteria Pane specify the field that gets updated. Double-click PurchaseOrderAmount in tblPurchaseOrder.
4. The Update To row specifies the table and attribute where the information comes from. Type [tblSumOfPOLineExtensionsByPO].[SumOfPurchaseOrderLineExtension]. Be sure to type the dot between the table name and field name.
5. Save your query as qryUpdatePurchaseOrderAmount. Close the query.
6. Test your Update query. Open tblPurchaseOrder in Datasheet view. Change the value of PurchaseOrderAmount for Purchase Order # 100001 to 0. Tab to the next record because Access does not update records until you either tab to the next record or close the table. Leave the table open.
7. Double-click qrySumOfPOLineExtensionsByPO to run the Make-table query. Click Yes in the warning dialog boxes. Type 100001 for the PO #. Double-click qryUpdatePurchaseOrderAmount to run the query. Click Yes in warning dialog boxes. Click anywhere in tblPurchaseOrder to **Repaint** the table, which updates PurchaseOrderAmount for PO #100001 to $3,812.75. Close the table.

EXERCISE 9.25: CREATING A MACRO TO AUTOMATE THE MAKE-TABLE AND UPDATE QUERIES

1. Click the Create tab and click Macro in the Other group. Click Show All Actions in the Show/Hide group because the Set Warnings action is not available in the default set of actions.
2. In the Action column of the first row, start typing SetWarnings. Access will recognize the action after you type SetW because no other action begins with the same four characters (see Figure 9.23). The SetWarnings action specifies whether system messages are displayed. When set to No (default setting) the warning dialog boxes you saw when running the Action queries are not displayed.

3. One way to run a query and view it in Datasheet view is to double-click it in the Navigation Pane. The OpenQuery action can perform the same function. Select OpenQuery in the Action column on the second row. When you know which Macro action you want, it is often quicker to start typing the action name instead of scrolling through the list.

4. Click on the Query Name cell in the Action Arguments Pane. Notice that the combo box arrow appears in the cell when you click on it. Select qrySumOfPOLineExtensionsByPO to run the first of the two queries you created to update PurchaseOrderAmount. Leave the View argument set to Datasheet, which will cause the OpenQuery action work like double-clicking a query in the Navigation Pane. Leave the Data Mode set to its default setting, Edit, which allows editing of existing records or new records to be added.

5. Add a second OpenQuery action in the Action Builder Pane. Move your cursor to the Action Arguments Pane. Select qryUpdatePurchaseOrderAmount in the Query Name cell. Leave the View argument set to Datasheet and the Data Mode set to Edit.

6. The last step to update the PurchaseOrderAmount in the form is to repaint the form, which will update the value in PurchaseOrderAmount the same way you repainted *tblPurchaseOrder* by clicking on it after running the Update query. Start typing RepaintObject in the next available Action cell until the full Macro action name appears.

7. Select Form as the Object Type in the Action Arguments Pane. Select frmPurchaseOrder from the list of Object Names. The completed macro appears in Figure 9.24.

8. Close the macro. In the Save As dialog box name your macro mcrUpdatePurchaseOrderAmount.

Fig. 9.23 Macro Builder.

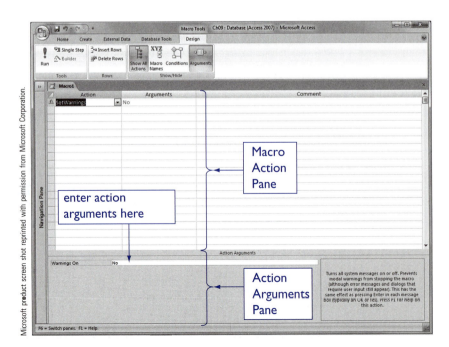

Fig. 9.24 Completed
Macro *mcrUpdate-*
PurchaseOrderAmount.

mcrUpdatePurchaseOrderAmount	
Action	**Arguments**
⚠ SetWarnings	No
OpenQuery	qrySumOfPOLineExtensionsByPO, Datasheet, Edit
OpenQuery	qryUpdatePurchaseOrderAmount, Datasheet, Edit
RepaintObject	Form, frmPurchaseOrder

EXERCISE 9.26: ADDING A BUTTON TO *FRMPURCHASEORDER* TO RUN THE MACRO

1. Open frmPurchaseOrder in Design view.
2. Make room for the Macro button at the bottom of the form. Click the subform to select it. Use the Up Arrow key to move the subform up, eliminating the space between it and the Primary Contact control. Grab the handle on the bottom of the subform and drag it up until you have 1/2-inch of space between the bottom of the subform and the Form Footer bar.
3. Click Button in the Controls group. Move your cursor to your newly created blank space at the bottom of the form's Detail section. Double-click to start the Command Button Wizard. The Command Button Wizard dialog boxes are reproduced in Figure 9.25 to help guide you through the process.
4. In the first dialog box, click Miscellaneous in the Category list, and then click Run Macro in the Actions list. Click Next.
5. Double-click mcrUpdatePurchaseOrderAmount in the next dialog box. Double-clicking selects the macro you want the button to run and advances you to the next dialog box.
6. To make it easy for a user to understand the purpose of a button, use a short, clear description of the button's function unless you have a picture that clearly illustrates the button's purpose. Since you may not have such a picture, click the Text radio button, type Update PO Amount in the Text box, and click Next.
7. In the last dialog box, type cmdUpdatePOAmount. Notice the *cmd* prefix for Command Buttons. Click Finish.
8. Click the PurchaseOrderAmount control, open the Property Sheet, and select the Data tab. To prevent users from entering incorrect Purchase Order totals change the Default Value to 0, change Enabled to No, and change Locked to Yes. Because this is a Required field, adding the Default Value allows the current record to be written to *tblPurchaseOrder* before the user runs the UpdatePOAmount macro.
9. Make it clear to users that PurchaseOrderAmount is not editable. On the Other tab, change the Tab Stop property to No. Click the Format tab and change both the Back Style and Border Style to Transparent.
10. Save your changes and close the form.

TRY IT

Test the Purchase Order Entry form. Double-click frmPurchaseOrder in the Navigation Pane. Enter the information from Figure 9.26. After you enter the data, press the UpdatePOAmount Command Button. Type 999999 in the dialog box and click OK. The PurchaseOrderAmount value should change from $0.00 to $552.00.

Use the Record Selectors to delete the data you just entered. Click a Record Selector in the subform and press the Delete key. Repeat this process for the remaining items in the subform, and then use the form's Record Selector to delete the form data.

Fig. 9.25 **Command Button Wizard dialog boxes.**

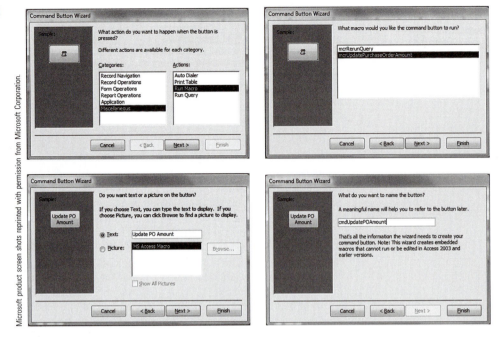

Microsoft product screen shots reprinted with permission from Microsoft Corporation.

Fig. 9.26 **Purchase Order Entry form with test data.**

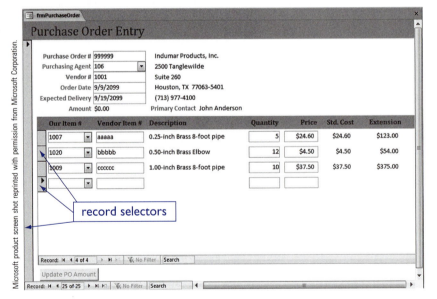

Microsoft product screen shot reprinted with permission from Microsoft Corporation.

Recording Purchases (Inventory Receipts)

Once Pipefitters Supply Company enters its purchase order data and transmits its purchase order data to vendors (by mail, fax, e-mail, or a vendor's Web site), *tblReservation-PurchaseOrderInventory* will contain the detailed line item information about what it expects vendors to ship. When merchandise arrives on the receiving dock, Pipefitters will want to record the quantity and identity of each item in each shipment. Materials handlers enter this receiving report information directly into the firm's accounting system using a database form. This electronic receiving report enters data directly into the Purchase table.

Many firms use bar code scanners that read inventory identification codes on inventory packages. These scanners can also date- and time-stamp the inventory receipt record. The accounts payable department collects other information about inventory received, including vendor invoice number and each item's price, from vendor invoices and can enter that information directly into the Purchase table.

To capture Purchase data in your database, you will use the following tables as shown in Figure 9.4: *tblPurchase*, *tblInflow-PurchaseInventory*, *tblInventory*, *tblEmployee*, *tblVendor*, and *tblPurchaseOrder*. The only new tables you need to create are *tblPurchase* and *tblInflow-PurchaseInventory*. Since these tables are similar to *tblPurchaseOrder tblReservation-PurchaseOrderInventory*, you do not need to create them from scratch.

The Purchase Table

The purchase table stores information similar to the Purchase Order table. Figure 9.27 shows the similarities between the fields of the two tables. The main difference is that the primary key from *tblSaleOrder* is posted as a foreign key in *tblSale*. This link allows Pipefitters to determine which sale orders have been fulfilled, and, for the unfilled and partially filled orders, which inventory items still need to be delivered.

Fig. 9.27 Comparison of fields for *tblPurchaseOrder* and *tblPurchase*.

Table Name	tblPurchaseOrder	tblPurchase
Primary Key	PurchaseOrderID	InventoryReceiptID
Date	PurchaseOrderDate	InventoryReceiptDate
Other Date	ExpectedDeliveryDate	n/a
Amount	PurchaseOrderAmount	InventoryReceiptAmount
Other Attribute	n/a	VendorInvoiceID
Vendor (FK)	VendorID	VendorID
Employee (FK)	EmployeeID	EmployeeID
Other (FK)	n/a	PurchaseOrderID

EXERCISE 9.27: CREATING THE PURCHASE TABLE

1. Click tblPurchaseOrder in the Unassigned Objects section of the Navigation Pane. Press Ctrl+C and then Ctrl+V. Type tblPurchase in the text box of the Paste Table As dialog box, click the Structure Only Paste Option, and then click OK.
2. Open tblPurchase (in the Unassigned Objects section of the Navigation Pane) in Design view.
3. Copy PurchaseOrderID. Right-click the Primary Key field of PurchaseOrderID. Move your cursor to the first empty row, right-click, and then click Paste to create a copy of PurchaseOrderID. Change the Indexed property to Yes (Duplicates OK).
4. Make the following changes to the Field Names and Captions. Do NOT delete the fields
   - Change Field Name: PurchaseOrderID (the primary key) to InventoryReceiptID.
   - Change Caption property from Purchase Order # to Inventory Receipt #.

- Change Field Name from PurchaseOrderDate to InventoryReceiptDate.
  - Change Caption property from Date Ordered to Date Received.
- Change Field Name from PurchaseOrderAmount to InventoryReceiptAmount.
  - Change Validation Text property from Purchase Order amount... to Inventory Receipt amount...

5. Delete ExpectedDeliveryDate. Right-click on ExpectedDeliveryDate, click Delete Rows.

6. Add a new field, VendorInvoiceID.
   - Change Field Size to 20.
   - Type Vendor Invoice # in the Caption property cell.
   - Set the Required property to Yes.
   - Set the Allow Zero Length property to No.
   - Set the Indexed property to Yes (Duplicates OK) because it is likely that Pipefitters will lookup inventory receipts by the vendor's invoice number.

7. Move a Field Row by clicking the Record Selector next to the Field Name. Then click and drag it to its desired place. Move EmployeeID and PurchaseOrderID so your fields are in the same order as the table in Figure 9.28.

8. Open the Property Sheet. Delete the table-level Validation Rule and Validation Text that you created for *tblPurchaseOrder*.

9. Save and close the table.

10. Import data from the *Ch09.xlsx* Excel file for *tblPurchase*. Follow the instructions in Exercise 9.11, substituting *tblPurchase* for *tblPurchaseOrder*. When you finish importing the data, open *tblPurchase* to verify that all 27 records were imported.

Fig. 9.28 *tblPurchase* Field list.

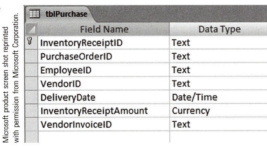

The Purchase-Inventory Table

The Purchase-Inventory table records the many-to-many inflow relationship between *tblPurchase* and *tblInventory*. These are the goods that Pipefitters actually receives from vendors. Therefore, *tblInflow-PurchaseInventory* will store four fields:

1. The primary key of *tblPurchase*.
2. The primary key of *tblInventory*.
3. The quantity of each inventory item received.
4. The price of each inventory item received.

The primary keys from *tblPurchase* and *tblInventory* will combine to form the composite primary key in *tblInflow-PurchaseInventory*. Before you begin the next exercise, close any open tables or forms.

EXERCISE 9.28: CREATING THE *TBLINFLOW-PURCHASEINVENTORY* RELATIONSHIP TABLE

1. Click tblReservation-PurchaseOrderInventory in the Unassigned Objects section of the Navigation Pane. Click Ctrl+C, then Ctrl+V. In the Paste Table As dialog box, type tblInflow-PurchaseInventory in the name box, and then click the Structure Only radio button and click OK.
2. Open tblInflow-PurchaseInventory in Design view.
3. Make the following changes to the Field Names and Captions. Do NOT delete the fields:
   - Change Field Name from PurchaseOrderID (the primary key) to Inventory-ReceiptID.
     - Change Caption property from Purchase Order # to Inventory Receipt #.
   - Change Field Name from QuantityOrdered to QuantityReceived.
   - Change Field Name from POPrice to InventoryReceiptPrice.
4. Delete VendorItemID.
5. Save and close the table.
6. Import data from the *Ch09.xlsx* Excel file for *tblInflow-PurchaseInventory*. Follow the instructions in Exercise 9.11, substituting tblInflow-PurchaseInventory for tblPurchaseOrder. When you finish importing the data, open tblInflow-PurchaseInventory to verify that all 173 records were imported.

The Inventory Receipt (Purchase) Entry Form

The Inventory Receipt Entry form closely resembles the Purchase Order Entry form that you created earlier in the chapter. The main difference is that the Inventory Receipt Entry form records what Pipefitters' actually receives from vendors, which may be only part of what they ordered. Although we refer to the form used to enter merchandise received as the Inventory Receipt Entry form, we named the underlying tables *tblPurchase* and *tblPurchaseLineItem* because taking title to the merchandise (when received) is the GAAP definition of a purchase event.

Creating Relationships with the Purchase Table

In Exercise 9.29 you will add the relationships with *tblPurchase* necessary to build the Inventory Receipt Entry form.

EXERCISE 9.29: CREATING RELATIONSHIPS RELATED TO THE PURCHASE EVENT

1. Close all open Access objects.
2. On the Database Tools tab, click Relationships in the Show/Hide group. Your Relationships window should look like how you left it at the end of Exercise 9.13 (see Figure 9.13).
3. Minimize the Navigation Pane by clicking the << at the top-right corner of the pane.
4. Click Show Table in the Relationships group (on the Design tab), double-click tblPurchase and tblInflow-SaleInventory. Then click Close.
5. Create your links the same way you did in Exercise 9.13. Drag from the primary key to the matching foreign key or from the primary key to the matching part of a composite primary key.

6. When the Edit Relationships dialog box appears make sure that the correct attributes appear in the tables you dragged from and to. The relationship type at the bottom of the dialog box should always be one-to-many. Check Enforce Referential Integrity and Cascade Update Related Fields. Finally, click Create in the dialog box.
7. Resize and move the newly added tables to look like the Relationships window in Figure 9.29. You may also refer back to Figure 9.4, which lists the primary and foreign keys for each table.
8. Close the Relationships window and click the Yes button in the dialog box to save your changes, then click >> on the Navigation Pane to restore it.

Fig. 9.29 Relationships window after adding Purchase event.

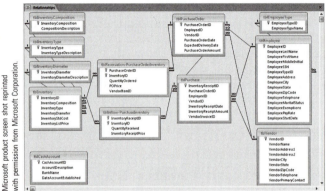

Microsoft product screen shot reprinted with permission from Microsoft Corporation.

Now that you have established the necessary foreign key and relationship table links, you can create an Inventory Receipt Entry form. Because the Inventory Receipt Entry form is similar to the Purchase Order Entry form, it is possible to use *frmPurchaseOrder* and *fsubPurchaseOrder* to create the Inventory Receipt Entry form. Although it is sometimes easier to create complex forms like this from scratch, we want you to modify existing Access objects to help you better understand what happens "behind the scenes," which will give you the ability to fix problems and make improvements to existing forms and other Access objects.

Creating a Query for Purchase Line Items

The main difference between the query for purchase order line items and the query for purchase line items is that *tblReservation-PurchaseOrderInventory* and its fields are replaced with *tblInflow-PurchaseInventory* and its fields. A minor difference is that Pipefitters does not record the VendorItemID on receipt of the inventory, just when it places the order.

EXERCISE 9.30: MODIFYING *QRYPURCHASEORDERLINEITEM* TO CREATE *QRYPURCHASELINEITEM*

In this exercise you will change the subform's Record Source and the Control Source for all existing fields.

1. Right-click qryPurchaseOrderLineItem in the Unassigned Objects section of the Navigation Pane. Click Copy. Right-click anywhere in the Navigation Pane. Click

Paste. In the Paste Table As dialog box, type qryPurchaseLineItem in the name box; click the Structure Only radio button and then click OK.

2. Open qryPurchaseLineItem in Design view.

3. Click Show Table in the Query Setup group, double-click tblInflow-PurchaseInventory, and click the Close button. You may need to move and resize *tblInflow-PurchaseInventory* in the Table Pane to see all field names.

4. On the Criteria Pane, change the table reference for InventoryID to tblInflow-PurchaseInventory.

5. Delete VendorItemID from the Criteria Pane.

6. Change the table reference for QuantityOrdered to tblInflow-PurchaseInventory. Change the Field from QuantityOrdered to QuantityReceived.

7. Change the table reference for POPrice to tblInflow-PurchaseInventory. Change the Field from POPrice to InventoryReceiptPrice.

8. Change the table reference for PurchaseOrderID to tblInflow-PurchaseInventory. Change the Field from PurchaseOrderID to InventoryReceiptID. Save your changes.

9. Click the PurchaseOrderLineExtension field on the Criteria Pane, and click Builder in the Query Setup group. In Expression Builder, change the expression to PurchaseLineExtension: [QuantityReceived]*[InventoryReceiptPrice]. Click OK.

10. Delete tblPurchaseOrderLineItem from the Table Pane. Save your changes.

11. Check your query. Click Run in the Results group. The dynaset should look similar to Figure 9.30, with 173 records. Close the query.

Fig. 9.30 *qry-PurchaseLineItem* **dynaset.**

Microsoft product screen shot reprinted with permission from Microsoft Corporation.

Item #	Description	Quantity	Price	Std. Cost	Extension	Inventory Receipt
1001	0.25-inch Brass 4-foot pipe	75	$13.20	$13.20	$990.00	100001
1001	0.25-inch Brass 4-foot pipe	75	$13.00	$13.20	$975.00	100010
1001	0.25-inch Brass 4-foot pipe	20	$13.00	$13.20	$260.00	100016
1001	0.25-inch Brass 4-foot pipe	60	$13.20	$13.20	$792.00	100020
1002	0.50-inch Brass 4-foot pipe	25	$15.95	$15.90	$398.75	100001
1002	0.50-inch Brass 4-foot pipe	60	$16.00	$15.90	$960.00	100010
1002	0.50-inch Brass 4-foot pipe	65	$16.00	$15.90	$1,040.00	100016
1002	0.50-inch Brass 4-foot pipe	40	$15.95	$15.90	$638.00	100020
1002	0.50-inch Brass 4-foot pipe	30	$16.00	$15.90	$480.00	100025
1003	1.00-inch Brass 4-foot pipe	15	$20.89	$20.90	$313.35	100001
1003	1.00-inch Brass 4-foot pipe	50	$21.00	$20.90	$1,050.00	100010
1003	1.00-inch Brass 4-foot pipe	15	$21.00	$20.90	$315.00	100016
1003	1.00-inch Brass 4-foot pipe	35	$20.89	$20.90	$731.15	100020
1004	2.00-inch Brass 4-foot pipe	15	$26.30	$26.30	$394.50	100004
1004	2.00-inch Brass 4-foot pipe	25	$26.30	$26.30	$657.50	100011
1004	2.00-inch Brass 4-foot pipe	15	$26.30	$26.30	$394.50	100015
1004	2.00-inch Brass 4-foot pipe	30	$26.30	$26.30	$789.00	100022
1005	3.00-inch Brass 4-foot pipe	15	$33.25	$33.20	$498.75	100011
1005	3.00-inch Brass 4-foot pipe	30	$33.20	$33.20	$996.00	100015
1005	3.00-inch Brass 4-foot pipe	40	$33.20	$33.20	$1,328.00	100022
1006	4.00-inch Brass 4-foot pipe	35	$39.25	$39.20	$1,373.75	100004
1006	4.00-inch Brass 4-foot pipe	10	$39.25	$39.20	$392.50	100011
1006	4.00-inch Brass 4-foot pipe	10	$39.20	$39.20	$392.00	100015
1007	0.25-inch Brass 8-foot pipe	25	$24.75	$24.60	$618.75	100007
1007	0.25-inch Brass 8-foot pipe	60	$24.50	$24.60	$1,470.00	100010
1007	0.25-inch Brass 8-foot pipe	50	$24.50	$24.60	$1,225.00	100016

Record: 1 of 173   No Filter   Search

TRY IT

How do you know that *qryPurchaseLineItem* should produce 173 records? Find where the data for the fields comes from and verify that you should have 173 records.

Modifying frmPurchaseOrder *and* fsubPurchaseOrder *to Create the Inventory Receipt Form* (frmPurchase)

Modifying the Since the Sale Entry form is similar in complexity to the Sale Order Entry form; you will use Form Wizard to create it. The main form is based on *tblSale* and *qryVendorInfo*, and the subform follows *qrySaleLineItem*. In addition to the controls used in the Sale Order Entry form, you will add controls to this form that resolve the following questions: How can a salesperson remember so many vendor numbers and avoid making typos even if he or she remembers some of them? How can a salesperson remember all inventory item IDs and how can typos be prevented?

EXERCISE 9.31: MODIFYING *FSUBPURCHASEORDER* TO CREATE *FSUBPURCHASE*

1. Click fsubPurchaseOrder in the Unassigned Objects section in the Navigation Pane. Press Ctrl+C and then Ctrl+V. Type fsubPurchase in the text box of the Paste Table As dialog box, then click OK.
2. Open fsubPurchase in Design view. Click Property Sheet in the Tools group; hide the Navigation Pane.
3. The Property Sheet should open to the Data tab with Form selected. Change the Record Source to qryPurchaseLineItem.
4. Click the Format tab. Change the Caption to fsubPurchase.
5. Delete the VendorItemID control from the Detail section and its label from the Form Header section.
6. Click the QuantityOrdered control. Change the Control Source property from QuantityOrdered to QuantityReceived in the Data tab. On the Other tab, change the Name to QuantityReceived.
7. Click the POPrice control. Change the Control Source on the Data tab to InventoryReceiptPrice. Change the Name on the Other tab to InventoryReceiptPrice.
8. Click the PurchaseOrderLineExtention control. Change the Control Source on the Data tab to PurchaseLineExtension. Change the Name on the Other tab to PurchaseLineExtention.
9. Adjust the spacing of the controls and labels. Close the Property Sheet. Press Ctrl+A. Press and hold the Shift and click the Our Item # label and the InventoryID combo box to unselect them. Press and hold the Left Arrow key, or just press it repeatedly to move all items selected to the left to eliminate the large blank space caused by deleting the VendorItemID control and label.
10. Eliminate blank space in the Form Header and Detail sections by moving the labels and controls to the top of their respective form sections and dragging the Detail and Form Footer bars upward (see Figure 9.31).
11. View the subform in Form view (see Figure 9.32). Save and close the subform.

Fig. 9.31 *fsub-Purchase* **in Design view.**

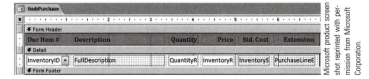

Fig. 9.32 *fsub-Purchase* in Form view.

Microsoft product screen shot reprinted with permission from Microsoft Corporation.

EXERCISE 9.32: MODIFYING *FRMPURCHASEORDER* TO CREATE *FRMPURCHASE*—PART 1

The main tasks you will perform in Part 1 will be to create a copy of *frmPurchaseOrder*, change captions, and change the data source for the subform.

1. Click frmPurchaseOrder Unassigned Objects section in the Navigation Pane. Press Ctrl+C and then Ctrl+V. Type frmPurchase in the text box of the Paste Table As dialog box, and then click OK.
2. Open frmPurchase in Design view.
3. Click on the title in the Header and change the title to Inventory Receipt Entry.
4. Reduce the width of the subform control. Click the subform, and grab one of the right handles (small box on the line surrounding the subform; cursor turns into a two-headed arrow) and drag handle to the left to reduce the size of the subform control. Then drag the edge of the Detail section to the edge of the subform control to eliminate empty space (see Figure 9.33).
5. Make room for an additional Control in the top of the form. Press and hold the Shift key. Click the subform and the Update PO Amount Command Button. Press the Down Arrow key repeatedly until you have room to insert an additional control above the subform.
6. Click Property Sheet in the Tools group. Hide the Navigation Pane. Select Form from the combo box at the top of the Property Sheet. Click the Format tab if it is not already showing. Change the Caption to frmPurchase.
7. Change the data source of the subform. Select fsubPurchaseOrder (you have not yet changed the name to *fsubPurchase*) from the combo box at the top of the Property Sheet. Click the Data tab. Click the combo box arrow in the Source Object property and select fsubPurchase. Type InventoryReceiptID in both the Link Master Fields property and the Link Child Fields property (you cannot use the Builder button because the Data Source of the form has not yet been changed).
8. Change the name of the subform in the Other tab to fsubPurchase.
9. Save your changes.

EXERCISE 9.33: MODIFYING *FRMPURCHASEORDER* TO CREATE *FRMPURCHASE*—PART 2

The next set of steps will lead you through the process of changing the query behind the form.

1. Select Form from the combo box at the top of the Property Sheet. Click the Data tab. Click the Builder button in the Record Source property. You should see a query window with frmPurchase: Query Builder on the tab.
2. Click Show Table in the Query Setup group. Double-click tblPurchase. Click the Close button.
3. Delete the ExpectedDeliveryDate column on the Criteria Pane.
4. Change all table cells for all fields currently set to tblPurchaseOrder to tblPurchase: PurchaseOrderID, EmployeeID, VendorID, PurchaseOrderDate, and PurchaseOrderAmount.
5. Change the following field cells:
   - From PurchaseOrderID to InventoryReceiptID
   - From PurchaseOrderDate to InventoryReceiptDate
   - From PurchaseOrderAmount to InventoryReceiptAmount
6. Drag PurchaseOrderID from the tblPurchase field roster into the Criteria Pane to the right of InventoryReceiptID.
7. Drag VendorInvoiceID from the tblPurchase field roster into the Criteria Pane to the right of PurchaseOrderID.
8. Delete tblPurchaseOrder from the Table Pane.
9. Click Run in the Results group to verify that the dynaset shows 27 records. Return to Datasheet view. Close the Query Builder. Click Yes in the Save Changes dialog box.

EXERCISE 9.34: MODIFYING *FRMPURCHASEORDER* TO CREATE *FRMPURCHASE*—PART 3

The main tasks in Part 3 are to change data sources and labels for existing controls and adding additional controls and labels.

1. Delete the ExpectedDeliveryDate control, which deletes its label, too.
2. Make room for PuchaseOrderID and VendorInvoiceID and their labels below InventoryReceiptID by moving EmployeeID, VendorID, InventoryReceiptDate, and InventoryReceiptAmount to just above the subform. Delete the blank space between the PurchaseOrderDate and PurchaseOrderAmount controls and related labels.
3. Add PurchaseOrderID to the form. Select InventoryReceiptID, press Ctrl+C, then press Ctrl+V twice. Click the Arrange tab. Select all of the controls and labels to the left of the Vendor information. Click Top in Control Alignment group to align the controls and labels. Change Field Controls and labels. You should have three copies of PurchaseOrderID. We will refer to them as PurchseOrderID 1, 2, and 3.
4. Click the PurchaseOrderID1 control. Change the Control Source on the Data tab to InventoryReceiptID. Click the Other tab and change the Name to InventoryReceiptID. Repeat this process with the following controls and labels:
   - Change Control Source and Name from PurchaseOrderID2 to PurchaseOrderID.
   - Change Control Source and Name from PurchaseOrderID3 to VendorInvoiceID. Delete the Input Mask on the Data tab.

- Change Control Source and Name from PurchaseOrderDate to InventoryReceiptDate.
- Change Control Source and Name from PurchaseOrderAmount to InventoryReceiptAmount.

5. Change the following labels:
   - From Purchase Order # (1) to Inventory Receipt #
   - From Purchase Order # (3) to Vendor Invoice #
   - From Purchasing Agent to Materials Handler
   - From Order Date to Date Received.
6. Click the EmployeeID combo box. Change the Row Source for EmployeeID on the Data tab to qryMaterialsHandler. Change the Name on the Other tab to cboMaterialsHandler.
7. Change the tab order. Click Tab Order on the Arrange ribbon. Move PurchaseOrderID into the second position and VendorInvoiceID into the third position. Click OK. Save your changes.
8. Eliminate the blank space at the top of the form so it looks like the form in Design view in Figure 9.33. Switch to Form view. Your form should look like Figure 9.34. Save your changes and close the form.

Fig. 9.33 *frmPurchase* in Design view after completing Exercise 9.34.

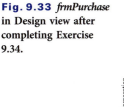

Microsoft product screen shot reprinted with permission from Microsoft Corporation.

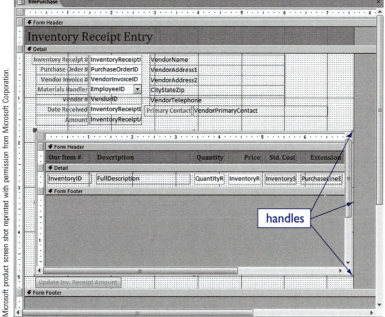

Fig. 9.34 *frm-Purchase* **in Form view after completing Exercise 9.34.**

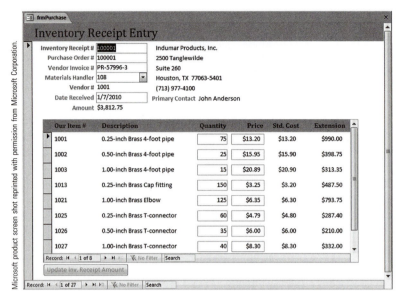

The Inventory Receipt Entry form you created in the last several exercises functions properly except for the Update PO Amount Command button. In Exercise 9.35, you will build a new set of queries to update InventoryReceiptAmount in *frmPurchase*, modify *mcrUpdatePurchaseOrderAmount*, and modify the *cmdUpdatePOAmount* Command button. Use the detailed instructions provided in Exercises 9.23 through 9.26 along with brief explanations in Exercise 9.35, below, and the accompanying figures.

EXERCISE 9.35: CREATE QUERIES, A MACRO, AND A BUTTON TO UPDATE *INVENTORYRECEIPTAMOUNT*

1. Create a Make-table query similar to *qrySumOfPOLineExtensionsByIR* to sum PurchaseLineExtensions by InventoryReceiptID. Click Query Design on the Create ribbon, add qryPurchaseLineItem from the Show Table dialog box. Click Totals in the Show/Hide group, add InventoryReceiptID and PurchaseLineExtension to the Criteria Pane, then make adjustments so your Criteria Pane looks like Figure 9.35. Click Make Table in the Query Type group and enter tblSumOfPurchLineExtensionsByIR as shown in the Make Table dialog box in Figure 9.35. Save the query as qrySumOfPurchLineExtensionsByIR and close the query. Double-click qrySumOfPurchLineExtensionsByIR in the Navigation Pane to run it. Type 100001 in the dialog box. Check tblSumOfPurchLineExtensionsByIR to verify that the total is $3,812.75.

2. Create an Update query similar to *qryUpdatePurchaseOrderAmount*. Click Query Design on the Create ribbon; add tblPurchase and tblSumOfPurchLineExtensionsByIR from the Show Table dialog box. Click Make Table in the Query Type group. Add InventoryReceiptAmount to the Criteria Pane. Type [tblSumOfPurchLineExtensionsByIR].[SumOfPurchaseLineExtension] (see Figure 9.36). Save your query as qryUpdateInventoryReceiptAmount. Test your query by opening *tblPurchase* and changing the InventoryReceiptAmount for InventoryReceiptID 100001 in to 0 and closing the table. Double-click qryUpdateInventoryReceiptAmount in the Navigation Pane to run the query. Check *tblPurchase* to verify that InventoryReceiptAmount for InventoryReceiptID 100001 was changed to $3,812.75.

3. Modify *mcrUpdatePurchaseOrderAmount*. Click mcrUpdatePurchaseOrderAmount in the Navigation Pane. Press Ctrl+C to copy the table. Press Ctrl+V to paste it and name it mcrUpdateInventoryReceiptAmount. Open mcrUpdateInventoryRe-

ceiptAmount in Design view. Change the Query Name (in the Action Arguments Pane) for the first OpenQuery action to qrySumOfPurchLineExtensionsByIR. Change the Query Name for the second OpenQuery action to qryUpdateInventoryReceiptAmount. Change the Object Name for the RepaintObject action to frmPurchase (see Figure 9.37). Save and close the macro.

4. Modify the Command Button in *frmPurchase*. Open frmPurchase in Design view. Open the Property Sheet and select cmdUpdatePOAmount. Change the Caption on the Format tab to Update Inv. Receipt Amount. Change the On Click property on the Event tab to mcrUpdateInventoryReceiptAmount. Change the Name on the Other tab to cmdUpdateInvReceiptAmount (see Figure 9.38). Click the Command button and drag the right handle to the right until the entire Caption is showing. Save and close the form.

5. Test the new Command button. Change InventoryReceiptAmount for InventoryReceiptID 100003 in *tblPurchase* to 0 and close the table, double-click qrySumOfPurchLinExtensionsByIR in the Navigation Pane to run the query, click Yes to the two warning dialog boxes, enter 100003 in the Inventory Receipt ID dialog box, and click Yes to the warning dialog box. Double-click qryUpdateInventoryReceiptAmount in the Navigation Pane to run the query, and click Yes to the warning dialog boxes. Check *tblPurchase* to verify that InventoryReceiptAmount for InventoryReceiptID 100003 was changed to $664.50.

Fig. 9.35 *qrySumPurchLineExtensionsByIR* in Design view.

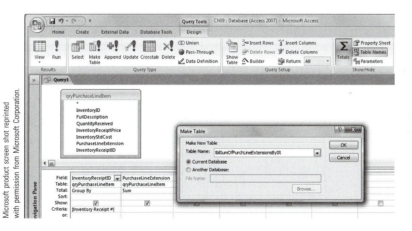

Microsoft product screen shot reprinted with permission from Microsoft Corporation.

Fig. 9.36 *qryUpdateInventoryReceiptAmount* in Design view.

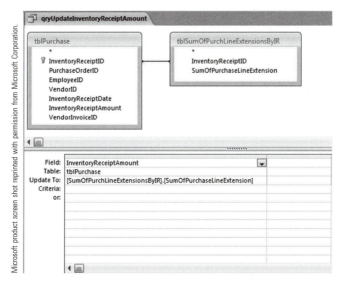

Microsoft product screen shot reprinted with permission from Microsoft Corporation.

Fig. 9.37 *mcrUpdate-InventoryReceipt-Amount* **in Design view.**

Microsoft product screen shot reprinted with permission from Microsoft Corporation.

Fig. 9.38 *frm-Purchase* **Property Sheet for** *cmdUpdate InvReceiptAmount.*

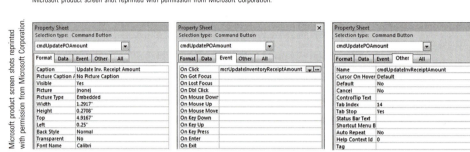

Microsoft product screen shots reprinted with permission from Microsoft Corporation.

Adding a Control for VendorID to Inventory Receipt Entry Form

Pipefitters Supply Company's accounting system links inventory receipts to specific purchase orders. Although the vendor for the inventory receipt must be the same as the vendor on the related purchase order, the current Inventory Receipt Entry form contains no control to ensure that the vendor on the purchase order is the same vendor recorded on the related inventory receipt(s). In the next set of exercises you will add a button to *frmPurchase* that updates the VendorID, which is similar to the button that updates InventoryReceiptAmount.

EXERCISE 9.36: CREATE AN UPDATE QUERY TO TRANSFER VENDORID FROM *TBLPURCHASEORDER* TO *TBLPURCHASE*

1. Before creating the Update query, you need to add a dummy Vendor to *tblVendor* so that it is easy to tell that VendorID has not yet been input into *frmPurchase*. Use *frmVendor* to add Vendor 9999 with the information provided in Figure 9.39.
2. Click Query Design on the Create ribbon. Add tblPurchase and tblPurchaseOrder from the Show Table dialog box. Click Update in the Query Type group.
3. Double-click VendorID in the tblPurchase field roster and double-click PurchaseOrderID in the tblPurchaseOrder field roster to add them to the Criteria Pane, type [tblPurchaseOrder].[VendorID] in the Update To cell for VendorID, and type "9999" in the Criteria cell (see Figure 9.40).
4. Double-click InventoryReceiptID in tblPurchase to add it to the Criteria Pane. In Chapter 8, you created queries for Accounts Receivable using date parameters that allow users to compute the Accounts Receivable balance for any date. However, when you used parameters in *qrySumOfPOLineExtensionsByPO* and *qrySumOfPurchLineExtensionsByIR*, the *Enter Parameter Value dialog box* requires the user to retype information that he or she just entered into the current record of a form. To eliminate this potential source of errors, the macro you will build in the next exercise creates a temporary variable from data in the current form record that will become the criteria in this query.
5. In the Criteria cell for InventoryReceiptID, type the location of the temporary variable created by the macro: [TempVars]![TempInventoryReceiptID] (see Figure 9.40). Using a Parameter query to search for a specific InventoryReceiptID will

save much computing time as the database gets larger. Otherwise, Access would have to search all records in *tblPurchase* for VendorIDs equal to 9999.

6. Save your query as qryUpdateVendorID. Close the query. Open frmPurchase in Design view, and open the Property Sheet and minimize the Navigation Pane.

7. Click VendorID to change its properties to have it look like a reference field such as VendorName. On the Format tab change both the Back Style and Border Style to Transparent. On the Data tab, change Enabled to No and Locked to Yes. Set the Default Value to 9999 so the dummy vendor information is automatically entered, just like the $0.00 default value is automatically entered as the PurchaseOrderAmount. Change the Tab Stop on the Other tab to No.

8. Save and close the form. Restore the Navigation Pane.

Fig. 9.39 Dummy vendor 9999 information entered in *frmVendor.*

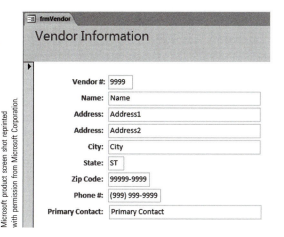

Fig. 9.40 *qryUpdate-VendorID* in Design view.

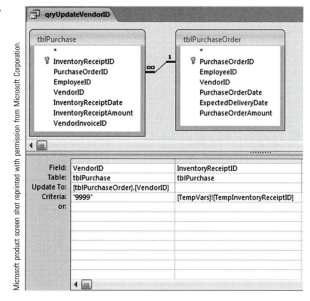

EXERCISE 9.37: CREATE A MACRO TO UPDATE THE VENDORID IN *FRMPURCHASE*

Refer back to Exercise 9.25 for additional discussion of Macro Actions used in that exercise: SetWarnings, OpenQuery, and RepaintObject.

1. Click the Create tab and click Macro in the Other group. Click Show All Actions in the Show/Hide group because some actions are not available in the default set of actions.

2. Type or select SetWarnings in the Action column of the first row. Leave the default Action Argument set to No to disable system messages.

3. Set the second Action to RunCommand and choose SaveRecord from the list of Commands in the Action Arguments Pane. This forces the current record to be saved. This will save the data you entered in *frmPurchase* into *tblPurchase*.

4. Create a temporary variable for InventoryReceiptID that will be used in qryUpdateVendorID. Type or select SetTempVar in the next available Action row. Type TempInventoryReceiptID in the Name argument text box. Click the Build button next to the Expression argument text box. In the Expression Builder, double-click Forms; double-click AllForms; double-click frmPurchase; and double-click InventoryReceiptID in the second column (see Figure 9.41). Click OK to close Expression Builder, and add your expression to the Expression argument box. This expression directs Access to set the temporary variable, TempInventoryReceiptID, equal to the current value in the InventoryReceiptID control of *frmPurchase*. Press the F1 key to find out more about the SetTempVar action.

5. Add an OpenQuery action to run *qryUpdateVendorID*, and select qryUpdateVendorID from the list of Query Names in the Action Arguments Pane. Leave the default values for View (Datasheet) and Data Mode (Edit).

6. Select or type RepaintObject in the next available Action cell. In the Action Arguments Pane, select Form as the Object Type and frmPurchase as the Object Name.

7. Finally, remove the temporary variable to prevent it from being accidentally used by another query or macro. Add a RemoveTempVar action to your macro. Type TempInventoryReceiptID for the name of the temporary variable you want to remove. The completed macro appears in Figure 9.42.

8. Close the macro. In the Save As dialog box, name your macro mcrUpdateVendorIDandInvItems. The *andInvItems* part of the name is necessary because you will add additional Actions to this macro in the next set of exercises to transfer inventory items ordered to the Inventory Receipt Entry form.

9. Test your query and macro by opening *tblPurchase* and changing VendorID for InventoryReceiptID 100002 in to 9999 and closing the table. Because the SaveRecord Command will not work unless it is activated from within the form (SaveRecord saves the record of the active object, which will NOT be the form when you double-click the macro in the Navigation Pane), delete that row from your macro before proceeding with your test. Open frmPurchase.and go to the record for InventoryReceiptID 100002. Double-click mcrUpdateVendorIDand InvItems in the Navigation Pane to run the macro. VendorID for InventoryReceiptID 100002 should now be 1008. Close the form and restore your macro (use the completed macro in Figure 9.42 as a guide).

Fig. 9.41 *Expression Builder* for *SetTempVar Expression* argument.

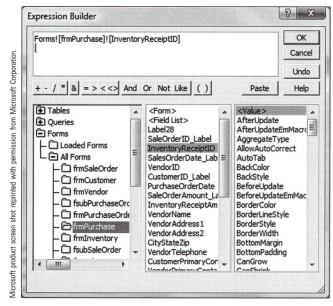

Fig. 9.42 *mcrUpdate-VendorID* in Design view.

EXERCISE 9.38: ADDING A BUTTON TO *FRMPURCHASE* TO RUN THE MACRO

We presented detailed steps to create a Command button in Exercise 9.26 and Figure 9.25. You may refer back to them for more detailed explanations.

1. Open frmPurchase in Design view. Click Button in the Controls group. Move your cursor to just below the Primary Contact label and double-click to start the Command Button Wizard.
2. In the first dialog box, click Miscellaneous in the Category list, then double-click Run Macro to advance to the next dialog box.
3. Double-click mcrUpdateInventoryIDandInvItems (not shown in Figure 9.25) in the next dialog box.
4. Click the Text radio button, type Update Vendor # and Inv. Items in the Text box, and click Next.
5. In the last dialog box, type cmdUpdateVendorIDandInvItems; click Finish.
6. Click Tab Order in the Control Layout group on the Arrange ribbon; move cmdUpdateVendorIDandInvItems to the place just above fsubPurchase. Click OK.
7. If you do not have room for the new Command button, move the subform and the Update Inventory Receipt Amount button down to make room. Your finished form in Design view should look like Figure 9.43. Save and close the form.
8. Test your new button. Open tblPurchase and change VendorID for InventoryReceiptID 100004 in to 9999 and close the table. Open frmPurchase and go to the record for InventoryReceiptID 100004. Click your new Command button to execute mcrUpdateVendorIDandInvItems. Verify that the VendorID for InventoryReceiptID 100004 changed from 9999 to 1007.

Fig. 9.43 *frm-Purchase* in Design view after completing Exercise 9.38.

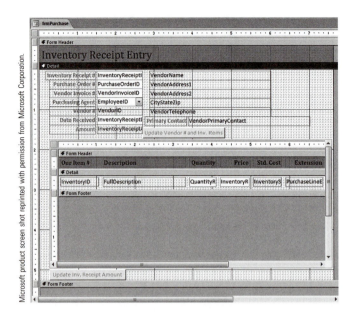

Microsoft product screen shot reprinted with permission from Microsoft Corporation.

Adding a Control Limiting Inventory Items Received to Items Ordered on the Inventory Receipt Entry Form

Ensuring that the proper vendor information appears on the Inventory Receipt Entry form allows Pipefitters Supply Company to have confidence that it will pay the correct vendor for merchandise received. It is equally important that Pipefitters only pays vendors for received merchandise that was actually ordered. Accounting staff in most enterprises are responsible for verifying that merchandise received is the same merchandise that was ordered. They compare the items and prices on the purchase order, vendor invoice, and inventory receipt. If the three documents do not agree an accounting clerk reconciles the differences. For example, if Pipefitters receives an item it did not order, an accounting clerk must contact the vendor and decide what to do with the unordered merchandise. This process takes time, and time is money.

In an effort to reduce the amount of time that accounting clerks spend reconciling purchase documents you will add a control to the Inventory Receipt Entry form in the next set of exercises. This control transfers the items from the related purchase order to the form. If Pipefitters instructs its materials handlers (and informs its vendors) to fill out the Inventory Receipt Entry form at the time of delivery, they will simply refuse to accept delivery of any merchandise not listed on the form. If it is not practical to record the contents of shipments while the delivery truck is still at Pipefitters, materials handlers simply set aside unordered merchandise and fill out an Unordered Merchandise form. Either procedure will save the accountants valuable time.

EXERCISE 9.39: CREATE APPEND QUERY QRYADDORDEREDITEMSTOPURCHINV

1. Click the Create tab and click Query Design in the Other group.
2. Select the following tables in the Show Table dialog box by double-clicking them: tblPurchase, tblPurchaseOrder, and tblReservation-PurchaseOrderInventory. Click the Close button. Move and resize the field rosters to make all field names visible.
3. Click Append in the Query Type group, select tblInflow-PurchaseInventory from the combo box in the Append dialog box, and click OK.
4. Double-click InventoryReceiptID from the tblPurchase field roster to add it to the Criteria Pane. Type [TempVars]![TempInventoryReceiptID] in the Criteria cell to use the temporary variable created by *mcrUpdateVendorIDandInvItems*.

5. Double-click InventoryID from the tblReservation-PurchaseOrder-Inventory field roster to add it to the Criteria Pane. Notice that Access automatically fills in fields with matching names from *tblInflow-PurchaseInventory* in the Append To cells (see Figure 9.44). You have to manually select the Append To fields if the names are different. To illustrate, double-click POPrice in the tblReservation-PurchaseOrder-Inventory field roster. Notice that the Append To cell for POPrice is blank. Delete POPrice from the Criteria Pane as you do not need it for this query.

6. Save your query as qryAddOrderedItemsToPurchInv. Close the query.

7. Open tblInflow-PurchaseInventory in Design view, set default values for QuantityReceived and InventoryReceiptPrice to 0. When the Append query adds the Purchase Order Line Items to this table, your default value settings automatically populate QuantityReceived and InventoryReceiptPrice with zeros. The zero values serve two purposes. First, they add values to required fields not populated by the Append query—all required fields must have a value before Access can save the record. Second, the zero values indicate that the materials handlers have not yet physically counted the inventory or entered a price from the vendor's invoice.

8. To test your query, you must delete the RemoveTempVar Action from *mcrUpdateVendorIDandInvItems* to keep the value of TempInventoryReceiptID in memory so it can be used by *qryAddOrderedItemsToPurchInv*. Double-click frmPurchase to open it in Form view. Go to a New Record. Enter the information in Figure 9.45. Tab to the Update Vendor # and Inv. Items button and click it to run *mcrUpdateVendorIDandInvItems*, which will update VendorID to 1009 (and set the value of TempInventoryReceiptID to 999999). Double-click qryAddOrdered-ItemsToPurchInv to add the Inventory Line Items; click Yes in the Warning dialog boxes. To see the changes go to the previous record and then back to your newly created record. You should see two inventory items, 1032 and 1045, added to the subform. Delete the test record. Close the form. Open mcrUpdateVendorIDandInvItems in Design view and replace the RemoveTempVar Action (see Exercise 9.37, Step 7).

Fig. 9.44 *qryAdd-OrderedItemsToPurch-Inv* **in Design view.**

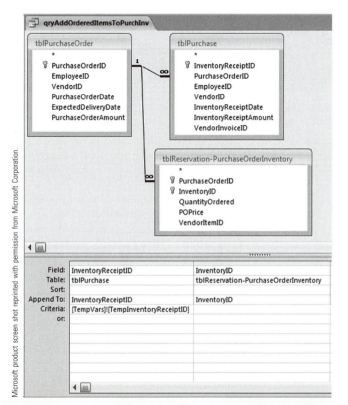

Fig. 9.45 Inventory Receipt Entry form with test record.

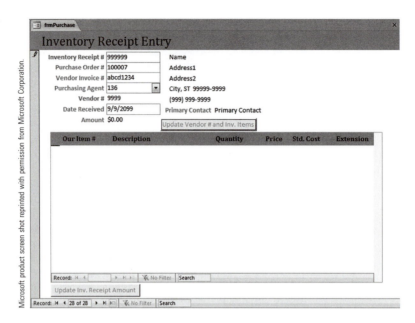

Microsoft product screen shot reprinted with permission from Microsoft Corporation.

EXERCISE 9.40: ADD ACTIONS IN *MCRUPDATEVENDORID* TO ADD ORDERED ITEMS TO THE CURRENT RECORD OF THE INVENTORY RECEIPT ENTRY FORM

Use Figure 9.46 as a guide for this exercise.

1. Open mcrUpdateInventoryIDandInvItems in Design view. Click the record selector for the RemoveTempVar Action and drag it down until you have at least four blank rows between OpenQuery and RemoveTempVar.

2. Add the OpenForm Action in the first blank row in the Macro Action Pane (necessary to allow *fsubPurchase* to be repainted after *qryAddOrderedItems-ToPurchInv* adds records to *tblInflow-PurchaseInventory*). Select the following Argument values:
   - Form Name—fsubPurchase
   - View—Form (default value)
   - Data Mode—Edit
   - Window Mode—Hidden (subform does not open in a new tab)

3. Add an OpenQuery Action; set the Query Name argument to qryAddOrderedItemsToPurchInv. Leave the other Arguments set to their default values.

4. Repaint the subform. Add RepaintObject to the Macro Action Pane; set Object Type to Form and Object Name to fsubPurchase.

5. Close the subform running in hidden Window Mode. Add a Close Action. Set Object Type to Form, Object Name to fsubPurchase, and Save to No.

6. If necessary, move the RemoveTempVar Action to eliminate blank rows between Actions. Save and close the macro. Beware if you run this macro on a record that previously had inventory items added to it, the list of inventory items will *not* be updated until you leave the current record. Eliminating the need to leave the current record to update the inventory list requires coding that is beyond the scope of this textbook.

Fig. 9.46 *mcr-UpdateVendorIDand-InvItems* after adding actions to add inventory items to the current record.

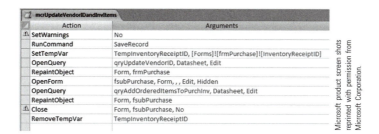

EXERCISE 9.41: ADD CONTROLS TO *FSUBPURCHASE* TO PREVENT USERS FROM ADDING UNORDERED ITEMS TO THE INVENTORY RECEIPT ENTRY FORM

Now that you have a macro that transfers items ordered to the Inventory Receipt Entry form, you need to prevent users from changing InventoryItemIDs or adding additional inventory items to the form.

1. Open fsubPurchase in Design view; open the Property Sheet.
2. Delete the InventoryID combo box. Click Text Box in the Controls group and double-click in the Detail section under the # sign of the Our Item # header.
3. On the Format tab, change the Back Style and Border Style to Transparent.
4. On the Data tab, set the Control Source to InventoryID; change Enabled to No and Locked to Yes.
5. Change the Name on the Other tab to InventoryID. Change the Tab Stop to No.
6. Delete the Label. Use the buttons in the Control Alignment group on the Arrange Ribbon to help you line up the new Control. Save and close the form.
7. Select Form from the combo box on the Property Sheet. Click the Data tab. Change the Allow Additions property to No. Save your changes and switch to Form view. Notice that the *New Record Selector has been removed from the Detail section of the subform (see Figure 9.47). Also, the New Record navigation button on the Navigation bar has been removed. Close the subform.*
8. Test your macro by opening *frmPurchase*, entering the test record in Figure 9.45, and clicking the Update Vendor # and Inv. Items button. VendorID should change to 1009 and two inventory items, 1032 and 1045, should have been added to the form. Use the record selectors on the subform and form to delete the test data. Close the form.

Recording Cash Paid to Vendors

Thus far, in this chapter, you have learned how Pipefitters Supply Company can maintain vendor records, maintain inventory records, prepare purchase orders, and record receipts of ordered inventory items. Once Pipefitters receives inventory items, its vendors would like it to pay for those items. This section describes one of the many ways to use the information you have gathered in your acquisition/payment process tables to write checks. Since *tblPurchase* contains the total cost of each shipment of inventory received (thanks to the objects you created to sum the inventory receipt line extensions and transfer those totals to the Purchase table), you can use that table as a basis for payments.

Fig. 9.47 Inventory Receipt Entry form after completing Exercise 9.41.

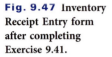

Cash Account Information

You created a Cash Account table in Chapter 8. It contains details about each one of Pipefitters' cash accounts, including a primary key to link it to other tables. We will use the same Cash Account table for the remaining chapters without modification.

The Cash Disbursements Table

The Cash Disbursements table is very similar to the Cash Receipts table. They both contain information about a cash event, and contain foreign keys to the cash resource, economic event (purchase or sale), employee and external agent (vendor or customer) tables. We will assume that Pipefitters makes all cash disbursements by check. Therefore, a check number would make a good primary key because they are numbered sequentially as a control and a check number is used only once. However, if you open *tblCashAccount* you notice that Pipefitters already has two checking accounts—a primary checking account and a payroll account. Also, the Cash Account table allows for Pipefitters to add additional cash accounts that may also be checking accounts. Because different accounts may use the same check number, Pipefitters will use a ***composite*** primary key—cash account number and check number.

In addition to the composite primary key, you will want to include fields for the date the check was written, for the amount of the check, for the inventory receipt it relates to, for the vendor number, and for the employee number of the accountant who wrote the check. Figure 9.4 shows the foreign keys that link the cash disbursement event to the related economic event (*tblPurchase*), resource (*tblCashAccount*), and agents (*tblEmployee* and *tblVendor*). Figure 9.48 shows just how similar the attributes in *tblCashReceipt* and *tblCashDisbursement* are. These similarities will allow you to quickly modify *tblCashReceipt* to create *tblCashDisbursement*.

Fig. 9.48 Comparison
of fields for *tblCash-
Receipt* and *tblCash-
Disbursement.*

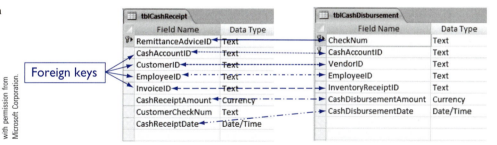

EXERCISE 9.42: **MODIFYING THE CASH RECEIPT TABLE TO
CREATE THE CASH DISBURSEMENT TABLE**

1. Click tblCashReceipt in the Chapter 8 Tables section of the Navigation Pane. Press Ctrl+C and then Ctrl+V; type tblCashDisbursement in the name box; click the Structure Only radio button and then click OK.
2. Open tblCashDisbursement in Design view. It will be located in the Unassigned Objects section of the Navigation Pane.
3. Change the Field names as indicated in Figure 9.48. Be sure to delete CustomerCheckNum, as there is no such Field in *tblCashDisbursement.*
4. Set the composite primary key. Press and hold the Shift key and click the record selector for CheckNum and CashAccountID. Click Primary Key in the Tools group.
5. Change the properties for all Fields as indicated in Figure 9.49.
6. Save your changes and close the table.
7. Import data from the *Ch09.xlsx* Excel file for *tblCashDisbursement.* Follow the instructions in Exercise 9.11, substituting tblCashDisbursement for tblPurchase-Order. When you finish importing the data, open tblCashDisbursement to verify that all 31 records were imported.

Fig. 9.49 Field
Properties for
tblCashDisbursement.

Field Name	CheckNum	CashAccountID	CashDisbursementAmount	CashDisbursementDate
Data Type	Text	Text	Currency	Date/Time
Field Size (or Decimal Places)	5	3	2	
Format			Currency	Short Date
Input Mask	00000;;_	000;;_		99/99/0000;;_
Caption	Check #	Cash Account #	Amount Paid	Date Paid
Default Value			0	Date ()
Required	Yes	Yes	Yes	Yes
Allow Zero Length	No	No		
Indexed	Yes (Duplicates OK)	Yes (Duplicates OK)	No	No

Primary Key and Attributes

Field Name	VendorID	EmployeeID	InventoryReceiptID
Data Type	Text	Text	Text
Field Size (or Decimal Places)	4	3	6
Format			
Input Mask	0000;;_	000;;_	000000;;_
Caption	Vendor #	Employee #	Inventory Receipt #
Default Value			
Required	Yes	Yes	Yes
Allow Zero Length	No	No	No
Indexed	Yes (Duplicates OK)	Yes (Duplicates OK)	Yes (Duplicates OK)

Foreign Keys

Creating Relationships with the Cash Disbursement Table

Look at Figure 9.4. Are there any many-to-many relationships with the Cash Disbursement table? Since there are none, you are ready to create the relationships with *tblCashDisbursement*.

EXERCISE 9.43: CREATING RELATIONSHIPS RELATED TO THE CASH DISBURSEMENT EVENT

1. Close all open Access objects.
2. In the Database Tools tab, click Relationships in the Show/Hide group. Your Relationships tab should look like how you left it at the end of Exercise 9.29 (see Figure 9.29).
3. Minimize the Navigation Pane.
4. Click Show Table in the Relationships group (on the Design tab). Double-click tblCashDisbursement. Click Close. Resize tblCashDisbursemsent so that the entire table name and all field names are visible. Move it below *tblPurchase*.
5. Create your links the same way you did in Exercises 9.13 and 9.29. Drag from the primary key to the matching foreign key or from the primary key to the matching part of a composite primary key. Use Figure 9.4 as a guide.
6. When the Edit Relationships dialog box appears, make sure that the correct attributes appear in the tables you dragged from and to. The relationship type at the bottom of the dialog box should always be one-to-many. Check Enforce Referential Integrity and Cascade Update Related Fields. Finally, click Create in the dialog box.
7. Your completed set of relationships should look like Figure 9.50.
8. Close the Relationships window and click the Yes button in the dialog box to save your changes, and then click >> on the Navigation Pane to restore it.

Fig. 9.50 Relationships window after adding Cash Disbursement event.

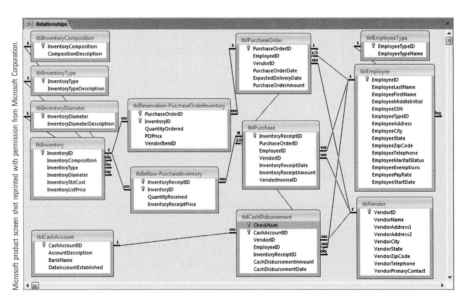

Microsoft product screen shot reprinted with permission from Microsoft Corporation.

The Cash Disbursement Entry Form

Pipefitters Supply Company's payment policy with vendors is to pay the full balance up to $5,000 within ten days and pay any remaining balance within ten days after the first payment. When one of Pipefitters' accountants writes a check to a vendor, he or she should be able to view the inventory receipt amount and the sum of prior payments made for that inventory receipt as well as the balance due. If the sum of prior payments is greater than the inventory receipt amount, the accountant needs to find the source of the error. Additionally, it is helpful to see the payment history related to the inventory receipt. If prior payments are less than the inventory receipt amount, the accountant applies the rules for making payments. You will build a query to compute the current balance due by inventory receipt. The balance due will be used in the Cash Disbursement Entry form as a control. Because the balance due will not be updated until the Balance Due query is run again by closing and opening the form, you will add a button on the form to update the balance due.

EXERCISE 9.44: CREATING TWO QUERIES TO COMPUTE BALANCE DUE TO VENDORS

The two queries you will create in this exercise are very similar to the queries you created for the Cash Receipts Entry form in Exercises 8.40 and 8.41. Due to their similarity, the steps in Exercise 9.44 are condensed. Refer to Exercises 8.40 and 8.41 for additional guidance. In this exercise you will build two queries. The first query uses an *aggregate function* to sum the cash disbursements for each inventory receipt on or before the date of the current cash disbursement. The second query uses a *horizontal computation* to subtract the sum of the cash paid from the inventory receipt amount to arrive at the balance due to the vendor.

Create the first query.

1. Click the Create tab and click Query Design in the Other group. Add tblCashDisbursement to the Table Pane. Add InentoryReceiptID and CashDisbursementAmount, respectively, to the Criteria Pane.
2. Click Totals in the Show/Hide group, leave the InvoiceID Total cell set to Group By, change the Total cell for CashDisbursementAmount to Sum.
3. Open the Property Sheet. Type Prior Payments as the caption for the sum of cash disbursements. Close the property sheet.
4. Save the query as qrySumOfCDByInventoryReceipt.

Create the second query.

5. Create a new query using Query Design. Add tblPurchase and qrySumOfCDByInventoryReceipt to the Table Pane. Add to the Criteria Pane InventoryReceiptID, InventoryReceiptAmount, and VendorID, respectively, from the *tblPurchase* field roster; add SumOfCashDisbursementAmount from the *qrySumOfCDByInventoryReceipt* field roster to the Criteria Pane.
6. Change join properties of the link between the tblPurchase and qrySumOfCDByInventoryReceipt field rosters to include ALL records from *tblPurchase* and only those records from *qrySumOfCDByInventoryReceipt* where the values of InventoryReceiptID are equal (Radio Button 2 in the Join Properties dialog box). The link, an outer join, should now be an arrow pointing to the *qrySumOfCDByInventoryReceipt* field roster (see Figure 9.51).
7. Save your query as qryBalanceDueToVendor.
8. Use Builder to add the following expression to the Criteria Pane: BalanceDue: [InventoryReceiptAmount]-Nz([SumOfCashDisbursementAmount],0). On the Property Sheet, type Balance Due in the Caption cell for your newly created field, BalanceDue.
9. Add InventoryReceiptDate from the *tblPurchase* field roster to the Criteria Pane.
10. Save and close your query.

Fig. 9.51 *qryBal-anceDueToVendor* in Design view.

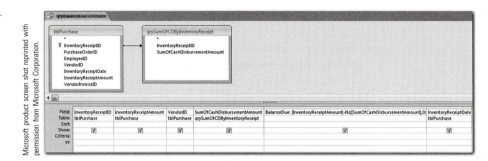

The Cash Disbursement Entry form uses the form/subform design. The top portion of the Cash Disbursement Entry form will contain inventory receipt-related data from *qryBalanceDueToVendor*. None of these fields will be editable because they are for reference only. The main form will also show vendor information (i.e., name and address), which you will have to add to the query behind the form. The subform contains all fields from *tblCashDisbursement*. The VendorID and InventoryReceiptID fields will be linked to the main form, which will automatically populate these fields and ensure that cash disbursements are recorded for the correct vendor and inventory receipt. Using data from the purchase table serves as a control because cash disbursements can only be recorded for inventory receipts that exist in *tblPurchase*. Because of the similarity between the Cash Receipt Entry form and the Cash Disbursement Entry form, you will start with copies of *frmCashReceipt* and *fsubCashReceipt* instead of using the Form Wizard.

EXERCISE 9.45: CREATE THE CASH DISBURSEMENT ENTRY FORM—MAKING CHANGES TO *FSUBCASHRECEIPT*

1. Click fsubCashReceipt in the Chapter 8 Forms section of the Navigation Pane, press Ctrl+C, then Ctrl+V. In the Paste As dialog box, type fsubCashDisbursement. Open fsubCashDisbursement in Design view. It will be located in the Unassigned Objects section of the Navigation Pane. Minimize the Navigation Pane.
2. Open the Property Sheet. Select Form from the combo box at the top of the property sheet. On the Data tab, change the Record Source to tblCashDisbursement. On the Format tab, change the Caption to fsubCashDisbursement.
3. Make the changes indicated in Figure 9.52 to the controls and labels in the Detail section of the subform.
4. View the form in Datasheet view. This is how the subform will look in the main form. Click the Datasheet Selector. Click the More menu in the Records group on the Home ribbon. Click Column Width and click the Best Fit button to make both the column headers and data visible.
5. Close the subform.

Fig. 9.52 Changes to controls and labels in *fsubCashDisbursement*.

Old Control Name	New Control/Caption Name	New Input Mask
RemittanceAdviceID	CheckNum	00000;;_
CashAccountID	CashAccountID	
Customer #	VendorID	0000;;_
EmployeeID	EmployeeID	
InvoiceID	InventoryReceiptID	
CashReceiptAmount	CashDisbursementAmount	
CustomerCheckNum	DELETE	
ShippingDate	CashDisbursementDate	

Old Label Name	New Label name
RA #	Check #
Cash Acct. #	Cash Acct. #
Customer #	Vendor #
Employee #	Employee #
Invoice #	Inv. Receipt #
Amount	Amount
Date	Date

EXERCISE 9.46: CREATE THE CASH DISBURSEMENT ENTRY FORM—MAKING CHANGES TO *FRMCASHRECEIPT*

Modify *qryBalanceDueToVendor* to be used as the form's Record Source.

1. Click qryBalanceDueToVendor in the Unassigned Objects section of the Navigation Pane, press Ctrl+C, then Ctrl+V. In the Paste As dialog box, type qryFormCDRecordSourceData. Open qryFormCDRecordSourceData in Design view.
2. Click Show Table in the Query Setup group to add qryVendorInfo to the Table Pane. Link qryVendorInfo to tblPurchase by clicking and dragging VendorID from the qryVendorInfo field roster to the tblPurchase field roster. Add the following fields to the Criteria Pane: VendorName, VendorAddress1, VendorAddress2, CityStateZip, VendorTelephone, and VendorPrimaryContact. Save your changes and close the query.

Copy *frmCashReceipt* to make a starting place to create *frmCashDisbursement*.

3. Click frmCashReceipt in the Chapter 8 Forms section of the Navigation Pane, press Ctrl+C, then Ctrl+V. In the Paste As dialog box, type frmCashDisbursement. Open frmCashDisbursement in Design view. It will be located in the Unassigned Objects section of the Navigation Pane. Minimize the Navigation Pane.
4. Change the Form Header to Cash Disbursement Entry.

Change the data sources of the form and its controls.

5. Open the Property Sheet. Select Form from the combo box at the top of the property sheet. On the Data tab, change the Record Source to qryFormCDRecordSourceData. On the Format tab, change the Caption to frmCashDisbursement.

6. Make the changes indicated in Figure 9.53 to the controls and labels in the Detail section of the form. Before you start making these changes, select all of the controls and labels above the subform and move them 1/4- inch to the right to make room for longer label names.

Make changes to the subform.

7. Select fsubCashReceipt from the combo box at the top of the property sheet. On the Data tab, change the Source Object to fsubCashDisbursement. On the Format tab, change the Caption to fsubCashDisbursement.

8. Link InventoryReceiptID and VendorID from the subform to the form. Click the Builder button next to the Link Master Fields Property box to open the Subform Field Linker. Click OK on the Information dialog box. Add InventoryReceiptID to the first row of both the Master Fields column and Child Fields column, and add VendorID the second row in both columns; click OK.

9. Close the Property Sheet. Change to Layout view. Grab the right side of the subform and narrow the width to remove the excess blank space.

10. Save the form. Your completed form should look like the Cash Disbursement Entry form in Figure 9.54.

Fig. 9.53 Changes to controls and labels in *frmCashDisbursement.*

Old Control Name	New Control/Caption Name	New Input Mask
InvoiceID	InventoryReceiptID	
SaleAmount	InventoryReceiptAmount	
CustomerID	VendorID	0000;;_
SumOfCashReceiptAmount	SumOfCashDisbursementAmount	
BalanceDue	BalanceDue	
ShippingDate	InventoryReceiptDate	
CustomerName	VendorName	
CustomerAddress1	VendorAddress1	
CustomerAddress2	VendorAddress2	
CityStateZip	CityStateZip	
CustomerPrimaryContact	VendorPrimaryContact	

Old Label Name	New Label name
Invoice #	Inv. Receipt #
Invoice Amount	Inv. Receipt Amount
Customer #	Vendor #
Prior Receipts	Prior Payments
Balance Due	Balance Due
Invoice Date	Inv. Receipt Date
Primary Contact	Primary Contact

Fig. 9.54 Cash
Receipt Entry form
in Form view.

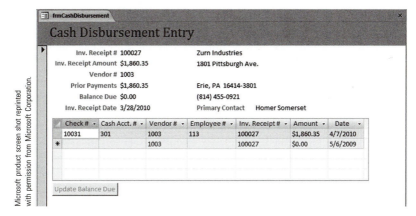

There is no need to make any changes to the Update Balance Due button because the macro behind button, Requery, reruns the query behind the open form. As discussed in Chapter 8, the Requery Macro Action returns to the first record of the form after rerunning the query behind the form. Returning to the current record requires coding that is beyond the scope of this textbook.

TRY IT

Test the Cash Disbursement Entry form and its Update Balance Due button. Double-click frmCashDisbursement in the Navigation Pane. Go to the last record (Inv. Receipt # 100027). The Invoice Amount is $1,860.35. Prior Payments are $1,860.35, so the Balance Due is $0.00. Add a test record: Check # 99999, Cash Acct. # 301, Employee # 136, Amount $500, and Date 9/9/2010. Click the Update Balance Due button. Notice that the form returns to the first record. Go to the last record. Prior Payments is now $2,360.35. The Balance Due has been updated to its current balance of ($500.00), meaning that we overpaid for this inventory receipt by $500.00. Delete Check # 99999 by clicking on the Record selector and pressing the Delete key.

Acquisition and Payment Process for Non-Inventory Items

Most firms acquire resources other than inventory. The acquisition of labor in the human resources process is covered in Chapter 10. Resources acquired such as advertising and utilities have a short useful life. These types of resources are immediately expensed for financial accounting purposes. Other items acquired such as equipment, furniture, and insurance policies have a longer useful life. Resources with long useful lives are recorded as assets and expensed throughout their useful lives.

Recording Information for Non-Inventory Resources with Short Useful Lives

Acquisition of resources with short useful lives are recorded similarly to the way you recorded the acquisition of inventory. The same Purchase Order table you created to record inventory orders could be used to record ordering advertising or a package delivery, though many acquisitions of short-lived non-inventory items would likely not require a purchase order. Similarly, the same Purchase table used to record inventory receipts could be used to record receipt of non-inventory items if the Inventory Receipt ID were replaced with a generic Resource Receipt ID. Likewise, the Cash Disbursements table described in this chapter could also record payments for non-inventory items.

The resource table would look like a chart of accounts for the expense section of an income statement. It would likely contain a Resource Type ID, a Resource Type Name, and a Resource Type description. Resource Type/Category tables classify resources by how they are aggregated on an income statement, such as selling expenses, administrative expenses, and non-operating expenses.

Acquisition of short-lived non-inventory items would require Reservation and Inflow relationship tables separate from the Reservation and Inflow tables for inventory. These non-inventory relationship tables would contain the primary keys of the resource and event tables they join, the quantity acquired, cost per unit acquired, and a detailed description of the items acquired.

Recording Information for Non-Inventory Resources with Long Useful Lives

Non-inventory items with long useful lives would be recorded similarly to resources with short useful lives. The main difference is that information about the resources' useful lives needs to be stored as well as the method used to allocate the cost over the resource's useful life. The useful life and expense allocation method can be recorded in the Inflow relationship table, especially if the firm does not have standard useful lives or expense allocation methods. However, if either attribute is based on the type of resource and not the specific resource acquired, then a firm will avoid data redundancy by storing useful life and/or expense allocation method in the resource table.

Deriving Financial Statement Information

You have now successfully created a working acquisition/payment business process in Access for merchandise inventory that allows you to enter all information into the system related to purchase orders, inventory receipts (purchases), and cash disbursements. By properly linking the tables through foreign keys and relationship tables, you are ready to produce financial statement information. The two main financial statement items that depend only on the activities in the acquisition/payment process are Sales and Accounts Receivable.

We will use the same naming conventions discussed in Chapter 8 for financial statement queries, which often require multiple queries to achieve the final result.

Accounts Payable

Accounts Payable, like Accounts Receivable, is merely a timing difference between duality events. For Accounts Payable, the timing difference is between purchases and related cash disbursements. Therefore, Accounts Payable can be determined by computing the sum of the purchases and subtracting the sum of the cash disbursements related to those purchases. Since a horizontal computation (e.g., [sum of purchases] − [sum of cash disbursements]) cannot use the result of an aggregate function from the same query (e.g., sum of sales, sum of cash receipts), the computation of Accounts Payable will require three queries: summing purchases, summing cash disbursements related to purchases, and subtracting the total cash disbursements from total purchases.

What kind of date constraints do we need to compute balance sheet items like Accounts Payable? Remember that a balance sheet reports the account balances of assets, liabilities, and equities at a specified point in time. You have to sum the purchases and related cash disbursements from the company's inception through the balance sheet date. Therefore, balance sheet queries only have an ending date constraint. Income statement queries have both a beginning date constraint and an ending date constraint.

EXERCISE 9.47: USING QUERIES TO COMPUTE ACCOUNTS RECEIVABLE—SUM OF PURCHASES AND SUM OF CASH DISBURSEMENTS RELATED TO PURCHASES

The first query sums purchases through the balance sheet date.

1. Click the Create tab and click Query Design in the Other group. Double-click tblPurchase in the Show Table dialog box. Close the dialog box.
2. Add InventoryReceiptAmount and InventoryReceiptDate, respectively, to the Criteria Pane. Click Totals in the Show/Hide group. Change the Total cell for InventoryReceiptAmount to Sum. Open the Property Sheet and type Purchases in the Caption property.
3. Change the InventoryReceiptDate Total to Where. In the Criteria cell of InventoryReceiptDate, type <=[End of Period Date] to sum all purchases up through the balance sheet date.
4. Check your query. Click Run in the Results group. Use 1/31/2010 for the end of period date, which is the balance sheet date. Total sales for the date ended should be $43,074.30. Save your query as qryAccPay1-SumOfPurchases and close the query.

Create the second query to sum cash disbursements related to purchases. Although you will not use any fields from *tblPurchase*, the inner join between *tblPurchase* and *tblCashDisbursement* insures that only cash disbursements related to purchases are summed. Even though the *Ch09.accdb* database has only one source of cash disbursements, you will add this step because it is critical in full accounting database systems where there are multiple sources of cash disbursements.

5. Click the Create tab and click Query Design in the Other group. Double-click tblPurchase and tblCashDisbursement in the Show Table dialog box. Close the dialog box.
6. Add to the Criteria Pane CashDisbursementAmount and CashDisbursementDate, respectively, from the tblCashDisbursement field roster. Click Totals in the Show/Hide group.
7. Change the Total cell for CashDisbursementAmount to Sum. Open the Property Sheet. Type Cash Disbursements in the Caption property.
8. Change the Total cell for CashDisbursementDate to Where. In the Criteria cell type <= [End of Period Date].
9. Save the query as qryAccPay2-SumOfCD. Check your query. Click Run in the Results group. Use 1/31/2010 for balance sheet date. Total cash receipts related to sales for the date ended should be $22,455.05.

EXERCISE 9.48: USING QUERIES TO COMPUTE ACCOUNTS PAYABLE

The third and final query uses the results of the two queries in Exercise 9.47 to compute Accounts Payable. It is similar to the query in Exercise 8.47 that computes Accounts Receivable.

1. Click the Create tab and click Query Design in the Other group. Add qryAccPay1-SumOfPurchases and qryAccPay2-SumOfCD to the Table Pane. The fields in these two queries are independent of one another and do not need to be joined. If they did need to be joined you would include a common field in each query to have a way to join them.

2. Add to the Criteria Pane SumOfInventoryReceiptAmount from the qryAccPay1-SumOfPurchases field roster and SumOfCashDisbursementAmount from the qryAccPay2-SumOfCD field roster. Save your query as qryAccPay3-AccountsPayable.

3. Click the first available Field on the Criteria Pane. Click Builder in the Query Setup group. Enter AccountsPayable: [SumOfInventoryReceiptAmount]-Nz([SumOfCashDisbursementAmount],0). If there are no cash disbursements for the period covered by your query, the Nz function replaces the null value with the second argument in the function, 0, so that the computation will have a valid result.

4. Open the Property Sheet. Type Accounts Payable as the caption for your newly created field, AccountsPayable. Save your query.

5. Test the Nz function by running the query and using 1/17/2010 as the balance sheet date. Your result should be $11,286.00. See Figure 9.55.

6. Now rerun your query using 1/31/2010 as the balance sheet date. Your result should be $20,619.25. Notice that purchases and cash disbursements in Figure 9.55 match the results from the individual queries.

Fig. 9.55
qryAccPay3-AccountsPayable **dynasets.**

Microsoft product screen shots reprinted with permission from Microsoft Corporation.

qryAccPay3-AccountsPayable		
Purchases	Cash Disbursements	Accounts Payable
$11,286.00		$11,286.00

Dynaset for 1/17/2010

qryAccPay3-AccountsPayable		
Purchases	Cash Disbursements	Accounts Payable
$43,074.30	$22,455.05	$20,619.25

Dynaset for 1/31/2010

Deriving other Information Useful for Decision Making

Database accounting information systems include much information that is useful to non-accountants. Traditional accounting records contained only the date and dollar amount of each purchase and cash disbursement. A database accounting system contains much more information about each purchase and cash disbursement. The purchase, purchase order, inventory, and vendor tables we described in this chapter can be combined in many ways to provide useful information to the marketing and strategic management functions.

Accounts Payable by Vendor

In addition to computing Accounts Payable in the aggregate for financial reporting purposes, firms also need to track how much they owe individual vendors. This can be accomplished by making modifications to your existing Accounts Payable queries. The steps involved are virtually identical to the steps in Exercises 8.48 and 8.49 to compute Accounts Receivable by customer. Use the detailed instructions provided in Exercises 8.48 and 8.49 along with brief explanations in the exercise below and the accompanying figures to guide you.

EXERCISE 9.49: MODIFYING ACCOUNTS PAYABLE QUERIES TO GENERATE ACCOUNTS RECEIVABLE FOR INDIVIDUAL VENDORS

Create the first query by copying and modifying *qryAccPay1-SumOfPurchases*.

1. Make a copy of qryAccPay1-SumOfPurchases and name it qryAPByVendor1-SumOfPurchases. Open qryAPByVendor1-SumOfPurchases in Design view. Click and drag VendorID to the first column of the Criteria Pane to group purchases by vendor.
2. Save your changes. Check your query. Click Run in the Results group. Use 1/31/2010 for the balance sheet date. The totals are now listed by VendorID. You should have 7 vendors in your result. Close the query.

Create the second query by copying and modifying *qryAccPay2-SumOfCD*.

1. Make a copy of qryAccPay2-SumOfCD and name it qryAPByVendor2-SumOfCD. Open qryAPByVendor2-SumOfCD in Design view. Click and drag VendorID from the tblCashDisbursement field roster to the first column of the Criteria Pane to group cash disbursements by vendor.
2. Save your changes. Check your query. Click Run in the Results group. Use 1/31/2010 for the balance sheet date. The totals are now listed by VendorID. You should have 4 vendors in your result. Close the query.

Create the third and final query, which will be similar to *qryAccPay3-AccountsPayable*. Since some vendors in the database have no purchases or cash disbursements, and other vendors have purchases and no cash disbursements, you will need outer joins like you created in Exercise 9.44.

1. Click the Create tab and click Query Design in the Other group. In the Show Table dialog box click the Queries tab, double-click qryVendorInfo, qryAPByVendor1-SumOfPurchases, and qryAPByVendor2-SumOfCD. Close the dialog box.
2. Double-click VendorID and VendorName from qryVendorInfo, SumOfInventoryReceiptAmount from the qryAPByVendor1-SumOfPurchases field roster, and SumOfCashDisbursementAmount from the qryAPByVendor2-SumOfCD field roster.
3. Save your query as qryAPByVendor3-AccountsPayable.
4. Add the following expression to the next available row on the Criteria Pane: AccountsPayable: Nz([SumOfInventoryReceiptAmount],0)-Nz([SumOfCashDisbursementAmount],0). Open the Property Sheet, type Accounts Payable as the caption for AccountsPayable, and set the Format property to Currency.
5. Use VendorID to create a Left Outer Join from qryVendorInfo to qryAPByVendor1-SumOfPurchases, and from qryAPByVendor1-SumOfPurchases to qryAPByVendor2-SumOfCD. See Figure 9.56. Exercise 8.49 provides a detailed explanation.

6. Save your changes. Check your query. Click Run in the Results group. Use 1/31/2010 for the balance sheet date. The dynaset is shown in Figure 8.57. Notice that there are now 15 vendors listed because all vendors in the database are included, even the dummy vendor (9999) and vendors from whom Pipefitters made no purchases on or before 2/28/2010. Close the query.

Fig. 9.56
qryAPByVendor3-
AccountsPayable **in**
Design view.

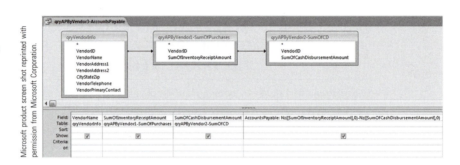

Fig. 9.57 Dynaset
for *qryAPByVendor3-*
AccountsPayable **on**
1/31/2010.

Vendor #	Name	Purchases	Cash Disbursements	Accounts Payable
1001	Indumar Products, Inc.	$6,008.80	$6,008.80	$0.00
1002	Binford Products, Inc.			$0.00
1003	Zurn Industries	$9,943.25	$5,664.50	$4,278.75
1004	Technical Alloys, Inc.	$317.00		$317.00
1005	Fittube, Inc.			$0.00
1006	Flow Master			$0.00
1007	Allied Brass Mfg. Co.	$8,407.00	$2,108.25	$6,298.75
1008	Lasco Fittings, Inc.	$8,673.50	$8,673.50	$0.00
1009	Modine Mfg., Co.	$426.00		$426.00
1010	Quality Pipe Products, Inc.			$0.00
1011	Chase Brass & Copper Co., Inc.	$9,298.75		$9,298.75
1012	Westflex Pipe Manufacturing			$0.00
1013	Hach Co.			$0.00
1014	Copper Brite Inc.			$0.00
9999	Name			$0.00

Record: ◄ ◄ 1 of 15 ► ►◄ No Filter   Search

TRY IT

Prevent the dummy vendor from showing up in the Accounts Payable by Vendor query. Open qryAPByVendor3-AccountsPayable in Design view. In the Criteria cell for VendorID, type <>9999. Rerun the query. Notice that VendorID 9999 is now absent from the dynaset.

Summary

This chapter described how to design and implement the acquisition/payment business process in Access. In the design phase, you identified the duality of economic events, added the purchase order event, and identified and linked the resources and agents associated with the events. After that you added primary keys, foreign keys, and relationship tables. You also used the design phase to enforce business rules and add controls.

While designing the acquisition/payment process, you likely noticed similarities between the data models for the acquisition/payment process and the sales/collection process. The similarities exist because you applied the resources, events, and agents methodology for creating databases. Designing the acquisition/payment process should have been significantly easier than designing the sales/collection process because you are following the same steps to identify events, the resources and agents related to them, and other events to which they are related.

After designing the database, you implemented it in Access by building tables and creating relationships between them. Once again, due to the similarity of the database design you were able to reuse many of the tables you created for the sales/collection process. Reusing sales/collection tables gave you the opportunity to see how making changes to Field properties affect the look and functionality of various fields.

Once the tables and relationships were completed, you gained much experience in making changes to existing queries and creating new, more complex queries. Hopefully, you have a better feel of when it is best to create a query from scratch versus making changes to an existing query. You also spent much more time working with action queries. You created make-table queries to temporarily store the result of aggregate functions (e.g., sum of purchase order line extensions), and you used a make-table query to temporarily store inventory line items from the purchase order so they could be added to the Inventory Receipt Entry form with an append query. Additionally, you used update queries in conjunction to the make-table queries to ensure that the sum of the inventory line extensions (i.e., purchase order line extensions and inventory receipt line extensions) equaled the total amount in the related event tables.

After you created a set of queries to accomplish a task, you automated tasks and added additional controls through the use of macros. You saw how you could use the SetTempVars action to take a value from one form control and use it to populate other controls to prevent input errors. In addition to learning what macros can accomplish, you also learned about some of their limitations (e.g., executing the Requery action in a form takes you back to the first record).

Finally, you built queries from acquisition/payment data for external financial reporting and for internal use. You used parameters to set the balance sheet date for Accounts Payable in total and by vendor. Hopefully, you saw how easy it is to convert sales/collection-related queries for use in the acquisition/payment process. For example, you should be able to take the Open Sale Orders query and use it to create an Open Purchase Order query.

Questions and Problems for Review

Multiple-Choice Questions

1. The purchase event is linked to which other events?
   a. Inventory and cash.
   b. Sale and purchase order.
   c. Vendor and employee.
   d. Purchase order and cash disbursement.
2. In which table will you find the quantity of Item #1021 ordered on Purchase Order # 100017?
   a. *tblPurchaseOrder*.
   b. *tblPurchase*.
   c. *tblReservation-PurchaseOrderInventory*.
   d. *tblInflow-PurchaseInventory*.
3. The Vendor table described in this chapter, *tblVendor*, is not in third normal form because
   a. its primary key, VendorNumber, is not unique.
   b. it contains VendorAddress1 and VendorAddress2, which are repeating fields.
   c. the VendorState field is transitively dependent on the VendorZipCode field.
   d. the VendorCity field is functionally dependent on the VendorState field.
4. Purchase process activities include all of the following except
   a. recording payments received from customers.
   b. keeping vendor information current.
   c. recording the cost of materials purchased.
   d. printing purchase orders.

5. The Append query *qryAddOrderedItemsToPurchInv* creates a control to
   a. automatically add items from the related Purchase Order to the Inventory Receipt Entry form.
   b. prevent a materials handling clerk from recording unordered items received into the database.
   c. help ensure that the inventory handling clerk counts the items received.
   d. *qryAddOrderedItemsToPurchInv* is used to create all of the above controls.

6. The primary key in *tblCashDisbursement* is
   a. CashAccountID and CheckNum.
   b. CheckNum.
   c. CheckNum and VendorID.
   d. CashAccountID, CheckNum, and VendorID.

7. The Make-table query, *qrySumOfPOLineExtensionsByPO*
   a. requires you to create a primary key in the query design.
   b. creates a new table the first time the query is run, and running the query again merely adds records to the existing table.
   c. deletes the existing table and creates a new table every time the query is run.
   d. a and b are correct.

8. Enforcing referential integrity on VendorNumber from *tblVendor* to *tblPurchaseOrder* is a good way to ensure that
   a. the VendorID in *tblVendor* is valid.
   b. the VendorID in *tblPurchaseOrder* is valid.
   c. the VendorID must be entered into *tblPurchaseOrder* when initially entering Purchase Order information.
   d. both a and c are correct.

9. What date constraint parameters should be used in the criteria when computing balance sheet items like accounts payable?
   a. <=[Beginning of Period Date].
   b. <=[End of Period Date].
   c. Between [Beginning of Period Date] and [End of Period Date].
   d. [Beginning of Period Date] <= [End of Period Date].

10. What does the following macro action accomplish?

ACTION	ARGUMENTS
OpenQuery	qryUpdateVendorID, Datasheet, Edit

   a. Opens *qryUpdateVendorID* in Design view to be edited.
   b. Runs *qryUpdateVendorID* just like double-clicking it in the Navigation Pane.
   c. Opens *qryUpdateVendorID* in Datasheet view without running the query.
   d. None of the above answers are correct.

Discussion Questions

1. In Pipefitters Supply Company's *tblInventory* table, you used a foreign key link with referential integrity on the InventoryComposition field to the *tblInventoryComposition* table to control input to the InventoryComposition field. You could have achieved the same result by creating the following Validation Rule for InventoryComposition instead of creating a separate inventory composition table: = **"B" or "C".** Discuss the advantages and disadvantages of each approach.

2. How could you use the tables in this chapter to measure vendor price and delivery performance?

3. How would you add quality measurements to the purchase cycle system described in the chapter?

4. In *tblPurchaseOrder* why was it necessary to use a table-level validation rule to ensure that the expected delivery date occurs on or after the purchase order date?

5. Your completed database in this chapter contains all tables from the acquisition/payment process and the sales/collection process. What balance sheet and income statement items can be computed by using tables from both business processes? Describe how you would compute these amounts.

Practice Exercises

Note: Before attempting any of the following practice exercises, save a new copy *Ch09.accdb* from the Companion Web site to use for the Practice Exercises. Then, clear the copied database's Read-only file attribute. Begin the names of all Access objects you create in the Practice Exercises with PE#-. Replace # with the Practice Exercise number.

1. Create a query that identifies vendors by name from whom Pipefitters Supply Company has purchased ½-inch brass inventory items. Name your query PE1-qry050BrassVendors.

2. Create a Check Register report like the one in Figure 9.58. It is grouped by CashAccountID and sorted by CheckNum. First create a query with the following fields from *tblCashDisbursement*: cash account number, check number, check date, payee (vendor), and check amount; and VendorName from *tblVendor*. Use begin date and end date parameters in your query so the user can generate a check register for any desired period of time. Use the same parameters in the Report Header to show the time period covered by the report Name the query PE2-qryCheckRegister, and the report PE2-rptCheckRegister.

Fig. 9.58 *rptCheck-Register* in **Report view for the period 2/1/2010 to 2/7/2010.**

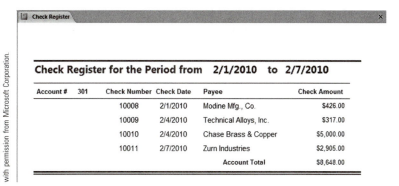

Microsoft product screen shot reprinted with permission from Microsoft Corporation.

3. Create a query that lists all open items—items that have been ordered, but not yet received. Use the three Chapter 8 Open Sale Order queries as your guide. Since you will have three queries, begin the query names with PE3-1qry..., PE3-2qry..., and PE3-3qry.... Make sure that you include VendorID in the third query (you may need to first add VendorID to one of your earlier queries) so you can complete Practice Exercise 4.

4. Compute the average number of days to receive items by vendor. You will need two queries because you have to separate the horizontal computation to compute days to receive each item from the aggregate function to compute the average of the result of your horizontal computation. Start your first query by making a copy of your final query from Practice Exercise 3 and renaming it PE4-1qryDaysToReceiveItems. Use it to compute days to receive items. Name the second query to compute the average days to ship items by vendor PE4-2qryAvgDaysToReceiveItems.

5. Use the Query Wizard to create a query that will find purchase orders with expected delivery dates at least seven days before today that you have not received even a partial shipment as of today. Hint: Microsoft Access includes a Date() function that you might find helpful. Name the query PE5-qryPOWithoutMatchingReceipt. Test your query by adding a new purchase order with an expected delivery at least seven days prior to the current date.

6. Replace the VendorID control in *frmPurchaseOrder* with a combo box that lists vendors alphabetically. Be sure to update the tab order after adding the combo box. To get started, make a copy of *frmPurchaseOrder* and name it PE6-frmPurchaseOrder.

Problems

1. The Bayside Falafel Hut (BFH) is a restaurant owned by Dima Jhari that specializes in Middle Eastern cuisine. BFH has grown rapidly and has found that managing its purchasing function is essential to controlling costs and operating profitably. BFH has asked you to design a database that will help it control its purchasing operation. BFH buys ingredients and supplies from several different food products wholesalers. Amit Kamir is the restaurant's executive chef and functions as its purchasing agent. All orders with vendors are placed by Amit and are confirmed with a printed purchase order. Vendors sometimes send several orders to BFH in only one shipment. When the shipments arrive, one of three or four kitchen staff members counts the items and fills out a receiving report. These staff members sign each report at the bottom on the "receiving clerk" line. Vendors mail invoices within a few days of shipping the orders to BFH. At the end of each month, Dima matches copies of the purchase orders, receiving reports, the invoices received from the vendors, and writes checks for the amounts due. Dima always pays the outstanding balances at the end of each month, even if she has to borrow money to do so. She always pays each vendor with one check, even if that vendor has sent multiple shipments during the month. Assume that all check numbers are unique, regardless of which cash account is used. List the events, resources, and agents (internal and external) that exist in the BFH acquisition/payment process. State any assumptions you needed to make.

2. Refer to the BFH case described in Problem 1, and create a business process model similar to that shown in Figure 9.2 for the restaurant. The diagram should show the entities you identified in Problem 1 along with the relationships between those entities and their cardinalities.

3. Refer to the BFH case described in Problem 1 and the work you did in Problem 2. Use Access to build the tables and create the relationships you have defined. Populate the tables with sample data that you create and test the tables to make certain that the relationships operate to enforce referential integrity as appropriate.

4. Refer to the work you have done in the preceding three problems. Create data entry forms for the BFH acquisition/payment process that allow you to enter data into every table without opening the table itself. Use the forms in the *Ch09.accdb* database as guides. You are not required to add elaborate controls. Add combo boxes where appropriate, and lock fields that populate automatically.

5. Refer to the work you have done in the preceding four problems. Create reports for the BFH acquisition/ payment process below. You can display the date as "month, year" by using the expression =Format$([PurchaseOrderDate],"mmmm yyyy",0,0).

    a. Create a monthly report that shows purchases by vendor and, within vendor, by product.

    b. Create a monthly report that shows items received organized by receiving clerk (that is, your report will have a Receiving Clerk header section).

    c. Create a monthly Purchases Summary report that lists all items purchased, sorted by total quantity purchased.

    d. Create any additional specific reports that your instructor assigns.

CHAPTER 10

Human Resources Process

CHAPTER OBJECTIVES

The human resources (HR) business process includes both human resource management (HRM) and payroll functions. Typical HRM functions include recruiting, hiring, training, benefits management, and terminating employees. An enterprise's payroll activities are often referred to as the payroll cycle because they encompass transaction processing and reporting activities. These activities include calculating employee earnings, recording payments to employees, and maintaining payroll records. These records must satisfy a complex array of government regulations pertaining to time and pay records. Firms also use HR (both HRM and payroll) information to create management reports and financial statements. This chapter shows you how to use Microsoft Access tables, queries, forms, and reports to:

- **Create a model of the human resources business process.**

- **Create a Microsoft Access database based on the business process model.**

- **Create controls to enforce business rules.**

- **Create and maintain employee records.**

- **Create and maintain records of time worked.**

- **Calculate gross and net pay.**

- **Record payments to employees.**

- **Produce information for financial statements.**

- **Produce information for internal purposes.**

Introduction

This chapter describes the human resources (HR) business process of an accounting information system. We illustrate many components of this process using example data for the Pipefitters Supply Company. As mentioned earlier, the HR process includes both human resource management (HRM) activities and payroll activities. We will focus on the payroll activities, which include everything from a requisition for some type of labor operation all the way through to paying employees.

Accountants sometimes consider payroll activities to be a part of the acquisition/ payment process. Payroll activities can also be integrated into the conversion process in manufacturing firms. However, treating the payroll activities as part of the HR process— separate from both acquisition/payment and conversion processes—helps highlight some of its interesting and unique characteristics. Designing and implementing an integrated HRM and payroll system is a complex undertaking. In this chapter you will learn the fundamental integrated accounting components related to payroll activities. These fundamental elements form the basis of even the most complex integrated accounting and HRM systems.

All but the very smallest enterprises have payroll activity. In this chapter you will learn about payroll activities that virtually all firms undertake. In service and merchandising firms, payroll cost appears as an expense item on the income statement. In manufacturing firms, the portion of payroll expenditures that is related to manufacturing activities becomes a part of the cost of goods manufactured. This cost appears on the financial statements in the cost of goods sold and in the cost of finished goods and work-in-progress inventories.

Pipefitters Supply Company's Human Resources Business Process

Pipefitters Supply Company employs fifty people in six functional areas. Employees are grouped based on function: accountant, administrator (includes supervisors and managers), salesperson, maintenance staff, materials handler, and purchasing agent.

Pipefitters has a relatively stable work force. Some employees have been with the company for over thirty years. Pipefitters has been growing recently and its work force has grown significantly during the current year. Supervisors or managers identify a need to hire one or more additional employees for their functional area. The company then advertises for the position in various print and online media. After an initial screening of the job applications, the appropriate functional manager interviews the candidates and makes the final hiring decision.

On each Thursday, Pipefitters' administrators meet to create the work schedule for the coming week. Each week a different administrator leads the meeting and assumes responsibility for the schedule. In the meeting, the administrators decide how many hours of which type of employees they need and then create a detailed schedule that includes each employee and his or her scheduled hours for during the coming week. At the present time, Pipefitters only differentiates labor by function and not by labor operation type. For example, the work schedule only shows the number of hours for each accountant, not the type of work they are scheduled to do—payroll, general ledger, accounts receivable, accounts payable, etc. After the schedule is made, each employee initials the schedule next to their name to indicate that they have been informed as to their upcoming schedule. The work schedule is a paper document that is not currently recorded in Pipefitters' accounting information systems (AIS).

Pipefitters calculates employee pay by the hour, and pays employees on the last day of each month for all hours worked during that month. No employees are on a fixed salary. The normal work week at Pipefitters is forty hours, and employees earn overtime at 1.5 times their normal pay rate for any hours they work beyond the normal work week. All employees are paid on the second day of the following month based on monthly time cards that are approved by employees' supervisors or managers, who input the hours-worked data into the system.

An accountant prepares payroll checks for one of the owners to sign. Each employee receives only one payroll check for the month. Payroll checks use funds drawn from the payroll account.

Duality of Economic Events

EXERCISE 10.1: MODELING THE DUALITY RELATIONSHIP FOR PIPEFITTERS SUPPLY COMPANY'S SALES/COLLECTION PROCESS

1. Based on the narrative for Pipefitters' HR process, draw the entities and relationship involved in the duality.
2. What is the event or activity that causes an increase in a resource? Identify this economic increment event with a "+" sign.
3. Since the HR process is a special type of acquisition/payment process, they will have an economic event in common; which event is it? Identify the economic decrement event with a "−" sign.
4. Add the cardinalities to your drawing.

Figure 10.1 shows the duality for the HR process. Labor acquisition is the economic increment event. This is measured by the number of hours that employees work. The economic decrement event is cash disbursement, just like in the acquisition/payment process. As noted in the sales and acquisition processes, the two events do not need to occur at the same time. Employees are paid after their labor has been acquired. If the accounting period ends a day other than the last day of the pay period, accrued payroll

Fig. 10.1 Pipefitters Supply Company human resources duality.

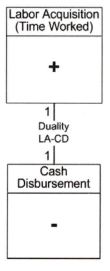

expenses can be derived by running the payroll queries based on hours worked since the last pay period.

Since Pipefitters' pays employees with one check for each month of time worked (each record in the labor acquisition table), a cash disbursement can have only one instance of labor acquisition associated with it. Therefore, the labor acquisition side of the duality relationship is 1. Also, since an instance of labor acquisition is associated with only one cash disbursement, the cash disbursement side of the relationship is 1.

Basic Human Resources Data Model

In the following exercise you will draw a diagram of Pipefitters' basic HR process: the duality events that make up the economic duality, and the resources and agents to which each event is linked. What is the resource that has an *inflow* relationship with labor acquisition? Which resource has an *outflow* relationship with cash disbursement? Which agent has an *external participation* with the duality events? Which agent has an *internal participation* relationship with the economic events? The resulting data model forms the core of most HR business processes.

EXERCISE 10.2: CREATING THE BASIC HR DATA MODEL

1. Add to Figure 10.1 the resource and agent(s) for the labor acquisition event and their relationships with labor acquisition.
2. Add cardinalities to the relationships with labor acquisition.
3. Add to your model the resource and agent(s) for the cash disbursement event and their relationships with cash disbursement.
4. Add cardinalities to the relationships with cash disbursement.

Labor Acquisition (Time Worked) Event

The data model in Figure 10.2 shows that a labor acquisition results in an inflow of labor (the labor type resource). The labor type resource and inflow relationship are shown as dashed lines because Pipefitters does not track specific types of labor acquired. For example, Pipefitters does not record what type of accounting work (e.g., payroll, general ledger, accounts receivable) accountants perform. However, we included labor type in the model to illustrate what the model would look like for enterprises that track labor by the specific type of work performed.

The inflow of labor comes from an employee acting as an external agent. An employee acting as an internal agent also participates in the relationship. The one-to-many relationship between employee-as-external-agent and labor acquisition is a typical set of cardinalities between events and external agents; the relationship indicates that a particular employee-as-external-agent can participate in many labor acquisitions and that a labor acquisition has at most one employee-as-external-agent.

Likewise, the one-to-many relationship between employee-as-internal-agent and labor acquisition indicates that a specific employee-as-internal-agent may participate in many labor acquisitions and that a labor acquisition participates with only one employee-as-internal-agent.

If Pipefitters tracked labor by detailed type of work performed, the inflow relationship between labor acquisition and labor type would be many-to-many because a particular labor type (e.g., unloading incoming inventory) can be involved with many labor acquisitions (time worked) and a particular labor acquisition can have many different labor types (e.g., fourteen hours of unloading incoming inventory and sixty-six hours of loading outgoing inventory).

Fig. 10.2 Pipefitters Supply Company HR duality with resources and agents.

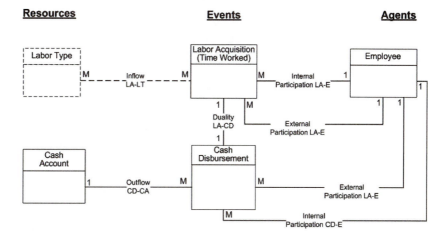

Cash Disbursement Event

Figure 10.2 shows that a cash disbursement results in an outflow of cash to an employee-as-external-agent and that an employee-as-internal-agent also participates in the relationship. Like the labor acquisition event, both participations with cash disbursement are one-to-many. Also, the one-to-many cardinalities involving the cash account resource indicate that a cash account may participate in many cash disbursement events and that any particular cash disbursement will come from a single cash account.

Compare the data models in Figure 10.2 and Figure 9.1. Notice the similarities and differences between the acquisition/payment process and the HR process. The main difference is that employees in the HR process participate as external agents whereas outside vendors are the external agents in the acquisition/payment process. Another difference is that recording inventory inflows from the acquisition/payment process is critical to Pipefitters' success, although recording the inflow of labor type in the HR process is not.

Work Schedule Event

Pipefitters' HR process begins when the administrators (with one administrator assuming responsibility) create the coming week's work schedule for Pipefitters' employees. This event, once approved by employees, commits Pipefitters to pay employees for the scheduled number of hours and also commits employees to work the number of hours specified by the work schedule.

When Pipefitters creates a work schedule, it has a *reservation* to receive labor from employees-as-external agents: a *reservation* relationship between work schedule and labor type (not currently tracked by Pipefitters). Also, since administrators (employees-as-internal-agents) make work schedules for employees-as-external-agents, the work schedule is related to employee-as-internal-agent and employee-as-external-agent. Finally, a work schedule is *fulfilled* by labor acquired (labor acquisition event) from employees-as-external-agents, so the relationship between a work schedule and labor acquisition is a *fulfillment* relationship. Even though Pipefitters does not have a work schedule event or labor type resource in its AIS, add the work schedule event and its relationships to Pipefitters' HR model.

EXERCISE 10.3: ADDING THE WORK SCHEDULE EVENT TO PIPEFITTERS SUPPLY COMPANY'S HR DATA MODEL

1. Add work schedule to the HR data model in Figure 10.2 and the appropriate relationships. Be sure to add the employee type entity that was included in the sales/collection and acquisition/payment processes (Chapters 8 and 9, respectively).
2. Add the cardinalities to the relationships.

Figure 10.3 shows the complete HR data model for Pipefitters Supply Company. It includes two type/category entities not previously discussed—exemptions and withholding—which we will discuss in the next section. The fulfillment relationship between work schedule and labor acquisition is one-to-many because a work schedule is for Pipefitters' entire staff (many labor acquisition events for each work schedule). The reservation relationship (if Pipefitters tracked it) between work schedule and labor type has the same many-to-many relationship as the actual inflow of labor type (if it were tracked) because a work schedule will be for many different types of work tasks (labor type) and a labor type (if it were tracked) likely will be scheduled many times. Also, like the labor acquisition event, work schedule participates with only one employee-as-internal-agent (the responsible administrator) and an employee-as-internal-agent may participate with (have responsibility for) many work schedules. However, unlike the labor acquisition event, the cardinalities for the participation relationship between work schedule and employee-as-external-agent is many-to-many because a single work schedule, even though

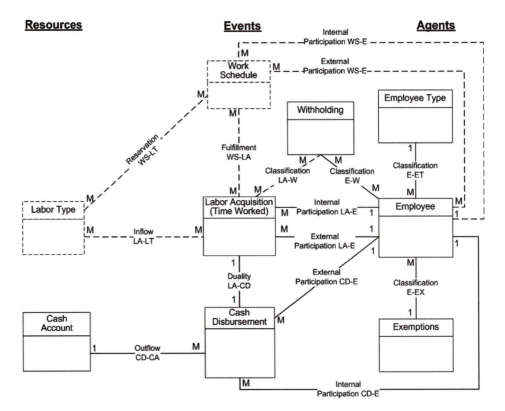

Fig. 10.3 Pipefitters Supply Company HR process with all entities.

not part of the AIS, has many employees-as-outside-agents, and an employee-as-outside-agent will likely participate with many work schedules (one schedule for each week).

Exemptions and Withholding Entities

The payroll portion of the HR process requires withholding computations based in part on the number of exemptions employees claim on their W-4 forms. Each employee has only one value for number of exemptions, which is why the exemptions side of the employee-exemptions relationship is "1". Many employees may claim the same number of exemptions so the employee side of the relationship is "M".

The tax bracket used in withholding computations is based in part on gross pay for the period and marital status. That is, there are two sets of withholding brackets: one set for single persons (persons not classified as married for federal tax purposes) and another set for married persons. The relationships with withholding are more complex than with other entities we have modeled in this textbook.

Notice that the withholding entity has a relationship with both employee *and* labor acquisition. The employee-withholding relationship is based on marital status. Since a particular withholding bracket may be associated with many employees the employee side of the relationship is "M." Unlike the other classification relationships we have discussed, an employee is related to the whole set of withholding brackets—either the set for single persons or the set for married persons. Therefore, the withholding side of the relationship is "M," creating a many-to-many relationship.

A similar line of reasoning applies to the relationship between labor acquisition (hours worked) and withholding. A withholding bracket may be associated with many labor acquisitions; a labor acquisition (if gross pay minus the allowance amount* were directly recorded for each labor acquisition) will be associated with two tax brackets— one for single persons and one for married persons. The resulting many-to-many labor acquisition-withholding relationship, along with the other classification relationships, is shown in Figure 10.3.

Completing the HR Model

To complete the HR data model we chose primary keys for each entity (see Figure 10.4). Notice that withholding has a composite primary key, just like you use for relationship tables. We chose a composite primary key for a similar reason: Each record in the withholding table is based on information that comes from the employee table and could come from the labor acquisition table (if we captured gross income minus allowance amount in the labor acquisition table). Based on the primary keys and participation cardinalities, you can create the foreign keys and relationship tables.

EXERCISE 10.4: MAKING RELATIONSHIPS WITH FOREIGN KEYS AND RELATIONSHIP TABLES

1. Using the primary keys provided for Pipefitters' data model in Figure 10.4, create foreign keys for the one-to-many relationships.
2. Add relationship tables and composite primary keys for the many-to-many relationships.

---

*One factor in determining the federal withholding tax bracket is gross pay less an amount based on the amount of allowances an employee claims. We will cover withholding computations in detail later in the chapter.

Fig. 10.4 HR process with primary keys.

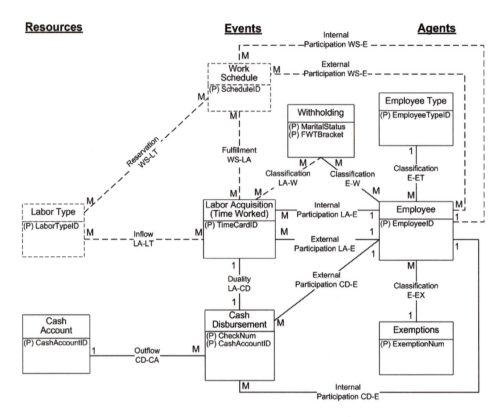

Notice that we posted MaritalStatus as a foreign key in the employee table instead creating a relationship table. This was done for two reasons. First, because we are not recording FWTBracket in the labor acquisition table (we will assign the value for FWTBracket in the payroll withholding computation queries), we do not have a complete primary key to record in a relationship table. Second, we do not need to enforce referential integrity between the two tables as a control, which is discussed when we create input forms. If your foreign keys and relationship tables do not match those in Figure 10.5, review the "Relational Database Management Systems" section in Chapter 2.

Like the acquisition/payment process described in Chapter 9, the HR process portion of an accounting system maintains information about external agents (employees) and resources (cash accounts). However, Pipefitters does not track information about specific types of labor, the resource acquired. Also, Pipefitters does not yet track work schedules, the commitment event, in its database either. The entities that we will actually use in Access appear in Figure 10.6 along with their primary and foreign keys.

Employee Information

The basic building block for any payroll system is employee information. At a minimum, Pipefitters will need employee names, Social Security numbers, and pay rates. To calculate net pay amounts, it will need number of exemptions and marital status information. Pipefitters will also need employee addresses for mailing paychecks and

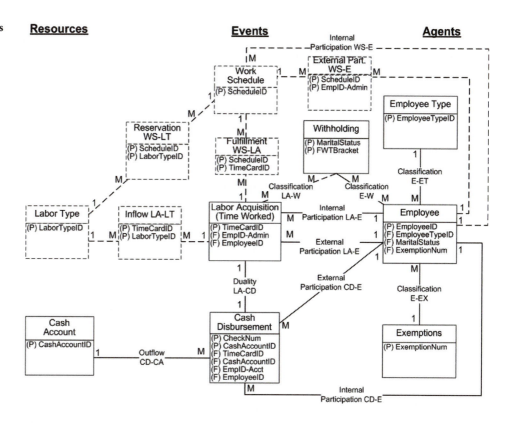

Fig. 10.5 HR process with primary keys, foreign keys, and relationship tables.

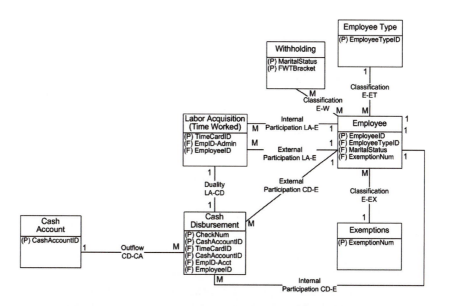

Fig. 10.6 HR process with entities that will be used in Access database.

employee start dates for determining eligibility for pension and other benefit plans. These are only a few examples of the types of employee information stored in payroll databases. Indeed, some firms track hundreds of individual data items for each employee!

Integrated HRM systems are the end product of an evolutionary process. Originally, HR systems and payroll systems were separate in most companies. When firms began adopting database approaches to reduce data redundancy in their information processing activities, these two systems were ideal targets for integration. However, to enhance internal control, even today's integrated HRM systems limit accounting personnel's access to employee data—additions, deletions, and changes to employee records are typically handled by the HR department.

The Employee Table

The first HR table that we will describe is the Employee table. The Employee table provides a central location for storing all information about each employee. This makes the human resources job of adding, deleting, and updating employee information easy and efficient. It also eliminates data redundancy; human resources creates and maintains data in this table, yet the accounting department can use information stored in the table to calculate payroll and print paychecks. The Employee table will include a fairly large number of fields. You will need to identify a good primary key field and then add fields to store employee names, addresses, Social Security numbers, pay rates, and start dates. You will also need to store other information in the Employee table (e.g., marital status and number of exemptions) that Pipefitters will need to calculate withholding tax amounts.

The first field you will include in the Employee table is its primary key, the employee number. Recall that a table's primary key must be a unique identifier that exists for every record in the table. One tempting primary key candidate for the Employee table is the employee Social Security number; however, privacy laws discourage firms from using Social Security numbers to identify employees. Also, large companies have found that the Social Security Administration occasionally assigns the same number to more than one person and sometimes assigns a person more than one number. By creating its own employee numbering scheme, Pipefitters can maintain complete control over the integrity of its Employee table's primary key.

Some firms use the employee number to store information implicitly. For example, a firm could make all managers' numbers begin with the digit 4. What happens when an employee gets promoted or is assigned to a new job function? Pipefitters has decided to use a simple sequential numbering scheme to ensure that each employee number is unique and that the number contains no implicit information about an employee that might change. In a sequential number scheme, you assign each new employee a number that is one greater than the largest employee number already assigned. You do not reuse old employee numbers after employees leave because the employee number provides a permanent access path to past employees' records. Although specific rules and practices vary from state to state, employers often are required to keep data about past employees for many years.

As you design the fields that will store employee names, keep in mind what you have learned in earlier chapters about good database design practices. For example, you will store the employee name data in the most atomic form possible; that is, in the smallest possible logical chunks. Pipefitters has decided to break employee names into three logical pieces: first name, middle initial, and last name. Other firms might also include separate fields to store titles, such as Mr. and Ms., or surname suffixes, such as Sr., Jr., and III.

The next set of fields in Pipefitters' Employee table is the address and telephone number fields. Designing these fields should be a familiar task for you by now, since you have already created address and telephone number fields for customers and vendors in

Chapters 8 and 9, respectively. The address and telephone number fields for the Employee table and their properties are similar to those of the Customer and Vendor tables you have already built.

The final group of fields will store information that Pipefitters Supply Company needs to calculate employees' gross and net pay. This information includes employees' pay rates, number of exemptions claimed, and marital status. You also will need a field to store employees' start dates. Pipefitters organizes its employees by job function, so we will include a job function identifier in the Employee table. Note that storing the job function number in the Employee table works only because Pipefitters permanently assigns employees to job functions and employees do not perform more than one job function. Other companies that do not have such a policy must store the employee-job function link in a relationship table to accommodate the many-to-many relationships that can arise.

In the next exercise, you will create an Employee table for Pipefitters Supply Company. Since the Customer and Employee tables have many fields in common, we will start with a copy of the Customer table to save some time creating a table with sixteen fields.

EXERCISE 10.5: CREATING *TBLEMPLOYEE*

1. Start Microsoft Access. Open the *Ch10.accdb* database you downloaded from the Companion Web site.
2. Right-click tblCustomer in the Chapter 8 Tables section of the Navigation Pane. Click Copy. Right-click anywhere in the Navigation Pane. Click Paste. Since the Employee table already exists in the database, type tblMyEmployee in the Paste Table As dialog name box. Click the Structure Only radio button; then click OK. Due to the length of this exercise be sure to save your work periodically.
3. Open tblMyEmployee in Design view. It will be located in the Unassigned Objects section of the Navigation Pane.
4. Change the Primary Key name from CustomerID to EmployeeID. Change the Field Size to 3, the Input Mask to 000;0_, and the Caption to Employee #. If Pipefitters begins employee numbers with 101, how many employees can they have in their database?
5. Change the second field name from CustomerName to EmployeeLastName. Change the Field Size to 30, and the Caption to Last Name.
6. Add four blank rows to make room for EmployeeFirstName, EmployeeMiddleInitial, and EmployeeSSN. Click the Record Selector next to CustomerAddress1 to select where the first row will be added. Press and hold the Shift key and press the Down Arrow three times to highlight the next three rows. Click Insert Rows in the Tools group to insert four blank rows between EmployeeLastName and CustomerAddress1.
7. Copy EmployeeLastName to the first blank row. Click the Record Selector next to CustomerAddress1. Press Ctrl+C to copy; click the Record Selector next to first blank row. Press Ctrl+V to paste. Change the field name to EmployeeFirstName. Change the Field Size to 15, and the Caption to First Name.
8. Enter EmployeeMiddleInitial in the next blank row of the Field Name column and leave its Data Type set to Text. Set its Field Size property to 1 and its Input Mask property to >L. This will permit a one-letter middle initial and force it to be capitalized, even if a user enters it in lower case. Set this field's Caption property to MI. Why should you leave the Required field property set to No?
9. In the third blank row you created, enter a Field Name of EmployeeSSN for the Social Security number field, and leave its Data Type set to Text. Set its Field Size property to 11 to store nine digits and two hyphens for each Social Security number. Set its Input Mask property to 000\ -00\ -0000;0;_ to help users enter the

field values in the U.S. Social Security System's format, set its Caption property to SSN, and set the Required property to Yes.

10. Since all of the address fields and phone number field properties are identical for customers and employees, the only change you need to make is to change Customer in each of the address and phone number Field Names to Employee.

11. Delete CustomerCreditLimit and CustomerPrimaryContact. Select both fields by using the Record Selectors as you did in Step 6. Press the Delete key to delete the two rows selected.

12. Enter EmployeeMaritalStatus as the next Field Name. Leave its Data Type set to Text, set its Field Size property to 1, its Input Mask property to >L, its Caption property to Marital Status, and its Required property to Yes. If an employee does not declare a marital status, U.S. law requires employers to withhold at the single person rate. Therefore, we can set the Default Value property to S. Note that Access automatically encloses the value with quotation marks when you leave the Default Value property.

Since an employee must be either single or married, the only permissible values for this field are M and S. You can use the Validation properties to limit data entry to these values. Set the Validation Rule property for the EmployeeMaritalStatus field to =M Or S. Once again, quotation marks automatically enclose the stated values when you leave the property box.

Set the Validation Text property to Please enter an M for Married or an S for Single.

13. Another information item that Pipefitters needs to calculate its employees' federal income tax withholding amounts is the number of exemptions each employee claims. In the next open row of the Field Name column, type EmployeeExemptions.

14. Since Pipefitters will use the EmployeeExemptions value in calculating net pay, you must store it as a number. The value for this field will always be a whole number (an integer) and will never exceed 255. Set the EmployeeExemptions Data Type to Number. Change its Field Size property to Byte, and its Decimal Places property to 0. Set the Input Mask property to 0 and the Caption property to Exemptions.

TRY IT

To save storage space and increase database access speed, you should try to use the smallest storage space on the disk for number fields. In this case, a Byte field size is the most efficient. To learn more about the Field Size property settings that Microsoft Access provides for Number fields, select Help, Microsoft Access Help Topics from the menu; enter field size property; click Search; double-click Set the field size in the Topics Found; and then click the Change the field size of a number field link. This Help Topic provides detailed information about the available Field Size property settings including range, decimal precision, and storage requirements.

15. If an employee does not specify a number of exemptions, U.S. tax law requires withholding at the rate for zero exemptions; therefore, set the EmployeeExemptions Default Value property to 0. Note that Microsoft Access does not automatically enclose the 0 in quotation marks, because it is a Number Data Type, not a Text Data Type. The quotation marks are necessary only for character values, not number values. When you set the Default Value property for a field with a Number Data Type, Microsoft Access knows to store the default value as a number.

16. To calculate employees' gross pay, we must know what their pay rates are. Pipefitters Supply Company pays all of its employees by the hour; so, we can store each employee's pay rate in a field in an EmployeePayRate field. In the next open row of the Field Name column, type EmployeePayRate. Set its Data Type to Currency, its Decimal Places property to 2, its Caption property to Pay Rate, and its Required property to Yes.

17. The U.S. government and many states have established minimum hourly wages. You can use the Validation Rule property to prevent entry of a value in the EmployeePayRate field that is less than the minimum wage. Using the Validation Rule property this way is an example of a limit check, an internal control procedure that limits the range of values that a field will accept. You can also use the Validation Rule property to set a maximum value on the field. One way that a data entry person can perpetrate payroll fraud is to change an accomplice's pay rate to a large number and issue him or her one paycheck. The accomplice then quits and disappears. A data entry person could also commit an unintentional error that overpays an employee. Although you cannot completely prevent this type of fraud or error, you can reduce the impact by setting a maximum limit on the EmployeePayRate value. If you assume that the legal minimum wage is $7.50 per hour and the highest wage Pipefitters expects to pay is $40.00 per hour, you can set minimum and maximum limits on the EmployeePayRate field. Set the EmployeePayRate Validation Rule property to > 7.49 And < 40.01, and set its Validation Text property to The Pay Rate you have entered is not within the allowed range of Pay Rate values. This Validation Rule property requires that any EmployeePayRate value be within the limit check values. The Validation Text property includes the error message that will appear in a dialog box if a user attempts to enter an out-of-range value.

18. Enter a Field Name of EmployeeTypeID in the next blank row and leave its Data Type set to Text. Set its Field Size property to 2, its Input Mask property to 00;0;_, its Caption property to Type, and its Required property to Yes.

19. The last field will store the date each employee began work. Enter a Field Name of EmployeeStartDate; set its Data Type to Date/Time, its Input Mask property to 99/99/0000;0;_, its Caption property to Start Date, its Default Value to Date() (the current date), and its Required property to Yes.

20. Save your changes. Switch to Datasheet viewtblMyEmployee. so you can copy the records from tblEmployee into your table. Open tblEmployee in Datasheet view. Press Ctrl+A to select all records. Press Ctrl+C to copy the records. Switch to tblMyEmployee. Click the New Record Selector and press Ctrl+V to add all 50 records to your table.

Now, open tblEmployee in Design view and compare your table to *tblEmployee*. Figure 10.7 shows a sample records in Datasheet view for the fifty Pipefitters Supply Company employees. Due to the width of the table, not all fields can be displayed in Figure 10.7.

Although the Employee table you just built includes sixteen fields, it is actually less complex than the employee tables you will encounter in practice. In addition to the information included in this example, employee tables often include fields that store title, job skill, education level, insurance and pension plan participation codes, direct-deposit bank account information, and even the name of a person to call in case of an emergency.

Many firms associate particular employees with job function, projects, or departments. For example, Pipefitters Supply Company tracks employees to job function (employee type). In the preceding exercise, you avoided wasting storage space by using a field to store the employee type number rather than the employee type name. Using an

Fig. 10.7 *tblEmployee* in Datasheet view.

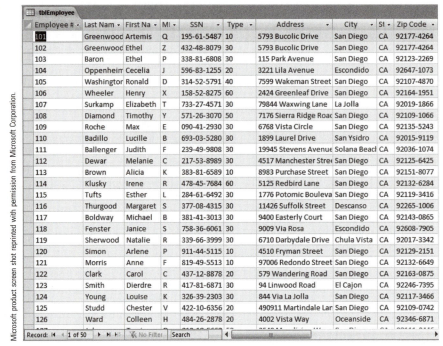

Employee #	Last Nam	First Na	MI	SSN	Type	Address	City	St	Zip Code
101	Greenwood	Artemis	Q	195-61-5487	10	5793 Bucolic Drive	San Diego	CA	92177-4264
102	Greenwood	Ethel	Z	432-48-8079	30	5793 Bucolic Drive	San Diego	CA	92177-4264
103	Baron	Ethel	P	338-81-6808	30	115 Park Avenue	San Diego	CA	92123-2269
104	Oppenheim	Cecelia	J	596-83-1255	20	3221 Lila Avenue	Escondido	CA	92647-1073
105	Washington	Ronald	D	314-52-5791	40	7599 Wakeman Street	San Diego	CA	92107-4870
106	Wheeler	Henry	X	158-52-8275	60	2424 Greenleaf Drive	San Diego	CA	92164-1951
107	Surkamp	Elizabeth	T	733-27-4571	30	79844 Waxwing Lane	La Jolla	CA	92019-1866
108	Diamond	Timothy	Y	571-26-3070	50	7176 Sierra Ridge Road	San Diego	CA	92109-1066
109	Roche	Max	E	090-41-2930	30	6768 Vista Circle	San Diego	CA	92135-5243
110	Badillo	Lucille	B	693-03-5280	30	1899 Laurel Drive	San Ysidro	CA	92015-9119
111	Ballenger	Judith	F	239-49-9808	30	19945 Stevens Avenue	Solana Beach	CA	92036-1074
112	Dewar	Melanie	C	217-53-8989	30	4517 Manchester Stre	San Diego	CA	92125-6425
113	Brown	Alicia	K	383-81-6589	10	8983 Purchase Street	San Diego	CA	92151-8077
114	Klusky	Irene	R	478-45-7684	60	5125 Redbird Lane	San Diego	CA	92132-6284
115	Tufts	Esther	L	284-61-6492	30	1776 Potomic Bouleva	San Diego	CA	92119-3416
116	Thurgood	Margaret	S	377-08-4315	30	11426 Suffolk Street	Descanso	CA	92265-1006
117	Boldway	Michael	B	381-41-3013	30	9400 Easterly Court	San Diego	CA	92143-0865
118	Fenster	Janice	S	758-36-6061	30	9009 Via Rosa	Escondido	CA	92608-7905
119	Sherwood	Natalie	R	339-66-3999	30	6710 Darbydale Drive	Chula Vista	CA	92017-3342
120	Simon	Arlene	P	911-44-5115	10	4510 Fryman Street	San Diego	CA	92129-2151
121	Morris	Anne	F	819-49-5513	10	97006 Redondo Street	San Diego	CA	92132-6649
122	Clark	Carol	C	437-12-8878	20	579 Wandering Road	San Diego	CA	92163-0875
123	Smith	Dierdre	R	417-81-6871	30	94 Linwood Road	El Cajon	CA	92246-7395
124	Young	Louise	K	326-39-2303	30	844 Via La Jolla	San Diego	CA	92117-3466
125	Studd	Chester	V	422-10-6356	20	490911 Martindale Lar	San Diego	CA	92109-0742
126	Ward	Colleen	H	484-26-2878	20	4002 Vista Way	Oceanside	CA	92346-6871

Record: 1 of 50   No Filter   Search

employee type number makes data entry easier and less error-prone. The next section describes an employee type table in which you can store employee type names.

The Employee Type Table

The Pipefitters Supply Company Employee type table is similar to the inventory type tables. It only needs two fields: a two-digit primary key for each employee type. The second field will store the employee type names. Exercise 10.6 provides step-by-step instructions for building this table.

EXERCISE 10.6: BUILDING AN EMPLOYEE TYPE TABLE

1. Click the Create tab; click Table in the Tables group and click the Design View command that appears in the Datasheet context tab. Access asks you to name the table.
2. To create the primary key, type EmployeeTypeID in the first row of the Field Name column and click Primary Key in the Tools group. Leave the Data Type set to Text.
3. Set the field properties: Field Size—2; Input Mask—00;0;_ Caption—EmployeeType #; Required—Yes; Allow Zero Length—No; Indexed—Yes (No Duplicates).
4. Enter EmployeeTypeName in second row of the Field Name column. Leave the Data Type set to Text.
5. Set the following field properties: Field Size—50; Caption—Employee Type Name; Required—Yes; Allow Zero Length—No; Indexed—No. Save your work and close the table.
6. Save the table. Since the Employee Type table already exists in the database, type tblMyEmployeeType in the Save As dialog box and then click OK to save your table. Close the table.

EXERCISE 10.7: LINKING *TBLEMPLOYEE* AND *TBLEMPLOYEETYPE*

1. Close all open tables. In the Database Tools tab, click Relationships in the Show/Hide group and minimize the Navigation Pane.
2. Add *tblEmployee* and *tblEmployeeType* to the Relationships window. Click Show Table in the Relationships group; double-click tblEmployee and tblEmployeeType and then click Close.
3. Resize your tables to show the entire table name and all of the attributes. Move the two agent tables to the extreme right side of the Relationships window to be consistent with the REA model format.
4. Create links between tables. Drag from the primary key in *tblEmployeeType* to the matching foreign key in *tblEmployee*.
5. After you click and drag the primary key to the foreign key, the Edit Relationships dialog box appears. Make sure that the correct attributes appear in the tables you dragged from and to. The relationship type at the bottom of the dialog box is should always be one-to-many. Check Enforce Referential Integrity and Cascade Update Related Fields. Finally, click Create in the dialog box. When you are finished, your Relationship window should look like the one in Figure 10.8.
6. Close the Relationship window and click the Yes button in the dialog box to save your changes.

Fig. 10.8 Linking *tblEmployee* and *tblEmployeeType* in the Relationship window.

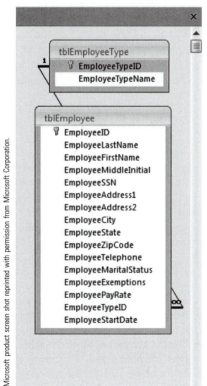

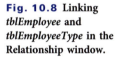

Microsoft product screen shot reprinted with permission from Microsoft Corporation.

The Employee Information Entry Form

The number and size of the fields in the Employee table make the task of entering data directly into the table in Datasheet view cumbersome. In this section, you will learn how to build a form for the Employee table that will make entering, changing, and deleting employee information much easier.

The Employee Information Entry form must include controls for the sixteen fields in *tblEmployee*. One way to make data entry easier in a form with so many fields is to reduce visual clutter. You can do that on this form by grouping related fields into separate sections of the form. Pipefitters' Employee table includes information that you can sort into four logical groups: employee identification fields, employee name fields, employee address fields, and payroll calculation information fields.

The employee identification fields are EmployeeID, EmployeeType, and Employee-StartDate. The employee name fields are EmployeeLastName, EmployeeFirstName, and EmployeeMiddleInitial. The employee address fields are EmployeeAddress1, Employee-Address2, EmployeeCity, EmployeeState, EmployeeZipCode, and EmployeeTelephone. The payroll calculation fields are EmployeeSSN, EmployeeMaritalStatus, Employee-Exemptions, and EmployeePayRate.

You will learn how to arrange controls in logical sections for this employee information form in the next two exercises. These exercises will also give you valuable practice in creating a form from scratch; that is, starting with a blank form. You will construct all of the form elements without using the Form Wizard. You can use Figures 10.10 and 10.11 as guides for sizing and placing the graphics objects, labels, and controls on the form as you complete the next three exercises. Close all tables to begin this exercise.

EXERCISE 10.8: USING FORM WIZARD TO ADD ALL FIELDS FROM *TBLEMPLOYEE* TO A NEW FORM

1. Click tblEmployee in the Unassigned Objects group of the Navigation Pane to highlight the table name.
2. Click the Create tab and click MoreForms in the Forms group and then click Form Wizard.
3. Click the >> button to move all available table fields to the Selected Fields panel.
4. Click the Next button to get to the Layout dialog box. Click Columnar if it is not already selected to create a form that displays all of the selected fields for each record in a single column.
5. Click the Next button twice to enter a form name. Type frmEmployee in the text box.
6. Click the Finish button which closes the dialog box and opens *frmEmployee* in Form view.
7. Switch to Design view. Click the Arrange tab. Press Ctrl+A to select all controls and labels on *frmEmployee*. Click Remove in the Control Layout group to allow each object to be adjusted independently. Click an empty part of the form to unselect all objects.
8. Click the Design tab, select all labels by clicking just above the Employee # label and dragging the cursor down until the select box (it will look like a vertical line if you drag straight down) touches all label boxes. Click Bold and Right Justify in the Font group. Eliminate excess space in the label boxes by dragging the left side of each label to the right.
9. Switch to Layout view. Eliminate excess space in the field controls for all fields with a fixed length by dragging the right side of the box to the left: Employee #, MI, SSN, State, Zip Code, Phone, Marital Status, Exemptions (maximum of two digits), Pay Rate (Maximum $40.00), Type, and Start Date. Use Figure 10.9 as a guide.
10. Switch to Design view. Delete the header frmEmployee; then drag the Detail Bar up to the top to remove the header area from the form.

Fig. 10.9 Employee Information form after sizing labels and controls.

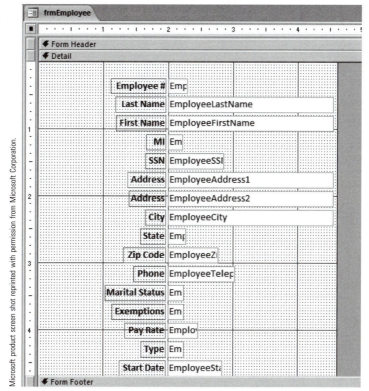

In the next exercise you are going to create four separate areas which you will use to group the employee fields: identification, name, payroll information, and address.

EXERCISE 10.9: GROUPING EMPLOYEE INFORMATION ON THE EMPLOYEE INFORMATION FORM

1. Minimize the Navigation Pane and close the Property Sheet if it is open. The form should still be in Design view. Make room to add additional objects to the form by clicking on the right edge of the Detail portion of the form and dragging it to the right until the form is nine inches wide.

2. Click the Rectangle tool in the Controls group; move your cursor just to the right of EmployeeID; click and drag to create a box 4-inches wide and 1-1/2-inches tall. Click the Special Effect menu in the Controls group and select Raised. Click Fill/Back Color in the Font group and select an appropriate color for the rectangle. Right-click the Rectangle; move your cursor to Position and select Send to Back so that the labels and controls you drag onto the rectangle sit on top of it.

3. Add a label to the box. Click Label in the Controls group; move your cursor about 1/2 inch below the top of the box, double click, and type Name. Click a blank area of the Detail section, then click the Name label. Click Bold and Center in the Font group. Click the Special Effect menu in the Controls group and select Raised. Use Figure 10.10 to position your label.

4. Click and drag the following controls and labels to the name rectangle EmployeeFirstName, EmployeeLastName, and EmployeeMiddleInitial. Use Figure 10.10 as a guide.

5. Click the Name label; press and hold the shift key and click the Rectangle. Press Ctrl+C and press Ctrl+V to create a new data grouping area. Increase the height of the rectangle to 2 inches. Right-click the Rectangle; move your cursor to Position and select Send to Back. Change the label name to Address.

6. Click and drag the following controls and labels into the Address rectangle: EmployeeAddress1, EmployeeAddress2, EmployeeCity, EmployeeState, EmployeeZipCode, and EmployeePhone. Use Figure 10.10 as a guide.

7. Click and drag EmployeeSSN until it is just above EmployeeMaritalStatus. Make another copy of the Name label and rectangle and move it to the left of and even with the top of the Name area of the form. Right-click the Rectangle; move your cursor to Position and select Send to Back. Change the label name to Identification. Grab the left side of the Rectangle and drag it to the right until the rectangle is only 2 inches wide. Reposition the label. Using Figure 10.10 as a guide, the form by dragging in the following controls and labels into the group: EmployeeID, EmployeeType, and EmployeeStartDate.

8. Repeat Steps 5 and 6 by copying the Address label and rectangle.

9. Repeat Step 7 with the remaining controls and labels: EmployeeSSN, EmployeeMaritalStatus, EmployeeExemptions, and EmployeePayRate. Use Figure 10.10 as a guide.

10. Move all objects to 1/4 inch below and to the right of the top-left corner of the form. Reduce the size of the Detail section until it is 1/4 inch wider and longer than the data entry area. Save your work.

11. Switch to Form view. Notice that only one record is displayed at a time. Tab through form. Notice that the tab order is based on the field order of *tblEmployee*. Return to Design view. Open the Property Sheet. Select Form in the Property Sheet combo box if it is not already selected. Change the Default View to Continuous so that you can display as many records as your screen size will allow.

12. Click the Arrange tab; click Tab Order in the Control Layout group. Click the Auto Order button. Notice that the tab stops are re-ordered from left-to-right and top-to-bottom. Manually re-order the tab stops to move from the first item to the last item in each group in the following group order: Identification, Name, Payroll Information, and Address. Save your work.

Fig. 10.10 Employee Information form in Design view.

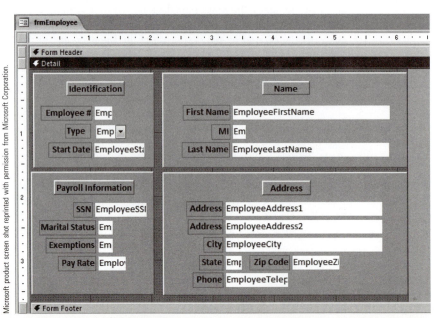

EXERCISE 10.10: COMPLETING THE EMPLOYEE INFORMATION FORM

In Chapters 8 and 9 we showed you how to use combo boxes as preventive controls by reducing the likelihood that erroneous identification codes are entered into the AIS. You will add a similar control to the Employee Information form. See Exercise 8.16 for detailed instructions for creating combo boxes. Additionally, you will make changes to the Form and Detail format properties to increase the form's ease of use.

1. Open *frmEmployee* in Design view if it is not already open. Click the EmployeeTypeID control box and press the Delete key to delete the control and label. Click Combo Box in the Controls group; move your cursor to where the EmployeeTypeID control should be and double-click to start the Combo Box Wizard. In the first dialog box click the Next button to select the default option *I want the combo box to lookup the values in a table or query*.
2. Double-click tblEmployeeType in the next dialog box to select it and advance to the next dialog box.
3. Click >> to move both attributes to the Selected Fields column. In this dialog box, click on the field CompositionDescription and then click > to select it. Click the Next button.
4. Sort by EmployeeTypeName. Ascending order is the default option. Click the Next button.
5. Double-click the right edge of each column to get the best fit for each column. Click the *Hide key column (recommended)* check box to uncheck it. In this form, we do want to display *tblEmployeeType*'s key field. Click the Next button.
6. Double-click EmployeeTypeID to store its value and advance to the next dialog box.
7. Click the combo box arrow and select EmployeeTypeID to store the value from the combo box you are creating into the EmployeeTypeID field in *tblEmployee*. Click the Next button.
8. In the last dialog box, enter Type for the label name and click the Finish button.
9. Bold the label font; resize the control box and switch to Layout view to make sure the data fits within the box.
10. Click the Arrange tab; click Tab Order and move comboXX (where XX is a number) from the bottom (it was the most recent control with a tab stop added to the form) to the second row from the top.
11. Select a contrasting color to make the data entry groups stand out. Return to Design view and click Property Sheet in the Tools group; select Detail from the Property Sheet combo box; click the Format tab on the Property Sheet. Then click the Back Color control box to bring up the color palette. Select a contrasting color. Set Alternate Back Color to No Color.
12. Select Form from the Property Sheet combo box and click the Format tab on the Property Sheet. Set the Default View to Continuous Forms; set Record Selectors to No; set Dividing Lines to Yes and set Scroll Bars to Neither.
13. Save your work. View the form in Form view. It should look like Figure 10.10.

In addition to learning more about the payroll cycle in this exercise, you learned how to use color, control properties, and object grouping to create a form that contains many fields but is still easy to read and to use for data entry and editing tasks.

Maintaining Employee Records

Now that you have an Employee table and a form that makes using that table easy, you can efficiently and effectively maintain employee information. With the Employee

Information form, Pipefitters can enter new employee information easily and update records as employees move, change their number of exemptions or marital status, get new telephone numbers, and change other information items they have entered in the Employee table.

Notice how the combo box control for the EmployeeType field makes data entry easier. When you click the combo box button, a list of all the EmployeeTypeID and EmployeeTypeDescription values that are in the Employee Type table appears as shown in Figure 10.11.

When a user selects a particular EmployeeTypeDescription value, the combo box control enters the related EmployeeTypeID value into the EmployeeTypeID field of the Employee table. The advantages of using a combo box control here include:

- *Data entry clerks do not need to memorize lists of employee type numbers.*
- *Only valid type numbers can be entered in the Employee table.*
- *It reduces storage needs in the Employee table by storing type numbers instead of descriptions.*
- *New types can be added easily to the Employee Type table, and they will automatically appear in the Employee Information form combo box.*

Note how the Default Value property settings you incorporated into the Employee table operate in the form. For example, immediately after you create a new record by entering a new EmployeeID, EmployeeStartDate becomes the current date, EmployeeMaritalStatus value becomes *S*, and the EmployeeExemptions value becomes *0*.

Fig. 10.11 Employee Information form with combo box in Form view.

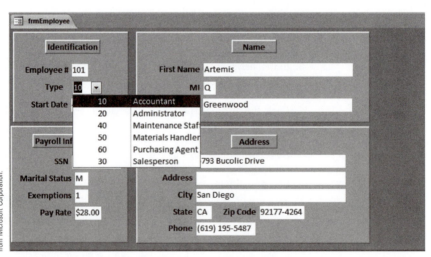

TRY IT

You can test the operation of the other internal control features you built into the table's design. For example, try entering illegal values in the EmployeePayRate field. If you attempt to enter a value less than 7.5 or greater than 40 in the field, a dialog box appears with the error message we entered as the Validation Text property. Note that the form will not permit you to leave the record until you enter an acceptable value in the EmployeePayRate field.

Updating existing employee records to reflect pay rate changes, new addresses, new telephone numbers, and other changes is straightforward. The navigation buttons at the bottom of the form make it easy to find and display any employee record you want to change. The form will let a user move through the individual fields in the displayed record using the Up and Down arrow keys, the Tab and Shift+Tab keys, or the Enter key. Also, remember that any internal control features that you built into the table's structure will limit changes to existing field values. That is, the changes you make cannot result in a value that would violate any of the controls.

To summarize, you now have a table that contains information about Pipefitter Supply Company's employees. The table relates each piece of information to a particular employee through the employee number—a primary key that uniquely identifies each employee. All information about a particular employee appears in one row of *tblEmployee* and depends on the primary key value for that row. You also have a form that facilitates entering, deleting, and changing employee information. You can use the information in this Employee table to construct HR process forms, queries, and reports for Pipefitters Supply Company.

Recording Labor Acquisition (Time Worked)

The economic increment event in the HR process is an event that measures the work of each employee. Often this measure is the time that employees have worked. Pipefitters Supply pays employees by the hour, as many companies do. However, not all organizations pay their employees on the basis of time worked. For example, firms may pay salespersons a percentage of their sales as a commission. Similarly, companies sometimes pay their managers bonuses based on their departments' profit, production, or efficiency. Even when firms calculate pay using time worked, the methods they use to capture time data vary tremendously. Some have their workers punch a time clock, others use automated bar code scanners that read employee badges, and still others have workers fill out hard copy or electronic time sheets. Regardless of how firms capture time worked data, they must store the data by employee and by pay period before calculating payroll. In the Pipefitters Supply Company HR database, you will store this information in the Labor Acquisition table.

The Labor Acquisition Table

In this section, you will learn how to build a time worked table that stores regular and overtime hours worked by each employee for each pay period. We have made two key simplifying assumptions: that Pipefitters calculates all pay on an hourly basis, and that Pipefitters pays all of its employees once each month with a single check.

You will need a primary key that uniquely identifies each employee's time worked in each pay period. Pipefitters uses time cards to record employee time worked and the time cards are numbered sequentially with a five digit number, we will use the time card number as the primary key.

There are other ways to create a primary key for the Labor Acquisition table. Since Pipefitters already has an employee number for each employee and each employee has only one record for each pay period, you could build a composite primary key that includes the employee number field and the pay period field to uniquely identify each pay record. However, we prefer to use the time card number because having sequentially numbered documents is an added control. The time cards for any pay period should form an unbroken sequence, and the first time card of the next pay period should be the next number in the sequence. Queries can be run to discover any time card that violates these conditions—indicating either an error or an irregularity.

The Labor Acquisition table will also include two fields that will store the hours employees have worked—one field for regular hours, the other field for overtime hours. Pipefitters uses only one overtime pay rate and that rate is one and one-half times the regular pay rate. Further, you can assume that when Pipefitters' supervisors and managers (Administrator employee type) enter the time worked data in this table, they have already calculated regular and overtime hours from workers' time cards.

In Exercise 10.11 you will create a Labor Acquisition table for Pipefitters Supply Company that accomplishes the necessary data storage objectives. The Labor Acquisition table also illustrates some internal control features that can help reduce potential losses from errors or irregularities as Pipefitters processes its payroll. You should have the Database window open on the Access desktop to begin this exercise.

EXERCISE 10.11: BUILDING THE LABOR ACQUISITION TABLE

1. Click the Create tab; click Table Design in the Tables group. Enter a Field Name of TimeCardID, leave its Data Type set to Text, and set its Field Size to 5. Enter an Input Mask property of 0000;0;_ and enter a Caption property of Time Card #. Set the Required property to Yes, Allow Zero Length to No, and set the Indexed property of Yes (No Duplicates). Click Primary Key in the Tools group to set the table's primary key.

2. Add the remaining five fields and properties listed in Figure 10.12.

   Notice that both EmployeeID and EmployeeSupervisorID are both foreign keys from *tblEmployee*. As depicted in Figure 10.6, EmployeeID is the link to the employee-as-external-agent in *tblEmployee*, while EmployeeSupervisorID provides the internal participation link between *tblLaborAcquisition* and *tblEmployee*. Also LAPayPeriodEnded is indexed to make queries keying on pay period faster. Finally, The validation rule for both regular and overtime hours worked not only prevents hours greater than allowed to be entered (185 = 23 days × 8 hours per day for regular time; and 200 hours of overtime is a company policy), the validation rule also prevents administrators from accidentally entering negative numbers.

3. Save the file. Name it tblLaborAcquisition. Close the table.

4. Import data from the *Ch10.xlsx* Excel file for *tblLaborAcquisition*. Click the Browse button to find the location where you stored *Ch10.xlsx*. Double-click Ch10.xlsx.

5. Import the Labor Acquisition data from *Ch10.xlsx*. Click Excel on the External Data ribbon.

6. Click the radio button for the second option Append a copy of the records to the table:. Select tblLaborAcquisition from the combo box. Click OK.

7. In the next dialog box, highlight the worksheet tblLaborAcquisition. Click Next twice.

8. In the last dialog box, tblLaborAcquisition should already be entered in the *Import to Table:* textbox. Click Finish. Open tblLaborAcquisition in datasheet view to verify that all 143 records were imported into the database (see Figure 10.13).

Fig. 10.12 Foreign keys and attributes for *tblLaborAcquisition.*

Field Name	EmployeeID	EmployeeSupervisorID
Data Type	Text	Text
Field Size	3	3
Format (or Decimal Places)		
Input Mask	000;;_	000;;_
Caption	Employee #	Supervisor #
Validation Rule		
Validation Text		
Default Value		
Required	Yes	Yes
Allow Zero Length	No	No
Indexed	Yes (Duplicates OK)	Yes (Duplicates OK)

Foreign Keys

Field Name	LAPayPeriodEnded	LARegularTime	LAOverTime
Data Type	Date/Time	Number	Number
Field Size		Integer	Integer
Format (or Decimal Places)		Auto	Auto
Input Mask	99/99/0000;0;_		
Caption	Month Ended	Regular Hours	Overtime Hours
Validation Rule		>=0 And <185	>=0 And <20 I
Validation Text		The number of regular hours you entered is too large.	The number of overtime hours you entered is too large.
Default Value		0	0
Required		Yes	Yes
Allow Zero Length		No	No
Indexed	Yes (Duplicates OK)	No	No

Attributes

Figure 10.6 shows two links between Pipefitters Supply Company's Labor Acquisition table Employee table. Both foreign keys in *tblLaborLaborAcquisition*, EmployeeID, and EmployeeSupervisorID link to EmployeeID in *tblEmployee*. In the next exercise, you will enforce referential integrity on these links to prevent users from entering time worked for employee numbers that do not exist in *tblEmployee*. This internal control feature, often called an ***existence check*** or a ***validity check,*** can reduce the threat of errors and irregularities in payroll processing. Exercise 10.12 reinforces how to create this control feature. Be sure you have closed *tblLaborAcquisition* before you begin this exercise.

Fig. 10.13 *tblLabor-Acquisition* in Data-sheet view.

Time Card #	Employee #	Supervisor #	Month Ended	Regular Hours	Overtime Hours
10001	101	128	1/31/2010	168	0
10002	102	140	1/31/2010	168	0
10003	103	140	1/31/2010	168	0
10004	104	126	1/31/2010	168	4
10005	105	122	1/31/2010	168	8
10006	106	104	1/31/2010	168	11
10007	107	140	1/31/2010	168	0
10008	108	122	1/31/2010	142	0
10009	109	125	1/31/2010	87	0
10010	110	125	1/31/2010	168	0
10011	111	140	1/31/2010	168	7
10012	112	125	1/31/2010	126	0
10013	113	128	1/31/2010	147	0
10014	114	104	1/31/2010	168	0
10015	115	140	1/31/2010	168	3
10016	116	125	1/31/2010	168	0
10017	117	140	1/31/2010	146	0
10018	118	140	1/31/2010	98	0
10019	119	140	1/31/2010	132	0
10020	120	128	1/31/2010	168	2
10021	121	128	1/31/2010	60	0
10022	122	126	1/31/2010	141	2
10023	123	140	1/31/2010	168	0
10024	124	125	1/31/2010	168	14
10025	125	126	1/31/2010	112	0
10026	126	140	1/31/2010	168	3

Record: 1 of 143   No Filter   Search

EXERCISE 10.12: LINKING *TBLLABORACQUISITION* TO *TBLEMPLOYEE*

1. In the Database Tools tab, click Relationships in the Show/Hide group and minimize the Navigation Pane.
2. Add *tblLaborAcquisition* to the Relationship window. Click Show Table in the Relationships group; double-click tblLaborAcquisition; then click Close.
3. Resize your event table, *tblLaborAcquisition*, to show the entire table name and all of its attributes. Move the table to the center of the Relationship window to be consistent with the resources, events, and agents (REA) model format. Use Figures 10.14 and 10.15 as guides.
4. Create the first link between tables. Drag from the primary key in *tblEmployee* to the matching foreign key, EmployeeID, in *tblLaborAcquisition*.
5. After you click and drag the primary key to the foreign key the Edit Relationships dialog box appears. Make sure that the correct attributes appear in the tables you dragged from and to. The relationship type at the bottom of the dialog box should always be one-to-many. Check Enforce Referential Integrity and Cascade Update Related Fields. Finally, click Create in the dialog box.
6. Repeat Steps 4 and 5, substituting EmployeeSupervisorID for EmployeeID in *tblLaborAcquisition*. Notice that the dialog box shown in Figure 10.14 appears when you try to add a second relationship between the same two tables. Click No to create the second relationship. Also notice that Access generates a second field roster for *tblEmployee* instead of showing both relationship links between the *tblLaborAcquisition* field roster and *tblEmployee* field roster. When you are finished your Relationship window should look like the one in Figure 10.15.
7. Close the Relationship window and click the Yes button in the dialog box to save your changes.

Fig. 10.14 Dialog box when creating a second relationship between *tblEmployee* and *tblLaborAcquisition*.

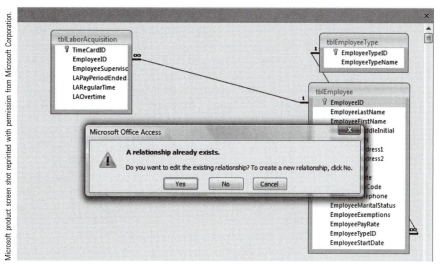

Fig. 10.15 Relationship window after adding links between *tblEmployee* and *tblLaborAcquisition*.

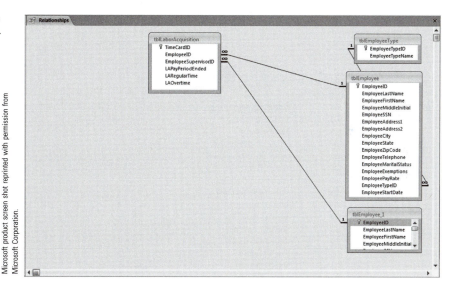

The Labor Acquisition (Time Worked) Entry Form

You can build a data entry form for the Labor Acquisition table that will ease the task of entering employees' time records. The Labor Acquisition Entry form will use the employee name fields in the Employee table to provide another validity check that can help data entry clerks detect errors. You can design the Labor Acquisition Entry form so that it displays the employee's name when a user enters an employee number. This lets the user check the displayed name against the employee name on the time card source document. In Exercise 10.13 you will create a query to concatenate Employee-FirstName, EmployeeMiddleInitial, and EmployeeLastName, which you will use in Exercise 10.14 to build a Labor Acquisition Entry form that includes this control feature.

EXERCISE 10.13: BUILDING A QUERY TO CONCATENATE THE EMPLOYEE NAME FIELDS

1. Click the Create tab and click Query Design in the Other group.
2. The only table you need for this query is *tblEmployee*. Double-click tblEmployee from the list presented in the Show Table dialog box and click the Close button.
3. Double-click EmployeeID in the tblEmployee Field Roster to add it to the Criteria Pane.
4. Move your cursor to the Field cell in the next column on the Criteria Pane; right-click to bring the shortcut menu and select Zoom. The Zoom box allows you to see everything you are entering in the Field cell. Enter EmployeeName: EmployeeFirstName & " " & EmployeeMiddleInitial & ". " & EmployeeLastName in the Zoom box. Click OK to close the Zoom box.
5. Click Property Sheet in the Show/Hide group. Type Name in the Caption property cell.
6. Save the query as qryEmployeeName. Run the query. After adjusting the column width for EmployeeName, your query result should look like Figure 10.16. Close the query.

Fig. 10.16 *qry-EmplolyeeName in Datasheet* view.

Microsoft product screen shot reprinted with permission from Microsoft Corporation.

Employee #	Name
101	Artemis Q. Greenwood
102	Ethel Z. Greenwood
103	Ethel P. Baron
104	Cecelia J. Oppenheim
105	Ronald D. Washington
106	Henry X. Wheeler
107	Elizabeth T. Surkamp
108	Timothy Y. Diamond
109	Max E. Roche
110	Lucille B. Badillo
111	Judith F. Ballenger
112	Melanie C. Dewar
113	Alicia K. Brown
114	Irene R. Klusky
115	Esther L. Tufts
116	Margaret S. Thurgood
117	Michael B. Boldway
118	Janice S. Fenster
119	Natalie R. Sherwood
120	Arlene P. Simon
121	Anne F. Morris
122	Carol C. Clark
123	Dierdre R. Smith
124	Louise K. Young
125	Chester V. Studd
126	Colleen H. Ward

Record: 1 of 50   No Filter

Fig. 10.17 *frm-LaborAcquisition* in Form view after using the Form Wizard.

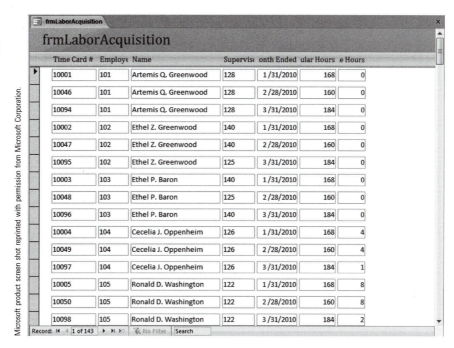

EXERCISE 10.14: CREATING A LABOR ACQUISITION ENTRY FORM

1. Click tblLaborAcquisition in the Unassigned Objects group of the Navigation Pane. Click the Create tab and click MoreForms in the Forms group, and click Form Wizard. The first of a few Form Wizard dialog boxes appears.
2. The fields for *tblLaborAcquisition* appear in the first dialog box. Click the >> button to send all available table fields to the Selected Fields panel.
3. Select Query: qryEmployeeName from the Tables/Queries combo box. Click EmployeeID in the Selected Fields panel. Double-click EmployeeName in the Available Fields panel to add it to the selected items right below EmployeeID. Click the Next button.
4. Click Next again to accept the default of viewing the data by *tblLaborAcquisition*.
5. Click the Tabular option button and then click the Next button to continue.
6. Click Office from the list of form styles. Click Next, and name the form. Type frmLaborAcquisition in the text box.
7. Click the Finish button to view your form in Form view. It should look like the form if Figure 10.17.

EXERCISE 10.15: IMPROVING THE WIZARD-GENERATED LABOR ACQUISITION ENTRY FORM

1. Open *frmLaborAcquisition* in Design view. Click Property Sheet in the Tools group if it is not already open.

Edit the query behind the form.

2. Select Form from the Property Sheet combo box and click the Data tab. Click the Data Source Builder button to open the query behind the form.
3. Scroll to the right to find LAPayPeriodEnded. Click and drag it to the leftmost column of the *QBE grid* (another name for the Criteria Pane). Set the sort values

for both LAPayPeriodEnded and TimeCardID to Ascending. This will make it easy to spot time cards that are out of sequence. Save your changes. If you are curious you can run the query and see that the result contains the same fields that are in the form. Close the Query Builder.

Add a combo box for employee supervisor to make it easier to enter EmployeeSupervisorID and to verify that the supervisor's name and EmployeeID on the time card are correct.

4. Make a copy of *qryMaterialsHandler* in the Chapter 8 Queries section of the Navigation Pane. Click qryMaterialsHandler in the Navigation Pane. Press Ctrl+C to copy the query. Press Ctrl+V to paste it and name it qryAdministrator. Open qryAdministrator in Design view (in the Unassigned Objects section of the Navigation Pane). Change the criteria for EmployeeTypeID to 20, the EmployeeTypeID for administrators. Save and close the query.

5. Return to *frmLaborAcquisition*. Minimize the Navigation Pane. Click Combo Box in the Controls group. Move your cursor next to the EmployeeSupervisorID control and click to start the Combo Box Wizard. Click the Next button. Click the Queries radio button and double-click qryAdministrator from the list of queries. In the next dialog box select all fields except EmployeeTypeID. Click Next twice. Resize the column and click the Next button twice. Click the second radio button and select EmployeeSupervisorID from the combo box list. Click the Next button. Click Finish.

6. Press Ctrl+A to select all form objects. Click the Arrange tab and click Remove in the Control Layout group. Move the cursor to an empty spot on the form and click to unselect all form objects. Delete the combo box label and also delete the original EmployeeSupervisorID control. Move the combo box under the original label.

Using Figure 10.18 as a guide, make the final appearance and function modifications to the form, which include the items listed in the next set of steps. Remember that you can make formatting changes in Layout view, which allows you to see the data as you change the appearance of your form.

7. Change the form header to Time Worked Data Entry.

8. Modify the captions. Minimize the Navigation Pane to view the whole form and make the form 7-1/2 inches wide. Bold and center the captions. Make the horizontal space between the labels equidistant using the Position tools on the Arrange ribbon.

9. Modify the field controls. Resize the field controls by using the Size to Fit tool. In Layout view Size to Fit is on the Arrange ribbon in the Position group (or in the Size group if you are in Design view). Center the controls under their respective labels.

10. Center ID numbers. Change the Special Effect for all active controls to Sunken.

11. Add an Alternate Back Color to the detail section (in the Format tab for the Detail section) to create rows of alternating colors. This makes it easier for the eye to follow the same record across the screen. We used #99CCFF in Figure 10.18, but you can experiment with different combinations of Back Color and Alternate Back Color.

12. Make EmployeeName inaccessible. See Steps 8 and 9 in Exercise 9.26 for a detailed description.

13. Reorder the tab stops. View your changes in Form view.

14. Save your changes and close the form.

The Pipefitters Supply Company example includes some simplifying assumptions. The sample data includes only three months of data for fifty employees. All employees are paid on an hourly basis that includes regular hours and only one class of overtime hours. A more sophisticated HR part of an AIS would track accrual and use of vacation time,

Fig. 10.18 Completed *frmLaborAcquisition* in Design view and Form view.

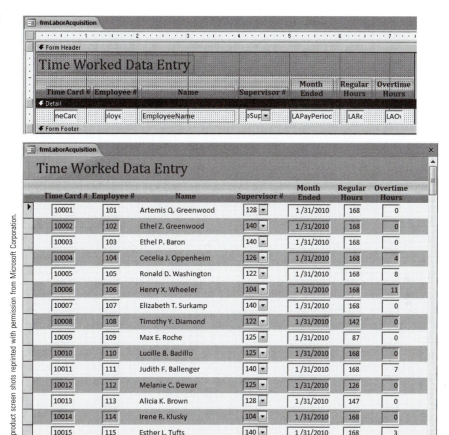

paid time off, unpaid time off, and sick days. AISs for Payroll often must track several types of overtime (for example, over eight hours per day, over forty hours per week, hours worked on holidays) and calculate pay using measures other than hours. However, even with the limited example components included in this chapter, you can generate useful information for internal and external reporting purposes.

Recording Cash Paid to Employees

Thus far in this chapter, you have learned how Pipefitters Supply Company can maintain employee records and enter time card data into its AIS to record labor acquisition events. At the end of each pay period, after Pipefitters has received labor from its employees, its employees would like to get paid for their time worked. This section describes one of the many ways to use the information you have gathered in your HR process tables to write checks. However, unlike the acquisition/payment process, determining the amount to pay its employees requires a series of complex computations and two category tables that you have not yet created. But before we explain how to compute payroll, we need to address how to change Pipefitters AIS to allow for the Cash Disbursement event to have duality relationships with more than one type of economic increment event (e.g., purchases, labor acquisitions) and more than one type of external agent (e.g., vendors, employees as labor providers).

The Cash Disbursement Table

You constructed the Cash Disbursement table in Chapter 9. Like other events, it is connected to a resource, cash account. As explained in Chapter 9, we will use the same Cash Account table for the remaining chapters.

In the data modeling portion of this chapter you created a duality relationship between labor acquisition and cash disbursement as well as an external participation relationship between cash disbursement and employee (see Figure 10.6). However, cash disbursement already has a duality relationship with purchase and an external participation relationship with vendor (see Figure 9.4). Figure 10.19 shows the design of Pipefitters' AIS related to cash disbursement based on the data models for the acquisition/payment process (Figure 9.4) and the HR process (Figure 10.6). We eliminated the internal participation relationships with employee, the inventory resource, and the inflow relationship between purchase and inventory as they are not relevant to this discussion.

Notice in Figure 10.19 that the Cash Disbursement table has a foreign key for each duality event: TimeCardID and InventoryReceiptID. To accommodate the data models from both business processes we will make an ***implementation compromise***. We could simply add a field for TimeCardID to the current Cash Disbursement table. But, then half of the cells in these fields would be empty, which is poor database design. Also, in Chapter 11 we will add cash disbursement for loan repayments (debt financing) and for dividend payments (equity financing). We could add two more fields to the table, but then three-fourths of the foreign key cells would be empty! Another option would be to create relationship tables for payroll cash disbursements, but that makes the database more complex and makes querying the database more difficult. The only advantage of

Fig. 10.19 Combined acquisition/payment and HR data model.

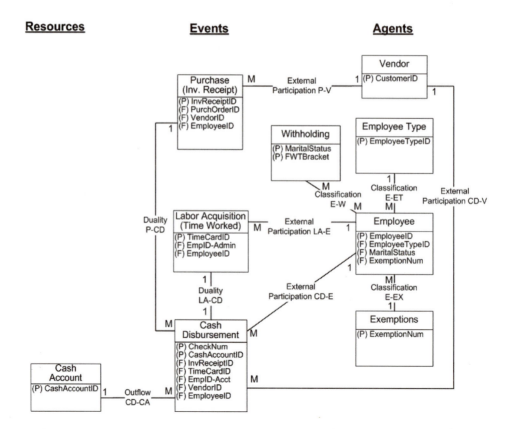

these two alternatives is that you can still enforce referential integrity, which is an effective internal control. But, you cannot set the Required field property to yes for these foreign keys, which is also an effective internal control.

However, we can eliminate the problems of the above two solutions by using a generic field, EventID, for the duality event foreign key. This will allow the field to contain an InventoryReceiptID, a TimeCardID, a LoanID, or a StockIssueID. The same reasoning applies to changing the VendorID field to a generic PayeeID field. Although referential integrity cannot be enforced—an EventID (or PayeeID) may come from several different tables—combo boxes (or other controls) can be added to input forms to compensate for the lack of referential integrity.

One other problem of using generic foreign key fields in *tblCashDisbursement* is how to distinguish one type of cash disbursement from another. The solution is to add a Cash Disbursement type table and add a field to the Cash Disbursement table for Cash Disbursement type. The Cash Disbursement Type table will have a primary key, the type of event the cash disbursement relates to, and the type of external agent that participates with that cash disbursement type.

The revised data model is shown in Figure 10.20. Notice that the two event foreign key fields, InventoryReceiptID and TimeCardID, were replaced with a single field, EventID. This same field will be used in Chapter 11 for financing events that are linked to cash disbursement. Also notice that the two external agent foreign key fields, VendorID and EmployeeID, were replaced with a single field, PayeeID. PayeeID will also be used in Chapter 11 to store foreign keys for creditors and investors. We eliminated the need for a Payee Type table because each cash disbursement type also specifies the payee type in addition to the related event type.

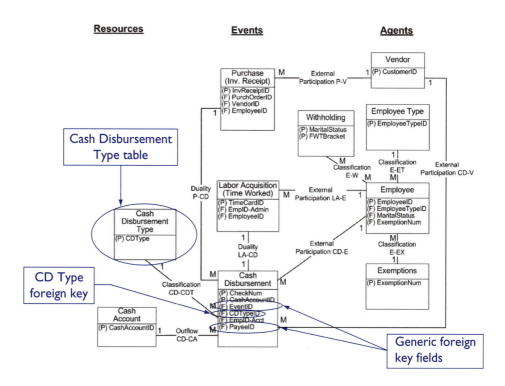

Fig. 10.20 Combined data model with Cash Disbursement Type table implementation compromise.

EXERCISE 10.16: MODIFYING THE CASH DISBURSEMENT TABLE

1. Open tblCashDisbursement in Design view. It is located in the Unassigned Objects section of the Navigation Pane.
2. Make the following changes to the VendorID field and its properties:
   - Change the Field name to PayeeID.
   - Change the input mask to 9999;;_ to allow for up to four digits to be entered—the length size of Pipefitters longest PayeeID field.
   - Change the caption to Payee #.
3. Make the following changes to the InventoryReceiptID field and its properties:
   - Change the Field name to EventID.
   - Change the input mask to 999999;;_ to allow for up to six digits to be entered—the length size of Pipefitters longest EventID field.
   - Change the caption to Event #.
4. Add the CDTypeID field and enter the CDTypeID for cash disbursements:
   - Insert a blank row after CashAccountID. Click the PayeeID Record Selector, right-click and select Insert Row.
   - In the new row type CDTypeID in the Field Name cell. Leave the Data Type set to Text.
   - Set the Field Size to 2 and set the Input Mask to 00;;_.
   - Enter CD Type # for the Caption. Save your changes and switch to Datasheet view.
   - Enter 01 in the CD Type for each of the 31 records. Return to Design view.
   - Set the Required property to Yes, the Allow Zero Length property to No, and leave the Indexed property set to Yes (Duplicates OK).
5. Check to see that you have all of the fields listed in Figure 10.21. Save your changes and close the table.

Fig. 10.21 Final Cash Disbursement table in Design view and Datasheet view.

tblCashDisbursement	
Field Name	**Data Type**
CheckNum	Text
CashAccountID	Text
CDTypeID	Text
PayeeID	Text
EmployeeID	Text
EventID	Text
CashDisbursementAmount	Currency
CashDisbursementDate	Date/Time

tblCashDisbursement

Check #	Cash Account #	CD Type #	Payee #	Employee #	Event #	Amount Paid	Date Paid
10001	301	01	1001	113	100001	$3,812.75	1/18/2010
10002	301	01	1008	113	100002	$4,700.50	1/25/2010
10003	301	01	1003	113	100003	$664.50	1/26/2010
10004	301	01	1007	101	100004	$2,108.25	1/27/2010
10005	301	01	1003	101	100005	$5,000.00	1/28/2010
10006	301	01	1008	135	100006	$3,973.00	1/29/2010
10007	301	01	1001	135	100007	$2,196.05	1/29/2010
10008	301	01	1009	131	100008	$426.00	2/1/2010
10009	301	01	1004	131	100009	$317.00	2/4/2010
10010	301	01	1011	101	100010	$5,000.00	2/4/2010

Next, you will create the Cash Disbursement Type table. It is similar to the Employee Type table you built earlier in the chapter. It has a two-digit primary key and a name field, EventTypeName. It also has a name field for the external participant type, PayeeTypeName.

EXERCISE 10.17: CREATING THE CASH DISBURSEMENT TYPE TABLE

1. Click the Create tab, click Table Design in the Tables group, and click Design View. To create the primary key, type CDTypeID in the first row of the Field Name column and click Primary Key in the Tools group. Leave the Data Type set to Text.
2. Set the field properties: Field Size—2; Input Mask—00;0; Caption—CDType #; Required—Yes; Allow Zero Length—No; Indexed—Yes (No Duplicates).
3. Enter EventTypeName in second row of the Field Name column. Leave the Data Type set to Text.
4. Set the following field properties: Field Size—25; Caption—Related Event; Required—Yes; Allow Zero Length—No; Indexed—No.
5. Enter PayeeTypeName in the third row of the Field Name column. Leave the Data Type set to Text.
6. Set the following field properties: Field Size—25; Caption—Payee Type; Required —Yes; Allow Zero Length—No; Indexed—No.
7. Save the table. Type tblCashDisbursementType in the Save As dialog box and then click OK to save your table.
8. Switch to Datasheet view to enter the Cash Disbursement Type records in Figure 10.22.
9. Close the table.

Fig. 10.22 Data for *tblCashDisbursement-Type* displayed in Datasheet view.

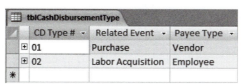

Microsoft product screen shot reprinted with permission from Microsoft Corporation.

EXERCISE 10.18: CREATING AND UPDATING RELATIONSHIPS WITH *TBLCASHDISBURSEMENT*

1. Close all open tables. In the Database Tools tab, click Relationships in the Show/ Hide group and minimize the Navigation Pane. Your Relationship window should look like Figure 10.15.
2. Click Show Table in the Relationships group, add the following tables by double-clicking them: tblCashDisbursement, tblCashDisbursementType, tblPurchase, and tblVendor. Click the Close button.
3. Right-click on the Menu Bar and click Minimize the Ribbon to make your Relationship window larger. Move and resize your tables until they are arranged like Figure 10.23.
4. Remove Referential Integrity from the Purchase-Cash Disbursement link and the Vendor-Cash Disbursement link. Right-click the link; then click Edit Relationships, uncheck the Enforce Referential Integrity box, and click OK. Notice that you cannot cascade update related fields without enforcing referential integrity. Although cascading changes in a primary key to all related fields is a good

database practice, it should rarely be necessary. However, one could use update queries to accomplish the same thing, though it is less efficient.

5. Create new links between *tblCashDisbursement* and the following tables: *tblCashDisbursementType*, *tblLaborAcquisition*, and *tblEmployee*. Remember to drag from the primary key to the appropriate foreign key.

6. After you click and drag the primary key to the foreign key the Edit Relationships dialog box appears. (When you drag from EmployeeID in *tblEmployee* to PayeeID in *tblCashDisbursement*, click No in the dialog box to create a new relationship.) Make sure that the correct attributes appear in the tables you dragged from and to. The relationship type at the bottom of the dialog box is should always be one-to-many. Only check Enforce Referential Integrity and Cascade Update Related Fields for the link between *tblCashDisbursement* and *tblCashDisbursementType*. Click Create in the dialog box when you are done. After completing this exercise your Relationship window should look like the one in Figure 10.24.

7. Close the Relationships window and click the Yes button in the dialog box to save your changes.

Fig. 10.23 Relationship window after adding Field Rosters.

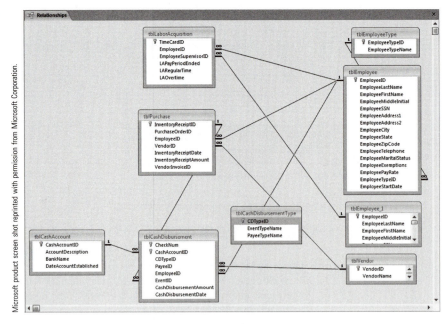

Microsoft product screen shot reprinted with permission from Microsoft Corporation.

Although the Cash Disbursement table is complete, you cannot make the Cash Disbursement Payroll form yet because you first need to create queries for gross pay, FICA tax, Medicare tax, and federal withholding tax (FWT). These payroll items will be explained in the next section.

Fig. 10.24 Relationship window after relationships have been added or updated.

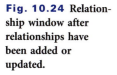

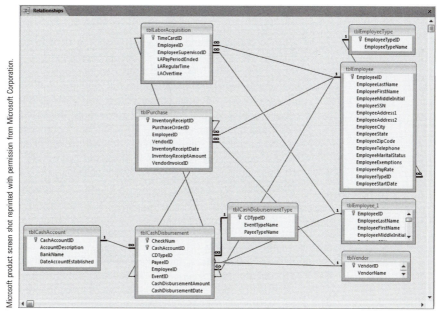

Calculating Payroll

Thus far in this chapter you have learned how to enter and maintain HR information. However, the main transaction processing objective of the HR process is to calculate payroll (e.g., gross wages, amounts withheld, net pay) and capture cash disbursement data for payroll checks.

Queries are useful tools for performing payroll calculations. Indeed, if relational database management software lacked a query language, you could not use it to calculate payroll. Because payroll calculations can be very complex, you will learn how to build several queries that each accomplishes a step in calculating payroll. Then you will learn how to use these queries to build payroll register reports, employee earnings record reports, and payroll check reports. You can extend this step-by-step approach to more complex payroll systems as you encounter them in your future studies or in your practice of accounting.

Payroll Calculation Queries

Gross pay has two components. The first is the regular calculation. To do this, you need only multiply each employee's pay rate by the number of regular hours he or she worked in the pay period. Since you have pay rates in *tblEmployee* and regular hours by pay period in *tblLaborAcquisition*, you can query these two tables to calculate regular pay. The computation of overtime pay is only a little bit more complex as the overtime pay rate is 1.5 times an employee's pay rate.

You can use the Pipefitters Supply Company sample data to learn how to build these queries. Pipefitters' Employee table has fifty employee records, and its Labor Acquisition table includes three monthly pay periods of labor acquisition time data. You will use the January payroll period for the example calculations in these exercises.

EXERCISE 10.19: CALCULATING GROSS PAY

1. Click the Create tab and click Query Design in the Other group.
2. Double-click tblEmployee and tblLaborAcquisition from the list presented in the Show Table dialog box, and click the Close button.
3. The link between EmployeeID in *tblEmployee* and EmployeeSupervisorID in *tblLaborAcquisition* must be deleted to perform this query because Access will enforce both inner join rules at the same time. The only records that would meet these requirements are Labor Acquisition records where the employee and supervisor are the same person! Since we do not need supervisor information for this query, click the link and press the Delete key. Now, *tblEmployee* and *tblLaborAcquisition* will be linked only by EmployeeID.
4. Double-click EmployeeID, TimeCardID, and LAPayPeriodEnded, respectively, in the *tblLaborAcquisition* field roster to add them to the QBE grid. Set the Sort cell of EmployeeID to Ascending.
5. Since gross pay is used in many computations in addition to calculating the amount of employees' paychecks (e.g., wages expense on the income statement), the criteria for LAPayPeriodEnded needs to cover a period of time (e.g., month, quarter, year). Just like you have done with queries for income statement items, you will use the between function with a begin date parameter and an end date parameter. Type Between [Beginning of Period Date] and [End of Period Date] as the Criteria for LAPayPeriodEnded cell for in the QBE grid.
6. Add the data for the regular pay and overtime pay computations. Double-click EmployeePayRate from the *tblEmployee* field roster. Double-click LARegularTime and double-click LAOvertime, respectively from the *tblLaborAcquisition* field roster. Save your query as qryGrossPay.
7. In the first empty column, click the Field cell; right-click and select Build... to open the Expression Builder to build the following expression RegularPay: [EmployeePayRate] * [LARegularTime]. Remember that you can double-click the field names in the second column to add them to the expression box. Click OK when you are done.
8. Notice that the RegularPay expression is highlighted. Press Ctrl+C; click the next empty Field cell and press Ctrl+V. Edit the RegularPay expression to compute overtime pay. Press Shift+F2 to open the Zoom box. Edit the expression in the Zoom box to read OvertimePay: [EmployeePayRate] * 1.5 * [LAOvertime], and then click OK. Save the query.
9. Use Expression Builder to create the gross pay expression in the next Field cell: GrossPay: [RegularPay] + [OvertimePay]. Click OK when you are done.
10. Add captions to the three expressions you created. Click RegularPay; open the Property Sheet and type Regular Pay as the Caption. Click OvertimePay and add Overtime Pay as its Caption. Click GrossPay and type Gross Pay as its Caption. Save your query.
11. Verify that the pay calculations are correct by running the query and computing gross pay by hand for one or two employees who worked overtime during January 2010. When you run the query, type 1/1/2010 for the beginning of the period date and type 1/31/2010 for the end of the period date (see Figure 10.25). Although you could have typed 1/31/2010 for both dates, specifying the whole month of January will alert the user to an error if a date other than 1/31/2010 appears in the dynaset. If some of the labels are not completely visible you can adjust all column widths at once by clicking the Datasheet Selector, selecting Column Width from the More menu in the Records group, and clicking the Best Fit button. If any of the currency amounts are not in currency format, return to Design view and set the Format property to Currency and Decimal Places to 2. Save and close your query.

Fig. 10.25 Gross Pay
query dynaset.

Datasheet Selector

Employee #	Time Card #	Month Ended	Pay Rate	Regular Hours	Overtime Hours	Regular Pay	Overtime Pay	Gross Pay
101	10001	1/31/2010	$28.00	168	0	$4,704.00	$0.00	$4,704.00
102	10002	1/31/2010	$28.00	168	0	$4,704.00	$0.00	$4,704.00
103	10003	1/31/2010	$8.20	168	0	$1,377.60	$0.00	$1,377.60
104	10004	1/31/2010	$19.40	168	4	$3,259.20	$116.40	$3,375.60
105	10005	1/31/2010	$7.50	168	8	$1,260.00	$90.00	$1,350.00
106	10006	1/31/2010	$15.40	168	11	$2,587.20	$254.10	$2,841.30
107	10007	1/31/2010	$22.40	168	0	$3,763.20	$0.00	$3,763.20
108	10008	1/31/2010	$9.20	142	0	$1,306.40	$0.00	$1,306.40
109	10009	1/31/2010	$7.75	87	0	$674.25	$0.00	$674.25
110	10010	1/31/2010	$12.90	168	0	$2,167.20	$0.00	$2,167.20
111	10011	1/31/2010	$18.00	168	7	$3,024.00	$189.00	$3,213.00
112	10012	1/31/2010	$9.80	126	0	$1,234.80	$0.00	$1,234.80
113	10013	1/31/2010	$10.60	147	0	$1,558.20	$0.00	$1,558.20
114	10014	1/31/2010	$9.00	168	0	$1,512.00	$0.00	$1,512.00
115	10015	1/31/2010	$16.60	168	3	$2,788.80	$74.70	$2,863.50
116	10016	1/31/2010	$24.00	168	0	$4,032.00	$0.00	$4,032.00
117	10017	1/31/2010	$10.20	146	0	$1,489.20	$0.00	$1,489.20
118	10018	1/31/2010	$14.00	98	0	$1,372.00	$0.00	$1,372.00
119	10019	1/31/2010	$12.80	132	0	$1,689.60	$0.00	$1,689.60
120	10020	1/31/2010	$17.90	168	2	$3,007.20	$53.70	$3,060.90
121	10021	1/31/2010	$12.50	60	0	$750.00	$0.00	$750.00
122	10022	1/31/2010	$8.20	141	2	$1,156.20	$24.60	$1,180.80
123	10023	1/31/2010	$21.50	168	0	$3,612.00	$0.00	$3,612.00
124	10024	1/31/2010	$14.20	168	14	$2,385.60	$298.20	$2,683.80
125	10025	1/31/2010	$13.60	112	0	$1,523.20	$0.00	$1,523.20
126	10026	1/31/2010	$32.20	168	3	$5,409.60	$144.90	$5,554.50

Record: 1 of 45   No Filter   Search

Of course, calculating gross pay is only the first part of the payroll calculation. The second and more complex part is to calculate the deductions from gross pay that determine net pay. Your next step will be to revise *qryGrossPay* so that it calculates deductions and net pay. Payroll deductions include taxes, insurance, profit-sharing contributions, and many other items. The rules for calculating each of these deductions generally fall into one of four categories:

1. *Fixed Amount Deductions.* These deductions are easy to calculate because they are a fixed amount each pay period. Examples of these include deductions for health insurance premiums, group life insurance premiums, and employee-approved donations to charitable organizations such as the United Way.

2. *Fixed Percentage Deductions.* These deductions are a fixed percentage of gross income each pay period. Examples of these include deductions for Medicare tax, and employer-withheld city and county earnings taxes in many parts of the United States. Some state income taxes are also calculated as a fixed percentage of all earned income.

3. *Varying Percentage Deductions.* These deductions are similar to the fixed percentage deduction except that the percentage changes with variables such as level of income, marital status, and number of exemptions claimed. The U.S. federal income tax payment that employers must withhold from employee pay is the most common example of this type of tax. Many states have income tax withholding rules that are similar to the federal rules and, therefore, also fall within this category.

4. *Fixed Percentage Deductions Subject to a Ceiling.* These deductions are a fixed percentage of gross income each pay period until a ceiling amount is reached. The most common example of this deduction type is the deductions under the U.S. Federal Insurance Contributions Act (FICA), which is commonly called the **Social Security tax.** Employers deduct a fixed percentage of gross pay only until the FICA limit for the year is reached. Some states, such as California, require employee contributions to unemployment insurance funds that are calculated this way, too.

The first type of deduction, a fixed amount each pay period, is easy to model. You need only one additional Employee table field—a binary indicator of whether the employee was subject to the deduction—to trigger the calculation. The second type of deduction, a fixed percentage, is even easier to implement. You simply build the fixed percentage into the payroll calculation query. The third type of deduction, a varying percentage, can be difficult to implement because it requires one or more additional tables. These tables contain the various percentages and the points at which they change from one value to another. The fourth type of deduction, a fixed percentage subject to a ceiling, is even more difficult to implement. It requires an additional query to calculate year-to-date totals and compare the calculated totals to the ceiling amounts. The ceiling amounts may be stored in a separate table or included in the query.

The Pipefitters Supply Company example payroll calculation includes the second and third types of deductions. The fixed percentage calculations are the Medicare and the Social Security, or FICA, tax. A deduction for FICA tax is actually the fourth type, since it is a fixed rate up to a maximum pay amount per year. However, we have designed the Pipefitters Supply Company sample data so that none of the employees exceed the FICA ceiling. Therefore, you can model the FICA tax for Pipefitters as a fixed percentage deduction. The deduction for the federal income tax that Pipefitters must withhold from its employees' pay shows some of the intricacies of modeling the third type of deduction. This deduction is usually called *federal withholding tax (FWT)* or *federal income tax (FIT) withheld*.

Please note that the tax deduction calculations we model in this chapter are not intended to be complete or accurate. Employer tax laws change constantly and vary by state. Our purpose here is to give you some practice building tables and queries that you can adapt to specific user needs and to the ever-changing requirements of government regulators.

Before you create the query that will calculate net pay, you will build two tables that contain data necessary to compute the amount of FWT: one table for FWT rates and a second table for exemption amounts. You could include exemption rates and amounts in *qryNetPay*, but placing them in a separate table makes updating and modifying the amounts much easier. And remember, tax laws change even more frequently than software versions!

EXERCISE 10.20: BUILDING THE EXEMPTION TABLE

The FWT rates depend in part on gross pay less the exemption amount. In this exercise you will create a lookup table to find employees' exemption amounts based on the number of exemptions they claim, which is recorded in *tblEmployee*.

1. Click the Create tab; click Table Design in the Tables group and click Design View. Type ExemptionNumber in the first row of the Field Name column and click Primary Key in the Tools group. Set the Data Type to Number.
2. Set the following field properties: Field Size—Byte; Decimal Places—0; Input Mask —99; Caption—Num. of Exempts; Required—Yes; Indexed—Yes (No Duplicates).
3. Enter ExemptionAmount in second row of the Field Name column. Set the Data Type to Currency.
4. Set the field properties: Format—Currency; Decimal Places—2; Caption— Exemption Amt.; Required—Yes; Indexed—No.
5. Save the table. Type tblExemption in the Save As dialog box and then click OK to save your table.
6. Enter the data. You can either switch to Datasheet view and manually enter the data in Figure 10.26 or import it from the *Ch10.xlsx* file like you did for *tblLaborAcquisition* in Exercise 10.11.
7. Close the table.

Fig. 10.26 Data for *tblExemption* displayed in Datasheet view.

Number of Exempt	Exemption Amt.
0	$0.00
1	$304.17
2	$608.34
3	$912.51
4	$1,216.68
5	$1,520.85
6	$1,825.02
7	$2,129.19
8	$2,433.36
9	$2,737.53
10	$3,041.70
11	$3,345.87
12	$3,650.04
13	$3,954.21
14	$4,258.38
15	$4,562.55
0	$0.00

Notice that the Exemption amounts are all multiples of $304.17. You could easily compute the exemption amount in the Net Pay query by multiplying an employee's number of exemptions by $304.17. However, many payroll taxing authorities decrease the value of additional exemptions beyond a certain number, sometimes down to $0. This is another reason why we showed you how to model exemptions as a lookup table.

EXERCISE 10.21: BUILDING THE WITHHOLDING TABLE

The other table you need to determine the FWT rate to compute the amount of FWT is the Withholding table. It is a more complex lookup table. The tax bracket information used to compute each employee's FWT amount is based on his or her marital status (stored in *tblEmployee*) and gross pay less his or her exemption amount.

1. Click the Create tab; click Table Design in the Tables group and click Design View. Type MaritalStatus in the first row of the Field Name column. In the second row, type FWTBRacket in the Field Name column.
2. Set the concatenated primary key. Click the Record Selector for MaritalStatus, then press and hold the Ctrl key and click the Record Selector for FWTBracket. Click Primary Key in the Tools group.
3. Use the Figure 10.27 table to set the data types and field properties for MaritalStatus and FWTBracket. Add the attributes in the bottom section of Figure 10.27. Why is the Input Mask for MaritalStatus >L?
4. Save the table. Type tblWithholding in the Save As dialog box and then click OK to save your table.
5. Enter the data. You can either switch to Datasheet view and manually enter the data in Figure 10.28 or import it from the *Ch10.xlsx* file like you did for *tblLaborAcquisition* in Exercise 10.11.
6. Close the table.

Notice in Figure 10.28 that we are actually storing two separate tables, one for each filing status. This is one of the benefits of using a concatenated primary key. You can even accommodate more than two marital or other statuses. For example, the U.S. Tax Code contains four tax bracket tables based on marital status: married filing jointly, married filing separately, head of household, and single. Also, you can easily add more tax brackets for each marital status just by adding additional rows to the table. Being able to

Fig. 10.27 Primary keys and attributes for *tblWithholding*.

Field Name	Marital Status	FWTBracket
Data Type	Text	Text
Field Size	1	2
Input Mask	>L	
Caption	Marital Status	Tax Bracket
Required	Yes	Yes
Allow Zero Length	No	No
Indexed	Yes (Duplicates OK)	Yes (Duplicates OK)

Primary Keys

Field Name	FWTLowerLimit	FWTUpperLimit	FWTRate	FWTBracketBaseAmt
Data Type	Currency	Currency	Number	Currency
Field Size			Double	
Format	Currency	Currency	Percent	Currency
Decimal Places	2	2	2	2
Caption	Lower Limit	Upper Limit	FWT Rate	FWT Base Amt.
Required	Yes	Yes	Yes	Yes
Indexed	No	No	No	No

Attributes

Fig. 10.28 Data for *tblWithholding* displayed in Datasheet view.

Marital Status	Tax Bracket	Lower Limit	Upper Limit	FWT Rate	FWT Base Amt.
M	1	$0.00	$1,313.00	0.00%	$0.00
M	2	$1,313.01	$2,038.00	10.00%	$0.00
M	3	$2,038.01	$6,304.00	15.00%	$72.50
M	4	$6,304.01	$9,844.00	25.00%	$712.40
M	5	$9,844.01	$18,050.00	28.00%	$1,597.40
M	6	$18,050.01	$31,725.00	33.00%	$3,895.08
M	7	$31,725.01	$1,000,000.00	35.00%	$8,407.83
S	1	$0.00	$598.00	0.00%	$0.00
S	2	$598.01	$867.00	15.00%	$29.80
S	3	$867.01	$3,017.00	25.00%	$165.55
S	4	$3,017.01	$5,544.00	28.00%	$563.80
S	5	$5,544.01	$14,467.00	33.00%	$1,522.80
S	6	$14,467.01	$31,250.00	35.00%	$3,946.98
S	7	$31,250.01	$1,000,000.00	35.00%	$9,017.98
*					

easily expand the capability of this table (e.g., without changing the table structure or adding additional tables) is referred to as *scalability*.

EXERCISE 10.22: LINKING *TBLEXEMPTION* AND *TBLWITHHOLDING* TO *TBLEMPLOYEE*

1. Close all open tables. In the Database Tools tab, click Relationships in the Show/Hide group and minimize the Navigation Pane. Your Relationship window should look like Figure 10.24.

2. Add *tblEmployee* and *tblEmployeeType* to the Relationship window. Click Show Table in the Relationships group; double-click tblExemption and tblWithholding and then click Close.

3. Minimize the Ribbon to bring all Field Rosters into full view. Right-click on the Menu Bar and click Minimize the Ribbon.

4. Resize your tables to show the entire table name and all of the attributes. Move the Withholding and Exemption field rosters next to the Employee table field roster.

5. Create the Exemption-Employee link. Drag from the primary key in *tblExemption*, ExemptionNumber, to the related foreign key, EmployeeExemptions, in *tblEmployee*.

6. Make sure that the correct attributes appear in the tables you dragged from and to. The relationship type at the bottom of the dialog box is should be one-to-many. Check Enforce Referential Integrity and Cascade Update Related Fields. Click the Create button.

7. Create the Withholding-Employee link. Drag from the partial primary key, MaritalStatus in *tblWithholding* to the related foreign key, EmployeeMaritalStatus, in *tblEmployee*.

8. Make sure that the correct attributes appear in the tables you dragged from and to. MaritalStatus in *tblWithholding* is not unique because is part of a concatenated primary key. MaritalStatus in *tblEmployee* is not unique either because it is a foreign key. Therefore, the relationship type is many-to-many. However, Access shows the Relationship type at the bottom of the dialog box as Indeterminate. You cannot enforce referential integrity for an indeterminate relationship. Click the Create button.

9. Remove tables and relationships that are unrelated to the HR process. Click the tblPurchase field roster and press the Delete key. tblPurchase and its relationships are no longer displayed, but the links you created still exist. Delete the tblVentor in the same manner.

10. When you are finished, your Relationship window should look like the one in Figure 10.29.

11. Close the Relationship window and click the Yes button in the dialog box to save your changes.

Fig. 10.29 Final Relationship window for the HR process.

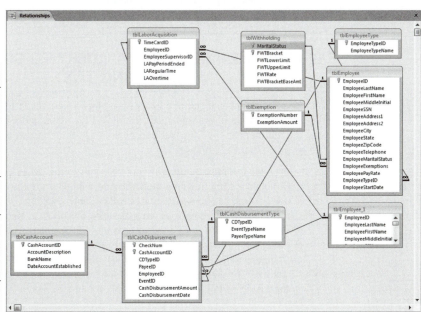

In the next three exercises you will add a computation for gross wages less exemption amount to *qryGrossPay*, create a query to compute FWT, and finally create a Net Pay query.

EXERCISE 10.23: ADDING THE GROSS PAY LESS EXEMPTION AMOUNT COMPUTATION TO *QRYGROSSPAY*

1. Restore the Navigation Pane and the Ribbon if you have not done so already. Open qryGrossPay in Design view. It is located in the Other Objects section of the Navigation Pane.
2. Add the *tblExemption* field roster to the Table Pane. Right-click an empty place on the Table Pane, click Show Table, double-click tblExemption and click the Close button.
3. Use the scroll bar in the Criteria Pane (same as the QBE grid) to scroll to the right until you can see the GrossPay field column and at least two blank columns. Double-click ExemptionAmount to add it to the first available column in the Criteria Pane. Save your query.
4. Create an expression to subtract ExemptionAmount from GrossPay. However, your result cannot be less than zero. Otherwise, the result will not fall between the lower limit and upper limit of any tax bracket in *tblWithholding* (see Figure 10.28). Therefore, you will add the **IIF** function to your expression to disallow negative numbers. The IIF function looks like this: **IIF (expr, truepart, falsepart)**. IIF evaluates an expression. If it is true, the value or expression in **truepart** is returned. If the expression is false, it returns the value or expression in **falsepart**. Click Builder in the Query Setup group and add the following expression. GrossLessExempt: IIf(([GrossPay]-[ExemptionAmount])>0, ([GrossPay]-[ExemptionAmount]),0). Remember that you can double-click on the fields in the second column to save typing time. Be sure to enter the parentheses exactly as shown. Save the query.
5. Run the query for the month of January 2010 and verify that the query is correctly calculating GrossLessExempt. For example the highlighted rows in Figure 10.30 show exemption amounts in excess of gross pay. Therefore, the IIF statement returned $0.00 instead of negative amounts. Close the query.

EXERCISE 10.24: CREATING A QUERY TO COMPUTE FEDERAL WITHHOLDING TAX

In this exercise you will create a query that mimics the Lookup function in Excel. You will use a combination of an employee's MaritalStatus value and GrossLessExempt to identify the appropriate FWT bracket and make a series of computations using values from fields within that FWT bracket.

1. Click the Create tab and click Query Design in the Other group.
2. Double-click tblEmployee and tblWithholding from the list of tables, click the Queries tab, double-click qryGrossPay, and click the Close button. Resize and move the field rosters so you can see all fields in each field roster. You can expand the Table Pane by grabbing the bar between it and the Criteria Pane and dragging it downward.
3. Double-click EmployeeID, TimeCardID, and LAPayPeriodEnded, respectively, in the *qryGrossPay* field roster to add them to the Criteria Pane. Sort EmployeeID in Ascending order.

4. Add EmployeeMaritalStatus from the *tblEmployee* field roster to limit FWT brackets to those with the employee's marital status.
5. Based on an employee's marital status, select the FWT bracket where GrossLessExempt falls within the FWT lower limit and FWT upper limit. Add GrossLessExempt from *qryGrossPay* and FWTBracket from *tblWithholding* to the Criteria Pane. To specify the correct FWT bracket add the following to the Criteria cell of GrossLessExempt: Between [tblWithholding].[FWTLowerLimit] And [tblWithholding].[FWTUpperLimit]. Open the Zoom box by clicking the Criteria cell and pressing Shift+F2 so you can see the entire expression as you type it.
6. Select the data from FWT bracket to compute the FWT amount. Add FWTLowerLimit, FWTRate, and FWTBracketBaseAmt from the *tblWithholding* field roster.
7. Save the query as qryFWT. Run the query for the month of January 2010. Using Figure 10.28 verify the accuracy of the Tax Bracket, Lower Limit, and FWT Base Amt for the first five employees.
8. Compute the FWT amount. Click the field cell in the first empty column of the Criteria Pane and click Builder in the Query Setup group. Enter FWT: ((([GrossLessExempt]-[FWTLowerLimit])*[FWTRate])+[FWTBracketBaseAmt]. Click OK when you are done.
9. Save the query and run it for January 2010 to verify that the FWT amounts are correct. Figure 10.31 shows the dynaset. Close the query.

Fig. 10.30 Partial view of *qryGrossPay* dynaset.

qryGrossPay				
Regular Pay	Overtime Pay	Gross Pay	Exemption Amt.	GrossLessExempt
$4,704.00	$0.00	$4,704.00	$304.17	$4,399.83
$4,704.00	$0.00	$4,704.00	$304.17	$4,399.83
$1,377.60	$0.00	$1,377.60	$608.34	$769.26
$3,259.20	$116.40	$3,375.60	$912.51	$2,463.09
$1,260.00	$90.00	$1,350.00	$608.34	$741.66
$2,587.20	$254.10	$2,841.30	$0.00	$2,841.30
$3,763.20	$0.00	$3,763.20	$304.17	$3,459.03
$1,306.40	$0.00	$1,306.40	$1,520.85	$0.00
$674.25	$0.00	$674.25	$912.51	$0.00
$2,167.20	$0.00	$2,167.20	$304.17	$1,863.03
$3,024.00	$189.00	$3,213.00	$0.00	$3,213.00
$1,234.80	$0.00	$1,234.80	$1,216.68	$18.12
$1,558.20	$0.00	$1,558.20	$304.17	$1,254.03
$1,512.00	$0.00	$1,512.00	$304.17	$1,207.83
$2,788.80	$74.70	$2,863.50	$304.17	$2,559.33
$4,032.00	$0.00	$4,032.00	$608.34	$3,423.66
$1,489.20	$0.00	$1,489.20	$0.00	$1,489.20
$1,372.00	$0.00	$1,372.00	$304.17	$1,067.83
$1,689.60	$0.00	$1,689.60	$304.17	$1,385.43
$3,007.20	$53.70	$3,060.90	$0.00	$3,060.90
$750.00	$0.00	$750.00	$304.17	$445.83
$1,156.20	$24.60	$1,180.80	$1,216.68	$0.00
$3,612.00	$0.00	$3,612.00	$608.34	$3,003.66
$2,385.60	$298.20	$2,683.80	$304.17	$2,379.63
$1,523.20	$0.00	$1,523.20	$304.17	$1,219.03
$5,409.60	$144.90	$5,554.50	$0.00	$5,554.50

Record: ◄ ◄ 8 of 45 ► ►► ►* No Filter Search

Fig. 10.31 *qryFWT* dynaset.

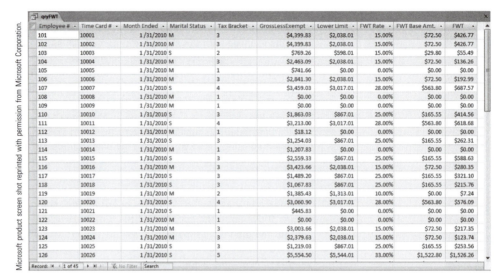

Microsoft product screen shot reprinted with permission from Microsoft Corporation.

The computation for net pay is Gross Pay – FWT – FICA – Medicare. You computed gross pay in Exercise 10.18 and FWT in Exercise 10.23. Since FICA and Medicare are based on fixed percentages of gross pay—the FICA percentage is 6.2% and Medicare is 1.45%—you have all the information you need to compute net pay. Remember that we are ignoring the FICA ceiling limit to simplify the computations.

EXERCISE 10.25: CREATING A QUERY TO COMPUTE NET PAY

1. Click the Create tab and click Query Design in the Other group.
2. Click the Queries tab, double-click qryFWT and qryGrossPay, and click the Close button. Resize and move the field rosters so you can see all fields in each field roster.
3. Create a link between the two queries by clicking and dragging TimeCardID from one field roster to TimeCardID in the other field roster. You should see a link between *qryFWT* and *qryGrossPay*.
4. Double-click EmployeeID, TimeCardID, LAPayPeriodEnded, and GrossPay from the *qryGrossPay* field roster to add them to the Criteria Pane. Sort EmployeeID in Ascending order.
5. Double-click FWT from the *qryFWT* field roster to add it to the Criteria Pane.
6. Save your query as qryNetPay.
7. Enter the FICA expression in the next open Field cell in the QBE grid: FICA: [GrossPay]*0.062. Run the query to test the expression.
8. Notice that some of the calculated values for FICA have more than two decimal places (see the dynaset in the top portion of Figure 10.32). Rounding errors can create many hours of extra work in accounting systems, and payroll calculations are perhaps the most infamous source of those rounding errors. To eliminate rounding errors at the calculation point, accounting systems designers have developed a number of tricks. You can use one of these tricks to make sure FICA values are stored with two decimal places. The trick is to multiply the result by 100, use an integer function to round the value, and then divide the rounded

value by 100. You can incorporate this rounding procedure into this query by revising the FICA calculation so that it reads FICA: Int([GrossPay]*0.062*100)/100. Press Shift+F2 if you want to use the Zoom Box to modify the FICA expression.

9. Run the query to test the revised expression. The FICA column values in the resulting dynaset should now have no more than two decimal places (see the bottom portion of Figure 10.32). You could have revised the expression to read: FICA: Int([GrossPay] * 6.2) and it would have worked just as well. However, the expression you used has the advantage of being self-documenting—it reveals what you were thinking when you wrote the expression. This can be important if someone else may need to revise the expression in the future—a likely occurrence in HR systems!

10. Enter the Medicare Expression in the Field cell next to FICA: Medicare: Int ([GrossPay]*0.0145*100)/100.

11. Open the Property Sheet and set Format to Currency for both FICA and Medicare. Save your query.

12. Use the Expression Builder to enter the Net Pay expression: NetPay: [GrossPay] – [FWT] – [FICA] – [Medicare]. Click OK to close the Expression Builder. Set the Caption to Net Pay.

13. Save your query and run it for January 2010. Your dynaset should look like the one in Figure 10.33. Close the query.

Fig. 10.32 Dynaset containing FICA computation with and without the Int function.

qryNetPay				
Employee # ▾	Month Ended ▾	Gross Pay ▾	FWT ▾	FICA ▾
101	1/31/2010	$4,704.00	$426.77	291.648
102	1/31/2010	$4,704.00	$426.77	291.648
103	1/31/2010	$1,377.60	$55.49	85.4112
104	1/31/2010	$3,375.60	$136.26	209.2872
105	1/31/2010	$1,350.00	$0.00	83.7
106	1/31/2010	$2,841.30	$192.99	176.1606
107	1/31/2010	$3,763.20	$687.57	233.3184
108	1/31/2010	$1,306.40	$0.00	80.9968
109	1/31/2010	$674.25	$0.00	41.8035
110	1/31/2010	$2,167.20	$414.56	134.3664

FICA computation without Int function

qryNetPay				
Employee # ▾	Month Ended ▾	Gross Pay ▾	FWT ▾	FICA ▾
101	1/31/2010	$4,704.00	$426.77	291.64
102	1/31/2010	$4,704.00	$426.77	291.64
103	1/31/2010	$1,377.60	$55.49	85.41
104	1/31/2010	$3,375.60	$136.26	209.28
105	1/31/2010	$1,350.00	$0.00	83.7
106	1/31/2010	$2,841.30	$192.99	176.16
107	1/31/2010	$3,763.20	$687.57	233.31
108	1/31/2010	$1,306.40	$0.00	80.99
109	1/31/2010	$674.25	$0.00	41.8
110	1/31/2010	$2,167.20	$414.56	134.36

FICA computation with Int function

Fig. 10.33 *qryNet-Pay* Dynaset.

Employee #	Time Card #	Month Ended	Gross Pay	FWT	FICA	Medicare	Net Pay
101	10001	1/31/2010	$4,704.00	$426.77	$291.64	$68.20	$3,917.39
102	10002	1/31/2010	$4,704.00	$426.77	$291.64	$68.20	$3,917.39
103	10003	1/31/2010	$1,377.60	$55.49	$85.41	$19.97	$1,216.73
104	10004	1/31/2010	$3,375.60	$136.26	$209.28	$48.94	$2,981.12
105	10005	1/31/2010	$1,350.00	$0.00	$83.70	$19.57	$1,246.73
106	10006	1/31/2010	$2,841.30	$192.99	$176.16	$41.19	$2,430.96
107	10007	1/31/2010	$3,763.20	$687.57	$233.31	$54.56	$2,787.76
108	10008	1/31/2010	$1,306.40	$0.00	$80.99	$18.94	$1,206.47
109	10009	1/31/2010	$674.25	$0.00	$41.80	$9.77	$622.68
110	10010	1/31/2010	$2,167.20	$414.56	$134.36	$31.42	$1,586.87
111	10011	1/31/2010	$3,213.00	$618.68	$199.20	$46.58	$2,348.54
112	10012	1/31/2010	$1,234.80	$0.00	$76.55	$17.90	$1,140.35
113	10013	1/31/2010	$1,558.20	$262.31	$96.60	$22.59	$1,176.71
114	10014	1/31/2010	$1,512.00	$0.00	$93.74	$21.92	$1,396.34
115	10015	1/31/2010	$2,863.50	$588.63	$177.53	$41.52	$2,055.82
116	10016	1/31/2010	$4,032.00	$280.35	$249.98	$58.46	$3,443.21
117	10017	1/31/2010	$1,489.20	$321.10	$92.33	$21.59	$1,054.18
118	10018	1/31/2010	$1,372.00	$215.76	$85.06	$19.89	$1,051.30
119	10019	1/31/2010	$1,689.60	$7.24	$104.75	$24.49	$1,553.12
120	10020	1/31/2010	$3,060.90	$576.09	$189.77	$44.38	$2,250.66
121	10021	1/31/2010	$750.00	$0.00	$46.50	$10.87	$692.63
122	10022	1/31/2010	$1,180.80	$0.00	$73.20	$17.12	$1,090.48
123	10023	1/31/2010	$3,612.00	$217.35	$223.94	$52.37	$3,118.34
124	10024	1/31/2010	$2,683.80	$123.74	$166.39	$38.91	$2,354.76
125	10025	1/31/2010	$1,523.20	$253.56	$94.43	$22.08	$1,153.14
126	10026	1/31/2010	$5,554.50	$1,526.26	$344.37	$80.54	$3,603.33

Record: 1 of 45　No Filter　Search

The Cash Disbursement Entry Form for Payroll Checks

Pipefitters Supply Company pays its employees on the second day after the payroll date. If this day falls on a weekend or holiday, the payroll checks will be stored in the company safe and distributed on the next business day. The Payroll Data Entry form will look similar to the Cash Disbursement Entry form you created in Chapter 9 for payments to vendors (see Figure 9.54). The main difference is that the top portion of the form will contain employee payroll information instead of the inventory receipt and vendor contact information. You will build a query containing all employee payroll fields you will need for the top portion of the form.

EXERCISE 10.26: CREATING THE EMPLOYEE PAYROLL INFORMATION QUERY

1. Click the Create tab and click Query Design in the Other group. Click the Queries tab. Add *qryEmployeeName*, *qryGrossPay*, and *qryNetPay* to the Table Pane, and click Close. Link *qryEmployeeName* to *qryGrossPay* by dragging EmployeeID from one field roster to the other. Link *qryNetPay* to *qryGrossPay* by dragging TimeCardID from one field roster to the other.
2. Add the fields listed in Figure 10.34 to the Criteria Pane. As you fill up the Criteria Pane use the scroll bar to reveal additional empty columns.
3. Sort TimeCardID in Ascending order.
4. Save your query as qryFormCDPayrollRecordSourceData.
5. Run the query for January 2010. The first five records are shown in Figure 10.35. Close your query.

Fig. 10.34 Fields for *qryFormCDPayroll RecordSourceData.*

Field Name	Field Roster
TimeCardID	qryGrossPay
EmployeeID	qryGrossPay
EmployeeName	qryEmployeeName
EmployeePayRate	qryGrossPay
LAPayPeriodEnded	qryGrossPay
RegularPay	qryGrossPay
OvertimePay	qryGrossPay
GrossPay	qryGrossPay
FWT	qryNetPay
FICA	qryNetPay
Medicare	qryNetPay
NetPay	qryNetPay

Fig. 10.35 *qry-FormCDPayrollRecord-SourceData* in Datasheet view.

Microsoft product screen shots reprinted with permission from Microsoft Corporation.

qryFormCDPayrollRecordSourceData

Time Card #	Employee #	Name	Pay Rate	Month Ende
10001	101	Artemis Q. Greenwood	$28.00	1/31/2010
10002	102	Ethel Z. Greenwood	$28.00	1/31/2010
10003	103	Ethel P. Baron	$8.20	1/31/2010
10004	104	Cecelia J. Oppenheim	$19.40	1/31/2010
10005	105	Ronald D. Washington	$7.50	1/31/2010

Regular Pay	Overtime Pay	Gross Pay	FWT	FICA	Medicare	Net Pay
$4,704.00	$0.00	$4,704.00	$426.77	$291.64	$68.20	$3,917.39
$4,704.00	$0.00	$4,704.00	$426.77	$291.64	$68.20	$3,917.39
$1,377.60	$0.00	$1,377.60	$55.49	$85.41	$19.97	$1,216.73
$3,259.20	$116.40	$3,375.60	$136.26	$209.28	$48.94	$2,981.12
$1,260.00	$90.00	$1,350.00	$0.00	$83.70	$19.57	$1,246.73

The Payroll Check Data Entry form uses the form/subform design. The top portion of the form will contain the payroll information from *qryFormCDPayrollRecordSourceData*. None of these fields will be editable because they are for reference only. The subform contains all of the fields from *tblCashDisbursement*. The PayeeID and EventID fields will be linked to the main form which will automatically populate EventID. PayeeID does not automatically populate, due to multiple links with EmployeeID within the same table. Using data derived from *tblLaborAcquisition* serves as a control because payroll cash disbursements can only be recorded for labor acquisitions that exist in *tblLaborAcquisition*.

EXERCISE 10.27: USING FORM WIZARD TO CREATE THE PAYROLL CHECK DATA ENTRY FORM

1. Click qryFormCDPayrollRecordSourceData in the Unassigned Objects group of the Navigation Pane to highlight the table name. Click the Create tab and click MoreForms in the Forms group and then click Form Wizard.

2. Click the >> button to move all available fields from *qryFormCDPayrollRecord SourceData* to the Selected Field*s* panel.
3. Select tblCashDisbursement from the Tables/Queries combo box. Click the >> button to move all available fields to the Selected Fields panel.
4. Click the Next button, click byqryFormCDPayrollRecordSource, which will put the query fields in the top portion of the form and the Cash Disbursement fields in the subform, just like the Cash Disbursement Entry form for vendors you created in Chapter 9.
5. Click the Next button three times, which brings you to the form names dialog box. Type frmCashDisbursementPayroll in the Form text box and fsubCashDisbursementPayroll in the Subform text box.
6. Click the Finish button to close the dialog box and open *frmCashDisbursementPayroll* in Form view.
7. Type 1/1/2010 in the Beginning of Period Date dialog box and 1/31/2010 in the End or Period Date dialog box. You may receive a Form Wizard warning that the form cannot be opened in Form view or Datasheet view. This occurred because date parameter dialog box prevented the form from immediately opening. Just click OK and you will see that the form opens in Form view and the subform opens in Datasheet view as illustrated in Figure 10.36.
8. Close the form.

Although this form is functional, we will improve its look and function, and add some input controls in the next two exercises.

Fig. 10.36 *frmCash-DisbursementPayroll* in **Form view after using Form Wizard.**

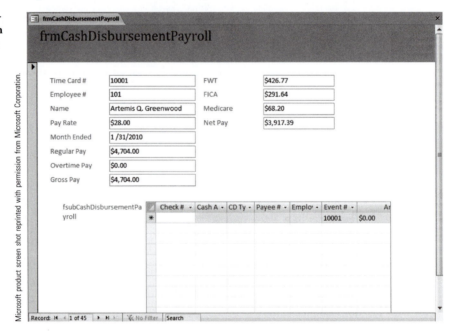

Microsoft product screen shot reprinted with permission from Microsoft Corporation.

EXERCISE 10.28: IMPROVING THE PAYROLL CHECK DATA ENTRY SUBFORM

1. Open fsubCashDisbursementPayroll in Design view. It is located in the Unassigned Objects group of the Navigation Pane. Click Property Sheet in the

Tools group and click the Format tab. Select Form from the Property Sheet combo box if it is not already selected.

2. Since only one payroll check will be written for each time card, you will eliminate many of the subform's navigation controls by making the following changes to its Format properties:
   - Set Record Selectors to No.
   - Set Navigation Button to No.
   - Set Scroll Bars to Neither.
   - Set Close Button to No.
   - Set Min Max Buttons to None.

3. All payroll checks are drawn from the payroll account, CashAccountID 302. Click the CashAccountID control which will select it in the Property Sheet combo box. Click the Data tab and set Default Value property to "302". Since users should not write a payroll check from any other account, change the Enabled property to No and Locked to Yes. Click the Other tab and change Tab Stop to No. These changes prevent users from entering the wrong cash account for payroll checks.

4. Click the CDTypeID control. Click the Data tab and set Default Value property to "02", which is the Cash Disbursement Type number for payroll cash disbursements. Make the same changes for CDTypeID as you did in Step 3 for CashAccountID.

5. The values of PayeeID and EventID will be set by the link between the subform and form. Make them unavailable like you did in Step 3.

6. View the subform in Datasheet view. Click the Datasheet Selector; click the More menu in the Records group; click Column Width; then click the Best Fit button to adjust all column widths.

7. Close the subform. Notice that you cannot use the Close Button (the X in the right-hand corner of the form) because you disabled it. Right-click the fsubCashDisbursementPayroll tab; click Close. and click Yes to save your changes.

EXERCISE 10.29: IMPROVING THE PAYROLL CHECK DATA ENTRY FORM

Use Figure 10.37 as a guide for how your form should look.

1. Open frmCashDisbursementPayroll in Design view, open the Property Sheet. Press Ctrl+A to select all form objects; click the Arrange tab and click Remove in the Control Layout group to allow each object to move independently. Click an empty place on the form to unselect all objects.

2. Change the Header to Payroll Check Data Entry. Click and drag the Detail bar down so you can grab the bottom grab handle of the Header label and remove the excess height of the label box. Drag the detail bar back up until it touches the Header label box.

3. Open the Property Sheet on the Design ribbon, or right-click and select Properties. Click and drag the cursor through all of the controls and labels in the Detail section above the subform. Change the following Format properties on the Property Sheet to make the controls appear inaccessible:
   - Set Back Style to Transparent.
   - Set Border Style to Transparent.

4. Click an empty space on the form to unselect the objects. Select all text boxes (not the labels) in the detail section of the form by holding down the Shift key and clicking each text box. Click the Property Sheet Data tab. Change the Enabled property to No and the Locked property to Yes. Click the Other tab and set Tab Stop to No. Switch to Form view. The controls look inaccessible and are inaccessible. Only the subform controls are active.

5. Notice that PayeeID does not automatically populate in the subform because Form Wizard did not create a link between EmployeeID in the form and PayeeID in the subform. Therefore, you will add this link. Return to Design view. Click fsubCashDisbursementPayroll to select it. Click the Data tab on the Property Sheet, click the the Builder button in the Link Master Fields control box, select EmployeeID in the second Master Fields combo box and PayeeID in the second Child Fields combo box, and click OK.

6. Resize and rearrange the form labels and controls to look like Figure 10.37. All labels are aligned right. Layout view allows you to see the subform in Datasheet view and gives you the ability to move and resize it.

7. Save your changes to the form and close it.

8. Import the *tblCashDisbursement* data for the payroll checks from *Ch10.xlsx* using the same method as in Exercise 10.11. *tblCashDisbusement* should have 174 records after importing the data. Open *frmCashDisbursementPayroll* in Form view to see how the form looks with data entered.

Fig. 10.37 Completed *frmCashDisbursement-Payroll* in Design view and Form view.

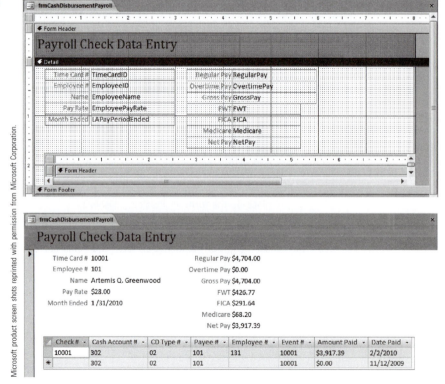

Now that you have finished creating input forms to gather data from HR process activities, we will show you how to derive useful information for internal and external reporting purposes.

Deriving Financial Statement Information

Human Resource activities create financial items on both the balance sheet and income statement. We will first show you how to derive information for the balance sheet. The balance sheet items you can produce from Pipefitters Supply Company's HR portion of its AIS are current liabilities: Wages Payable and Payroll Taxes Payable. We can report the Payroll Taxes Payable in the aggregate or as individual components—FWT Payable, FICA Payable, and Medicare Payable.

After producing the balance sheet items, you will modify your income statement queries to generate Wages Expense and Payroll Tax Expense (as individual components or in the aggregate). We continue using the same naming conventions as in Chapters 8 and 9 for financial statement queries, which often require multiple queries to get the final result.

Wages and FWT Payable

Wages Payable, like Accounts Payable, is based on imbalances between duality events. It is the sum of the net pay from all labor acquisitions less all cash disbursements for labor acquisitions. Unpaid wages also give rise to payables for FWT, FICA, and Medicare. In the process of computing Wages Payable, you will also compute FWT Payable, which is the sum of the FWT amounts deducted from employees' pay. However, because FICA and Medicare also have an employer contribution, you will compute FICA Payable and Medicare Payable in a separate set of queries.

EXERCISE 10.30: BUILDING WAGES AND FWT PAYABLE QUERIES

The Wages and FWT Payable computations require six queries.
The first three queries are identical to *qryGrossPay*, *qryFWT*, and *qryNetPay*, except that the *Between* date constraint is replaced with a *less than or equal to* date constraint.

1. Click qryGrossPay in the Navigation Pane. Press Ctrl+C to copy the query. Press Ctrl+V to paste it and name it qryWagesPayable1-GrossPay. Open qryWagesPayable1-GrossPay in Design view (in the Unassigned Objects section of the Navigation Pane). Change the criteria for LAPayPeriodEnded to <=[End of Period Date]. Run the query and try using an end date of 3/31/2010. You should have 143 records in your dynaset. Save and close the query.

2. Make a copy of qryFWT, name it qryWagesPayable2-FWT, and open qryWagesPayable2-FWT in Design view. Click Show Table in the Query Setup group, click the Queries tab, and add qryWagesPayable1-GrossPay to the Table Pane. For all field columns on the QBE grid with qryGrossPay as the Table property, change the Table property to qryWagesPayable1-GrossPay. Delete qryGrossPay from the Table Pane. Run the query and try using an end date of 3/31/2010. You should have 143 records in your dynaset. Save and close the query.

3. Make a copy of qryNetPay; name it qryWagesPayable3-NetPay and open qryWagesPayable3-NetPay in Design view. Click Show Table in the Query Setup group; click the Queries tab; then add qryWagesPayable1-GrossPay and qryWagesPayable2-FWT to the Table Pane. Link *qryWagesPayable1-GrossPay* to *qryWagesPayable2-FWT* by clicking and dragging TimeCardID from one field

roster to the other. Make the appropriate Table property substitutions. Delete qryGrossPay and qryFWT from the Table Pane. Run the query and try using an end date of 3/31/2010. You should have 143 records in your dynaset. Save and close the query.

Sum FWT, FICA, Medicare, and NetPay. If we assume that Pipefitters has not yet remitted any payroll taxes to the Federal government, the sum of FWT for the period will be the FWT Payable amount for the balance sheet.

4. Click the Create tab and click Query Design in the Other group. Click the Queries tab; double-click qryWagesPayable3-NetPay and click the Close button. Add FWT, FICA, Medicare, and NetPay to the QBE grid. Click Totals in the Show/Hide group. Change the Total property for each field to Sum. Open the Property Sheet. Add the Captions in Figure 10.38. Set the Format and Decimal Places for FICA and Medicare to Currency and 2. Save your query as qryWagesPayable4-SumOfNetPay. Run the query for 3/31/2010. You should have the same totals as in Figure 10.38.

Create a new query to sum all payroll cash disbursements on or before the end date. In Chapter 9, we linked *tblCashDisbursement* to *tblPurchase* in the query to get cash disbursements related to purchases. With the addition of a Cash Disbursement Type table in the database, you can use the CDTypeID attribute to select specific types of cash disbursements.

5. Click the Create tab and click Query Design in the Other group. Double-click tblCashDisbursement and click the Close button. Add CashDisbursementAmount, CashDisbursementDate, and CDTypeID, respectively to the QBE grid. Click Totals in the Show/Hide group. Change the Total property for CashDisbursementAmount to Sum. Change the Total property for CashDisbursementDate to Where, and set its Criteria to <=[End of Period Date]. Change the Total property for CDTypeID to Where, and set its Criteria to 02. You can verify the CDTypeID by opening *tblCashDisbursementType* in Datasheet view. Enter 3/31/2010 for the End of Period Date.

6. Open the Property Sheet. Enter CD Payroll for the CashDisbursementAmount Caption property. Save your query as qryWagesPayable5-SumOfCDPayroll. Run the query for 3/31/2010. The dynaset is in Figure 10.38. Close the query.

Create a query to subtract the sum of cash disbursements from the sum of net pay. You will use the Nz function just like you did to compute other financial statement items such as Accounts Receivable and Accounts Payable.

7. Click the Create tab and click Query Design in the Other group. Click the Queries tab; double-click qryWagesPayable4-SumOfNetPay qryWagesPayable5-SumOfCDPayroll and click the Close button. Add SumOfNetPay to the QBE grid. Create a null-to-zero expression for the sum of cash disbursements in the second Field cell on the QBE grid. Press Shift+F2 to open the Zoom Box. Type CDPayroll: Nz([SumOfCashDisbursementAmount],0) and click OK.

Click the next open field cell, open the Zoom Box, and enter the Wages Payable expression: WagesPayable: [SumOfNetPay] - [CDPayroll]. Open the property sheet and add the captions. Save your query as qryWagesPayable6-WagesPayable. Run the query using 3/31/2010 for the end of period date. The result is in Figure 10.38. Rerun the query using 1/31/2010 for the end of period date. The Nz function returns a value of zero, which allows Wages Payable to be computed. Close your query.

Fig. 10.38 Dynasets for FWT and Wages Payables queries.

qryWagesPayable4-SumOfNetPay

FWT Payable	FICA Withheld	Medicare Withheld	Net Pay
$41,357.20	$20,416.25	$4,774.30	$262,756.72

End of Period Date 3/31/2010

qryWagesPayable5-SumOfCDPayroll

CD Payroll
$162,193.81

End of Period Date 3/31/2010

qryWagesPayable6-WagesPayable

Net Pay	CD Payroll	Wages Payable
$262,756.72	162193.8118	$100,562.91

End of Period Date 3/31/2010

qryWagesPayable6-WagesPayable

Net Pay	CD Payroll	Wages Payable
$76,917.31	0	$76,917.31

End of Period Date 1/31/2010

Microsoft product screen shots reprinted with permission from Microsoft Corporation.

TRY IT

Notice that CD Payroll is not in currency format. Normally you can fix this by opening the Property Sheet and selecting Currency as the format. However, once in a while there are no options in the Format combo box and the Decimal Places property is missing! The bad news is that Access occasionally misinterprets or cannot determine the data type of an expression, as it did for the CDPayroll expression. The good news is that you can add a *Type Conversion Function* to your expression. *CCur* converts an expression to Currency. The format of the expression is CCur(expr), where expr is the expression you want to convert to Currency. Open qryWagesPayable6-WagesPayable in Design view. Add the Ccur function to CDPayroll: CDPayroll: Ccur(Nz([SumOfCashDisbursementAmount],0)). Rerun the query for 3/31/2010. Compare your result (see Figure 10.39) to the same query in Figure 10.38 without the Ccur function.

Fig. 10.39 *qryWages-Payable6-WagesPayable* for 3/31/2010 using Ccur function for CDPayroll expression.

qryWagesPayable6-WagesPayable

Net Pay	CD Payroll	Wages Payable
$262,756.72	$162,193.81	$100,562.91

Microsoft product screen shot reprinted with permission from Microsoft Corporation.

FICA and Medicare Payable

The tax burden for FICA and Medicare taxes is shared equally by an employer and the employees. Pipefitters Supply Company and all employers incur a FICA Tax expense of

6.2% and Medicare Tax expense of 1.45% of the total employee gross income (ignoring the FICA ceiling amount). Therefore, FICA Payable (FICA Withheld + FICA Tax Expense) and Medicare Payable (Medicare Withheld + Medicare Tax Expense) are two times the amount withheld. Since you have already done all the hard work building HR into Pipefitters' AIS, all that remains is a single query to compute FICA and Medicare Payable.

EXERCISE 10.31: BUILDING A FICA AND MEDICARE PAYABLE QUERY

1. Click the Create tab and click Query Design in the Other group. Click the Queries tab. Add qryWagesPayable4-SumOfNetPay to the Table Pane, and click Close.
2. Add the FICA Payable expression to the first Field cell: FICAPayable: [SumOfFICA] * 2. Open the Property Sheet. Set Format to Currency. Type FICA Payable for the Caption property.
3. Add the Medicare Payable expression to the second Field cell: MedicarePayable: [SumOfMedicare] * 2. In the Property Sheet, set Format to Currency. Type Medicare Payable for the Caption property.
4. Save your query as qryFICAandMedicarePayable. Run the query for 3/31/2010. Compare your result with Figure 10.40.

Fig. 10.40 *qryFICA-andMedicarePayable* dynaset for 3/31/2010.

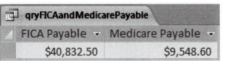

Microsoft product screen shot reprinted with permission from Microsoft Corporation.

Income Statement Items

The income statement items associated with Pipefitters Supply Company's HR process are Wages Expense and Payroll Tax Expense. Payroll Tax Expense can be reported in its aggregate or its components. We chose the two most common payroll tax components: FICA Tax Expense and Medicare Tax Expense. You only need one additional query to compute all of Pipefitters' HR-related income statement items.

EXERCISE 10.32: CREATING THE PAYROLL EXPENSE QUERY

1. Click the Create tab and click Query Design in the Other group. Click the Queries tab. Add qryNetPay to the Table Pane, and click Close. Add GrossPay, FICA, and Medicare, respectively, to the QBE grid.
2. Click Totals in the Show/Hide group. Change the Total property for each field to Sum.
3. Open the Property Sheet. Add the Captions in Figure 10.41. Set the Format to Currency and Decimal Places to 2 for FICA and Medicare. Save your query as qryPayrollExpenses. Run the query for the period beginning 1/1/2010 and ending 3/31/2010. You should have the same totals as in Figure 10.41. Close the query.

Fig. 10.41 *qryPay-rollExpenses* dynaset for 3/31/2010.

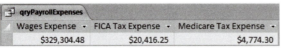

Microsoft product screen shot reprinted with permission from Microsoft Corporation.

Deriving Other Information Useful for Decision Making

Employee Information Reports

You can build a variety of reports using information in *tblEmployee*. The example report that you will build in the next exercise shows one possibility. This example Employee Pay report will list employee names, start dates, and pay rates. The report will group employee records by department and show the average pay rate for each department.

EXERCISE 10.33: BUILDING AN EMPLOYEE PAY RATE REPORT

1. Create a query for the report. Click the Create tab and click Query Design in the Other group. Add tblEmployee and tblEmployeeType, to the Table Pane. Click the Queries tab, add qryEmployeeName to the Table Pane and click Close.
2. Add the following fields to the QBE grid in the specified order:
   - EmployeeTypeID and EmployeeTypeName from the *tblEmployeeType* field roster. Set EmployeeTypeID Sort property to Ascending.
   - EmployeeID from the *tblEmployee* field roster. Set the Sort property to Ascending.
   - EmployeeName from the *qryEmployeeName* field roster.
   - EmployeeStartDate and EmployeePayRate from the *tblEmployeeType* field roster.
3. Save the query as qryEmployeePayRateRptInfo. Close the query.
4. Click qryEmployeePayRateRptInfo in the Unassigned Objects section of the Navigation Pane. Click the Create tab and click Report Wizard in the Reports group. Click >> to select all available fields. Click Next. Click Next again to accept the default view of the data (by *tblEmployeeType*).
5. Click Next to move to the Sort Order dialog box. Sort the detail records by EmployeeID. Click the Summary Options button. Click the Avg check box and the Summary Only radio button. Click OK. Click Next.
6. Click the Outline Layout radio button. Click Next twice. Name the report rptEmployeePayRate and click Finish to preview the report. Click Close Print Preview on the right side of the Print Preview ribbon to return to Design view (see Figures 10.42 and 10.43).

Fig. 10.42 Design view of *rptEmployee-PayRate* created with Report Wizard.

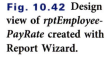

Fig. 10.43 Report view of *rptEmployeePayRate* created with Report Wizard.

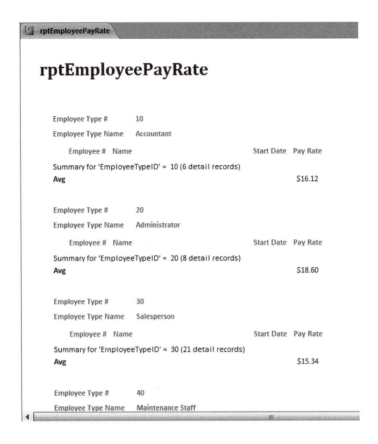

EXERCISE 10.34: IMPROVING THE EMPLOYEE PAY RATE REPORT

Use Figures 10.44 and 10.45 to guide you through this exercise.

1. Click Group and Sort in the Grouping & Totals group on the Design ribbon. Group by EmployeeTypeID should be highlighted. Click More. Click the arrow next to *do not keep group together on one page* and select keep whole group together on one page. Click the X at the top right to close the Group, Sort, and Total panel.

2. Click and drag the bottom of the Page Header bar downward to create a Page Header area. Drag the Header title to the Page Header section. Change the title name as indicated in Figure 10.44. Make copies for each of the titles in the Page Header. Experiment with fonts and font sizes. Change the fill color of the page area.

3. Remove the Report Header by clicking and dragging the top of the Page Header bar upward. Click and delete the objects in the Page Footer.

4. You should now have four sections on the report: Page Header, EmployeeTypeID Header, Detail, and EmployeeTypeID Page Footer. You can click and drag the bottom edges of these sections to change the size of each. This will give you room to include all of the controls that the report requires. Click OK. Move and resize the control as indicated in Figure 10.44.

5. Add a page number to the Page Header area. Click Insert Page Number in the Controls group (next to Logo). In the Page Numbers dialog box select Page N Format, Top of Page Position, and Right Alignment.

6. Allow the objects to move independently by pressing Ctrl+A to select all objects. Click the Arrange tab and click Remove in the Control Layout group. Switch to Layout view to help you move and resize the objects in the EmployeeTypeID Header.

7. Rename the label for Average Pay Rate. Move the label and control into the EmployeeTypeID Header. Delete the remaining summary information in the EmployeeTypeID Footer.
8. Add the lines. Click Line in the Controls group on the Design ribbon. Click and drag from one side of the form to the other. Drawing a straight line with a mouse or touch pad can be tricky. Make your line 2 points thick. Once you have a straight line it is easier to copy, move, and resize the lines than creating new lines.
9. Switch between Layout view and Design view as necessary. Save your report after you complete it. Close the report.

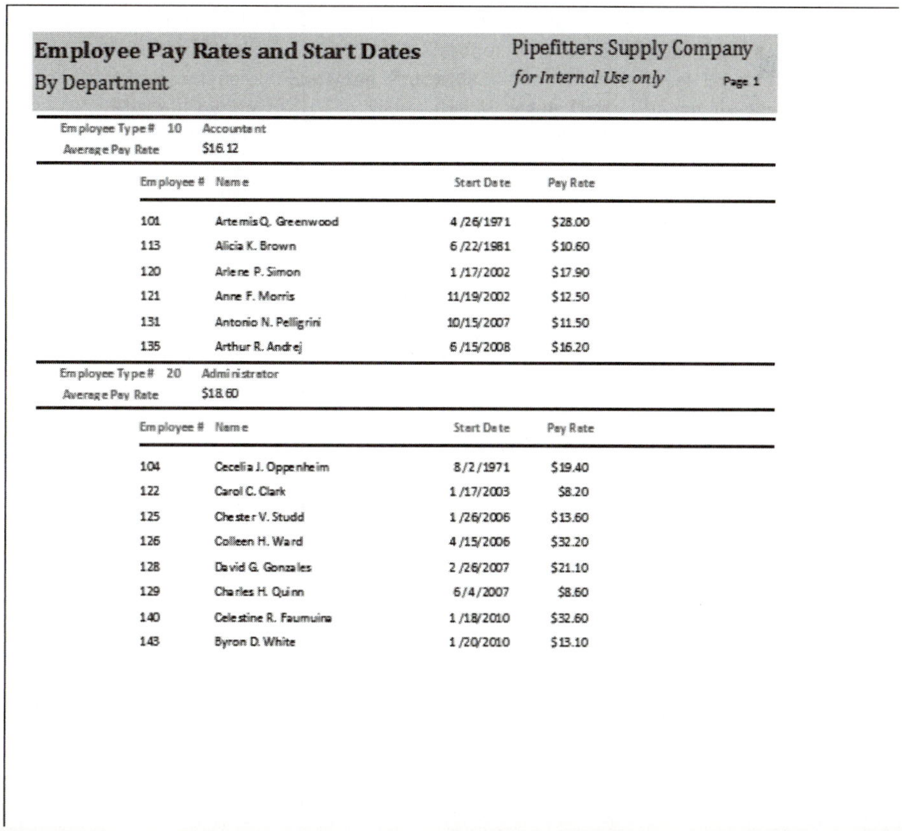

Fig. 10.44 Improved *rptEmployeePayRate* in Design view.

Microsoft product screen shot reprinted with permission from Microsoft Corporation.

Fig. 10.45 Page 1 of Improved *rptEmployeePayRate*.

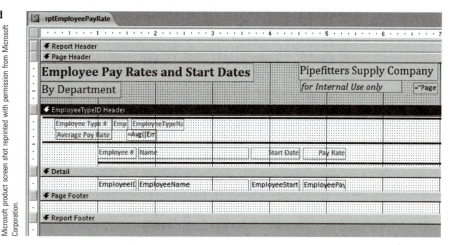

Time Worked Report

In the next two exercises you will build a report that displays total regular and overtime hours worked, regular pay, overtime pay, and gross pay, all by department. This kind of report can direct managers' attention to departments that might have staffing or work scheduling problems. You will build this report in two steps. First, you will design a query that links the Labor Acquisition, Employee, and Employee Type tables. In the second step, you will build a report based on this query.

EXERCISE 10.35: BUILDING A TIME WORKED REPORT

Create a query for the report.

1. Make a copy of qryGrossPay. Click qryGrossPay in the Navigation Pane. Press Ctrl+C; press Ctrl+V and name it qryTimeWorked. Open qryTimeWorked in Design view. Add tblEmployeeType to the Table Pane and click Close.
2. Delete the following field columns from the QBE grid: EmployeeID, TimeCardID, EmployeePayRate, and GrossLessExempt. Delete the tblExemption field roster from the Table Pane.
3. Drag EmployeeTypeName from the *tblEmployeeType* field roster to the first column in the QBE grid. Save and run your query from 1/1/2010 to 3/31/2010. You should have 143 records. Close your query.

Create the Time Worked and Gross Pay by Department report.

4. Click qryTimeWorked in the Unassigned Objects section of the Navigation Pane. Click the Create tab and click Report Wizard in the Reports group. Click >> to select all available fields. Highlight LAPayPeriodEnded in the Selected Fields panel and click the < button to remove it. Click Next.
5. Click the > button to group the report by EmployeeTypeName. Click Next.
6. Click the Summary Options button. Click the Sum check box for all five fields listed; select the Summary Only radio button. Click OK. Click Next.
7. Click the Stepped Layout radio button. Click Next.
8. Click Next to accept the style already selected, or you can change it to something you like better.
9. Name the report rptTimeWorked and click Finish to preview the report. Enter 1/1/2010 for the beginning of period date and 3/31/2010 for the end of period date. Click Close Print Preview on the right side of the Print Preview ribbon to return to Design view, which should look like the report in Figures 10.46 and 10.47.

Fig. 10.46 Design view of *rptTimeWorked* created with Report Wizard.

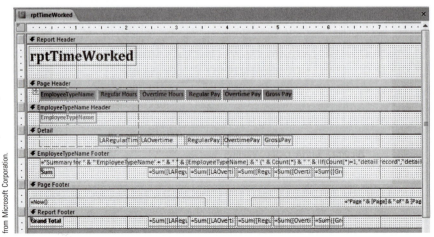

Fig. 10.47 Report view of *rptTimeWorked* created with Report Wizard.

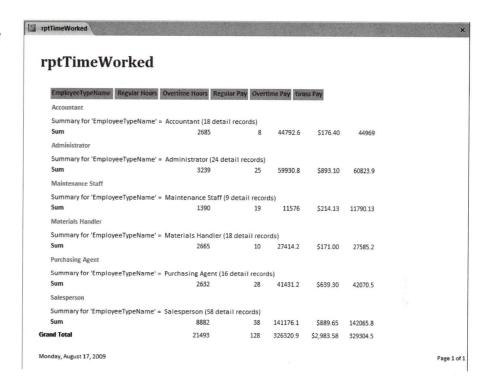

EmployeeTypeName	Regular Hours	Overtime Hours	Regular Pay	Overtime Pay	Gross Pay
Accountant					
Summary for 'EmployeeTypeName' = Accountant (18 detail records)					
Sum	2685	8	44792.6	$176.40	44969
Administrator					
Summary for 'EmployeeTypeName' = Administrator (24 detail records)					
Sum	3239	25	59930.8	$893.10	60823.9
Maintenance Staff					
Summary for 'EmployeeTypeName' = Maintenance Staff (9 detail records)					
Sum	1390	19	11576	$214.13	11790.13
Materials Handler					
Summary for 'EmployeeTypeName' = Materials Handler (18 detail records)					
Sum	2665	10	27414.2	$171.00	27585.2
Purchasing Agent					
Summary for 'EmployeeTypeName' = Purchasing Agent (16 detail records)					
Sum	2632	28	41431.2	$639.30	42070.5
Salesperson					
Summary for 'EmployeeTypeName' = Salesperson (58 detail records)					
Sum	8882	38	141176.1	$889.65	142065.8
Grand Total	21493	128	326320.9	$2,983.58	329304.5

Monday, August 17, 2009   Page 1 of 1

EXERCISE 10.36: IMPROVING THE TIME WORKED REPORT

Use Figures 10.48 and 10.49 to guide you through this exercise. Also, we will show you how to use objects from *rptEmployeePayRate* in this report to save you time and effort.

1. Click and drag the bottom of the Report Header bar downward to increase its size. Click the Header Title and delete it (press the Delete key). Open *rptEmployeePayRate* in Design view. Click an open area of the Page Header just below the *for Internal Use only* box and drag the cursor through all four title boxes (not the page number) to select them. Click Ctrl+C to copy these objects. Click the rptTimeWorked tab to return to *rptTimeWorked*. Click an empty part of the Report Header and press Ctrl+V to paste. With all four title boxes still selected, use the down arrow key to make room at the top of the Report Header for the time period information and the separator line (see Figure 10.48).

2. After you finish adjusting the title text boxes, copy and paste the Time Worked & Gross Pay title box and move it into the top left-hand corner of the Report Header. Change the title to For the Period between. Add the Date Parameter controls. Click Text Box in the Controls group and double-click in the Report Header where you want to place the control. Type the first date parameter in the control [Beginning of Period Date]. Delete the label; change the font to match the title. Add the and title by making a copy of the first date title and adjusting it. Make a copy of the first date parameter. Move it into place and edit the text to read [End of Period Date]. Use Layout view to help size the parameter controls. Whenever you go from Design view to any of the other views Access reruns the query behind the report. Therefore, you will be required to enter the date parameters again.

3. Copy the top line from the Page Header in *rptEmployeePayRate* and paste it into the *rptTimeWorked* Report Header. Be sure to click in the Report Header area

before you paste. After you resize the line, make a copy of it to use for the bottom in the Report Header.

4. Allow the objects to move independently by pressing Ctrl+A to select all objects; click the Arrange tab and click Remove in the Control Layout group.

5. Click the EmployeeTypeName label in the Page Header and press the Delete key. Click and drag the selection box through the remaining five labels to select them. Click and drag the labels into the Report Header (see Figure 10.48). Click and drag the top of the employeeTypeName Header bar up to eliminate the Page Header from the report.

6. Select the controls in the Detail section and delete them. Click and drag the top of the Detail bar up to eliminate the Detail section from the report.

7. Delete the Summary control in the top of the EmployeeTypeName Footer and delete the Sum label below it. Select the five aggregate totals in the EmployeeTypeName Footer and drag them into the EmployeeTypeName Header directly under their respective labels in the Report Header.

8. Eliminate the EmployeeTypeName Footer. Delete the controls in the Page Footer and eliminate the Page Footer.

9. Format all totals. Open the Property Sheet. In Layout view you need to select it from the **shortcut menu**, which is the menu that appears when you right-click in any application. Use Standard Format and 0 Decimal Places for hours worked totals. Use Currency Format and 2 Decimal Places for pay totals.

10. Use Layout view to make final adjustments to the aggregate labels and controls. Whenever you go from Design view to any of the other views Access reruns the query behind the report. Therefore, you will be required to enter the date parameters again.

11. Switch between Layout view and Design view as necessary. Save your report after you complete it. Close the report.

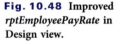

Fig. 10.48 Improved *rptEmployeePayRate* in Design view.

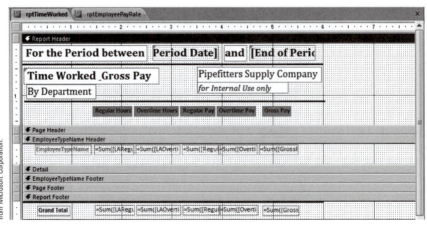

This report illustrates how you can arrange the HR data to obtain some interesting information. By examining the ratio of overtime hours to regular hours shown in this report, managers at Pipefitters Supply Company can identify employee types that are improperly staffed or that have scheduling problems.

Fig. 10.49 Improved *rptEmployeePayRate* in Report view.

	For the Period between	1/1/2010 and 3/31/2010			
Time Worked_Gross Pay By Department			Pipefitters Supply Company *for Internal Use only*		
	Regular Hours	Overtime Hours	Regular Pay	Overtime Pay	Gross Pay
Accountant	2,685	8	$44,792.60	$176.40	$44,969.00
Administrator	3,239	25	$59,930.80	$893.10	$60,823.90
Maintenance Staff	1,390	19	$11,576.00	$214.13	$11,790.13
Materials Handler	2,665	10	$27,414.20	$171.00	$27,585.20
Purchasing Agent	2,632	28	$41,431.20	$639.30	$42,070.50
Salesperson	8,882	38	$141,176.10	$889.65	$142,065.75
Grand Total	21,493	128	$326,320.90	$2,983.58	$329,304.48

Summary

This chapter described how to design and implement the HR business process in Access. In the design phase you identified the duality of economic events, added the work schedule event, and identified and linked the resources and agents associated with the events. Work schedule is not in the actual database because Pipefitters has not yet integrated work scheduling into the electronic portion of its AIS. Also, the HR resource acquired, labor type, is not in the AIS because Pipefitters does not yet track the specific tasks its employees perform. After that you added primary keys, foreign keys, and relationship tables. You also used the design phase to enforce business rules and add controls.

In the process of designing the HR process you likely noticed the similarities and differences between the data models for the HR process and the acquisition/payment process. Similarities exist because you applied the resources, events, and agents methodology for creating databases and both databases have a cash disbursement event. The differences in the two processes are what likely made the database design more difficult. For example, just determining the resource acquired or the outside agent was challenging. However, following the same steps to identify events, the resources and agents related to them, and other events to which they are related enabled you to ask the right questions.

After designing the database you implemented it in Access by building the tables and creating relationships between them. One of the most significant challenges in this part of the database design was to accommodate tables and relationships from other business processes. You added new tables, changed field properties, and even changed relationship properties.

Once the tables and relationships were completed, you gained experience in making creating complex computations. Especially difficult was the computation of FWT. The data for the computation came from multiple tables and you even used a query result to determine one of the keys in a lookup table.

You built queries from HR process data for external financial statements. Finally, you spent considerable effort constructing reports to produce useful information for internal consumption.

Questions and Problems for Review

Multiple-Choice Questions

1. The labor acquisition event is linked to which resource?
   a. Cash.
   b. Inventory.
   c. Labor type.
   d. Employee.

2. A good primary key for an employee table in a firm that pays fixed monthly salaries would be
   a. employee number.
   b. number month.
   c. employee number and month.
   d. employee number or month.

3. Human resources process activities include all of the following except
   a. keeping employee addresses current.
   b. recording changes in employee pay rates.
   c. recording employee time billed to clients.
   d. All of the above activities are part of the HR process.

4. To make a data entry form that contains a large number of fields easier to use, a designer might
   a. put the fields in alphabetical or numeric order.
   b. use a sharply contrasting background color.
   c. group related fields together on the form.
   d. specify a tabular form design in the Form Wizard.

5. To prevent an unintentional violation of state minimum wage laws, a designer who is creating an employee data entry form could
   a. set the Input Mask property of the EmployeePayRate text box control to an appropriate limit.
   b. set the Validation Rule property of the EmployeePayRate text box control to an appropriate limit.
   c. set the OnUpdate property of the EmployeePayRate text box control to an appropriate limit.
   d. any of the above.

6. The EmployeeTypeID field in *tblEmployee* is a
   a. lookup key.
   b. primary key.
   c. foreign key.
   d. relationship key.

7. The external agent for the Cash Disbursement event is
   a. customer.
   b. vendor.
   c. employee.
   d. b and c are correct.

8. The Labor Acquisition table has two relationships with the Employee table. Which of the following is true regarding enforcing referential integrity?
   a. Referential integrity cannot be enforced on either relationship.
   b. Referential integrity can only be enforced either relationships, but not both.
   c. Referential integrity can only be enforced if both fields in the relationship have identical names.
   d. Referential integrity can be enforced on both relationships.

9. A good way to handle multiple calculations in Access reports that are based on queries is to
   a. perform the horizontal calculations in the query and the vertical calculations in the report.
   b. perform the vertical calculations in the query and the horizontal calculations in the report.
   c. perform all calculations in the query and use the report tools to make the report look better.
   d. perform all calculations in the report and use the query to gather the underlying information from the tables.

10. Wages Payable equals
    a. Net pay.
    b. Net pay plus FWT.
    c. Net pay plus FICA Withheld plus Medicare Withheld.
    d. Gross pay.

Discussion Questions

1. If you wanted to add employees to whom you pay a percentage commission to the payroll system described in this chapter, you would need to store the commission rate in a table. Discuss which table(s) you might use and why.
2. Describe how you could modify *tblLaborAcquisition* to include hourly time records. What would be primary key candidates for the modified table?
3. Why are the purchase process and the HR process often discussed separately?
4. How could you modify the time worked by department report to make it more useful to Pipefitters Supply Company?
5. Discuss the advantages and disadvantages of storing employee names in *tblEmployee* in three parts.

Practice Exercises

Note: Before attempting any of the following practice exercises, save a new copy *Ch10.accdb* from the Companion Web site to use for the Practice Exercises. Then, clear the copied database's Read-only file attribute. Begin the names of all Access objects you create in the Practice Exercises with PE#-. Replace # with the Practice Exercise number.

1. Write a query that independently verifies the gross pay calculation that *qryGrossPay* performs. You can use the queries in *Ch10.accdb* as a starting point for your query design. Name your query PE1-qryGrossPay.
2. Create a report that uses the tables in *Ch10.accdb* to print a payroll check and earnings statement for any one employee. Start with *qryFormCDRecordPayrollSourceData*. Name the query PE2-qryPayrollCheck, and the report PE2-rptPayrollCheck.
3. Add any necessary tables to *Ch10.accdb* and revise *qryNetPay* to include a deduction for medical insurance. Clearly state any assumptions you must make to accomplish this task.
4. Modify *Ch10.accdb* to include employees that earn a fixed salary each pay period. (Hint: Think of the salary as a pay rate and the pay period as a unit of time worked.)
5. Create a report in *Ch10.accdb* to show the monthly payroll accrual journal entry at the end of each month (before the checks are written) for Pipefitters Supply Company's general ledger. The journal entry does NOT include the employer's portion of FICA and Medicare. Report Payroll Taxes Payable and Payroll Tax Expense in the aggregate. Use the financial statement queries you derived at the end of the chapter to create a single query named PE5-qryPayrollJournalEntry. Name the report PE5-rptPayrollJournalEntry.

Problems

1. Garcia Intermodal Transport (GIT) is a freight and distribution company that operates local delivery trucks and long-distance tractor-trailer rigs from its location in El Paso, Texas. GIT would like you to design an Access database that it can use to manage its payroll function. The company has thirty employees who perform a wide variety of functions. All of GIT's employees are qualified to operate all of the company's vehicles, and all are qualified to drive interstate and international routes. Employees also perform dispatch, truck loading and unloading, and administrative work. GIT pays its employees every week on Saturday based on the work they have completed through Friday of that week. Because all employees are capable of all job functions in the business, and because the value of the work performed depends on the function performed, GIT pays a rate based on the work performed rather than paying each employee a set pay rate for all work performed. The company has pay rates for local driving, interstate driving, international driving, dispatch,

truck loading/unloading, and administrative work. List the entities that exist in the GIT HR process. State any assumptions you believe are necessary.

2. Refer to the GIT case described in Problem 1, and create a diagram similar to that shown in Figure 10.4 for the transport company. The diagram should show the entities you identified in Problem 1 along with the relationships between those entities and their cardinalities.

3. Refer to the GIT case described in Problem 1 and the work you did in Problem 2. Use Access to build the tables and create the relationships you have defined. Populate the tables with sample data that you create, and test the tables to make certain that the relationships operate to enforce referential integrity as appropriate. You can copy tables from the *Ch10.accdb* database to save time. Unlike the Pipefitters Supply Company example, you do not need to worry about tables from other business processes.

4. Refer to the work you have done in the preceding three problems. Create data entry forms for the GIT HR process database that allow you to enter data into every table without opening the table itself. You can use the forms in the *Ch10.accdb* database as guides.

5. Refer to the work you have done in the preceding four problems. Create reports for the GIT payroll database as follows:

a. Create queries that calculate gross pay and net pay.

b. Create an employee pay rate and start date report.

c. Create a time worked report by job function.

d. Create any additional reports that your instructor assigns.

CHAPTER 11

Financing Process

CHAPTER OBJECTIVES

The financing business process includes both debt financing activities and equity financing activities. Debt financing activities include making loan agreements, issuing debt instruments (cash receipt), and repaying the debt (cash disbursements). Equity financing activities include issuing stock (receiving cash), declaring dividends, paying dividends (cash disbursement), and repurchasing stock (cash disbursement). Information about these events are recorded for decision making, financial reporting, and maintaining records of the resource involved in these events (cash) as well as the agents involved (owners/investors, creditors, and employees). In this chapter, you will learn how to use Microsoft Access to design tables, queries, forms, and reports that can help you:

- **Create a model of the financing business process.**
- **Create a Microsoft Access database based on the business process model.**
- **Create controls to enforce business rules.**
- **Create and maintain owner/investor and creditor records.**
- **Create and maintain cash records.**
- **Record loan agreements.**
- **Record debt issue proceeds received from creditors.**
- **Record debt payments of principal and interest to creditors.**
- **Record stock subscriptions.**
- **Record stock issue proceeds received from owners/investors.**
- **Record dividend declarations.**
- **Record dividends paid to owners/investors.**
- **Produce information for financial statements.**
- **Produce information for internal purposes.**

Introduction

This chapter describes the financing business process of an accounting information system. We illustrate many components of this process using example data for the Pipefitters Supply Company. The financing process includes activities related to the issuance of debt and equity securities. These activities include everything from requisitions for external financing all the way through repaying loans and paying dividends. Whether firms are manufacturers, merchandisers, or service businesses, their financing processes are similar. Debt financing starts with a loan agreement between the firm and a creditor, which states the terms of the loan. The firm then issues the debt—giving a promissory note and receiving the loan proceeds. Then, the loan is repaid with interest in one or more payments. Equity financing begins with a stock subscription between the firm and a stockholder, which states the terms of the stock issue. The firm then issues stock to a stockholder and the firm receives cash. Dividends are often paid to stockholders throughout the life of the corporation (only corporations may issue stock).

Differences in financing activities are often due to the size of the firm, its growth rate, and the length of its cash conversion cycle (time from purchasing merchandise until cash collected from customers) For example, small corporations may only issue stock to active owners, not passive investors. They may handle the stock issue themselves. Large corporations will likely use a brokerage firm to handle the stock issue, offering the stock for sale on an organized stock exchange primarily to passive investors.

Download to your computer or other storage device the Access database from the book's companion Web site. The unzipped database is named *Ch11.accdb*. It contains all the objects that you will need to follow the illustrations in this chapter as well as to complete the end-of-chapter exercises and problems.

Pipefitters Supply Company's Financing Business Process

Pipefitters Supply Company occasionally needs to obtain external funding. Its primary source of external funding comes from banks. When it borrows money from a bank, one of Pipefitters three owners negotiates the loan agreement, but assigns responsibility to one of the accountants for ensuring that the written terms of the agreement are consistent with oral negotiations. The debt issue (cash receipt of loan proceeds) usually occurs within 10 days of the agreement. One of the accountants is responsible for making sure that the loan is deposited into a non-operating account. Cash is transferred from the non-operating account as it is needed. Each loan agreement is associated with one loan issue. Pipefitters Supply Company always uses installment loans because it makes their cash flows much more predictable. Loan payments (cash disbursements) are made monthly, consisting of both principal and interest. Each loan payment is for only one loan, even if Pipefitters has multiple loans with the same bank. An accountant makes loan payments. Loan payments are paid out of the operating account.

Pipefitters initially only issued stock to its owners, but recently it issued shares to outside investors as an alternative to debt financing. **Stock subscription** are for various numbers of shares at a price per share negotiated prior to the time of issue. The negotiated terms, including number of shares and proceeds due are part of the stock subscription information. All stock subscriptions are for no par value common stock. A stock subscription involves only one stockholder. As with the loan agreement, an owner[1] negotiates the stock subscription and assigns responsibility for each stock subscription to

---

[1]Although all stockholders are owners of a corporation, we use the term *owner* to refer to stockholders (often the company founders) who actively manage the business rather than passive investors.

one of the accountants. Stock issues (cash receipts) usually take place within 30 days of the stock subscription. One of the accountants is responsible for the stock-issue cash receipt, depositing the cash into a non-operating account and transferring it into the operating account as needed. Dividends are generally paid monthly out of the operating account. Dividends are paid at the same rate (amount per share of stock) on all shares outstanding. The dividend amount per share depends on the firm's profitability and their currently liquidity. Dividends are paid by one of the firm's accountants. Pipefitters has never repurchased stock from an owner/investor and has no policy for such an event.

Duality of Economic Events

EXERCISE 11.1: MODELING THE DUALITY RELATIONSHIP FOR PIPEFITTERS SUPPLY COMPANY'S SALES/ COLLECTION PROCESS

1. Based on the narrative for Pipefitters' financing process, draw the entities and relationship involved in the duality. Recall from Chapter 10 that *making payroll* (paying employees for labor acquired) and paying vendors for merchandise are both cash disbursement events. They are just different types of cash disbursements.
2. Identify the economic increment event with a "+" sign.
3. Identify the economic decrement event with a "−" sign.
4. Add the cardinalities to your drawing.

Figure 11.1 shows the duality for the financing process. Cash receipt is the economic increment event; and cash is received from a creditor in a debt issue event, and cash is also received from a stockholder in a stock issue event. Cash disbursement is the economic decrement event, which may be for loan payments to creditors or for dividend payments to stockholders. The cash receipt almost always occurs prior to the cash disbursement.

Fig. 11.1 Pipefitters Supply Company financing duality.

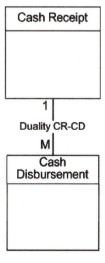

Both types of financing cash receipt events may participate with many (M) cash disbursements. Therefore, the cash disbursement side of the relationship is M. Additionally, since a cash disbursement pertains to only one debt issue or stock issue (cash receipt events), the cash receipt side of the relationship is 1.

Basic Financing Data Model

In the following exercise you will add resources and agents to each event in the duality relationship. Economic increment events have an *inflow* relationship with a resource and economic decrement events have an *outflow* relationship with a resource. Events generally participate with at least one internal agent in an *internal participation* relationship, and with only one external agent in an *external participation* relationship. The resulting data model forms the core of the financing process.

EXERCISE 11.2: ADDING RESOURCES AND AGENTS TO THE FINANCING DUALITY OF EVENTS

1. Add to your model the resource and agents for the cash receipt event and their relationships with cash receipt.
2. Add cardinalities to the relationships with cash receipt.
3. Add to your model the resource and agents for the cash disbursement event and their relationships with cash disbursement.
4. Add cardinalities to the relationships with cash disbursement.

Cash Receipt Event

The cash receipt event in Figure 11.2 is virtually identical to the cash receipt event modeled in the sales/collection process in Chapter 8. A cash receipt results in an inflow of cash from a stockholder or creditor (external agent) and that an employee (internal agent) also participates in the relationship. Both participation events are one-to-many.

The resource, cash account, is used because we track information about cash accounts, including the date and amount of inflows and outflows. The one-to-many cardinalities indicate that a cash account may have inflows from many cash receipt events and that any particular cash receipt will be deposited into only one cash account.

Cash Disbursement Event

This is the same cash disbursement event that was modeled in the acquisition/payment process in Chapter 9 and the HR process in Chapter 10. The data model in Figure 11.2 shows that a cash disbursement results in an outflow of cash to the external agent, stockholder, or creditor, and that an employee (internal agent) also participates in the relationship. Again, you see the typical one-to-many participation relationships.

The outflow relationship between cash disbursement and cash is also one-to-many because a cash account may have outflows from many cash disbursements and that any particular cash disbursement will be come from only one cash account.

Fig. 11.2 Pipefitters Supply Company financing duality with resource and agents.

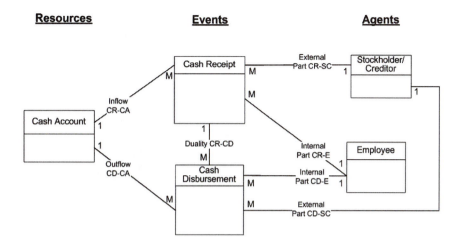

Commitment Events

In Exercise 11.3, you are going to add not one, but two commitment events. Unlike the data models in other business processes modeled in this textbook, each commitment event is linked to both economic events.

Loan Agreement

A loan agreement specifies terms of the future cash receipt of the loan amount, which is a debt-issue type of cash receipt. The same loan agreement also specifies the interest rate, as well as the timing and amount of each cash disbursement allocated to principal and interest.

Stock Subscription

A stock subscription also specifies the terms of the cash receipt, including the number of shares to be issued and the price of those shares. It will also specify the type of stock. However, because Pipefitters only issues common stock, the stock subscription is not specific as to the timing and amount of future cash disbursements for dividends. If Pipefitters did issue preferred stock, the dividend rate (specified as a percentage of par value) would provide much more certainty about future cash disbursements, provided there were sufficient profits to pay preferred dividends.

Simplifying Assumptions

To simplify the example, we are purposely ignoring the dividend declaration event for now, which would be modeled as another commitment event. It would be linked to cash disbursement and to the stock subscription. Stock issue would no longer be directly linked to cash disbursement.

The other simplifying assumption is that we are not linking the commitment events to the resource, cash account, through reservation relationships. Recall the reservation relationships from prior chapters: the sale order-inventory relationship in the sales/collection process (Chapter 8), the purchase order-inventory relationship in the acquisition/payment process (Chapter 9), and the work schedule-labor type relationship in the HR process (Chapter 10).

EXERCISE 11.3: ADDING THE COMMITMENT EVENTS TO PIPEFITTERS SUPPLY COMPANY'S FINANCING DATA MODEL

1. Add loan agreement and stock subscription to the financing data model in Figure 11.2 and the appropriate relationships.
2. Add the cardinalities to the relationships.

Figure 11.3 shows the complete financing process data model for Pipefitters Supply Company. We use the term *Stock Agreement* instead of *Stock Subscription* in the data model (and later in the database) to make it easier to relate the loan commitment event (loan agreement) to the stock commitment event (stock subscription). The fulfillment relationships between the commitment events (loan agreement and stock agreement) and cash receipt are one-to-one because we stated in the narrative that each financing agreement has only one cash receipt. The fulfillment relationships between each of the two financing agreements and cash disbursement are one-to-many. Each installment loan agreement will have many loan-payment cash disbursements, and each loan-payment cash disbursement will be for only one loan. The same reasoning holds true between stock agreement and dividend-payment cash disbursements. Also the participation relationships between commitment events and agents (both internal and external agents) are one-to-many because only one internal agent and one external agent participate with each commitment event, and agents may participate in many commitment events over time.

Fig. 11.3 Pipefitters Supply Company financing process with all resources, events, and agents.

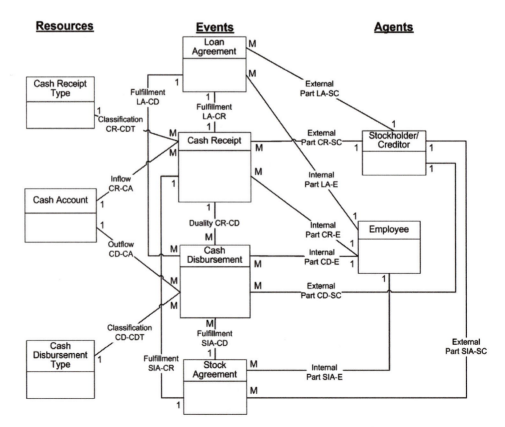

Notice that we included the cash disbursement type entity introduced in Chapter 10. We used the same logic to add a cash receipt type entity to Pipefitters' financing data model as Pipefitters has at least three cash receipt types: customer collections, debt issues, and stock issues. Finally, we omitted the three employee category entities (employee type, exemption, and withholding) from the model to make the diagram easier to read. Imagine how cluttered the data model would be with three additional tables and relationships!

Completing the Financing Model

To complete the model, we identified primary keys for each entity (see Figure 11.4). Based on the primary keys and participation cardinalities, you can create the foreign keys and relationship tables. What participation cardinalities require you to link two entities with a relationship table instead of a foreign key? Review the "Relational Database Management Systems" section in Chapter 2 if you are unsure.

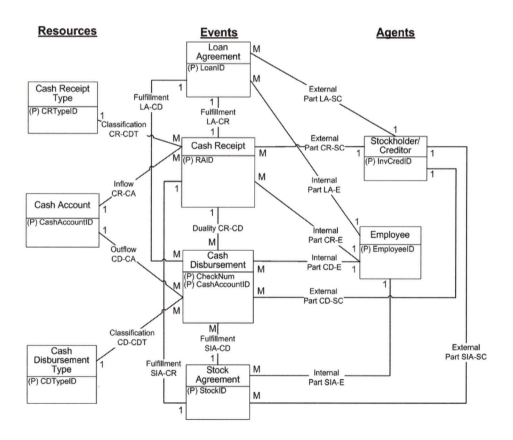

Fig. 11.4 Financing process with primary keys.

EXERCISE 11.4: MAKING RELATIONSHIPS WITH FOREIGN KEYS AND RELATIONSHIP TABLES

1. Using the primary keys provided for Pipefitters' data model in Figure 11.4, create foreign keys for the one-to-many relationships.
2. Create foreign keys for the one-to-one relationships.

If your foreign keys for the one-to-many relationships do not match those in Figure 11.5, review the "Relational Database Management Systems" section in Chapter 2.

Fig. 11.5 Financing process with primary keys, foreign keys, and relationship tables.

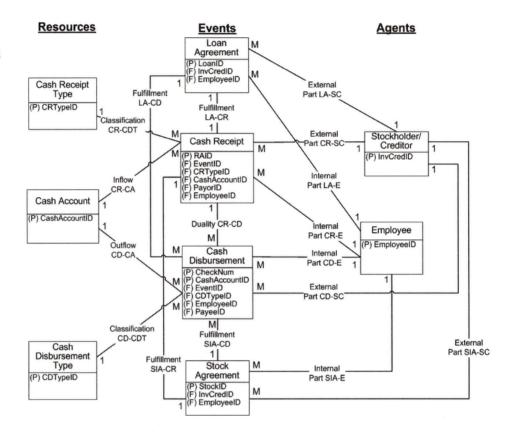

How do you create the link for a one-to-one relationship? You can post from a foreign key into either the table on side of a one-to-one relationship, but you cannot post foreign keys into both tables. The general rule about which table to choose is to choose the one that makes sense. If there is a temporal relationship, as there is between commitment events and the related economic event, create a foreign key in the event that occurs later. This avoids having null values in a table. In Figure 11.5 LoanID from the Loan Agreement table is posted in the EventID field in the Cash Receipt table. This way, when the cash receipt is recorded, the foreign key, LoanID, already exists. If RAID, the primary key for the Cash Receipt table, were posted as a foreign key in the Loan Agreement table then the RAID foreign key field could not be a required field, which is an internal control weakness. Both internal auditors and external auditors would have to perform extra work to determine which null values for the RAID foreign key are correct and which ones indicate errors or irregularities.

Creating Pipefitters' Financing Process in Access
Stockholder and Creditor Information

Firms need easy and reliable access to information about their stockholders and creditors. Access to this information should be restricted to only those individuals who need it. Imagine if all employees at Wal-Mart had access to the contact information for all of Wal-Mart's creditors! Accountants and managers involved in financing activities need stockholder and creditor names, addresses, telephone numbers, and contact people. They also need to know how many shares of stock they own or for which loans they are creditors. Like information about customers, vendors, and employees, all stockholder and creditor information is kept in one table to ensure that stockholder and creditor information is consistent wherever it is used. If, for example, a creditor moves to a new location, the creditor's address is changed only once. In a Pipefitters' relational database accounting information system (AIS), stockholder and creditor information resides in a stockholder/creditor table.

The Stockholder/Creditor Table

The first table in the financing process that we will describe is the Stockholder/Creditor table. It contains the same fields as the Vendor table. Since we will gather the same data for both vendors and stockholders/creditors, we could simply add stockholders/creditors to the Vendor table. However, we would need to add an External Agent Type table, and link the two tables by adding a field in the Vendor table for ExternalAgentTypeID. Moreover, we should rename the table and the attributes to more accurately reflect the content of the table and its fields. Renaming tables and attributes does not sound like a big deal until you realize that fields and expressions in queries and other Access objects will need to be changed manually. The other option is to simply add a separate Stockholder/Creditor table.

EXERCISE 11.5: CREATING *TBLSTOCKHOLDERCREDITOR* FROM *TBLVENDOR*

1. Start Microsoft Access. Open the *Ch11.accdb* database you downloaded from the Companion Web site.
2. Click tblVendor in the Chapter 9 Tables section of the Navigation Pane. Press Ctrl+C, press Ctrl+V, type tblStockholderCreditor in the Paste Table As dialog name box, click the Structure Only radio button, and click OK.
3. Open tblStockholderCreditor in Design view. It will be located in the Unassigned Objects section of the Navigation Pane.
4. Change the Primary Key name from VendorID to FinancierID. We chose **Financier** instead of StockholderCreditor for the prefix for *tblStockholderCreditor* field names because it is much shorter and its meaning is similar. Change the FinancierID caption to Financier #.
5. Change the prefix on the remaining fields from Vendor to Financier.
6. Save your changes and close the table. Wait until you create the Stockholder/Creditor form to enter the stockholder/creditor data in Figure 11.6.

Fig. 11.6 *tbl-Stockholder-Creditor* in **Datasheet view.**

Microsoft product screen shot reprinted with permission from Microsoft Corporation.

	Financier #	Name	Address	Address	City	State	Zip Code	Phone #	Primary Contact
	1001	Arthur Kamedes	5332 Outrigger Way		Oxnard	CA	93035-1825	(805) 856-4639	Arthur Kamedes
	1002	Paul Van Cleave	821 Mandalay Beach Rd.		Oxnard	CA	93035-1076	(415) 288-4260	Patrick J. Crocker
	1003	California Bank and Trust	1690 South El Camino Real		San Mateo	CA	94402-3042	(650) 573-8543	Sylvia Sanz
	1004	Crescendo Ventures	480 Cowper Street	Suite 300	Palo Alto	CA	94301-1504	(650) 470-1200	Clint Korver
	1005	Rocky Mountain Bank	8165 Montana Hwy 35	P.O. Box 144	Bigfork	MT	59911-3590	(406) 751-7060	Denise Benson

The Stockholder/Creditor Information Form

The Stockholder/Creditor Information form contains the same data as the Vendor Information form you created in Chapter 9. Therefore, you will start with a copy of the Vendor Information form and simply change the source of the data from *tblVendor* to *tblStockholderCreditor*.

EXERCISE 11.6: USING THE CUSTOMER INFORMATION FORM TO CREATE THE STOCKHOLDER/ CREDITOR INFORMATION FORM

1. Click frmVendor in the Chapter 9 Forms section of the Navigation Pane. Then press Ctrl+C, then Ctrl+V. In the Paste As dialog box, type frmStockholder Creditor.
2. Open frmStockholderCreditor in Design view. It will be located in the Unassigned Objects section of the Navigation Pane.
3. Click Property Sheet in the Tools group if the property sheet is not already open.
4. Select Form from the combo box at the top of the property sheet. On the Data tab, change the Record Source to tblStockholderCreditor.
5. Change VendorID to FinancierID. Click the VendorID control. On the property sheet change the Control Source to FinancierID by clicking on the combo box arrow. Click the Other tab. Change the Name to FinancierID.
6. Change the label in the Detail section of the form to Financier #.
7. Change the Control Source of the remaining fields to the appropriate fields from *tblStockholderCreditor*. For example, change the source from VendorName to FinancierName. Also, change the Name in the Other tab to begin with Financier instead of Vendor.
8. Change the header to Stockholder/Creditor Information.
9. Save the form. View the form in Form view. It should look like Figure 11.7 after you enter the financing agents' data from Figure 11.6.

Fig. 11.7 Stockholder/Creditor Information form in Form view.

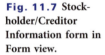

Microsoft product screen shot reprinted with permission from Microsoft Corporation.

frmStockholderCreditor

Stockholder/Creditor Information

Financier #:	1001
Name:	Arthur Kamedes
Address:	5332 Outrigger Way
Address:	
City:	Oxnard
State:	CA
Zip Code:	93035-1825
Phone #:	(805) 856-4639
Primary Contact:	Arthur Kamedes

Maintaining Stockholder/Creditor Records

You have now built a Stockholder/Creditor table to store financing agent information and a Stockholder/Creditor Information form that makes it easy to enter and view data in that table. With the Stockholder/Creditor Information form, you can create records for new stockholders and creditors. You can also update records as stockholders and creditors move, get new telephone numbers, and change other items of information you have stored in the table.

TRY IT

There are few circumstances in which you would delete a former stockholder or creditor from the database because these transactions are usually for very large dollar amounts. Also, there may be regulatory requirements to keep records of all current and past stockholders. Open frmStockholderCreditor in Design view. Click Property Sheet in the Tools group if the property sheet is not already open. Select Form from the combo box at the top of the property sheet. On the Data tab, change Allow Deletions to No (see Figure 11.8). Save your changes and switch to Form view. Click on the record selector and press the Delete key. Instead of deleting the record you hear the Windows error sound. Close the form.

Fig. 11.8 Using form properties to disallow record deletions in *frmStockholderCreditor*.

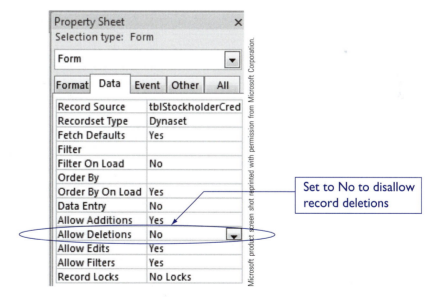

Microsoft product screen shot reprinted with permission from Microsoft Corporation.

Set to No to disallow record deletions

Recording the Loan Agreement Event

When Pipefitters Supply Company decides to borrow money, one of the owners makes preliminary inquiries with one or several banks and/or other creditors. When a suitable creditor is identified, an owner negotiates the exact terms of the loan and the creditor and one of Pipefitters' accountants draws up a *loan agreement*. This agreement specifies all of the information relevant to the loan, including the parties involved, amount of money to be received by Pipefitters, the date the loan proceeds will be transferred, the annual rate, duration of the loan, and schedule of loan payments.

The Loan Agreement Table

A loan agreement is a commitment event that leads to an economic event. Loan agreements initially lead to a cash receipt (receiving the loan proceeds), and later to cash disbursements to repay the loan. As you can see in Figure 11.5, a loan agreement is linked to one employee and one creditor. These two participation relationships are implemented by adding foreign keys to *tblLoanAgreement*. Notice in Figure 11.5 that we chose to omit the reservation relationship with the Cash Account table to simplify the database. If we included this reservation relationship, we could easily compute the expected cash available because we could add the pending cash receipt to the actual cash balance.

Figure 11.9 shows the eight fields for *tblLoanAgreement*. Notice that *tblLoanAgreement* has one date field for the start of the loan, and a second date field for maturity date. You will create a table-level validation rule, like you did for the Purchase Order table in Chapter 9, to prevent a user from accidentally entering a maturity date that is earlier than the loan date.

Fig. 11.9 Fields for *tblLoanAgreement*.

Field Name	LoanID	FinancierID	EmployeeID
Data Type	Text	Text	Text
Field Size	4	4	3
Format			
Input Mask	0000;;_	0000;;_	000;;_
Caption	Loan #	Creditor #	Employee #
Default Value			
Validation Rule			
Validation Text			
Required	Yes	Yes	Yes
Allow Zero Length	No	No	No
Indexed	Yes (No Duplicates)	Yes (DuplicatesOK)	Yes (DuplicatesOK)

Primary Keys and Foreign Keys

Field Name	LoanAmount	InterestRate	LoanDate	MaturityDate	Pmts Per Year
Data Type	Currency	Number	Date/Time	Date/Time	Number
Field Size		Single			Byte
Format	Currency	Percent	Short Date	Short Date	
Decimal Places	2	4			0
Input Mask			99/99/0000;;_	99/99/0000;;_	
Caption	Amount	Interest Rate	Loan Date	Maturity Date	Pmts Per Year
Default Value	0	0			
Validation Rule	>0	>0			
Validation Text	Loan amounts must be positive	Interest rate must be positive			
Required	Yes	Yes	Yes	Yes	Yes
Allow Zero Length					
Indexed	No	No	No	No	No

Attributes

EXERCISE 11.7: CREATING THE LOAN AGREEMENT TABLE

1. Create a new table. Click the Create tab and click Table Design in the Tables group.
2. Create the primary key. Type LoanID in first Field Name box and then click Primary Key in the Tools group.
3. Press F6 to move to the Field Properties section of the window. Enter the Field Properties for LoanID listed in Figure 11.9.
4. Enter the remaining Data Types and Field Properties for the foreign keys FinancierID and EmployeeID and as listed in Figure 11.9.
5. Enter the remaining attributes in Figure 11.9. Unlike other date fields in Pipefitters' AIS, you will leave the default value blank instead of using the current date function because loans generally begin up to ten days after the loan agreement is finalized. The final attribute, PaymentsPerYear is included to facilitate interest computations. For example, a loan with monthly payments will have 12 payments per year. Since loan interest rates are always stated as an annual rate, you can easily compute the monthly interest rate by dividing InterestRate by PaymentsPerYear.
6. Save the table as tblLoanAgreement.

This completes the basic design of *tblLoanAgreement*.

EXERCISE 11.8: CREATING A TABLE-LEVEL VALIDATION RULE FOR MATURITY DATE

1. Open tblLoanAgreement in Design view if it is not already open. It will be located in the Unassigned Objects section of the Navigation Pane.
2. Click Property Sheet in the Show/Hide group to bring up the table-level properties.
3. On the Property Sheet click the Validation Rule Control box to activate the Expression Builder button. Click the Expression Builder button to open Expression Builder.
4. Enter [MaturityDate] > [LoanDate]. Remember to double-click the field names in the second panel of the Expression Builder to save time and ensure accuracy. Click OK to close Expression Builder.
5. Add the following validation text: Maturity date must be later than loan date.
6. Save and close the table.

TRY IT

Open *tblLoanAgreement* and enter a new record. Enter 9999 for LoanID, 9999 for FinancierID, and 999 for EmployeeID. You are allowed to enter these values even though they do not exist in the related tables because you have not yet linked *tblLoanAgreement* to its related tables and enforced referential integrity. Enter $50,000 for LoanAmount, and 9 for the interest rate. Type 05/01/2010 in the LoanDate field. In the MaturityDate field enter 03/01/2010. Tab to PaymentsPerYear and type 12. Tab to the next record. Notice that a dialog box with your validation text appears when you try to go to the next record. After clicking OK, you can either delete the current record by pressing the Esc key or entering a valid date for MaturityDate. Delete the record and close the table.

EXERCISE 11.9: CREATING RELATIONSHIPS WITH *TBLLOANAGREEMENT*

1. In the Database Tools tab, click Relationships in the Show/Hide group and minimize the Navigation Pane. Minimize the Ribbon to increase the Relationship window by right-clicking on the Menu Bar and selecting Minimize the Ribbon. Your relationship window should look like the one in Figure 11.10.

2. Add *tblLoanAgreement* and *tblStockholderCreditor* to the Relationships window. Right-click an empty spot in the Relationship window and select Show Table. Double-click tblLoanAgreement and tblStockholderCreditor; then click Close.

3. Use Figure 11.11 as a guide. Resize and move *tblLoanAgreement* and *tblStockholderCreditor* into place as shown in Figure 11.11, which is consistent with the resource, event, agent (REA) model format.

4. Create the links between the agent tables and *tblLoanAgreement*. Remember to drag from the table with the primary key to the table with the foreign key.

5. After you click and drag the primary key to the foreign key the Edit Relationships dialog box appears. Make sure that the correct attributes appear in the tables you dragged from and to. The relationship type at the bottom of the dialog box should always be one-to-many. Check Enforce Referential Integrity and Cascade Update Related Fields. Finally, click Create in the dialog box.

6. When you are finished your Relationship window should look like the one in Figure 11.11.

7. Close the Relationships window and click the Yes button in the dialog box to save your changes. Right-click the Menu Bar and select Minimize the Ribbon, which has a check mark next to it, indicating that the ribbon is already minimized. If you right-click the menu bar after restoring the ribbon, you will see that the check mark has been removed.

Fig. 11.10 Relationship window before adding *tblLoan-Agreement* and *tblStockholderCreditor*, and relationships.

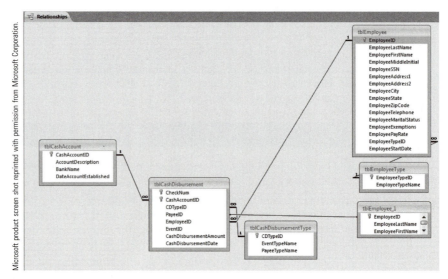

Microsoft product screen shot reprinted with permission from Microsoft Corporation.

Fig. 11.11 Relationship window after adding *tblLoanAgreement* and *tblStockholderCreditor*, and relationships.

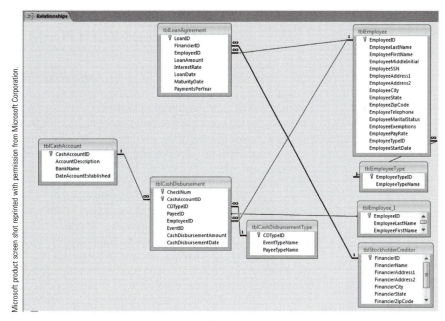

The Loan Agreement Entry Form

The Loan Agreement Entry form is relatively simple. The form looks similar to the form portion of the Purchase Order form from Chapter 9. The form populates a single table, *tblLoanAgreement*, and the reference data comes from the Stockholder/Creditor table.

EXERCISE 11.10: CREATING *QRYSTOCKHOLDERCREDITORINFO* FOR THE LOAN AGREEMENT ENTRY FORM

1. Click the Create tab and click Query Design in the Other group.
2. Double-click tblStockholderCreditor from the list presented in the Show Table dialog box, and click the Close button.
3. Double-click all fields in the *tblStockholderCreditor* field roster to move them to the Criteria Pane except FinancierCity, FinancierState, and FinancierZipCode.
4. Click the Field cell in the first empty column on the Criteria pane and press Shift+F2 to open the Zoom Box. Concatenate city, state, and zip code. Type CityStateZip: [FinancierCity] &", " & [FinancierState] &" " & [FinancierZip Code].
5. Highlight the CityStateZip column and move it to the right of FinancierAddress2 by clicking the column when the cursor turns into a down arrow and dragging it.
6. Save the query as qryStockholderCreditorInfo. Run the query to view the resulting dynaset (see Figure 11.12). You see stockholders and creditors listed because sometimes a stockholder later becomes a creditor and vice versa. Close the query.

Fig. 11.12 *qryStockholderCreditor* in Datasheet view.

Financier #	Name	Address	Address	CityStateZip	Phone #	Primary Contact
1001	Arthur Kamedes	5332 Outrigger Way		Oxnard, CA 93035-1825	(805) 856-4639	Arthur Kamedes
1002	Paul Van Cleave	821 Mandalay Beach Rd.		Oxnard, CA 93035-1076	(415) 288-4260	Patrick J. Crocker
1003	California Bank and Trust	1690 South El Camino Real		San Mateo, CA 94402-3042	(650) 573-8543	Sylvia Sanz
1004	Crescendo Ventures	480 Cowper Street	Suite 300	Palo Alto, CA 94301-1504	(650) 470-1200	Clint Korver
1005	Rocky Mountain Bank	8165 Montana Hwy 35	P.O. Box 1440	Bigfork, MT 59911-3590	(406) 751-7060	Denise Benson

EXERCISE 11.11: CREATING THE LOAN AGREEMENT ENTRY FORM WITH FORM WIZARD

1. Click tblLoanAgreement in the Unassigned Objects section in the Navigation Pane. Click More Forms in the Forms group of the Create tab. Click Form Wizard.
2. You should see tblLoanAgreement in the Tables/Queries list box. If not, click the list box arrow, and click Table: tblLoanAgreement in the list. Click the >> button to move all fields into the Selected Fields panel.
3. Click the Tables/Queries list box arrow, and click Query: qryStockholderCreditorInfo from the list. Select all fields except FinancierID. Before you click the >> button to place all Available Fields into the Selected Fields list, be sure that PaymentsPerYear is highlighted in the Selected Fields panel. Click qryStockholderCreditorInfo. FinancierID (Access attaches the table/query name to a field when two fields in the *Selected Fields list* have the same name). Click the < button to remove qryStockholderCreditorInfo.FinancierID from the Selected Fields panel.
4. Click Next. Access should select by tblLoanAgreement to view the data by default.
5. Click Next. Click Next again to accept the default layout, Columnar.
6. Click Next. Click the Office style if it is not already selected, and click Next.
7. Save your form as frmLoanAgreement. Click the Finish button. Enter the data in Figure 11.13. This will make formatting easier because you can see the data in Layout view, which allows you to resize the controls to fit the data. Close the form.

Fig. 11.13 *frmLoanAgreement* in **Form view after using the Form Wizard.**

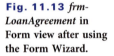

Microsoft product screen shot reprinted with permission from Microsoft Corporation.

frmLoanAgreement	
frmLoanAgreement	
Loan #	1001
Creditor #	1003
Employee #	101
Amount	$50,000.00
Interest Rate	8.6250%
Loan Date	2/1/2010
Maturity Date	2/1/2011
Pmts Per Year	12
Name	California Bank and Trust
Address	1690 South El Camino Real
Address	
CityStateZip	San Mateo, CA 94402-3042
Phone #	(650) 573-8543
Primary Contact	Sylvia Sanz

Record: ◄ ◄ 1 of 1 ► ►I ►⊠   No Filter   Search

Although this Wizard-generated form is certainly usable and includes many basic controls needed to enter, delete, and modify sale order information, you know from your experience in the last three chapters that this form needs improvement in form, function, and controls.

Fig. 11.14 Partially improved Loan Agreement Entry form in Design view and Form view.

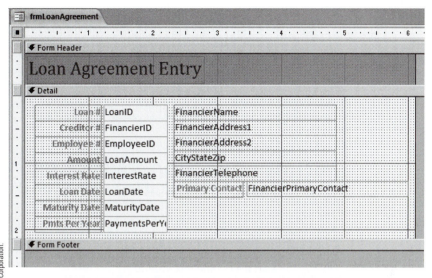

EXERCISE 11.12: IMPROVING THE LOAN AGREEMENT ENTRY FORM

1. Open frmLoanAgreement in Design view. Press Ctrl+A, click the Arrange ribbon, and click Remove in the Control Layout group. Use Figure 11.14 as format guides.
2. Change the Form Header to Loan Agreement Entry and resize both the text box and header to eliminate excess vertical space.
3. Delete the labels for FinancierName, FinancierAddress1, FinancierAddress2, CityStateZip, and FinancierTelephone.
4. Bold and right-justify the remaining labels.
5. Resize and align the fields in the form to look like the examples in Figures 11.14 and 11.14. Some tasks may be easier to accomplish in Layout view and others may be easier in Design view.
6. Switch to Design view. Click Property Sheet in the Tools group.
7. Click the empty Detail space just above the FinancierName control box and drag down to select FinancierName, FinancierAddress1, FinancierAddress2, CityStateZip, FinancierTelephone, and FinancierPrimaryContact. Format these fields to blend in with the background. Click the Format tab on the Property Sheet if it is not already visible. Change the Back Style and Border Style properties to Transparent.

8. Lock the controls to prevent users from changing creditor data in the Loan Agreement Entry form. Click the Data tab on the Property Sheet. Change the Enabled property to No and the Locked property to Yes. Remove the tab stop to prevent users from moving the cursor to fields that cannot be changed. Click the Other tab on the Property Sheet. Change the Tab Stop property to No.
9. Save and close the form.

EXERCISE 11.13: ADDING COMBO BOXES FOR FINANCIERID AND EMPLOYEEID

Add a combo box for FinancierID.

1. Open frmLoanAgreement in Design view. Click the Combo Box button in the Controls group. Move the cursor to the empty area of the Detail section and click to start the Combo Box Wizard.
2. Click Next. In the first dialog box click the first option button with the caption *I want the combo box to lookup the values in a table or query;* then click the button.
3. Click the Queries radio button and double-click qryStockholderCreditorInfo to select where the data will come from and advance to the next dialog box.
4. Double-click the following fields to add them to the Selected Fields panel: FinancierID, FinancierName, and FinancierPrimaryContact. Click the Next button. Sort in ascending order first by FinancierName and second by FinancierPrimaryContact. Click the Next button.
5. Adjust the column sizes by double-clicking on the right edge of each column. Click Next. Click Next again to store the value of the highlighted field, FinancierID, in the database and advance to the store value dialog box.
6. Click the second Radio button and select the FinancierID field. Click the Next twice and click the Finish button.
7. Click the Combo Box label and press the Delete key. Associate the Creditor # label with the combo box by holding the Shift key and clicking the label and the combo box. Click the warning label next to the combo box and select Associate FinancierID_Label with Combo## (## is a number that is part of the combo box name). Click the original FinancierID control and delete it. Move the combo box into place and resize it (see Figure 11.15).

Create an Accountant query.

8. Make a copy of qryAdministrator in the Chapter 10 Queries section of the Navigation Pane. Click qryAdministrator in the Navigation Pane. Press Ctrl+C to copy the query. Press Ctrl+V to paste it and name it qryAccountant. Open qryAccountant in Design view (in the Unassigned Objects section of the Navigation Pane). Change the criteria for EmployeeTypeID to 10, the EmployeeTypeID for accountants. Save and close the query.
9. Return to frmLoanAgreement. Click Combo Box in the Controls group. Move your cursor next to and empty part of the Detail section and click to start the Combo Box Wizard. Click the Next button. Click the Queries Radio button and double-click qryAccountant from the list of queries. In the next dialog box select all fields except EmployeeTypeID. Click Next twice. Resize the columns and click the Next button twice. Click the second radio button and select EmployeeID from the combo box list. Click the Next button. Click Finish. Repeat Step 7 for EmployeeID.
10. Change the tab order. Click the Arrange tab. Click Tab Order in the Control Layout group to open the Tab Order window. Click Detail in the Section column if it is not already selected. In the Custom Order panel move the combo boxes into the correct order. Click the OK button.

11. Save the form and view it in Form view. Check the tab order. Check the combo boxes. If the width is too narrow, return to Design view, open the Property Sheet, click the combo box to select it, and click the Format tab in the Property sheet. Make the Column Width values large enough to accommodate each column. Adjust the List Width value to equal the sum of the column widths. You may need to go back and forth between Form view and Design view a couple of times until you are satisfied with the width. Set the Column Heads property to display column headings in your combo boxes (see Figure 11.16).

12. Save the form. Enter the loan agreement for the two loans displayed in Figure 11.17.

Fig. 11.15 Associating original Creditor # label with FinancierID combo box.

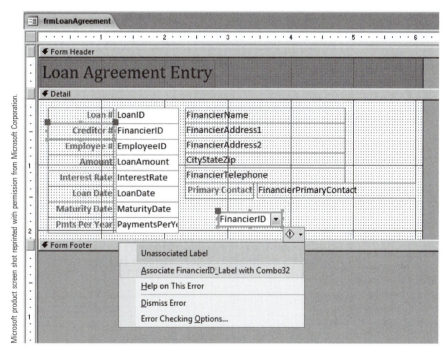

Fig. 11.16 Combo box properties.

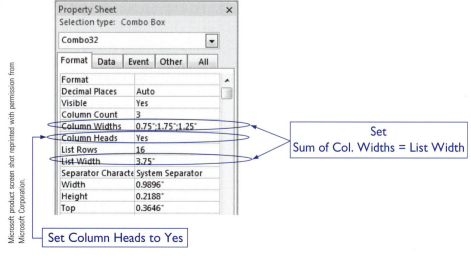

Fig. 11.17 Completed Loan Agreement Entry form in Form view.

Microsoft product screen shot reprinted with permission from Microsoft Corporation.

Recording Cash Receipts from Debt Issues

In Chapter 10, we showed you how to create a Cash Disbursement Type table, add an extra field to the Cash Disbursement table, and alter existing relationships to enable Pipefitters AIS to distinguish one type of cash disbursement from another. In this section, we will make a similar set of changes to the cash receipt portion of the AIS to enable Pipefitters Supply Company to distinguish between cash receipts from sale collections, from debt issues, and from stock issues. The data model in Figure 11.5 shows the Cash Receipt Type table and its link to the Cash Receipt table.

Cash Account Information

The importance of having control over cash cannot be overstated, especially for cash receipts related to financing activities due to the large monetary value of each cash receipt event. In Chapter 8 you created the Cash Account table to show into which cash account a cash receipt is deposited. Open the Cash Account table and add the following account information:

- *Account #: 303.*
- *Description: Financing Proceeds.*
- *Bank Name First Bank.*
- *Date Established 12/20/2009.*

The Cash Receipt Table

You constructed the Cash Receipt table and its related resource table, *tblCashAccount*, in Chapter 8. In the data modeling portion of this chapter you created a fulfillment relationship between loan agreement and cash receipt as well as an external participation relationship between cash receipt and stockholder/creditor (see Figure 11.4). However, cash receipt already has a relationship with another event, sale, and an external participation relationship with vendor (see Figure 8.5). Figure 11.18 shows the design of Pipefitters' AIS related to cash receipts based on the data models for the sales/collection process (Figure 8.5) and the financing process (Figure 11.5). We eliminated the internal participation relationships with employee, the inventory resource, and the outflow relationship between sale and inventory as they are not relevant to this discussion.

The data model in Figure 11.18 shows how we replaced InvoiceID and CustomerID in the Cash Receipt table with generic fields, EventID and PayorID, to accommodate cash receipts from any event. The type of cash receipt cannot be determined by the foreign key field names because the foreign key field may contain an Invoice ID, a Loan ID, or

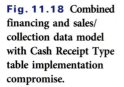

Fig. 11.18 Combined financing and sales/collection data model with Cash Receipt Type table implementation compromise.

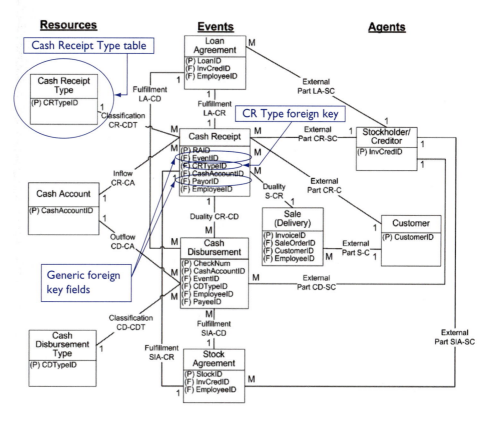

an ID number from another type of cash receipt event. Therefore, we added the Cash Receipt Type table to store the event name and external agent type associated with each cash-receipt event type, and linked it to the Cash Receipt table by adding a foreign key for event type ID.

The downside to using this kind of ***implementation compromise*** is that you cannot enforce referential integrity on links with the generic foreign keys. For example, if PayorID in *tblCashReceipt* has a link to *tblCustomer* and to *tblStockholderCreditor* and referential integrity were enforced on both links, you could not enter any data in the PayorID field: entering a CustomerID would violate referential integrity with *tblStockholderCreditor* because customer numbers are not kept in *tblStockholderCreditor*, and vice versa. You will build additional controls into your input forms to compensate for the lack of referential integrity. See Chapter 10 for an extended discussion on alternative implementation compromises.

EXERCISE 11.14: MODIFYING THE CASH RECEIPT TABLE

1. Open tblCashReceipt in Design view. It is located in the Unassigned Objects section of the Navigation Pane. Use Figure 11.19 as a guide.
2. Make the following changes to the Customer field and its properties:
   - Change the Field name to PayorID.
   - Change the input mask to 99999;;_, to allow for up to five digits to be entered—the length size of Pipefitters longest PayorID field.
   - Change the caption to Payor #.
3. Make the following changes to the InvoiceID field and its properties:
   - Change the Field name to EventID.

- Change the input mask to 999999;;_, to allow for up to six digits to be entered
  —the length size of Pipefitters longest EventID field.
- Change the caption to Event #.

4. Make the following changes to the CustomerCheckNum field and its properties:

- Change the Field name to PayorCheckNum.
- Change the caption to Payor Check #.

5. Add the CRTypeID field and enter the CRTypeID for cash receipts:

- Insert a blank row after CashAccountID. Click the PayorID Record Selector,
  right click and select Insert Row.
- In the new row type CRTypeID in the Field Name cell. Leave the Data Type set to
  Text.
- Set the Field Size to 2 and set the Input Mask to 00;;_.
- Enter CR Type # for the Caption. Save your changes and switch to Datasheet
  view.
- Enter 01 in the CR Type for each of the 81 records. Return to Design view.
- Set the Required property to Yes, the Allow Zero Length property to No, and
  leave the Indexed property set to Yes (Duplicates OK).

6. Save your changes and close the table.

Fig. 11.19 Final Cash Receipts table in Design view and Datasheet view.

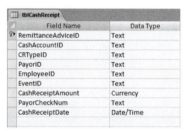

Microsoft product screen shots reprinted with permission from Microsoft Corporation.

Next, you will create the Cash Receipt Type table. Since it is identical to *tblCash-DisbursementType* except for the field names and captions, you will make a copy of *tblCashDisbursementType* and make a few minor changes to create *tblCashReceiptType*.

EXERCISE 11.15: CREATING THE CASH RECEIPT TYPE TABLE FROM *TBLCASHDISBURSEMENTTYPE*

1. Click the tblCashDisbursementType in the Unassigned Objects section of the
   Navigation Pane, press Ctrl+C, and then press Ctrl+V. In the Save Table As
   dialog box, type tblCashReceiptType in the text box of the Paste Table As dialog
   box, click the Structure Only Paste Option, and then click OK.

2. Open tblCashReceiptType in Design view. Change the Primary Key field name to CRTypeID; change the Caption to CR Type #.
3. Save the table and switch to Datasheet view to enter the Cash Receipt Type records in Figure 11.20.
4. Close the table.

Fig. 11.20 Data for *tblCashReceiptType* displayed in Datasheet view.

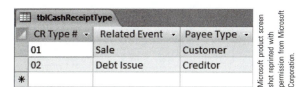

CR Type #	Related Event	Payee Type
01	Sale	Customer
02	Debt Issue	Creditor

EXERCISE 11.16: CREATING AND UPDATING RELATIONSHIPS WITH *TBLCASHRECEIPT*

1. Close all open tables. In the Database Tools tab, click Relationships in the Show/Hide group and minimize the Navigation Pane. Your Relationship window should look like Figure 11.11.
2. Click Show Table in the Relationships group, add the following tables by double-clicking them: tblCashReceipt, tblCashReceiptType, tblSale, and tblCustomer. Click the Close button.
3. Right-click on the Menu Bar and click Minimize the Ribbon to make your Relationship window larger. Move and resize your tables to until they are arranged like Figure 11.21.
4. Remove Referential Integrity from the Sale-Cash Receipt link and the Customer-Cash Receipt link. Right click the link, click Edit Relationships, uncheck the Enforce Referential Integrity box, and click OK. Notice that you cannot cascade update related fields without enforcing referential integrity. Although cascading changes in a primary key to all related fields is a good database practice, it should rarely be necessary.
5. Create new links between *tblCashReceipt* and the following tables: *tblCashReceiptType*, *tblLoanAgreement*, and *tblStockholderCreditor*. Remember to drag from the primary key to the appropriate foreign key.
6. After you click and drag the primary key to the foreign key the Edit Relationships dialog box appears. Make sure that the correct attributes appear in the tables you dragged from and to. Only check Enforce Referential Integrity and Cascade Update Related Fields for the link between *tblCashReceipt* and *tblCashReceiptType*. Click Create in the dialog box when you are done. After completing this exercise your Relationship window should look like the one in Figure 11.22.
7. Close the Relationships window and click the Yes button in the dialog box to save your changes.

The Cash Receipt Loan Issue Entry Form

The Cash Receipt Loan Issue form is similar to the Cash Receipt Sale form. When one of Pipefitters' accountants receives a creditor's check, he or she should be able to compare the amount received to the amount stated in the related loan agreement. We stated that there is only one cash receipt associated with each loan agreement to simplify the form; you do not need to compute prior collections and balance due like you did in Chapter 8 for the Cash Receipt Sale form.

Fig. 11.21 Relationship window after adding Field Rosters.

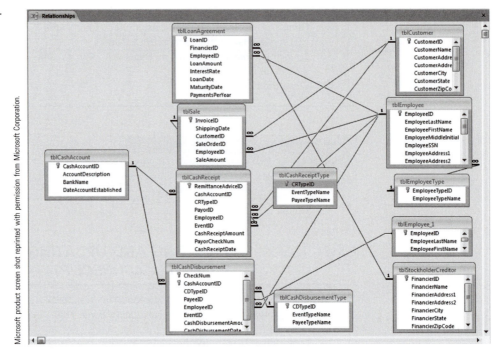

Fig. 11.22 Relationship window after relationships have been added or updated.

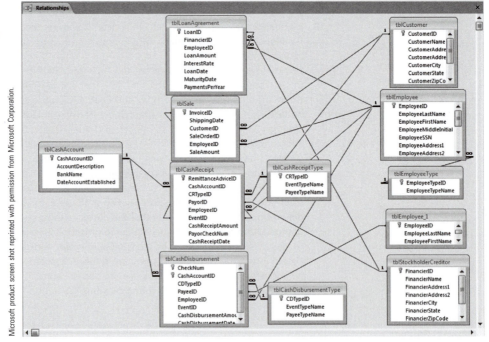

Before creating the Cash Receipt Loan Issue form, you will adjust the original Cash Receipt form to accommodate the extra Cash Receipt Type field. You will then create a separate form to record cash receipts from loan issues by modifying the Cash Receipt Sale form. Even though you already have a Cash Receipt form to record cash received from customers, it cannot be easily modified to display reference information from both sales and loan issues. Moreover, creating separate forms for financing activities can be an effective internal control by limiting user access to financing activity data.

EXERCISE 11.17: MAKING CHANGES TO THE CASH RECEIPT SALE ENTRY FORM

1. Rename the Cash Receipt subform to differentiate the Cash Receipt Sale Entry form from other cash receipt forms. Click the triangle next to Objects by Chapter at the top of the Navigation Pane and click Object Type. Right-click fsubCashReceipt in the Forms section of the Navigation Pane; click Rename and change the name to fsubCashReceiptSale. Right-click the triangle next to All Access Objects at the top of the Navigation Pane and click Objects by Chapter. Open fsubCashReceiptSale in Design view located in the Chapter Forms section of the Navigation Pane. Minimize the Navigation Pane.

2. Add CRTypeID to the subform. Click Add Existing Fields in the Tools section on the Design ribbon. Click CRTypeID in the Field List panel. Click and drag CRTypeID from the Field List panel to just below the CashAccountID field and label.

3. Click Property Sheet on the Design ribbon; click the CRTypeID control on the form to select it and click the Format tab on the Property Sheet. To make this control inaccessible, change the Back Style and the Border Style to Transparent. On the Data tab set the Default value to "01"; change Enabled to No and Locked to Yes. On the Other tab, change Tab Stop to No.

4. Make PayorID and EventID active controls because the links to these fields no longer have referential integrity enforced. Therefore the fields are not automatically populated through their links to *tblSale*. Click Property Sheet on the Design ribbon; click the PayorID control on the form to select it and click the Format tab on the Property Sheet. To activate this control change the Back Style to Normal and the Border Style to Solid. On the Data tab change Enabled to Yes and Locked to No, and change the Input Mask to 99999;;_. On the Other tab, change Tab Stop to Yes. Repeat the same steps for EventID, except change the Input Mask to 999999;;_.

5. Close the Property Sheet and minimize the Navigation Pane.

6. Save your changes. Switch to Form view. Scroll to the bottom of the form to see the default values in the New Record row (see Figure 11.23). Close the form.

7. Rename the Cash Receipt subform to differentiate the Cash Receipt Sale Entry form from other cash receipt forms. Restore the Navigation Pane. Click the triangle next to Objects by Chapter at the top of the Navigation Pane and click Object Type. Right-click frmCashReceipt in the Forms section of the Navigation Pane; click Rename and change the name to frmCashReceiptSale. Right-click the triangle next to All Access Objects at the top of the Navigation Pane and click Objects by Chapter.

8. Open frmCashReceiptSale in Design view, located in the Chapter Forms section of the Navigation Pane. Minimize the Navigation Pane. An Information dialog box appears because you changed the subform name, so *fsubCashReceipt* no longer exists. Click OK to close the dialog box.

9. Change the header to Cash Receipt Entry - Sales.

10. Change the source for the subform. Open the Property Sheet; click the subform in the Detail section of the form; click the Data tab and change the Source Object to fsubCashReceiptSale. Click the Link Master Fields property box. A Subform Field Linker dialog box appears because the original field names in the subform, InvoiceID and CustomerID, no longer exist. Click OK to close the dialog box and open the Subform Field Linker. Select InvoiceID and CustomerID, respectively in the Master Fields boxes. Select EventID and PayorID, respectively in the Child Fields boxes, and click OK.

11. Click the Other tab and change the name to frmCashReceiptSale.

12. Close the Property Sheet, minimize the Navigation Pane and switch to Layout view. You should be able to see the entire subform. Click the subform to select

it. Click and drag the right-hand edge to expose the entire Date field. Click and drag the title to the right until the entire title is visible. Save your changes and close the form.

Fig. 11.23 *fsub-CashReceiptSale* in Datasheet view after adding CRTypeID field.

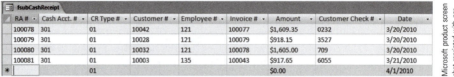

Use Figures 11.24 and 11.25 as guides for Exercises 11.18 and 11.19.

EXERCISE 11.18: CREATING THE CASH RECEIPT LOAN ISSUE ENTRY FORM—MAKING CHANGES TO THE CASH RECEIPT SALE FORM—PART 1

Create a Creditor Information query to list only creditor information.

1. Click qryStockholderCreditorInfo in the Unassigned Objects section of the Navigation Pane. Press Ctrl+C, then Ctrl+V to copy and paste it. Name the new query qryCreditorInfo.
2. Open qryCreditorInfo in Design view (in the Unassigned Objects section). Right-click an empty spot in the Table Pane and select Show Table. Double-click tblLoanAgreement and click Close. Double-click LoanID to add it to the QBE (Query by Example) grid. Adding LoanID to the query limits the dynaset to only creditors because only creditors participate in loan agreements. Join the two field rosters on FinancierID. Save and close the query.

Make changes to the Cash Receipt Sale Entry subform.

3. Make a copy of *fsubCashReceiptSale*. Click the fsubCashReceiptSale in the Chapter Forms section of the Navigation Pane, press Ctrl+C, then press Ctrl+V. In the Save Form As dialog box, change the name to fsubCashReceiptLoanAgreement, then click OK.
4. Open fsubCashReceiptLoanAgreement in Design view, located in the Unassigned Objects section of the Navigation Pane. Change the Customer # label to Creditor #. Change the Invoice # label to Loan #. Change the Customer Check # label to Creditor Check #.
5. Open the Property Sheet, select Form from the combo box if it is not already selected, click the Data tab and click the Query Builder button in the Record Source property control box. Click Yes to build a query based on the table. Add all fields from *tblCashReceipt* to the QBE grid. Set the Criteria for CRTypeID to "02" to limit the cash receipts displayed to receipts from loan issues. Close the query and accept the changes.
6. Press and hold the Shift key and click the CashAccountID, PayorID, and EventID controls in the form's Detail section; on the Data tab change Enabled to No and Locked to Yes. On the Other tab, change Tab Stop to No.
7. Set default values. Click the CRTypeID control in the form's Detail section, and change the Default Value on the Property Sheet's Data tab to "02". Use the same method to set the CashAccountID to 303.
8. Select Form from the Property Sheet combo box; click the Format tab and change the caption to fsubCashReceiptLoanAgreement. Save and close the form.

EXERCISE 11.19: CREATING THE CASH RECEIPT LOAN ISSUE ENTRY FORM—MAKING CHANGES TO THE CASH RECEIPT SALE FORM—PART 2

1. Make a copy of *frmCashReceiptSale*. Click the frmCashReceiptSale in the Chapter Forms section of the Navigation Pane; press Ctrl+C and then press Ctrl+V. In the Save Form As dialog box, change the name to frmCashReceiptLoanAgreement and then click OK.
2. Open frmCashReceiptLoanAgreement in Design view, located in the Unassigned Objects section of the Navigation Pane.
3. Change the header to Cash Receipt Entry – Loan Issue.
4. Delete the Update Balance Due button by clicking on it and pressing the Delete key.
5. Change the source for the subform. Open the Property Sheet, click the subform in the form's Detail section, click the Data tab, and change the Source Object to fsubCashReceiptLoanAgreement. Click the Other tab and change the name to fsubCashReceiptLoanAgreement.
6. Select Form in the Property Sheet combo box; click the Format tab and change the Caption to frmCashReceiptLoanAgreement. Click the Data tab, and choose tblLoanAgreement from the list in the Record Source control box. Click the Record Source Builder button to open the query behind the form. Click Yes to the dialog box because you want to build a query. Click Show Table in the Query Setup group; click the Queries tab; scroll down the list; double-click qryCreditorInfo and click Close. Create a link between the two field rosters on FinancierID, and create another link between the two field rosters on LoanID.
7. Add the following fields to the QBE grid from the tblLoanAgreement field roster: LoanID, FinancierID, LoanAmount, LoanDate, and MaturityDate.
8. Add the following fields to the QBE grid from the qryCreditorInfo field roster: FinancierName, FinancierAddress1, FinancierAddress2, CityStateZip, FinancierTelephone, and FinancierPrimaryContact. Close the query and save your changes.
9. Notice that all of the controls in the Form detail have the green triangle in the upper left-hand corner to indicate that the controls are invalid. Change the labels as indicated in Figure 11.24.
10. Delete the Prior Receipts and Balance Due controls and labels. Change the Invoice Date label to Loan Date, and move it up as indicated in Figure 11.24.
11. On the Design tab, click Add Existing Fields, click MaturityDate, and click and drag it to just below the LoanDate control in the form's Detail section. Use Figure 11.24 as a guide for formatting and sizing the label and control. Use the same property values in Exercise 11.18, Step 3, to make MaturityDate a reference field. Close the Add Existing Fields panel and open the Property Sheet.
12. Change the source and names for each of the form's Field controls as indicated in Figure 11.24. Change the Control Source on the Data tab, and change the Name on the Other tab.
13. Update the tab order. Click Tab Order in the Control Layout on the Arrange tab. Move MaturityDate up until it is just below LoanDate. Click OK. Save your changes and switch to Form view.
14. Enter the cash receipt information in Figure 11.25. If you sort *tblCashReceipt* by date, you will notice that the remittance advice (RA) number for loan issue is out of sequence. Normally, this would indicate an error or irregularity. In our case, however, the RA #s are out of sequence because we recorded all of the cash receipts from sales long before we introduced the financing process. Close the form when you are done.

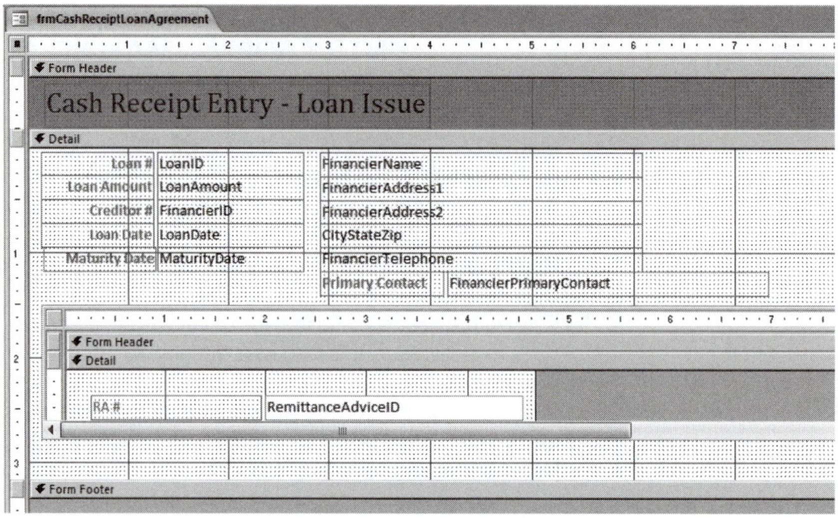

Fig. 11.24 Cash Receipt Loan Issue Entry form in Design view.

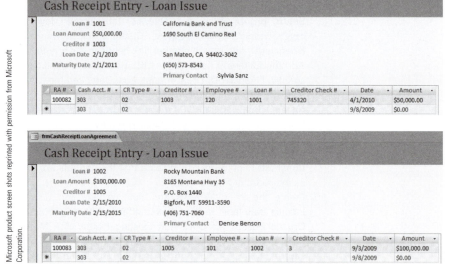

Microsoft product screen shot reprinted with permission from Microsoft Corporation.

Fig. 11.25 Cash Receipt Loan Issue Entry form in Form view with cash receipt information.

Microsoft product screen shots reprinted with permission from Microsoft Corporation.

Recording Cash Paid to Creditors

When Pipefitters Supply Company makes loan payments to its creditors, each cash disbursement is for only one loan, even if Pipefitters has more than one loan payment due to the same creditor on the same day. Loan payments, in general, may be a payment of principal, interest, or a combination of principal and interest. Since Pipefitters uses only installment loans, each payment has a principal component and an interest component. Principal and interest are determined by the terms of the loan agreement: loan amount (the principal), annual interest rate, and the frequency of the payments. Since principal plus interest equals the amount of the cash disbursement, a separate fulfillment table containing the principal and interest information for each scheduled payment will link the Loan Agreement table to the Cash Disbursement table. You can use the loan agreement information to construct a ***loan amortization table*** in Excel, which computes the total payment, the principal amount, the interest amount, and the remaining principal balance.

tblFulfillment-LACD will store LoanID as a foreign key to link it to *tblLoanAgreement*. Also, the primary key of *tblFulfillment-LACD* will be stored as a foreign key in *tblCashDisbursement* to provide the link between those two tables. Figure 11.26 shows the addition of the Fulfillment table to the financing process data model.[2]

Fig. 11.26 Financing process data model with *tblFulfillment-LACD.*

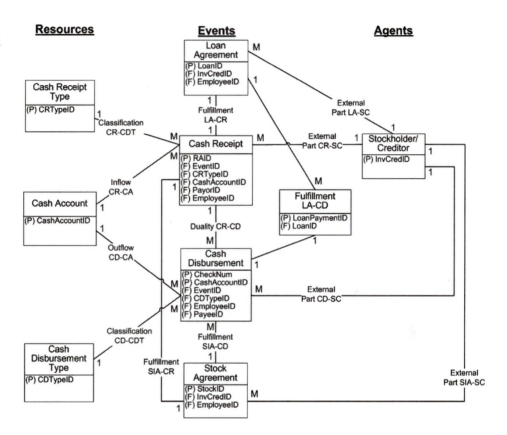

Cash Disbursement Table

In Chapter 10, you made changes to the Cash Disbursement table similar to the changes you made to the Cash Receipt table earlier in this chapter. You added a foreign key for Cash Disbursement Type, made the external agent and event foreign keys generic and removed referential integrity from links to them, and you created a Cash Disbursement Type table, which enables Pipefitters to capture data about many types of cash disbursements. Since you already experienced the ripple effect from adding a Cash Receipt Type table in this chapter—having to change other Access objects due to object name changes as well as structural changes—we took care of making similar changes related to the cash disbursement event revisions.

---

[2]Normally, a fulfillment relationship-table that links *tblLoanAgreement* to *tblCashDisbursement* contains the primary keys of the two tables it links. However, since the relationship table links a one-to-many relationship, we can maintain the Required field property for the EventID foreign key in *tblCashDisbusrement* by using LoanPaymentID as the EventID foreign key.

Cash Disbursement Type Table

As mentioned above, you created the Cash Disbursement Type table in Chapter 10 to enable the Cash Disbursement table to capture cash payments from both purchases and labor acquisitions. Now you need to add a third Cash Disbursement Type to the table for loan payments. Add the data in the last row of the Cash Disbursement Type table shown in Figure 11.27.

Fig. 11.27 Loan Payment type added to *tblCash-DisbursementType* in Datasheet.

Microsoft product screen shot reprinted with permission from Microsoft Corporation.

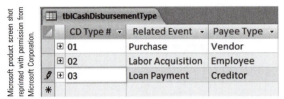

CD Type #	Related Event	Payee Type
01	Purchase	Vendor
02	Labor Acquisition	Employee
03	Loan Payment	Creditor

Fulfillment Loan Agreement-Cash Disbursement Table and Its Relationships

The Fulfillment Loan Agreement-Cash Disbursement table is where the amounts of each loan payment allocated to principal and interest will be stored. The table will have a primary key, LoanPaymentID, a foreign key (LoanID) to link it to *tblLoanAgreement*, scheduled payment date, payment number, and the principal and interest amounts. Additionally, the primary key from *tblFulfillment-LACD* will be stored in *tblCashDisbursement* as a foreign key, completing the link between *tblLoanAgreement* and *tblCashDisbursement*.

EXERCISE 11.20: CREATING THE FULFILLMENT LOAN AGREEMENT-CASH DISBURSEMENT TABLE

Create a new table.

1. Click the Create tab, and click Table Design in the Tables group.
2. Enter the Field Names, Data Types, and Properties for the five attributes of this table in Figure 11.28. LoanPaymentID is the Primary Key.
3. Close the table and name it tblFulfillment-LACD.
4. Save your work and close the table.

Import the Loan Payment Schedule data for *tblFulfillment-LACD* from *Ch11.xlsx*.

5. Click Excel on the External Data ribbon. Click the Browse button to find the location where you stored *Ch11.xlsx*. Double-click Ch11.xlsx.
6. Click the Radio Button for the second option Append a copy of the records to the table: and select tblFulfillment-LACD from the combo box. Click OK.
7. In the next dialog box, highlight the worksheet tblFulfillment-LACD. Click Next twice.
8. In the last dialog box, tblFulfillment-LACD should already be entered in the *Import to Table:* textbox. Click Finish. Open tblFulfillment-LACD in datasheet view to verify that all 72 records were imported into the database.

Fig. 11.28
tblFulfillment-LACD
**Fields and completed
table in Datasheet view.**

Field Name	LoanPaymentID	LoanID	PaymentDueDate
Data Type		Text	Date/Time
Field Size	5	4	
Format			Short Date
Input Mask	00000;;_	0000;;_	99/99/0000;;_
Caption	Loan Payment ID	Loan #	Due Date
Required	Yes	Yes	Yes
Allow Zero Length	No	No	
Indexed	Yes (No Duplicates)	Yes (Duplicates OK)	No

Field Name	PaymentNum	PrincipalAmount	InterestAmount
Data Type	Number	Currency	Currency
Format / Field Size	Integer	Currency	Currency
Decimal Places	0	2	2
Caption	Payment #	Principal	Interest
Default Value		0	0
Validation Rule	>0	>=0	>=0
Validation Text	Payment # must be an integer greater than zero.	Principal amount cannot be negative.	Interest amount cannot be negative.
Required	Yes	Yes	Yes
Indexed	No	No	No

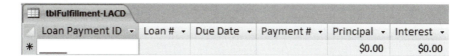

EXERCISE 11.21: CREATING RELATIONSHIPS WITH *TBLFULFILLMENT-LACD*

1. Click the Database Tools tab, click Relationships in the Show/Hide group, and minimize the Navigation Pane and the Ribbon. Your Relationship window should look like Figure 11.22.
2. Hide the tables that are not part of the financing process by clicking them and pressing the Delete key: *tblCustomer*, *tblEmployee_1* (employee-as-external agent), and *tblSale*.
3. Right-click an empty space in the Relationship window, click Show Table, double-click tblFulfillment-LACD to add it to the Relationship window. Click the Close button.
4. Move and resize tblFulfillment-LACD as indicated in Figure 11.29.
5. Create the link between *tblLoanAgreement* and *tblFulfillment-LACD*. Click LoanID in the tblLoanAgreement field roster and drag it onto LoanID in the

6. Create the link between *tblFulfillment-LACD* and *tblCashDisbursement*. Click LoanPaymentID in the tblFulfillment-LACD field roster and drag it onto EventID in the tblCashDisbursement field roster. Do **not** check Enforce Referential Integrity. Click Create in the dialog box.

7. Finally, create the participation relationship between *tblStockholderCreditor* and *tblCashDisbursement* by dragging FinancierID from *tblStockholderCreditor* to EventID in *tblCashDisbursement*. Do **not** check Enforce Referential Integrity. Click Create in the dialog box when you are done. Your Relationship window should look like the one in Figure 11.29.

8. Close the Relationship window and click the Yes button in the dialog box to save your changes.

Fig. 11.29 Relationship window for financing process after addition of *tblFulfillment-LACD.*

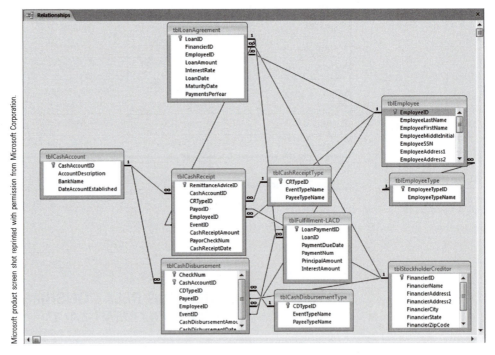

Microsoft product screen shot reprinted with permission from Microsoft Corporation.

The Loan Payment Entry Form

Pipefitters Supply Company pays its loans in accordance with the terms of the loan agreement, which are stored in *tblLoanAgreement*. Details of each scheduled payment are stored in *tblFulfillment-LACD*. Creditor information is stored in *tblStockholderCreditor*, and Cash Disbursement information is stored in *tblCashDisbursement*.

Unlike other forms you have created for Pipefitters Supply Company, the Loan Payment Entry form will be organized by creditor, and it will have three subforms. The first subform contains the *tblLoanAgreement* fields, and it is linked to the main form by FinancierID. The second subform, *tblFulfillment-LACD*, is linked to the Loan Agreement subform by LoanID. The third subform, *tblCashDisbursement*, contains the only active fields. It is linked to the main form by PayeeID/FinancierID. You will first use Form Wizard to build the *tblStockholderCreditor/tblLoanAgreement/tblFulfillment-LACD* form. You will then add a third subform control for *tblCashDisbursement*.

EXERCISE 11.22: USING FORM WIZARD TO CREATE THE LOAN PAYMENT ENTRY FORM

1. Open qryCreditorInfo in Design view. Click the column selector (just above the field cell on the QBE grid) for LoanID. Press the Delete key to delete LoanID from the QBE grid. Save and close the query.
2. Click qryCreditorInfo in the Unassigned Objects section in the Navigation Pane. Click More Forms in the Forms group of the Create tab. Click Form Wizard.
3. You should see qryCreditorInfo in the Tables/Queries list box. If not, click the list box arrow, and click Query: qryCreditorInfo in the list. Click the >> button to move all fields into the Selected Fields panel.
4. Click the Tables/Queries list box arrow, and click Table: LoanAgreement from the list. Select all fields. Before you click the >> button to place all Available Fields into the Selected Fields list, be sure that FinancierPrimaryContact is highlighted in the Selected Fields panel.
5. Select Table: Fulfillment-LACD from the Tables/Queries list. Make sure that PaymentsPerYear is highlighted in the Selected Fields panel before adding all fields in *tblFulfillment-LACD* to the Selected Fields list. Click Next. Access should select by qryCreditorInfo to view the data by default. Notice that the illustration shows creditor information in the form subforms for loan agreement information and fulfillment (scheduled loan payment detail) information.
6. Click Next. Select Tabular format for both subforms.
7. Click Next. Click the Office style if it is not already selected, and click Next.
8. Save your form and subforms as frmCashDisbursementLoan, fsub1CashDisbursementLoan, and fsub2CashDisbursementLoan, respectively. Click the Finish button. Your form should look like the one illustrated in Figure 11.30.
9. Switch to Design view. Press Ctrl+A, click the Arrange ribbon, and click Remove in the Control Layout group. Use Figure 11.31 as a guide to make the changes described in the following steps.
10. Change the header on the form as indicated. Make a copy of the form title and paste it into each of the subforms. Reduce the font on the subform titles and change the names accordingly.
11. Change the Financier # label to Creditor #. Delete all the form labels except Creditor # and Primary Contact. Bold the labels and Align Right. Resize and move the creditor information controls as indicated in Figure 11.31, and make them reference fields.
    - Click Property Sheet on the Design ribbon.
    - Select all of the creditor information controls and click the Format tab on the Property Sheet. Change the Back Style and the Border Style to Transparent.
    - On the Data tab set Enabled to No and Locked to Yes.
    - On the Other tab, change Tab Stop to No.
12. Save and close the form.
13. Open qryCreditorInfo in Design view. Double-Click LoanID in the tblLoanAgreement field roster to add it to the QBE grid. Save and close the query.

Fig. 11.30 *frm-CashDisbursementLoan* in Form view after using Form Wizard.

Fig. 11.31 Completed Loan Repayment Entry form in Design view.

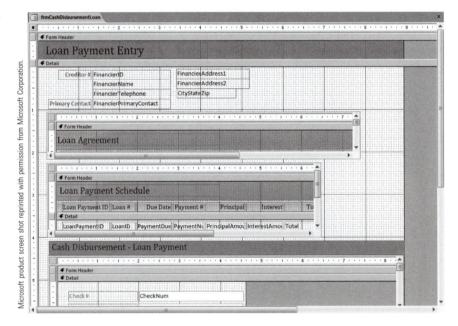

EXERCISE 11.23: MAKING IMPROVEMENTS TO *FRMCASHDISBURSEMENTLOAN* AND THE FIRST TWO SUBFORMS

1. Open fsub1CashDisbursementLoan, the Loan Agreement subform, in Layout view. Resize the labels and controls as indicated in Figures 11.31 and 11.32.

2. Switch to Design view. Select all of the controls and make them reference fields by following Exercise 11.22, Step 10.

3. With the Property Sheet still open, select Form from the Property Sheet combo box and click the Format tab. Change the Default View to Single Form because each record in the Cash Disbursement Loan Entry form will contain only one of a creditor's loan agreements—creditors with multiple loan agreements will have multiple records in the Cash Disbursement Loan Entry form.

4. Eliminate many of the subform's navigation controls by making the following changes to the Form Format properties:
   - Set Record Selectors to No.
   - Set Navigation Button to No.
   - Set Scroll Bars to Neither because only one loan agreement will be visible for each record in the form.
   - Set Close Button to No.
   - Set Min Max Buttons to None.

5. On the Data tab set the following properties to No: Allow Additions, Allow Deletions, and Allow Edits.

6. Save and close fsub1CashDisbursementLoan.

7. Alter the query behind the form to add a Total Payment Due field based on a horizontal computation. Although creating computational queries outside of a form and using them as a Record Source (like *qryCreditorInfo*) is a best practice (easier to access the query), you will add a computational field in a query behind the form to enhance your database knowledge and skill. Open fsub2CashDisbursementLoan, the Loan Payment Schedule subform, in Design view. Follow Step 5 in Exercise 11.19 to open the Query Builder. Add all of the fields from the *tblFulfillment-LACD* field roster to the QBE grid. Scroll to the first empty column in the QBE grid and click the Field cell. Using either the Zoom Box (Shift+F2) or Expression Builder (on the Design ribbon in the Query Setup group) enter the following expression to compute the total payment due: Total: [tblFulfillment-LACD]! [PrincipalAmount] + [tblFulfillment-LACD]![InterestAmount]. Close the query and save your changes.

8. Click and drag the right edge of the Form Detail area to make room for your new field, Total.

9. Make a copy of the Interest Amount control and label by holding the Shift key, clicking the Interest Amount control and label, and pressing Ctrl+C, Ctrl+V. You may use the tools in the Control Alignment group on the Arrange ribbon to help you move and align the Interest Amount label.

10. Change the label to Total. Click the copy of InterestAmount; open the Property Sheet to the Data tab; change the control Source to Total; click the Other tab and change the name to Total.

11. Follow Steps 1–5 for fsub2CashDisbursementLoan to limit the form's navigation capability, except leave the Form's Default View set to Continuous Forms. Add a line just below the field controls to clearly separate the scheduled loan payments. You will need to grab the Form Footer bar at the top and drag it down a little bit to make room for the line. Save and close the form.

Fig. 11.32 Completed
Loan Repayment Entry
form in Form view.

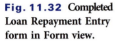

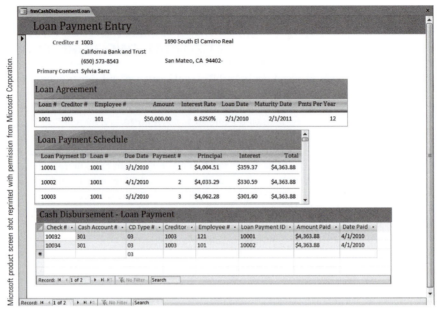

EXERCISE 11.24: ADDING THE CASH DISBURSEMENT SUBFORM TO *FRMCASHDISBURSEMENTLOAN*

Add the Cash Disbursement Loan Payment subform to *frmCashDisbursementLoan*.

1. Open frmCashDisbursementLoan in Design view; minimize the Navigation Pane; open the Property Sheet and click the Data tab. Add a Cash Disbursement Loan Payment subform. Return to Design view. Make room for another subform by dragging the top of the Form Footer bar down 1-1/2 inches. Click Subform/ Subreport in the Controls group, move your cursor just below the bottom-left corner of the Loan Payment Schedule subform and click to start the Subform Wizard.

    • Leave the Use existing Tables and Queries radio button selected, click Next.
    • Select Table: tblCashDisbursement from the Tables/Queries combo box, and add all available fields to the Selected Fields panel. Select Table: tblFulfill-ment-LACD and add LoanID to the Selected Fields panel.
    • Click Next; click the Define my own radio button because you want to link the subform to the form on two fields (the "select from a list" option only allows for one link). Select FinancierID and LoanID, respectively for the Form/Report fields. Select PayeeID and LoanID, respectively for the Subform/Subreport fields.
    • Click Next; name the subform fsub3CashDisbursementLoan and click Finish.

2. Delete the fsub3CashDisbursementLoan label and move the subform down to make room for a title. Make a copy of the Loan Payment Schedule title, move it right above the new subform, and make it the same size as the fsub3CashDisbursementLoan. Change the name to Cash Disbursement – Loan Payment., and change the Fill color to match the Form Header color

    • Select Form Header in the Property Sheet combo box; click the Back Color Builder button; click More Colors and write down the RGB values: Red 121, Green 167, and Blue 227.
    • Click the Cash Disbursement – Loan Payment label and use the Back Color Builder to enter RGB color values. Switch to Form view to verify that the colors match.

3. Save and close the form.

Make changes to *fsub3CashDisbursementLoan*.

4. Restore the Navigation Pane and open fsub3CashDisbursementLoan in Datasheet view. Change the Event # label to Loan Payment ID and the Payee # label to Creditor #. Click the Datasheet Selector; click the More menu in the Records group; click Column Width and click the Best Fit button to resize the columns.
5. Open the Query Builder like you did in Step 1 for *frmCashDisbursementLoan*. Change the Criteria for CDTypeID to 03 to limit the cash disbursements displayed to loan payments. Close the query and accept the changes.
6. Click the CDTypeID control and set the Default Value (on the Data tab of the Property Sheet) to "03".
7. Disable CDTypeID and PayeeID. Press and hold the Shift key and click PayeeID to select both CDTypeID and PayeeID. On the Data tab on the Property Sheet change the Enabled property to No and the Locked property to Yes. Click the Other tab on the Property Sheet and change the Tab Stop property to No.
8. Save and close the form.

Make final changes to *frmCashDisbursementLoan*.

9. Open frmCashDisbursementLoan in Layout view; minimize the Navigation Pane and move and resize all three subforms as illustrated in Figures 11.31 and 11.32 to display all of the data. Resize the Cash Disbursement – Loan Payment title to match width of the subform.
10. Switch to Design view. Open the Property Sheet; click CashDisbursementAmount in *fsub3CashDisbusrsementLoan* to select it (use the horizontal scroll bar on the form and both scroll bars on the subform to make CashDisbursementAmount visible); click the Data tab; click the Default Value control to show the Builder button and click the button (see Figure 11.33). Drag the edge of the Expression Builder to make it wider so you can see the names of the forms in the first panel. Double-click Forms in the first panel; double-click Loaded Forms; double-click frmCashDisbursementLoan and double-click fsub2CashDisbursementLoan to display the subform's list of controls in the second panel. Scroll down the second panel and double-click Total to add its complete path to the Expression Pane; click OK to make this expression the default value for CashDisbursementAmount.
11. Add a second link between *fsub1CashDisbursementLoan* and *frmCash DisbursementLoan*. Click fsub1CashDisbursementLoan in the Detail section. Click the Data tab; change the Link Master Fields by clicking the Builder button to open the Subform Field Linker. Add LoanID as a second Master Field and Child Field, which will cause the subform to only show one loan agreement for each record of the main form. This is another reason that you added LoanID to *qryCreditorInfo*.
12. Change the Link Master Field for *fsub2CashDisbursementLoan*. Click fsub2CashDisbursementLoan in the Detail section. Click the Data tab; change the Link Master Fields property to LoanID to link it directly to the main form, yet another reason that you added LoanID to *qryCreditorInfo*.
13. Save your changes and close the form.
14. Open frmCashDisbursementLoan in Form view, and minimize the ribbon to see the entire form. Enter the first two loan payments for each of the two loans using the following data:
    - Rocky Mountain Bank (Creditor # 1003), Loan # 1001, Payment #1: Check # 10032; Cash Account # 301; Employee # 121; Loan Payment ID 10001; Amount Paid $4,363.88; Date Paid 3/1/2010.
    - Rocky Mountain Bank (Creditor # 1005), Loan # 1002, Payment #1: Check # 10033; Cash Account # 301; Employee # 101; Loan Payment ID 10013; Amount Paid $1,991.94; Date Paid 3/15/2010.

- California Bank and Trust (Creditor # 1003), Loan # 1001, Payment #2: Check # 10034; Cash Account # 301; Employee # 121; Loan Payment ID 10002; Amount Paid $4,363.88; Date Paid 4/1/2010.
- Rocky Mountain Bank (Creditor # 1005), Loan # 1001, Payment #2: Check # 10035; Cash Account # 301; Employee # 121; Loan Payment ID 10014; Amount Paid $1,991.94; Date Paid 4/15/2010.

15. Close the form.

Fig. 11.33 Expression Builder for CashDisbursement-Amount default value.

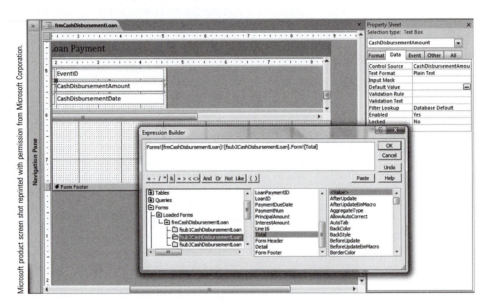

Microsoft product screen shot reprinted with permission from Microsoft Corporation.

You have completed the debt financing portion of the financing process.

Recording the Stock Agreement Event

Pipefitters Supply Company raised its initial capital by issuing stock to its two original owners, and also issued additional shares of stock for subsequent contributions by the owners. They recently began contacting potential investors about investing in Pipefitters Supply Company. When they find a suitable investor and agree on the basic terms of the stock issue, Pipefitters' accountants draws up a ***stock subscription***. A stock subscription is the agreement between the issuing company and the pending stockholder that specifies all of the information relevant to the stock issue, including the parties involved, number of shares to be issued, price per share, and the issue date. Even though the agreement is called a stock subscription, we refer to it as a stock agreement to make comparisons between debt financing and equity financing database objects easier to follow.

The Stock Subscription Table (tblStockAgreement)

Like a loan agreement, a stock subscription is a commitment event that leads to a cash receipt (receiving the stock issue proceeds), and later to cash disbursements for dividend payments. Figure 11.5, shows a stock subscription linked to one employee and one investor. These two participation relationships are implemented by adding foreign keys to the stock subscription table, *tblStockAgreement*. We omitted the reservation relationship with Cash Account to simplify the database. Figure 11.34 shows the six fields for *tblStockAgreement*.

EXERCISE 11.25: CREATING THE STOCK AGREEMENT TABLE

1. Create a new table. Click the Create tab, and click Table Design in the Tables group.
2. Create the primary key. Type StockID in first Field Name box and then click Primary Key in the Tools group.
3. Press F6 to move to the Field Properties section of the window. Enter the Field Properties for StockID listed in Figure 11.34.
4. Enter the remaining Data Types and Field Properties for the foreign keys FinancierID and EmployeeID as listed in Figure 11.34.
5. Enter the remaining attributes in Figure 11.34. Leave the IssueDate default value blank instead of using the current date function because stock issues may not take place for days or weeks after the agreement is negotiated.
6. Save the table as tblStockAgreement.

Fig. 11.34 Fields for *tblStockAgreement.*

Field Name	Stock ID	FinancierID	EmployeeID
Data Type	Text	Text	Text
Field Size	4	4	3
Format			
Input Mask	0000;;_	0000;;_	000;;_
Caption	Stock #	Stockholder #	Employee #
Required	Yes	Yes	Yes
Allow Zero Length	No	No	No
Indexed	Yes (No Duplicates)	Yes (DuplicatesOK)	Yes (DuplicatesOK)

Primary Keys and Foreign Keys

Field Name	SharesIssued	PricePerShare	StockIssueDate
Data Type	Number	Currency	Date/Time
Field Size	Long Integer		
Format		Currency	Short Date
Decimal Places	0	2	
Input Mask			99/99/0000;;_
Caption	# of Shares	$ Per Share	Issue Date
Default Value			
Validation Rule	>0	>0	
Validation Text	Number of shares issued must be positive integers.	Price per share must be positive.	
Required	Yes	Yes	Yes
Indexed	No	No	No

Attributes

EXERCISE 11.26: CREATING RELATIONSHIPS WITH
TBLSTOCKAGREEMENT

1. In the Database Tools tab, click Relationships in the Show/Hide group and minimize the Navigation Pane. Minimize the Ribbon to increase the Relationship window by right-clicking on the Menu Bar and selecting Minimize the Ribbon. Your Relationship window should look like the one in Figure 11.29.
2. Add *tblStockAgreement* to the Relationship window. Right-click an empty spot in the Relationship window and select Show Table. Double-click tblStockAgreement and then click Close.
3. Use Figure 11.35 as a guide. Resize and move tblStockAgreement into place as shown in Figure 11.35.
4. Create the links between the agent tables and *tblStockAgreement*. Remember to drag from the table with the primary key to the table with the foreign key.
5. After you click and drag the primary key to the foreign key, the Edit Relationships dialog box appears. Make sure that the correct attributes appear in the tables you dragged from and to. The relationship type at the bottom of the dialog box should always be one-to-many. Check Enforce Referential Integrity and Cascade Update Related Fields. Finally, click Create in the dialog box.
6. Link *tblStockAgreement* (StockID) to *tblCashReceipt* (EventID) using Steps 4 and 5 as a guide, but do **not** enforce referential integrity.
7. When you are finished, your Relationship window should look like the one in Figure 11.35.
8. Close the Relationship window and click the Yes button in the dialog box to save your changes. Right-click the Menu Bar and select Minimize the Ribbon to uncheck the box and restore the ribbon.

Fig. 11.35 Relationship window after adding *tblStockAgreement* and relationships.

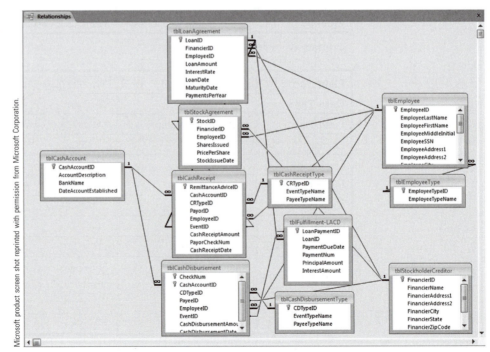

Microsoft product screen shot reprinted with permission from Microsoft Corporation.

The Stock Subscription Entry Form

The Stock Subscription Entry form is relatively simple. It is similar to the Loan Agreement Entry form you created earlier in the chapter. The form populates a single table, *tblStockAgreement*, and the reference data comes from the Stockholder/Creditor table.

EXERCISE 11.27: CREATING QUERIES FOR THE STOCK SUBSCRIPTION ENTRY FORM

1. Click the Create tab and click Query Design in the Other group. Double-click tblStockAgreement in the Show Table dialog box. Close the dialog box.
2. Add all of the attributes from the field roster to the QBE grid.
3. Click the first empty Field cell on the QBE grid. Use either the Zoom Box (Shift+F2) or Expression Builder (on the Ribbon in the Query Setup group) to enter the following expression: Total: [SharesIssued] * [PricePerShare]. Save your query as qryStockAgreement and close the query.

EXERCISE 11.28: ALTERING THE LOAN AGREEMENT FORM TO CREATE THE STOCK AGREEMENT ENTRY FORM

1. Click frmLoanAgreement in the Unassigned Objects section of the Navigation Pane. Press Ctrl+C, then Ctrl+V to copy and paste it. Name the new form frmStockAgreement. Open frmStockAgreement in Design view (in the Unassigned Objects section). Use Figure 11.36 as a guide.
2. Change the Form Header title to Stock Subscription Entry. Change the Loan # label to Stock #. Change the Creditor # label to Stockholder #. Change the Amount label to Expected Proceeds. Change the Interest Rate label to $ Per Share. Change the Loan Date label to Issue Date. Change the Pmts Per Year label to # of Shares.
3. Open the Property Sheet and select Form from the combo box. Click the Format tab and change the Caption to frmStockAgreement. Click the Data tab and click the Record Source Builder button to open the Query Builder. Delete the tblLoanAgreement field roster from the Table Pane; click Show Table in the Query Setup group; click the Queries tab; double-click qryStockAgreement and click Close. Add all of the *qryStockAgreement* attributes to the QBE grid to the left of the FinancierName.
4. Join the two field rosters on FinancierID. Close the query and save your changes. Click the Format tab on the Property Sheet (select Form from the combo box if it is not already selected) and change the Caption to frmStockAgreement.
5. Click the LoanID control; click the Property Sheet Data tab; change the Control Source to StockID; click the Other tab and change the name to StockID.
6. Repeat Step 5, with the following controls:
   - Change LoanAmount to Total.
   - Change InterestRate to PricePerShare. On the Format tab change the Format to Currency and Decimal Places to 2.
   - Change LoanDate to StockIssueDate.
   - Change PaymentsPerYear to SharesIssued. On the Format tab change the Format to Standard and leave the Decimal Places set to 0.
7. Delete the MaturityDate control and label.

8. Rearrange the controls and their labels to be consistent with Figure 11.36. Change the Tab Stop order (in the Control Layout group on the Arrange ribbon) to reflect the new order of the controls.
9. Drag the Form Footer Bar upward to eliminate blank space below the form's controls.
10. Save your changes and switch to Form view to enter the following Stock Agreement data.
    * Stock # 1001; Stockholder # 1001; Employee # 101; # of Shares 50000; $ Per Share 1; Issue Date 9/3/2009.
    * Stock # 1002; Stockholder # 1002; Employee # 101; # of Shares 50000; $ Per Share 1; Issue Date 9/3/2009.
    * Stock # 1003; Stockholder # 1001; Employee # 101; # of Shares 25000; $ Per Share 1; Issue Date 11/1/2009.
    * Stock # 1004; Stockholder # 1002; Employee # 101; # of Shares 10000; $ Per Share 1; Issue Date 11/1/2009.
    * Stock # 1005; Stockholder # 1004; Employee # 101; # of Shares 35000; $ Per Share 3; Issue Date 3/10/2010.
11. Close the form.

Fig. 11.36 Stock Agreement Entry form in Design view and Form view.

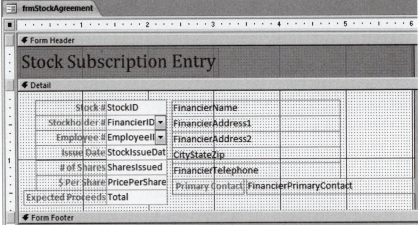

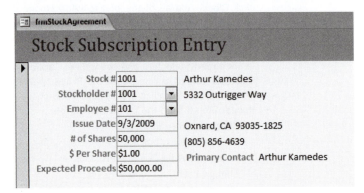

Microsoft product screen shots reprinted with permission from Microsoft Corporation.

Recording Cash Receipts from Stock Issues

Earlier in the chapter you added a Cash Receipt Type table, made changes to the Cash Receipt table, and removed referential integrity from some relationships with the Cash Receipt table to allow *tblCashReceipt* to capture data from many types of Cash Receipt events. These changes also accommodate the recording of different types of external agents, customers, stockholders, and creditors, whose data are kept in separate tables.

The Cash Receipt Stock Issue Entry Form

The Cash Receipt Stock Issue form is similar to the Cash Receipt Loan Issue form. When one of Pipefitters' accountants receives a stockholder's check, he or she should be able to compare the amount received to the product of the number of shares issued times the price per share stated in the related stock agreement. To simplify the form there is only one cash receipt associated with each stock agreement; you do not need to compute prior collections and balance due. You will create a form to record cash receipts from stock issues by modifying the Cash Receipt Loan Agreement form.

EXERCISE 11.29: CREATING THE CASH RECEIPT STOCK ISSUE ENTRY FORM—PART 1

Before creating the Cash Receipt Stock Issue Entry form, add the following Cash Receipt Type record to *tblCashReceiptType*: CR Type # 03; Related Event Stock Issue; Payee Type Stockholder.

Use Figure 11.37 and 11.38 as guides for this exercise.

1. Make a copy of *fsubCashReceiptLoanAgreement*. Click the fsubCashReceiptLoan Agreement in the Unassigned Objects section of the Navigation Pane, press Ctrl +C, then press Ctrl+V. In the Save Form As dialog box, change the name to fsubCashReceiptStockIssue and then click OK.
2. Open fsubCashReceiptStockIssue in Design view, located in the Unassigned Objects section of the Navigation Pane. Change the following labels: Loan # to Stock #, Loan Amount to Issue Amount, and Creditor # to Stockholder #.
3. Open the Property Sheet, select Form from the combo box if it is not already selected; click the Data tab and click the Query Builder button in the Record Source property control box. Click Yes to build a query based on the table. Add all fields from *tblCashReceipt* to the QBE grid. Set the Criteria for CRTypeID to "03" to limit the cash receipts displayed to receipts from stock issues. Close the query and accept the changes.
4. Press and hold the Shift key and click the CashAccountID, PayorID, and EventID controls in the form's Detail section; on the Data tab change Enabled to No and Locked to Yes. On the Other tab, change Tab Stop to No.
5. Set default values. Click the CRTypeID control in the form's Detail section, and change the Default Value on the Property Sheet's Data tab to "03". Use the same method to set the CashAccountID Default Value to 303. Save your changes and close the form.

Fig. 11.37 Cash Receipt Stock Issue Entry form in Design view and Form view.

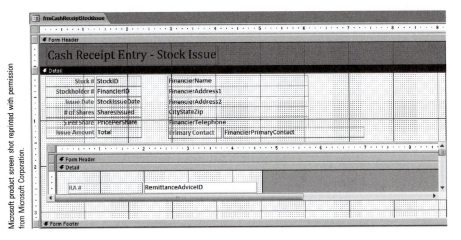

Fig. 11.38 Cash Receipt Stock Issue Entry form in Design view.

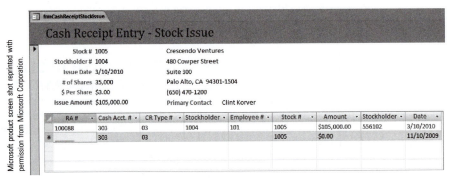

EXERCISE 11.30: CREATING THE CASH RECEIPT STOCK ISSUE ENTRY FORM—PART 2

Create the Stockholder Information query to list only stockholder information.

1. Click qryStockholderCreditorInfo in the Unassigned Objects section of the Navigation Pane. Press Ctrl+C, then Ctrl+V to copy and paste it. Name the new query qryStockholderInfo.

2. Open qryStockholderInfo in Design view (in the Unassigned Objects section). Click Show Table in the Show/Hide group; double-click tblStockAgreement to add it to the Table Pane; double-click StockID in the tblStockAgreement field roster to add it to the QBE grid and click Close. Adding StockID to the query limits the dynaset to only stockholders because only stockholders participate in stock agreements. Join the two field rosters on FinancierID. Save and close the query.

Make a copy of *frmCashReceiptLoanAgreement*.

3. Click frmCashReceiptLoanAgreement in the Unassigned Objects section of the Navigation Pane; press Ctrl+C and then press Ctrl+V. In the Save Form As dialog box, change the name to frmCashReceiptStockIssue; click OK.

Make changes to *frmCashReceiptLoanAgreement*.

4. Open frmCashReceiptStockIssue in Design view, located in the Unassigned Objects section of the Navigation Pane.

5. Change the header to Cash Receipt Entry – Stock Issue.

6. Delete the MaturityDate control and its label from the Detail section. Change the following labels: Creditor # to Stockholder #, Loan # to Stock #, Creditor Check # to Stockholder Check #, and Loan Date to Issue Date.

7. Select Form in the Property Sheet combo box; click the Format tab and change the Caption to frmCashReceiptStockIssue. Click the Data tab, and click the Record Source Builder button to open the query behind the form. Delete both field rosters. Click Show Table in the Query Setup group; click the Queries tab; scroll down the list and double-click qryStockAgreement and qryStockholder and then click OK. Create a link between the two field rosters on FinancierID. Create a second link between the field rosters on StockID.

8. Add all of the qryStockAgreement fields to the QBE grid. Then add all fields except FinancierID from the qryStockholderInfo field roster. Close the query and save your changes.

9. For the three controls with a green triangle in the upper left-hand corner (indicating that the controls are invalid), change the Control Source in the Data tab and Name in the Other tab. Change LoanID to StockID. Change LoanAmount to Total. Change LoanDate to StockIssueDate.

10. On the Design tab, click Add Existing Fields; click SharesIssued, and click and drag it to just below the IssueDate control in the form's Detail section. Click PricePerShare in the Field List and drag it to just below SharesIssued. Close the Add Existing Fields panel. Remove users' ability to edit these fields as you did in Step 8 of Exercise 11.22. Use Figure 11.37 as a guide for formatting and sizing the labels and controls.

11. Open the Property Sheet. Change the source for the subform. Open the Property Sheet if it is not already open; click the subform in the form's Detail section; click the Data tab and change the Source Object to fsubCashReceiptStockIssue. Click the Other tab and change the name to frmCashReceiptStockIssue. Use the Subform Field Linker like you did in Step 10 of Exercise 11.17 to change the Link Master Fields to StockID and FinancierID, and the corresponding Link Child Fields to EventID and PayorID, respectively.

12. Enter the cash receipt information in Figure 11.39. Close the form when you are done.

Fig. 11.39 Cash Receipt information for Stock Issues.

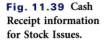

Microsoft product screen shot reprinted with permission from Microsoft Corporation.

Cash Receipt Entry - Stock Issue

Stock # 1001   Arthur Kamedes

RA #	Cash Acct. #	CR Type #	Stockholder #	Employee #	Stock #	Amount	Stockholder Check #	Date
100084	303	03	1001	101	1001	$50,000.00	2305	9/3/2009

Stock # 1002   Paul Van Cleave

RA #	Cash Acct. #	CR Type #	Stockholder #	Employee #	Stock #	Amount	Stockholder Check #	Date
100085	303	03	1002	101	1002	$50,000.00	3150	9/3/2009

Stock # 1003   Arthur Kamedes

RA #	Cash Acct. #	CR Type #	Stockholder #	Employee #	Stock #	Amount	Stockholder Check #	Date
100086	303	03	1001	101	1003	$25,000.00	2187	11/1/2009

Stock # 1004   Paul Van Cleave

RA #	Cash Acct. #	CR Type #	Stockholder #	Employee #	Stock #	Amount	Stockholder Check #	Date
100087	303	03	1002	101	1004	$10,000.00	3199	11/1/2009

Stock # 1005   Crescendo Ventures

RA #	Cash Acct. #	CR Type #	Stockholder #	Employee #	Stock #	Amount	Stockholder Check #	Date
100088	303	03	1004	101	1005	$105,000.00	556102	3/10/2010

Recording Dividends (Cash) Paid to Stockholders

When Pipefitters Supply Company pays dividends to stockholders, we make the simplifying assumption that each cash disbursement is for only one stock issue, even when two or more stock issues come from the same owner. Since Pipefitters only issues common stock, dividends paid for each stock issue is computed by multiplying the dividend per share by the number of shares in each stock issue. Although number of shares for each stock issue is stored in the Stock Agreement table, you need a fulfillment table similar to *tblfulfillment-LACD* to store the dividend payment rate. The new table will be named *tblFulfillment-SACD.*

   tblFulfillment-SACD will store StockID as a foreign key to link it to *tblStockAgreement.* Also, the primary key of *tblFulfillment-SACD* will be stored as a foreign key in *tblCashDisbursement* to provide the link between those two tables. Figure 11.40 shows the addition of the Fulfillment table to the financing process data model.[3]

Cash Disbursement Table and Cash Disbursement Type Table

You already made the necessary changes to the Cash Disbursement table and Cash Disbursement Type table, so no additional structural changes are needed. The only alteration to either table necessary to allow Pipefitters' AIS to record dividend payments is to add an additional record to the Cash Disbursement Type table: CD Type # 04, Related Event Dividend Payment, and Payee Type Stockholder.

Fig. 11.40 Financing process data model with *tblFulfillment-SICD.*

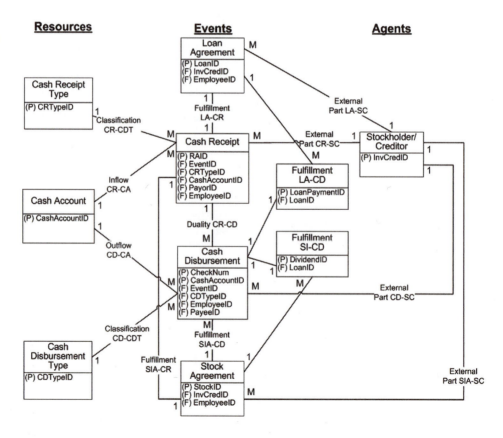

Fulfillment Stock Agreement-Cash Disbursement Table and Its Relationships

The Fulfillment Stock Agreement-Cash Disbursement table is where the dividend per share will be stored. The table will have a primary key (DividendID), a foreign key (StockID) to link it to *tblStockAgreement*, and the scheduled payment date. Additionally, the primary key from *tblFulfillment-SACD* will be stored in *tblCashDisbursement* as a foreign key, completing the link between *tblStockAgreement* and *tblCashDisbursement*.

EXERCISE 11.31: CREATING THE FULFILLMENT STOCK AGREEMENT-CASH DISBURSEMENT TABLE AND RELATIONSHIPS

1. Make a copy of *tblFulfillment-LACD*. Click tblFulfillment-LACD in the Unassigned Objects section of the Navigation Pane. Press Ctrl+C and then Ctrl+V. Type tblFulfillment-SACD in the Paste Table As dialog name box; click the Structure Only radio button and click OK.

2. Open tblFulfillment-SACD in Design view, also located in the Unassigned Objects section of the Navigation Pane. Change the following fields and properties:
   - Change the LoanPaymentID field to DividendID. Change the Caption to Dividend #.
   - Change the LoanID field to StockID. Change the Caption to Stock #.
   - Change the PaymentDueDate field to DividendDeclarationDate. Change the Caption to Date Declared.
   - Change the PrincipalAmount field to DividendPerShare. Change the Caption to Div. Per Share. Change the Validation Text to Dividend per share cannot be negative.

3. Delete PaymentNum and InterestAmount by clicking each one's Record Selector and pressing the Delete key.

4. Save your changes and close the table.

5. Import Dividend Declaration data for *tblFulfillment-SACD* from *Ch11.xlsx*.

6. Click the Database Tools tab, click Relationships in the Show/Hide group, and minimize the Navigation Pane and the Ribbon. Your Relationship window should look like Figure 11.35.

7. Hide *tblEmployee_1* (employee-as-external agent) by clicking it and pressing the Delete key.

8. Right-click and empty space in the Relationship window, click Show Table, double-click tblFulfillment-SACD to add it to the Relationship window. Click the Close button.

9. Move and resize tblFulfillment-SACD as indicated in Figure 11.41.

10. Create the link between *tblStockAgreement* and *tblFulfillment-SACD* by dragging LoanID from the tblStockAgreement field roster onto LoanID in the tblFulfillment-SACD field roster. Check Enforce Referential Integrity and Cascade Update Related Fields, and click Create in the dialog box when you are done.

11. Create the link between *tblFulfillment-SACD* and *tblCashDisbursement*. Click DividendID in the tblFulfillment-SACD field roster and drag it onto EventID in the tblCashDisbursement field roster. Do not check Enforce Referential Integrity. Click Create in the dialog box.

12. Since you already created the participation relationship between *tblStockholderCreditor* and *tblCashDisbursement* you are done creating relationships. Your Relationship window should look like the one in Figure 11.41. Close the Relationship window and click the Yes button in the dialog box to save your changes.

Fig. 11.41 Relationship window after adding *tblFulfillment-SACD* and relationships.

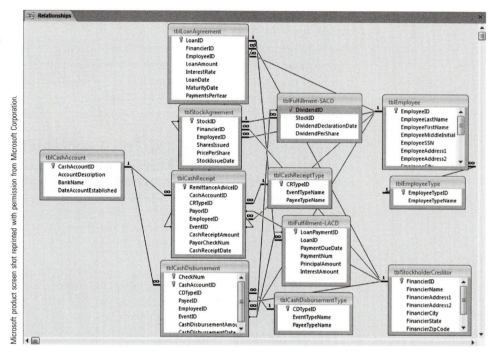

The Dividend Payment Entry Form

Pipefitters Supply Company pays a monthly dividend based on the number of shares outstanding as of the dividend date—we are ignoring corporate dividend rules such as declaration date, date of record, etc., to keep the complexity of the database to a manageable level. Details of each scheduled payment are stored in *tblFulfillment-SACD*. Stockholder information is stored in *tblStockholderCreditor*, and Cash Disbursement information is stored in *tblCashDisbursement*.

The Dividend Payment Entry form is similar to the Loan Payment Entry form. It will be organized by stockholder, and it will have three subforms. The first subform contains the *tblStockAgreement* fields, and it is linked to the main form by FinancierID. The second subform, *tblFulfillment-SACD*, is linked to the main form containing the stockholder information by StockID, which you added to *qryStockholderInfo*. The third subform, *tblCashDisbursement*, contains the only active fields. It is linked to the main form by PayeeID/FinancierID. You will use the Loan Payment Entry form as a starting place for *frmCashDisbursementDividend*.

EXERCISE 11.32: CREATING THE DIVIDEND PAYMENT ENTRY FORM—PART 1

In this exercise you will make copies of the Cash Disbursement Loan Payment form and its subforms. Next, you will make the necessary changes to the Cash Disbursement subform. Then you will create a Fulfillment query to compute the dividend payable to each stockholder, and make the necessary changes to the Fulfillment subform.

1. Make copies of *frmCashDisbursementLoan* and its three subforms. Name the new forms frmCashDisbursementDividend, fsub1CashDisbursementDividend, fsub2Cash DisbursementDividend, and fsub3CashDisbursementDividend, respectively.

Make changes to the Cash Disbursement subform. Use Figure 11.42 as a guide.

2. Open fsub3CashDisbursementDividend in Design view; open the Property Sheet; select Form from the Property Sheet combo box and click the Record Source Query Builder button. Change the Criteria for CDTypeID to "04" to display only cash disbursements for dividends. Delete tblFulfillment-LACD and add tblFulfillment-SACD to the Table Pane. Double-click StockID to add it to the QBE grid. Close the Query Builder and accept the changes. Click the Format tab and change the form's Caption to fsub3CashDisbursementDividend.
3. Click CDTypeID and change the Default Value on the Data tab to "04".
4. Click CashDisbursementDate; click the Data tab and delete the Default Value.
5. Change the Creditor # label to Stockholder # and change the Loan Payment ID label to Dividend #. Save and close the form.

Create a query for the Fulfillment subform.

6. Click the Create tab and click Query Design in the Other group. Double-click tblFulfillment-SACD and tblStockAgreement in the Show Table dialog box. Close the dialog box.
7. Add all of the *tblFulfillment-SACD* attributes to the QBE grid. Add SharesIssued from the *tblStockAgreement* field roster to the QBE grid.
8. Click the first empty Field cell on the QBE grid. Use either the Zoom Box (Shift +F2) or Expression Builder (on the Ribbon in the Query Setup group) to enter the following expression: Total: [SharesIssued] * [PricePerShare]. Save your query as qryFulfillment-SACD and close the query.

Make changes to the Fulfillment subform.

9. Open fsub2CashDisbursementDividend Design view; minimize the Navigation Pane; open the Property Sheet; select Form from the Property Sheet combo box and change the Record Source to qryFulfillment-SACD. Click the Format tab and change the form's Caption to fsub2CashDisbursementDividend.
10. Delete the Payment Num control and its label.
11. Using the Property Sheet, change the Record Source on the Data tab and Name on the Other tab for all six controls:
    - From LoanPaymentID to DividendID.
    - From LoanID to StockID.
    - From PaymentDueDate to DividendDeclarationDate.
    - From PrincipalAmount to DividendPerShare.
    - From InterestAmount to SharesIssued. On the Format tab change the Format to Standard and leave the Decimal Places set to 0.
    - From Total to DividendPayable.
12. Change the title and labels, and resize and move them as indicated in Figure 11.43. You do not need to remove the layout currently applied to the controls—no need to use the Remove icon on the Arrange tab.
13. Save and close the form.

Fig. 11.42 *fsub3-CashDisbursement-Dividend* in Design view.

fsub3CashDisbursementDividend

Form Header	
Detail	
Check #	CheckNum
Cash Account #	CashAccountID
CD Type #	CDTypeID
Stockholder #	PayeeID
Employee #	EmployeeID
Dividend #	EventID
Amount Paid	CashDisbursementAmount
Date Paid	CashDisbursementDate
Form Footer	

Fig. 11.43 *fsub2-CashDisbursement-Dividend* in Design view and Form view.

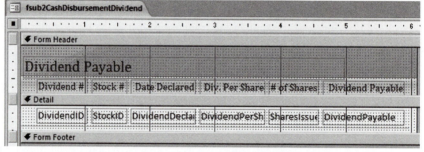

fsub2CashDisbursementDividend

Form Header

Dividend Payable

Dividend #	Stock #	Date Declared	Div. Per Share	# of Shares	Dividend Payable
Detail					
DividendID	StockID	DividendDeclar	DividendPerSh	SharesIssue	DividendPayable

Form Footer

fsub2CashDisbursementDividend

Dividend Payable

Dividend #	Stock #	Date Declared	Div. Per Share	# of Shares	Dividend Payable
10001	1001	1/15/2010	$0.05	50000	$2,500.00
10005	1001	2/15/2010	$0.05	50000	$2,500.00
10009	1001	3/15/2010	$0.05	50000	$2,500.00
10002	1002	1/15/2010	$0.05	50000	$2,500.00
10006	1002	2/15/2010	$0.05	50000	$2,500.00
10010	1002	3/15/2010	$0.05	50000	$2,500.00

EXERCISE 11.33: CREATING THE DIVIDEND PAYMENT ENTRY FORM—PART 2

In this exercise you will make the necessary changes to the Stock Agreement subform. Use Figure 11.44 as a guide.

1. Open fsub1CashDisbursementDividend in Design view; minimize the Navigation Pane; open the Property Sheet; select Form from the Property Sheet combo box and change the Record Source on the Data tab to qryStockAgreement. Click the Format tab and change the form's Caption to fsub1CashDisbursementDividend. Change the Default View to Single Form because each record in the Cash Disbursement Dividend Entry form will contain only one of a stockholder's stock agreements—stockholders with multiple stock agreements will have multiple records in the Cash Disbursement Dividend Entry form.
2. Delete the Payment Num control and its label.
3. Click the LoanID control; click the Property Sheet Data tab; change the Control Source to StockID; click the Other tab and change the name to StockID.
4. Repeat Step 3, with the following controls:
   - Change LoanAmount to Total.
   - Change InterestRate to PricePerShare. On the Format tab change the Format to Currency and Decimal Places to 2.
   - Change LoanDate to StockIssueDate.
   - Change PaymentsPerYear to SharesIssued.
5. Delete the MaturityDate control and label.
6. Change the title and labels, and resize and move them as indicated in Figure 11.44. Remove the layout currently applied to the controls by pressing Ctrl+A and clicking Remove in the Control Layout group on the Arrange tab. This will enable you to easily move the controls and labels.
7. Save and close the form.

Fig. 11.44 *fsub1-CashDisbursement-Dividend* in **Design view and Form view.**

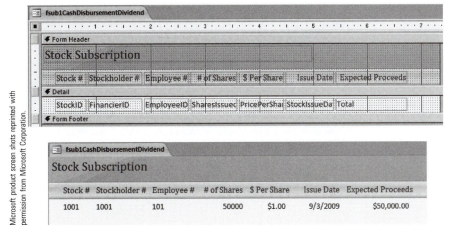

EXERCISE 11.34: CREATING THE DIVIDEND PAYMENT ENTRY FORM—PART 3

In this exercise you will complete the Cash Disbursement Dividend Entry form by making changes to the Cash Disbursement form, including changing the Record Source for the subforms. Use Figures 11.45 and 11.46 as guides.

1. Open frmCashDisbursementDividend in Design view; minimize the Navigation Pane; open the Property Sheet and select Form from the Property Sheet combo box. Change the Record Source on the Data tab to qryStockholderInfo. Click the Format tab and change the form's Caption to frmCashDisbursementDividend.

2. Change the source for *fsub1CashDisbursementDividend*. Click fsub1CashDisbursementLoan in the form's Detail section; click the Data tab and change the Source Object to fsub1CashDisbursementDividend. Click the Other tab and change the name to fsub1CashDisbursementDividend. Click the Data tab. Change the second Link Master Fields and Link Child Fields properties to StockID by editing the text boxes rather than opening the Subform Field Linker.

3. Change the source for *fsub2CashDisbursementDividend*. Click fsub2CashDisbursementLoan in the form's Detail section, click the Data tab, and change the Source Object to fsub2CashDisbursementDividend. Click the Other tab and change the name to fsub2CashDisbursementDividend. Click the Data tab. Change the Link Master Fields and Link Child Fields properties to StockID by editing the text boxes.

4. Change the source for *fsub3CashDisbursementDividend*. Click fsub3CashDisbursementLoan in the form's Detail section; click the Data tab and change the Source Object to fsub3CashDisbursementDividend. Click the Other tab and change the name to fsub3CashDisbursementDividend. Click the Data tab. Change the second Link Master Fields property to StockID by editing the text box.

5. Change titles and labels on the form as indicated in Figures 11.44 and 11.45. Use Design view and Layout view as necessary to resize and move the subforms.

6. Save your changes and close the form.

Import the Dividend Payment data for *tblCashDisbursement* from *Ch11.xlsx* by following the steps below or enter the data by hand using the Dividend Payment Entry form.

7. Click Excel on the External Data ribbon. Click the Browse button to find the location where you stored *Ch11.xlsx*. Double-click Ch11.xlsx.

8. Click the Radio Button for the second option Append a copy of the records to the table: and select tblCashDisbursement from the combo box. Click OK.

9. In the next dialog box, highlight the worksheet tblCashDisbursement. Click Next twice.

10. In the last dialog box, tblCashDisbursement should already be entered in the *Import to Table:* textbox. Click Finish. Open tblCashDisbursement in Datasheet view to verify that all 13 records were imported into the database for a total of 191 cash disbursement records. Open frmCashDisbursementLoan to see that the dividend payment data matches the related reference data in each record of the form.

You now have a complete financing process in your AIS.

Fig. 11.45 Completed Dividend Entry form in Design view.

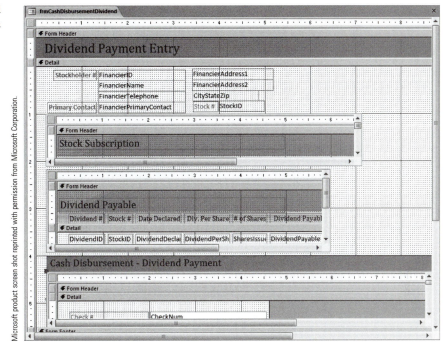

Microsoft product screen shot reprinted with permission from Microsoft Corporation.

Fig. 11.46 Completed Dividend Entry form in Form view.

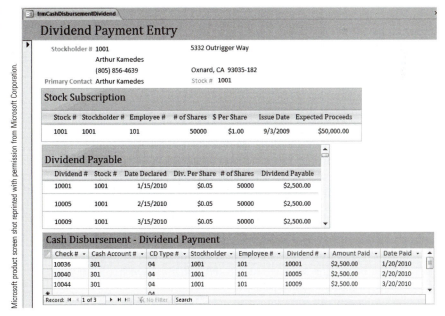

Microsoft product screen shot reprinted with permission from Microsoft Corporation.

We leave the derivation of financial statement information and information for internal purposes to the end-of-chapter exercises.

Summary

This chapter described how to design and implement the financing business process in Access. In the design phase you identified the duality of economic events, added the loan agreement and stock agreement (stock subscription) events, and identified and linked the resource and agents associated with the events. After that you added primary keys, foreign keys, and relationship tables. You also used the design phase to enforce business rules and add controls.

Although the design of the financing process was straightforward, integrating the financing process proved challenging. You added new tables, changed field properties, and even changed relationship properties. You saw how a minor change to a single table structure, such as adding CRTypeID to the Cash Receipt table, caused a lot of extra work in changing database objects you had already finished. This is one reason why one cannot develop parts of a database in isolation. Moreover, you now understand the importance of building scalability into the original database design, such as adding Cash Receipt Type and Cash Disbursement Type tables to allow for cash receipts and disbursements from many different types of events.

Once the tables and relationships were completed, you created queries to be used in forms and in combo boxes. You also created and edited the queries behind forms. You also created forms similar to those in other business processes. The most complex forms you created were for loan payments and dividend payments. These forms contained three subforms. You gained much experience in linking forms and subforms as well as using various formatting properties to manipulate the look and functionality of the subforms.

Questions and Problems for Review

Multiple-Choice Questions

1. The financing process includes all of the following except
   a. keeping creditor information current.
   b. recording cash receipts from stockholders.
   c. recording payments to vendors.
   d. computing interest expense.
2. What event is captured by *tblStockAgreement*?
   a. Issuing stock to stockholders.
   b. Declaring dividends.
   c. Receiving money from stockholders.
   d. None of the above.
3. The Pipefitters Supply Company database described in this chapter uses Event Type tables instead of
   a. enforcing referential integrity.
   b. creating separate tables for each type of cash receipt and cash disbursement.
   c. both a and b are correct.
   d. neither a nor b is correct.
4. The duality relationship in Pipefitters' financing process is
   a. not materialized in the Access database.
   b. implemented by posting a foreign key in *tblCashReceipt*.
   c. implemented by posting a foreign key in *tblCashDisbursement*.
   d. implemented with a relationship table.
5. How does the query for the Creditor # combo box in the Loan Agreement Entry form limit the FinancierID choices to creditors only?
   a. The criteria for FinancierType is set to "10".
   b. The FinancierID choices are not limited to creditors.
   c. Referential integrity is enforced between *tblEmployee* and *tblLoanAgreement*.
   d. EmployeeType in *tblEmployee* uses a validation rule.

6. For data entry subforms that are for reference only, like the Stock Subscription subform in the Dividend Payment Entry form, which of the following form-level property settings does NOT help prevent the addition of new records?
   a. Navigation Buttons set to No.
   b. Scroll Bars set to None.
   c. Close button set to No.
   d. Allow additions set to No.

7. Why does the query to compute balance due from customer by invoice, *qryBalanceDueFromCustomer*, use a left outer-join between *tblSale* and *qrySumOfCash-ReceiptsByInvoice*?
   a. We need to compute the balance due only for sales that have related cash receipts.
   b. Balance due needs to be computed for all customers, even if there are no sales for that customer.
   c. We need to compute balance due for each cash receipt, even if there is no related sale for a particular cash receipt.
   d. We need to compute the balance due for all sales, even if they do not have related cash receipts.

8. If customers could make partial payments for sales and customers could also pay for all sales made during a particular month with a single check, the relationship between *tblSale* and *tblCashReceipt* would be represented by
   a. posting the primary key from *tblSale* into *tblCashReceipt*.
   b. enforcing referential integrity between *tblSale* and *tblCashReceipt*.
   c. posting the primary key from *tblCashReceipt* into *tblSale*.
   d. creating a relationship table.

9. Which Field property, validation rule or input mask, disallows data from being entered into a field ***before*** moving to the next field?
   a. Validation rule only.
   b. Input mask only.
   c. Both validation rule and input mask.
   d. Neither validation rule nor input mask.

10. Which are the tables you would need to provide a listing of open sale order items?
    a. *tblSaleOrder, tblReservation-SaleOrderInventory, tblSale,* and *tblOutflow-SaleInventory.*
    b. *tblReservation-SaleOrderInventory, tblSale,* and *tblOutflow-SaleInventor.*
    c. *tblCustomer, tblSaleOrder, tblSale,* and *tblInventory.*
    d. *tblCustomer, tblSaleOrder, tblReservation-SaleOrderInventory, tblSale, tblOutflow- SaleInventory,* and *tblInventory.*

Discussion Questions

1. If *qryCreditorInfo* were used as the record source for a form to record creditor information, would a user be able to add new creditors with this form? Why or why not?

2. What would happen if the Link Master Fields and Link Child Fields properties StockID was removed from the Cash Disbursement – Dividend Payment subform (*fsub3CashDisbursementDividend*) in the Dividend Payment Entry form? Why?

3. How would you change Pipefitters Supply Company's database to allow for preferred stock to be issued in addition to common stock? For dividend payments on both preferred and common stock?

4. How would you change Pipefitters Supply Company's database to allow for bonds to be issued at a discount? That is, the cash receipt from the loan issue is less than the amount of principal due at the end of the loan. Bonds are loans that can be sold like stock. Interest payments are generally made twice a year and the principal is due at maturity. The difference between the issue price and the face value (amount due at maturity) of a discounted bond represents additional interest expense.

5. What information do you feel is missing from the Loan Agreement table? Why is it important?

Practice Exercises

Note: Before attempting any of the following practice exercises, save a new copy *Ch11.accdb* from the Companion Web site to use for the Practice Exercises. Then, clear the copied database's Read-only file attribute. Begin the names of all Access objects you create in the Practice Exercises with PE#-. Replace # with the Practice Exercise number.

1. Create a set of queries to compute total Loans Payable as of any balance sheet date. Assume that all loans are issued at face value (no discounts or premiums). First, compute the sum of the loan amounts received. Second, compute the sum of cash payments allocated to principal. Third, subtract the sum of the principal payments from the sum of loan proceeds. Begin the name of each query with PE1-XqryLoansPayable-Query-Description, where X is the xth query in the set, and QueryDescription describes what the query accomplishes.

2. Compute interest expense for any period of time using the cash method of accounting (do not accrue interest expense). Name your query PE2-XqryInterestExpense.

3. Create a set of queries to compute total Dividends Payable as of any balance sheet date. First, compute the sum of the dividends declared. Second, compute the sum of dividends paid. Third, subtract the sum of the dividends paid from the sum of dividends declared. Begin the name of each query with PE3-XqryDividendsPayable-QueryDescription.

4. Create a query to determine the total shares of stock issued and the total dollar amount of shares issued. Since Pipefitters Supply Company does not have any stock repurchases (Treasury Stock), shares issued equal shares outstanding. Name your query PE4-qryDividends-.

5. Create a report to list total shares owned and total issue amount by stockholder on a specific date, and show a list of dividends paid to each stockholder for any period of time. The end date is the date on which total shares issued is computed. Name your report PE5-rptDividends, and name your related queries PE5-XqryDividends-.

Index

Note: Italicized pages numbers followed by the letter *f* refer to figures.

& (Ampersand), 174
1–1 (One-to-one) relationship, 78, 159, 538
1–M (One-to-many) relationship, 78, 145, 147, 159, 398–399
1NF (First normal form), 73–74

A

Abs function, 165
Access. *See* Microsoft Access
Access Options dialog box, 8, *9f*, 236
Accounting information systems (AISs), 63–64
Accounts payable
   defined, 397
   deriving information, 458–460
   using queries to compute, *460f*
   by vendor, 461–462, *462f*
Accounts receivable
   by customer, 385–387
   deriving, 383–385
   using queries to compute, 459
Acquisition/payment process, 395–463
   cash disbursements
      cash account information, 450
      Cash Disbursement Entry form, 452–457
      Cash Disbursements table, 450–452
      overview, 449–450
   data model
      cash disbursement events, 399
      completing, 400–402
      purchase events, 398–399
      purchase order events, 399–400
   deriving information
      accounts payable, 458–460
      accounts payable by vendor, 461–462
   duality, *302f–305f, 307f,* 397, 496
   inventory information
      Inventory form, 406–408

Inventory table, 405–406
inventory receipts
   Inventory Receipt (Purchase) Entry form, 433, 436–449
   overview, 430–431
   Purchase line items, 434–435
   Purchase table, 431–432
   Purchase-Inventory Table, 432–433
for non-inventory items
   with long useful lives, 458
   with short useful lives, 457–458
overview, 61–62, 395–397
purchase orders
   Employee table, 409
   overview, 408–409
   Purchase Order Entry form, 413–430
   Purchase Order line items, 416–417
   Purchase Order table, 409–412, 414–415
   Purchase Order-Inventory table, 412–413
vendor information
   maintaining vendor records, 404–405
   Vendor Information form, 403–404
   Vendor table, 402–403
Action queries
   Append query, 190–191
   defined, 142–143
   Delete query, 189–190
   Make Table query, 187
   overview, 186–187
   Update query, 187–189
Administrator, database, 58
Advanced Filter/Sort, table, 25–26
Agents
   creating, 301–304
   external, 298, 302
   internal, 302
Aggregate function, 378, 453

Aggregate operations, *173f,* 174–176
AISs (accounting information systems), 63–64
Alias, 271
Allow Zero Length field property, 107, 331
Ampersand (&), 174
And logical operator, 32–34, *33f,* 172
Append query, 143, 187, 190–191, 446–447, *447f*
Application development, 131–132
Arithmetic operators, 160
Asterisk wildcards, 36, 171–172
Attachment data type, *91f*
Attributes, 2, 11, 68–70, 83, 306–308
AutoCorrect feature, 98–99, 104
AutoForm tool, 332–333
AutoFormat group, 251
AutoNumber data type, *91f*
Available Fields list, 254
Averages, computing, 174

B

Backing up databases, 16–17
Balance due to vendors, 453
Bar code scanners, 431
Basic acquisition/payment data model, *398f*
Behind-the-form queries, 225–226
Blocked content, in Access, 5
Bound controls, 208, 261, 274, 276
Boyce-Codd normal form, 73
Bridge table, 83, 111–112
Business entrepreneur's script, 299
Business process model
   adding attributes to, 306–308
   adding relationship cardinalities to, 304–306
   converting to logical database, 308–309
   creating, 301

Business processes
acquisition/payment process, 61–62
financing process, 62–63
human resources process, 62
overview, 59–60, 296
sales/collection process, 60–61
Buttons
adding to frmPurchaseOrder to run
macro, 429
Inventory Receipt form, 440–442
limiting choices with, 222–225
option, 224, *225f*
to run macro updating VendorID, 445

C

Calculated controls, 208, 261, 277–281, *281f*
Calculated fields, 56, 161
Calculated results. *See* Expressions
Calculations, adding to reports, 264–266
Capitalization in queries, 36
Caption property, 106
Cash Account table, 375
Cash Disbursement Dividend subform,
580–581f
Cash Disbursement Entry form, 452–454
making changes to frmCashReceipt,
455–457f
for payroll checks, 512
Cash Disbursement Loan form, *564f*, 565
Cash Disbursement table
Cash Disbursement Type table and, 576
creating relationships with, 452
overview, 450–451, 496–501
Cash Disbursement Type table, 552–553,
560, 576
Cash disbursements
acquisition/payment process, 298
to creditors
Cash Disbursement table, 559
Cash Disbursement Type table, 560
Fulfillment Loan Agreement-Cash
Disbursement table and relationships, 560–562
Loan Payment Entry form, 562–568
overview, 558–559
to employees
cash disbursement events, 471
Cash Disbursement table, 496–501
overview, 495
financing process, 533–535
to stockholders
Cash Disbursement table, 576
Cash Disbursement Type table, 576
Dividend Payment Entry form,
578–583
Fulfillment Stock Agreement-Cash
Disbursement table and
relationships, 577–578
overview, 576
to vendors
cash account information, 450

Cash Disbursement Entry form,
452–457
cash disbursement events, 399
Cash Disbursements table, 450–452
overview, 449–450
Cash Receipt Entry form, 377–382
Cash Receipt Loan Issue Entry form,
553–558f
Cash Receipt Sale Entry form, 555–557, *556f*
Cash Receipt Stock Issue entry form,
573–575
Cash Receipt table
creating relationships with, 376–377
modifying, 550–553
modifying to create Cash Disbursements
table, 451
overview, 375–376
Cash Receipt Type table, *551f*, 552, *553f*
Cash receipts
cash account information, 374–375, 550
Cash Receipt Entry form, 377–382
Cash Receipt Loan Issue Entry form,
553–558
Cash Receipt table
creating relationships with, 376–377
overview, 375–376, 550–553
defined, 301
events, 323, 534
recording cash receipts from debt issues,
550
recording from stock issues, 573
Categories
Access Navigation Pane, 6
table, 127–131, 339
Chain, value, 59
Child table, 159
Clipboard group, 21
Closed set, 142
Closing
Access, 46
database, 46
reports, 245
Coffee Merchant tables, 70–73
Colors, formatting, 121–122
Column fields, pivot table, 178
Column Width dialog box, 150, *150f*
Columns
adding
overview, 94–95
using lookup field, 95–97
altering display properties, 150
altering order and size of, 149–150
defining in table, 93–94
deleting, 98, 246–248
designating as composite primary key,
112, *113f*
displaying totals, 122–123
formatting, 122
freezing, 119–121
hiding, 119–121
moving, 99, 246–248

overview, 68
query, formatting, 165
rearranging, 118–119
in relational databases, 2
removing primary key designation from,
112
renaming, 98
resizing, 118–119, 246–248
searching for values in, 22
in tables, 10–11
titles, modifying, 248–249
unhiding and unfreezing, 121
Combo Box Wizard, 344–345, *346f*, 485,
494
Combo boxes
EmployeeID, 364, 423, *424f*
Inventory Composition, 344–345
inventory lookup, 424–425, *425f*
salesperson, 363–364
Command Button Wizard, 382, 429, *430f*
Command tabs, Access ribbon, 5
Commands
adding to Quick Access Toolbar, 9
on ribbon, 20–21
using KeyTips for, 21
Commitment event, 323, 399, 535
Comparison operators, *34f*, 160, *170–171f*
Complex primary key, 111
Composite primary key
Cash Disbursements table, 450
designating two columns as, 112, *113f*
first normal form, 74
many-to-many relationship, 160, 308
overview, 55–56, 111
Compound primary key, 111
Conditional formatting, 252, *269f*
Conditional Formatting dialog box, 216,
217f
Conditions, in queries, 170
Contacts table template, 92
Contextual command tab, 19
Control Layout move handle, *264f*
Control properties, changing, 361–362
Controls
applying conditional formatting to,
216–217, 252, 268–269
bound, 208, 261, 274, 276
calculated, 208, 261, 277–281, *281f*
Cash Disbursement Entry form, *455–456f*
control layouts, 217–218
corrective, 327
inserting to limit choices, 222–225
moving, 218–220
report, formatting, 251–252
sizing, 218–220
types of, 261
Conversion process, 60
Copying tables, 104
Corrective controls, 327
Cost of disk storage, 66–67
Created Date category, 8

Creditors, recording cash paid to
  Cash Disbursement table, 559
  Cash Disbursement Type table, 560
  Fulfillment Loan Agreement-Cash
    Disbursement table and
    relationships, 560–562
  Loan Payment Entry form, 562–568
  overview, 558–559
Criteria, in queries, 168–173
Crosstab queries, 151–153, *152f*, 187
Currency data type, *91f*
Currency format, 519
Custom category, 6–7
Custom groups, 6–7, 128–129
Customer Data Entry form, 332–334
Customer information
  Customer Data Entry form, 332–334
  Customer table
    adding controls to, 327–331
    overview, 326–327
  maintaining records, 334–335
Customer Information form
  creating Vendor Information form from,
    403–404
  using to create Stockholder/Creditor
    Information form, 540
Customer report
  adding group to, 250
  modifying column titles, 248–249, *249f*
Customer table
  adding controls to
    Indexed field property, 331
    input masks versus validation rules,
      327–330
    Required field property, 330–331
  overview, 326–327
Cycles, transaction, 59

D

Data acquisition, 64–65
Data consistency, enforcing, 220
Data dictionary, 70, 309
Data entry form, 196, *197f*
Data fields, pivot table, 178
Data inconsistencies, 57, 65
Data independence, 66
Data integrity, enforcing, 220
Data mining, 56
Data modeling, 295–316
  Access database, creating, 309–315
  acquisition/payment process
    cash disbursement events, 399
    completing, 400–402
    purchase events, 398–399
    purchase order events, 399–400
  agents, creating, 301–304
  business process model
    adding attributes to, 306–308
    adding relationship cardinalities to,
      304–306
    converting to logical database, 308–309

business process model, creating, 301
defined, 67
events, creating, 301–304
financing process
  cash disbursement events, 534–535
  cash receipt events, 534
  commitment events, 535
  completing, 537–538
  loan agreements, 535
  simplifying assumptions, 535–537
  stock subscriptions, 535
human resources process
  cash disbursement event, 471
  completing, 473–474
  exemptions and withholding entities,
    473
  labor acquisition (time worked) event,
    470–471
  work schedule event, 471–473
overview, 296
relationships, creating, 301–304
resources, creating, 301–304
sales/collection process
  cash receipt event, 323
  completing, 324–326
  overview, 321–322
  sale event, 322–323
  sale order event, 323–324
value chain model, creating, 298–301
value system model, creating, 296–298
Data redundancy, 65
Data reporting, 64–65
Data types, *91f*
Data validation
  forms, 220–221
  table-level, 108–111
Database accounting
  accounting information systems, 63–64
  advantages of, 57–58
  business processes
    acquisition/payment process, 61–62
    financing process, 62–63
    human resources process, 62
    overview, 59–60
    sales/collection process, 60–61
  Coffee Merchant tables, 70–73
  database management systems
    advantages of, 66
    data acquisition and reporting, 64–65
    defined, 2
    disadvantages of, 66–67
    functions of, 65–66
    overview, 64
  defined, 65
  design, 82–83
  disadvantages of, 58–59
  double-entry bookkeeping versus, 53–57
  entity-relationship models, 83–84
  events-based theories of accounting,
    52–53
  normalization

first normal form, 74
  overview, 73
  second normal form, 74–76
  table relationships, 78–79
  third normal form, 76–77
  overview, 51–52
  REA modeling, 84
  relational database management systems
    data dictionary, 70
    database objects, 67–68
    join operation, 79–82
    overview, 67, 79
    primary and foreign key attributes,
      68–70
    project operation, 79
    schema of a relation, 70
    select operation, 79
Database administrator, 58
Database Documenter command, Database
    Tools tab, 115
Database management systems (DBMS)
  See also Microsoft Access
  advantages of, 66
  data acquisition and reporting, 64–65
  defined, 2
  disadvantages of, 66–67
  functions of, 65–66
  overview, 64
Databases
  backing up, 16–17
  closing, 46
  design overview, 82–83
  online, Microsoft, 15
  opening, 16
  relational, defined, 2
  templates, 14–15
Datasheet
  formatting, 121
  modifying, 118
Datasheet contextual tab, 19–20, 23
Datasheet view
  adding Total row, 123
  Cash Disbursement table, *498f*
  deleting columns in, 98
  exemption table, *505f*
  formatting, 121–122
  freezing columns, 120
  hiding columns, 119–120
  inventory table in, *337f*
  moving columns in, 99
  overview, 18–19
  queries in, 143, *143f*
  renaming columns in, 98
  resizing and rearranging columns in,
    118–119
  unhiding columns in, 121
Date( ) function, 166–168
DateDiff function, 167–168, *168–169f*
DatePart function, 166, *167f*
Dates, 258
Date/Time data type, *91f*

DBMS. *See* Database management systems
Debt financing, 532
Decrement, economic, 298, 300–301
Deductions, payroll, 503
Default Value property, 107
Default View property, 113, 156
Delete query, 142–143, 187, 189–190, *190f*
Deleting
    columns, 98, 246–248
    labels associated with bound controls, 276
    records from Customer Data Entry form,
      335
    records in accounting databases, 405
    reports, 46
    tables, 104
Deletion anomaly, 75
Dependencies
    functional, 76
    transitive, 76–77
Description property, 113
Design contextual tab
    Primary Key command, 112
    Property Sheet command, 113
Design, query, 11, *12f*, *28f*, *30f*
Design ribbon, *345f*
Design view
    Cash Disbursement table, *498f*
    deleting columns in, 98
    Employee Information form, *484f*
    forms, 207–208
    versus Layout view, 245
    moving columns in, 99
    opening new, blank report in, 259, *260f*
    queries in, 143, *143f*
    renaming columns in, 98
    reports, 44, 259
Detail band, report, 274–276, *275f*
Detail section of forms, 197, *198f*
Detective controls, 327
Determinants, 76
Dimming table objects, 127
Disbursement, cash, 298
Disk storage, 66–67
Display characteristics, tables, 23–24
Display Control property, 108
Display properties, table, *24f*
Dividend Payment Entry form, 578–583,
    583f
Dividends, 533
Documenter dialog box, 26, *27f*, 115, 213
Domain-Key normal form, 73
Double-entry bookkeeping, 53–57
Duality
    acquisition/payment process, *302f–305f*,
      307f, 397, 496
    financing process, 533–534
    human resources process, 469–470
    sales/collection process, 321–322
Dynasets
    Accounts Payable, *460f*
    Accounts Payable for vendors, *462f*

altering column display properties, 150
altering order and size of columns,
    149–150
example of, *28f*
inability to save, 31
one-table query, *31f*, *148f*
overview, 11, *12f*, 142, 148–149
parameter query, *155f*
printing, 37–38, 151
producing sorted query results, 149
QBE, 27
sorting, 31–32
SQL statements, *186f*

E

Economic decrement, 298, 300–301
Economic increment, 298
Edit Relationships dialog box
    creating relationships relating to Cash
      Receipt event, 377
    linking category tables, 340
    linking tables, 314, *315f*
    Sale event tables, 368
    Sale Order event tables, 354
Edit Switchboard Item window, 233
Edit Switchboard Page dialog box, 234
E-mail, publishing reports to, 287
Employee commission field, 108–109
Employee Information Entry form, 481–485
Employee pay rate report, 521–523
Employee payroll information query,
    512–513
Employee table, 409, 476–480
Employee Type table, 480–481
EmployeeID combo box, 364, 423, *424f*
Employees
    adding to database, 348
    Employee Information Entry form,
      481–485
    Employee table, 476–480
    Employee Type table, 480–481
    information reports, 521–523
    maintaining employee records, 485–487
    overview, 474–476
    recording cash paid to
      cash disbursement events, 471
      Cash Disbursement table, 496–501
      overview, 495
Enable this content radio button, Access, 5
End of Period Date dialog box, 385
Entity-relationship models, 83–84
Equijoins, 81–82
Equity financing, 532
Events, 301–304
Events accounting, defined, 63
Events-based theories of accounting, 52–53
Excel, Microsoft
    creating access database by importing
      data from, 310
    importing data from into Purchase Order
      table (tblPurchaseOrder), 411

importing data from into Vendor table,
    403
Exemption table, 504, *505f*
Exemptions, 473
Existence check, 489
Exit icon, Access, 4
Exiting Access, 4
Expand indicator, 102
Exporting reports to Word, 285
Expression Builder, 162–164, *163f*, 356–358,
    445f, *568f*
Expressions
    including in queries, 36–37, *38f*
    inserting in text box controls source
      property, 232
    null fields referenced in, 166
    in queries, 160–161
Extensions, line, 56
External agents, 298, 302
External participation relationship, 302, 322,
    398, 470, 534

F

Federal income tax (FIT), 504
Federal Insurance Contributions Act
    (FICA), 503–504
Federal withholding tax (FWT), 504,
    508–509
FICA (Federal Insurance Contributions
    Act), 503–504
FICA payable, 519–520
Field alias, 161
Field labels, form, 202
Field List pane, 273, *274f*
Field Properties panel
    Allow Zero Length option, 107
    Caption property, 106
    Default Value property, 107
    Field Size property, 106
    Format property, 106
    Indexed property, 107
    Input Mask property, 106
    Lookup properties, 107–108
    overview, 106
    Required property, 107
    setting, 109–110
    validation rule, 107
    Validation Text line, 107
Field Size property, 106
Field-level validation rule, 410
Fields
    See also Columns
    adding, 259, 273–274
    deleting from Customer Data Entry form,
      335
    filter, 178
    manually adding, *274f*
    order of, 258
    overview, 68
    pivot table, 178
    rearranging, 275–277

reorganizing, 275–277
selecting from related tables, 260
Fifth normal form, 73
File Open dialog box, *312f*
Files
  flat, 64
  synonymous terms, 68
Filter fields, 178
Filter On Load property, 113
Filter property, 113, 157
Filtering
  mailing labels, with query behind report,
    289–290
  report rows, 252–253, *253f–254f*
  rows, 24–26
  table rows, 24, *25f*
Financing duality of events, 534
Financing process
  cash receipts
    cash account information, 550
    Cash Receipt Loan Issue Entry form,
      553–558
    Cash Receipt table, 550–553
    recording cash receipts from debt
      issues, 550
  data model
    cash disbursement events, 534–535
    cash receipt events, 534
    commitment events, 535
    completing, 537–538
    loan agreements, 535
    simplifying assumptions, 535–537
    stock subscriptions, 535
  duality, 533–534
  loan agreements
    Loan Agreement Entry form, 545–550
    Loan Agreement table, 542–545
    recording events, 541
  overview, 62–63, 532–533
  recording cash paid to creditors
    Cash Disbursement table, 559
    Cash Disbursement Type table, 560
    Fulfillment Loan Agreement-Cash
      Disbursement table, 560–562
    Loan Payment Entry form, 562–568
    recording cash paid to creditors,
      558–559
  recording cash paid to stockholders
    Cash Disbursement table, 576
    Cash Disbursement Type table, 576
    Dividend Payment Entry form,
      578–583
    Fulfillment Stock Agreement-Cash
      Disbursement table, 577–578
    recording dividends paid to
      stockholders, 576
  stock subscriptions
    Cash Receipt Stock Issue entry form,
      573–575
    recording cash receipts from stock
      issues, 573

recording stock agreement event, 568
Stock Subscription Entry form,
  571–572
Stock Subscription table
  (tblStockAgreement), 568–570
stockholder and creditor information
  maintaining stockholder/creditor
    records, 541
  overview, 538–539
  Stockholder/Creditor Information
    form, 540
  Stockholder/Creditor table, 539
  versus transaction cycle, 59
Find Duplicates queries, 153, *153f*
First normal form (1NF), 73–74
First record navigation button, 22
FIT (federal income tax), 504
Fix function, 165
Fixed amount deductions, 503
Fixed percentage deductions, 503
Flat files, 64, 158–159, *158f*
  defined, 2
FOB destination, 397
FOB shipping point, 320
Font Color command, 121–122
Font group, 21
Footer section, form, 197, *198f*
Footers, group, 250, *263f*, 265
Force New Page property, 266, *267f*
Foreign keys
  acquisition/payment process, 400, *401f*
  adding to Business Process Model, 308,
    309f
  financing model, 537–538, *538f*
  HR model, 473, *475f*
  making relationships with, 324
  overview, 55, 68–70
  Sales/Collection process, *325f*
  in two-table queries, 144
Form design window, 202
Form view, 17
Form Wizard
  basic forms, 206–207
  Cash Receipt Entry form, 379–380
  Employee Information Entry form,
    483
  Inventory Data Entry form, 342, *343f*
  Labor Acquisition Entry form, 493–494
  Loan Agreement Entry form, 546
  Loan Entry Payment form, 563
  multiple-table forms, 227, 229
  one-table forms, 200, *201f*
  Payroll Check Data Entry form,
    513–514
  Sale Entry form, 369–370
  Sale Order Entry form, 359–365
Format function, 165
Format property, 106
Formatting
  calculated controls, *280f*
  Customer Data Entry form, 333

datasheets, 121–122
reports, 251–252
Sale Order Entry form, 361
static, 268
Forms
  adding logos to, 209–210
  adding titles to, 209
  automatically created, *41f*
  behind-the-form queries, 225–226
  building, 199–200
  controls
    applying conditional formatting to,
      216–217
    control layouts, 217–218
    inserting to limit choices, 222–225
    moving, 218–220
    sizing, 218–220
  creating quickly, 40–41
  data validation, 220–221
  design guidelines, 205–206
  Design view, 207–208
  designating startup form, 235–237
  editing data with, 42
  enforcing data integrity and consistency
    with, 220
  example of, *13f*
  Form Wizard, 206–207
  Layout view, 214
  modifying default view, 214–215
  mortgage calculation form, 230–233
  multiple items form, 204–205
  multiple-table form, 227–228
  navigating, 211
  opening existing, 39
  overview, 12, 38, 195–197
  printing, 43–44, 212–214
  query-based, *40f*
  saving, 41
  special purpose forms, 230
  split, 42–43
  split form, 203–204
  standard form, 200–202
  subform, 228–230
  switchboard, 233–235
  types of, 197–199
  viewing queries through, 40
  viewing tables through, 38–40
Fourth normal form, 73
Freezing columns, 119–121
FrmPurchaseOrder
  adding buttons to run macro, 429
  modifying to create Inventory Receipt
    (Purchase) Entry form, 436–442
FsubPurchaseOrder, 436–442
Fulfillment Loan Agreement-Cash
  Disbursement table, 560–562, *561f*
Fulfillment relationship, 323, 399, 471
Fulfillment Stock Agreement-Cash
  Disbursement table, 577–578, *578f*
Fulfillment table, 559, *559f*, 576, *576f*
Functional dependencies, 76

Functions
  date, 166–168
  math, 164–165
  null fields referenced in expressions, 166
  overview, 164
FWT (federal withholding tax), 504,
    508–509
FWT payable, 517–519

G

Get External Data dialog box, 133, *134f*, *312f*
Getting Started window, *311f*
Getting Started with Microsoft Access
    window, 3
Go To command, 22
Grand totals, 176
Graphics
  adding to reports, 281–284
  report, *283f*
Grid, adjusting report, 264
Gross pay, 501–503, 508
Group footers, 250, *263f*, 265
Group headers, 250, 263–264
Group on list, *263f*
Group, Sort, and Total pane, 250, 262, *263f*,
    265
Grouping
  data, 173–174, 176
  field, *256f*
  reports, 249–251, 258, 261–264
Groups
  Access Navigation Pane, 6, 8
  Access ribbon, 5
  adding to customer report, 250
  custom, 6–7, 128–129
  on ribbon, 20–21
  sorting within, *251f*

H

Header section, form, 197, *198f*, 208
Headers, group, 250, 263–264
Help resources
  obtaining, 3
  printing, 4
Hidden objects in Navigation Pane, 270–271
Hiding
  columns, 119–121
  groups, 8, 130
  object names, 127
  tables, 104–105
Hierarchical model, 67
Home tab, Access, 5
Horizontal computation, 378, 453
Human resources process, 467–527
  data model
    cash disbursement event, 471
    completing HR Model, 473–474
    exemptions and withholding entities, 473
    labor acquisition (time worked) event,
      470–471
    work schedule event, 471–473

deriving information
  employee information reports, 521–523
  FICA payable, 519–520
  FWT payable, 517–519
  income statement items, 520
  Medicare payable, 519–520
  Time Worked report, 524–527
  wages payable, 517–519
duality, 469–470
employee information
  Employee Information Entry form,
    481–485
  Employee table, 476–480
  Employee Type table, 480–481
  maintaining employee records,
    485–487
  overview, 474–476
labor acquisition (time worked)
  Labor Acquisition Entry form, 491–495
  Labor Acquisition table, 487–491
  overview, 60, 62, 468–469
payroll calculation
  Cash Disbursement Entry form for
    payroll checks, 512
  queries for, 501–512
recording cash paid to employees
  Cash Disbursement table, 496–501
  overview, 495
Hyperlink data type, *91f*

I

Icons, adding to Quick Access Toolbar, 9
Identifiers, 169–170
Implementation compromise, 496, 551
Import Spreadsheet Wizard, 310, *312f–313f*
Income statement items, 520
Inconsistencies, data, 57, 65
Increment, economic, 298
Independence, data, 66
Indexed field property, 107, 331
Indicator, expand, 102
Infinity symbol, 101
Inflow relationship, 302, 321, 398, 470, 534
Inner joins, 176, 383
Input Mask property, 106, 110, 327–330
Input Mask Wizard, 330
Insert Picture dialog box, 209
Insert Subdatasheet dialog box, 102
Insertion anomaly, 75
Internal agents, 302
Internal participation relationship, 302, 322,
    398, 470, 534
Inventory Composition Combo Box,
    344–345
Inventory Data Entry form, 341–347,
    407f–408f
Inventory Form, 406–408
Inventory information
  Inventory Data Entry form, 341–347
  Inventory form, 406–408
  Inventory table, 336–341, 405–406

Inventory input forms, 196, *197f*
Inventory lookup combo box, 424–425,
    425f
Inventory Receipt Entry form, 434,
    448–450f, 449
  adding control for VendorID to, 442–446
  modifying frmPurchaseOrder and
    fsubPurchaseOrder to create,
    436–442
  overview, 433
Inventory receipts
  Inventory Receipt (Purchase) Entry form
    adding control for VendorID to,
      442–446
    adding control limiting inventory items
      received to items ordered on,
      446–449
    modifying frmPurchaseOrder and
      fsubPurchaseOrder to create,
      436–442
    overview, 433
  overview, 430–431
  purchase events, 398–399
  Purchase line items, 434–435
  Purchase table
    creating relationships with, 433–434
    overview, 431–432
  Purchase-Inventory Table, 432–433
Inventory table, 336–341, 405–406
Invoice balances, outstanding, 378
Invoice reports, 272, *273f*, *284f*
Items, pivot table, 178

J

JIT (just-in-time) production control
    system, 396
Join operation, 79–82
Join Properties dialog box, 378, *379f*
Joining tables, 157–158
Joins
  equijoins, 81–82
  inner, 176, 383
  outer, 81, 176–177, *177f*
Junction table, 78, 83
Just-in-time (JIT) production control
    system, 396

K

Keyboard shortcuts, 21, 22
KeyTips, 21

L

Label Wizard, 288
Labels
  adding to reports, 281–284
  altering, 277
  associated with bound controls, deleting,
    276
  calculated control, 280
  Cash Disbursement Entry form, *455–456f*
  creating mailing, 287–290

mailing, *289–290f*
modifying in Layout view, 215–216
report, *282f*
Labor acquisition (time worked)
  events, 470–471
  Labor Acquisition (Time Worked) Entry
    form, 491–495
  Labor Acquisition table, 487–491
Last record navigation button, 22
Layout change, defined, 118
Layout, pivot table, 178
Layout view
  adding logo to report, 246
  adjusting columns, 246–248
  forms, 210, *211f*, 214
  modifying labels in, 215–216
  modifying report title, 246
  one-table report in, *244f*
  overview, 244–245
  reports, 245
Layout View command button, *334f*
Line extensions, 56
Link Tables dialog box, 133, *134f*
Linked table design warning dialog box, 134,
  135f
Linked tables, 131
Linking
  in access database, 314, *315f*
  category tables, 339–340
  exemption table and employee table,
    506–507
  HR model tables, 481
  Labor Acquisition table, 490
  tables to external tables, 133–135
List Box Wizard, 222–223
List boxes, 222–225
Literal operands, 168–169
Literal values, 168
Literals, defined, 328
Loan Agreement Entry form, 545–550,
  571–572
Loan Agreement table, 542–545
Loan agreements
  Loan Agreement Entry form,
    545–550
  Loan Agreement table, 542–545
  overview, 535
  recording loan agreement events, 541
Loan amortization table, 559
Loan Payment Entry form, 562–568
Logical database, converting business
  process model to, 308–309
Logical model, 308
Logical operators, *34f*, 172–173
Logos
  adding to forms, 209–210
  adding to reports, 245–246
Lookup field, adding columns using,
  95–97
Lookup properties, 107–108
Lookup Wizard data type, *91f*, 95–97

M
Macros
  completed, *429f*
  creating to automate make-table and
    update queries, 427–428
  Inventory Receipt form, 440–442
  to update VendorID, 444, *445f*
  updating balance due in Cash Receipt
    Entry form, 381–382
Mailing labels, *289–290f*
Maintaining vendor records, 404–405
Make Table query, 142, 187, *188f*, *372f*,
  426–427
Many-to-many (M–M) relationships, 78–79,
  147, 159–160
Materials requirement planning (MRP)
  system, 396
Math functions, 164–165
Medicare payable, 519–520
Memo data type, *91f*
Microsoft Access
  closing, 46
  customizing, 8
  databases
    backing up, 16–17
    creating, 309–315
    opening, 16
    relational, 2
    templates, 14–15
  defined, 2
  environment
    objects, 9–14
    overview, 5
    work surface, 5–9
  exiting, 4
  forms
    creating quickly, 40–41
    editing data with, 42
    overview, 38
    printing, 43–44
    saving, 41
    split, 42–43
    viewing query through, 40
    viewing table through, 38–40
  help resources
    obtaining, 3
    printing, 4
  overview, 1
  queries
    expressions, including in,
      36–37
    one-table, 29–30
    overview, 27
    printing dynasets, 37–38
    saving, 30–31
    selection criteria, 32–36
    sorting results, 31–32
    using, 28–29
  reports
    creating quickly, 44–45
    overview, 44

    previewing, 44
    printing, 47
    saving, 45–46
  starting, 3
  tables
    changing display characteristics, 23–24
    navigating, 22
    opening, 18–22
    printing, 26
    printing structure, 26–27
    searching for values in columns, 22
    sorting and filtering rows, 24–26
    viewing data through different tabs,
      17–18
  work area, 18
Microsoft Excel
  creating Access database by importing
    data from, 310
  importing data from into Purchase Order
    table, 411
  importing data from into Vendor table,
    403
Mining, data, 56
M–M (many-to-many) relationships, 78–79,
  147, 159–160
Modal dialog box, 198
Modeling. *See* Data modeling
Modified Date category, 8
Mortgage calculation forms, 230–233
Moving
  columns, 99
  controls, 218–220
MRP (materials requirement planning)
  system, 396
Multiple Items Form wizard, 204–205
Multiple items forms, 197, 204–205
Multiple-table forms, 227–228
Multiple-table queries, 157–158
Multi-table reports, 269

N
Naming, forms, 209
Navigating
  forms, 39–40, 211, 405
  tables, 22
Navigation Options dialog box, 127–131,
  231
Navigation Pane
  Created Date category, 8
  Custom category, 6–7
  dimming and showing objects, 105
  hidden objects in, 270–271
  hiding tables, 105
  information displayed in, 16
  Modified Date category, 8
  Object Type setting, 7
  organizing tables in, 125–126
  overview, 6
  Tables and Related Views category,
    7–8, 104
Net pay, 510–511

Network model, 67
New (blank) record button, 22
Non-inventory items
    with long useful lives, 458
    with short useful lives, 457–458
Normal form, 73
Normalization
    first normal form, 74
    overview, 73
    second normal form, 74–76
    table relationships, 78–79
    third normal form, 76–77
Northwind 2007 database, 15
Null attributes, 75
Null fields, 166
Null literal operand, 169
Null values, 10
Number data type, *91f*
Nz function, 166

O

Object Type category, 7, 125–126
Office Access. *See* Microsoft Access
Office fluent interface, 5
OLE Object data type, *91f*
One-dimensional pivot tables, 179–180
One-table queries, 29–30, *31f*, 146–148, *148f*
One-table reports, *244f*
One-to-many (1–M) relationship, 78, 145,
        147, 159, 398–399
One-to-one (1–1) relationship, 78, 159, 538
Online databases, Microsoft, 15
Online templates, Microsoft, 14
Open sale orders, 387–390
Open/Close button, Access Navigation
        Pane, 6
Opening
    databases, 16
    tables, 18–22
Operators, in queries, 161–162
Option buttons, 224, *225f*
Or logical operator, *35f*, 147–148, *148f*
OR operator, 34–36
ORDER BY clause, 183
Order By On Load property, 113
Order By property, 157
Order By table property, 113
Orientation property, 156–157
Outer joins, 81, 176–177, *177f*
Outflow relationship, 302, 321, 398, 470, 534
Output All Fields property, 156
Outstanding invoice balances, 378

P

Page breaks, adding to reports, 266–267
Page dates, 258
Page Footer section, 197, *198f*
Page header, adding labels to, 281–282
Page Header section, 197, *198f*, 208
Page Layout ribbon, Excel, 310, *311f*
Page numbers, 258
Page times, 258

Paper reports, 258, 284
Parameter queries, 153–155, *155f*
Parent table, 159
Pay rate report, employee, 521–523
Payroll calculation
    Cash Disbursement Entry form for
        payroll checks, 512
    queries for, 501–512
Payroll Check Data Entry form, 513–516
Payroll deductions, 503
Payroll Expense query, 520
PDF-format, 285–287
Pencil symbol, 117
Pivot tables
    defined, 178
    one-dimensional, 179–180
    overview, 177–178
    terminology, 178
    two-dimensional, 180–181
PivotChart view, 143–144, *143f*
PivotTable query, *180–181f*
PivotTable view, 143–144, *143f*
Populating tables, 115, 117
Preventive internal controls, 327
Previewing reports, 44, 252
Primary Key command, Design contextual
        tab, 112
Primary key field, 24
Primary keys
    acquisition/payment process, *401f*
    attributes, 68–70
    composite
        designating two columns as, 112, *113f*
        first normal form, 74
        M–M relationships, 160, 307–308
        overview, 55–56, 111
    establishing, 111–113
    financing model, 537, *537f–538f*
    HR process with, *474f*
    overview, 55
    Sales/Collection process with, *325f*
    in tables, 11
    in two-table queries, 144
Print dialog box, 26, 115
Print Preview, 44, 151, 252, 266, 284
Print width warning dialog box, 213
Printing
    dynasets, 37–38, 151
    forms, 43–44, 212–214
    help resources, 4
    records, 124–125
    reports, 47, 284
    table structure, 26–27, 115
    tables, 26
Products form, 38–39, *39f*
Project operation, 79, *80f*
Property Sheet
    Default View property, 156
    Filter property, 157
    Order By property, 157
    Orientation property, 157
    Output All Fields property, 156

    overview, 156
    query, 156–157, *156f*
    query column, *150f*
    Top Values property, 156–157
    Unique Rows property, 157
    Unique Values property, 157
Property Sheet command, Design contextual
        tab, 113
Property Sheet dialog box, 221, *346f*
Property Sheet tabs, 361–362
Publishing reports
    e-mail, 287
    exporting to Word, 285
    overview, 284
    PDF- or XPS-format, 285–287
    printing, 284
Purchase line items, 434–435
Purchase order, 347, 396
Purchase Order Entry form
    creating query for vendor data used in,
        415–416
    Form view, *420f*, *422–423f*
    overview, 413–414
    using Sale Order Entry form to create,
        417–430
Purchase Order line items, 416–417, *418f*
Purchase Order table
    creating relationships with, 414–415
    overview, 409–412
    versus Purchase table, *431f*
Purchase Order-Inventory table, 412–413
Purchase orders
    Employee table, 409
    events, 399–400
    overview, 408–409
    Purchase Order Entry form, 413–414
        creating query for vendor data used in,
            415–416
        using Sale Order Entry form to create,
            417–430
    Purchase Order line items, 416–417
    Purchase Order table, 409–412,
        414–415
    Purchase Order-Inventory table,
        412–413
Purchase requisition, 396
Purchase table, *432f*
    creating relationships with, 433–434
    overview, 431–432
Purchase-Inventory Table, 432–433

Q

QBE (Query by Example), 27, 29, 142
Queries
    Accounts Payable for vendors, 461–462
    action
        Append query, 190–191
        Delete query, 189–190
        Make Table query, 187
        overview, 186–187
        Update query, 187–189
    behind-the-form, 225–226

to compute balance due to vendors, 453, *454f*
to compute outstanding invoice balances, 378
computing accounts receivable, 383–386
for concatenating employee name fields, 492
creating for customer data used in Sale Order Entry form, 355–357
creating for Purchase line items, 434–435
creating for Purchase Order line items, 416–417
creating for Sale line items, 368–369
creating for Sale Order line items, 357–359
creating for sales, 383
creating for salesperson combo box, 363
creating for vendor data used in Purchase Order Entry form, 415–416
creating one-table, *31f*
creating pivot table from, 180, *181f*
creating report based on, 272
creating select, 144–146
creating subforms from, 228–230
criteria in, 168–173
dynasets
  altering column display properties, 150
  altering order and size of columns, 149–150
  overview, 148–149
  printing, 151
  producing sorted query results, 149
employee payroll information, 512–513
Expression Builder, 162–164
expressions in, 36–37, 160–161
FICA and Medicare Payable, 520
filtering mailing labels with, 289–290
formatting columns, 165
forms based on, *40f*
functions
  date, 166–168
  math, 164–165
for FWT, 508–509
FWT Payable, 517–518, *519f*
grouping data, 173–174, 176
including expressions in, *38f*
Inventory Receipt form, 440–442
multiple-table, 157–158
multitable reports based on, 269
for net pay, 510–511
null fields referenced in expressions, 166
one-table, 29–30
operators in, 161–162
outer join, 176–177
overview, 11–12, 27–29, 58, 141–142
parameter, 153–155
for payroll calculation, 501–512
Payroll Expense, 520
pivot table
  defined, 178
  one-dimensional, 179–180
  overview, 177–178

terminology, 178
two-dimensional, 180–181
printing dynasets, 37–38
for printing invoices, 371
producing list of open sale order items, 388–389
Property Sheet
  Default View property, 156
  Filter property, 157
  Order By property, 157
  Orientation property, 157
  Output All Fields property, 156
  overview, 156
  Top Values property, 156–157
  Unique Rows property, 157
  Unique Values property, 157
for purchase line items, *435f*
Query Wizards
  crosstab queries, 151–153
  Find Duplicates query, 153
  overview, 151
relationships, table
  many-to-many (M-M), 159–160
  one-to-many (1-M), 159
  one-to-one (1-1), 159
  overview, 158–159
retrieving selected rows from table, 146–148
saving, 30–31, 151
selection criteria
  complex, 32–34
  creating using OR operator, 34–36
sorting results, 31–32
SQL view
  finding employees with longer than average tenure, 185–186
  overview, 181–182
  select statement syntax, 182–183
  self-join queries with, 183
  using subquery to find customers without invoices, 183–185
Stock Subscription Entry form, 571
summarizing data, 173–174, 176
supplying report data, examining, 269–272, *270f*
types of, 142–143
used to build pivot table, 179
using to compute Accounts Payable, 460
using to compute Accounts Receivable, 459
viewing through forms, 40
views, 143–144
wages, 517–518, *519f*
writing basic, 162
Query by Example (QBE), 27, 29, 142
Query Wizards
  crosstab queries, 151–153
  Find Duplicates queries, 153
  overview, 151
Question mark icon, 3
Quick Access Toolbar, 8–9

R
Radio buttons, 224, *225f*
RDBMS. *See* Relational database management system
REA (resources, events, agents) modeling, 84, 296
Rearranging
  columns, 118–119
  fields, 275–277
Record selector, 22
Recording sales
  Sale Entry form
    overview, 367
    using Form Wizard to build, 369–370
  sale events, 322–323
  Sale line items, creating query for, 368–369
  Sale table
    creating relationships with, 367–368
    overview, 365–366
  Sale-Inventory table, 366–367
Records, 68, 124–125. *See also* Rows
Records group, 21
Recursive relationship, 84
Redundancy, data, 65
Reference data, 361–362
Referential integrity, 99–103, 314, 341
Relation, defined, 67
Relational database management system (RDBMS). *See* also *entries beginning with "database"*
  data dictionary, 70
  foreign key attributes, 68–70
  functions of, 65–66
  objects, 67–68
  operations
    join, 79–82
    overview, 79
    project, 79
    select, 79
  overview, 2, 67
  primary key attributes, 68–70
  schema of a relation, 70
Relational model, 67
Relationship cardinalities, adding to business process model, 304–306
Relationship tables
  acquisition/payment process with, *401f*
  adding to Business Process Model, 308, *309f*
  creating, 351–352
  entity-relationship diagram, 83
  financing model, 537–538
  HR model, 473, *475f*
  making relationships with, 324, 400
  overview, 56, 78
  Sales/Collection process, *325f*
Relationship window, HR process, 506–507
Relationships
  among tables, 145–146
  Cash Receipt table, 553, *554f*

Relationships (*continued*)
creating with Cash Disbursements table,
452
creating with Cash Receipt table, 376–377
creating with Purchase Order Table,
414–415
creating with Purchase table, 433–434
creating with Sale Order table, 353–355
creating with Sale table, 367–368
editing and removing, 103
Fulfillment Loan Agreement-Cash
Disbursement table, 560–562
Fulfillment Stock Agreement-Cash
Disbursement table, 577–578
HR model, 473
Loan Agreement table, 544, *545f*
making with foreign keys, 400
many-to-many (M-M), 159–160
one-to-many (1-M), 159
one-to-one (1-1), 159
overview, 18, *19f*, 78–79, 83, 158–159
Purchase table, *434f*
removing, 103
rules for creating, 308
updating, 499
Relationships window
creating relationships relating to Cash
Receipt event, 376–377
creating relationships relating to sales
events, 367–368
establishing referential integrity, 100–101
joining tables in, 158
Labor Acquisition tables, *491f*
linking category tables, 339–340, *341f*
linking tables, 314, *315f*
removing relationships, 103–104
Sale Order Table, 353–354, *355f*
Remittance advice number, 375
Removing table relationships, 103
Renaming
columns, 98
tables, 104
Report Header, 245
Report view, 17, 44, *45f*, 245, 252–253
Report Wizard, 253–257, 272, 521, *522f*,
524f–525f
Reports
adding logos to, 245–246
adding page breaks, 266–267
calculations, adding, 264–266
closing, 245
columns
deleting, 246–248
moving, 246–248
resizing, 246–248
titles, modifying, 248–249
controls
adding calculated, 277–281
applying conditional formatting to,
252, 268–269
creating quickly, 44–45, 244–245
deleting, 46

design guidelines
existing paper reports, 258
field order, 258
overview, 257–258
page numbers, dates, and times, 258
simplicity, 258–259
sorting and grouping, 258
Design view, 259
examining query supplying report data,
269–272
example of, *14f*
fields
adding, 259, 273–274
rearranging, 275–277
reorganizing, 275–277
selecting from related tables, 260
fine-tuning, 269
formatting, 251–252
graphics, adding, 281–284
grouping, 249–251, 261–264
invoice report, 272
labels
adding, 281–284
creating mailing, 287–290
Layout view, 245
loading, 44
modifying properties, 267–268
multitable report based on queries, 269
overview, 12–14, 44, 58, 243
previewing, 44, 252
printing, 47, 284
publishing
e-mail, 287
exporting to Word, 285
overview, 284
PDF format, 285–287
printing, 284
XPS format, 285–287
Report Wizard, 253–257
saving, 45–46, 245, 277
sorting, 249–251, 261–264
tabular control layout, 261
titles, adding to, 245–246
Required field property, 107, 330–331
Reservation relationship, 323, 399, 471
Resizing
columns, 118–119, *248f*
controls in layout groups, 218–219
individual controls, 219
objects, 202
Resources
adding to Sales/Collection duality
relationship, 322
creating, 301–304
Resources, events, agents (REA) modeling,
84, 296
Ribbon
interface, 5–6
tabs and groups on, 20–21
Rich Text Format (rtf) format reports, 285, *286f*
Rich Text group, 21
Rnd function, 165

Round function, 164–165, *165f*, 228
Row fields, pivot table, 178
Rows
filtering, 24–26
filtering report, 252–253, *253–254f*
in relational databases, 2
retrieving selected from tables, 146–148
sorting, 24–26
synonymous terms for, 67
in tables, 10–11
Rtf (Rich Text Format) format reports, 285,
286f
Running query, 29

S
Sale Entry form
overview, 367
using Form Wizard to build, 369–370
Sale line items, 368–369
Sale Order Entry form
creating query for customer data used in,
355–357
overview, 353
using Form Wizard to build, 359–365
using to create Purchase Order Entry
form, 417–430
Sale Order line items, 357–359
Sale Order table
creating relationships with, 353–355
overview, 348–351
Sale Order-Inventory table, 351–353
Sale orders
adding employees to database, 348
open, 387–390
overview, 347–348
Sale Order Entry form
creating query for customer data used
in, 355–357
overview, 353
using Form Wizard to build, 359–365
sale order events, 323–324
Sale Order line items, creating query for,
357–359
Sale Order table
creating relationships with, 353–355
overview, 348–351
Sale Order-Inventory table, 351–353
Sale table
creating relationships with, 367–368
overview, 365–366
Sale-Inventory table, 366–367
Sales/collection process
customer information
Customer Data Entry form, 332–334
Customer table, 326–331
maintaining customer records, 334–335
data model
cash receipt events, 323
completing, 324–326
overview, 321–322
sale events, 322–323
sale order events, 323–324

deriving information
  accounts receivable, 383–385
  accounts receivable by customer, 385–387
  open sale orders, 387–390
  sales, 382–383
duality, 321–322
inventory information
  Inventory Data Entry form, 341–347
  Inventory table, 336–341
overview, 60–61, 320
printing invoices, 371–374
recording cash received from customers
  cash account information, 374–375
  Cash Receipt Entry form, 377–382
  Cash Receipt table, 375–377
recording sales
  Sale Entry form, 367, 369–370
  Sale line items, 368–369
  Sale table, 365–368
  Sale-Inventory table, 366–367
sale orders
  adding employees to database, 348
  overview, 347–348
  Sale Order Entry form, 353, 355–357, 359–365
  Sale Order line items, 357–359
  Sale Order table, 348–351, 353–355
  Sale Order-Inventory table, 351–353
Salesperson combo box, 363–364
Saving
  forms, 41
  queries, 30–31, 151
  reports, 45–46, 245, 277
  tables, 114
Scalability, 506
Schema of a relation, 70
Scroll bar, 21–22
Second normal form, 73–76, *77f*
Security control functions, centralization of, 58
Security Warning bar, Access, 5
Select operation, 79, *80f*
Select queries, 144–146
SELECT statement, 182–183, *184f*
Selected Fields list, 254, *256f*
Selection criteria, 11
  complex, 32–34
  creating using OR operator, 34–36
  defined, 79
Selection queries, 11, 27, 142. *See also* Queries
Self-join queries, 183
Shift-clicking controls, 276
Shortcuts
  Access, 5–6
  adding to Custom groups, *130f*
  Custom categories and, 129
  KeyTips, 21
Show Hidden Objects check box, Navigation Pane, 105
Show Table dialog box, 100, *101f*
Showing

object names, 127
  tables, 104–105
Shutter Bar, 125
Since the Sale Entry form, 436, *436–437f*
Sizing, controls, 218–220
Social Security tax, 503–504
Sort & Filter group, 21
Sort order, frmSaleOrder, 363
Sorting
  query results, 31–32
  reports, 249–251, 258, 261–264
  rows, 24–26
  tables, *115f*
Source property, text box controls, 232
Special purpose forms, 230
Split Form Wizard, 203–204
Split forms, 17, 42–43, *43f*, 199, 203–204
Spreadsheet page, 68
SQL view. *See* Structured Query Language view
Stacked control layout, 217–219
Standard cost, defined, 406–407
Standard forms, 200–202
Starting Access, 3
Startup forms, 235–237
Static formatting, 268
Status bar, Datasheet view, 20
Stock Agreement Entry form, 571–572, *572f*
Stock Agreement table, *569–570f*, 570
Stock Subscription Entry form, 571–572
Stock Subscription table (tblStockAgreement), 568–570
Stock subscriptions
  Cash Receipt Stock Issue entry form, 573–575
  defined, 532–533
  overview, 535
  recording cash receipts from stock issues, 573
  recording stock agreement events, 568
  Stock Subscription Entry form, 571–572
  Stock Subscription table (tblStockAgreement), 568–570
Stockholder and creditor information
  maintaining stockholder/creditor records, 541
  overview, 538–539
  Stockholder/Creditor Information form, 540
  Stockholder/Creditor table, 539
Stockholder/Creditor Information form, *539–541f*, 540
Stockholder/Creditor table, 539, 545
Stockholders, recording dividends (cash) paid to
  Cash Disbursement table, 576
  Cash Disbursement Type table, 576
  Dividend Payment Entry form, 578–583
  Fulfillment Stock Agreement-Cash Disbursement table and relationships, 577–578
  overview, 576

Structure changes, table, 66
Structured Query Language (SQL) view, *143f*, 144
  finding employees with longer than average tenure, 185–186
  overview, 181–182
  SELECT statement syntax, 182–183
  self-join queries with, 183
  using subquery to find customers without invoices, 183–185
Subdatasheets, 102, *103f*
Subforms
  creating, 227
  creating from queries, 228–230
  defined, 199
  example, *200f*
Subschema, 66
Summarizing data, 173–174, 176
Summary functions, 174–176
Summary options, *257f*
Switchboard, 233–236
Switchboard Manager, 233–234

T
Tab order, 211–212, 363
Tab Order dialog box, 212
Table Name dialog box, *313f*
Table structure, 66, 70
Table view, 17
Table-level validation rule, 410–411, *411f*, 543
Tables
  adding columns to, 96
  adding lookup column to, 97–98
  attributes of, 68
  bridge, 111–112
  categories, 127–129
  changing display characteristics, 23–24
  columns
    adding, 94–97
    deleting, 98
    displaying totals, 122–123
    freezing, 119–121
    hiding, 119–121
    inserting, 95
    moving, 99
    rearranging, 118–119
    renaming, 98
    resizing, 118–119
  copying, 104
  creating
    from scratch, 93–94
    from templates, 90–92
  datasheet
    formatting, 121
    modifying, 118
  deleting, 104, 118
  display properties, *24f*
  expand indicators, 102
  Field Properties panel
    Allow Zero Length option, 107
    Caption property, 106

Tables (*continued*)
Default Value property, 107
Field Size property, 106
Format property, 106
Indexed property, 107
Input Mask property, 106
Lookup properties, 107–108
overview, 106
Required property, 107
validation rule, 107
Validation Text line, 107
fields, selecting from related, 260
hiding, 104–105
intertable relationships, 103
joining, 157–158
linking to external tables, 133–135
navigating, 22
object names
hiding, 127
showing, 127
opening, 18–22
organizing in Navigation Pane, 125–126
organizing into custom categories, 129–131
overview, 10–11, 67, 89–90
pivot
defined, 178
one-dimensional, 179–180
overview, 177–178
terminology, 178
two-dimensional, 180–181
populating, 115, 117
primary key, establishing, 111–113
printing, 26
printing records, 124–125
printing structure, 26–27, 115
properties, 113–114
in queries, 144–145
referential integrity, 99–103
in relational databases, 2
relationships among, 145–146, *145f*, 400
renaming, 104
resizing and rearranging columns, 118–119
retrieving selected rows from, 146–148
saving, 114
searching for values in columns, 22
separating from other database objects, 131–133
showing, 104–105
sorting and filtering rows, 24–26
sorting automatically, *115f*
table-level data validation, 108–111
transition, 111–112
unnormalized, 74
viewing data through different tabs, 17–18
viewing through forms, 38–40
Tables and Related Views category, 7–8, 125–126
Tabular control layout, 217, 261, *262f*
TblStockAgreement, 568–570

Templates
creating tables from, 90–92
database, 14–15
Text box controls
inserting expressions in source property, 232
replacing with list boxes, 222–223
Text boxes, 277–279, *279f*
Text data type, *91f*
Third normal form, 73, 76–77
Time worked (labor acquisition)
events, 470–471
Labor Acquisition (Time Worked) Entry form, 491–495
Labor Acquisition table, 487–491
Time worked report, 524–527
Times, 258
Titles
adding to forms, 209
columns, 248–249
form, 202
reports, 245–246, *246f*
Toggle key, Access Ribbon, 6
Top Values property, 156–157
Total row, 174
Totals command, 122
Totals list, 265
Totals queries, 173
Transaction cycles, 59
Transition table, 111–112
Transitive dependencies, 76–77
Tuple, 67
Two-dimensional pivot tables, 180–181, *182f*
Two-table queries, 144
Type tables, 339
Typification relationship, 302

U
Unbound controls, 208, 261
Undo command, 16, 247
Unfreezing columns, 121
Unhide Columns dialog box, 121
Unhiding columns, 121
Unique Rows property, 157
Unique Values property, 157
Unnormalized table, 74
Update PO Amount Command button, 439–440
Update query, 143, 187–189, 427, 442–443

V
Val function, 165
Validation Rule property, 479
Validation rules, 107, *116f*, 327–330
Validation Text line, 107
Validity check, 489
Value chain model, 59, 296, 298–301
Value system model, 296–298

Values
literal, 168
null, 10
searching for in columns, 22
Varying percentage deductions, 503
Vendor information
maintaining vendor records, 404–405
Vendor Information form, 403–404
Vendor table, 402–403
Vendor Information form, 403–405, *404f*
Vendor Information query, 415–416, *416f*
Vendor table, 402–405, 539
VendorID, 442–446
Vendors, recording cash paid to
cash account information, 450
Cash Disbursement Entry form, 452–457
cash disbursement events, 399
Cash Disbursements table, 450–452
overview, 449–450
View group, 21
Viewing
data through different tabs, 17–18
queries through forms, 40
tables through forms, 38–40
Views, 143–144. *See also names of specific views*

W
Wage queries, 517–518, *519f*
Wages payable, 517–519
WHERE clause, 183
Wildcard characters, 36, 171–172, *171f–172f*
Withholding entities, 473
Withholding table, 505, *506f*
Word, exporting reports to, 285
Work area, Access, 18
Work schedule events, 471–473
Work surface
Navigation Pane
Created Date category, 8
Custom category, 6–7
Modified Date category, 8
Object Type setting, 7
overview, 6
Tables and Related Views category, 7–8
overview, 5
Quick Access Toolbar, 8–9
ribbon interface, 5–6
setting options, 8

X
XPS-format, publishing reports in, 285–287

Y
Yes/No data type, *91f*

Z
Zoom dialog box, 117, 271
Zoom scroll control, *46f*